THE PENGUIN DICTIONARY
OF SURNAMES

Basil Cottle was born at Cardiff in 1917, a collateral descendant
of Joseph Cottle, the first effective publisher of Wordsworth,
Coleridge, Lamb, and Southey. After taking 'Firsts' in Classics
and English in 1938 he trained as a schoolmaster; during the war
he spent three years in the Army and three in the Foreign Office
(as a member of the 'Enigma' team at Bletchley), and in 1946
entered the English Department of the University of Bristol,
where he is now Reader in Mediaeval Studies. Among his other
publications are *The Life of a University* (with J. W. Sherborne,
1951), *Thomas Chatterton* (1963), *The Triumph of English:
1350–1400* (1969), *The Plight of English* (1975), and many re-
views in the *Review of English Studies* and the *Journal of English
& Germanic Philology*.

Dr Cottle describes himself as an 'Anglican, Liberal, Welshman, antiquarian, poet, and amateur artist'.

THE PENGUIN
DICTIONARY OF SURNAMES

BASIL COTTLE

SECOND EDITION

PENGUIN BOOKS

Penguin Books Ltd, Harmondsworth, Middlesex, England
Penguin Books, 625 Madison Avenue, New York, New York, 10022 U.S.A.
Penguin Books Australia Ltd, Ringwood, Victoria, Australia
Penguin Books Canada Ltd, 2801 John Street, Markham, Ontario, Canada L3R 1B4
Penguin Books (N.Z.) Ltd, 182–190 Wairau Road, Auckland 10, New Zealand

—

First published 1967
Reprinted 1969
Second edition 1978

—

Made and printed in Great Britain
by Hazell Watson & Viney Ltd
Aylesbury, Bucks
Set in Monotype Plantin

TO

BILL HOLLIDAY

OF WHITEHAVEN

AND DORIS, LESLIE AND MICHAEL

PREFACE TO THE SECOND EDITION

Since the publication of the first edition of this Dictionary in 1967, great progress has been made in the study of the surnames of the British Isles. A working conference, organized by Herbert Voitl, was held at Erlangen on 21–4 September 1975, and was attended by eleven of the fifteen invited workers in this field; it became clear that hopes for a definitive dictionary of surnames must centre on the combined findings of the Erlangen archive, whose 300,000 punch-cards in general work back from present-day surnames, the Lund archive, which works forward from the earliest documentation, and the Leicester *English Surnames Series*, which had already started publication with George Redmonds's *Yorkshire West Riding*, arguably the best book on regional surnames yet written. Meanwhile P. H. Reaney's Dictionary has been published in an expanded second edition (1976) by R. M. Wilson, and studies in specialist aspects have been produced by some of the Erlangen party, notably Gillian Fellows Jensen, Gillis Kristensson, Bo Seltén, and W. F. H. Nicolaisen. It is wholly relevant that the English Place-Name Society's volumes have reached new accuracy and exhaustiveness with J. McN. Dodgson's *Cheshire* and Margaret Gelling's *Berkshire*; and the Michigan *Middle English Dictionary* has limped on from H to M.

This new edition of *The Penguin Dictionary of Surnames* has enlarged the first from about 8,000 to about 12,000 names; and, because the first included all the commonest insular names in the British Commonwealth and the United States, the second has been enabled to draw on many which are rare and odd. This new word-hoard was largely built up by my mother, Cecile Mary Cottle, who almost until her death in her ninety-third year went on diligently listing, from the local and national newspaper, all names not in my first volume, along with the provenance of their bearers; this labour of love I here lovingly acknowledge. I must also thank William H. Vodrey, of East Liverpool, Ohio, who for ten years has faithfully sent me cuttings of genuine American surnames in their settings; some of these (like Turnipseed and Cabbagestalk) are of a whimsical or rueful modernity which debars them from the corpus, and some are probable exotics (like Cashdollar, Clapsaddle, and Vulgamore), but most of them fit into the pattern already established and are a happy link between our two countries.

I have had no second thoughts about the Introduction, which is unchanged, and hardly any about the original entries, though a very few have been a little expanded; but I think Charles Manning of

PREFACE TO THE SECOND EDITION

Seaton has saved me from further error over **Chenevix** I have ignored the new 'counties'. As before, my friend Leslie A. Ll. Matthews of Caerffili has given me expert help with the proofs.

BASIL COTTLE

31 August 1977

INTRODUCTION

The surnames of the British Isles, and those of British ethnic stock in the Commonwealth and the United States of America, fall into only four broad classes. This is the first neat and simple fact about surnames, and almost the last; but the simplicity of the fourfold division is not deceiving, and the many essays that have begun with a statement of it are on the only sure ground. Within the classes the thousands of names have reached us after a toilsome march of centuries, assailed by human ignorance and smartness, by the English inability to spell, by the decay of medieval trades and medieval grammar, by droll humour that makes the sensible name turn silly, by squeamishness that gives a veneer to obscenity, and of course by the biological fact that some families of fine name and fine lineage grind to a halt whereas others, slight or splendid, ripple or surge onwards; thus when Captain Wilson **Kettle** died in Canada in January 1963, aged 102, he left alive 584 descendants, and those of his name among them would make nonsense of any distribution-map of Canadian surnames previously compiled. But the four great classes are a constant and a comfort, and they shall be plainly set out forthwith; not enumerated, but designated by those four letters, FLON, one of which will stand immediately after the name in almost every entry in this dictionary:

F Surnames taking, or based on, the First-name of the ancestor or his father or mother (who are likewise ancestors). Since surnames arose in medieval days, when scepticism and heterodoxy were confined mainly to childless clergy, and the family man was orthodox and receptive, this class might just as well be remembered as Font-names, too, and their medieval Christian bias is strikingly emphatic.

L Surnames recording Localities or places where ancestors originated; although most of these spots are villages from Unst to the Loire valley, 'P' for 'place-names' would be unsatisfactory, as taking no account of the many names of mere features – the odd **Tree** or **Green** or **Mill** – which were not originally 'names' at all.

O Surnames recording the Occupation or status of the ancestor; 'status' must be mentioned, because being a **Lord** (even if the name be taken literally) did not involve what we should normally call an occupation.

N Surnames that are Nicknames, descriptive of the ancestor's face, figure, temper, morals, tastes, clothes, and the rest.

The purpose of each entry in this dictionary will be to assign the name to one of the four classes (or to several where there are several origins), to give it as accurate a meaning as will still make sense after a lapse of 500–1,000 years since its genesis, to state the language stock from which it immediately came (and sometimes, when the fact is fascinating, that from which it ultimately came also), and when possible to give some idea of the present distribution of the name. Any other information will be of a quite miscellaneous nature, but it will hardly ever be genealogy, which is the province of the genealogist; names, not their bearers, are the characters in this book, and something other than fame or notoriety is needed to secure inclusion for the transient holders of a lasting name. But when a surname seems oddly apt for some human performance (like **Butlin**), or oddly otherwise (like **Christie**); when an inventor's surname is depersonalized into merely the name of his brain-child (whether it be biscuit or hearse); when the metaphysics of the subject gets to work and poor George **Abbot** has a grim adventure while holding an office that he wouldn't have held a hundred years before, when real abbots were around – then the paradox or overtone may give warm life to a name that records a forgotten concept in a dead language.

I have promised the 'meaning' of each surname; and I must at once define 'the meaning of meaning' in this context. No philosophical niceties are needed for this: once again, the material subdivides with the utmost tidiness, and the vast majority of names in the first two categories (F and L) fall under one head, while the O and N names, rarer and easier than they, and curiously junior to them, fall under another. The two heads are as follows, and it will be simpler to start with the second. When the O and N surnames were bestowed on, or adopted by, the ancestor, they meant literally and bluntly what they mean to us; in many cases they are within our grasp immediately, if they say to us such things as **Carpenter** or **Strong**, because these concepts are unchanged since the Middle Ages, and we may be forgiven or justified if we look for a hereditary knack or physique in the bearers of these names. Even if they puzzle us, and only recourse to a dictionary of earlier English or French will solve the problem, the meaning given to us by the scholar will be the meaning intended at the time of bestowal or adoption.

Now with the other two classes, the F and L, things are usually quite the reverse; when surnames began to be fixed in the high Middle Ages, the exact or even rough meaning of many Old English stems had been forgotten, and first-names from that source were misinterpreted or often, perhaps, just shrugged away as meaningless; when the name went back a little farther, to our Germanic ancestors abroad, the chances of deception or oblivion were even greater, and a tough, horsey name like **Rosamond** got mixed up with the cult of the Blessed Virgin and (stopping short only of *rosa mystica*) was assumed to come from Latin *rosa munda* 'immaculate rose'. For even the knowledge of Latin, the one studied and standardized tongue, was imperfect; it was devoutly believed that Latin, and all other languages, were descended from Hebrew (which, by the way, is quite untrue), and scholars, who were nearly all churchmen, tended to find Latin stems wherever a godly lesson could be drawn from them. When Toki and Sunniva **Flower** (which probably didn't mean *flower*), good citizens of York, had a son, of early promise and of solid fulfilment as Saint Robert of Knaresborough, his verse biographer commends their choice of name, **Robert**, 'because he was both stalwart and valiant'; a glance at the entry will show that it is made up of two Germanic stems, meaning 'fame' and 'bright', polished by the Normans and important in their dynasty – but to the poet it was Latin *robur* 'heart of oak', and he rejoiced at the prescience of those who had chosen so well. When their own tongue – English – and their only vehicle of study – Latin – were so mishandled, it is not surprising to see the mess they made of Hebrew and Greek, both so vitally necessary for the interpretation of names from the Bible. The attitude to the Jews was such that their available scholarship was not reaching Englishmen at all; and Greek, which had been studied in Northumbria before the Viking invasions, was soon almost unknown. In any case, we didn't like the Greeks – were we not the British, descended and named from Brutus the Trojan? And their church was schismatic, and far beyond our horizon.

Thus in the F category the *true* meaning of the name is usually not the *intended* meaning; and the same applies, almost as sweepingly, to the L category. Admittedly, the brief feature-names ('locality') like *Hill* and *Brook* have the same immediacy as they had at their origin; but most of this great class are place-names proper, and it is a notorious fact that the study of English place-names is one from which the amateur must modestly shrink and which engenders flyting-matches between the experts. Nowadays we are armed with records of the earliest forms, with an Old English lexicon and even with a Middle English one as far as H, and rational interpretations can be given; but by surname-times our place-names had been so pounded by generations of mispronunciation, by Norman-trained Domesday clerks, and by meddling priests, who thought that 'Ryme Intrinseca' would make a posh name for a bucolic Dorset village, that the chances of hitting on the meaning must have been slight indeed. So when we say that the F **Giles** and the L **Tarvin** mean 'kid' and 'boundary', and cite Greek and Old French, and Latin and Welsh, in support, we must add that this is what they 'mean' to *us* with our books of reference, and that to their first users they 'meant' something different or nothing whatever.

Before examining the special features of each of the classes, it will be as well to consider why and when our surname system began. Family pride may be dismayed and dashed to find long and Frenchified and came-over-with-the-Conqueror names lumped with the generality. But length is not significant – **Cholmondeley** is intrinsically as humble as **Nye**; and French origin confers no distinction – **Butcher** is down-to-earth and French, **Kemp** is resonant and English. The alleged age of a surname is trickier, but even if it can be proved to have arrived just after 1066 it is puzzling that decent Englishmen should so covet a link with the mercenaries of the carpet-bagging pirate, usurper, and tanner's daughter's bastard. If one *must* have a foreign name, a more rational choice would be from the stock of those late arrivals, the 50,000 or so Huguenots, who sought Britain for their faith's sake, and not for spoil.

Many factors contributed to the establishment of a surname system. For generations after the Conquest a very few dynasts and magnates passed on hereditary names, but the main of the population, with a wide choice of first-names out of Keltic and Old English and Norman and church Latin and church Greek, avoided ambiguity without the need for surnames. Many had two names in their lifetimes, but when John (the) **Smith's** son Robert took up carpentry and styled himself, or was styled, Robert (the) **Carpenter**, and when Edward **Black** (who had black hair) left a son Stephen **Brown** (who had brown hair), the age of surnames had clearly not yet arrived. But society became stabilized; there was property to leave in wills; the towns grew; and the labels that served to distinguish a handful of folk in a friendly village were not adequate for a teeming slum where perhaps most of the householders were engaged in the same monotonous trade, so that not even their occupations could distinguish them; and some first-names were gaining a tiresome popularity, especially **Thomas** after 1170. The hereditary principle in surnames gained currency first in the South, and the poorer folk were slower to apply it; but in a few cases in the 1200s, in many more in the 1300s, and in most of the remainder in the 1400s, our present family names received their first forms. This applies to England (though the North was tenacious of older methods) and to the Scots Lowlands, which spoke and speak a dialect of English, but in the Scots Highlands and the Hebrides the magnificent system of Gaelic patronymics already obtained, and even now the eloquent *Mac-* and *Mc-* forms show little sign of modification and none of decay. In

Ireland, too, an even more elaborate statement of one's family tree, with *Mac-* and *O* showing both sonship and descent, was the rule until the English made an all-out attempt to change it: the statute of 1465 (5 Edward IV, cap. 3) is one of the very first comments on English surnames, standing back from them and seeing what shape they had taken, since it required every Irishman in the counties around Dublin to adopt a surname of English form – it could be a town, or a colour (the examples are descriptive of hair or complexion), or an art or science (like **Smith, Carpenter**), or an office (like **Cook, Butler**). This, of course, belongs to prescriptive rather than descriptive linguistics, but it is really listing L, N, and two kinds of O; it will be seen that F is omitted, the English no doubt feeling that the Irish were too exclusively given to this type of name already. As a result of this statute, and of factors much older and much more recent – flattering the invader or defying him, crudely 'translating' a name from one language into another, the recent systematic revival of the study of Irish Gaelic – Ireland now has a rich and complex array of native (patronymic) and English-type surnames, though ten of the twelve commonest are Gaelic.

The surnames of Wales are of late formation, and are a grave disappointment; as a means of distinguishing neighbours who already bear the same biblical or Welsh first-names, their limited numbers are powerless. A long terrace of colliery cottages, or a whole dairy-farming village, may be more or less shared by the surnames **Jones, Thomas, Williams, Davies** (none of them of Welsh origin, either!), with a repetitious set of first-names to go with them. As a result, an extra surname often lifts the bearer out of the ruck and does a good job during his lifetime: F John **Jones** Olwen (it was his mother's name), L Owen **Owen** Maesteg (he used to live there), O Evan **Evans** the Box (he is an undertaker), N Thomas **Thomas** Salem Baptist Church (which sums up his religion). Most Welsh surnames are of the F class, and this goes back to the wonderfully rich and proud patronymic system that was still vigorous in the 1500s but dying in the next century; it is impressive to read such early parish registers as those of Grosmont, Monmouthshire, where the entries take the baptized or wedded or buried villagers back by the leaps of *ap (son)—ap—ap—ap—* or *verch (daughter)—ap—ap—ap—* to half a dozen generations before, and there is pathos in the list of forbears that grace the baptism even of the illegitimate baby. How many of us could now name our great-great-grandfathers? The present system is a ruin, patched by the unofficial 'lifetime' surnames and by the ugly and long-winded makeshift of hyphenation, whereby an appellation like **Williams-**

Thomas just looks twice as non-Welsh as each of its parts. I heard recently of a very Welsh-minded girl who contemplated translating her English surname **Middleton** into *Canoldref*; and I am sure that Wales would gain from having many well-rounded native surnames of this type.

But the surnames of England, more varied and haphazard than those of her neighbours, are the norm, and most of those now existing must have been fixed in the couple of hundred years between 1250 and 1450. There are hardly any contemporary comments on the process, and the 1389 Guild Return of the Barbers of Norwich, authorized by Philip Barbur, James Barbir, and Thomas Barbyr-at-the-Preachers', shows a disregard for uniformity of spelling, and conveys the threat that Thomas will emerge as either **Barber** or **Barbour** or **Thomas** (or something based on that) or even **Church** or **Frere**. Even the word *surname* was used loosely, to mean an extra name, and 'Mandeville', late in the 1300s, lets Jesus take His *surname* from Nazareth; but already little jokes could be made on people's surnames, as if they were now accepted as part of society, and the 1386 Petition of the Mercers to Parliament jests bitterly about the wicked mayor Nicholas Brembre, calling him 'the forsaid brere or Brembre', since *brembre* could mean 'briar, bramble'. And since those days a surname has been a part of every Englishman's identity, and pride and mockery and speculation have grown up around it. That fine old antiquarian Camden, in his essay on the subject, said: 'I protest in all sincerity, that I purpose nothing less than to wrong any whosoever'; the awful ambiguity here was unintentional, but too many later writers have been at pains to deflate pride and poke fun at the innocent pleasure of bearing a winsome name. It is true, however, that 'superior' names usually disappoint when analysed, and are sometimes seamy; and if a list of the surnames of an ordinary modern community is examined it will prove a great social equalizer, wearing the aspect of a normal village of a few hundred years ago, with its trades and humble professions, its favourites and its Ishmaels, the far-travelled and the stay-at-homes. As speech elements, surnames keep their isolation from the mere vocabulary; fossilized and superficially meaningless, they obey laws and assume shapes unknown to dictionary words – in the Isle of Man Telephone Directory the abjectly dependent *Q*– (though still propped by its satellite –*u*–) comes into its own, and six students of the Engineering Faculty of the University of Bristol in 1959–60 bore the names **Fox, Hix, Rix,** Blix, Phoenix, and Merckx.

The characteristics and problems of the four classes (starting with the two older and bigger) must now be considered:

F First-names and local names share the bulk of the population of England and Wales; in some areas (certainly Wales, and less strikingly parts of the North) the former are in a comfortable majority, but even if it is true that F surnames are somewhat in excess of L names they occur with much less variety, and with a tiresome sameness of origin. A browse around the entries **Ph–**, **Sim–/Sym–**, **Thom–/Tom–**, will show how repetitive this material is, and the more popular first-names were turned into surnames by a formula which will soon become familiar to the user of this dictionary:

(1) Leave it as it is: **Andrew**.

(2) Add the Middle English genitive (possessive) singular inflexion *–es* to show the relationship '(son) of Andrew': **Andrewes**. These genitives must sometimes mean 'servant of', 'dweller at the house of'.

(3) Modernize this by eliding the *–e–*, but don't bother with the apostrophe by which, in a phrase such as 'the boy's hat', we signalize the omission: **Andrews**.

(4) Make the relationship clearer by adding *–son*, the *–s–* of which swallows up the *–es* or simplified *–s* of the father's first-name: **Robertson**; *son* is an Old English word, but this fact will not normally be mentioned in the entries.

(5) Use a pet form of the F: **Thom** (for **Thomas**). These pet forms, or diminutives (young Thomas, jolly old Thomas, little Thomas), will be defined throughout the dictionary as (dim.) **'Thomas'** (or whatever the F may be), and in case 'dim.' seems a graceless word to use I can honestly say that I mean no offence.

(6) Make the diminutive even more diminutive by adding a suffix or two – often out of Old French, whatever the language of the original F: **Tomkin** (the last bit was Flemish), Tom-el-in (with two Old French suffixes) giving **Tomlin**, which is really a treble diminutive.

(7) Add *–es* to the diminutive: **Symes**;

(8) or *–s*: **Sims**;

(9) or such a genitive to the double or treble diminutive: **Simpkins**;

(10) or *–son* to the diminutive: **Simpson**;

(11) or *–son* to the double or treble diminutive: **Simpkinson** – these last five being from the F **Simon**.

We must except the Gaelic patronymics from this formula; but the effect of *Mac–* and *O* on names they precede is somewhat similar to that of the English inflexions. *O* (which should never be followed by an apostrophe) means 'grandson/descendant of'; *Mac–* (which is always correct, though I have throughout risked the solecism *Mc–* so as to mark off these Gaelic names from **Machen, Macy**, etc., and to give them a block of their own between **Ma–** and **Me–**) means 'son of'. And in Welsh names the prefix *Ap–*, usually run into the F as in **Price** and **Powell** and even **Bowen**, means 'son of' likewise.

The first-names that receive this formulaic treatment are, however, a rich and varied array. The oldest ones in continuous use in these islands are Keltic (which will always be so spelt herein, to avoid mispronunciation and confusion with a Glasgow soccer team). The Britons, Keltic ancestors of the **Welsh** (that ugly word) and Cornish and Bretons, variously welcomed and opposed the Roman invaders after A.D. 43, and borrowed from them Latin names which they moulded to their own speech-habits, while still retaining an ancient Keltic stock of names; these, the purely British (like **Rhys**) and the assimilated Latin (like **Kay**), survive, though their numbers are few. In Scotland a form of Primitive Welsh existed, as did the mysterious Pictish, but the pattern there was utterly shattered by the arrival of another Keltic race, the Gaelic-speaking Scots, from Ireland; the ranks of **Mc–** names given here are witnesses of this new common culture.

From about 400 onwards the pattern in England was revolutionized by Germanic invasions. In the first of these, which eventually penned the Welsh in Wales and Cornwall and a few smaller pockets, we are told that the Jutes grabbed rich Kent and the Isle of Wight, the Saxons much of the bland South, the Angles a lion's share in the Midlands and North. They naturally brought their own personal names, grim with their savage religion and the titles of their gods; the wolf and eagle haunt them, but they include gracious attributes as well, and all have a real virility and purposefulness. What marks them off from so many other first-names is their tendency to have two elements, the first often alliterating with the father's name or even sharing its first element, but the conjunction of the two not necessarily offering any 'sense'; thus although **Woolgar** 'wolf spear' may call up a valid little picture, 'faith fortress' in **Warburton** doesn't. The reader will find many of these, and think them disappointing and silly; he will prefer the 'monothematic' (single-element) names, but the later Anglo-Saxons held to the dithematics, so that the simpler forms lost face and were left for the poorer classes.

Through all the trying centuries of Germanic settlement, the dispossessed Welsh held on to something precious besides their primitive names – the Christian religion; beleaguered and chastened, the church was still at work on the fringe of 'England' when Augustine came in 597 to start the conversion of the English, and the names of its primeval saints – the Apostles, the crucial Martin – must long have been familiar in Wales. But although the English quickly and with converts' gusto accepted Roman Christianity in the South and Keltic Christianity in the North, they kept to their pagan names, and only the occasional monk or priest is recorded with a name out of the new religion. And soon the second wave of Germanic first-names broke on our shores, those of the Vikings – Danes by 800, Norwegians in the North-West after 900; their Scandinavian spellings, and some of their elements, were new, but in general they resembled the West Germanic forms that had irrupted into Britain four centuries earlier. Again there was conquest, this time of Germanics by Germanics; then reconquest, peace, assimilation, unity within a structure of different laws and dialects, until the death of the Anglo-Saxon King Edward the Confessor in 1066. What happened in that year strategically and politically is well known; linguistically, it brought French speech from Normandy, but in its first-name aspect it occasioned the third great onset of Germanic names, since the Normans were Northmen, our second set of Scandinavian visitors, and they had kept their family names even while adopting the more cosmopolitan tongue of the France they had invaded. These three waves will be shown in this dictionary as (with due abbreviations) 'Old English', 'Old Norse', and 'Germanic normanized'; but not all can be thus pin-pointed, and some must remain plain 'Germanic'.

Although the Conquest brought us the last pre-surname wave of names – **Richard** and **Robert** and **Roger** and the rest – the font was extending its scope, mainly at the expense of the tough old Anglo-Saxon names. More and more children were being called after figures in the Old Testament, with their names (sometimes whole statements, or even questions like **Michael**) from Hebrew and other Semitic tongues, and in the New Testament, where the nomenclature was variously Hebrew and Greek and Latin. The later, non-scriptural saints, with their crazy martyrdoms and incredible miracles, were just as popular in a superstitious age, and here the civilisations and their languages mingled, as hardy old Teutonic names like those of Saints **Gilbert** and **Ledger** will show. Female saints, Margaret and Barbara and Cecilia and others, have likewise formed surnames, and it is customary to accuse the ancestor of illegitimacy if his descendants be called **Maggs** or **Babbs** or **Sisson**; this (as if it matters) must often be the case, but a posthumous infant took its mother's name, and a wife's dominant personality or more interesting name might be thus immortalized.

L Local names are a much livelier set. It has already been mentioned that they name somewhat fewer of the population than do the previous class, and none of them figures among the dozen commonest surnames in England; but whereas a lot of people bear a few overdone first-names, a lot of others bear a vast number of different local names, with their varied information on soil and situation, crops and beasts, wild birds and pretty weeds, mills and fish-dams, butter, whitewash, quarrels, water-pipes, goblins, and trysts. Of all our surnames, the biggest consistent set is of those based on the names of English villages and (less often) towns, usually in the surviving form of the place-name (such as **Newton**), sometimes with a slight simplification (as from –*leigh* to –*ley*, giving **Cranley**), sometimes with a grotesque respelling such as **Shufflebottom**; in cases like the last, a folksy sense of humour has doubtless conspired with illiteracy against the more accurate spelling, and has nearly ousted it. Or ignorance, and a family tradition, will confirm such spellings as **Faircloth**, which I have seen above a draper's; if the village-name **Havercroft** had come into use as a surname first in the 1960s, it would surely have been corrupted early to *Hovercraft*, and in just the same way the post-Conquest centuries altered names whose original meaning was camouflaged, and gave them instead a shape that had some contemporary meaning.

The language stocks that contributed to these place-names are those outlined under the F heading, but Old English in its different – and increasingly different – dialects hugely preponderates. The oldest elements will be Keltic, which covered most of the British Isles before the arrival of the Romans; such place-names as **London** already had enough currency and authority to survive the Roman linguistic on-slaught and those that were to follow. The next – Latin – layer was available during three centuries to Romans and romanized Britons not only for speech, writing, and personal names, but also for naming or renaming places; respect for (or, more probably, the mere convenience of) British names secured their retention as the first elements of hy-brids such as *Ebu*(or *o*)*racum* (see **York**). The Anglo-Saxon invaders in general built on new ground; Roman sites, whether taken over, or casually squatted in, or neglected, by the newcomers, were often given the tag –*chester* (itself from Latin *castra*); some 'built-up areas' may have been avoided through superstitious awe, and at some the timber-building barbarians may have felt admiration for the workmanship, as at Fawler, Oxfordshire, which means the 'spotty floor' or tessellated pavement rediscovered 100 years ago. But the map of our place-names is mainly Old English, with the vital exception of the frequent (in some areas, dominant) Keltic names for waterways and hills. How these have persisted has never been made quite clear; did the Saxon ask the Briton (in what tongue?) the name of the feature, and take his word for it? Certainly the information, whether given by this method or not, was dull enough; the Keltic element is usually no *name* at all, but simply 'river, water' or 'hill, top', and the Saxon, as if it *were* a name, put his own absolutely equivalent topographical word before or after it. Thus *River Avon* means 'river river', and even double woods and valleys will be seen under **Chetwode** and **Cundall**; **Pendle** Hill, Lancashire, is a grosser tautology, meaning 'hill hill hill' in Keltic and Old English and Old English. We are told that British cartographers at work in Africa, upon asking the natives (again, in what tongue?) the names of hill or river, have accepted as *names* such answers as 'hill' or 'hill, of course' or 'I don't know' or 'You'll have to ask the chief', and have incorporated them on maps. Neither story seems credible; but at least it is noticeable that there are far fewer of these Keltic survivals in the East (especially the South-East), where the fate of the Welsh was speedy massacre and expulsion by the Germanic spearhead, than in the West and North, where the pattern was more slowly evolved.

The later invasion altered the map somewhat less. After the presence of the Scandinavian raiders had been accepted as inevitable and permanent, and the Danelaw had been set its bounds north and east of Watling Street, the influence of Old Norse (most strikingly perhaps in its many names in *–by*) was stamped all over the North and the North Midlands, though many of the older names lasted and the two Germanic languages, cousins and now neighbours, tainted each other's forms in a way reflected in a few of the place-names occurring as surnames in these pages. For interpreting these Danish and Norwegian settlement-names, we have the huge corpus of words extant in the saga literature, but it must be remembered that this mostly belongs to far Iceland and to the period of early Middle English, not to England in the 800s and 900s, and modifications must be allowed for. Finally, the Normans did little to our place-name nomenclature; their foreign-trained scribes jibbed at our spelling, especially our *–gh–* and *–th–*, and probably hated our concatenations of consonants (see **Nicol**), but apart from the odd 'beautiful place' like **Bewley**, their language does not lie heavy on our earth.

The place-names that yield surnames are usually of small communities – villages, hamlets, some so insignificant that they are now lost to the map – rather than of towns. A place-name, it is reasonable to suppose, was a handy surname only when a man moved from his place of origin (where the place-name would make a futile addition to his name) elsewhere, and his new neighbours bestowed it, or he himself adopted it. This is borne out by **Bristow**; and, strictly speaking, a name like **Cornwallis** is pointless and unlikely in Cornwall, but useful and likely in Devon or further afield. It would seem that movements of individuals, bearing the names of their birthplaces or of their ancestral holdings, were in general between villages or from village to town, and not out from the towns; and town-names as surnames remain somewhat rare. Scots places (so differently interpreted by Johnston in 1892 and 1934, and by Watson in 1926) contribute plenty of surnames, often with a primitive British stratum lying beneath a Gaelic revision; French places, chiefly the springboards of Normans in the *départements* Calvados, Eure, Manche, and Seine-Maritime, survive in many weird misspellings; a memory of more distant places is seen in **Lubbock** and **Rome,** and astonishingly in **Baldock.**

Of course, from which place a surname derives, when many places bear the same name, can be proved only by the possession of authentic family documents. With a common place-name like **Newton**, many families must have arisen, and in many areas. In a case (one of many) like **Bagley**, the name of four places straddling in a great square over more than half England, it has been felt best to list the counties in which the places occur; a striking incidence of the surname in one of these areas will then *suggest* an origin there, but the other localities cannot always be excluded. Welsh counties hardly figure in the entries, since their places are so rarely influential in the formation of surnames.

The easy, and not very exciting, sub-class of local surnames, the mere topographical features such as **Tree, Green, Mill,** was mentioned at the outset; they will be entered as 'locality'. One of their oddities is the frequent addition of an –*s*, which I have taken as a genitive and rendered as 'of (i.e. at)', though this will often be a shorthand expedient; but certainly a plural cannot always be intended. Bearers of these names were not wanderers; their homes were fixed at some feature in or near the community. Yet it is important to realize that the nature of these names is close to the original nature of many place-names proper; a reading of any Anglo-Saxon charter relating to land or boundaries will show that most of the 'place-names' were in fact little more than map-references – the preposition *at/in/by*, etc. + a defining or descriptive adjective + a noun, the two latter words being typically in the dative case then needed after prepositions (as it still is with pronouns, e.g. *by me, to him*). Some of these phrases, like **Hendon** and **Newnham** with their datives still showing, lasted into place-names, and some even retain prepositions like **Under—** and **By—,** but it is clear that usually the idea of a place-name as one single noun that could be the grammatical subject of a sentence, saying things like **'Priddy** is a nice place', was a late development. Some such surnames, then, are primitive indeed; and many are still the repositories of Old

English variations in dialect, since they have resisted the levelling that standard *speech* has always tended to impose on dialects. Their present cosy aspect as plump, euphonious nouns, Havering-atte-Bower and Saint Anthony in Roseland, is new; they were not named with ono-matopoeia in mind, though the police training centre at Chantmarle in Dorset was able to exploit the rustic music of Dorset village-names by substituting them for room-numbers, with Melplash and Tolpuddle for bathrooms, and places on the banks of a certain river for the even smaller rooms. Paul Jennings has gone further, seeing place-names as inhabiting mysterious corners of the dictionary; his obsolete third person singular verbs in the phrase 'Man erith, woman morpeth' will be seen (under **Morpeth**) to have a grisly basis.

A few seemingly L names can have no relevance save to employment, and they will be found under an O head; **Spence** clearly cannot mean that the ancestor lived in a larder, but that he worked there. (The name also shows that a child of my acquaintance who referred to 'Marks and Spensive' was philologically not wide of the mark). Another group of latish names, formerly held to be L, prove to be a mixed bag – the so-called 'sign'-names; anything that could have formed a sign outside an inn or shop or house (beasts, plants, humans, angels, symbols) is demonstrably a sign-name only if medieval forms are found preceded by *atte* and the like. It is clear that L names teem with difficulties, and any expert in the field will deplore the heretical casualness of my 'farm' for –**ton**; 'place' is the only safe rendering (for what even meant 'vil-lage/township/town'), but I have varied it with 'farm' to avoid colour-lessness and because there are plenty of places where 'farm' is the livelier and likelier meaning.

O Despite the primacy of **Smith**, and the high incidence of **Taylor**, occupational names form a much smaller class than the F and L; and they are far less complicated. What the ancestor did for a living is sometimes what the descendant is still doing for a living, and few of the trades and skills have utterly perished. The amount of specializa-tion shown is astonishing; the hackneyed picture of a medieval com-munity improvising all its needs, the families making their own garments *ab ove*, everyone a jack of all trades, is clearly not quite accurate. The makers of little things, and the doers of seasonal jobs, are recorded along with the workaday folk; but **Mather** may have been a very Stakhanovite at his mowing. The small processes of some trades, especially cloth-making, are meticulously covered in surviving names, and even when a craft is obsolete its exact nature is easily recoverable from a good dictionary. In British India this method of forming surnames continued; two eminent cricketers, Contractor and Engineer, were from the sub-continent, and I noticed in a 1963 newspaper the name Canteenwallah. One class of o names is puzzling at first sight – the names of animals, or commodities, or various single objects, as metonyms for the people who bred them, sold them, or made them (the 'Jones the milk' type); but with many of these, which could also be descriptive nicknames, it is impossible to dogmatize.

N Nicknames form the smallest and easiest class. They shade from simple colour-names through those descriptive of looks, physique, character, clothes, preferences, all expressed by one word, to quasi-similes like **Vidler**, who had a 'face like a wolf'. Or a creature's name alone was cited to illustrate the bearer's shape or voice or morals; and this, in the case of such as **Bull**, could be an occupational metonym. Among surnames, the briefer the harder; few could be more straight-forward than the delightful **Haythornthwaite**, but many ugly little monosyllables must be nonce-words, nicknames applied through some lost anecdote to the ancestor, and subsequently clipped beyond hope of our recovering their secrets. Obscene and unkind names have usu-ally been disguised, and a few of these euphemisms hide in this dictionary; some fatuous and garrulous characters, who kept using the same mild oaths and cheery greetings, will be found under their favourite exclamations. Tiny clauses of the **Shakespeare** type, though potentially amusing, are now not always clear.

> Said Liddell to Scott,
> 'Well, that's the lot.'

No surname lexicographer could say this of his compilation: the vast number of extant surnames (figures between 30,000 and 100,000 have been mentioned as their tally), the contorted spelling that any family is liable (and entitled) to adopt, the difficulty of discovering tiny pockets of an all-but-perished name, and the dispersal of British names as far as the Antipodes are obvious reasons for imperfection; but just as important is the lack of early documentation. Many names may be correctly interpreted simply by recourse to dictionaries of the older state of the contributory languages, but no *proof* of the authenticity of these readings is possible without a thread of documentary evidence taking the family back to the days of surname-making, and a plentiful supply of good early spellings that leave the first 'meaning' in no doubt. The first writer on surnames to recognize this and put it into practice was the Rev. C. W. Bardsley, whose posthumous *Dictionary of English and Welsh Surnames* (1901) diligently collected early spellings of the many names, together with their dates and locations; his etymologies were often mistaken and his guesses wide of the mark, and 'meanings' were not given for the place-names, but as a name-list for later students to work on it is admirable. At last, in 1958, Dr P. H. Reaney, using the necessary method and bringing to it a full store of linguistic apparatus, produced his superb *Dictionary of British Surnames*, 366 big double-columned pages covering about 20,000 names. To save space, he deliberately omitted most of the English place-names, but these can be construed in Professor Ekwall's *Concise Oxford Dictionary of English Place-Names* or (in the case of tiny spots, even fields, or names now effaced) in the appropriate county volume of the *English Place-Name Society*, which, like Professor Pevsner in another endeavour, is gradually clothing the shires of England with a white robe of facts. Dr Reaney's work contains many brilliant little articles, and is sure to remain the standard on the subject; in special fields, such as occupational names and Old English names, authoritative studies have been made by Fransson, Tengvik, von Feilitzen, and others, and Dauzat is available for names of French origin, but Dr Reaney's is the only book to assemble all the classes of surnames along with unambiguous evidence for their interpretation. The present volume may seem to fall under Ernest Weekley's ban (on page 330 of his charming and discursive *Surnames*): 'compilations which dispense with evidence are not to be taken seriously'. But quoting the evidence would double the size of the book while adding nothing to the 'meaning' save confirmation; the evidence lies in archaic spellings, and in documents that are the province of the scholar, not of the 'common reader'; the conclusions reached by the English Place-Name Society were reached too meticulously to need sifting; and a latecomer in this field may be excused for being an eclectic, weighing the enthusiasm or prejudice or ponderousness of the pioneers, in any cases of doubt, against the common sense and up-to-date scholarship of Dr Reaney.

Family pride quite apart, the fascinations of surname study are many. It takes us back to days when English had strange sounds like initial *fn*– and *wl*– and *hn*– and *hl*–, and spelt initial *wh*– far more sensibly as *hw*–; when the *k*– of *kn*– was a reality (cf. the insensitive 'NITCRAFT' above a Monmouthshire wool-shop); when single letters existed for *gh* (see **Menzies**) and *th* (cf. Ye Olde Tea-Shoppe); and when our grammar, though more complicated and Latinate than now, was not guilty of some of the imprecisions of Modern English. A student of mine, whose grasp of linguistics was but languid, improved considerably on learning that she was a dative singular; the inflexion she bore (which will usually be entered here as showing 'dative after lost preposition') is no great loss, any more than the *-e* of the adjective when it found itself in the 'weak' position after *the* ('weak adjective after lost definite article'). Other waifs of inflexion show how we once suffered from that curse of civilized languages, grammatical gender: the *-r-* of the feminine dative singular of the definite article after a lost preposition in **Rock**, the *-n-* of the masculine in **Nash**. The dative plural, once in *-um*, will often figure in these pages, with a few genitive plurals and other signs of lost riches.

Further, the importance of surnames as a reflex of history – especially social history – is obvious; many O and N names hint at the jobs, clothes, habits, and failings of a past age, and a L name such as **Earnshaw** shows how dangerous it once was to leave baby outside. Some of the traits can be curiously lasting: a man living at Cranleigh (see the surname **Cranley**) told me casually in the train that his goldfish-pond had been depopulated by herons; and the bearer of an O name is entitled to an atavistic hope for some lurking skill – a **Crowther** might possess unexploited musical talent, and the fine old rhythms of the scythe perhaps await their consummation in a **Mather**. I hope that this book may thus afford help in planning a career; it could certainly be a wily weapon for wives who wanted to prove that, historically at any rate, they had married beneath them.

Hyphenations as such cannot be dealt with in this dictionary, but will be dismembered; most of them are very recent, some are mutually contradictory (e.g., **Dale-Hill**), some rather puckish (e.g., Fife–Dance), some hideously cacophonous (e.g., **Cox–Cox**), some biologically baffling (e.g., **Finch–Kite**).

There are over 8,000 different surnames in the following pages, many of them referred back to a head-form; over 2,100 occur in the *Dictionary of American Biography*, which has about 4,250 different names of British ethnic stock among its 16,000 entries. The omissions are of various kinds: rare and dull names, recent importations from abroad, rare and inferior spellings, a host of place-names where the feature owned means just 'place' and the owner's name defies certain interpretation, monosyllabic nonce-names from which the laughter has died, and the thousands that for various reasons defy analysis; the tremendous frequency of **Ryan**, and the august, seemingly informative richness of **Prendergast**, are no armour against obscurity of derivation, and only their special character has won them inclusion.

The incidence and distribution of the principal surnames is a matter of some interest and even of some clarity. Frequency-counts published by H M Stationery Office exist for the commonest names of the British Isles, and there is a similar compilation for the United States (1939);

the Scottish lists are very pleasing, inasmuch as they give the positions for 1858 and 1958, but in so small a country the use merely of the general indexes of births, deaths, and marriages is not quite as conclusive as could be wished; the Irish count is for 1890, but that for England and Wales lags badly, and nothing official has been published since the 1853 figures. Fortunately, in 1890 Henry Brougham Guppy, former naval surgeon and amateur geologist and antiquarian, brought out his curious *Homes of Family Names*, in which, for reasons more solid than snobbish, he counted the incidence, county by county, of the names of one wide-spread class – the 'yeoman' farmer; this rather arbitrary limitation deprives the book of some of its value, but his figures are often patterned and sometimes explanatory of the meaning, and I have incorporated their evidence as often as possible. Thus when a surname has been assigned to one of the classes FLON, given its meaning (in single quotation marks), derived from its language stock (the chief ones shown by two capital letters, OE OF ON), located – if a place-name – in its county, guppied, and put in its place in a national table if it is so common, then its little monograph must be considered complete.

*

In the preparation of this book, I owe particular thanks to five of my colleagues at the University of Bristol – Miss Susie I. Tucker, Professor J. C. J. Metford, Mr F. J. Warne, Mr G. Mellor, and Dr A. J. Willis; to my friend the Reverend G. Neville Boundy; and to kind correspondents, especially Professor Sir Ifor Williams, Professor Melville Richards, Professor Yves Lefèvre of the University of Bordeaux, Dr Edward MacLysaght of the Irish Manuscripts Commission, and Mr N. Y. Sandwith of the Royal Botanic Gardens, Kew. My friend Mr L. A. Ll. Matthews of Caerffili has helped me expertly with the proofs.

BASIL COTTLE

Bristol, 31 October 1964

NOTES ON USING THIS DICTIONARY

Order of Information. Surnames adding **–e**, **–s**, or **–son** to a headword will normally be found in the same entry as the headword, regardless of strict alphabetical order.

The information in each entry is given in the following order:

> **Headword**
> I. Class of name (F, L, O, N: see page 9)
>   (i) meaning (in single quotes)
>   (ii) linguistic derivation (O E, O N, etc.)
>   (iii) location, frequency, remarks
>   (iv) alternative meanings
> II. Alternative classes
> III. **Dependent words**
> IV. Overall general remarks

† = died

— or – after an initial abbreviates the whole name.

In noting the distribution of surnames, contiguous counties are linked by dashes.

In noting the distribution of places, a number in brackets after the county-name shows how many times the place-name occurs in it; occurrence less than thrice will not normally be shown.

/ separates alternative meanings or forms.

Omissions. Completeness in a work of this kind is, of course, impossible. However, the basic reason for not including a name has been either that it is not English, or else that there is nothing useful or interesting to say about it (see page 24 of the Introduction).

ABBREVIATIONS

Aberdeens	Aberdeenshire
Argylls	Argyllshire
A S	Anglo-Saxon
Ayrs	Ayrshire
Banffs	Banffshire
Beds	Bedfordshire
Berks	Berkshire
Berwicks	Berwickshire
Bucks	Buckinghamshire
c.	*circa*
Caern	Caernarvonshire
Cambs	Cambridgeshire
cf..	compare
Ches	Cheshire
DAB	*Dictionary of American Biography*
Denb	Denbighshire
Derbys	Derbyshire
dim.	diminutive
DNB	*Dictionary of National Biography*
Dumfs	Dumfriesshire
Dunbartons	Dunbartonshire
Co. Durham	County Durham
F	first-name (see page 9)
Fifes	Fifeshire
Flints	Flintshire
Glam	Glamorganshire
Glos	Gloucestershire
Hants	Hampshire
Herefords	Herefordshire
Herts	Hertfordshire
Hunts	Huntingdonshire
Inverness	Invernessshire
IoW	Isle of Wight
Kincardines	Kincardineshire
Kirkcudbrs	Kirkcudbrightshire
L	local name (see page 9)
Lanarks	Lanarkshire
Lancs	Lancashire
Leics	Leicestershire

Lincs	Lincolnshire
ME	Middle English
MED	*Middle English Dictionary*
Middx	Middlesex
Mon	Monmouthshire
Montgoms	Montgomeryshire
N	nickname (see page 9)
Nairns	Nairnshire
Northants	Northamptonshire
Northd	Northumberland
Notts	Nottinghamshire
O	occupational name (see page 9)
ODCN	*Oxford Dictionary of English Christian Names*
OE	Old English
OED	*Oxford English Dictionary*
OF	Old French
ON	Old Norse
OW	Old Welsh
Oxon	Oxfordshire
Peebles	Peebleshire
Pemb	Pembrokeshire
Perths	Perthshire
Radnors	Radnorshire
Renfrews	Renfrewshire
Ross & Crom	Ross & Cromarty
Roxbs	Roxburghshire
Salop	Shropshire
Selkirks	Selkirkshire
Staffs	Staffordshire
Stirlings	Stirlingshire
TD	Telephone Directory
Warwicks	Warwickshire
Wigtowns	Wigtownshire
Wilts	Wiltshire
Worcs	Worcestershire
East Yorks	East Riding of Yorkshire
North Yorks	North Riding of Yorkshire
West Yorks	West Riding of Yorkshire
Yorks	Yorkshire

A

Abbatt, Abbett See **Abbot**.

Abberley L 'clearing of (an A S called) Prosperity/Happiness Bold' O E; place in Worcs.

Abbey L 'abbey' O F; presumably for a layman employed there.

Abbiss L Not 'abbess', but '(of, i.e.) at the **Abbey**'.

Abbot(t) O 'abbot' O E from Latin, ultimately from Aramaic *abba* 'father'; his servant rather than his offspring. Or ?N based on some lost joke. –**tt** much commoner than –**t**. George **Abbot** (†1633) was the only archbishop of Canterbury to shoot a gamekeeper.

Abd(e)y, Abdie L '**Abbey**' M E from Latin.

Abel(l) F 'son' Hebrew; the name of the first murder victim was a popular F here in the 13th century. –**l** much commoner than –**ll**.

Abercrombie, Abercromby L 'mouth of the crooked stream' Scots Gaelic; place in Fifes.

Abernethy L 'mouth/confluence of the Nethy (= ?pure)' Scots Gaelic + British; places in Perths and Inverness. The A— Biscuit so called ?from Dr John A— (†1831), surgeon and dietician.

Able See **Abel**.

Ablett, Ablitt, Ablott F dim. '**Abel**', with Old French suffix –*ot* (often feminine).

Abraham F 'father of a multitude' Hebrew; the name of the Patriarch as changed from *Abram* 'high father' – so that **Abram** is nearer the original. Neither as F nor surname is it confined to Jews. **Abrahams (on)** '(son)/son of A—'.

Abram, Abrams(on) See **Abraham**.

Absalom, Absolom, Absolon, Absolum F 'father of peace' or 'the father is peace' Hebrew; the ill-fated son of David.

Ace See **Aze**.

Acfield L 'open country with oaks' O E.

Acford L 'ford at the oaks' O E.

Acheson F Scots and Border form of **Atkinson**. Family name of the earls of Gosford.

Acker L 'plot of arable land' O E (cf. *acre*). **Ackerman** L 'farmer (literally plot-man)' O E – first letter short, not long as suggested by spelling **Akerman**. **Ackers** L '(of, i.e.) at the plot'.

Ackford See **Acford**.

Acklam L 'at the oak woods/clearings' O E dative plural after lost preposition; places in East and North Yorks.

Ackland See **Acland**.

Ackroyd L 'oak clearing' OE; place in West Yorks, and a Yorks surname; cf. **Royds**.

Acland L 'lane of (an AS called) Acca' OE; place in Devon.

A'Court L 'at the court-house/manor/castle' OF.

Acres See **Ackers**. Counted by Guppy only in Herts.

Acroyd See **Ackroyd**.

Acton L 'place at the oak(s)' OE; places in six counties (but first element of some others is ?from AS owner's name).

Acum L 'at the oaks' OE dative plural after lost preposition.

Adair F (older *Edʒear*) Scots version of **Edgar**.

Adam F 'red' Hebrew (from the colour of the skin). The F very popular in 13th century. Origin of many surnames in **Ad–** and **At–**. **Adams** (rarely **Addams**) F '(son) of A—'; 26th commonest surname in USA in 1939, and seventh commonest in *DAB*. **Adamson** F 'son of A—'.

Adcock F dim. '**Adam**'+**Cock**.

Addams; Addey, Addie See **Adams**; and dim. '**Adam**'.

Addis(on) F '(son)/son of **Addie**'; –is is chiefly of Mon–Herefords, –ison is found early in Yorks.

Addy See **Addie**; chiefly a West Yorks surname.

Adeane L 'at the valley' OE; see **Dean**.

Adie F dim. '**Adam**'.

Adkin(s) Rarer, but more nearly original, form of **Atkin(s)**.

Adlam F 'noble helmet' Germanic (a form more strictly derived from Old English would be *Athelhelm*).

Adlard F 'noble hard' OE or continental Germanic.

Adlington L 'place/farm of the family/folk of (an AS called) Prosperity Wolf' OE; places in Ches, Lancs, but surname chiefly of Notts–Derbys.

Adlum See **Adlam**.

Adney L 'island of (an AS woman called) Prosperity Joy' OE; place in Salop.

Adrain L 'at the drain/drainage-channel' from OE verb; Johannes atte Drene appears in Somerset in 1327. But USA notable born in Carrickfergus, Northern Ireland, of Huguenot stock, may have been F; see **Adrian**.

Adrian F 'of the Adriatic (Sea)' Latin (with H–); the name of a Roman emperor and some popes, including Nicholas **Breakspear**.

Affleck L 'field of the (flat) stone' Scots Gaelic; places in Angus and Lanarks, and (Auchinleck, Boswell's lairdship) Ayrs and Wigtowns.

F: *first name*   L: *local name*   N: *nickname*   O: *occupational name*

Agar See **Algar**; commonest in North Yorks–East Yorks. Family name of the earls of Normanton.

Agate L 'at the gate' OE (–g– from plural; for original singular see **Yates**).

Agg, Agget(t) F dim. and double dim. '**Agnes**', or from a version of the saint's name Agatha 'good' Greek.

Agnes F 'chaste' Greek, but popularly associated with Latin *agnus* 'lamb'; Roman martyr saint.

Agnew N 'lamb' OF. Or ?L, from Agneaux ?'lambs'; place in Manche.

Aguila(r) O 'needle-maker' OF; –r is the better spelling.

Agutter L 'at' OE 'the gutter/drain/watercourse' OF.

Ahern(e) F (for O A—) 'descendant of Horse Lord' Irish.

Aiken(s), Aikin(s) Scots forms (even further from the original **Adam** than are those in **Aitk**–) of **Atkin(s)**.

Aimes See **Ames**.

Ainsdale L 'valley of (an A S called) Own Wolf' OE; place in Lancs.

Ainsley See **An(ne)sley**.

Ainsworth L '**Ewan**'s enclosure' OW+OE; Ekwall read *Eogan/Eugain* as the name of the possessor; place in Lancs, and still a surname there.

Aish See **Ash**.

Aistrope L 'eastern **Thorp**' OE; place (Aisthorpe) in Lincs.

Aitken(s), Aitkin(s) Scots forms of **Atkin(s)**. –en was the 93rd commonest surname in Scotland in 1958.

Aizlewood See **Hazelwood**.

Akehurst L 'oak **Hirst**' OE; chiefly a Sussex surname.

Akeley L 'oak wood/glade/clearing' OE; place in Bucks.

Akerman, Akers Inferior spellings of **Ackerman, Ackers**.

Akroyd See **Ackroyd**.

Alabaster Corruption of OF *alblaster* (for meaning, see **Ballester**), by folk-etymology.

Alan F 'the Alan', i.e. member of a nomadic Scythian tribe; a Welsh–Breton saint, bishop of Quimper; especially popular as F in Lincs, where many of William I's Bretons settled; frequency as a surname in Scotland is by confusion with a Scots Gaelic F derived from *ail* 'stone'. But early Breton stem *Alamn*– suggests an origin in Germanic tribal *Alemann*– 'all men', as in French name for Germany.

Alban F 'of Alba' (one of the Roman cities of Italy and Gaul called Alba 'white' Latin; cf. the white cliffs of Albion and the vestment *alb*). First British martyr (his death was as likely to have been outside Caerleon as at Saint A—s, Herts).

Albert F 'noble bright' Germanic; reached us before 1066, reappeared in the normalized form **Aubert,** had a wearisome vogue owing to the Prince Consort; now means a watch-chain or an Australian tramp's toe-rag.

Albone See **Alban.**

Allbright F 'noble bright' O E; of the same meaning as **Albert,** but the vowel and the –r– have changed places by metathesis.

Al(l)cock F dim. '**Alan**'+**Cock,** though the first element may be a diminutive of other names in *Athel*–, *Alf*–; –l– and –ll– chiefly Staffs, Notts surnames.

Alcott L 'old cottage/hut' O E; but involved with **Alcock.**

Alden F 'old friend' O E (cf. **Alwin**). Or N, see **Haldane.**

Alder L 'alder-tree' O E; counted by Guppy only in Northd.

Alderman O 'alderman, head of a guild' O E.

Alderton L 'farm in the alders' O E, places in Salop, Suffolk; but places in Glos, Northants, Wilts, are 'farm of Old Army's people' O E; and place in Essex is 'Elf Guardian's farm' O E.

Aldis, Aldous F Pet form of some woman's name beginning with *Ald*– 'old' O E. But **Aldous** may sometimes be L 'old house' O E; chiefly a Suffolk surname.

Aldred F 'old counsel' O E.

Aldren L '(at) the alders' O E dative plural –*um* after lost preposition; occurs early in Somerset.

Aldrich F 'old/elf/noble rule' O E; first element figures in other Fs variously as *Ald*–/*Alf*–/*Athel*–. Or = **Aldridge,** with which it occurs in Home Counties, East Anglia, Glos.

Aldridge L 'dairy-farm in the alders' O E, place in Staffs; or 'ridge of the alders/elders/(A S pioneer called) Old' O E, place in Bucks. Or = **Aldrich.**

Alexander F 'defender of men' Greek; popularized in Middle Ages by spread of apocryphal A— Romances; current in Scotland after English-born Queen Margaret named a son A—, and A—s II and III reigned 1214–85; hence generic name *Sandy* for a Scot. 83rd commonest surname in Scotland in 1958. Family name of the earls of Caledon.

Alford L 'ford of (an A S woman called) Old War' O E, place in Somerset; a Devon surname, so this is likelier than 'ford by the alders/ (heathen) temple' O E, place in Lincs.

Alfred F 'elf counsel' O E (Ethel*red* the Un*ready* lacked the second element); the king's fame, and proverbs fathered on to him, preserved the F even after 1066, but the surname is rare.

F: *first name*   L: *local name*   N: *nickname*   O: *occupational name*

Algar F 'noble/elf/old spear' OE (or, if family originated in a county with Scandinavian traditions, 'elf spear' ON); = **Elgar**, and also normanized to forms in **Au–**.

Alger With –g– as in *gag* = **Algar**. But with –g– as in *George* F 'temple army' OE, second element (OE *here* 'army') as in *harry*, Hereford. Normanized to **Au–**.

Alis(s) F 'Alice' OF version of 'noble kind/sort' (cf. *–hood*) Germanic; modern F *Adelaide*.

Alison F dim. 'Alice'; see **Alis**; the heroine of one of England's prettiest medieval lyrics, Chaucer's Wife of Bath and her crony, and his Carpenter's wanton wife were called A—; or 'son of Alice/**Alan**'.

Allan See **Alan**. This surname, with other spellings, was the 43rd commonest in Scotland in 1958.

Allard(e), Allart See **Adlard**. **Allars** '(son) of A–'.

Allaun L 'at the glade' OF; cf. *lawn* and Welsh *llan*.

Allchurch L 'old church' OE.

Allcock See **Alcock**.

Allcot(t) L 'old cottage' OE. Chiefly a Herts surname.

Allder Form of **Alder** seen in Herts.

Alldis and **Allebone** See **Aldis** and **Alban**.

Allen See **Alan**, of which it is the commonest form as a surname: 38th in England and Wales in 1853, 19th in USA in 1939.

Allenby L 'Agyllun's (N = 'point/thorn' OF)/**Alan**'s farm' second element ON; places (Aglionby, Allonby) in Cumberland.

Allerton L 'place in the alders', places in Lancs, West Yorks; or 'Elf Guardian's place', place in Somerset; or 'Elf Counsel's place', place in West Yorks (and cf. **Alfred**); all OE.

Allibon(d), Allibone Corruptions of **Alban**.

Alline Version of **Alan**, early settled in USA. **Allinson** F 'son of **Alan**'. Found chiefly in Co. Durham–North Yorks.

Allis(h), Alliss; Allison See **Alis; Alison**.

Allister See **McAlaster**. But Reaney found it also as a corruption of L *Alcester* 'Roman site' OE from Latin 'on the River Alne (= very white)' OW.

Allmark See **Hallmark**.

Allnutt F The second element is 'boldness' OE, the first 'noble/elf/ old/temple' OE.

Allport L 'old (market–) town' OE, place in Derbys; cf. the church of St Mary-le-Port (i.e., 'in the market'), Bristol. A Staffs surname.

Allright See **Allwright**; *–ric* spelt to look like **–right**.

Allsop(p) See **Alsop**.

Allston See **Alston**.

Allwright F 'old rule' OE; –*ric* spelt to look like **Wright**.

Allyn See **Alan**.

Almond F 'temple/noble protector' OE (cf. *Athel*– in **Aldrich**).

Alred F 'noble/old counsel' OE.

Alsop(p) L 'Ælle's (F related to ?"all" or "noble") valley' OE; place (–op) in Derbys, and Derbys–Notts–Staffs surnames.

Alston(e) F 'noble (*Athel*–)/elf/old/temple stone' OE. Or L 'Old ?Bearcub's place', place in Cumberland; or 'Elf Friend's place', place in Devon; or 'Elf Victory's place', places in Lancs, Glos; or 'Noble Boldness's place', place in Surrey; or '**Alfred**'s place', place in Staffs. All OE. Guppy counted –**n** only in Suffolk.

Altham L 'river-meadow with swans' OE; place in Lancs.

Alton L 'old/stream-source/Elf's/Ælle's (cf. **Alsop**) place' OE; places in seven counties.

Alveston L 'Ēan-Wolf's/All-Battle's farm' OE, places in Warwicks, Glos; or 'Temple-Rule's/Elf-Rule's farm' OE, places (Alvaston) in Derbys, Ches.

Alvey F 'elf war' OE.

Alvord = **Alford**, with West Country voicing of –**f**– to –**v**–.

Alwin, Alwyn (and sometimes **Alwen**) F 'old/noble/elf friend' OE.

Ambler O 'ambling horse/mule' OF; ?for a keeper of them, but a York fuller in 1400 was called it for fun; or 'enameller', by corruption from OF. Still a West Yorks surname.

Ambrose F 'immortal' Greek; the **m** and **r** occur in our *mortal*. Popularity of F due to Saint A—, bishop of Milan. Welsh form is *Emrys*. Common in Cambs–Essex.

Ambury Despite the L appearance, probably a version of **Amery**.

Amery F 'work rule' OF from Germanic *Amalric*. Common form (especially in Devon) of a numerous group beginning with **Am–, Em–, Emb–** (and ?**Im–, Hem–**).

Ames See **Amis**. But some of the USA bearers go back to an **Eames**.

Amey F A tangle of **Amis**, 'friend' OF, and 'loved' OF. Chiefly a Hants surname.

Amis(s) F 'friend' OF from Latin *amicus*; rarer than its form **Ames**.

Amlot F dim. '**Amis**'; but the **Amis**–**Amos**–Amyas–Hamo–**Amery**–**Emery** complex is very ambiguous.

Ammon F 'awe/terror protector' Germanic. **Ammon(d)s** '(son) of A—'.

Amor N 'love' OF, though the exact reason is hard to fix.

Amory See **Amery**; a Bristol and south-west form.

F: *first name*   L: *local name*   N: *nickname*   O: *occupational name*

Amos Corruption of **Amis** to F 'carried' Hebrew; the minor prophet; a F not used in England before the Reformation, and never popular (cf. Byron's rude remark, 'Oh, Amos Cottle! – Phoebus! what a name'; but cf. **Byron**). Counted by Guppy only in Kent, Northants.

Ampleford L 'ford where sorrel/dock grows' OE; place (–forth) in North Yorks.

Anderson F 'son of (dim.) **Andrew**'. Ninth commonest surname in Scotland in 1958, eighth in USA in 1939. Family name of the viscounts Waverley.

Andrew F 'manly' Greek; the first-called disciple; his bones brought by Saint Regulus to Scotland, of which he is patron, and where the F is popular – but the surname is found chiefly in Cornwall and Devon. **Andrew(e)s** '(son) of A—'; –ws common from Hants to Devon.

Andrewartha L 'the upper place' Cornish; **an** is the Cornish definite article.

Angel(l) F 'angel' (originally = 'messenger') Greek; used as F in Middle Ages (and for Tess's husband). Or L as sign-name ('at the sign of the Angel') or by confusion with **Angle**. Or O through playing this (easy) part in a religious play. Or as a flattering/sarcastic N. Form in –ll is by far the commoner, but Thos **Angell** who emigrated to Boston in 1631 had descendants called **Angel**.

Angle L 'nook, corner (of buildings), point of land, outlying district' OF; early forms with *in the A—* and *del A—* prove this. But sometimes ?confused with **Angel**, like Pope Gregory's little joke.

Anglezark L 'shieling of (a Norseman called) Relic of the Gods' ON (cf. **Olliffe**); place in Lancs.

Angove O 'the **Smith**' Cornish; **an** is the Cornish definite article.

Angus F 'one choice' Scots Gaelic. Or L, from the county – once Forfar – now called after an 8th-century Pictish king.

Anker(s) Though there is a F *Anchier* OF, the derivation may sometimes be N 'anchorite, recluse' OE and L '(of, i.e.) at the anchorite's'. Chiefly a Ches surname.

Ann(e) F '(God) has favoured me' Hebrew = *Hannah*; said in an apocryphal gospel to be the Blessed Virgin's mother. **Anns** '(son) of **Ann**'. But the F is not recorded in England until the 1200s, and may often be dim. '**Agnes**'.

Annesley L 'clearing of (an AS whose name is related to) *One*' OE; place in Notts.

Annett F dim. '**Agnes/Ann**'; chiefly a Northd surname. **Annetts** '(son) of A—'.

Annis(s) F dim. 'Agnes/Ann'.

Ansell F '(pagan) god helmet' Germanic; F usually **Anselm** (once in London TD).

Ansford L 'Temple Protector's ford' OE; place in Somerset.

Ansley L 'clearing with a hermitage' OE, place in Warwicks; first element was originally *ān-setl* 'solitary dwelling'. **Anslow** in Staffs was once of the same form.

Anson F 'son of **Agnes/Ann**'.

Anstey (or **Anstee**) L 'one path, single track' (with suggestion of steepness also) OE; places in over nine counties. South Midlands and south-west surname. But cf. **Ansteys**.

Ansteys See **Anstice**; and there may be interchange with **Anstey**.

Anstice F (adjective from) 'Resurrection' Greek. The male Saint Anastasius didn't catch on in the West, but the female Saint Anastasia did, and her F was even bestowed on the Virgin's midwife.

Anstie See **Anstey**.

Anstis(s) See **Anstice**.

Anstruther L 'the stream' Scots Gaelic (**an** the definite article); place in Fifes.

Antcliff(e) L 'eagles' cliff' OE; one of the places called Arn(e)cliff(e) in West and North Yorks.

Ant(h)ony F Latin *Antonius*, a family name of unknown origin; –**th**-spelling is vicious (based on false derivation from Greek *anthos* 'flower'). From the Egyptian hermit are derived *Saint A—'s Fire* (erysipelas) and the *tantony pig* (the runt of the farrow).

Antrobus L 'bush of (a Norseman called) Sole Ruler' ON; place in Ches.

Anyan, Anyon Versions of **Ennion**; **Anyan** is found in Lincs.

Aplin See **Applin**; chiefly a Somerset surname.

Appelbe(e) See **Appleby**.

Apperley L 'wood/clearing with apple trees' OE; places in Glos, Northd, West Yorks (but it is chiefly a Herefords surname, so the Glos origin is likeliest).

Appleby L 'apple farm' OE+ON; places in Westmorland, Leics, Lincs (but it is chiefly a Northd surname, so the Westmorland origin is likeliest).

Applegarth, Applegate, Applegath L 'apple enclosure, orchard' ON; locality, or places (all –rth) in Cumberland, East and North Yorks.

Appleton L 'apple farm' OE; places in five counties (five in Yorks), and surname found chiefly in Yorks–Lancs.

F: *first name*   L: *local name*   N: *nickname*   O: *occupational name*

Applewhite L 'clearing with apples' OE+ON; places (Applethwaite) in Cumberland and Westmorland.

Appleyard L 'apple enclosure, orchard' OE.

Applin L '(among) the apples' OE dative plural in *–um*.

Apps L 'aspen-tree' OE.

Apsimon F 'son' (Welsh *Ap–*) 'of **Simon**'.

Arber(r)y See **Arbury**.

Arblaster An OF spelling of **Ballester**, **Alabaster**.

Arbon F 'eagle bear' ON, a Danelaw F and surname.

Arbrey, **Arbury** L 'earth fortification' OE; Roman and other forts in Cambs, Herts, Warwicks.

Arbuthnot(t) L 'mouth of the little holy/healing (stream)' Scots Gaelic; place (–ot) in Kincardines. But Johnston (1934) wanted to make it 'marsh of the silly fellow' Scots Gaelic.

Archbald, **Archbell**, **Archbo(u)ld**, **Archbutt** See **Archibald**.

Archdeacon O 'archdeacon' OE from Latin; the bishop's right–hand man – who should have been celibate.

Archer O 'bowman' OF; either professional or – since most males could handle a bow – notably skilled. A universal surname.

Archibald, **Archibo(u)ld** F 'precious bold' Germanic, the original *Ercan–* being influenced by Greek names in *Archi–*; common only in Scotland as a F, especially for the families Douglas and Campbell.

Arden, **Ardern** L 'dwelling-place' OE, places (–en) in four counties; or 'gravel/eagle valley' OE, place in North Yorks. **–ern** chiefly a Ches surname, and that of a brilliant medieval surgeon.

Argent N 'silver' OF; from possession, occupation, or hair-colour.

Arkell, **Arkill**, **Arkle** (also **Argall**) F 'eagle cauldron' ON; **–ell** is chiefly a Glos surname, **–le** Northd.

Arkwright O 'ark-/chest-/bin-maker' OE. Among its variants is the sporty **Hattrick**.

Arlet(t), **Arlette** See **Arlott**.

Arley L 'eagle wood' OE; places in Ches, Lancs, Warwicks, Worcs.

Arlott(e) N 'fellow, chap, rogue' OF (cf. *harlot*, a later meaning).

Armer See **Armour**.

Armistead (commoner than **Armitstead**) L 'hermitage (literally hermit place)' OF+OE; first element shows *er–* becoming **ar–** as in **Clark**, second is as in *bedstead/instead*. Chiefly a Cumberland–Westmorland–Lancs surname.

Armitage L 'hermitage' OF; cf. **Armistead**; locality, or place in Staffs.

Armour O 'armourer' OF.

Armstrong N 'strong in the arm' OE. Abundant in Northd, then

Cumberland–Co. Durham and south Scotland; a tough Border surname.

Arne L 'house' OE; place in Dorset.

Arnell See **Arnold**.

Arnold F 'eagle power' Germanic. Or L 'eagle **Haugh** (*halh*)' OE; places in Notts, East Yorks. Chiefly a south Midlands and Mon surname.

Arnot(t) See **Arnold**.

Arram L 'at the shielings/hill-pastures/huts' ON (from Irish) dative plural after lost preposition; place in East Yorks.

Arrindell See **Arundel**.

Arrington L 'place of the family/folk of (an A S called) Eagle' OE; place in Cambs (unless it be for the far more frequent **Harrington**).

Arrowsmith O 'arrow-maker' OE.

Arsnell See **Horsenail**.

Arthur F Arthur, (?king or) general against the A S invaders, was presumably a romanized Briton with a F derived from a Latin family name *Artorius*, ?related even to *Arcturus* 'bear-guardian' Greek, the bright star in the constellation Boötes; but Keltic sources have been suggested – 'bear' also, and 'stone'. **Arthurs** '(son) of A—'.

Arundel(l), Arundale L 'horehound valley' OE; place (–el) in Sussex. But (as the six silver swallows, on black, of their arms suggest) the post-1066 Somerset and Dorset settlers must have had a N 'swallow' OF *arondel* (now *hirondelle*).

Asbee L 'farm in the ash-trees' ON; places (Asby) in Cumberland and Westmorland.

Asbury L Probably for **Astbury** 'eastern fort' OE, place in Ches, rather than one of the places Ashbury 'fort in the ash-trees' OE, place in Devon, or 'fort of (an A S called) Spear' OE, place in Berks.

Asch(e) See **Ash**; –e could show dative after lost preposition.

Ascott L 'eastern cottage/hut' OE; places (–ott/–ot) in five counties.

Ash(e) L 'ash-tree' OE; locality, or places in seven counties; also the source of many surnames like **Dash**, **Nash**, **Rash**, **Tash**. (It was also the name of the Old English letter æ.) –e could show dative after lost preposition.

Ashbridge L 'bridge at the ash-trees' OE, unless it is a corruption of Ashridge 'ash-tree ridge' OE in Herts.

Ashbrook L 'eastern brook' OE; place in Glos.

Ashburner O 'burner of ashes' (who made potash by burning ashes of wood, weeds, or straw) OE.

Ashby L 'ash-tree farm' ON (an Old Norse owner *Aski* may sometimes be involved); places (nearly twenty) in Midlands, the biggest being A— de la Zouch, Leics. The surname spread beyond the Danelaw.

Ashcombe L 'ash-tree valley' OE; places in Devon, Somerset.

Ashcroft L '**Croft** in the ash-trees' OE; locality, or place in Berks.

Ashdown L 'ash-tree hill' OE, forest in Sussex; or '(A S called) Ash/Spear/Ship's hill' OE, place in Berks.

Ashenden L 'hill covered with ash-trees' OE; place in Bucks.

Ashfield L 'open land with ash-trees' OE; places in five counties.

Ashford L 'ash-tree ford' OE; places in Derbys, Devon, Salop; origins of the Kent and Middx places are dully complicated. Found in Warwicks, Devon–Cornwall, Suffolk.

Ashhurst A more pedantic spelling, instanced in *D A B*, of **Ashurst**.

Ashill L 'ash-tree hill' OE; locality, or place in Somerset. But place in Norfolk was originally 'ash-tree clearing' OE.

Ashkettle F 'god cauldron' ON, the first element being pagan and the second sacrificial; nearest surviving surname to Old Norse *Asketill*, though **Askell** preserves a later Old Norse form.

Ashley L 'ash-tree wood/glade/clearing' OE; places in fifteen counties.

Ashman O 'shipman, sailor', even 'pirate' OE. Chiefly a Somerset surname.

Ashmead L 'ash-tree meadow' OE; locality, or place in Glos.

Ashmore L 'lake in the ash-trees' or 'boundary (it is near the Wilts border) in the ash-trees' or '(A S called) Spear's boundary' OE; place in Dorset, yet Guppy found the surname chiefly in Derbys, Worcs.

Ashness L 'headland/(projecting) ridge with an ash-tree copse' ON; place in Cumberland.

Ashplant Grotesque corruption of **Absalom**.

Ashton L 'ash-tree farm/place' OE; places in many counties (five in Wilts). A more southern version of Danish **Ashby**.

Ashurst L 'ash-tree **Hirst**' OE; places in Hants, Kent, Sussex.

Ashwell L 'spring/stream in the ash-trees' OE; places in six counties including Herts, and a Herts surname.

Ashwick L '**Wick** in the ash-trees' OE; place in Somerset.

Ashwin F 'spear friend' OE.

Ashwood L 'ash-tree wood' OE; locality, or place in Staffs.

Ashworth L '**Worth** in the ash-trees' OE; place in Lancs, and a Lancs–West Yorks surname.

Aske L 'ash-tree' ON; locality, or place in North Yorks.

Askell See **Ashkettle**.

Askew L 'oak wood' ON; place in North Yorks; the surname variant **Ayscough** is nearer the original, and **Askey** further away.

Askham L 'homestead in the ash-trees' OE; places in Notts, West

Yorks; but place in Westmorland is 'at the ash-trees' OE/ON dative plural after lost preposition – also ?the meaning of Askam, Lancs.

Askwith L 'ash-tree wood' ON; place in West Yorks.

Aspinal(l), Aspinell, Aspinwall L 'spring/stream in the aspens (trembling poplars)' OE (second element is our *well*); place (–wall) in Lancs. **Asmall** imitates a Lancs pronunciation.

Aspley L 'aspen wood/clearing' OE (cf. **Aspinal**); places in five counties.

Asquith See **Askwith**.

Astbury See **Asbury**. A Ches surname.

Astel(l) See **Astle**.

Asterley L 'eastern clearing' OE; place in Salop, and still a Salop surname. Sometimes perhaps from place Asterleigh (same meaning) in Oxon.

Astle L 'eastern hill' OE; locality, or place in Ches.

Astley L 'eastern wood/clearing' OE; places in five counties; but place in West Yorks is '**Askell**'s **Haugh** (*halh*)' ON+OE. Family name of the barons Hastings.

Aston L 'eastern place' OE; places in over a dozen English counties, including ten in Salop, but places in Glos, Herefords, Salop are the same as **Ashton**.

Astrop L 'eastern **Thorp**' first element OE; place in Northants.

Astwood L 'eastern wood' OE; places in Bucks, Worcs (four).

Atcheson, Atchison See **Acheson**.

Atherton L '(A S called) Noble Army's place' OE; place in Lancs, and still a Lancs surname.

Athol(l) L 'new Ireland' Scots Gaelic; the district of Scotland.

Atkin F double dim. '**Adam**'. **Atkins(on)** '(son)/son of A—'. Whereas –s is typically a Midlands surname, **–son** is overwhelmingly northern.

Atlay, Atlee, Atley See **Attlee**.

Attack L 'at (the) oak' OE.

Attenborough L 'at the mound/hill' OE or 'at the grove' OE (cf. **Burgh, Bear**) or even 'at the fort' OE (cf. **Burrough**); for the –en cf. **Nash**. The place in Notts is neither the origin nor of the same derivation. Chiefly a surname of Northants–Notts–Derbys and Essex.

Atterbury L 'at the **Bury**' OE; –ter– represents the feminine dative singular of the definite article after the preposition **at**.

Atthey L 'at the enclosure' OE.

F: *first name*   L: *local name*   N: *nickname*   O: *occupational name*

Atthill L 'at the hill' OE.

Attlee, Attley L 'at the wood/clearing' OE, the second –t– being the remains of the definite article.

Attridge Though formally it might sometimes be L 'at the ridge' OE, it is likelier to be F 'noble powerful' OE.

Attwater L 'at the water' OE (cf. **Attlee**).

Attwell, Attwill L 'at the spring/stream' OE (cf. **Attlee**); –i– a Devon–Somerset surname.

Attwick L 'at the dairy-farm' OE.

Attwood L 'at the wood' OE (cf. **Attlee**).

Attwool(l) Dorset form of **Attwell**.

Atwater, Atwell, Atwick, Atwill, Atwood Inferior spellings of Att–.

Atyeo L 'at the river/stream' OE; a south-west dialect form.

Aubert See **Albert**.

Aubin F 'Albinus (from *albus* "white")' Latin, through OF.

Aubray, Aubrey, Aubry F 'elf ruler/counsel' Germanic.

Auchmuty L 'field (?rising ground) of the swine-pen' Scots Gaelic; place (Auchtermuchty) in Fifes; USA family is of Fifes stock.

Auckland L Formerly something like *Alclyde* (original name of Dumbarton), 'cliff/rock on the Clyde (= ?washer/cleanser)' British, transferred to the site in Co. Durham and later confused with *aukland* 'additional land' ON.

Auger See **Alger**.

Aughton L 'place in the oaks' or 'place at the oak' OE; several places in Lancs, also in Wilts, East and West Yorks.

Augur See **Algar**. It was no doubt learnedly (but wrongly) associated with Latin *augur* 'soothsayer, diviner'.

Augustin(e) F dim. 'Augustus (= venerable, consecrated)' Latin; F popular through Saints A— of Hippo and Canterbury, but a rare surname.

Ault N 'old' OE. Or L 'hill' Welsh *allt*, pronounced *olt* on the English side of the Border.

Austen, Austin F dim. '**Augustine**' OF version of Latin, and usual ME form of the saint's name. In the *DAB* there are eleven –in to one –en; in the London TD the proportion is 430:50.

Avent F 'fitting, suitable, handsome' OF *avenant*.

Averell USA notable descended from William A— or **Avery**; and cf. **Averill**.

Averill N 'April' OF. A month-name rarely keeps its meaning as a surname (cf. **January**), but Reaney suggests the hint of 'changeable, vacillating'; Chaucer's Anelida compares her lover with April. *ODCN*'s F *Everild* 'boar battle' OE (which should become *Everil*) is only barely possible.

Avery The chief surname survival of **Alfred**, which the Normans found hard to pronounce (it even occurs as *Arflet*); chiefly a southern surname.

Awber(r)y See **Aubray**.

Awre L ?'alder-tree' OE; place in Glos.

Axtell See **Ashkettle**; –sk– has become –x– as in 'I axed him'.

Ayckbourn L 'stream in the oaks' OE.

Ayer N 'heir' OF. Or F reduced from such a F as **Alger**; or the same as **Hair**. Hence many surnames in Air–, **Eyr–**, Eyer–, **Ayr–** (which may be from the Scots burgh Ayr, ?'smooth river' Scots Gaelic, or ?a vaguer Keltic meaning connected with the Oare Water, Somerset, and the Rhine tributaries Ahr and Aar). **Ayers** '(son) of A—'.

Aykroyd See **Ackroyd**.

Ayler O 'garlic-seller' OF.

Ayliffe F ?one of the many OE *Æthel–* names; or the mysterious Ailef/Ailof which figures in Domesday Book. No connection with the village of Aycliffe, Co. Durham.

Aylmer, Aylmore F 'noble famous' OE (first element *Athel–/Ethel–*, cf. **Aldrich**.

Aylward F 'noble guardian' OE.

Aylwin F 'noble friend' or '?elf friend' OE; these involve normalization of the first elements *Athel–*, *Alf–*. Chiefly a Sussex surname.

Aynsley See **Annesley, Ansley**.

Ayre(s) See **Ayer(s)**.

Ayscough See **Askew**.

Aysh See **Ash, Aish**.

Aze F 'Azo' Germanic, with the element seen in OE *Æthel–* 'noble'.

F: *first name*   L: *local name*   N: *nickname*   O: *occupational name*

B

Babb(itt) F (double) dim. 'Barbara' (see **Barbary**); but some USA **Babbitts** claim descent from settler Bobet. **Babbs** '(son) of B—'.

Babcock F dim. 'Barbara' (see **Barbary**)+**Cock**; or a further perversion of **Badcock**.

Bable F double dim. 'Barbara' (see **Barbary**).

Bacchus This bibulous surname is a corruption of **Backhouse**;. Weekley says one bearer was 'fined for intoxication, Jan. 5, 1911'.

Bach(e) L 'stream' OE (the word had an –*e*).

Bachelor O 'young knight, novice in arms' OF.

Back L 'ridge, hill'. Or N 'bat' (?from dim sight or nocturnal habits); or 'back' (from some deformity). Or F *Bacca* ' ?hunchback, fatty'. All OE.

Backhouse (corrupted to **Backus**) L 'bakehouse' OE.

Bacon O 'bacon(-seller), pork(-butcher)' OF, a metonym. Dauzat also cites a Germanic F connected with verb *bag*–'to fight'.

Badcock F dim. '**Bartholomew**'+**Cock**, or ?'*Bada* (= ?war/ ?bloated/?bad)' OE+**Cock**; chiefly a Berks, Devon–Somerset surname.

Badman F dim. '**Bartholomew**'+dim. **–man** as in **Jackman**; chiefly a Somerset surname.

Badrick F 'battle rule' OE.

Bagg(e) N 'money-bag, pack, bundle' ME; but a Germanic F based on *bag*–'fight' existed. Chiefly a Somerset surname.

Bagley L ' ?badger wood/clearing' OE; places in Berks, Salop, Somerset, West Yorks. Or from **Baguley** (with same meaning) in Ches; surname also spelt **Bagguley**.

Bagshaw L ' ?badger copse' OE; Derbys place and surname.

Bail L 'outer-court wall of a castle' OF; from residence/authority therein. Sometimes spelt *bailey* as in *Old Bailey*, London.

Bailey, Baillie O 'bailiff' OF; crown official, king's officer in county/ hundred/town, keeper of a royal building or demesne, sheriff's deputy, or even agent/factor; a Scots alderman is still a *bailie*. Or L = **Bail**; or 'berry wood/glade/clearing' OE, place in Lancs. Common south of the line Ches–Yorks, and **–ley** was the 34th commonest surname in USA in 1939. **Bailey** is the family name of the barons Glanusk.

Bain(e) L '(public) bath' OF; for an attendant thereat. Or N 'white, fair' Scots Gaelic; or 'bone' OE in its northern form retaining *ā*; or 'direct, obliging, hospitable' ON; **Bain(e)s** '(son) of B—'.

Bainbridge L 'straight/direct/handy bridge' ON, places in Co. Durham, West Yorks; or 'ridge over (River) Bain (= short)' ON, place in North Yorks. A Cumberland–Westmorland–Co. Durham–Yorks surname.

Baird O Scots version of *bard* 'singer, minstrel' Keltic. Family name of the viscounts Stonehaven.

Bairnsfather N 'child's father' OE; but the meaning may be that of **Barnfather**, based on an ON compound, meaning '(illegitimate) child's alleged father'.

Baisbrown(e) L 'cowshed edge' ON, place (–e) in Westmorland.

Baker O 'baker' OE; occurs all over England, though rarer in the north. 33rd commonest surname in England and Wales in 1853, 23rd in USA in 1939.

Bakewell L 'stream/spring of (an AS called) Badeca (a name connected with ?'pledge')' OE; place in Derbys.

Balch See **Belch**. A Wilts–Somerset surname.

Balderston(e) L 'farm of (an AS called) Bold Army' OE; two places (–n and –ne) in Lancs.

Balding F 'bold man' OE, related to **Bold** as **Harding** is to *hard*.

Baldock L 'Baghdad' in an Old French form. The Knights Templars held the manor in Herts, naming it from some fancied resemblance to the Middle Eastern city, now capital of Iraq and meaning ?'city of (a Muslim dervish called) Dat' Arabic. Guppy found it only in Kent, Notts.

Baldree, Baldrick, Baldr(e)y F 'bold ruler' Germanic (–**rick** is nearest to the original).

Baldwin F 'bold friend' Germanic. Though both elements exist in Old English, the F was brought to England about the time of the Conquest.

Bale(s) See **Bail**; and '(of, i.e.) at the **Bail**'.

Balfe N 'stammering, dumb' Irish.

Balfour L 'village with pasture' Scots Gaelic (second element from British); places in Kincardines and Angus (one in Orkney is modern). Family name of the barons Kinross and the barons Riverdale.

Balhatchet N 'give the axe' OF, for an executioner.

Balkwell, Balkwill Versions of **Bakewell**, though chiefly in Bucks, Glos.

Ball N '(fat as a) ball' ME or 'bald' (a *ball* being a bare patch or white streak) ?OE. Or L 'round hill, knoll' OE. Or F *Balle* ON.

Ballamy Version of **Bellamy** seen in Devon.

Ballard N 'bald' ?OE+OF suffix; cf. **Ball**. Chiefly a Worcs surname.

F: *first name*   L: *local name*   N: *nickname*   O: *occupational name*

Ballester O 'crossbowman' OF (original best seen in Channel Islands surname **Larbalestier**, where **L–** shows definite article); ultimately from *ballista* 'military catapult' Latin (cf. *ballistics*).

Ballinger Corruption of **Beringer**. Mainly a Glos surname.

Ballister See **Ballester**.

Balmer O 'spicer, ointment-seller' OF.

Balsden L 'Bold's valley' OE; place (Balsdean) in Sussex. But **Balsdon** is chiefly a Devon surname, and may be from some '–hill' name unidentified.

Balshaw L 'rounded/smooth **Shaw**' OE; place in Lancs.

Bamford L 'ford with a footbridge (literally beam)' OE; places in Derbys, Lancs.

Bampfylde L 'bean field' OE.

Bancroft See **Bencroft**; place in Cambs, and common as field-name in Northants, but surname found chiefly in Ches–Derbys–West Yorks.

Banfield L 'bean field' OE; chiefly a Herefords surname.

Banham L 'homestead where beans grow' OE; place in Norfolk.

Banister O 'basket (-maker)' OF, a metonym. No connection with the *banister* of a stairs, but ?sometimes from **Ballester**.

Banker L 'dweller on a hillside/bank' ON+**–er**.

Bank(e)s L 'of (i.e. at) the hillside/bank' ON, or a plural; but surnames such as **Bankhouse** existed, and may have been reduced. A Danelaw surname.

Bannar, Banner O 'banner-/standard-bearer' OF; or 'one who summons/proclaims/heralds' OE and OF; **–ar** appears in the north more than **–er**.

Bannerman O 'one who carries a banner, standard-bearer' OF+OE. Chiefly a Scots surname.

Bannister See **Banister**.

Baragwanath N 'wheaten bread' Cornish.

Barbary F Usual medieval English form of *Barbara* 'foreign/barbarian woman' Greek – the kind of foreigner who could make only unGreek noises like *ba-ba*; virgin martyr, the saint efficacious against lightning.

Barber (and Scots **Barbour**) O 'barber' OF, who was also liable to take surgery and dentistry in his stride. Very common in Ches.

Barclay L 'birch wood' OE; places Berkeley, Glos, Berkley, Somerset, and Barklye, Sussex; **–er–** becomes **–ar–** as in **Clark**. Now chiefly a Scots surname – descendants of a Glos **Berkeley** who settled in David I's reign.

Bardell Corruption of **Bardolph**.

Barden L 'barley valley' OE; place in West Yorks, but place in North Yorks might equally be 'barn valley' OE.

Bardolph F ' ?bright wolf' Germanic; now tainted by its disreputable connection with Falstaff.

Bardsley L 'clearing of (an AS called) Warrior Counsel' OE; place in Lancs.

Barford L 'barley ford' (i.e. used in its transport) OE; places in five counties. But Little B—, Beds, is 'ford at the birches' OE; and place in Surrey is '(AS called) Bear's ford' OE. Chiefly a Northants surname, and a place in Northants.

Barker O 'tanner' ON+–**er**; he stripped bark from trees for tanning, and prepared it; or 'shepherd' OF (Modern French *berger*), with –*er*– becoming –**ar**– as in **Clark**. Very common in Yorks.

Barkham L 'river-meadow with birches' OE; places in Berks, Sussex.

Barkway L 'track through birches' OE; place in Herts.

Barlow(e) L 'barley hill' OE, place in Lancs; or 'barley/barn clearing' OE, place in West Yorks; or 'boar wood' or 'barley clearing' OE, place in Derbys; all –ow; last two would be better spelt –ley. Chiefly a Ches–Lancs, Notts surname, but –**e** is rare.

Barnabe(e), **Barnaby** F dim. 'Barnabas (= son of consolation)' Hebrew; Saint Paul's missionary companion.

Barnard Commoner version of **Bernard**, –**er**– becoming –**ar**– as in **Clark**. Guppy found it abundantly in Essex.

Barne N 'child, youngster, young knight' ON (cf. Modern Scots *bairn*); or 'warrior' OE. Or F 'bear' ON. Or L 'barn', see **Barnes**.

Barnes L 'barns' (strictly speaking, *barley* houses) OE, locality, or place in Surrey; or 'of (i.e. at) the barn', genitive rather than plural. Or F '(son) of (one of the first three suggested meanings of) **Barne**'. Family name of the barons Gorell.

Barnet(t) F dim. '**Barnard**'. Or L '(place cleared by) burning' OE; locality, or places in Herts, Middx.

Barney L 'barley/barn island' OE; place in Norfolk.

Barnfather See **Bairnsfather**.

Barnfield L 'barn (strictly speaking *barley* house) field' OE.

Barnham L 'homestead of Warrior/Bear' OE/ON+OE; places in Norfolk, Suffolk, Sussex. The showman **Barnum** claimed descent from an English titled family B—.

Barnstable L Ekwall suggests either '**Staple** belonging to (an AS called) Beard' OE or 'post for mooring warships' OE; town (–aple) in Devon.

F: *first name*   L: *local name*   N: *nickname*   O: *occupational name*

Barnwell L 'spring/stream of the warriors' or 'of (an A S called) Warrior' OE, place in Cambs; or 'stream by a burial-mound' OE, two places in Northants.

Baron O 'baron' OF; from rank or title, or from service in a baronial household, or from the courtesy title of certain freemen of the Cinque Ports, London, and York. But ?sometimes N, from pride or haughty bearing. Mainly a Lancs–Yorks surname.

Barraby L 'farm on the hill(s)' ON; places (Barrowby) in Lincs and (two) West Yorks.

Barraclough L 'dell with a grove' (cf. **Bear**, **Clough**) OE; lost place in ?West Yorks.

Barrat(t) N 'commerce, chaffering' or 'trouble' or 'fraud' or 'contention, strife' OF – all these meanings could lead to Ns. But ?sometimes O 'cap-/bonnet-(maker)' OF, a metonym.

Barrell O 'barrel(-maker)' OF, a metonym. Or N for a fat man, or for a sozzled one. Sometimes a reduced form of **Barwell**.

Barrett See **Barratt**, of which it is the far commoner form.

Barringer Form of **Beringer**.

Barrington L The Glos place is 'farm of the followers of (an A S called) Warrior' OE; the Cambs and Somerset places belonged to tribal leaders of more evasive names. Chiefly a Somerset surname.

Barron See **Baron**.

Barrow L 'at the grove' or 'at the hill/mound' OE, relics of a dative noun after a lost preposition; places in nine counties and mostly meaning the former. But Barrow-in-Furness was ??fancifully named from Barra in the Outer Hebrides ('St Barr's Island' ON) +'island' ON. Surname of Sussex–Kent, Lancs.

Barry L 'rampart, suburb under a rampart' OF – the origin of Madame **Dubarry** (= 'of the rampart'); or ?'birch, brushwood' or ??'height in the field' Scots Gaelic, place in Angus; and Nest de Barri, in Sussex 1185, sounds Welsh (as if from Barry, Glam). Or N 'fair head' Irish or 'like a spear' Irish. 71st commonest surname in Ireland in 1890.

Barsby L 'farm of (a Norseman called) Child' ON; place in Leics.

Barson F 'son of (dim). **Bartholomew**'.

Barter O 'barterer, exchanger' OF (cf. **Barratt**); or in sense of N 'squabbler'.

Bartholomew F 'son of Talmai (= abounding in furrows)' Hebrew; the Apostle, whose first name was Nathanael. Guppy counted it only in Kent, Lincs.

Bartle F dim. '**Bartholomew**'; surname of Notts, Cornwall.

Bartlet(t) F double dim. '**Bartholomew**'; common in Dorset–Somerset, Oxon.

Bartley L 'birch wood/clearing' OE; places in Hants, Worcs.

Barton L 'barley farm' OE, but in Middle English 'demesne farm kept for the lord's use, grange for storing his crop'; still used in the south for 'farmyard' OE. There are places of this name in two dozen English counties.

Bartram See **Bertram**; –er– becomes –ar– as in **Clark**. A Notts surname. Also spelt **Bartrum**.

Barwell L 'boar stream' OE; place in Leics.

Barwick L 'barley/corn farm, grange' OE; places in Norfolk, Somerset, West Yorks; from **Berwick**, –er– becoming –ar– as in **Clark**.

Baseley Feminine form of **Basil**.

Basil F 'kingly' Greek, via Latin, to Old French; normally a feminine F in medieval England, but occasionally male, ?with reference to Saint Gregory of Nyssa's great brother (†379).

Baskerville, Basketfield, Baskwell L 'place in the bushes' OF; place (Boscherville) in Eure. Counted by Guppy only in Ches.

Bass(e) N 'short, dwarfish, lowly' OE. **Basset(t)** dim. '**B—**'.

Bassil(l) See **Basil**.

Bassingthwai(gh)te L '**Thwaite**' ON 'of (a Norman nicknamed) Bastun (= stick)' OF; place (Bassenthwaite) in Cumberland.

Bastable Form of **Barnstable**, seen chiefly in Dorset.

Bastard N 'bastard' OF.

Basten, Bastian, Bastien, Basti(o)n F dim. '**Sebastian**'; –tion no doubt linked by folk-etymology with fortification.

Batchelar, Batchelder, Batcheldor, Batchel(l)er, Batchel(l)or, Batchelour See **Bachelor**.

Bate F dim. '**Bartholomew**'. Or O 'boat(man)' OE, in a northern dialect form. Or N 'profit, gain, good husbandry' OE or ON. Occurrence in 13th century of surname preceded by *of* or *de* suggests a transferred meaning like L 'good pasture'. **Bates(on)** '(son)/son of **B—**'; –s mostly a Midlands surname.

Bateman O 'servant of **Bate**'; such –**man** surnames were common in Yorks. Or O 'boatman' OE (cf. **Bate**).

Bath Must sometimes be L, from the Somerset city, 'baths' OE; but Reaney's five variants of a Welsh *Ap*– surname are impressive. Guppy counted it only in Kent and Cornwall.

Bather F 'son of Atha' Welsh; **Bathers**, '(son) of **B—**', is still found in North Wales, and **Batho** in Salop.

F: *first name*   L: *local name*   N: *nickname*   O: *occupational name*

Batram, Batrim, Batrum Forms of **Bartram.**

Batt Of many possible origins. Each of the meanings of **Bate** suggests itself. Or N 'bat' (but this is a late word, and the Middle English word for the beast was *bakke*) or 'cudgel' ?OE/?OF/?Welsh. Or whatever the Old English F *Bata* meant. Guppy counted it only in Somerset. **Batts** '(son) of **B**—'.

Batten F double dim. '**Bartholomew**'; a south-west surname.

Batt(e)rick See **Badrick.**

Batterson F Early spelling suggests that this is 'son of **Batten**'.

Battey, Battie, Batty(e) dim. '**Batt**'; **-ty** a West Yorks surname.

Baud N 'sprightly, cheerful' OF.

Bax N '(son) of **Back**'. Or L 'of (i.e. at) the ridge' OE.

Baxenden, Baxendine L 'valley where (good flat) bakestones are found' OE; place (**-den**) in Lancs.

Baxter O 'baker' (especially female; cf. *spinster*, a female spinner) OE.

Bayl(e)y, Baylie(s), Baylis(s) See **Bailey**; **-s** may show '(son) of/at the' F/L meanings; but **-lis(s)** may be from *baillis* 'bailiff' OF.

Baynton F 'farm of (an A S called) Bǣga (= ?ring, bracelet)' OE; place in Glos.

Bazel(e)y, Bazell(e), Bazley Feminine forms of **Basil**; **-zely** and **-zley** are Northants surnames.

Beach, Beacham See **Beech, Beauchamp.**

Beachcroft L '**Croft** at the beech-tree/brook' OE.

Beacon L 'beacon (usually on a hilltop)' OE.

Beade F 'Bede', an Old English F connected with verb meaning 'proclaim, announce'; popularized by the great Northumbrian scholar.

Beadel, Beadell, Beadle O 'beadle, town-crier, apparitor' OE; **Beadles** will be '(son) of/(at the house) of the beadle'.

Beal(e) must usually be N 'beautiful' OF; but in the north-east it may be L, from Beal (Northumberland) 'hill with bees' OE or Beal (West Yorks) 'nook by loops (of the River Aire)' OE.

Beaman, Beamand, Beament See **Beaumont**; **Beaman** could also be for **Beeman.**

Beamer O 'trumpeter' OE.

Beamish L 'beautiful mansion' OF; place in Co. Durham.

Bean O 'bean(-seller/-grower)' OE, a metonym. Or N 'bean' as a thing of no worth; or 'pleasant, kindly' ME from ?OF (cf. Modern French adverb *bien*); or 'ready, willing, obedient' ON (spelt in Middle English *bain, bein, beane*). Scots surname is sometimes ?F dim. 'life' Scots Gaelic.

Bear(e) L 'pasture, (especially) swine-pasture' or 'grove' or 'barley' all OE; –e may sometimes show a dative after a lost preposition. The incidence of this surname, and of **Beer**, in the south-west involves also the town of Beer, Devon, and numerous places called Bere/Beer in Devon, Dorset, Hants, Somerset. Rarely, N 'bear' (the animal) OE may be the origin.

Beard N 'beard' OE; generations after the Conquest were in general clean-shaven. A Midlands surname, and incidence in Derbys suggests also L 'bank, hillside' OE; place in Derbys.

Beaton F dim. 'Beatrice (= bringer of joy)' Latin; but a family tradition claims L ' ?gravel, cement, bitumen' OF, place (Béthune) in Pas-de-Calais. Mrs **Beeton**'s name is a variant, and the defeatist **Beaten**.

Beatson F 'son of (dim.) Beatrice' (see **Beaton**).

Beattie, **Beatty** Scots and Cumberland–Westmorland versions of (dim.) **Bate**.

Beauchamp L 'lovely field' OF; various places in France; earliest settlers were from Beauchamps, Manche. Often perverted to **Beacham**, **Beecham**.

Beauclerk N 'fine' OF '**Clark**'. Family name of the dukes of St Albans.

Beaumont L 'lovely hill' OF; five places in Normandy; earliest settlers were from Beaumont-le-Roger, Eure. Family name of the viscounts Allendale.

Beavan, **Beaven** Forms of **Bevan** ?influenced by *heaven*.

Beaver L 'beautiful view' OF; place (Belvoir) in Leics. Or N 'beaver' OE (cf. **Beverley**).

Beaves, **Beavis** N (early used as F) 'handsome/dear son' OF. Or L 'Beauvais' (capital of the Gaulish tribe *Bellovaci*) OF from Gaulish; place in Oise.

Bebb F from OE masculine *Bebba* or feminine *Bebbe* (the town of Bamborough is named after Queen Bebbe, wife of King Æthelfrith), of unknown meaning and not related to 15th-century *bebbing* 'tippling', which is from Latin *bib–*. Chiefly a North Wales surname.

Bebbington L 'farm of **Bebb**'s people' OE; Ches place (Bebington) and surname.

Beck L 'stream' ON; or from one of the places Bec in Normandy, with same ON meaning. Or N 'beak, big-nose' OF; or 'pick-axe, mattock' OE, sometimes in use as a F, sometimes O for a maker/seller.

Becket(t) N 'little mouth/beak' OF (Saint Thomas **Becket**'s spurious arms, three Cornish choughs or becquets OF, are simply a heraldic pun). Sometimes L 'bee cottage/hive' OE, place in Berks; or '(AS called) Bicca's cottage' OE, place in Devon; very doubtfully 'top of

---

F: *first name* L: *local name* N: *nickname* O: *occupational name*

the stream (literally beck-head)' ON. **Beckett** is the family name of the barons Grimthorpe.

Beckford L 'ford of (an AS called) Becca' OE; the personal name occurs in the oldest English poem, *Widsith*, and may mean 'pick-axe, mattock' or 'beck, stream'; place in Worcs.

Beckles L 'pasture on a stream' ON+OE; place (Beccles) in Suffolk.

Beckwith L 'beech wood' OE+ON; place in West Yorks.

Bedale L 'Bede's nook' OE (see **Beade**); place in North Yorks.

Beddoe(s), Beddow, Beddow(e)s F dim. '**Meredith**', and '(son) of B–'. Chiefly Salop surnames.

Bedford L 'Bede's ford' OE (cf. **Beade**), the Beds town; and a Hunts and Herts surname.

Bedward F 'son' (from Welsh *Ap–*) 'of **Edward**'.

Bedwell L 'spring/stream with a bucket/butt' OE; places in Essex, Herts, Middx.

Beech L 'beech-tree' or 'stream' OE, hard to tell apart. **Beecher** 'dweller at the **B—**'.

Beecham See **Beauchamp**.

Beecher L As with other –er names, the force of the suffix appears to be 'one who lives by a beech-tree' OE.

Beechey L 'beech-hedge/-enclosure' OE.

Beechwood L 'beech wood' OE.

Beedell See **Beadel**. Chiefly a Devon surname.

Beeman O 'beekeeper' OE. Or see **Beaumont**.

Beer(e) See **Bear**, with no reference to strong drink. Mainly a Devon surname.

Beeton See **Beaton**.

Belch N 'belch' OE, for a man given to eructation, or (from same origin) 'pride, arrogance'. But sometimes L (as in our *balk*) 'beam, bank, ridge' OE.

Belcher Possibly N 'belcher' or L 'dweller at the ridge' (see **Belch**); but more likely to be N 'good sir(e), grandfather' OF, or 'nice face' OF (cf. *cheer*). A Berks–Bucks–Oxon surname. Also **Belchier**.

Beld(h)am, Beldom N 'fine lady' OF, eventually a sneer for a hag.

Belgian N 'handsome leg' OF.

Belgrave L Originally 'grove where martens live' OE, but *merde* (OE *mearth* 'marten') was misunderstood as 'dung' OF and euphemized to *bel* 'lovely' OF; place in Leics.

Belham N 'handsome man' OF, despite its looking like a place-name.

Bell F dim. 'Isabel', see **Isabell**. Or L '(at the Sign of the) Bell' OE, or for residence by the town bell. Or O, from being the bell-ringer or bellman. Or (especially) N 'handsome, beautiful' OF. So the originator of the surname could be styled variously; F *fitz Bell*; L *atte Belle*; O *de la Belle*; N *le Bel*. Common in Northd–Co. Durham, the north, and east Midlands. 45th commonest surname in Scotland in 1958, 89th in Ireland in 1890, 33rd in USA in 1939.

Bellamy N 'handsome friend' OF. Guppy found it only in Lincs–Notts and Hunts.

Bellasis L 'lovely site' OF; places (–is and –ize) in three north-eastern counties.

Bellchamber O 'bell-chamber' OE+OF, rather than L, since the ringer would hardly live *in* the church tower.

Bellerby L 'farm of (a Norseman called) Bag' ON; place in North Yorks.

Bellhanger Corruption of **Beringer**, by folk-etymology.

Bellis(s) L 'bell-house, campanile' OE. Or O 'bellows' OE, for a worker/maker of them. Or F 'son' (from Welsh *Ap*–) 'of **Ellis**'.

Bellmaine N 'beautiful hands' OF.

Belt N or O, for a wearer or maker of a 'belt' OE.

Beman(d), Bement See **Beaumont**; –man could also be for **Beeman**.

Bembridge L 'beam/plank bridge' OE, place in IoW; but there is no early form to prove this meaning.

Benbough, Benbow N 'bend-bow' OE, for an archer.

Bence F '(son) of **Benn**'.

Bench L 'riverbank' (as at Stonebench in Glos, on the Severn) or 'terrace' OE.

Bencroft L 'bean **Croft**' OE; place in Northants.

Bendall L 'bean nook' OE; places (Benhall) in Suffolk and (Bendall) in Derbys, but it is chiefly a Suffolk surname, so Benthall 'bent-grass nook' OE, place in Salop, is not a likely origin.

Bendish L 'bean enclosure' OE; places in Essex, Herts. The form **Bendix** has the misleading look of being '(son) of **Benedict**'.

Bendle See **Bendall**.

Benedict F 'blessed' Latin, from the 6th-century saint and founder of the chief monastic order; whence many surnames in **Ben**–. Or sometimes ?N 'bless (you/us)!' Latin *benedicite*, from a favourite exclamation.

Benfield L 'open country with bent-grass' OE or 'bean field' OE.

Benger Version of **Beringer**.

Benjamin F 'son of the south' Hebrew, the youngest of Jacob's sons; found early as a F and surname, and not confined to Jews.

Benn F dim. '**Benedict**'. Rarely ?N 'plump, lumpish' Germanic.

Bennell See **Bendall**.

Bennet(t) F Usual Middle English dims. of **Benedict**, based on Old French forms and much commoner than the original. **–ett** is chiefly found south of the Mersey and Humber; it was the 46th commonest surname in England and Wales in 1853, and 36th in USA in 1939. **Bennet** is the family name of the earls of Tankerville. **Bennetts** '(son) of **B—**'.

Bennion See **Beynon**. Chiefly a surname of Salop–Staffs–Ches.

Bennison F '(son) of **Bennet**', made to look and sound like *benison* 'blessing'; found early in Yorks.

Bennitt(s) See **Bennet(t)**.

Benson F 'son of (dim.) **Benedict**'. Or L 'place of the family/folk of (an AS pioneer called) Benesa' (whose F is connected with *bane* 'slayer') OE; place in Oxon. A Cumberland–Westmorland–Yorks– Lancs surname, so the first element may sometimes be F *Bjorn* 'bear' ON.

Benste(a)d L 'place where beans grow' OE; chiefly a Kent surname.

Bentley L 'clearing covered with bent-grass' OE; places in ten scattered counties with surnames as scattered.

Bentoft L '**Toft** where beans are grown' OE + ON.

Benton L 'place in the bent-grass' (which sounds wretched) or 'bean place/farm' OE; two places in Northants – but Guppy's distribution in Cambs, Kent, Lincs suggests locality names.

Benwell L 'inside the wall' OE; place in Northd between Hadrian's Wall and the Tyne.

Beringer F 'bear (the animal) spear' Germanic (Beringar was one of Charlemagne's Twelve Paladins). Whence, by confusion of consonants, various surnames in **Ba–/Be**+*r/l/n*, and even **Bellhanger**. The feminine form *Berengaria* was the name of Richard I's queen and the famous liner.

Berkeley Older, rarer, and non-Scots form of **Barclay**.

Bernard F 'bear brave' Germanic (or first element may be *beorn* 'warrior' OE). Used long before Saint B— of Clairvaux (†1153) augmented its vogue. Family name of the earls of Bandon.

Berridge L Scots version of **Beveridge**, but also found in Leics– Rutland.

Berrington L 'place attached to a fort/manor' OE; places in Glos– Herefords–Salop–Worcs; but place in Northd is 'hill with a (prehistoric) camp' OE.

Berry See **Bury**. Common in Lancs (from the town of Bury), and further south. Family name of the viscounts Camrose and the viscounts Kemsley.

Berryman O 'man/servant at the manor' OE; common in Cornwall.

Bertalot The OF double dim. which normally yields **Bartlett**.

Bertenshaw See **Birkenshaw**.

Bertram, Bertrand F 'bright raven' Germanic; OF version was –*n*/–*nd*. Much commoner form is **Bartram**.

Berwick See **Barwick**; places in seven counties.

Bes(s)ant, Besent See **Bez(z)ant**; **Besent** a Dorset surname.

Bessemer O 'besom-/broom-maker' OE. But its greatest son invented a process for 'decarbonizing and desiliconizing pig-iron' (*OED*).

Best N 'beast' OF, for animal savagery or stupidity; or ?'best' OE. Family name of the barons Wynford.

Best(i)man O 'man who looks after beasts' OF+OE.

Betchley L 'clearing of (an A S called) Betti' OE; place (Beachley) in Glos, earlier known as *Bettesley*.

Bethel(l) F 'son' (from Welsh *Ap*–) 'of Ithel' (see *Idle*); or dim. 'Elizabeth' (see **Isabell**). No connection with Jacob. **Bethell** is the family name of the barons Westbury.

Betteridge Despite the L look, see **Badrick**.

Betterson, Bettison F 'son of **Beaton**'.

Betton L 'farm of (an A S called) Ring' OE, place (B—Abbots) in Salop; or 'farm by a stream' OE, place (B— in Hales) in Salop. Or a form of **Beaton**.

Bevan F 'son' (from Welsh *Ap*–) 'of Evan' (see **Evans**). Welsh and Border surname.

Beveridge N 'drink, liquor to clinch a bargain, liquor by way of a tip' OF; the bestower or recipient in these well-documented customs.

Beverley L 'beaver stream' OE; place in East Yorks. The beaver was not yet extinct in England in the medieval period.

Bevin N 'drink wine' OF. But sometimes for **Bevan**.

Bew N 'handsome, beautiful' OF.

Bewick L 'bee farm' OE; places in Northd, East Yorks, and a Northd surname.

Bewley L 'beautiful place' OF; places in Co. Durham, Kent, Westmorland, and (Beaulieu) Hants; but place in Wilts is 'clearing with gadflies' OE.

Bewsher See **Belcher**, in its last two meanings.

Bexley L 'box-tree wood/clearing' OE; place in Kent.

Beynon F 'son' (from Welsh *Ap*–) 'of Eynon' (see **Ennion**). Chiefly a South Wales surname.

Bez(z)ant N 'gold coin of a type first minted at Byzantium, city of Byzas' (the leader of the Megarian expedition that founded it *c.*

F: *first name*   L: *local name*   N: *nickname*   O: *occupational name*

658 B.C.) Greek; in heraldry, a golden roundel – three make a pawn-broker's sign.

Bibb(e)y F double dim. '**Isabell**'; found in Staffs and Yorks in 1200s, and now chiefly in Lancs.

Bible F dim. '**Isabell**'.

Bickerstaff(e), **Bickersteth** L 'beekeepers' staithe/landing-place' OE; place (–affe) in Lancs.

Bickerton L 'beekeepers' place' OE; places in five counties.

Biddick L 'by the ditch' OE; place in Co. Durham. But a Cornwall surname.

Biddle See **Beadel**; chiefly a Glos surname.

Biddulph L 'by the digging/mine' OE; place in Staffs.

Bigg N 'big, strong' ME; but some early forms are preceded by *de* and *atte* (though no topographical term survives in *MED*), and there is ?a connection with ON stems meaning 'build' and 'inhabitant'. **Biggs** F '(son) of **B**—'; much commoner than –g, especially in Bucks.

Biggerstaff See **Bickerstaff**.

Biggin L 'building, house' ME from ON; locality, or places in six counties.

Bighead N 'big head' OE – physically rather than temperamentally.

Billingsley L 'clearing of (an A S called) ?Swollen/Incensed' OE; place in Salop.

Bindless, **Bindloss** O 'wolf-binder/-catcher' OE+OF.

Bindon L 'inside the hills' OE; place in Dorset.

Bing L 'hollow' OE, or 'stall, bin; slag/refuse heap' ON.

Bingham L 'homestead at a **Bing**' OE, or the first element may contain an owner's name; place in Notts, and a surname of Notts–Derbys–Lincs.

Bingley L 'clearing with a hollow' OE or 'clearing with a (slag/refuse) heap' ON+OE; place in West Yorks.

Binks L 'of (i.e. at) the bank' OE, or a plural; cf. *bench*.

Binns L 'of (i.e. at) the bin/manger/stall' OE, or a plural as at **B**—, in Southowram, West Yorks, the origin of the local family; or ?a topographical use as 'hollows'. Or O 'bin(-maker)', a metonym.

Binste(a)d L 'place where beans grow' OE; places in Hants, IoW, Sussex, all originally beginning Bene–; cf. **Benste(a)d**.

Birbeck Form of place-name and surname **Birkbeck**.

Birch L 'birch-tree' OE; southern surname of which the northern form is **Birk**.

Birchall L 'nook with birch-trees' OE; locality, or place (now Birtles 'little birches' OE) in Ches. Chiefly a Lancs–Ches surname.

Birchenall L 'birch nook/hill' OE.

Bircumshaw See **Birkenshaw**.

Bird N 'fledgeling, bird' OE, from occupation or resemblance; or 'woman, damsel, sempstress' OE (appears in Middle English as *burd, bird*, etc., and often confused with *bride*). Common from Staffs–Leics–Northants–Norfolk south.

Birk L 'birch-tree' ON; see **Birch**. **Birks** L 'of (i.e. at) the birch-tree', or a plural.

Birkbeck L 'stream in the birches' ON; place in Westmorland.

Birkby L 'Britons' farm' ON; places in Cumberland, Lancs, Yorks.

Birkenshaw L '**Shaw** of birch-trees' OE; place in West Yorks. Reaney lists twenty-two grotesque variants.

Birkett L 'birch-covered hill' OE; places in Cumberland, Lancs.

Birkin L 'birch wood' OE; locality, or place in West Yorks.

Birley L 'clearing with a byre/cowshed', or 'clearing by a fort/manor' OE; three places in Derbys, one (of latter meaning) in Herefords.

Birmingham L 'homestead of the family of (an A S called) ?Warrior/ Protector' OE, the Warwicks city.

Birt See **Bright**. But it may sometimes stand for **Bret**/**Brit** 'Breton', as in the Glos place Westonbirt.

Birtle(s) L 'birch hill(s)' OE; places in Lancs, Ches; –s a Ches surname.

Birtw(h)istle L '(A S called) Chicken's/Fledgeling's river-fork' OE; lost place in Padiham, Lancs.

Bisgood N Reaney assigns this to **Peascod**.

Bish L 'thicket' OE (cf. *bush* and Shelley's second F *Bysshe*); locality, or place in Sussex.

Bishop O 'bishop' OE; not, we hope, the son of a celibate medieval prelate, but one who worked in his household. Or N from appearance or bearing, or from taking the part in a play, or from being a boy-bishop in that absurd ceremony. Mostly a southern surname.

Bishton L 'bishop's farm/manor' OE; places in Glos, Salop, Staffs, Mon.

Bismire N 'disgrace' OE, and therefore a bad character.

Bisp See **Bishop**.

Bispham L 'episcopal estate (literally bishop's homestead)' OE; several places in Lancs, including one in Blackpool.

Biss N 'fine linen' OF, ultimately from Greek; or 'dull/brownish grey' OF (cf. the paintbox colour *green bice*).

Bisset(t) N 'darkish, brownish, greyish' OF.

Bithell See **Bethel(l)**.

F: *first name*   L: *local name*   N: *nickname*   O: *occupational name*

Black N 'black(-haired), dark-complexioned' O E; and cf. **Blake**. 46th commonest surname in Scotland in 1958, 49th in U S A in 1939.

Blackadder L 'black ?swift (stream)' O E + Scots Gaelic; river and place in Berwicks.

Blackborrow L 'black hill' O E; places (–borough) in Devon, Norfolk.

Blackbourn(e), **Blackburn(e)** L 'black stream' O E; Lancs town and places in Cumberland, Co. Durham, West Yorks; or locality names in various spellings.

Blacker must usually be O 'bleacher' O E, the opposite of what it looks like.

Blackford L 'black ford' O E; places in Cumberland, Lancs, Salop, Somerset, and a Somerset surname.

Blacklee, **Blackley** L 'black clearing/wood' O E; locality, or place (–ey) in Lancs.

Blacklock N 'black hair/tress/lock' O E.

Blackman F 'black-haired/dark man' O E, early in use as a F.

Blackmore L 'black moor/forest' O E, places in five counties; or 'black mere/pool' O E, places in Herts, Hants. A Devon–Somerset surname.

Blackshaw L 'black **Shaw**' O E; place in West Yorks. Counted by Guppy only in Ches.

Blackwell L 'black spring/stream' O E; places in seven counties.

Blackwood L 'black wood' O E; locality, or places in West and East Yorks.

Blagden, **Blagdon** L 'black hill' O E; places in Dorset, Devon, Somerset; but place in Northd is 'black valley' O E.

Blagrave, **Blagrove** L 'black grove' O E; locality, or place (–ave) in Berks.

Blake N 'pale' O E (cf. *bleak*); or '**Black**', with another form of the adjective producing a long vowel; thus two contradictory meanings are possible. Guppy found it only in Surrey–Bucks–Berks–Oxon–Hants–Wilts and Cornwall–Devon.

Blakemore L 'black moor/forest' O E, places in Devon, Herts; or 'black mere/pool' O E, places in Ches, Herefords; and cf. **Blackmore**.

Blaker See **Blacker**.

Blamire L 'dark mire' O N. **Blamires** 'of (i.e. at) the **B**—', or a plural, or a place in West Yorks.

Blamphin N 'white bread' O F, for a seller/baker of it.

Blampied, **Blampey** N 'white foot' O F.

Blanchard N 'whitish' O F; it was even the F of the Arthurian Sir Launfal's horse.

Blanchflower N 'white flower' OF, the heroine of a swooning medieval romance with young Floris; mocking when applied to males.

Bland L ?'windy/stormy place' OE, place in West Yorks; the gentle, coaxing adjective arrived far too late to form a surname. Scattered from Cambs to Cumberland.

Blandamore N 'full of love' OF (cf. Modern French *plein*) – the same sort of love as in **Fullalove**.

Blandford L 'ford where blays/gudgeons could be fished' OE; place in Dorset. Even if the story be true that many unclaimed orphans were so named after the total destruction of B— by fire in 1731, the meaning of the surname is unchanged.

Blank N 'white/fair (of skin or hair)' OF.

Blankhorn See **Blenkiron**.

Blatherwick L '(dairy-)farm where ?bladderwort/cardamine grows' OE; place (–wycke) in Northants, and a Notts surname.

Blaxter O 'bleacher' (especially female) OE.

Blaxton L 'black stone' OE; place in West Yorks.

Blaymire(s) See **Blamire(s)**.

Bleakman F 'black(-haired) man' OE.

Bleasdale L 'valley with a white/bare spot' ON (cf. *blaze*); place and surname in Lancs.

Blecher O 'bleacher' OE.

Blencowe L '?top of the ?hill' Welsh+ON; place in Cumberland.

Blenkinship, Blenkinsop(p) L '?top' Welsh+ ? +'**Hope**', or first eight letters may be an owner's name in the genitive; place (–opp) in Northd.

Blenkiron L 'hilltop with a cairn' Welsh; place (Blencarn) in Cumberland. Chiefly a North and East Yorks surname.

Blennerhassett L 'hill farm' Welsh+'hay shieling' ON; place in Cumberland. Oddly dismembered by USA scholar Roland **Blenner-Hassett**.

Blessed N 'blessed, fortunate' OE.

Blewett, Blewitt N 'bluish, pale' OF.

Bligh ME variant of **Blyth(e)**, and thus a strange surname for the uncompromising Captain; sometimes ?N 'starer' ON. Family name of the earls of Darnley.

Blight See **Blyth(e)**; an ugly piece of folk-etymology, but there are nineteen **Blights** to sixteen **Blighs** in the London TD. Chiefly a Cornwall–Devon surname.

Blinman N 'blind man' OE, the *–ndm–* simplified.

F: *first name*   L: *local name*   N: *nickname*   O: *occupational name*

Bliss N 'joy, happiness' OE. But Reaney also takes it back *via Blez* to L 'Blay' in Normandy, of unknown meaning.

Blomfield See **Bloomfield**.

Blondell N dim. 'blond' OF, normally occurring as **Blundell**.

Blood N 'blood' OE, for ?a blood-letter or ?a blood-relative. But also F 'son' (from Welsh *Ap*–) 'of Lloyd', which has reached Ireland.

Bloom O By metonymy for **Bloomer**; but now usually a Jewish N 'flower' German.

Bloomer O 'maker of blooms (iron/steel ingots)' OE; hence the garments devised by Mrs Amelia Jenks **B**— of New York.

Bloomfield L 'Blonville-sur-Mer' in Calvados; the owner's name meant 'fair, blond'. English hamlets meaning 'field of flowers' OE may have contributed no surname. Chiefly surname of Essex–Norfolk–Suffolk.

Bloor(e), Blore L ' ?hill (literally swelling, blister)' OE; place (Blore) in Staffs, and a Staffs group of surnames.

Blount Same as **Blunt**, but imitating the OF nasal.

Bloxham L 'homestead of (an AS called) Blocc' OE; places (–ham, –holm) in Oxon, Lincs.

Bloxon Despite the suggestion of '–son', probably from **Bloxham**.

Bluett See **Blewett**.

Blundell N dim. 'blond, fair-headed' OF. See **Blunt**.

Blunden N dim. 'blond' OF, as in surname Blondin found especially in Midi. Every surname in **–den** looks L (*–dene* 'valley' OE), but no place is known.

Blunt N 'blond, fair-headed' OF.

Bly ME variant of **Blyth(e)**

Blyth(e) N 'cheerful, gentle' OE. Or L, with reference to 'gentle/pleasant (streams)'; places in five counties. Pathetically, this was the original first syllable of Bethnal Green.

Blythin, Blythyn F ?'wolf-cub' Welsh.

Boar N 'boar' OE.

Boatswain O 'boatman, bosun' ON and OE.

Boatwright O 'boat-builder' OE; Reaney shows its long stay in Suffolk.

Boddington L 'farm/down of Bōta's people' OE (his name may be connected with *bōt* 'help'), places in Glos and Northants; chiefly a Warwicks surname.

Bodenham L 'homestead of (an AS called) Boda' OE (?of similar meaning to **Beade**); places in Herefords, Wilts, and chiefly a Herefords surname.

Body N 'body' OE, perhaps for striking physique.

Bodycote L 'cottage(s) of Boda' (see **Bodenham**) or 'cottage(s) of Boda's people' OE; place (Bodicote) in Oxon.

Bogg L 'bog' Irish. Or N 'puffed-up, saucy' ME.

Bokenham L 'homestead of (an A S called) He-Goat' OE; four places (Buckenham) in Norfolk.

Bolam L 'at the tree-trunks/planks (forming a bridge)' OE or ON, dative plural after lost preposition; places in Co. Durham, Northd, and a Northd surname.

Bold N 'bold, brave' OE. Or L, see **Bolton**; locality, or places in Lancs, Salop.

Boldero(e) F See **Baldree**.

Bolderson See **Balderston**.

Boldon L 'knob/?house hill' OE (cf. **Bolton**); places in Co. Durham, Northd.

Bolingbroke L 'brook of the family/folk of (an A S called) Bull' OE; place in Lincs.

Bolland L 'land by a river (Ribble)-bend' OE; place (Bolland/Bowland in Lancs–West Yorks; surname found in these counties.

Bollen See **Bullen**.

Bollom L 'at the tree-trunks/planks' (cf. *bole*) OE dative plural; locality, or one of the places (Bolam, Bolham) in Co. Durham, Northants, Northd.

Bolt L 'dwelling' OE, as in **Bolton**. An O name for a 'maker of bolts/ bars/missiles' OE is much less likely. Guppy counted it only in Devon.

Bolton L 'place with houses/huts, group of buildings, centre of a village' OE (the first element occurring as bothel/bottle/bold); places in four northern counties (many in Yorks); yet found as a surname even away from the north.

Bompas, Bompus L 'good passage/crossing' OF. Or N 'good pace' OF.

Bonamy N 'good friend' OF; especially a Guernsey surname.

Bond O 'husbandman, peasant', eventually 'serf' OE or ON.

Bondfield See **Bonfield**.

Bone N 'good' OF. **Bones** may be '(son) of B—' or a N of the **Smallbones** type.

Boney is probably a N 'bony' OE, or 'long-legged'.

Bonfield L From one of the three places Bonneville 'nice place' OF in Normandy. Chiefly a Herts surname.

Bonger N from a favourite exclamation 'good day!' OF.

F: *first name* L: *local name* N: *nickname* O: *occupational name*

Bonham, Bonhomme N 'good man' OF; there was a religious order of *Bonshommes*, who had the fine church at Edington, Wilts. But also L, since there was a William de **Bonham** in 1225, 1269; no place now known, but **–ham** is 'homestead/river-meadow' OE.

Boniface F 'good fate' Latin; martyr of Tarsus, several popes, and above all the name in religion of the great English saint, Winfrid (†755), apostle of the Germans. Generic term for an inn-keeper since Farquhar so named his in *The Beaux' Stratagem* (1707).

Bonner N 'gentle, gracious, courteous' OF (cf. *debonair*, which now too often means suave and foppish). Also **Bonnar**.

Bonser N 'good sir' OF. Counted by Guppy only in Northants, Notts.

Boocock See **Bowcott**.

Boodle L See first element of **Bolton**; a far cry from a London club.

Bookbinder O 'book-binder' OE.

Booker O 'maker of books' OE or one who *bouked*, a 'bleacher' ME.

Bool See **Bull**.

Boon N 'good' OF. Or L 'Bohun', from Bohon (meaning unknown) in Manche. Chiefly a Staffs surname.

Boorman O '**Bower** servant' OE.

Boosey L 'cow-shed' OE.

Boot(e) O 'boot(-maker/seller)' OF, a metonym.

Booth L 'hut, shed, shelter' ON; its dative plural, '(at) the huts', appears in Bootham Bar, York. A northern surname, especially Ches.

Boothby L 'farm with huts/sheds' ON; places in Cumberland, Lincs.

Boothman O 'worker at a **Booth**' ON+OE.

Boothroyd L 'clearing with huts/sheds' ON+OE; place in West Yorks.

Bootle L 'house, dwelling' OE (cf. **Bolton**); places in Cumberland, Lancs.

Bore See **Boar**.

Borland L 'board land (i.e. land held on the rental of a food supply or table)' ON+OE; various places in Scotland spelt Bor–/Bord–/Bore–, one with a final –s, and chiefly a Scots surname.

Borley L 'boar wood' OE; places in Essex (with a much-haunted rectory) and (–rel–) Worcs.

Borton See **Burton**. Still a Staffs surname, and Northants.

Boscawen L 'house by the elder-tree' Cornish; place in Cornwall. Family name of the viscounts Falmouth.

Boss(e)y N 'hunch-backed' OF.

Boston L '(Saint) Botulf's stone (?cross from which he preached)', place in Lincs; his F is Germanic, ?from Slav, or with second element ?'wolf', and 'stone' is OE.

Bosworth L Two places in Leics; but whereas (Husbands) B— means 'enclosure of (an AS called) Boar' OE, the owner of (Market) B— was called Bōsa; surname of Leics–Rutland and Beds.

Bothamley L See **Bottomley**. But sometimes perhaps = Barthomley 'clearing of the dwellers at the **Barton**' OE; place in Ches.

Bott N 'toad' OF. Rarely ? OE *Botta*, pet form of some F in *Bot*– 'remedy' – cf. *bootless*.

Bottom(e) L 'dell, valley-bottom' OE. **Bottoms** 'of (i.e. in) the dell', or plural. Stress on the second syllable is a hapless attempt to conceal a perfectly respectable meaning.

Bottomley L 'clearing in a dell' OE;' place and surname in West Yorks.

Bottomshaw See **Birkenshaw**.

Boucher O 'butcher' OF.

Bough L 'arched bridge' OE – one of the meanings of *bow*; locality, or places in Devon, Middx. The only member of the family in *DNB* came from Somerset. Sometimes pronounced *Boff*.

Boughton L 'place in the beeches' OE; places in Ches, Kent (four); but places in other counties are '(AS called) Stag's place' OE, and B— Park, Worcs, seems to have been the same as **Bolton**. Chiefly a Bucks surname.

Boult See **Bolt**.

Boulter O 'meal-sifter' OF. Chiefly a Worcs surname.

Boulton L See **Bolton**; or 'farm of (an AS called) Bola (= ?bull)' OE; place in Derbys – but Guppy counted it only in Glos–Worcs–Salop.

Boumphrey F 'son' (from Welsh *Ap*–) of **Humphrey**'.

Bound(s) Usually a version of **Bond** (cf. **Boundy**); and '(son) of B—'; –s is chiefly a Herefords surname.

Boundy See **Bond**; –y reproduces the –*i* inflexion of the Old Norse form.

Bourn(e) See **Burn**; the –e can derive from the organic final vowel of the Old English nominative, or be dative singular after a lost preposition; locality, or places in several counties.

Boutflour N 'sift flour' OF, for a miller.

Bouverie L 'ox farm' OF. A Huguenot surname.

Bovey L From B— Tracy or from North B—, Devon, on the River Bovey, a Keltic word which Ekwall compares with Bobbio in Italy. Chiefly a Devon surname.

Bow L 'arch, vault, bridge' OE; locality, or places in Berks, Devon, London.

F: *first name*   L: *local name*   N: *nickname*   O: *occupational name*

Bowcher See **Butcher** and perhaps **Belcher**.

Bowcott F dim. '**Baldwin**'+familiar **Cock**.

Bowden L Many places are called Bowden/din/don: Devon (eighteen) and Derbys, 'curved hill' OE; Wilts, 'above the hill' OE; Ches, from AS hill-owner called *Boga* (?related to *boy*); Leics, from feminine AS hill-owner called *Bugge*(= ? 'big, proud'; or 'bug'; or cf. **Bugg**). Rarely ?F see **Bowdoin**. Found in Devon–Cornwall and Derbys–Ches.

Bowdoin F 'bold friend' Germanic; cf. *Baudouin*, OF version of our **Baldwin**. Huguenot surname established in USA.

Bowen F 'son' (from Welsh *Ap*-) 'of **Owen**'. Chiefly a South Wales and Border surname.

Bower L 'dwelling, chamber, woman's room' OE, perhaps from service equivalent to that of **Chambers**; when Fair Rosamund received Henry II it was not, we regret to say, in an arbour or pergola in the garden; also places in Somerset, Sussex, etc. Sometimes ?O for **Bowyer**. **Bowers** is plural or 'of (i.e. at) the **Bower**'.

Bowerman O 'one who works in a **Bower**' OE.

Bowes L 'bows, curves (i.e. ?river-bends, curving valleys)' OE; place in North Yorks, and a North Yorks surname.

Bowie N 'yellow(-haired)' Scots Gaelic. The horrible knife was invented by Colonel James **B**— of Texas (†1836) or ?his brother.

Bowker, Bowkett, Bowland See **Butcher, Bowcott, Bolland**.

Bowler O 'bowl-maker/-seller', or N 'hard drinker'; both from 'bowl' OE. A surname of Derbys–Ches–Lancs.

Bowles L 'courtyards, huts, hovels' OF; place (Bouelles) in Seine-Maritime. Guppy counted it in Wilts, Kent.

Bowley L 'bullock pasture' OE; locality, or place in Herefords.

Bowmaker O 'bow-maker' OE.

Bowman O 'bowman, archer' OE.

Bown has the same origins as **Boon**, perhaps with an extra force of ME *boun* 'ready', from ON. Guppy counted it in Somerset, Derbys.

Bowness L 'bow (i.e. rounded) headland' ON, place in Cumberland; or 'bulls' headland' ON, place in Westmorland; each may contain Old English elements.

Bowra(h) L 'dweller at the **Bower**' OE (+–*er* corrupted); Kent surnames.

Bowring O 'dweller/servant at a **Bower**' OE.

Bowser N 'fair sir, grandfather' OF; cf. **Belcher**. Guppy counted it only in Lincs.

Bowyer O 'maker/seller of bows' OE.

Box L 'box-tree' OE; locality, or places in Glos, Herts, Wilts. Sometimes ?N, as boxwood was associated in Middle English with the colour 'yellow'.

Boxley L 'box-tree wood/clearing' OE; place in Kent.

Boxwell L 'spring/stream in the box-trees' OE; place in Glos.

Boyce L 'wood' OF. Or a Germanic F related to *boy* and meaning 'youth, servant, knave'.

Boyd N 'yellow(-haired)' Scots Gaelic, the F of Lady Macbeth's brother. 90th commonest surname in Scotland in 1958. Family name of the barons Kilmarnock.

Boyes See **Boyce**; or '(son) of the youth/servant'. A surname of Yorks and Hants.

Boyle F (for O B—) 'descendant of ?Having Profitable Pledges' Irish. 47th commonest surname in Ireland in 1890, and (through Irish immigration) 81st in Scotland in 1958. Family name of the earls of Cork and Orrery, Glasgow and Shannon.

Boyter O 'box-maker' OF.

Brabazon L 'man from Brabant (= wooded territory)' OF from Gaulish. The surname may be disreputable; 13th-century Brabançons were thuggish mercenaries who beat up French provinces. Family name of the earls of Meath.

Brabbin, Brabbyn, Braben, Brabham, Brabin L 'Brabant', see **Brabazon**; **Brabner** 'man of Brabant'.

Bracegirdle N 'trouser-belt' OF *braie* or OE *brec* (cf. *breeches*)+OE; early forms do not support the fancy that it denotes a protector wrapped around an archer's 'arm' OF *bras*. Perhaps O, for a manufacturer. Chiefly a Ches surname.

Brackenborough, Brackenbury L 'hill covered with bracken' OE; place (–ough) in Lincs, and –y is a Lincs surname.

Brackenridge L 'ridge overgrown with bracken' OE; locality, or five places (–rigg) in Cumberland.

Bradbourne L 'broad stream' OE; places in Derbys, Kent; cf. **Bourne**.

Bradbrook L 'wide brook' OE.

Bradburn(e) See **Bradbourne**.

Bradbury L 'fort made of boards/planks' OE; place in Co. Durham.

Braddock L 'broad oak' OE. Counted by Guppy only in Ches.

Bradfer N 'arm of iron' OF. No doubt often corrupted to **Bradford**.

Bradfield L 'broad open land' OE; places in five counties.

Bradford L 'wide ford' OE; places in seven counties including Dorset,

F: *first name*   L: *local name*   N: *nickname*   O: *occupational name*

66

Somerset. But see also **Bradfer**. Counted by Guppy only in Dorset–Somerset.

Bradgate L 'wide gate/gap' OE; place in Leics.

Bradley L 'broad wood/clearing' OE; many places in over a dozen counties.

Bradman L See **Bradnam**. Or N 'broad man' OE.

Bradnam L 'at the wide river-meadow/homestead' OE, –n– showing weak dative of adjective after lost preposition and definite article; places (Bradenham) in Berks, Norfolk.

Bradshaw L 'broad **Shaw**' OE; places in Derbys, Lancs, West Yorks.

Bradstreet L 'broad **Street**/(Roman) road' OE.

Bradwell L 'broad stream' OE; places in five counties.

Bragg(e) N 'proud, arrogant; brisk, brave' ME from ?Keltic; –e could show weak adjective after lost definite article. Common Devon surnames.

Braham L Reaney shows how (as with **Graham** from Grantham) this can derive from 'homestead/river-meadow with broom-bushes' OE, places in Cambs and (Bramham) West Yorks; or from Brantham, Suffolk, where the first element is an owner's name; or from elsewhere.

Braithwaite L 'broad **Thwaite**' ON; places in Cumberland, North and West Yorks.

Brake L 'thicket, spinney' OE. Chiefly a Dorset–Somerset surname.

Brakspear See **Breakspear**.

Bramah, Bram(h)all L '**Haugh** (*halh*) where broom grows' OE; place (–hall) in Ches. The surname of Ernest **Bramah** (†1942), despite his *Kai Lung* stories, has no connection with *Brahmin* or any other oriental word.

Brambell L 'bramble' OE, or a version of **Bramhall**.

Bramford L 'ford by the broom-bushes' OE; place in Suffolk.

Bramley L 'clearing/field overgrown with broom' (but sometimes ?'with bramble') OE; places in four counties. A Leics–Lincs–West Yorks surname.

Brampton L 'place where broom grows' OE; places in ten counties.

Bran(n) F 'raven' Scots Gaelic (and Irish, Welsh, Breton).

Branchflower See **Blanchflower**.

Brand F 'sword; torch, firebrand' ON.

Brandon L 'hill covered with broom' OE; places in six counties, though the first element of the Lincs place may be the River Brant 'steep(-sided)' OE. Irish name may be F 'Brendan (= stinking hair)' Irish.

Brandreth L 'burnt clearing' OE (cf. noun *ride*); place in Kent.

Brangwyn(ne) F 'white/fair raven' OW, F of two ladies in Keltic legend, one with the risky job of being Isolde's maid.

Bran(n)igan F (for O B—) 'descendant of (dim.) Raven' Irish.

Brannan (a worse spelling is **Brannon**) (for O/McB—) F anglicized version of Irish names, descendants of men whose names meant '(dim.) sadness' and '(dim.) raven'.

Branthwaite L '**Thwaite** overgrown with broom' OE+ON; two places in Cumberland. Also spelt **Branwhite**.

Brasher, Brasier O 'brazier, brassfounder' OE; but **Brasher** may sometimes be the same as **Brasseur.**

Brasseur O 'brewer' OF.

Bratcher L 'dweller at a **Breach**' OE.

Bratton L 'newly cultivated/broken-up farm' OE; places in Devon, Somerset, Wilts; but places in Salop and Somerset are 'place on a brook' OE.

Braund Chiefly a Devon version of **Brand.**

Bray L 'brow (of a hill)' OE or 'hill' OW; places in Cornwall, Devon; but place in Berks is ?'mud' OF.

Braybrook(e) L 'broad brook' OE; place (–e) in Northants.

Brayer O 'pestle-maker/-seller' OF.

Brayshaw, Brayshay L Yorks versions of **Bradshaw.**

Brayton L 'broad place' ON+OE; places in Cumberland, West Yorks.

Brazier See **Brasher.**

Breach L 'opening, spinney left as a boundary, newly broken/tilled land' OE. Chiefly a Wilts surname.

Breakspear N 'break spear' OE, from some actual feat or blunder in battle or tournament. Nicholas B— was England's only pope, Adrian IV (†1159).

Bream N 'famous, splendid, fierce' OE. Or L, formerly Braham, Essex, West Yorks, 'river-meadow overgrown with broom' OE.

Brearley See **Brierley.**

Brede, Breed(e) L 'plain, broad open space' OE.

Breen L 'hill' Welsh; locality, or place (Brean) in Somerset.

Breese N 'gadfly' OE – but why? Late and near Wales, ?F 'son' (from Welsh *Ap*-) 'of **Rees**'. Counted by Guppy only in North Wales and Norfolk–Suffolk. Also occurs as **Breeze.**

Brelsford L 'ford at the burial/tumulus' OE; place (Brailsford) in Derbys.

Bremner See **Brabham**; from early settlers in east Scotland.

F: *first name*   L: *local name*   N: *nickname*   O: *occupational name*

Brend N 'branded (as a criminal)' OE. But Reaney shows that it is sometimes L 'land cleared by burning' OE.

Brennan If of Irish descent (for O/McB—) see **Brannan**. Otherwise N 'burn-hand' (from the official who executed this savage penalty) ON/OE+OE, or 'burnt-hand' (the victim). 28th commonest surname in Ireland in 1890.

Brent L 'high place' Keltic, or ?'steep' OE; places and eminences in Devon, Somerset; sometimes ?'burnt (place)' OE, from a site so cleared.

Brereton L 'place/farm in the briars' OE, places in Ches and (Brierton) Co. Durham – but the USA family was from Malpas, Ches; or 'hill covered with briars' OE, place in Staffs. A Salop–Ches surname.

Bretherton L 'the brothers' farm' ON+OE; place and surname in Lancs.

Bret(on), Brett(on) L 'Breton' or (as opposed to 'AS') 'Briton' OF – the latter used of Welshmen or Strathclyde Britons. But **Bretton** could be L 'Britons' place' OE, places in Derbys, West Yorks; or = **Bratton**. **Brett** is the family name of the viscounts Esher.

Brew O 'son of the judge' Manx contraction of a *Mc*- name.

Brewer, Brewster O 'brewer' OE. **-ster** is strictly a feminine suffix, but the surname is early used for men. **Brewer** may also be L 'heath' OF or (with same meaning) from place Bruyère in Calvados.

Brian F Keltic (OW/Irish) name containing element *bre* 'hill'; brought by Norsemen to the north from Ireland and by Bretons to the south.

Brice F ?Keltic, of unknown meaning; Saint B— (†444) was successor as bishop of Tours to the ever-popular Saint Martin. Now, alas, he is remembered as the saint on whose day the Danes were massacred.

Bridewell L 'spring/stream with birds' OE; or 'spring dedicated to Saint Bridget' (see **McBride**). The London building was named from the latter; it became a prison too late to make a surname.

Bridge L 'bridge' OE, from dwelling or duties thereat. Commoner in the south than **Briggs**, but counted by Guppy only in Lancs–Derbys. **Bridges** L 'of (i.e. at) the bridge' (rather than a plural); or 'Bruges (= heath, heather)' French version of Flemish, Belgian city.

Bridgeford L 'ford by a bridge' OE; places in Staffs and (–dgf–) Notts.

Bridgeman O 'bridgekeeper' or sometimes 'man living at the bridge' OE; maintenance of a bridge often devolved upon a hermit – or the bridgeman could be a tollkeeper. Family name of the earls of Bradford.

Bridger O 'bridgekeeper' OE. **Bridgers** '(son) of B—', though this may be an illiteracy for **Bridges**; no evidence for meaning 'bridge-builder'.

Bridgewood L 'wood at a bridge' OE or 'birch wood' OE.

Bridgman See **Bridgeman**, which outnumbers it. Found in Devon.

Bridgewater L '**Bridge** of **Walter**' (de Douai, in whose fee it was). The F was pronounced like our *water*, and abbreviated *Wat*; the dropping of –l– in the name of the Somerset town is therefore a good example of folk-etymology.

Bridle O 'bridle' OE, from being expert in making them.

Brierl(e)y L 'clearing with briars' OE; places in Staffs, West Yorks.

Briers L 'briars, brambles' OE.

Brierton and **Brigenshaw** See **Brereton** and **Birkenshaw**.

Brigg(s) L See **Bridge** and **Bridges**, of which these are ON versions and so found chiefly in the Danelaw. (Lincs town Brigg is ?too late a formation to be the origin.)

Brigham L 'homestead by a bridge' OE scandinavianized; places in Cumberland, East Yorks, and a Yorks surname.

Brighouse L 'houses by a bridge' ON+OE; place in West Yorks.

Bright N 'bright, handsome' OE; another form, with –r– in its original place after the vowel, is seen in **Birt/Burt** and Bert–/Bart– Fs.

Brighton L Too early to be from the contracted place-name of Brighton, Sussex; it is from Breighton, East Yorks, 'farm by a bridge' OE.

Brightwell L 'bright spring/stream' OE; places in Berks, Oxon, Suffolk.

Briginshaw and **Briley** See **Birkenshaw** and **Brierley**.

Brill L 'hill hill' OW+OE, tautologically; places in Bucks, Cornwall.

Brimble L 'bramble, blackberry-bush' OE. Chiefly a Somerset surname.

Brimblecombe L 'bramble valley' OE; place in Devon.

Brimmell See **Brimble**.

Brind L 'burnt place, place cleared by burning' OE; place in East Yorks.

Brindley L 'burnt wood/clearing' OE; place in Ches, and a Staffs surname.

Brine Bardsley exhibits a Wilts family spelt thus and also **Bryan** (and **Bryne**).

Brisbane N 'break-bone' OF+OE. The Queensland city was named after a Scots baronet.

Brisco(e) L 'birch wood' ON; places in Cumberland (–o), North Yorks; but place –oe in Cumberland is 'Britons' wood' ON.

F: *first name*   L: *local name*   N: *nickname*   O: *occupational name*

Brisley L 'wood/clearing full of gadflies' OE; place in Norfolk.

Brison F 'son of **Brice**'.

Bristol(l) L 'fort site' OE; places in West Yorks (Birstal), Leics (Birstall), Suffolk, East Yorks (Burstall); corrupted by the familiar city-name – but cities rarely give surnames, the citizens staying put and not taking them elsewhere. Oddly, cf. **Bristow**.

Bristow(e) L '(assembling-)place at the bridge' OE, the city and county of Bristol (originally –stow). The inhabitants still add –*l* to a final vowel (especially to –*a*), as in *pneumonial, Russial, Veronical, etceteral* – but when a native moved elsewhere his new neighbours pronounced his place of origin 'correctly'. Interpretations of the city name as '(Saint) Brig's (sister of Saint Brendan) place', 'bright place', 'breach/gorge place' are frivolous. Sometimes place **Burstow**, Surrey, 'fort place' OE may be involved. See, paradoxically, **Bristol**, and Guppy's count in Lincs.

Brittain, Brittan, Britten, Britt(on) See **Bret(on)**. The high incidence of surname **Britton** in Essex suggests the Bretons who settled in the east after the Conquest.

Broad N 'broad, stout' OE.

Broadbent L 'broad grassy place' OE; cf. **Bentley**. A West Yorks surname.

Broadfoot N 'broad foot' OE.

Broadhead L 'wide headland/hilltop' OE. Or N 'broad head' OE. Chiefly a West Yorks surname.

Broadley L 'broad clearing' OE; a spelling with less historical warrant than **Bradley**. Guppy counted it only in Kent.

Broadribb N 'broad rib(s)' OE.

Broadrick See **Broderick**.

Broadwater L 'wide stream' OE; places in Essex, Sussex.

Broadway L 'wide road' OE; places from Staffs to Kent and Somerset; but place in Dorset is 'great Wey', a Welsh river-name meaning ?'water'.

Broadwood L 'wide wood' OE; places in Devon, Somerset.

Broatch See **Brooch**; a form found in West Yorks.

Broben, Brobin, Brobyn F 'son' (from Welsh *Ap–*) 'of Robin' (see **Robert**).

Brock N 'badger' (because they stink) OE; or ?'young stag' OF. But often L 'brook' OE or (in Kent, Sussex, says Reaney) 'river-meadow'.

Brockhurst L 'badger **Hirst**' OE; place in Warwicks.

Brocklesby L 'farm of (a Norseman) called Trouserless' ON; place in Lincs.

Brockless, Brockliss N 'having no breeches' ON.

Brockton L 'place on a brook' OE; places in Salop (four) and (Brocton) Staffs.

Brockus See **Brookhouse**.

Brockway L 'road by a brook' OE.

Broder F (for O B—) Connected with 'dream' Irish.

Broderick F 'son' (from Welsh *Ap*–) 'of **Roderick**'.

Brodribb See **Broadribb**. The real surname of the actor Sir Henry Irving.

Brogden L 'brook valley' OE; place in West Yorks.

Broke See **Brooke**.

Brokenbrow L 'broken/uneven hill' OE; places in Glos and (with the Avon cutting a deep valley) Wilts, both Brokenborough.

Brome See **Broom**; –e perhaps shows dative after lost preposition.

Bromfield, Bromhall, Bromham, Bromley, Brompton, Bromwich L 'open country/**Haugh**/homestead (or river-meadow)/clearing/farm/dairy-farm where broom grows' OE; places in over a dozen counties; but –ley, Kent, is 'clearing with brambles' OE; and the two places –ton in Somerset are 'place by the Brendons (= brown hills)' OE.

Bromhead See **Broomhead**.

Brommage L Corruption of the Staffs or Warwicks **Bromwich**.

Brooch N of O type 'brooch, pin, lance' OF, for making them.

Brook L 'brook' OE, probably as many origins as there are streams; places in Kent, Rutland, Norfolk may have contributed. **Brooke** is either **Brook** with an –e for swank; or '(at the) brook' OE showing dative after lost preposition. **Brook(e)s** L 'of (i.e. at) the brook' (rather than a plural); –es is the older form of our genitive 's. Both common south of Ches–Lincs, and **Brooks** was the 46th commonest surname in USA in 1939. **Brooks** is the family name of the barons Crawshaw.

Brooker L 'dweller at the brook' OE+–er denoting not an agent but the same relationship as in *cottager*, *villager*. A Kent–Sussex surname.

Brookhouse L 'house by a brook' OE.

Brooksbank L 'bank of the brook' OE.

Broom L 'broom' (the bush) OE; locality, or places in many counties (some Broome and Brome). And cf. **Brougham**.

Brooman N 'brown(-skinned/-haired) man' OE.

Broome See **Broom** and **Brome**.

Broomfield, Broomhall See **Bromfield**; places in Essex, Kent, Somerset, and (–hall) Ches.

F: *first name*   L: *local name*   N: *nickname*   O: *occupational name*

Broomhead L 'hilltop with broom-bushes' OE; place in West Yorks, and chiefly a Derbys surname.

Brothers F '(son) of Brother' ON. Or N '(son) of a brother/kinsman' OE. Or even O '(son) of a fellow-guildsman' OE.

Brotherton L 'farm belonging to a (?younger) brother (or to a Norseman called Brother)' OE (or ON+OE), places in Suffolk, West Yorks.

Brough L 'fort' (usually an ancient camp) OE; places in four northern counties, and a Derbys–Staffs surname.

Brougham L 'homestead by the fort' OE; place in Westmorland, the fort (cf. *borough*) being the Roman station Brocavum. Sometimes, in view of the pronunciation, ?a pretentious spelling of **Broom**.

Broughton L 'place on a brook' OE, twenty places in twelve counties from Cumberland to Wilts; or (with same meaning as **Burton**) eight places from Lancs to Sussex; or 'place on a hill/mound' OE, places in Hants, Lincs.

Brown(e) N 'brown(-haired/-skinned)' OE (or sometimes OF); also an Old English F of the same meaning. The –e shows either a rise in the social scale or a weak adjective after a lost definite article. –n was the sixth commonest surname in England and Wales in 1853 (and now ?fourth), second in Scotland in 1958, 37th in Ireland in 1890, and third in USA in 1939. **Browne** is the family name of the marquesses of Sligo and of two barons.

Brownhill L 'brown hill' OE; locality, or places in Lancs, Salop, but place in West Yorks is someone's 'hall' OE.

Browning N dim. '**Brown**'; no evidence for the frequent –ing meaning 'family/folk of'. Counted by Guppy only in Glos, Beds–Northants.

Brownjohn N 'brown(-haired/-skinned)' OE or OF '**John**'.

Brownlie L 'brown clearing' OE.

Brownsmith O 'copper-/brass- (literally brown-) smith' OE.

Broxholm(e) L 'island in a brook' OE; place in Lincs.

Bruce L Some place in Normandy – ?'Briouze', Orne; ?'Le Brus', Calvados; not, apparently, 'Brix', Manche; the first is ?'muddy' OF from Gaulish, the second ?'heath' Gaulish or ??'maple' OF. 79th commonest surname in Scotland in 1958. Family name of the earls of Elgin and of three other peers.

Brundish L 'park/pasture/estate on a stream' OE; place in Suffolk.

Brunker F 'brown/burnished spear' OE.

Brunton L 'place on a stream' OE; four places in Northd.

Bruton L 'farm on the River Brue (= brisk)' OW+OE; place in Somerset.

Brutton Probably from one of the places **Broughton**.

Bryan(t) See **Brian**; **–t** is a parasitic dental as in **Hammond** and *varmint*, and **Bryant** is a thoroughly south-western surname.

Bryce, Bryne See **Brice, Brine**.

Bryson See **Brison**.

Buchan L '?calf' and '?little hut' Scots Gaelic; places in Aberdeens and Kirkcudbrs. Family name of the barons Tweedsmuir.

Buchanan L ?'low ground belonging to the canon' or ?'canon's house' Scots Gaelic; place in Stirlings. But in Pennsylvania it can be an anglicizing of German *Buchenhain* 'beech wood'.

Buck N 'stag' or 'he-goat' OE (or O, from employment with them). A Norfolk–Suffolk, Notts surname.

Buckden L 'stag valley' OE; place in Hunts (first element perhaps an A S owner's name).

Buckingham L 'river-meadow of Bucca's followers' OE (see **Buckminster**); place in Bucks.

Buckland L 'land held by charter (literally book-land)' OE; two dozen places in the south, and a lost one in Lincs.

Buckler O 'buckle-maker' or '(fencer with a) buckler' OF.

Buckley L 'buck (male deer) clearing' OE, place in Somerset; or 'he-goat field' OE. But the many Irish bearers are from **O Buhilly**; 99th commonest surname in Ireland in 1890. Family name of the barons Wrenbury.

Buckman O 'goat-/stag-keeper (literally -man)' OE; or 'one who studies/writes/binds books' OE.

Buckmaster See **Buckminster**, and cf. **Kittermaster**. Guppy found it chiefly in Beds.

Buckminster L 'church of Bucca' (an A S whose F is related to 'male deer' or 'he-goat') OE; place in Leics. This uncorrupted form (cf. **Buckmaster**) was taken to USA *c*. 1640.

Bucknall, Bucknell, Bucknill L 'Bucca's nook' OE (see **Buckminster**), places (–a–) in Lincs, Staffs; or 'Bucca's hill' OE, places (–e–) in Herefords, Oxon, Salop. But Guppy counted **–e–** only in Devon.

Buckton L 'farm of (an A S called) Stag/He-Goat' OE; places in Herefords, Northd, East Yorks.

Budd F 'beetle, tubby' OE *Budda*, or a later N. But as with many monosyllabic surnames, other forms such as dim. '**Baldwin**' may have fallen in with it. Counted by Guppy only in Hants.

Buffard N 'liable to puff/swell/rage' OF.

Bufton L 'above the farm/village' OE.

Bugby L Probably a corruption of Buckby, Northants, 'farm of (a man called) Stag/He-Goat' OE + ON.

F: *first name*   L: *local name*   N: *nickname*   O: *occupational name*

Bugden From **Buckden**, with a sense of humour (though a 'bug' was more a hobgoblin than a *cimex lectularius*).

Bugg N 'bogy, bugbear, spectre, hobgoblin, scarecrow' ?Welsh.

Bulger O 'wallet-/bag-maker' OF (cf. *budget*).

Bulkeley L 'bullock pasture' OE; place in Ches.

Bull N or O or (sign-name) L 'bull' OE. Midland and Wilts–Somerset surname.

Bullen L 'Boulogne' Latin *Bononia* from Keltic (Gaulish *bona* 'foundation').

Bullied N 'bull-headed' OE.

Bullin See **Bullen**.

Bullinger O 'baker' OF.

Bullock N or O 'bullock' OE; common in Ches–Staffs–Salop–Worcs–Glos–Mon.

Bullus L 'bull-house' OE, from employment there.

Bullworthy L 'bullock enclosure' (or first element as A S owner's name) OE; place in Devon.

Bulmer L 'bulls' lake' OE; places in Essex, North Yorks.

Bulpett, Bulpitt, Bulport, Bulputt L 'bull pit/hollow' OE, though the reference is not clear; the –e–/–i–/–u– are south-eastern, east Midland, and south-western forms of the –y– in OE *pytt*.

Bulpin L 'bull-pen' OE, from living/working there.

Bumphries F 'son' (from Welsh *Ap*–) 'of **Humphreys**'.

Bumstead L ' ?reedy place' OE; two places –mps– in Essex.

Bunclarke N 'good **Clark**' OF.

Buncombe L 'reedy valley' OE; whence (because of the political clap-trap of the member for B— county, North Carolina, in the mid 19th century) *bunkum*. Found as **Bunkham, Bunkum**.

Bunn(e)y Though early *de* forms are lacking, and Reaney's supposition of a N like 'swelling, bunion' (cf. **Bunyan**) is convincing, there may sometimes be a L origin from Bunny in Notts, 'reed island' or 'island in a stream once called *Bune*' OE.

Bunyan N or O Reaney's brilliant article shows how the bearer was either disfigured by a 'bunion' OF or something similar, or made 'buns' OF or other pastry.

Burbage, Burbidge L 'fort/manor brook' OE, places –age in Derbys, Wilts; or 'fort/manor ridge' OE, place –age in Leics. Misspelt **Burbridge**.

Burch See **Birch**, and sometimes **Burge**.

Burchard, Burchatt F 'fort hardy' OE.

Burchnall See **Birchenall**.

Burd N 'girl, maiden, ?sempstress' OE (cf. **Bird**). **Burdekin, Bur-**

75

dikin dim. 'girl, etc.'; probably rude. **-ikin** is a Derbys surname.

Burden, Burdon L 'fort hill' OE; places in Co. Durham, West Yorks; but another place in Co. Durham is 'valley with a byre/cowshed' OE.

Burfitt, Burfoot, Burford L 'ford by a fort/manor' OE; places (–ford) in Salop and (?'ford by a hill/mound' OE) Oxon.

Burgan, Burgin, Burgoin, Burgon, Burgoyne L 'Burgundian' OF. Guppy counted two of these in Devon.

Burge L 'bridge' OE, with metathesis of –r–, and with a –u– more likely in the west and south than in the east and north; chiefly a Somerset–Dorset surname.

Burgess O 'citizen, freeman, inhabitant of a borough' OF (same as the sneering word *bourgeois*).

Burgh L 'fort/manor' OE (cf. **Bury**), locality, or places in several counties; or 'mound/hill' OE, places in Norfolk, Surrey, etc.

Burghley L 'wood/clearing belonging to the fort/manor' OE; place in Northants.

Burgis Rarer, but more nearly original, form of **Burgess**.

Burk(e) L Despite resemblance to **Birk** (which may rarely be the origin), early forms suggest that this is a normanization of **Burgh** (especially the Suffolk place). Exported to Ireland, –e is now mainly an Irish surname, 29th commonest there in 1890, 45th in USA in 1939.

Burkett See **Birkett**.

Burl(e) O 'cup-bearer, butler' OE.

Burleigh, Burley L 'clearing belonging to a fort/manor' OE; at least seven places Burley from West Yorks to Hants, and also Burghley in Northants.

Burlington L 'farm of the family of (an AS whose name first appears spelt) Bret' OE; the local way of saying Bridlington, East Yorks.

Burman O 'servant in a **Bower**' OE, or status 'townsman, burgess' (from *borough*) OE; scattered, including Scotland and Worcs–Warwicks– Northants.

Burn L 'stream' OE; the word is now part only of the northern and Scots vocabulary, but was once common in the south (cf. Burnham, Bournemouth, Wimborne), where it eventually meant an intermittent stream, especially one flowing only in winter. **Burn(e)s, Burness** 'of (i.e. at) the B—', or plurals; –nes an older spelling than –ns. –ns found in Cumberland, Westmorland, Scotland; 61st commonest surname in Scotland in 1958, 68th in Ireland in 1890

F: *first name*   L: *local name*   N: *nickname*   O: *occupational name*

(but see **Byrne**). **Robert Burns**'s original surname was **Burness** from L Burnhouse 'house on the B—' OE, place in Argylls.

Burnage L ?'brown hedge' OE; place in Lancs.

Burnby L 'farm by a spring/well' ON; place in East Yorks.

Burnel(l) N dim. 'brown-haired/-skinned' OF. Chiefly a Bucks surname.

Burnes(s) See **Burns**. But –**ess** may also be from L Burnhouse (see **Burns**) or from the rare N 'burn-house' OE (?for one who carried out this punishment).

Burnet(t) N 'brownish' (of hair or hue) OF. Or O '(seller of) brown cloth (later, a good wool fabric)' OF, a metonym. Or L '(place cleared by) burning' OE, place in Somerset; and since **Becket** is doubtfully L 'beck-head', this might be 'head of the **Burn**'. Various families, from Scotland to Devon.

Burnham L Usually 'homestead on a **Burn**' OE, places in Bucks, Essex, Norfolk; but Somerset place is 'meadow on a **Burn**' OE; and two Lincs places are ?'at the springs' OE dative plural after lost preposition.

Burnley L 'clearing on a stream' or 'clearing on the River Brun (= brown)' OE; place in Lancs.

Burnside L Though this may sometimes be 'bank of a stream' OE, the Westmorland place is 'hill belonging to (an AS called) Brown Wolf' OE.

Burrell, Burrill N 'coarse woollen cloth' OF, or adjective 'reddish-brown'; but it came to mean 'coarse, unlettered, lay'. Peter Burel (c. 1242) gave his name to Langley Burrell, Wilts.

Burrough, Burrow L See **Burgh**. **Burroughs, Burrows** 'of (i.e. at) the fort/manor', or a plural; but these forms could be for '**Bower** house' OE. In Devon–Somerset–Wilts –**ough**/–**ow** are common, in Lancs –**ow**.

Burstall L 'site of a fort' (? a disused fort) OE; places in Suffolk, East Yorks.

Burstow L Metathesized form of **Bristow**, and still a Bristol surname. Place in Surrey, 'fort place' OE, may be a rarer origin.

Burt See **Bright**. Chiefly a south-west surname.

Burton L In the dozens of English places called B—, the commonest meaning is 'fort/manor-house enclosure', even 'fortified farm, farm near a fort' OE; in a couple of cases (especially the Staffs town) the first element is genitive, 'belonging to the fort'. But B— Bradstock, Dorset, is 'place/farm on the River Bredy (= ?boiler, throbber)' Keltic+OE; place in Sussex is 'Budeca's (an AS whose dim. N

77

meant ?'beetle/titch/fatty') place'; and B— Salmon, West Yorks, is 'broad place' ON+OE. **Bower** probably does not figure.

Burtonshaw See **Birkenshaw**.

Burwash L 'ploughland by a fort/manor' OE; place in Sussex.

Bury L (at) the fort/manor' OE, where the –y represents a dative after a lost preposition. Sometimes from the Lancs town, or B— St Edmunds, Suffolk, or Berry Pomeroy, Devon. But **Berry** is far commoner.

Busby L 'bush/shrub farm' ON; place in North Yorks, but an Oxon, Staffs surname.

Bush(e) L 'bush' ON (?and OE); –e may show dative after lost preposition.

Bushell O 'bushel' OF, for a user/maker of bushel-vessels.

Bushen L '(at) the bushes' ON (?and OE) dative plural after lost preposition. Chiefly a Devon–Somerset surname.

Buss O or N 'barrell, cask' OF, perhaps applied for the same reasons as **Barrell**. Chiefly a Kent surname.

Buszard See **Buzzard**.

Butcher O 'butcher' OF.

Butler O 'butler, wine-steward, head servant' OF (cf. *bottle*); in royal households, a high office epitomized in Archbishop Hubert Walter's brother, the first *Pincerna* of Ireland, and in the **Butler**s, dukes of Ormond. 37th commonest surname in USA in 1939. Still the family name of five Irish peers.

Butlin N 'hustle (the) churl' OF *boute-vilain*, a N suggesting ability to herd the common people. Chiefly a Northants surname.

Butner O 'button-maker' OF.

Butt Plenty of men in East Anglia and the south had But as a first-name from William II's time onwards; one of the twelve nouns in *OED* might suit, including 'cask, treetrunk, target or archery-ground, hillock, balk in ploughland' OF, or adjective 'thickset, stocky' ON. Chiefly Glos–Somerset–Dorset–Devon.

Butter(s) O from producing 'butter' OE or working in a **Buttery**; Reaney also supposes a N from the booming 'bittern' OF *butor*. And '(son) of B—'. Widespread family stocks in Perths, Kent, Cornwall.

Butterby L Despite its look of 'butter farm' OE+ON, this is 'beautiful find' OF; place in Co. Durham.

Butterfield L '**Field** where butter is produced' OE. A West Yorks–Lancs surname.

Butterwick L 'butter (dairy-)farm' OE; places in Dorset and six northern counties.

F: *first name* L: *local name* N: *nickname* O: *occupational name*

Butterworth L 'enclosure where butter is produced' OE; place in Lancs.

Buttery O for a worker in/controller of 'larder or liquor-store' OF. Surname of Notts–Yorks.

Button O 'button(-maker)' OF, a metonym.

Buxton L (originally with –s) 'rocking-stones, logan-stones' OE, place in Derbys; but place in Norfolk is ?'(AS called) Stag's/He-Goat's place' OE. A Derbys–Staffs–Ches surname.

Buzzard N 'buzzard' OF, the no-good hawk that couldn't be used for falconry; hence someone stupid and futile.

By L 'bend, corner' OE. Or ?N 'commerce, traffic' OE (cf. *buy*).

Byard, Byatt L 'by the yard, by the enclosure' OE.

Bye L 'at the **By**' or 'at the village' ON, dative after lost preposition.

Byers L 'byres, cowsheds' OE or 'of (i.e. at) the byre'; locality, or places in Co. Durham and (Byres) East Lothian, both plurals.

Byfield L 'open land in a river-bend' OE; or ?'by the open land' OE, place in Northants; in first case, **By**– is cognate with modern *bow* (arc).

Byfleet L 'by the stream' OE (cf. Fleet Street, London); place in Surrey.

Byford L 'commerce/traffic ford' OE (cf. *buy*), place in Herefords; or locality, 'by the ford' OE. Counted by Guppy only in Essex.

Bygrave L 'by the trench/ditch' OE; locality, like **Bygraves**, or place in Herts. But the meaning will sometimes be 'by the **Grove**' OE.

Byng See **Bing**.

Bynorth L 'living to the north' OE.

Byrne F (for O **B**—) 'descendant of Bear/Raven' Irish (from ON)/ Irish. Seventh commonest surname in Ireland in 1890. **Byrn(e)s** '(son) of **B**—'.

Byrom L '(at) the cowsheds' OE; locality, or places in Lancs and (Byram) West Yorks; originally –*um*, Old English dative plural after lost preposition. The source of the lordly name **Byron**.

Byron See **Byrom**. Resemblance to French *Biron* or Shakespeare's *Berowne* is fortuitous. Still a Notts surname.

Bysouth L 'living to the south' OE.

Bythesea L 'by the sea/pool/watercourse' OE.

Bytheway L 'by the road' OE.

Bywater(s) L 'by the water(s)' OE.

Bywood L 'by the wood' OE.

C

Caborne, Cabourn L 'stream with jackdaws' OE; place (–ourne) in Lincs.

Cadbury L Places in Somerset near Bristol and (North and South C—) near Wincanton, and in Devon; a form of *c.* 1000, *Cadanbyrig*, suggests 'fort of (an AS called) Cada (= ?lumpish)' OE, but the popular association of South C— with Arthur's Camelot makes *cad* 'battle' OW, or a British F associated with this, more attractive.

Caddick, Caddock N 'decrepit; epileptic, having the falling sickness' OF.

Caddow N 'jackdaw' (see **Coe, Daw**).

Cadwalad(e)r (anglicized to **Cadwallader**, especially in Salop) F 'battle leader' OW, a F as old as the 7th century; –**dr** is the best form.

Cadwgan F dim. 'Cadoc' Welsh *cad* 'battle'+suffix to make it adjectival; the commoner but inferior spelling is **Cadogan**.

Caesar F The dictator's family had borne this name long before he was born by Caesarian section, so it doesn't derive from Latin stem *caes*– 'cut'; it is '?fleece, head of hair' Latin, or ?'bluish-grey' Latin – but more probably of Etruscan origin. In England, fancifully given to children born by 'Caesarian' operations; but one family descend from an Italian whose F was *Cesare*, and who became physician to Queen Elizabeth I.

Caffin, Caffyn N dim. 'bald' OF (Norman).

Cager O or L, for a 'maker of cages' OF, or for duties or residence at the common cage for petty criminals.

Cahill F (for O C—) 'descendant of Powerful in Battle' Irish.

Cain(e) L 'Caen (= field of combat)' OF from Gaulish; place in Calvados. Or F (not of the first murderer, but) 'beautiful' OW (feminine) – the lady of Saint Keyne, Cornwall, but not of Keynsham, Somerset; or 'son of warrior' Manx contraction of a *Mc*-surname. This and **Cane** are surnames of Sussex–Hants.

Cain(e)s L 'juniper-trees' OF; places (Cahagnes, Cahaignes) in Calvados, Eure. Spelt **Keynes**, the family owned Combe K—, Dorset, in the 14th century and many Wilts estates later; still a Dorset surname.

Caird O 'craftsman, **Smith**' Scots Gaelic.

Caister, Caistor L 'Roman site' OE from Latin; places in Norfolk, Lincs.

F: *first name*   L: *local name*   N: *nickname*   O: *occupational name*

Cake O 'cake, flat bun' ON, for a maker of them.

Cakebread O 'flat loaf, griddlecake' ON+OE, for a baker.

Calcott, Calcutt L 'cold cottage/hut' OE; places in four counties; but places in Berks (–ot) and Wilts are ?'Cola's cottage' OE – the Old English N as in **Cole** – or 'coal-shed' OE.

Caldbeck L 'cold stream' ON; place in Cumberland.

Caldecot(t), Caldecourt L 'cold cottage(s)/hut(s)' OE; places in eleven counties (some –ecote and –icot).

Calder L '?rocky/?violent water' British river-name; places in Cumberland, Lancs, West Yorks.

Calderon O 'cauldron(-maker)' OF, a metonym.

Caldicot(t) See **Caldecot(t)**.

Caldwell L 'cold spring/stream' OE; places in Warwicks, North Yorks, Worcs (Caldewell), Renfrews. Counted by Guppy only in Lancs.

Calf(e), Callf N 'calf' OE; possibly O, for one who tended them.

Callaway L 'Caillouet (= pebbly place)' OF; place in Eure; a family from there must have established (Tytherington) Kellaways, Wilts.

Callcut See **Calcott**.

Callicott See **Caldecot**.

Callow N 'bald' OE. But sometimes ?L – the surname is frequent in Herefords, and the Herefords place means 'bald (hill)' also.

Calloway See **Callaway**. A Dorset surname.

Calthrop L By metathesis of –r– from either 'Kali's **Thorp**' ON+OE or 'charcoal/colt/cabbage **Thorp**' OE; places (Calthorpe) in Norfolk and Oxon.

Calton L 'calf farm' OE; places in Derbys, Staffs, West Yorks.

Calver L 'ridge for grazing calves' OE; place in Derbys, but a Suffolk surname.

Calverd O 'calf-herd' OE.

Calverley L 'clearing/pasture for calves' OE; place in West Yorks. Or (since the surname occurs in Dorset) 'clearing in a bare wood' OE, place (–leigh) in Dorset.

Calvert See **Calverd**. A Yorks surname.

Cam N 'crooked, cross-eyed' Scots Gaelic (cf. *gammy*). Or L 'crooked (river)' British river-name and place in Glos; or 'Caen', see **Cain**.

Camborne L 'crooked hill' Cornish; place in Cornwall.

Cambridge L 'bridge over the **Cam**' British+OE, place in Glos; the Cambs city was once 'bridge over the Granta (= ?muddy)' British+OE.

Camburn and **Came** See **Camborne** and **Camm**.

Camel N 'camel, ?porter, ?lumbering fellow' OE from Greek via

Latin, ultimately Semitic. Also L ?'rim/ridge hill' OW; two places (Queen and West C—) in Somerset, both doubtful claimants to be the site of Camelot.

Cameron N 'crooked nose, hook-nose' Scots Gaelic. Or, rarely, L – places in Fifes, Stirlings, of same meaning used topographically. 31st commonest surname in Scotland in 1958.

Camm L 'Caen' (see **Cain**) or 'crooked (river)' Welsh; place (Cam) in Glos. Or N 'crooked, cross-eyed, deformed' Scots Gaelic and Welsh, as in *game leg* and Davy Gam at Agincourt.

Cammamile N 'camomile' OF from Latin from Greek (= earth-apple). Its blossoms smell like apples, and it is used in pharmacy; but the reason for the N is obscure.

Camp(s) O 'warrior' OE (see **Kemp**), or a similar N 'battle' OE *camp*; and '(son) of C—'.

Campbell N 'crooked mouth' Scots Gaelic. Seventh commonest surname in Scotland in 1958 (as in 1858), and 31st in Ireland in 1890. Family name of the dukes of Argyll and of six other Scots peers.

Campin L 'open country, fertile land' OF; places (Campagne) in Oise, Pas-de-Calais, or the region Champagne (of the same meaning) normanized.

Campion Norman form of OF **Champion**; found in Northants–Lincs

Campton L 'place on the crooked (stream)' British+OE; place in Beds.

Candler Norman form of OF **Chandler**.

Cane See **Caine**.

Cann O 'can, pot, bucket, jar' OE, for a maker/seller. Or L 'deep valley (a topographical use of *can*)' OE; place in Dorset. The surname is common in Devon.

Cannan F (for O/McC–) 'descendant/son of White-Head' or 'of Wolfcub' Irish; anglicized spellings of two different Irish septs, often rendered **Cannon**.

Cannard N 'sluggard, wastrel' OF; the inn-sign at C—'s Grave near Shepton Mallet, Somerset, displays a hanged man. A surname of the Bristol area.

Cannel(l) O 'cinnamon(-seller)' OF. (*Atte* and *de* forms are lacking to make it L 'channel, river-bed, gutter, ditch' OF.) For Manx **Cannell** see **McConnal**. Guppy counted –ell only in Norfolk.

Cannington L 'farm by the Quantock (= ?rim of a circle) Hills' Keltic+OE; place in Somerset.

Cannon O 'canon, member of a communal house of clergy' OF

F: *first name*   L: *local name*   N: *nickname*   O: *occupational name*

(Norman dialect). **Cannons** '(son) of the canon' or 'dweller at the canons'. But for Irish bearers see **Cannan**.

Canonbury L 'manor of the (Augustinian) Canons (of St Bartholomew, Smithfield)' ME; place in Middx.

Cant Norman version of **Chant**.

Cantello(w), **Cantelo** L 'Canteloup/Canteleu (= song of the wolf)' OF – euphemism for something dreaded by the inhabitants; places in Calvados/Seine-Maritime. Most famous member of this stock was Saint Thomas de Cantelupe, bishop of Hereford (†1282).

Canter O 'singer' OF (Norman dialect), including the office of precentor.

Cantle L 'nook, corner, angle of land' OF (Norman dialect); but some lost –hill/–well/–hall/–**Haugh** place-name may be concealed here.

Capel, **Caple** L 'chapel' OF (Norman); locality, or places in four counties. Also sometimes N 'horse, nag' ME from ON and ultimately from Low Latin.

Caperon, **Capern**, **Capron** O 'hood, cap' OF (Norman dialect; cf. French *chapeau*), for a maker of them.

Capon O 'capon, neutered cockerel' OE, for a breeder and seller of them.

Capper O 'cap-maker' OE+–**er**.

Capstack, **Capstick** See **Copestake**. Guppy found –i– only in West Yorks.

Card(er) O 'carder/teaser of wool' OF.

Cardew L 'black fort' OW; place in Cumberland.

Careless, **Carey** See **Carless**, **Cary**.

Carface, **Carfax** L 'cross-roads (literally four ways)' OF, as at Oxford.

Carless N 'free from worry/responsibility' OE; it would now have much the same meaning if taken literally.

Carleton L Same as **Carlton**; places in four counties. Family name of the viscounts Dorchester.

Carli(s)le L 'Carlisle' in Cumberland; the Romano–British name meant 'belonging to Lugovalos', whose name meant 'strong as (the Keltic god) Lugus'; to this, 'fort/city' OW has been prefixed.

Carlton L Usually **Charlton** scandinavianized; dozens of places in a dozen counties, from Yorks to Beds. Another form is **Carleton**.

Carman N 'male person' ON (cf. **Charles**).

Carmichael L 'fort of **Michael**' first element British; place in Lanarks held by the **C—** family as early as 12th century. A Scots and Northd surname.

Carpenter O 'carpenter' Norman version of OF. Common from Oxon to Cornwall.

Carr L 'marsh, wet ground overgrown with brushwood' ON; frequent place-name element, especially in the Danelaw, and a northern surname.

Carruthers L ?'**Rhydderch**'s fort' OW, place in Dumfs.

Carsley L 'clearing of (an A S called) Bold Army' OE or 'clearing with cress' OE, place (Keresley) in Warwicks; places (Kearsley) in Lancs and Northd are of similar origin, though **Law** 'hill/mound' could have figured in both.

Carswell L 'spring/stream where cress grows' OE; places in Berks, Devon.

Carter O 'maker/driver of carts' OE (?from ON), or a similar meaning from an OF form in *char–*. 50th commonest surname in England and Wales in 1853.

Cartledge, Cartlidge L 'stream (see **Latch**) in rough stony ground' ON+OE; place (–e–) in Derbys.

Cartwright O 'cart-maker' OE (see **Carter** and **Wright**).

Carus L 'house in a **Carr**' ON+OE; locality, or places (Carhouse) in Lincs, West Yorks.

Carver O 'sculptor' OE+–er.

Carwardine L 'enclosure by a ?rock' OE; place (now Carden) in Ches.

Cary L ?'pleasant (stream)' Keltic; Somerset river on which stand Castle C—, C— Fitzpaine, Lytes C—, Babcary. Chiefly a Somerset surname. Family name of the viscounts Falkland.

Casbolt N ?'bald-headed' ME (Yorks dialect) *casbald*.

Case Probably the same as **Cass**. Chiefly a Norfolk surname.

Casement F 'son' (from Irish *Mc–*) 'of **Osmund**'.

Cash See **Cass**.

Cashen, Cashin N dim. 'crooked' Irish; or Manx 'son of C—', with the *Mc–* absorbed.

Cass F dim. 'Cassandra', the unfortunate Trojan princess whose F was ?a feminine form of **Alexander**; F popular in the Middle Ages, when we sympathized with our supposed ancestors from Troy. West Yorks surname.

Cassley See **Carsley**.

Casson F 'son of **Cass**'.

Casterton L 'place by a Roman site' OE; places in Rutland, Westmorland.

Castle L 'castle' Norman version of OF form in *ch–*.

Castleton L 'place by a **Castle**' OF (Norman)+OE; places in five counties.

F: *first name*   L: *local name*   N: *nickname*   O: *occupational name*

Caswall, Caswell L 'spring/stream where cress grows' OE; places in ten counties, originally spelt more like **Carswell**, also Crass–, Cress–, Carse–, Kers–.

Catcheside L 'cold-cheer hill' OE+OF+OE; place in Northd, and still a north-eastern surname.

Catchpole, Catchpoll, Catchpool(e) O 'chase-fowl' OF (cf. *pullet*), i.e. one who seizes poultry in lieu of debts, thence a tax-gatherer, a sheriff's official arresting on warrant for debt; the **C** is Norman dialect (cf. *chase* from Old French). Counted by Guppy only in Suffolk–Norfolk.

Cater O 'buyer' OF (Norman; cf. Modern French *acheter*), so 'caterer, purveyor for a household'.

Catford L '(wild) cats' ford' OE; place in Kent.

Cathcart L 'fort/wood' (early forms in Ker–/Ket– suggest that there were two places) 'on the (River) Cart (= ?cleanser, washer)' British; place in Renfrews.

Catley L '(wild) cats' wood/clearing' OE; places in four counties.

Catlin(g) F Derivative of 'pure' Greek, the legendary martyr St Katherine of Alexandria, one of the fourteen Holy Helpers and immensely popular in medieval England.

Catmore, Catmur L '(wild) cats' lake' OE (cf. *mere*); place in Berks (or first element is an A S owner with the N 'Cat').

Cator See **Cater**.

Catt N 'cat' OE, though why?

Cattanach, Cattenach F 'of the clan (Chattan) descended from the devotee of St Catan (= little cat)' Scots Gaelic.

Cattell F dim. 'Katherine'; see **Catlin**.

Catterall, Catterell L ?'cat's-tail' (long strip of land) ON – Ekwall quotes Katterall, Norway, as meaning this; place in Lancs, and chiefly a Lancs surname.

Catterick L ?'waterfall, cataract' Latin, kelticized; place in North Yorks.

Catterill, Catteroll See **Catterall**.

Cattle See **Cattell**.

Catton L '(wild) cats' valley' OE; place in Northd; but places in Derbys, Norfolk, East and North Yorks are from owners – 'Cat's/Cheerful's place' OE/ON+OE.

Caudle, Cauldwell L Same as **Caldwell**; places in five counties. But sometimes **Caudle** is 'caudle, sweet spiced gruel' OF – an invalid beverage, given as a N for some mocking reason.

Causey L Original form of 'causeway' OF from Latin; meaning 'surfaced with limestone' (cf. *calcium*); spelling –*way* is mistaken.

Cavanagh See **Kavanagh.**

Cave N 'bald' OF (Norman); cf. **Chaff.** But sometimes L, from places in East Yorks, named from a 'swift' OE stream nearby; rarely ?'cave' OF. Common in the line Dorset–Wilts–Oxon–Northants.

Cavell N dim. 'bald' OF (Norman); cf. **Cave.**

Cavendish L 'pasture of (an AS called) Bold or Bold-Daring' OE; place in Suffolk. Family name of the dukes of Devonshire and Portland, and of other peers.

Cavill L 'jackdaw field' OE; place (Cavil or Caville) in East Yorks.

Cawdell and **Cawdron** See **Caldwell** and **Calderon.**

Cawood L 'jackdaw wood' OE; places in Lancs, West Yorks.

Cawthorn(e) L 'cold/bleak/exposed thornbush' OE; places in West Yorks.

Cawton L 'calf farm' OE; place in North Yorks.

Cazalet, Cazaubon L dim. 'house-site', 'good house-site' OF; places in Dordogne, Basses-Pyrénées, Gers. Huguenot surnames.

Cecil F Latin *Caecilius*, derivative of *caecus* 'blind', early adopted in Welsh as *Sisyllt*. Family name of the marquesses of Exeter and of two barons.

Chadderton L 'place by a hill (literally chair)' British+OE (British word ultimately from Latin *cathedra*, itself from Greek); place in Lancs.

Chadwell L Same as **Caldwell**; places in Leics and (with an erroneous *Saint Chad's Well* on the map) Essex.

Chadwick L '**Wick** of (?Saint) Chad' (?same as first element of **Cadwaladr**); places in Lancs, Worcs; place in Warwicks is from an owner with a similar F.

Chafer O or L 'limekiln' OF.

Chaff(e) N 'bald' OF; –e shows weak adjective after lost definite article. –e chiefly a Devon surname. **Chaffin** dim. 'bald'.

Chainey and **Chalice** See **Chesnay** and **Challis.**

Chalk(e) L 'chalk/limestone' OE; locality, or places in Kent, Wilts.

Challen(s) L 'Châlons (-sur-Marne)' OF from a Gaulish tribe, the *Catalauni*; place in Marne where blankets and coverlets (called in England *shalloons*) were made – so the surname may be O, a metonym for a seller of them; or 'Châlon (-sur-Saône)' OF from Gaulish *Caladun*– (second element 'hill fort'); place in Saône-et-Loire.

Challenger O 'plaintiff, challenger, accuser' OF, unless by folk-etymology for **Challener, Challenor,** a 'blanket-maker' OF, from Châlons-sur-Marne (see Challen).

F: *first name*   L: *local name*   N: *nickname*   O: *occupational name*

Challis(s) L 'ladder, abrupt drop' OF (cf. *escalier*); place (Escalles) in Pas-de-Calais.

Chalmers Scots version of **Chambers**.

Chalton L 'place on chalk' OE, place in Hants; or 'calf farm' OE, two places in Beds.

Chamberlain(e), Chamberlayne, Chamberlin O 'private attendant of king or lord, one charged with control of private rooms' (eventually, a steward, and even a kind of male head chambermaid at an inn) OF form of Latin *camera* 'room' + Germanic *–ling* (as in *darling*, *hireling*, and other – often contemptuous – words).

Chambers L 'of (i.e. at) the chamber' OF, but really an O equivalent to **Chamberlain**.

Champernowne L 'Campernon (= field of Eagle Wolf)' OF + Germanic; place in Manche.

Champion O 'one who fights (for another, professionally) in wager of battle, athlete (especially boxer/wrestler)' OF from Latin *campus* 'field, arena'. But sometimes ?related to **Champness**.

Champness, Champney(s) L 'man from Champagne (= plain; flat country)' OF from Latin, the French province.

Chancellor O 'worker in a chancery, archivist, secretary' OF.

Chandler O 'candle-maker/-seller' OF. Chiefly a southern surname, common in Glos.

Chaney See **Chesnay**.

Channon The OF version of **Cannon**.

Chant N 'song' OF, for a professional or informal singer.

Chantr(e)y L 'singing (of mass)' OF, whence the 'chantry-chapel' where it was sung; locality, or place in Somerset.

Chaplain, Chaplin(g) O '(chantry-)priest, chaplain' OF; cf. **Chantry**.

Chapman O 'merchant, trader' OE (cf. *cheap*, *chaffer*, *chop and change*, slang *chap*, **Chipping**, Cheapside, Chepstow). A universal occupation and surname.

Chappel(l), Chapple L 'chapel' OF; from living near, or officiating.

Chard L See **Chart**; place in Somerset, and a Somerset surname.

Charity N '(Christian) love' OF or (from the same word) L or O 'house of refuge, hospital'.

Charles F 'man' OF version of Latin *Carolus*, from Germanic. Popularity of the F is based on the Charlemagne stories. It has sometimes ?absorbed O 'villein, serf, peasant' OE (see **Charlton**), which is ultimately from the same stem.

Charleston The various places called Charlestown are of too late foundation to form surnames, and perhaps a F Charleson 'son of **Charles**' lies behind the surname.

Charley L 'wood/clearing by a cairn/rock' British+OE; place in Leics.

Charlton L 'place of the free-peasants/villeins' OE (our *churl* has lost face). Quite fifteen counties have places of this name (there are seven in Somerset alone), but the surname is found chiefly in the north, especially Northd.

Charlwood L 'wood of the villeins, etc.' OE (see **Charlton**); place in Surrey.

Charnell L 'charnel-house, mortuary chapel, cemetery' OF, ultimately from Latin *carn*– 'flesh', ?for the gravedigger or custodian.

Charney L 'island on the (River) Charn (= stony, rocky)' British+ OE; place in Berks.

Chart L 'rough ground, common' OE; locality, or several places in Kent.

Charteris L 'Chartres' OF from a Gaulish tribe, the Carnutes (= ?'trumpet-people'); place in Eure-et-Loir. Also by confusion with **Chatteris**. Family name of the earls of Wemyss and March.

Chase O verb 'hunt' OF, here a metonym for 'hunter'. (Early forms do not support L 'unenclosed hunting-ground, chase'.) An odd choice of F to go with it is seen in the wanton name of Philander C—, USA Episcopal bishop (†1852).

Chaston L 'chestnut tree' OF.

Chatteris L 'strip of woodland' British+OE (cf. **Chetwode**); place in Cambs.

Chatterley L First element as in **Chadderton**; second 'wood/clearing' OE; place in Staffs.

Chatterton L See **Chadderton**; place in Lancs. Counted by Guppy only in Lincs.

Chaucer O 'maker of hose/breeches/leg-armour/boots/gaiters' OF.

Chawner See **Challener**.

Cheadle L ?'wood wood' British+OE, tautologically; places in Ches, Staffs.

Cheater O 'escheator' OF; his duty was to look after the king's escheats (the lapsing of heirless land to the Crown) in the county of his appointment.

Cheatham Misspelling of **Cheetham**.

Checkley L 'wood/clearing by a lump/hill' OE, though the first element may be an AS owner Ceacca (?related to 'cheek, jawbone'); places in Ches, Herefords, Staffs, but a surname of Bucks–Oxon– Warwicks.

F: *first name*   L: *local name*   N: *nickname*   O: *occupational name*

Chedzey, Chedzoy L 'island of (an AS called) Cedd' OE (see *Chad* under **Chadwick**), place (–o–) in Somerset.

Cheek N 'chops, jawbone' OE, for something striking in this feature.

Cheese O 'cheese' OE, a metonym. **Cheeseman, Cheese(w)right** of 'cheese-seller/-maker' OE.

Cheetham L 'homestead by a wood' British+OE; place in Lancs, and a Lancs–Ches, Notts surname.

Cheever N '(she-)goat' OF, because of nimbleness or some worse characteristic. **Cheevers** '(son) of C—'.

Chegwidden, later form of **Chegwin** L 'white house' Cornish.

Chenevix O 'hemp-seed' OF, grown for making sacks, ropes, nets, and coarse cloth – not for the cognate *cannabis*. A Huguenot surname.

Cheney See **Chesnay**. An ancient surname in East Anglia, Herts, Hunts, Leics.

Chenhalls L 'house by the ?stoneheap' Cornish (–n– from Cornish *an* 'the'); place in Cornwall.

Chenoweth L 'new house' Cornish.

Cheriton L 'church farm' OE; places in six counties; but place in Cornwall is the same as **Charlton**. A Devon surname.

Chermside, Chernside L ?'hill shaped like a churn' OE, place (Chirnside) in Berwicks, though the surnames are found in Dorset and elsewhere in the south.

Cherry N 'cherry' ME from OF; or O, from producing them. **Cherrison** 'son of C—'.

Cheshire L 'shire/county' OE 'of **Chester**'.

Chesnay, Chesney L 'oak grove' OF; locality, or places in France called Chenay, Chenoy, Chesnoy, Quesnay.

Chester L 'Roman site' OE from Latin *castra*; locality, or places in Ches, Derbys, Co. Durham.

Chesterfield L 'open land by a Roman site' OE; place in Derbys.

Chesterton L 'place by a Roman site' OE; places in seven counties.

Chestnut L 'chestnut-tree' OF+OE.

Chettle L 'deep valley locked in hills (literally kettle, cauldron)' OE; place in Dorset; but surname is chiefly Notts.

Chetwode, Chetwood L 'wood wood' British+OE, tautologically; place in Bucks.

Chick(en) N 'chicken' OE. Bardsley in 1901 feared that **Chicken** was extinct, but five were in the London TD in 1963.

Chidg(z)ey, Chidzey See **Chedzey**.

Chilcote L 'cottages of the children/young nobles/princes' OE; places in Leics, Northants.

Chilcott L 'cottages of (an AS called) Ship (cf. *keel*)' OE; place in Somerset, and a Dorset surname.

Child(e) O (or status) 'minor, youth awaiting knighthood, page' (like Childe Harold/Roland) OE (cf. **Chilton**). And ?L 'spring' OE. **Childs** '(son) of **C**—'.

Chilton L 'children's farm/manor' OE – first element may mean variously 'princes, young nobles, youths awaiting knighthood, retainers, young monks'; places in ten counties; but C— upon Polden, Somerset, is 'chalk-/limestone-hill farm' OE, and C—, IoW, is from an AS owner whose F is connected with 'keel/ship' OE; and Reaney shows how one 13th-century bearer was of Chilhampton, Wilts – 'children's village' OE.

Chilver(s) F 'ship (cf. *keel*) peace' OE; and '(son) of **C**—'.

Chin(n) N 'chin, beard' OE.

Chippendale, Chippindale, Chippindall L 'Chipping valley' OE +OE/ON, former name of Chipping, Lancs.

Chipping L 'market' OE; locality, or places in seven counties. See **Chapman**.

Chiselhurst L 'gravel hill' OE; place (**Chisle**–) in Kent.

Chisholm L 'meadow good for cheese' OE; place in Roxburghs.

Chislett L 'gravel place' OE; place (–et) in Kent.

Chisnall L 'gravelly nook' OE; place in Lancs.

Chiswick L 'cheese farm' OE; places in Cambs, Essex, Middx.

Chitty N 'whelp, pup, cub' Germanic, cognate with *kid*, *chitterlings*; chitty-faced means 'baby-faced'. Chiefly a Sussex surname.

Chivers Same as **Cheevers**, and much commoner, especially in Cambs.

Cholmondeley L 'wood/clearing of (an AS called) Ship (cf. *keel*) Protector' OE; place in Ches, pronounced **Chumley**. Family name of the barons Delamere.

Chorley L 'wood/clearing of the villeins, etc.' OE (see **Charlton**); places in six counties.

Chorlton L Same as **Charlton**; places in Ches, Lancs, Staffs.

Christey See **Christie**.

Christian F (more often female than male in Middle Ages) 'Christian' Latin; its derivatives may equally be from *Christiana*.

Christie, Christin(e) F dim. '**Christian**'; forms in –in(e) may go back to the OE spelling *cristen*; **Christie** (the woefully unsuitable surname of about the most frightful private murderer of the 20th century) was the 91st commonest surname in Scotland in 1958. **Christison** 'son of **C**—'.

F: *first name*   L: *local name*   N: *nickname*   O: *occupational name*

Christmas F For one born or baptized at 'Christmas' OE.

Christopher F 'bearing Christ' Greek. The F, once a declaration of personal witness, had foisted on to it the handsome and preposterous legend of the giant's ferrying the Christ-Child – whence the belief in Saint C— as a protector against accidents, and the motorists' trinkets. **Christophers(on)** '(son)/son of C—'.

Christy See **Christie**. The C— Minstrels named from their founder Edwin P. C— (†1862). Guppy counted it only in Essex.

Chrystal(l) F dim. 'Christopher', a Scots form.

Chubb N The 'chavender or chub' ME is a river-fish notably fat, lazy, and given to hovering in the sun or deep under roots; Thoreau says it tastes 'like brown paper salted'. Hence the senses of 'chubby, doltish, spiritless'. Family name of the barons Hayter, and chiefly a Devon surname.

Chum(b)ley See **Cholmondeley**.

Church L 'church' OE, from residence near, or duties such as those of verger/sexton.

Churcher, Churchman, Churchouse, Churchward, Churchyard are all mainly O; –er was 'connected with the church', –man kept it (like a modern sexton or verger), –house lived next to it or minded it, –ward looked after it, –yard kept up the churchyard; all the roots are OE.

Churchill L 'church hill' OE; locality, or places in four counties; the great C— family is ultimately derived from the Somerset place (and the name **Winston** from neighbouring Glos).

Churley L There is now no village so called, but it looks like 'villeins' wood/clearing' OE; cf. *churl*, **Charlton, Chorley**. There was an Adam Churleye in Somerset in 1327.

Churton L 'church farm' OE; place in Ches.

Chynoweth L 'new house' Cornish.

Cinnamon(d) N 'cinnamon' OF, the fragrant spice; perhaps mainly as a term of endearment – Absolon calls Alisoun 'sweet cinnamon' in *The Miller's Tale*.

Clachar O 'mason, builder in stone' Scots Gaelic.

Clanc(e)y F (for McC–) 'son of Ruddy Warrior' Irish.

Clapcott L '?hillock cottage' OE; but Clapcot, Berks, isn't so situated, and first element may be an A S owner with a N meaning something like 'lump'.

Clapham L 'hillock homestead' OE; places in Beds, London, Sussex.

Clapp N 'clumsy, heavily-built' OE, as in the various Clap–/Clop– place-names with humps and hillocks. Chiefly a Somerset surname.

Clapton L 'hillock farm' OE; places in six counties (three in Somerset).

Clare F (normally feminine, but cf. **St Clair**) 'bright, shining' Latin (cf. *clear*); whether as –*e* or –*a*, it was made more popular by Saint C— of Assisi (†1253). Or L 'clay slope' OE, place in Oxon; or stream-name ' ?gentle/?lukewarm/?bright' Keltic, place in Suffolk. Or O 'worker in clay' OE, for a worker in (wattle and) daub.

Clarewood L '**Worth** where clover grows' OE; place in Northd.

Clarges O '(?son/?servant) of the clergyman' OF; –**ar**– arising as in **Clark**, which is ultimately the same word.

Claridge F 'Clarice', a female name based on Latin *claritia* 'brightness'. Bardsley cleverly found a lady called alternately Claricie and Clarugge in Cambs in 1273. Chiefly a Beds surname.

Clark(e) O 'cleric, scholar, clerk, secretary' OF; especially a cleric in minor orders, and therefore not necessarily celibate; –*e* is merely an inferior spelling; –*er*– becomes –**ar**– as in Berkshire, Derby, Hertford, and the vulgarisms *varmint* and *varsity* for *vermin* and *university*. Formed the 27th (–**k**) and 41st (–**e**) commonest surnames in England and Wales in 1853 (together the 9th), 15th in Scotland in 1958, 32nd in Ireland in 1890.

Clatworthy L 'enclosure where burdock/goosegrass grows' OE; place in Somerset.

Clavering L 'clover field' OE; place in Essex.

Claybrooke L 'clayey brook' OE; place in Leics, and a surname of adjoining Warwicks.

Claydon L 'clay(ey) hill' OE; places in Bucks (four), Oxon, Suffolk.

Claypo(o)le L 'clayey pool' OE; place (–pole) in Lincs.

Clayton L 'place in the clay, place with good clay for pottery' OE; places in four counties, especially Lancs (five) and West Yorks (three), and a Ches–Derbys–Lincs–Lancs–West Yorks surname.

Cleal(e), Cleall L 'clayey hill' OE. Somerset–Dorset records of the family between 1539 and 1876 give these three spellings, as well as **Clehill, Cleyil, Cleel(e), Cleell, Clele.**

Clear(e) See **Clare.**

Cleary More frequent spelling of **Clery**; also found as O **C—.**

Cleave See **Cliff, Cleaves. Cleave** will be dative after lost preposition. **Cleaves** L 'of (i.e. at) the **Cliff**', or a plural.

Cleaveland See **Cleveland.**

Cleaver O Not from using the modern cleaver, but from being expert in splitting logs into planks; *cleave* is OE.

Clee L 'clay' OE, places in Lincs, Salop; but sometimes 'river-/road-fork' OE (cf. *claw*).

F: *first name*   L: *local name*   N: *nickname*   O: *occupational name*

Cleeve(s) L Same as **Cleave(s)**; places (–e) in Glos, Somerset, Worcs.

Clegg L '(haystack-shaped) hill' ON; place in Lancs, and a Lancs–West Yorks surname.

Cleghorn L 'clay house' OE; place in Lanarks.

Clemas, Clemens See **Clements**; but feminine F *Clemence* 'mildness' Latin existed.

Clement F 'mild, merciful' Latin; Saint, disciple of Saint Paul, sunk with an anchor; popular in England, with forty-odd churches; also the name of some popes. **Clements(on)** '(son)/son of C—'. **–ts** much commoner than **–t**.

Clemo(w) Cornish for **Clement**.

Clemson F 'son of (dim.) **Clement**' Cornish.

Clench See **Clinch**.

Clennell L 'clean hill (i.e. hill free from weeds/thorns)' OE; place in Northd.

Clent L 'rock, hill' OE; place in Worcs.

Clerk(e) Rare original forms of **Clark(e)**.

Clery O (for O C—) 'descendant of the clerk' Irish; see **Clark** and **McChlery**. C—, **Cleary**, and their O forms run to 5,000 in Ireland.

Cleve(s) See **Cleave(s)**.

Cleveland L 'hilly district' OE; place in North Yorks.

Cleveley L 'wood/clearing on a **Cliff**' OE; places in Oxon and (–leys) Lancs.

Clew See **Clough**. **Clew(e)s** L 'of (i.e. at) the C—'; **–ws** chiefly a Derbys surname.

Clewer L '**Cliff** dwellers' OE; places in Berks, Somerset.

Clewlow L ?'ball-shaped mound' OE; place (Cleulow) – with an AS cross on a mound – in Ches.

Cliff(e) L 'cliff, slope, river-bank' OE; **–e** is less correct than in **Clive**. Staffs–Ches–Lancs surnames.

Clifford L 'ford at a **Cliff**' OE; places in Glos, Herefords, West Yorks. Its use as a F is late and strange; and 'the little girl who was called Precipice after her Uncle Cliff' is even less funny than it looks.

Clifft, Clift See **Cliff**.

Clifton L 'place on a **Cliff**' OE, places in over two dozen counties from Northd to Dorset; or the usual pronunciation of Cliveden, Berks, 'valley among the **Cliff**s' OE. Guppy counted it only in Surrey, Oxon, Lincs.

Clinch L ?'ravine, crevice' OE (North Country *clink*); but place in Wilts also called **Clench** means 'lump, mass, hill' OE. Or O 'clinch, big nail, rivet' OE, a metonym for a maker/user of them.

Clink(er) O 'rivet(er), etc.'; see **Clinch**.

Clitheroe, Clitherow L 'hill/mound of loose stones' OE (cf. dialect *clider/clither* 'gravel, debris')+ON; place (–oe) in Lancs.

Clive L '(at) the **Cliff**'; –e shows dative after a lost preposition, with –ff– voiced to –v– between vowels; cf. *life* and *alive*.

Clopton L 'hill/hillock place' OE; places in four counties.

Close L 'enclosure' OF. Or N 'discreet, reserved' OF.

Clothier O 'cloth-worker/-seller' OE+–er.

Clotworthy See **Clatworthy**.

Cloud L 'hill, crag' OE; for instance, Temple C—, Somerset, is adjacent to **Clutton**.

Clough, Clow, Cluff L 'ravine, deep valley' OE; a common place-name element in the north, and chiefly a West Yorks surname.

Cloutman O 'codger, cobbler, patcher' OE (as in *Cast ne'er a clout till May be out*).

Cluelow, Clulee, Cluley, Clulow See **Clewlow**.

Clunes L 'meadow stance/resting-place' Scots Gaelic; places in Inverness and Perths.

Clutterbuck L A Glos family (leaving their name at C— Farm, Glos) said to have escaped from persecution in the Low Countries in the 1500s; but the name looks like an English place in –brook/–beck, especially Clitherbeck in North Yorks, 'stream at the debris/quarry' OE+ON, or Clouter Brook in Ches, '?noisy/clumsy brook' OE.

Clutton L '(rocky) hill place' OE; places in Ches, Somerset.

Coaley L 'clearing/wood in a recess' OE (cf. *cove*); place in Glos.

Coat(e), Coates See **Cote(s)**.

Cobbeldick, Cobbledick L Bardsley found it early and persistently in Lincs, and makes it '**Cobbold**'s ditch/dike' OE.

Cobbold F 'famed bold' OE.

Cobden L First element probably 'lump, knob' OE, second 'hill' OE (cf. **Down**); place in Todmorden, West Yorks. But in Cobdenhill, Herts, first two elements are 'lopped/polled thorn' OE.

Cobham L 'homestead at a ?river-bend' OE, place in Surrey; but first element may be an AS owner Cofa, just as Cobba 'big man' OE may have settled C—, Kent.

Cobleigh, Cobley L 'Cobba's clearing' OE (see **Cobham**); places (–ey) in Lapford and East Worlington, Devon, and a Devon surname.

Cobner See **Copner**.

Cochran(e) L ?'red brook' OW; place (–e) in Renfrews.

Cock A surname in which many possibilities meet, mostly jests (one

F: *first name*   L: *local name*   N: *nickname*   O: *occupational name*

94

of them ?obscene). A rare but real origin is L 'hillock, heap' OE (as in *haycock*) or '(at the Sign of the) Cock'. Or O 'ship's boat' OF, a metonym; or **Cook**. But above all it is a N 'cockerel' OE; or 'fatty' OE (if it be from OE F *Cocca*); or 'red' Welsh *coch*. The strutting barnyard fowl became a generic term for pert lads, and was attached as a suffix to dim. forms, as in **Simcock**. **Cocks** '(son) of C—'; rarer than its form **Cox**, but family name of the barons Somers.

Cockbaine N 'having legs like a cockerel, strutting' OE+OE (cf. **Langbain**).

Cockbill N 'cockerel's bill' OE+OE; there was a Ralph Cokkebill in Warwicks in 1332.

Cockcraft, Cockcroft See **Cockroft**.

Cocker(h)am L 'homestead on the River Cocker (= crooked)' Keltic+OE; place (–h–) in Lancs, and a surname of Lancs–Ches.

Cockfield L ?Sometimes 'open country with birds' OE, but the Suffolk and Co. Durham places had owners with Fs connected with ?*cough* and ?*cockerel*.

Cockgrove L 'wood with birds' OE.

Cocking F 'son/descendant of Cockerel' OE. Or L 'the people of (an A S called) Cockerel' OE; place in Sussex.

Cockram See **Cockerham**.

Cockroft L Unless this is a corruption of Carcroft '**Croft** in marshy ground' ON+OE, place in West Yorks, it is '**Croft** with birds/cockerels' OE.

Codrington L 'farm of the people of (an A S called) Famous Army' OE; place in Glos.

Coe N 'jackdaw' ON/OE. An East Anglian surname, and *coe* was a Norfolk dialect word for 'an odd old fellow'; cf. **Kay**.

Coffey F (for O C—) 'descendant of Victorious' Irish.

Coffin O 'basket, coffer' OF – ?a metonym for a maker/seller of them; the family gave its surname to Thorne C—, Somerset, and Hugh C— held Coffinswell, Devon, in 1185. But it may sometimes be for **Caffin**. Common in Devon, so Weekley connected it with 'red' Keltic (cf. **Gough**).

Cogswell L A welter of 'wild birds', 'hilltop', and an A S owner's F meaning 'Cockerel'; and 'spring' or 'nook' OE. Formally, the likeliest place is Coxwell, Berks, but Bardsley is emphatic that the surname existed only near Coggeshall, Essex.

Cohen O 'priest' Hebrew, and normally a Jewish surname.

Coker L 'crooked (river)' British; three places in Somerset.

Colborn(e), Colb(o)urn L This must usually be 'cool stream' OE; place (–burn) in North Yorks.

Colby L 'Cole's (ON or OE N) farm/village' ON; place in Norfolk.

Colclough L 'cold Clough' or 'Clough with coal/charcoal' OE; place in Staffs.

Coldham L 'cold homestead' OE; place in Cambs.

Coldstream L 'cold stream (the Tweed)' OE; place in Berwicks where the C— Guards were first recruited.

Coldwell L 'cold spring/stream' OE; places in four counties.

Cole F dim. 'Nicolas'. Or N 'coal(-black), swarthy' OE or 'pate, top-knot, crown of the head' ON – but the surname is far more southern than northern, so an Old Norse derivation is less likely. A couple are recorded as *atte Cole/Colle*, where the meaning is L ?'hill' OE. Or for **McDougall**. Family name of the earls of Enniskillen. **Coles** '(son) of C—'; common in the south-west.

Colebrook L 'cool brook' OE, part of Winchester once containing the city's washing-place. A surname of Hants and Sussex mainly.

Colefax See Colfax.

Coleman F Either Germanic, with sense of 'coal-black/swarthy man'; or dim. 'Nicolas', with –man added to mean ?'servant'; or Irish *Columbán* (a derivative of the F of Saint Columba 'dove' from Latin), which became **Colman** and was brought from Ireland by Vikings. Around the Weald of Kent–Sussex, it will be O 'charcoal-burner' OE– and the surname *is* chiefly found in Kent.

Coleridge L 'ridge where charcoal is burnt' OE; two places in Devon.

Colfax, Colfox N 'coal-fox, brant-fox' OE, a melanistic type – Chaucer tips its tail and ears with black; from some nasty trait.

Colin See **Collin**. **Colinson** F 'son of C—'.

Coll(s) Probably shares the various origins of **Cole(s)**.

Collard F double dim. 'Nicolas'; cf. **Collin**.

Colledge L 'Wich/Wick where charcoal is burnt' OE; places Colwich in Staffs (a salt area) and Colwick in Notts; in neither case is the –*w*– sounded. The meaning 'college (of priests/canons/students)' OF is barely possible.

Collen See **Collin**; a surname chiefly of Cambs.

Collet(t) F double dim. 'Nicolas'.

Colley N 'coaly, dusky, swarthy' OE.

Collier O 'charcoal-burner/-seller' OE. Commoner than **Collyer**. Family name of the barons Monkswell.

Collin(g) F double dim. 'Nicolas'; or ?from another meaning of **Cole/Coll**. **Collin(g)s** '(son) of C—'; but most of the **Collins**es in Ireland are for O Cullane 'descendant of ?Whelp' Irish; 30th commonest surname in Ireland in 1890. **Collinson** 'son of C—'.

F: *first name*　　L: *local name*　　N: *nickname*　　O: *occupational name*

Collingwood L 'challenge/dispute wood (i.e. wood whose ownership is disputed)' OF+OE; place in Staffs.

Collis(on) F '(son)/son of **Coll**'.

Collop N 'fried meat; bacon and eggs' OE from ?ON.

Collyer Surrey form of **Collier**.

Colman See **Coleman**.

Colthard, **Colthart** O 'colt-herd' OE.

Coltman O 'colt-keeper' OE.

Colwell, **Colwill** L 'cool spring/stream' OE, places (–well) in Northd, IoW and (–wall) Herefords; or 'Coly (= narrow) stream' British + OE, place (–well) in Devon – where –i– is common.

Colyer See **Collier**; still seen in the old charcoal-burning area of the Weald of Kent.

Combe L '(small) valley, valley in the flank of a hill, short valley running up from the sea' OE; the Old English word is usually derived from Welsh *cwm*, but this may not be the whole story. The –e may show a dative after a lost preposition. There are many places Co(o)mb(e) in the south – nine in Somerset, six in Devon, and in six other counties; and the associated surnames are mainly south-western. **Comb(e)s** L 'of (i.e. in) a **C—**'; –es is especially a Wilts surname.

Comber L 'dweller in a **Combe**'. Or ?O 'comb-maker' OE+–er. Also **Comer**.

Comfort N of a rare abstract type, 'encouragement, support' OF, for a rather nice person. Chiefly a Kent surname.

Comley N 'comely, handsome, admirable' OE. But more likely, in view of the –ley, is a L 'clearing in a **Combe**' OE, such as Combley in IoW.

Commin(s), **Commings** See **Cummin(s)**.

Compton L 'place in a **Combe**' OE; places in a dozen west Midland and southern counties, from Staffs to Devon, including eight in Somerset, and with an outlier in West Yorks. Family name of the marquesses of Northampton.

Comyns See **Cummins**.

Congreve L 'grove/wood in a **Combe**' OE; place in Staffs.

Conibear See **Conybear**.

Coningsby L 'king's farm' ON; place in Lincs.

Conisbee L From Conisby, Lincs, with same meaning as **Coningsby**.

Connell and O **C—** were the 25th commonest surname in Ireland in 1890; for meaning see **McConnal**.

Conner O '(ale-)conner, inspector, examiner' OE.

Conning N 'rabbit' OF; or 'clever, skilled' OE (cf. *cunning*).

Connolly F connected with Irish *Conall* 'high mighty'; 23rd commonest surname in Ireland in 1890.

Connor F (normally O **C—** or O **Conor**) 'descendant of High Will' Irish; they formed the ninth commonest surname in Ireland in 1890.

Considine F (for McC—) 'son of **Constantine**' in its Irish form.

Constable O From the chief executive officer of a king's court to a castle governor, a JP, or a parish constable (literally 'count of the stable') OF.

Constantine F dim. 'steadfast, constant' Latin, from the Emperor who made the Empire Christian.

Constaple See **Constable**.

Conway L North Wales (Caern) town and castle, garrisoned by Edward I with his Englishmen; named after River Conwy, where –wy is Welsh 'water' and Con– is ?'high/holy'. Hardly any Welsh place-names have given rise to surnames (whereas thousands of English places have), and the surname is usually an anglicization of two Irish names (in Mc– and O) meaning ?'head-smashing' and ?'yellow hound'.

Conybear(e) L 'rabbit-burrow, warren' OF+OE.

Conyers L 'Cogners/Coignières (= quince-trees)' OF; places in Sarthe/Seine-et-Oise.

Conyngham Same as **Cunningham**, but not normally found in Ireland.

Cooch See **Couch**.

Cook(e) O 'cook' OE. A good old surname that ought not to have the snobbish –e; Guppy found that sturdy farmers mostly did without it, and the national figures are usually 3 **Cook**:1 **Cooke**, but in parts of the north Midlands the position is reversed – Chester TD 2:5, Leicester 2:3, Manchester 2:nearly 3. **Cook** was the 42nd commonest surname in England and Wales in 1853. See also **Lequeux**.

Cooksey L 'island of (an AS called) Quick/Lively' OE; place in Worcs.

Coom(be), **Coom(b)er**, **Coomb(e)s** See **Combe**, **Comber**, **Comb(e)s**.

Cooper O 'wooden tub-/cask-/bucket-maker (or repairer)' ME from Germanic and Low Latin. Common everywhere save in the north, and 28th commonest surname in England and Wales in 1853. The variant **Coopper** is unpronounceable.

Coot(e) N 'coot' ME, from baldness or daftness.

Cope N 'cape, cope, cloak' OE, for a wearer – or O for a maker – of them.

F: *first name*   L: *local name*   N: *nickname*   O: *occupational name*

Copeland L 'bought land' ON (cf. **Chapman**); places in Cumberland, Co. Durham, or **Coupland** in Northd.

Copestake O 'woodcutter (literally cut-stake)' OF+OE. A Derbys surname.

Copland See **Copeland**.

Copleston(e) See **Copplestone**.

Copley L 'clearing by/on a hilltop' OE; ten places in West Yorks alone, and in other counties, though the Cambs place is 'round tumulus (**Low**)' OE.

Copner N 'illicit lover, adulterer, paramour' OE – unless proof could be adduced of L family origins at Copnor, Hants, 'landing-place of (an AS called) Top' OE.

Copp L Normally the 'hilltop' OE that figures in so many place-names. But also N 'crown of the head, topknot' (the same word).

Coppard N 'big-head' OE+OF suffix.

Coppersmith O 'worker in copper' OE+OE; a name established in USA.

Copperthwaite L '**Thwaite** of the **Cooper**'; place in North Yorks.

Copperwheat L Strange derivative of **Copperthwaite**, now much commoner than the original. Also **Copperwhite**.

Copplestone L '?stone like a crest (i.e. ?standing stone)' OE; two places in Devon, and a lost place in Suffolk.

Corb(in), **Corbet(t)** N 'raven' OF, from black hair or raucousness, and two forms of dim.; –tt is very common in the group Warwicks–Worcs–Glos–Herefords–Salop. **Corbett** is the family name of the barons Rowallan.

Corcoran N 'red-/purple-faced' Irish (also O **C—**, McC—).

Corden, **Cordon** O 'leather' OF, for a worker in it; see **Cordiner**.

Corder(e)y, **Corderoy** N '(having the) heart of a king' OF. Or L 'rope-walk' OF, probably for a ropemaker.

Cordiner O 'cordwainer, leather-worker, shoemaker' OF from Spanish city Córdoba (Latin Corduba; a Phoenician foundation); sometimes ?'maker of cord/ribbon' OF.

Corfe L 'cutting, pass' OE (cf. *carve*); places in Dorset (two), Somerset. But sometimes ?N 'raven' OF; cf. **Corb**.

Cork O Either 'cork' Spanish (ultimately from Latin) or 'cork (a purple dye prepared from lichens)' Irish and Scots Gaelic, from working in one of these materials. Whence also **Corker**.

Corlett F 'son of Thor People' Manx (the remains of *Mac*–)+ON.

Corley L 'wood with cranes/herons' OE; place in Warwicks.

Cormack See **McCormack**.

Cornelius F Roman family name perhaps derived from *cornu* 'horn';

the devout centurion in *Acts* x.1, and several martyred Popes. Not used as a F in medieval England, its introduction here being partly from the Low Countries and partly (to render names like Conchubhar) from Ireland.

Cornell L For **Cornwall**; or **Cornwell**; or **Cornall**, a lost place in Lancs; or **Cornhill**, Northd – '**Haugh** (*halh*) with cranes/herons' OE; or **Cornhill**, London (etc.) – 'hill where corn is sold' OE. Reaney adds N 'rook, crow' OF.

Corner L 'corner' OF. Or O 'horn-player' OF.

Corney L 'island with corn/cranes' OE, places in Cumberland, Herts; or a lost 'nook with cranes' OE, place in Lancs.

Cornford, Cornforth L 'mill ford' or 'ford where querns were to be got' OE, places (–d) in Dorset and (lost) near Fairford, Glos; or 'ford with cranes (the birds, of course)' OE, place (now –th) in Co. Durham. On the other hand, Guppy counted –d only in Sussex, and some lost or minor place meaning even 'ford near corn' OE is feasible.

Cornish L 'man from **Cornwall**'; OE suffix; naturally a Devon–Somerset surname.

Cornwall L **Corn**– from a British tribal name meaning ?'horn', –**wall** as in **Welsh**; thus the county name is a hybrid of British and OE. **Cornwallis** 'man from **C**–', with an OF suffix ?based on English –*ish*.

Cornwell L 'stream with cranes/herons' OE; place in Oxon.

Corp(e) N 'raven' OF (or ?ON). **Corps** '(son) of **Corp**'.

Corrick N 'dwarf, elf' Cornish or 'dwarfish' Breton; still a south-western name.

Cosh L 'hut, cabin, cottage, hovel' ?Keltic. Appears as a surname in Essex from 1248 on.

Costain F 'son of **Augustine**' Manx, with the *Mc*– absorbed; or dim. '**Constantine**'.

Costello F (for McC—) Probably 'son of **Jocelyn**' in an Irish form; 'first recorded instance of a Norman family assuming a Mac name', says MacLysaght.

Cote L 'cottage, hut, (sheep-)cote' OE. **Cotes** 'of (i.e. at) the **C**—,' or a plural. Locality, or places in thirteen counties (Cote, Cotes, Coat, Coate, Coates).

Coton See **Cotton**.

Cottam L 'at the cottages' OE dative plural –*um* after lost preposition; locality, or places in Notts, East Yorks, and others (in Notts, Bristol) called Cotham.

F: *first name*   L: *local name*   N: *nickname*   O: *occupational name*

Cotter O 'cottager, villein holding a cot through labour service' OF. But in Ireland and Man F (for McC—) 'son of Terrible Army' ON.

Cotterell, Cotterill O dim. 'cottager' OF; common in Warwicks–Worcs–Staffs–Ches–Derbys, Berks.

Cottier See **Cotter**; especially a surname of the Isle of Man, and pronounced *Cotcher*.

Cottle L 'wood (by the) estuary' Cornish, seat Cotehele in Cornwall, embowered in trees in a horseshoe bend of the River Tamar; there were Cottels at Cotehele in the 1200s – and even in 1120 Sir Robert de Cotel held the manor of Camerton, Somerset. But some of the Somerset–Dorset–Wilts bearers may be from O 'mailcoat' or 'dagger', both metonyms, or *cotel* (some sort of trader), all OF.

Cotton L '(at) the cottages/huts' OE dative plural after lost preposition; locality, or places (also Coton) in a dozen counties.

Cottrell, Cottrill See **Cotterell**.

Couch, Coucher, Couchman O From OF *couche* 'bed, couch, pallet, mattress, upholstery', for a maker of these. But a **Coucher** was also a 'bed-ridden person', or even ?'setter of jewels'. **Couchman** was mainly a surname of mid-Kent until recent times.

Coulson F 'son of (dim.) **Nicolas**' (cf. **Cole**). Chiefly a surname of Northd–Co. Durham–Yorks–Lincs, so places Coulston (Wilts) and Coulsdon (Surrey) are not involved.

Coulthard, Coulthart O See **Colthard**. Guppy counted **Coulthard** only in Cumberland–Co. Durham.

Coulton L '**Cole**'s place' or 'place with charcoal-burning/colts' all OE; place in North Yorks.

Counter O 'treasurer, one who keeps accounts' OF (Norman dialect).

Couper Scots form of **Cooper**; nearly half as many in Glasgow TD.

Coupland See **Copeland**.

Courage N 'heartiness, spirit, courage' OF.

Court L 'court, manor, castle' OF. Or N 'short' OF.

Courtauld N dim. 'short' OF; a Huguenot surname.

Courtenay N 'short nose' OF (though there is also a place in Loiret). A magnificent family that provided three emperors of Constantinople and the long line of the earls of Devon.

Courtiour O 'man working at a **Court**' OF (after all, every 'courtier' in *our* sense would already have some proud family name).

Courtnell L '**Haugh** of (an AS called) Short' OE, place (Courteenhall, pronounced Cortn-) in Northants.

Cousen, Cousin N 'relative, cousin, nephew' OF. **Cousens, Cousins, Couzens** '(son) of **C**—'.

Cove L Not from *a* cove, but (as family origins show) from the parishes of North and South C—, Suffolk, probably meaning 'cove' OE.

Cowan See **Cowen**.

Coward See **Cowherd**; a fine old bucolic surname made to look craven.

Cowder(o)y, Cowdray, Cowdrey L 'hazel copse' OF; place (–dray) in Sussex.

Cowen See **McOwen**. Or for **Cohen**.

Cowgill L Five places in West Yorks, meaning variously 'ravine' ON 'with cows/coal/a dam' OE, or 'ravine belonging to (a Norseman called) Kalli'.

Cowherd O 'cow-herd' OE; much rarer than **Coward** – one in London TD.

Cowley L 'cow pasture' OE, place in Glos; 'charcoal wood/clearing' OE, places in Derbys, Lancs; 'Cufa's (= ?fat, tubby) pasture' OE or '?hill (or ?log) wood/clearing' OE, places in Bucks, Devon, Oxon, Staffs; 'wood/clearing in a recess' OE or 'Cōfa's pasture' OE, place in Middx. But the forty-nine in the Isle of Man TD are no doubt F from **McAulay** or **McAuley**.

Cowlin(g) F double dim. '**Nicolas**' (see **Collin**). Or L 'place by (the hill called) Coll (= hill)' OE or ON; place (–g) in West Yorks.

Cowlinshaw L 'charcoal wood' OE; places (Cowlishaw) in Derbys, Lancs.

Cowmeadow L 'meadow with cows' OE.

Cowpe L 'cow valley' OE; place in Lancs.

Cowper See **Cooper**, which is pronounced the same.

Cowperthwaite See **Copperthwaite**; established in USA. Another version is **Cowpertwait**.

Cowslade L 'dell with cows' OE (cf. **Slade**). A Newbury, Berks, family said to have become extinct in 1931.

Cox(e) Respelling of **Cocks**, common in Dorset–Somerset–Glos–Oxon area. –e is very rare and affected.

Coxet(t)er O 'cock-setter' (who sets the cocks in cock-fighting) OE.

Coxon F 'son of **Cock**'.

Coxwell See **Cogswell**.

Coy N 'quiet, shy, coy' OF (from same stem as *quiet*).

Coysh See **Cosh**.

Crab, Crabb(e) N For being sharp as a 'crab-apple' ME (perhaps from the other *crab*), or for having a funny walk or a spiteful, crabby temper, from 'crab' OE.

Crabtree L 'crab-apple tree' ME+OE; chiefly a Lancs–West Yorks surname.

Craddock F 'amiable' Welsh *Caradawg* (cf. the brave *Caractacus* as

F: *first name*   L: *local name*   N: *nickname*   O: *occupational name*

respelt by the Romans who took him in bondage to Rome in A.D. 51). Rarely ?L, place in Devon, from a stream with the same sense, 'nice' Welsh. Occurs as **Cradick**, **Cradock**.

Crafton L 'place where (wild) saffron grows' OE (cf. *crocus*); place in Bucks.

Cragg L 'crag' Scots Gaelic or Welsh. **Craggs** 'of (i.e. at) the **C—**', or a plural.

Craig L Scots and Northd form of **Cragg**. 67th commonest surname in Scotland in 1958. Family name of the viscounts Craigavon.

Craigie L Places in a number of Scots counties, all derived from 'crag, rock' Scots Gaelic.

Cranage L 'stream with crows' OE; place in Ches.

Crandon L 'hill with cranes (the birds, of course)' OE; C—, Somerset, however, was spelt *Grene*– and *Gran*– in 1086 and 1212, and may once have been 'green hill' OE.

Crane N '(skinny and long-legged like a) crane' OE.

Cranfield, Cranford, Cranham L 'open land/ford/river-meadow with cranes' OE; places in Beds/Middx, Northants/Glos; but Cranham, Essex, was originally 'headland with crows' OE.

Crank N 'high-spirited, cocky' ME.

Crankshaw L 'wood with cranes' OE *cranuc*, not the usual *cran*; place (Cronkshaw) in Lancs.

Cranley, Cranmer, Cranwell L 'wood (or clearing)/pool/spring with cranes' OE; places in Suffolk and (–leigh) Surrey/Norfolk, Suffolk/Lincs.

Crass N 'fat' OF.

Craster L 'Roman site with crows' OE; place in Northd.

Crathorn L 'thorntree in a nook' ON, place (–e) in North Yorks, though Ekwall puts 'crows' or 'corncrakes' ON into it.

Craven L ?derived from Welsh *craf* 'garlic'; district of West Yorks. (No reference, we are glad to say, to cowardice.)

Crawcour N 'heart-breaker (literally break-heart)' OF. Or L from 'Crèvecœur' ('nicknamed from the dismay of the civilians at local fighting'); places in Calvados, Oise, Nord, etc.

Crawford L 'ford with crows' OE; places in Lanarks, Lancs, Dorset. Largely a Scots and North Country surname, but there are other stocks. 77th commonest surname in Scotland in 1958.

Crawhall L Formally, this looks like '*Haugh* with crows' OE, but no place is now known.

Crawley L 'wood/clearing with crows' OE. places in nine counties; but place in Northd is 'hill with crows' OE. A Beds–Northants surname.

Crawshaw, Crawshay L 'Shaw with crows' OE; place (–w) in Lancs, and West Yorks surnames.

Craze N 'fat' OF (cf. *crass* and **Crass**).

Creagh N Adjective from 'branch' Irish, from tradition of their having carried boughs in a battle against Norsemen at Limerick.

Crease N 'elegant, dainty' OE.

Creech L 'hill' British; places in Dorset, Somerset.

Crees(e) Forms of **Crease** common in Wilts–Somerset.

Creighton L 'rock/cliff place' OW+OE; place in Staffs.

Crerar O Scots Gaelic equivalent of **Sievewright**.

Cres(s)well L 'spring/stream where cress grows' OE; places in Northd, Staffs, Pemb, Derbys. Surname in –ss– common in Worcs, Derbys.

Crewe L 'ford, stepping-stones' OW; place in Ches.

Cribb O 'manger, stall for cattle' OE, from working at one.

Crichton L 'border/boundary place' Scots Gaelic+OE; place in Midlothian.

Crickett L 'little hill' Keltic+OF suffix; two places (–et) in Somerset.

Crippen, Cripps See **Crisp(in)**. **Cripps** is the family name of the barons Parmoor.

Crisp(e) N 'curly' OE from Latin; **Crispin** is a derived Roman F, especially that of the shoemakers' saint, martyred at Soissons *c.* 285.

Critchley L Probably a lost place in Lancs, 'hill hill' Keltic+OE, and still mainly a Lancs surname.

Croasdale Version of **Crossdale** found in Lancs.

Crocker O 'crockery-maker, potter' OE. Or form of **Crawcour**.

Croft L 'arable enclosure adjoining a house' OE, locality, or places in Herts, Lancs, Lincs, North Yorks; but place in Leics is 'machine, engine, mill' OE (cf. *craft*). Guppy counted it only in Warwicks, Lincs–Yorks–Lancs. **Crofts** 'of (i.e. at) the **C**—', or a plural.

Crofton L 'place with a **Croft**' OE, places in four counties; but place in Kent was once Cropton, ?'hump/hillock place' OE; and place in Lincs is ?'saffron place' OE.

Croker See **Crocker**.

Cromer L 'mere/pool with crows' OE; place in Norfolk.

Crompton L 'place in a stream-bend' OE; place in Lancs.

Cromwell L 'winding stream' OE; places in Notts, West Yorks.

Crook(e) F 'hook, crook'. Or a descriptive N for a hunchback or twister. Or L 'nook, bend'; place in Co. Durham. All from ON *krók-*. **Crook(e)s** L 'bends' ON; places in West Yorks and the north-east. –es is a Yorks–Derbys surname.

F: *first name*   L: *local name*   N: *nickname*   O: *occupational name*

Crookdale L 'crooked-oak valley' ON, place in Cumberland, and a Cumbrian surname.

Croom(e) L '(at) the nooks/side-valleys' OE dative plural after lost preposition, place in East Yorks; 'crooked stream' OW, three places in Worcs. Guppy counted **-m** only in Somerset.

Crosby (also **Crosbee**, **Crosbie**) L 'village/farm with cross(es)' ON; Old Norse *kross* is from Irish and ultimately from Latin; four places in Cumberland (where Crosscanonby was once Crosby-Canonby), and some in Lancs, Lincs, Westmorland, Yorks – all in the Scandinavian area.

Cross L 'cross' OE and ON (cf. **Crosby**); one who lived by a market/roadside cross, or ?a crossroads. A strongly Midland and East Anglian surname.

Crossdale L 'valley with crosses' ON; place in Cumberland.

Crossley L 'clearing with a cross' OE; two places in West Yorks, and still a West Yorks surname. Family name of the barons Somerleyton.

Crosthwaite L '**Thwaite** with a cross' ON; places in Cumberland, Westmorland, North Yorks.

Croston L 'place with a (market) cross' OE; place in Lancs.

Crouch L 'cross' OE. **Croucher** 'dweller at a **C—**'. Cf. **Cross**.

Croughton L 'saffron/river fork farm' OE; places in Ches, Northants.

Crow(e) N 'crow' OE.

Crowcombe L '**Combe** with crows' OE; place in Somerset.

Crowder See **Crowther**.

Crowhurst L '**Hirst** with crows' OE; place in Surrey.

Crowl(e) L 'curly (like the *crulle* locks of Chaucer's Squire), winding' OE – a lost river name, place in Lincs; but place in Worcs is ?'clearing at the bend/nook' OE. Alas, Guppy put it only in Cornwall.

Crowley L 'wood/clearing with crows' OE; locality, or places in Ches, Lancs. But Irish bearers are F (for O **C—**) 'descendant of Hard Hero' Irish.

Crowther O 'fiddler' Welsh *crwth*+**-er**. Chiefly a Lancs–West Yorks surname.

Croxall L 'hall of (a Norseman called) Hook' ON; place in Staffs.

Croyden, Croydon L 'saffron valley'/'hill with crows'/'valley with crows' all OE; places in Surrey/Somerset/Cambs.

Crozier O 'crosier' OF, with reference to carrying a bishop's or a cross; or L, as with so many **-er** names, from living near a cross; or again O, from selling them.

Cruickshank N 'bowlegged' ON (with Scots **-ui** from *-ō-*)+OE (cf. **Crook** and **Shank**). Chiefly a Scots surname.

Cruise See **Cruse**.

Crump N 'crooked, stooping' OE.

Cruse N 'ferocious' ME; or sometimes from **Cruwys**.

Crutch See **Crouch**; the Crutched Friars were so called from bearing or wearing a cross. Another possible derivation is from 'hill' Keltic; a place near Droitwich, Worcs.

Crutchley L Of the same meaning as **Critchley**.

Cruwys L Norman family from 'Cruys-Straëte' (meaning?); place in Nord.

Cubbin F Manx version of **McGibbon**.

Cuckow N 'cuckoo' OF, cf. **Gook**.

Cudbird, Cudding, Cuddy See **Cuthbert** (whose pet form *Cuddy* is now obsolete).

Cudlipp N This can hardly be anything but 'cut/cleft lip, hare-lip' OE + OE, though early forms are lacking. Yet Cudlippstown in Petertavy, Devon, was *Codelip(p)* in 1238 – 'the leap (over a stream) belonging to Cudda (cf. **Cudbird**)' OE.

Cuerden L 'ash-tree' OW; place in Lancs.

Cuff N ?'cuff, mittens' ME from Low Latin and first recorded about 1375. A Somerset–Wilts family, and (from the same stock) the family name of the Irish earls of Desart and barons Tyrawley.

Culcheth L 'recess in a wood' OW; place in Lancs.

Culham L 'river-meadow with a kiln' OE; place in Berks. But first element of place in Oxon is an AS owner with a N ?'cowl, hood' OE.

Cullen L 'Cologne (= colony)' OF from Latin, the German Rhineland city; or ?'at the back of the river' Scots Gaelic, place in Banffs. (But in south-west Scotland it is ?from Irish McC—.)

Culleton, Culliford L 'farm/ford on the narrow river' Keltic + OE; neighbouring places (Colyton, Colyford) in Devon.

Cullum See **Culham**. A man at Oxford in 1570 was called William Culhame or Colham or Culme.

Culpep(p)er O 'pepper-culler/-gatherer, spicer' OF + OE.

Culverhouse L 'dovecot' OE.

Culverwell L 'spring/stream frequented by doves' OE; no place is now recorded, but it is a south-western surname, and Culverswell (of the same meaning) is in Devon.

Cumberland L 'land of the Britons/Cymry (whom the English call **Welsh**)' OW + OE, the county. Guppy counted it only in Notts.

Cumberledge, Cumberlidge L Probably 'Welshman's/Welshmen's ridge/bank' OW + OE *hlinc*. Chiefly a Staffs surname.

Cumberworth L First element as in **Cumberledge**, second = 'enclosure' OE; places in Lincs, West Yorks.

F: *first name*　　L: *local name*　　N: *nickname*　　O: *occupational name*

Cumbes See **Combes**.

Cumine, Cuming(s) Forms of **Cummin(s)**.

Cummin(e), Cumming F dim. 'crooked, bent' Irish; a 7th-century abbot of Iona was *Cumin*. Also a Breton F (meaning?), which reached East Anglia by Breton settlement after 1066, and had already reached Bosc–Benard–Commin, Eure, whence ?came Robert Cumin, companion of the Conqueror and ancestor of Bruce's enemy the Red Comyn. Forms in **–ng** are mostly Scots. **Cummin(g)s** '(son) of **C—**'.

Cundall, Cundell, Cundill L 'valley valley' OE+ON, tautologically (cf. **Combe, Dale**); place (–a–) in North Yorks, and all Yorks surnames.

Cundy L 'conduit, waterpipe, pump, fountain' OF; found in Yorks in 1379, but Guppy counted it only in Cornwall.

Cunneber See **Conybear**.

Cunningham L Place in Ayrs; Johnston's derivation as ?'milk pails' Scots Gaelic sounds impossible; form *c.* 1150 was *Cunegan*, and the modern spelling, especially the **–ham** suffix, is the work of an anglicized scribe. But the Irish bearers are F (for O Cunigan) 'descendant of (dim.) Conn' Irish. 73rd commonest surname in Scotland in 1958, 74th in Ireland in 1890.

Curling N 'little curly' ME *crulling* from Germanic; found as Crullyng in 13th-century Sussex, and still a Kent surname.

Curnow L '**Cornwall**' Cornish, a late version of *Kernow*.

Curran Formerly Ó Curráin; in 1659 chiefly in Co. Waterford, but now spread evenly through the four provinces of Ireland; the meaning is quite unknown, and the background of the name unrecorded.

Currie L 'cauldron (i.e. ravine, glen)' Scots Gaelic; place (Corrie) in Dumfs – not, apparently, from place Currie ('wet plain' Scots Gaelic dative) in Midlothian. Black suggests also F, anglicizing of McVurich 'son of **Murdoch**'. 94th commonest surname in Scotland in 1958.

Curry L Either for **Currie**, or a British river-name on which stand the various places called Curry in Somerset. Also O 'kitchen' OF.

Curt(a)in N 'shorty' OF. Also standing for **McCurtin**.

Curthose, Curthoys Despite the first spelling, these will usually be forms of **Curtis**.

Curtis (rarely **Curtiss**) N 'courteous, educated, well-bred' OF. Some of the spellings support N 'short hose/stockings/breeches' OF+ Germanic, the name of William I's son Robert. There is nothing to suggest L 'court-house' OF+OE. Common from Lincs to Cornwall, especially in Bucks.

Curwen L ?'at the back of the hill' Scots Gaelic; place Colvend (once Culwen) in Kirkcudbrs.

Curzon L 'Courson (i.e. Curtius's place)' OF – Curtius a Roman family name ?related to Latin *curt*– 'short'; place in Calvados. Or N 'shortish' OF. Family name of the earls Howe and of two other peers.

Cushing, Cushion, Cussen(s), Cussins, Cussons See **Cousen(s)**.

Cuss O 'thigh-armour' OF, for a maker of it.

Custance F The usual English form of the female name *Constance* 'steadfastness' Latin, or a male name of the same meaning. But Reaney found that some were from Coutances, in Manche, named after the Emperor Constantius Chlorus, who fortified it in A.D. 305–6.

Cutbirth Corruption, no doubt with a family legend of Caesarian section, of **Cuthbert**.

Cuthbert(son) F 'famous bright' OE. Saint, bishop of Lindisfarne, and misogynist (†687); his cult was chiefly in north England and south Scotland, though Guppy counted the surname only in Lincs. And 'son of C—'.

Cutler O 'maker/vendor/sharpener of cutlery' OF.

Cutt F dim. '**Cuthbert**', or dim. of some other F with the same first element. **Cutts** '(son) of **C—**'. A Derbys surname.

Cutter O A craftsman who cuts various things, but especially 'tailor, barber' ME, from ?OE; perhaps also a wood-/stone-cutter. Painfully apt surname of Ephraim C—, eminent USA physician and surgeon.

Cutteridge F 'famed rule' OE, made to resemble a L –ridge name.

Cutting F 'son of **Cutt**'; –ing shows, as often, a patronymic. Chiefly an East Anglian surname.

Cypher N 'zero' OF from Arabic (ultimately from a verb meaning 'to be empty'). The term had reached England by 1400, but its application as a surname is ambiguous; there is certainly no reference to being an encoder or cryptanalyst.

Cyriax F '(son) of Cyriac (= lordly)' Greek; Saint Cyriac was the martyred baby son of Saint Julitta of Iconium, who usually shares his dedications (as at Capel Curig, North Wales).

F: *first name*   L: *local name*   N: *nickname*   O: *occupational name*

D

Dabb F dim. '**Robert**'. **Dabbs** '(son) of **D—**'.

Dabinett F double dim. '**Dabb**', with two OF suffixes.

Dabney See **Daubeny**.

Daboll USA corruption of **Dibell**.

Dacre L 'dropping/trickling stream' Keltic; place in Cumberland.

D'Aeth See **Death**.

Daft N 'meek, gentle' OE; but the rude meaning is medieval too. Chiefly Notts–Lincs.

Dagg N 'dagger' OF; but also (probably the same word) an ornamental scallop on a garment, or a pointed slash to show a brighter colour through; *Daggeberd* is a 1310 surname for a man with a pointed beard.

Dainty See **Dentith**. Chiefly a Northants surname.

Daish Form of **Dash**; cf. **Aish**.

Dakin(g) See **Daykin**. –n is found chiefly in the group Derbys–Ches–Staffs.

Dalby L 'valley farm' ON; places in Leics (three), Lincs, North Yorks, and a Leics surname.

Dale L 'valley, dale' OE and ON. A frequent and scattered surname, commoner than present-day *dales* would suggest.

Dall L 'dale, valley' ON/OE. Or N 'hand, paw' ME.

Dallas L 'meadow stance/resting-place' Scots Gaelic (both elements ?from British), places in Moray and Ross; or corruption of 'dale house' OE, locality, or place Dalehouse in North Yorks.

Dallimore See **De la Mare**.

Dalling L 'the gang of (an AS called) Proud/Resplendent' OE; place in Norfolk.

Dalli(n)son L 'from Alençon' (named ?after a F akin to **Alan**) Gaulish through OF; place in Orne.

Dalton, D'Alton L 'dale farm' OE; fourteen places in typical dale country – Co. Durham, Lancs, Northd, Westmorland, Yorks, yet, oddly, Guppy found the surname chiefly in Bucks. The spelling **D'—** must often be a mere affectation. The Daton and **Daughton** families of Co. Kilkenny were originally Norman 'from Autun/Authon' (named after the Roman Imperial title *Augustus*), but not from **Alton**, Hants.

Dalwood L 'wood in a valley' OE; place in Devon.

Dalyell See **Dalziel**.; both forms are now often sounded *Dee-ell*.

Dalziel(l) L Johnston poetically suggests 'field of the sungleam'

Scots Gaelic; place (–el) in Lanarks. The original ʒ ('yogh' – *y*
initially, spirant *gh* medially and finally) was wrongly written *z*,
leading to a spelling-pronunciation *Dalzeel*; **Dalyell** better (though
imperfectly) represents the sound. Surnames of the Scots Lowlands
and Border.

Damant See **Dammant**.

Damerall, Damerell L 'of' OF 'Aumale (= white marl)' Latin+
?Gaulish, place in Seine-Maritime, seen in fuller form in English
title Duke of *Albemarle* and Shakespeare's Aumerle. Chiefly a
Devon surname.

Damerham L 'river-meadow belonging to the judges' OE (cf. *doom*,
deem); place (once a royal manor) in Hants.

Dammant, Damment, Damont L Dauzat makes **Damont** 'up-
stream (from other houses)' OF; this is more satisfactory for the
short vowel *a* than the family tradition of F 'day protector' OE *Daeg-
mund*, but **Dayment** is probably for **Dayman**, with excrescent
dental (just as we turned *paysan* into *peasant* and *vermin* into *varmint*). The **Dammant** series are said to have had their heart-land
at Dallinghoo in Suffolk.

Dampier L 'Dampierre (= Saint **Peter**)' first element ultimately
Latin *dominus* 'master'; many places in France, including Normandy.

Damson N 'son of the lady/noblewoman/prioress/abbess' OF+OE;
though *dame* was used, with mock respect, of *any* woman.

Danby L 'Danes' farm' ON; three places in North Yorks, and a North
Yorks surname.

Dancer O '(professional) dancer' OF. Counted by Guppy only in
Bucks.

Dando L 'from Aunou (= "alder-tree"+suffix)' Latin through OF,
place in Orne. It does *not* mean an oath 'God's tooth!' (*dent-Dieu*),
as has been suggested.

Dane L 'valley' OE; see **Dean**.

Dangerfield L 'of' OF 'Angerville (= Ansgar/god-spear/Oscar's
place)' ON+OF from Latin *villa*, places in Calvados, Eure, Seine-
Maritime, Seine-et-Oise.

Daniel(l) F 'God has judged' Hebrew (a complete sentence, like
Michael), major prophet. **Daniel(l)s** '(son) of D—'. Both –l and
–ls are fairly common south of Worcs–Norfolk.

Danvers L 'from Antwerp (= at the wharf)' OF version of Flemish.

Darben N 'dear child (literally bairn)' OE.

Darby L Spelling from usual pronunciation of **Derby**, with –ar as

F: *first name*   L: *local name*   N: *nickname*   O: *occupational name*

in **Clark**. (But the D— of *D— and Joan* is a F, pet form of Irish Dermot, Diarmuid, 'free from envy'.) Guppy found it much shifted – Worcs, Essex, Somerset. Darbyites, or Exclusive Brethren, named after John Nelson **D—** (†1882).

Dargan F (for O **D—**) 'descendant of Red' Irish.

Dark(e) N 'dark' OE; **–e** could show weak adjective after lost definite article.

Darley L '(wild) animal/deer wood/clearing' OE; places in four counties; cf. **Derby**. Bardsley's first examples are in Yorks, Derbys, 1273, and two of the places are in these counties.

Darling N 'darling (literally little dear)' OE.

Darnell L 'hidden nook' OE; place (-all) in West Yorks. Also ?N – the plant 'darnel' OF was thought to be tipsifying.

Dart L Its frequency suggests that this is that rare thing, a (Devon) river surname, cognate with Darent(h), **Derwent**, **Darwen**.

Darton L 'deer enclosure' OE; place in West Yorks.

Darwen L Lancs town named from the River **D—**; see **Derwent**.

Darwin See **Darwen**. Or F 'dear friend' OE.

Dash L 'of (i.e. at)' OF 'the Ash'.

Dashwood L 'of' OF 'Ashwood'.

Dauben(e)y, Da(u)bney L 'from Aubigny (from F *Albinius* "white" +suffix)' Latin through OF, places in three départements of Normandy. **Daubney** was countable by Guppy in Lincs.

Dauber O He completed the 'wattle and daub' process, with clay/roughcast/plaster/whitewash; the word is OF.

Daughton See **Dalton**.

Daveis(s) Appear to be USA corruptions of **Davies**.

Davenport L 'town' OE 'on the (River) Dane (= trickler)' Keltic; place in Ches.

Davey See **Davie**.

David F Originally a lullaby word 'darling', then 'friend' generally, Hebrew. Popularity of the F here stems less from the Old Testament king than from the patron saint of Wales and two Scots kings. Fairly common surname in South Wales. **Davidson** 'son of **D—**'; utterly different from **Davies** in its distribution – mainly Northd–Cumberland–Westmorland–Co. Durham, and especially Scotland; 37th commonest surname there in 1958.

Davidge F '(son) of **David**', a perverse misspelling of *Davids*.

Davie, Dav(e)y F dim. '**David**'. **–ey** is the commonest, and **–ie** the rarest, of this group. All are found chiefly in Cornwall–Devon. **Davies(s)** '(son) of **D–**'. **–ies** is easily the commonest surname of the **David** family, and typically the Welsh spelling (English **Davis**);

Guppy found that about five and a half per cent of the farming population of Wales bore this surname; it was the fifth commonest surname in England and Wales in 1853; **–ss** is a USA corruption. **Davies** is the family name of the barons Darwen.

Davin Version (especially from County Tipperary) of **Devin**.

Davis See **Davies**, of which this is the more English spelling; common in Glos–Somerset–Oxon. London TD has 1800 **–is**; 1750 **–ies**, Bristol TD 356:310. 32nd commonest surname in England and Wales in 1853, seventh in USA in 1939.

Davison Rarer form of **Davidson** in Scotland, but outnumbering it in north-east England. Family name of the barons Broughshane.

Davy See **Davie**.

Daw(e) F dim. 'David', but probably linked in the popular mind with N 'jackdaw, foolish fellow' ?OE. Mainly a south-west surname. **Dawkins** '(son) of (dim.) D—', and so back to **David**. Mainly a Midland surname, especially Leics. **Daw(e)s** '(son) of D—'. **Dawson** 'son of D—'; very northern.

Dawlish L 'black stream' Keltic; place in Devon (cf. **Douglas**).

Dawtr(e)y L 'of Hauterive' OF (see **Hawtrey**).

Day O 'dairymaid, dairyman, servant' OE; originally '(loaf-)kneader' (which is what a *la-dy* was); hence *dairy*. Sometimes it may be a F dim. 'David'.

Daykin F double dim. 'David' (from second meaning of **Day**). Rarer than **Dakin**, but fairly common in Derbys.

Dayman O 'dairyman, herdsman' OE (cf. **Day**). Also, with excrescent dental, **Dayment** (see **Dammant**) and **Daymond**.

Daysh Form of **Dash**; cf. **Aysh**.

Deacon O 'deacon' OE, ultimately from Greek, meaning 'servant'; this dignitary, next below a priest, was officially celibate.

Deadman L 'deep(–river) homestead' OE; place (Debenham) in Suffolk.

Deakin, Deakon See **Deacon**.

Deal L 'valley' OE; locality, or place in Kent.

Dean(e) Two clear origins: surname once preceded by *de/in/at* is L 'valley' OE, where **–e** is correct (either as dative after lost preposition, or because even the nominative singular in OE ended in a vowel). But *le/the*+surname is O 'dean' OF from Latin word meaning 'chief of *ten*'; ?from service in a (celibate) dean's household. **Deane** is rare, but is the family name of the barons Muskerry.

Dear(e) N 'dear/brave/deer (or other wild beast)' all OE; the last N might be bestowed from swiftness, or hunting, or gamekeeping.

F: *first name*　　L: *local name*　　N: *nickname*　　O: *occupational name*

Also a F of the first meaning, or with 'dear' as first element. **–rson** 'son of **D—**'.

Dearman F 'dear person' OE.

Death (sometimes camouflaged as **D'Eath, De Ath**) N 'death' OE, ? for one who played the part in pageants and plays. Or ??O, the first element of **Deathridge**. Spellings with **D'** may rarely be L: there is a place Ath in Belgium.

Deathridge O Occurs as *Dethewright* in Essex in 1299; if this be not 'executioner, murderer' (from two OE stems), it may have as its first element a south-east form of OE *dyð*, 'fuel, tinder'; so 'fire-wood-seller'.

Debenham, Debnam See **Deadman**.

Debney N 'God bless!' OF, from a favourite exclamation.

De Courcy L 'of Courcy (= Curtius's place)' OF (cf. **Curzon**); places in Calvados, Manche, Loiret, Marne.

Deemer O 'judge' OE.

Deeping L 'deep place' OE; four places in Lincs in which the 'deep place' is a fen.

Deer(e) See **Dear(e)**.

Deighton L 'place with a dike/ditch round' OE; places in Yorks.

De la Bere L 'of the' OF 'swine-pasture' OE; see **Bear**.

Delafield L 'of the' OF 'Field', a hybrid like **De la Bere**.

De la Haye (or one word) L 'of the' OF 'Hay', another hybrid.

De la Mare, or **Delamar(e)**, **Delamere**, **Delamore** L 'of the' OF 'lake' OE; place (Delamere) in Ches; or third element could be any 'mere/moor/marsh' OE; and many places in France are called La Mare 'lake, pond' OF.

Delane, Delan(e)y F (for O **D—**) 'descendant of Black+(River) Slaney (= ?health-giving, safe)' Irish. Or **–y** might be L 'of the alder grove' OF.

De la Rue (or one word) L 'of the street' OF, from a house giving on to the highway. The first of the playing-card-making family was from Guernsey.

Delbridge L 'of the' OF 'bridge' OE, a hybrid like the **De la** surnames.

Delf, Delph L 'digging, ditch, quarry, pit' OE; places in Hunts, Kent, Lincs, West Yorks. Also **Delve**.

Dell L 'dell' OE. **Dellar, Deller** L 'one who lives in a dell'.

Dempsey F (for O **D—**) 'descendant of Proud' Irish.

Dempster O Female, later male 'judge' OE; cf. the Manx *deemsters* and the former *dempsters* in Scotland.

Denby L 'Danes' farm' ON; places in Derbys, West Yorks, and a West Yorks surname.

Denford L 'ford in a valley' OE; places in Berks, Northants.

Denham L 'valley homestead' OE, places in Bucks (near Uxbridge), Suffolk; but place in Bucks near Quainton is 'hill of the family/folk of **Dunn**' or 'hill of the hill people' OE.

Denis(e) F '(follower) of Dionysos/Bacchus, the god of wine' Greek; **Denise** was a popular female F based on this. The wholly inappropriate F of the Areopagite converted by Saint Paul in Athens, and of the decapitated bishop of Paris (†272). **Denison** 'son of D—'. But **Denis** can be L 'Danish', a mixture of *danais* OF and *denisc* OE, and **Denison** can be 'denizen' OF, one living in a city with all its attendant privileges (family name of the barons Londesborough).

Denley L 'clearing/wood in a valley' OE.

Denman L 'dweller in a **Dean**'.

Denmead L 'meadow in a valley' OE; place in Hants.

Denness See **Denis**.

Dennet(t) F dim. '**Denis**'.

Dennis(s), **Dennish**, **Dennison** See **Denis**; but –ish can be for **Devenish**.

Denson F 'son of **Denis**'. Or O 'son of the **Dean**'.

Dent N 'tooth' OF. Family name of the barons Furnivall.

Dentith, **Denty** N 'pleasure, speciality' OF from Latin stem *dignitāt–*, whence the –th (dropped in **Denty**, **Dainty**); or as adjective 'smart, handsome'.

Denton L 'valley place' OE, places in twelve counties; but place in Northants is from an owner.

Denver L 'Danes' crossing/ferry' OE; place in Norfolk.

Denwick L 'valley dairy farm' OE; place in Northd.

Derby L 'farm/village where (wild) animals/deer are seen' ON – either our *deer* or the 'mice and rats and such small deer' of *King Lear*; places in Derbys, Lancs.

Derbyshire L 'shire/county' OE 'of **Derby**'.

Derrick F 'people rule' Germanic. Counted by Guppy only in Somerset.

Derwent L 'oak (river)' OW, one that flowed through oak woods; four northern England rivers; for –ar– in **Dart**, **Darwen**, see **Clark**.

Desborough L 'hill where pennyroyal grows' OE; place in Berks; but place in Northants is '**Dear**'s fort/manor' OE. Counted by Guppy only in Beds.

Desmond L 'south Munster' Irish.

Devenish L 'man from Devon' OE (from British tribe *Dumnonii*).

Dever(e)aux, **Devereu(x)**, **Deveroux**, **Deverose** L 'of Evreux' OF

F: *first name*   L: *local name*   N: *nickname*   O: *occupational name*

(from Keltic tribe *Eburovices* 'dwellers on the (River) Ebura', from the Gaulish for 'yew'); place in Eure. (Saint Devereux, place in Herefords, is a mistake for *Saint Dyfrig's*.) **Devereux** is the family name of the viscounts Hereford.

Deverell, Deverill L 'river+fertile upland' Keltic (cf. **Yale**); places in Wilts (-ill), Cornwall (-al). Guppy found **-ell** only in Bucks–Oxon.

Devin(e), Devinn F (for O **D—**) 'descendant of (dim.) Poet/?(dim.) Black' Irish.

Dewar N 'pilgrim, custodian of a sacred relic' Scots Gaelic; cf. **McIndeor**. Or L, place in Midlothian, of same source, meaning 'relic'. Family name of the barons Forteviot.

Dewdney F 'God-given' OF, rendering Fs like Latin **Deodatus** and Greek *Theodore*; then rewritten as if an OE '–island' place-name.

Dewhurst L 'wet wood' OE; place in Blackburn, Lancs, and a Lancs surname.

Dewsall L '(Saint) **David**'s well/spring' Welsh (*Dewi*)+OE; place in Herefords.

Dexter O Female, but eventually also male 'dyer' OE (cf. *spinster*). A Suffolk, Leics–Warwicks surname.

Diamond Form of **Dayman**, with parasitic dental; the precious stone may not figure at all as the origin. A Devon surname, as are the variants **Diment, Dimond, Dimont, Dyment, Dymond**.

Dibble F dim. '**Theobald**'. Chiefly a Somerset surname.

Dibden, Dibdin L 'deep valley' OE; places (–en) in Hants, Kent.

Dibell, Dible, Diboll F dim. '**Theobald**'.

Diccox F '(son) of (double dim.) **Richard**'. See **Dick, Cox**.

Dick F dim. '**Richard**'. Whereas the pet form *Hick* is obsolete, and *Rick* rarish, **Dick** is still normal. **Dicks(on)** F '(son)/son of **D—**'. **-on** 66th commonest surname in Scotland in 1958, but in north England its respelling **Dixon** is much more usual.

Dicken F dim. '**Dick**'. **Dickens(on)** '(son)/son of **D—**'.

Dicker L 'ten' OE, ?from a rent paid by a bundle of ten iron rods; place in the Sussex iron-working area.

Dickin(s), Dickinson See **Dicken**. **–inson** is the commonest of these six, especially in the north.

Didcock L 'cottage(s) of (an AS called) Dudda' OE; place (Didcot) in Berks, and a Bucks surname. Tengvik offered 'rounded/lumpish, deceiving/rascally, cropped/hairless' as interpretations of the personal name, 'Dudda'.

Diddle Perhaps a pet-form of F 'Dudda' OE (see **Didcock**); certainly not 'cheat' as in current slang.

Digby L 'farm at a ditch/drain' ON; place in Lincs.

Diggens, Diggins Versions of **Dickens**.

Diggle(s) F double dim. '**Richard**', and '(son) of **D—**'.

Digweed O 'digger-up of weeds' ?OE+OE.

Dillon F Germanic *Dillo*, ?connected with word for 'destroy', normanized and taken to Ireland in 12th century.

Dilworth L '**Worth** where dill grows' OE; place in Lancs.

Dil(l)wyn L 'at the shady/secret places' OE dative plural after lost preposition; place (Dilwyn) in Herefords.

Dimblebee, Dimbleby L ' ?pool/?gorge farm' ON; place (Dembleby) in Lincs.

Diment (mostly Somerset), **Dimond, Dimont** See **Diamond**.

Dingle L 'dingle/dell' OE; places in Lancs, Warwicks.

Dingley L 'wood/clearing in a dingle/dell' OE; place in Northants.

Dingwall L 'parliament field' ON; place in Ross and Cromarty; cf. Tingwall (Orkney), Tingwall (Shetland), the Tynwald (Isle of Man), and the Icelandic Thingvellir – all in areas of Scandinavian settlement and administration.

Dinham L 'Dinan (= sacred valley)' Gaulish; place in Brittany.

Dinmore L 'big hill' OW (adjective second); place in Herefords.

Dinsdale L '**Haugh** (*halh*) belonging to **Deighton**'; places in Co. Durham, North Yorks.

Dinwiddie, Dinwiddy L first element 'fort' British (and Johnston sees 'shrubs' in second element); places in Dumfs, Roxbs.

Diplock L 'deep stream' OE. Counted by Guppy only in Sussex.

Dipple F dim. '**Theobald**'.

Disley L ?'dusty clearing' OE, says A. H. Smith; 'clearing with a mound' OE, says Gillis Kristensson; place in Ches.

Diss L 'ditch/dike' OE, normanized; place in Norfolk.

Ditchett L 'gate in the dike' (i.e. in the Fosse Way) OE; place (–eat) in Somerset.

Ditton L Same as **Deighton**; places in five counties.

Diver O 'rope-dancer, tight-rope walker, funambulist' ?OE (related to *dive*).

Dix F '(son) of **Dick**'. Guppy counted it only in Norfolk.

Dixey, Dixie N 'I have spoken' Latin; opening of the 39th Psalm, and so N for a chorister; this sounds incredible, but is supported by French surname **Dixi**.

Dix(s)on See **Dick**. Dixon is the family name of the barons Glentoran.

F: *first name*   L: *local name*   N: *nickname*   O: *occupational name*

Dobb, Dobb(i)e, Dobbin(g), Dobby(n) F dim. 'Robert'; –ie and –y are mainly Scots; F –in was applied to an old draught-horse. **Dobbs, Dobbin(g)s** '(son) of D—'. **Dobson, Dobbi(n)son** 'son of D—'. –bson mainly a northern surname.

Dobell, Doble N 'twin' OF (cf. *double*).

Dobois Corruption of *Dubois*. Bristol costumiers locally pronounced *Doughboys*.

Dobson F See **Dobb**.

Docherty See **Dougharty**. 55th commonest surname in Scotland in 1958 (by Irish immigration).

Dockeray, Dockery, Dockray, Dockree, Docwra L 'nook with dock/sorrel' OE+ON; places in Cumberland, Northd; –wra is an older spelling.

Dod(d) A F of this shape certainly existed. Various N meanings have been suggested, all Germanic in origin – 'fat/dowdy/dishonest/close-cropped'. The dialect *dod* 'rounded hilltop' at first seems likely, but the early surnames are not preceded by *de* or *at*, and the word is not recorded early. **Dod(d)s** '(son) of D—', a northern surname.

Dodge(n), Dodgeon, Dodgin, Dodgs(h)on, Dodgshun, Dodson F dim. '**Roger**' and thence dim. '**Dodge**' and 'son of **Dodge**'. **Dodgson** (the real surname of Lewis Carroll) sometimes made easier as **Dodson**.

Dodwell L 'stream/spring of (an AS called) Dodda (cf. **Dod**)' OE; place in Warwicks, and a Bucks–Oxon surname.

Doe N 'doe' OE – but why? Or L 'of Eu' (= 'city of Augustus'; originally *Augusta*; see **Augustine**) OF from Latin; place in Seine-Maritime.

Doherty See **Dougharty**. 15th commonest surname in Ireland in 1890.

Doidge F Mainly Devon form of **Dodge**.

Doig F '(devotee of Saint) Cadoc (= battle prince)' Scots Gaelic from OW.

Dolbear L 'Dola's grove' OE (his name is used in Devon as late as the 1300s); place (Dolbeare) in Ashburton, Devon.

Dolittle N 'do little, lounger, idler' OE.

Donaghy Ulster variant of **McDonaugh**.

Donald F 'world mighty' Scots Gaelic. **Donaldson** 'son of D—'; the 97th commonest surname in Scotland in 1958.

Donat F 'given' Latin past participle *donatus*, the F of martyrs, a schismatic, the popular medieval Latin grammarian, and a South

117

Wales Saint Dunawd now giving his name to two Glam places Saint Donat's.

Doncaster L 'Roman site' OE 'on the (River) Don (= water)' Keltic; place in West Yorks; cf. *Danube*.

Donkin See **Duncan**.

Donle(a)vy F ?' brown mountain' Irish.

Donnelly F (for O D—) 'descendant of Brown Valour' Irish. 65th commonest surname in Ireland in 1890.

Donoghue F (for O D—) 'descendant of **Duncan**' Irish.

Donovan See **O Donovan**. 67th commonest surname in Ireland in 1890.

Doolan F (for O D—) 'descendant of Black Defiance' Irish.

Dooley F (for O D—) 'descendant of Black Hero' Irish.

Doolittle N 'do little' OE, for a sluggard or idler. Chiefly a Worcs surname – it figures splendidly in the firm of **Doolittle** and Dalley, Estate Agents, Kidderminster.

Doorbar The compound (both elements OE) exists in ME, but makes little sense as a surname. Perhaps a corruption of **Dauber**. Found in Somerset.

Doran F (for O D—) 'descendant of (dim.) Exile/Stranger' Irish.

Dorchester L 'Roman site where ?fist-play/boxing was held' Keltic +OE, place in Dorset; or 'bright/splendid Roman site' Keltic+OE, place in Oxon.

Dore L 'door (i.e. pass)' OE; place in Derbys; but the element in Abbey D—, Herefords, is 'water, stream' Keltic.

Dorgan Munster version of Leinster **Dargan**.

Dormer N 'sleeper, lazybones' OF.

Dorrington L 'farm of **Dear**'s followers' OE, places in Lincs and (near Woore) Salop; or 'farm of Dodda's followers (cf. **Dod**)' OE, place (near Condover) in Salop. Chiefly a Herts and Hunts surname.

Dorton L 'place in a door (i.e. pass)' OE; place in Berks.

Dorward, Dorwood O 'doorkeeper' OE.

Dossetter Form of the Oxon **Dorchester**.

Doubtfire N 'put out the fire' OE, with *dout* respelt.

Douce N 'sweet, affable' OF, early in use as a F also.

Dougal(l), Dougill F 'dark stranger/foreigner' Irish – originally what the Irish called those blond beasts the Vikings.

Dougharty, Dougherty F (for O D—) 'descendant of Obstructive, Stern' Irish.

Doughty N 'tough, valiant' OE.

F: *first name*　　L: *local name*　　N: *nickname*　　O: *occupational name*

Douglas(s) L 'black water, dark stream' Scots Gaelic; place in Lanarks (cf. D—, Isle of Man; **Dawlish**; Dowlais, Glam). Lowland Scots and northern England surname. 84th commonest surname in Scotland in 1958. **Douglas** is the family name of nine peers. **–ss** corrupt.

Dovaston L 'Black's farm' OW+OE; place in Salop.

Dove N 'dove' OE/ON, for gentleness. But in Scotland ?for **Dow**.

Dover L 'waters' Keltic; place in Kent.

Dow N 'black' Scots Gaelic; and see **Dove**. Also F dim. '**David**'.

Doward L 'two hills' OW; places in Herefords.

Dowd F (for O **D**—) 'descendant of Black' Irish. Also a ME form of **David**.

Dowdeswell L 'stream/spring of (an AS called) Dogod (?derived from *dugan*, "to be useful, to avail")' OE; place in Glos, and a Glos surname.

Down(e) L 'down, hill' OE ?from Keltic; **–e** could show dative after lost preposition. Or F ?connected with 'dun, dark' OE. **Down(e)s** L 'of (i.e. at) the down', or a plural. Or F '(son) of **D**—', in its second meaning. **–ns** is the later form, with loss of the inflectional **–e–**.

Downend L 'end of the hill' or 'lower end' OE; locality or places in Berks, Cornwall, Glos, IoW, Somerset; two of the three Glos places have the second meaning.

Downham L 'hill homestead' OE; places in Cambs, Essex, Norfolk, Suffolk; or '(at) the hills' OE dative plural after lost preposition, places in Lancs, Northd and (–holme) North Yorks.

Downing F 'of the family of **Down/Dunn**' OE. Its two main areas have been Suffolk and Cornwall.

Downton L 'hill farm' OE; places in Herefords, Salop, Wilts.

Dowse See **Douce**. Chiefly a Lincs surname.

Dowsett N dim. 'sweet' OF.

Dowty See **Doughty**.

Doyle See **Dougal**. 12th commonest surname in Ireland in 1890.

D'Oyley (or one word) L 'of Ouilly (= ?fat/rich land)' OF; five places in Calvados. The non-U *doily* was named from a maker with a similar surname.

Drake N 'dragon' OE. Or O 'battle-standard (bearer)', a metonym of the same origin. Or even L '(at the Sign of the) Dragon'. (But unlikely ever to mean 'male duck'.) Found by Guppy only in Dorset–Devon, Norfolk, West Yorks.

Drane N 'drone, lazybones' OE.

Draper, Drapper O '(woollen) cloth-maker/-seller' OF.

Drawbridge L 'drawbridge' OE+OE.

Drawer O 'carrier, dragger, puller, transporter, drawer of things that get drawn (like wire)' OE.

Drax L 'portage' (overland between Rivers Ouse and Aire) OE (cf. *drag*); place in West Yorks.

Dray O 'dray, sled, wheelless cart' OE, for making or operating them. Ekwall shows that it could be L 'portage, place for drawing/dragging boats overland, ?steep hill requiring extra pull'.

Draycott L 'shed for keeping drays/sleds' OE; places in Berks, Derbys, Oxon, Somerset, Staffs, Wilts, Worcs, and a surname chiefly of Leics–Rutland and Staffs.

Drayton L 'portage/slipway/sled-track/(steep) hill (needing extra pull)+farm' OE (cf. **Drax**); places in about twenty Midland and southern counties.

Dreng Rarer original of **Dring**.

Drew F ?'ghost, phantom' Germanic *Drogo*, OF *Dru-*; or dim. '**Andrew**'. Or N 'lover, sweetheart, etc.' OF (cf. **Druce** and *Drury* Lane). Or ?L 'Dreux', as with **Druce**. Chiefly a Glos, Devon–Cornwall surname. **Dreweatt, Drewett, Drewitt** are pet forms.

Driffill L 'dirt/manure field' OE; places (Driffield) in Glos, East Yorks.

Dring O 'young man, servant, (later) free tenant holding by service and rent and military duty' ON (also used as ON F *Dreng-*); *-eng* has become *-ing* as in OE *streng* 'string'.

Drinkale, Drinkall N 'Drink health!' or 'Drink luck!' OE, the reply to 'Wassail!'; from a favourite exclamation.

Drinkwater N 'drink water' OE, either from the extreme poverty of one who could not afford ale, or sarcastically of a drunkard – Weekley quotes two Londoners in the 1320s: one the wife of Philip *le Tavener*, the other living at a tavern, and both **D—**. A correspondent has suggested to me that some bearers may have been, long before the discovery of insulin, diabetics with voracious unnatural thirsts.

Driscoll F (for O **D—**) 'descendant of Interpreter' Irish.

Driver O 'drover; driver of a team/vehicle' OE+**-er**; in ploughing, he urged oxen on with a lash, either at their side or by walking backwards in front of them, whereas the **Holder** OE actually held the plough-handles.

Druce L 'Dreux' (first element 'fortress/strong') OF from Gaulish *Durocasses*, place in Eure-et-Loir; or 'of Rieux ("streams")' OF, various places in northern France. Or N 'sturdy, stocky; lover, favourite' OF nominative *drus* from Keltic (cf. oblique case in **Drew**).

F: *first name*   L: *local name*   N: *nickname*   O: *occupational name*

Drummond L 'ridge' Scots Gaelic; places in Perths, Wigtowns. Family name of the earls of Perth.

Drury N 'love-affair, love-token, sweetheart' OF; see **Drew**.

Drysdale L 'Dryfesdale', Dumfs, second element 'valley' OE, first element tentatively linked by Johnston with verb 'drive' OE.

Dubarry See **Barry**.

Dubois L 'of the wood' OF; cf. **Boyce** and **Dobois**. A Huguenot surname.

Duck O 'duck(-breeder/-seller)' OE, a metonym. Or a N, for some baffling reason. Some confusion with **Duke**. Chiefly a Yorks surname.

Duckett Bardsley cleverly showed that this, in West Yorks especially, is F dim. '**Marmaduke**', but there are other more opaque origins in Reaney to account for the high incidence in Somerset.

Duckham L 'river-meadow/homestead with ?ducks' OE. Guppy counted it only in Mon.

Duckworth L 'enclosure with ?ducks' OE; two places in Lancs (in Oswaldtwistle and Bury), and a Lancs surname.

Dudbridge L 'Dudda's bridge' (see **Didcock**) OE; place in Glos, and a Glos surname.

Dudden L 'Dudda's hill' (see **Didcock**) OE; place (Duddon) in Ches.

Duddridge and **Dudgeon** See **Dudbridge** and **Dodgen**.

Dudley L 'Dudda's clearing' (see **Didcock**) OE; place in Worcs.

Duff N 'black, dark' Irish and Scots Gaelic. Family name of the dukes of Fife.

Duffey, Duffie F 'black man of peace' Irish and Scots Gaelic.

Duffield L 'open country with doves' OE; places in Derbys, East Yorks.

Duffus L ?'black stance/resting-place' Scots Gaelic; place in Moray. (Johnston made it 'dove-house' OE in 1892, 'dark water' Scots Gaelic in 1934.)

Duffy F (for O **D—**) See **Duffey**. 45th commonest surname in Ireland in 1890.

Dufton L 'place with doves' OE; place in Westmorland.

Dug(g)an F (for O **D—**) 'descendant of (dim.) Black' Irish and Manx.

Duguid N 'do good' OE; –ui– the Scots version of OE –ō–.

Duke O (or, rather, status) 'duke, captain of an army' OF. Often a N, from arrogance or from service in a ducal household. Some confusion with **Duck**, but generally found elsewhere – Sussex, Dorset. Certainly in Yorks the F **Marmaduke** was shortened to **Duke**. Family name of the barons Merrivale. **Dukes** '(son) of **D—**'.

Dulwich L 'dill meadow' OE; place in London.

Dummer L 'pool/mere by a hill' OE; places in Hants and (Dimmer) Somerset.

Duncalf(e) N 'grey-brown/dun calf' OE.

Duncan F 'brown warrior' Irish and Scots Gaelic. The 33rd commonest surname in Scotland in 1958, but occurs in northern England and Somerset, and also as **Donkin, Dunkin**.

Dungworth L '**Worth** with an underground room/house' OE, related to *dung*, the roof being ?covered with it; place in West Yorks.

Dunham L 'hill homestead' OE; places in Ches, Norfolk; but place in Notts was ?owned by an A S whose name meant 'brown' OE.

Dunkerton L 'hillfort-rock farm' OW+OE; place in Somerset.

Dunkin See **Duncan**.

Dunlop L ?'muddy hill' Scots Gaelic; place in Ayrs; cf. **Down**. In Ireland, sometimes ?for Mc**Donlevy**.

Dunmow L 'hill meadow' OE (cf. *mow*); place in Essex where the flitch is contested by the happily married.

Dunn(e) N 'brown, dark, swarthy' OE; –**nn** occurs throughout England. In Ireland, F (for O D—) 'descendant of Brown' Irish. –**e** was the 27th commonest surname in Ireland in 1890.

Dunphy Form of **Donoghue**.

Dunscombe L '**Dunn**'s valley' OE, an unidentified spot in the southwest.

Dunsford L '**Dunn**'s ford' OE; places in Devon and (–forth) West Yorks.

Dunstall L Same as **Tunstall**; places in Lincs, Staffs.

Dunstan, Dunston(e) F 'hill stone' OE (cf. **Down**); popular through Saint Dunstan, archbishop of Canterbury (†988). Also L '**Dunstan**'s farm' OE, place in Devon; 'stone on a hill' OE, place in Northd; '**Dunn**'s farm' OE, places in Lincs, Norfolk, Staffs; '**Dunn**'s stone' OE, place in Derbys.

Dunster L '**Dunn**'s tor/hill' OE; place in Somerset.

Duparc(q) L 'of the' OF '**Park**'.

Dupont L 'of the bridge' OF.

Dupuy L 'of the isolated peak' OF.

Duran(d), Durant N 'enduring, obstinate' OF. Huguenot and medieval stocks.

Durden N 'hard-tooth' OF.

Durham L (formerly *Dunholm*) 'hill peninsula' OE+ON; place in Co. Durham.

Durley L 'deer (but cf. **Derby**) wood/clearing' OE; places in Hants and (–leigh) Somerset.

F: *first name*   L: *local name*   N: *nickname*   O: *occupational name*

Durnford L 'hidden/secret ford' OE; place in Wilts.

Durran(t) See **Duran**.

Durston L 'Dear's farm' OE; place in Somerset, and a Somerset surname.

Durward See **Dorward**.

Dutch L 'German, Dutch, Flemish' Germanic.

Dwell(e)y N 'misled, erring, doting, in heresy' OE.

Dwerryhouse L 'dwarf's house' OE, a superstitious name for some odd natural feature; place in Lancs, and a Lancs surname.

Dybald, Dyball, Dybell, Dyble F dim. 'Theobald'.

Dye F dim. 'Dionysia', feminine of *Dionysius* (see **Denis**), so 'follower of Bacchus'. The fanciful L origin, *D'Eye* 'of Eye (= island)' OE, the Suffolk place, is at least borne out by occurrence in Norfolk. **Dyson** 'son of D—'; chiefly West Yorks surname.

Dyer O 'dyer' OE; cf. **Lister**.

Dyke L 'dike/ditch' OE. **Dykes** 'of (i.e. at) the D—', or a plural.

Dyment, Dymond See **Diamond**; **Dyment** is found chiefly in Somerset.

Dymock L ?'pigsty' OW; place in Glos.

Dyson See **Dye**.

E

Eac(c)hus (it rhymes with *teach us*) L This looks like a 'house' name, perhaps with a first element related to 'addition, increase' OE *ēaca* – ?'house on land added to an estate' OE. A Ches surname, recorded in the field-name Eachus Plan in Minshull Vernon.

Ead(e) F 'prosperity, happiness' OE – first element of a feminine F such as *Edith*. **Ead(e)s** '(son) of E—'.

Eager(s) See **Edgar(s)**.

Eam(e)s N '(son) of the uncle' (originally *maternal* only) OE, rather than a plural. **-es** counted by Guppy only in Beds and Somerset.

Eardley L 'dwelling–place clearing' OE; place in Staffs, and a Staffs surname.

Earl(e) O 'earl' OE (the only rank in the peerage from an OE word), from service in an earl's household, or from swagger, or from playing the part in a pageant; the **-e** is pointless. Chiefly Devon surnames.

Earley L 'ploughing–field' OE; place in Berks. Corrupted to **Early**, though this could be also N 'manly' (like an 'earl') OE.

Earnshaw L '**Shaw** with eagles' OE; place in Lancs, and a West Yorks surname.

Earwaker, Earwicker F 'wild-boar (cf. **York**) watchman' OE.

East L 'newcomer from the east, dweller to the east of the village' OE.

Eastabrook L 'to the east of the brook' OE.

Easter L 'sheepfold' OE (cf. *ewe*); two places in Essex. Or F from birth/baptism at the festival, which has an OE pagan name derived from a Germanic goddess of the *east* or dawn, whose festival was at the vernal equinox.

Easterbrook See **Eastabrook**.

Eastham L 'eastern homestead/river-meadow' OE; places in Ches, Somerset, Worcs, but commonest in Lancs.

Easthaugh L 'eastern **Haugh** (?*haga*)' OE; locality, or place in Norfolk.

Easthope, Eastop L 'eastern valley' OE; place in Salop.

Eastman, Eastment F 'grace protector' OE (reduced from *–mund*). Thackeray helped to revive as a F its derivative **Esmond**.

Easton L Normally 'eastern/east-facing place' (or 'to the east of the farm/village') OE; places in a dozen English counties. But E—, Devon, is 'Elf/Noble Ruler's place' OE; Great and Little E—, Essex, are 'stone(s) by the island' OE; and E— Neston, Northants, is '(A S called) Prosperity Stone's place' OE.

Eastwell L 'eastern spring/stream' OE; places in Kent, Leics.

Eastwood L 'eastern wood' OE, place in Essex; but D. H. Lawrence's birthplace in Notts is 'eastern **Thwaite**'.

Eaton L 'river/island farm' OE, according as the many places (around thirty in about fifteen counties) are derived from *ēa* or *ēg*; Eton, Bucks, of the first meaning, may be a source. Family name of the barons Cheylesmore.

Eaves L 'rim, edge, border (cf. *eaves* of a house)' OE *efes* (singular), especially the skirts of a wood. F '(son) of **Eve**' is far less likely. Mainly a Lancs surname; also occurs as **Eavis, Eves**.

Ebbetts F '(son) of (dim.) **Isabell**'.

Ebelthite See **Hebblethwaite**.

Eccles L 'church' OW/Irish, from Latin; places in Kent, Lancs, Norfolk.

Eccleston(e) L 'church farm' OW/Irish (cf. **Eccles**)+OE; places in Ches, Lancs (four).

Ecott L No place is now known, but –**cott** is normally 'cottage(s)' OE. A surname of Hants–Surrey–Sussex–Essex–Beds.

Eddis F '(son) of' the dim. of one of the Ed– names (see **Edds**).

Eddolls F '(son) of (an AS called) Prosperity/Happiness Wolf' OE.

Edds F '(son) of' the dim. of one of the male/female 'prosperity, happiness' names beginning with Ed–, from OE *ēad*.

Ede(s) See **Ead(e), Eades**.

Edenbridge L ?'Blessed Helmet's bridge' OE; place in Kent.

Edgar F 'prosperity/happiness spear' OE. **Edgars** '(son) of **E**—'.

Edge L 'crest, ridge, steep hill' OE.

Edgerton L '(AS called) Blade Army/Brave's place' OE, places (also Egerton) in four counties; or 'place of the folk/family of Blade Brave' OE, place in Kent.

Edg(e)ley L 'park/pasture clearing' OE; places (–e–) in Ches, Salop.

Edg(e)worth L '**Worth** on an **Edge**'; places in Glos, Lancs.

Edington L 'wasteland hill' OE, place in Wilts; or 'place belonging to (ASs called) Blessed Friend (male) or Blessed Joy (female)' OE, place in Somerset; or 'place of the family/folk of (an AS male called) Ida (= ?work, motion)' OE, place in Northd.

Edison F 'son of' the dim. of one of the Ed– names (see **Edds**).

Edman(s), Edmands, Edmond(s), Edmondson Forms of **Edmund, Edmunds(on)**.

Edmead, Edmead(e)s N 'good-hearted, humble-minded, gentle' OE. And '(son) of **E**—'. Also occurs as **Edmett**.

Edmund F 'prosperity/happiness protector' OE. Saint Edmund, king of the East Angles, and two other popular AS kings, gave the F an early currency, which Saint Edmund of Abingdon (†1240) prolonged. Forms with **–o–** are of OF type; **–man** may be 'man' OE rather than from *–mund*. **Edmunds(on)** '(son)/son of E—'. Whereas **–undson** is chiefly a Lancs–Yorks surname, **–unds/–onds** are west Midlands and South Wales. **Edmondson** is the family name of the barons Sandford.

Edrich, Edridge F 'prosperity/happiness powerful' OE.

Edward F 'prosperity/happiness guardian' OE. The Confessor preceded George as patron saint of England. **Edward(e)s** '(son) of E—'. **–s** was the 20th commonest surname in England and Wales in 1853 (it is found especially in Wales and the south), and 32nd in USA in 1939. **Edwardes** is the family name of the barons Kensington. **Edwardson** 'son of E—'.

Edwin(g) F 'prosperity/happiness friend' OE; the **–g** is illiterate.

Efemy See **Evemy**.

Efford L 'ford usable at ebb-tide' OE; places in Cornwall, Devon (three), Hants.

Egan F (for McE—) 'son of **Hugh**' Irish.

Egerton See **Edgerton**. Family name of the earls of Wilton and the earls of Ellesmere.

Egginton L '(AS called) Sword (or his folk)'s farm' OE, place in Derbys; or 'oak hill' OE, place (Eggington) in Beds.

Eggleton L '(AS called) ?Sword-Wolf's folk's farm' OE; place in Herefords, but a surname of Bucks–Berks.

Eglinton L Possibly has the same meaning as **Eggleton**; place in Ayrs, but a Norfolk surname (so perhaps from another place).

Eland L 'island' OE; place in Northd.

Eld N 'old' OE *eald*, in south-western dialect.

Elder N 'elder, senior' OE. (No reference to the tree.)

Eldridge See **Aldridge**.

Eley L See **Ely**. Or F dim. 'Elijah' (see **Elias**). Chiefly a Derbys surname.

Elford L 'Ella's/elder-tree ford' OE; places in Northd, Staffs. And see **Yelverton**.

Elgar See **Algar**.

Elias F Greek form of Hebrew *Elijah* 'Yahweh is God'. The vogue of the F was perhaps spread by Crusaders who had been to Mount Carmel, but the surname is very rare. **Eliason** 'son of E—'.

Eliot(t) See the far commoner **Elliot(t)**. **Eliot** is the family name of the earls of Saint Germans.

F: *first name*   L: *local name*   N: *nickname*   O: *occupational name*

Ellen F 'Helen (= bright)' Greek. Saint Helen was said to have found the True Cross, borne Constantine the Great, and been the daughter of Old King Cole of Colchester; this was enough to ensure her a cult in England. **Ellens** '(son) of E—'. Sometimes ?L 'elder-tree' OE and (–s) 'of (i.e. at) the elder-tree'.

Ellerbeck L 'alder brook' ON; place in North Yorks.

Ellerker L 'alder marsh' ON; place in East Yorks.

Ellerman See **Elliman**.

Ellerton L 'alder place' ON+OE, places in East and North Yorks; but place in Salop is '(AS called) Noble Hardy's place' OE.

Ellery See **Hilary**.

Elliman O 'oil-maker/-seller' OE; a fine surname for an embrocation-manufacturer.

Ellin(s), **Ellings** See **Ellen**.

Elliot(t) F dim. '**Elias**', with –tt far commoner than –t, but both evenly spread over England. They may sometimes, with the rarer **Eliot(t)**, have absorbed FS 'noble war' (feminine), 'noble Gēat' (one of the Swedish tribe to which Beowulf belonged – cf. **Merriott**), or 'elf ruler', all OE. –tt was the 48th commonest surname in USA in 1939. **Elliot** is the family name of the earls of Minto.

Ellis(s) ME form of **Elias**. –s is very common in the south and Midlands, and the 43rd commonest surname in USA in 1939. **Ellison** 'son of E—'. **Ellis** is also popular in Wales, perhaps by fusion with FS like Elised, from *elus* 'charitable, benevolent' Welsh.

Elm L 'elm-tree' OE; locality, or places in Cambs, Somerset. **Elm(e)s** 'of (i.e. at) the elm', or a plural; –s is later, with loss of inflectional –e–.

Elmar, **Elmer** See **Aylmer**. Also, rarely, L 'eel mere/pool' OE; place in Sussex. **Elmers** '(son) of E—'.

Elmore L 'river-bank with elms' OE; place in Glos. But see **Aylmer**.

Elphick F 'elf/fairy high' OE; saint, archbishop of Canterbury, martyred by Danes at Greenwich in 1012 and called by the Normans *Alphege*.

Elstob L 'elder-tree stump' OE, as befits the first female Old English scholar, the great Elizabeth E— (†1756); place in Co. Durham. Also spelt **Elstub**.

Elston L '(AS called) Noble Victory's farm' OE, place in Lancs; or '?(AS called) Elf's farm' OE, place in Notts; or 'Elias (Giffard)'s farm', place in Wilts. But Guppy counted the surname only in Devon, and a F 'old/temple stone' OE is just as likely.

Elvey F 'elf gift' OE.

Elvin F 'elf/noble friend' O E.

Elward F 'elf/noble guard' O E.

Elwell L 'wishing (literally omen, good luck) well' O E; place in Dorset.

Elwes F 'hale/healthy wide' Germanic; frenchified as Héloïse, the doomed love of Abélard.

Elwood F 'elf ruler' O E.

Ely L 'eel district' O E; place in Cambs.

Emanuel F 'God with us' Hebrew.

Emberson See **Emerson**.

Em(b)ery, Embry, Emrey See **Amery**.

Emerson F 'son of **Emery**'.

Emm(s) F 'Emma' (see **Emmet**). And '(son) of Emma'.

Emmanuel See **Emanuel**.

Emmerson is the commonest of the **Emerson** group, which also includes **Empson** (especially in Lincs) and **Emson** (in Essex). Guppy found **Em(m)erson** from Northd to Lincs–Notts.

Emmet(t), Emmot(t) F dim. 'Emma', a Germanic feminine F cut down from some double F with first element *ermin*– or *irmin*– 'whole/universal'; popularized by the daughter of Duke Richard I of Normandy, wife of (1) King Ethelred the Unready, (2) King Canute. But –**ott**, common in West Yorks, could also be L 'stream-meeting, confluence' O E; place in Lancs.

Endacott, Endicott L 'beyond the cottages' O E; place (–i–) in Cadbury, Devon.

Enfield L 'open country with lambs' O E (cf. *yean*); place in Middx.

England L 'England' O E, 'the country of the Angles' (ignoring the Saxons, etc.), who came from an *angle*-shaped area of Holstein; a curiously uninformative surname for use in England.

Englefield L 'open country of (an A S called) Ing (see **Ingham**) Rule' O E; place in Surrey.

English L 'English' O E; formerly referring to Angles (see **England**) as opposed to Saxons, but by surname times denoting an Englishman living among Borderers (Welsh, Strathclyde Welsh, Scots), or in the old Scandinavian areas of the north, or in intensely normanized districts; or one who had returned from being so nicknamed in France or elsewhere.

Ennion F Latin *Annianus*, from the family name *Annius*, adopted in O W and fathered on to such Welsh words as *anian* 'nature/genius', *einion* 'anvil', ?*uniawn* 'just, upright'; there was an early Welsh Saint Einiawn. And see **Kenyon** and **Onions**.

Enriched is a bizarre spelling of **Enright**.

F: *first name*   L: *local name*   N: *nickname*   O: *occupational name*

Enright F (for McE—) 'son of ?Unlawful/?(adjective related to verb meaning) attack' Irish.

Ensor L 'bank of (an AS called dim.) Blessed' OE; place (Edensor, pronounced Ensor) in Derbys, and an old Staffs surname. But Guppy found it countable only in Dorset, and the **Ensor** family of Rollesby Hall in Norfolk had similarly strayed.

Enticknap(p) L 'hillock (OE *cnæpp*) of (an AS called) Anneca' (derivative of male F *Anna*, ? ? cognate with OE verb *unnan* 'grant, favour') OE; or 'duck/ant hillock' OE; all these are according to whether early spellings with –*k*– or –*d*– or –*t*– are accepted. The surname survives in Enticknaps Copse, Surrey.

Entwis(t)le L 'waterhens'/ducks'/(AS called) Enna's river-fork' OE (cf. **Twistleton**); place (–isle) in Lancs, but –**istle** is the usual surname. Found in Ireland as **Entissle**.

Enwright is **Enright** made to look like a **Wright**/craftsman.

Equ(e)all ? ?N 'equable; equal/peer' Latin *aequalis*. Or ? ?L for *de Hakewell* (Essex, 1273), which survives as **Hakewill**.

Erith L 'gravelly landing–place' OE (cf. **Hythe**); places in Kent and (Ear–) Hunts.

Erridge L 'eagle ridge' OE; place (Eridge) in Sussex.

Erskine L Said by Johnston to be 'projecting height' Scots Gaelic; place in Renfrews.

Erwin F 'wild-boar friend' OE (cf. **York**).

Esbester Form of Orkney–Shetland **Isbister**, with a foothold in Bristol.

Escombe L 'at the parks/pastures' OE dative plural after lost preposition; place in Co. Durham with an AS church now in a drab colliery setting.

Escott L 'eastern cottage' OE; place (–ot) in Devon.

Esdaile L Simplified form of Eskdale, Dumfs, 'dale' ON/OE 'of the Esk (= water)' Keltic (cf. the rivers Exe, Axe, Usk, and *whiskey*).

Esh Form of **Ash**; also place of same meaning in Co. Durham.

Eskell See **Askell**.

Esmond(e) See **Eastman**.

Espley L 'aspen wood' OE; place in Northd.

Essex L 'East Saxons' OE, the county.

Esslemont L ?'low hill' (it is 219 ft) or ? ?'spell/incantation hill' Scots Gaelic version of British; place in Aberdeens.

Etheredge, **Etheridge** F 'noble rule' OE; cf. **Aldrich**.

Euden L 'yew valley' OE; places in Co. Durham, Northd.

Eustace, **Eustice**, **Eustis** F 'fruitful' Greek. The more famous of two Saints Eustace is a patron saint of hunters, having been converted by a stag with a crucifix in its horns. England nearly had a Bad King Eustace, Stephen's son, but 'Christ would not have it that he should rule long', says the Peterborough chronicler.

Evans F '(son) of Evan', one of the Welsh forms of **John**; see **Jones**. (It is possible that Evan sometimes absorbed the Romano-British F *Eugenius* 'well-born'.) Five per cent of Guppy's Welsh yeomen bore the surname in 1890, it was the eighth commonest surname in England and Wales in 1853, and the 29th in USA in 1939.

Evatt See **Evett**.

Eve(s) F Adam called his wife Eve 'because she was the mother of all living', says *Genesis*, but her name may have meant either 'lively' or 'serpent' in Hebrew. **Eves** is '(son) of Eve', though **Eaves** gives the much likelier meaning.

Eveleigh L Probably 'wild-boar wood' OE; place (Everley) in Wilts. The family are chiefly of Devon–Dorset, and John E— was a great architect of Georgian Bath.

Evemy F (Female) 'auspicious speech' Greek; in the apocryphal *Acts of Peter* Euphemia is one of the prefect Agrippa's four concubines, converted and martyred; a saint of the name was martyred in Bithynia in the 4th century.

Everard, Everatt F 'wild-boar hard' Germanic; cf. **York**. Mostly introduced after 1066, but an OE form may have contributed.

Everden(e) L 'wild-boar valley' OE; or from Everdon, Northants, 'wild-boar hill' OE; cf. **York**.

Evered Rarer (5:34 in London TD) form of **Everard**.

Everest L 'Evreux'; see **Deveraux**. The famous surname has travelled from Normandy to Nepal via Britain.

Everett (rarely **Everitt**) Commonest spelling of the **Everard** group, especially in East Anglia and Wilts.

Everhard See **Everard**.

Evershed N or (sign-name) L 'boar's head' OE. Found in Surrey in 1400s, and still a Sussex surname.

Everton L 'wild-boar place' OE; places in Berks, Lancs, Notts; cf. **York**.

Evett, Evitt F dim. '**Eve**'.

Ewan F Most probably 'well-born' Greek (cf. *eugenics* and *Eugene*), and thus equivalent to **Owen** and the Arthurian knight Ywain; the Greek much transformed in its passage through Keltic, whence emerge Irish and Welsh forms. (?Sometimes from a Welsh form of **John**; see **Jones**.)

Ewart L '**Worth** on a river' OE; place in Northd. Sometimes F

F: *first name*   L: *local name*   N: *nickname*   O: *occupational name*

'**Edward**' in an OF version. Or even O 'ewe-herd' OE, with a view to cheese.

Ewbank L 'hillside with yews' OE.

Ewer O 'water-bearer' OF (cf. French *eau*); the servant who brought ewers/basins of water for guests to wash at table between courses. **Ewers** '(son) of E—'.

Ewhurst L 'yew **Hirst**' OE; places in Hants, Surrey, Sussex.

Exelby L '**Askell**'s farm' ON; places in North Yorks and (now Asselby) East Yorks. It had reached Cornwall by the 1600s.

Ex(c)ell L 'church **Haugh**' OW + OE; two places (Exhall) in Warwicks.

Ex(t)on L '?ox farm' OE, place in Rutland; or 'East Saxons' place' OE, place in Hants; or 'place' OE 'on the (River) Exe (= water)' Keltic, place in Devon; all Exton. The *exons* or *exempts* of the Yeomen of the Guard were not appointed until 1668, too late to give rise to the surname.

Eye L 'island' OE (cf. the *i–* of *island*); locality, or places in five counties.

Eynon See **Ennion** and **Beynon**.

Eyre(s) See **Ayer(s)**.

Eyton L 'place on a river' OE; two places in Salop.

Ezard See **Isard**.

F

Faber O '**Smith**' Latin. Reinforced by persecuted Huguenots.

Fabian F From a Roman family name derived from 'bean' Latin; sainted pope of 3rd century.

Facey N One of Reaney's twenty-eight spellings (in F–, V–, Ph–) of a word meaning 'wanton, playful' OF, the most accurate form being **Lenfestey**.

Facit L Same as **Fawcett**; place in Lancs.

Fage N 'flattery, coaxing, deceit' ME.

Fagget(t)er, Faggotter O 'bundler/seller of sticks, dealer in faggots (not the type eaten with peas)' OF.

Fahy F (for O F—) 'descendant of ?(name related to) Foundation' Irish.

Fair N 'handsome, pretty' OE.

Fairbairn(e) N 'lovely child' OE; but sometimes ?corrupted from 'handsome warrior' OE (cf. **Barne**).

Fairbank(s) L 'lovely hillside(s)' OE+ON. –s is chiefly a north Midlands surname. Some USA –s are of Yorks origin, some Jewish.

Fairbourn L 'stream in the ferns' OE; places in Kent (-bourne), West Yorks (–burn).

Fairbrass N 'proud/fierce arm' OF *fier+bras*; a somewhat closer spelling is **Firebrace**.

Fairbrother N 'handsome/**Fair**'s brother' OE.

Fairchild N 'handsome **Child**' OE; sometimes ?a mocking 'pretty child'.

Faircliff(e), Faircloth, Fairclough L 'pretty ravine' OE (cf. **Clough**); **Fairclough** is common in Lancs. –cloth occurs aptly as the surname of a draper at Stromness, Orkney.

Fairfax N 'lovely hair' OE (since *fair* was not originally limited to 'blond'); *fax* survives in that lexicographer's tendon, *paxwax*.

Fairfield L 'beautiful **Field**' OE, locality, or place in Derbys; or 'pig field' OE (cf. *farrow*), place in Worcs.

Fairfoot N 'handsome foot' OE. But the location of early forms in Glos and Lincs suggests to Reaney that it can be L for Fairford, Glos ('clear ford' OE) or for **Farforth**.

Fairfoul(l), Fairfull N 'pretty bird' OE.

Fairhead N 'handsome head' OE. Chiefly an Essex surname.

Fairhurst L 'nice copse, nice wooded hill' OE.

Fairlee L 'beautiful wood/clearing' OE; place in IoW.

F: *first name*   L: *local name*   N: *nickname*   O: *occupational name*

Fairley L 'clearing with ferns' OE; place in Salop; or form of **Fairlee**.

Fairlie See **Fairlee** or **Fairley**.

Fairman N 'handsome man' OE (also ?confused with **Farman**).

Fairtlough L See **Faircliff**.

Fairweather N 'bright, calm weather' OE; perhaps from temperament or from a favourite greeting.

Faithful(l) N 'devout, sincere, loyal' OF+OE.

Falcon N 'falcon' OF. Or O, metonym for **Falconar**.

Falconar, Falconer, Falk(i)ner O 'hawker, falconer, keeper/trainer of falcons' OF –*auc*–; the –l– is a pedantic restoration from Latin, and shouldn't be pronounced. It could also mean 'crane-driver' – Reaney cites a 1257 carpenter who made a *faucon* 'crane/windlass' to be worked by *falconarii*. The London TD distribution of this group is: **Falconar** 2, **Falconer** 36, **Falkiner** 1, **Falkner** 21, **Faulconer** 1, **Faulkener** 1, **Faulkner** 146, **Faulknor** 1, **Fawkner** 1.

Falder O 'one who works at the (sheep-)folds or pens' OE. A northern surname retaining the long *ā* of OE, where midlands and south show **Folder** with a long *ō*.

Falk(us) F 'falcon' Germanic through French *Fauque(s)*, the objective case of which was *Faucon* (see **Fauchon**).

Fall, Falls, Faller L 'waterfall, fall in the ground, place with felled trees' OE; '(of, i.e.) at the F—'; and 'one who lives at a F—'. But **Faller** sounds very like L 'spotty floor, tessellated (Roman) pavement' OE; places (Fawler) in Berks, Oxon.

Fallow(s), Fallowes L 'land newly cultivated' OE; '(of, i.e.) at' such land; early forms prove the origin to be OE *fealg* rather than OE *fealu* 'fallow, yellowish'. Found in Staffs and further north.

Fallowfield L 'ploughed/harrowed/fallow/brownish **Field**' OE; places in Lancs, Northd; the earliest spellings are indecisive.

Fance L 'fens' or '(of, i.e.) at the fen' OE (see **Fann**). Found in Essex.

Fane N 'glad, eager, well-disposed' OE (cf. *fain*). Family name of the earls of Westmorland.

Fann L South-east, and south-east Midlands, form of **Fenn**.

Fant N 'child' OF (cf. *infant*), with loss of *en–*.

Farebrother See **Fairbrother**.

Farenden See **Far(r)ingdon**, **Farrington**.

Farewell L 'beautiful spring/stream' OE; places in Co. Durham, Staffs. Or N 'fare well, prosper' OE; or from a favourite exclamation 'Farewell!' OE.

Farfort(h), Farfor L 'journey/pig ford' OE; place (–th) in Lincs.

Fargher Manx version of **Farquhar**.

Faringdon L 'fern/bracken hill' OE; places in Berks, Dorset, Hants, and (Little F–) Oxon.

Farleigh, Farley L 'clearing with ferns' OE; places in nine counties; *–er–* becomes *–ar–* as in **Clark**.

Farlow L 'fern hill' OE.

Farman O 'traveller, hawker, pedlar' ON.

Farmborough L 'fern mound/hill' OE; place in Somerset; or for **Farnborough**.

Farmer O 'tax-collector, steward, bailiff' OF – not an English word, and not of the present sturdy meaning.

Farnall See **Farnill**.

Farnborough L 'fern mound/hill' OE; places in Berks, Hants, Kent, Warwicks.

Farncombe L 'fern valley' OE (cf. **Combe**); places in Surrey, North Yorks.

Farndon L 'fern hill' OE; places in Ches, Notts, Northants (two).

Farnell L Same as **Farnill**; places in Kent, Wilts.

Farnes L Hardly from the seventeen Farne Islands off the Northumberland coast, but 'ferns, bracken' OE.

Farnham L 'homestead/river-meadow in the ferns' OE; places in seven counties; but place in Northd is '(at) the thorns' OE dative plural.

Farnill L 'fern hill' OE; locality, or places (Farnhill, Fernhill) in eight counties.

Farnley L 'clearing with ferns' OE; two places in West Yorks.

Farnorth Corruption of **Farnworth**.

Farnworth L '**Worth** with ferns' OE; two places in Lancs.

Farqu(h)ar N 'very dear one' Scots Gaelic. **Farqu(h)arson** 'son of F—'.

Farr N 'bull' OE. Found by Guppy chiefly in Herefords, Herts.

Farrah, Farrar, Farrer, Farrey Variants of **Ferrar** (cf. **Clark**) chiefly from Yorks.

Farran, Farrant(s), Farrance, Farren, Farrin F 'journey risk/venture' OF smoothing of Germanic *Ferdinand*; but Hill Farrance, Somerset, is after a Norman landowner *Faron* 'pilferer, ferret' OF. **Farrant** was counted by Guppy in Sussex and Devon.

Farringdon See **Farrington**.

Farrington L 'farm in the ferns' OE, place in Somerset; but also confused with **Farringdon**, Devon, 'fern hill' OE, and with **Farndon**.

Farrow See **Farrar**.

Farthing N 'farthing' OE, ?based on rent or assessment. Or L 'quarter

F: *first name*   L: *local name*   N: *nickname*   O: *occupational name*

(of a virgate – i.e. of up to thirty acres)' OE. Or F *Farðegn* 'traveller' ON.

Farwell See **Farewell**.

Fatheringham Version of **Fotheringham**.

Fatt N 'fat' OE.

Faucett See **Fawcett**.

Fauchon N 'falchion, broadsword (though later applied also to a dagger)' OF from Latin *falx* 'sickle'. But it may sometimes be a version of F *Faucon* OF (see **Falk**).

Faulconer, Faulk(e)ner, Faulknor See **Falconar**.

Faulder Cumberland–Westmorland form of **Falder**.

Faulds See **Folds**.

Faulk(e)s F '(son) of **Falk**' or OF *Fauques* (see **Falk**).

Faull See **Fall**.

Faunt is **Fant** with the French nasal imitated with *u*.

Faux See **Faulkes**. And perhaps involved with **Folkes**.

Favel(l), Favill N 'tawny, fawn, fallow-coloured (horse)' OF *fauvel*; run together with 'flattery, insincerity, intrigue' OF *favele* from Latin *fabella* 'little yarn, fable'.

Fawcett L 'varicoloured hillside' OE; place in Westmorland.

Fawdon L 'varicoloured hill' OE; two places in Northd.

Fawkes See **Faux**. Chiefly a Glos surname.

Fawkner See **Falconar**.

Fawn N 'cub, young fallow deer' OF.

Fay L 'beech-tree' OF, or some place in France of that meaning. Or N 'fairy' OF. Some Irish bearers will be F (for O F—) 'descendant of Raven' Irish.

Faza(c)kerley L '?border strip (cf. *acre*) field' OE; place (–ak–) in Lancs.

Fear N 'fierce, proud, brave' OF; or 'comrade' OE. It can hardly ever mean 'fear' OE. **Fears** '(son) of **F**—', or direct from OF *fers, fiers*.

Fearing Probably a corruption of **Fearon**.

Fearn(e) See **Fern**.

Fearnehough, Fearnyhough See **Fernihough**.

Fearnley See **Fernley**.

Fearon O 'Smith' OF; cf. **Faber, Feaver**.

Feather(s) N for dressing, or O for trading, in 'feathers' OE, or as mockery of a lightweight body or mind. **–er** is chiefly a surname of West Yorks, and some claim to come from Feizor in that riding, 'Fech's shieling' ON – his name may be from Irish *Fiach* (whence, ultimately, the French word for a cab, *fiacre* – since Paris hackney-men first parked their cabs outside the church of S.-Fiacre).

Featherston(e), Featherston(e)haugh L 'tetralith, cromlech (literally four-stone)' OE – three uprights and a capstone; places (–stone) in Northd, Staffs, West Yorks; **–haugh** (from *halh*; see **Haugh**) is the former name of the Northd place.

Feaver O '**Smith**' OF; cf. **Faber**, **Fearon**.

Feehally F Liverpudlian Irish for 'son' (OF *fiz*) 'of **Harry**'.

Feilden Common version of **Fielden**.

Felgate See **Fieldgate**; locality, or places in Worcs and (Fell Gate) Co. Durham, the latter with the additional possibility 'fell, hill' ON. Chiefly an Essex surname.

Felix F 'happy' Latin, F of popes and of the Apostle of the East Angles; surname may also owe something to the feminine version *Felicia*; but the male F was killed by a film cat.

Fell L 'fell, mountain' ON; now chiefly a Cumberland–Westmorland– Lancs surname. In other areas it will usually be O 'skin, hide' OE (cf. *fellmonger*, *pelt*), from dealing in them.

Fellow(e)s N 'partners, companions' ON; or '(son) of the partner/ companion'. Reaney also supposes an intermediate form *Felhouse* from **Fieldhouse** (and, indeed, **Felthouse** exists). **Fellowes** is the family name of the barons Ailwyn and de Ramsey.

Felstead L 'site in a **Field**' OE; place (–sted) in Essex.

Feltham L 'hay meadow' OE, place in Somerset; or '**Field** homestead' OE, place in Middx.

Felthouse See **Fellowes**, **Fieldhouse**.

Felton L 'place in a **Field**' OE; places in four counties.

Femister O 'fee-master' OE+OF, i.e. 'shepherd, cowherd' (first element is to *fee* as Latin *pecus* is to Latin *pecunia*).

Fenby L 'fen farm' OE+ON; place in Lincs.

Fender O 'defender' OF (which is, of course, the function of a *fender* against the fall of the fire).

Fenemore (chiefly Oxon–Bucks), **Fenimore** See **Finnemore**.

Fen(e)lon F (for O **F—**) 'descendant of Fionnalan (first element "white, fair")' Irish; the family were chiefs in Co. Westmeath before the 1100s, but the name is now found mostly in Co. Carlow– Co. Wexford. Or L, if of English stock, since some Huguenots called *Fénelon* settled after 1685, named from a place in Dordogne.

Fenn L 'fen, marsh' OE.

Fennell O 'fennel' OE, a plant used in medicine and cookery. But Reaney also shows that a couple of landowners called Fitzneal ('son of **Neal**') were respelt as *Fennel* and the like.

Fenner L 'one who lives at a marsh/fen' OE. Chiefly a surname of

F: *first name*   L: *local name*   N: *nickname*   O: *occupational name*

Essex–Kent–Sussex. The resemblance to the word *venery* 'hunting' OF suggests another O meaning.

Fennimore See **Finnemore**.

Fenton L 'place in a fen' OE; places in eight counties.

Fenwick L 'dairy-farm in a fen' OE; place in Northd. A Northd Border family with its own repeated slogan or rallying-cry *A Fenwyke!* and a hectic record of fray and reprisal against the Scots.

Ferber See **Furber**.

Fergus(s) F 'man choice' Irish and Scots Gaelic. **Fergus(s)on** 'son of F—'; –uson, 38th commonest surname in Scotland in 1958, is common also in Cumberland–Westmorland–Northd.

Fermor Form, nearer to the original, of **Farmer**.

Fern L 'fern(s), bracken' OE.

Fernilee L 'clearing with bracken/fern' OE; place in Derbys.

Fernley L 'clearing with ferns' OE; place in West Yorks.

Fern(e)yhough, Fernihough L 'hollow with bracken' OE. Chiefly surnames of Staffs–Ches, but Lancs bearers may be L '**Haugh** with bracken' OE, from Fernyhalgh in Fulwood, Lancs.

Ferrar, Ferrer O '**Smith**, ironworker, farrier' OF.

Ferrier O 'ferryman' ON+–**er**.

Ferry L 'ferry' ON. Or for **Ferrier**.

Fettiplace N 'Make room! Give place!' OF, for an usher. An Oxon surname.

Feverel N 'February' OF (final –*r* changed to –**l** ?on analogy of *April*); from birth in the month, or frosty character.

Fewkes F '(son) of **Folk**'.

Fewster O 'maker of saddletrees' OF.

Fewtrell O 'keeper of hounds, who manages them in the chase' ME *veuterer* from OF. A Salop surname.

Fey Doubtfully N 'fairy' OF; or 'doomed' OE. Or L 'beech-tree' OF from Latin *fagus*, whence a few places Fay(e), Fey, in France.

ffinch, ffiske, ffitch, ffolkes (also **ffooks**), **fforde** See **Finch**, etc.; and cf. **ffoulkes**; these ridiculous forms can also be rendered **Ff—**.

ffoulke(s) Form of **Foulke(s)**. There is nothing 'superior' about the typographical absurdity of putting **ff** for initial **F**, an old medieval manuscript habit. The surname is common in North Wales – aptly enough, since Welsh *ff* is the English *f* sound, and *f* the *v*.

ffrench, ffytche See **French, Fitch**; and cf. **ffoulkes**.

Fick See **Fitch**.

Fickle N 'false, treacherous, fickle' OE.

Fiddes L 'wood stance/resting-place' Scots Gaelic; place in Aberdeens.

Fiddian See **Vivian**.

Fiddler O 'fiddle-player' OE. Reaney supposes also confusion with **Vidler**.

Fidge N See **Fitch**. **Fidgett** dim. '**Fidge**'. **Fidge** is south-eastern.

Fidge(o)n For **Vivian** or **Fitzjohn** or dim. '**Fidge**'.

Fidler Form of **Fiddler** counted by Guppy in Berks, Ches–Derbys.

Fido(e) N 'Son of God!' OF, from a favourite exclamation.

Field L 'field, cultivated land', but especially 'open country' OE, a common place-name element in areas that had been wooded. The surname is chiefly south Midlands and Sussex. **Fields** L 'of (i.e. at) the field', or a plural.

Fielden L 'in open country, in the fields' OE dative plural in –*um* after lost preposition. Surname of Lancs–West Yorks.

Fielder L, or O 'living/working in the fields (or in open country)' OE.

Fieldgate L 'gate into a field, gate into open country' OE; or in Norse-influenced areas 'road' ON 'to a field' or 'to open country'.

Fieldhouse L 'house in a field' or 'house in open country' OE.

Fielding L '**Field**-dweller' OE+associative suffix –*ing*.

Fiennes L 'flat open country' Germanic+suffix; place in Pas-de-Calais.

Fifehead, **Fifett**, **Fifoot** L 'five hides' (of land: see **Hyde**) OE; locality, or places in Dorset (three, Fifehead) and Somerset (Fivehead).

Figg See **Fitch**.

Fildes L 'fields, open country' OE.

Filer O 'one who files or makes files' OE *fil*+suffix; by 1674 it also means 'pickpocket'.

Fillary, or better, **Fillery** N 'son (of) the king' OF; same as **Fitzroy**.

Fillingham L 'homestead of Fygla's gang' OE – this AS had a name related to 'fowl, bird'.

Filson F 'son of (dim.) **Philip**'.

Finbow Possibly L 'woodpecker hill' OE; place (Finborough) in Suffolk, and a Suffolk surname.

Finch N 'finch' OE. In Chaucer, *to pull a finch* = 'to swindle a simpleton', and this may be the motive for the N. A Herts, Glos–Worcs surname.

Fincham L 'homestead frequented by finches' OE; place in Norfolk.

Finchley L 'clearing/wood with finches' OE; place in Middx.

Findlater L 'white hillside' Scots Gaelic; place in Banffs; the –**d**– is excrescent, and **Finlater** is nearer the original. A preposterous family belief exists that it denotes former holdings as far as the 'world's end' (French *fin de la terre*).

F: *first name*   L: *local name*   N: *nickname*   O: *occupational name*

Findlay, Findley, Findlow See **Finlay**; the –d– is excrescent, but Reaney shows it in Scotland as early as *c.* 1060. **Findlay** was the 96th commonest surname in Scotland in 1958.

Findon L 'woodpile hill' OE; place in Sussex.

Fine N 'refined, delicate' OF.

Finesilver O 'silver-refiner' OF+OE.

Fink See **Finch**, though the surname has also been recently brought by German Jews. One medieval London family left their name in both St Benet **Fink** church and **Finch** Lane.

Finlater, Finlator See **Findlater**.

Finlay, Finley, Finlow F 'fair hero' Scots Gaelic. Perhaps 'fair one of the god Lugus' (see **Carlisle**). **Finlayson** 'son of F—'.

Finn F (for O F—) 'descendant of White' Irish. But English bearers may be L 'the Finn' ON.

Finnegan F (for O F—) 'descendant of Fairheaded' Irish.

Finnemore N 'refined/dear love' OF.

Firbank L 'woodland hill' OE (cf. **Firth**); place in Westmorland.

Firebrace N 'proud/fierce arm' OF (cf. **Fairbrass**). Sir Aylmer F— was director of London's Second World War fire-fighting.

Firk L Defeatist spelling of **Firth**.

Firminger See **Furminger**.

Firth L 'woodland' OE. Reaney shows how the OE word (which should 'normally' develop into *firghth*) was corrupted through mis-spelling of its spirants, and metathesis of the –r–, into such forms as **Fright, Thrift, Freak, Frith, Firk**.

Fish N 'fish' OE, perhaps for a catcher or seller of them.

Fishbourne, Fishburn(e) L 'fish stream' OE; places in Co. Durham, Sussex, IoW.

Fisher O 'fisherman' OE (including the –er). But a couple were *de/ atte* F—, and this must be L 'fishery' OE (like 'fish-garth' ON). The surname is found everywhere, even inland, and was the 35th commonest surname in USA in 1939.

Fisherton L 'fishermen's place' OE; two places in Wilts.

Fishlock L 'fish-garth, fish-weir' OE, an enclosed piece of river for easy taking of fish.

Fishwick L 'dairy-farm where fish was sold' OE; place in Lancs; the effect on the milk is not recorded.

Fisk(e) ON forms of **Fish**.

Fitch N 'point, lance, spear' OF (not from 'fitchew, polecat').

Fitchett N dim. '**Fitch**'. Chiefly a Derbys surname.

Fitchew Reaney ignores any N origin in 'fitchew, polecat' OF, and assigns it to F *Fitzhugh* 'son' OF 'of **Hugh**'.

Fitter O ?'joiner, carpenter'; not a known ME word, and even the verb *to fit* is very late, but persons are called *le fittere* in the 1100s and 1200s in Warwicks, Glos, and Cambs.

Fitzgerald F 'son' OF 'of **Gerald**'. Gerald, Constable of Pembroke, married Nest, Princess of Wales; their line settled in Ireland, where the surname multiplied – 36th commonest there in 1890, and family name of the dukes of Leinster. See also **Fitzjohn**.

Fitzgibbon F 'son' OF 'of **Gibbon**'. Common in Ireland. See also **Fitzjohn**.

Fitzjames F 'son' OF *fiz* 'of **James**'. The principal family are descended from an illegitimate son of King James II.

Fitzjohn F 'son' OF 'of **John**'. It should be pointed out of all these **Fitz**– surnames that they do not prove the founder's illegitimacy, although the prefix distinguishes recent royal bastards.

Fitzmaurice F 'son' OF 'of **Maurice**'. See also **Fitzjohn**.

Fitzpatrick F 'son' OF 'of **Patrick**'; or, rather, 'son of the devotee of (Saint) **Patrick**' (see **Kilpatrick**). 61st commonest surname in Ireland in 1890. See also **Fitzjohn**.

Fitzroy N 'son (of the) king' OF; if meant seriously, this must imply illegitimacy. Family name of the dukes of Grafton.

Fitzsimmons, Fitzsimon(s) F 'son' OF 'of (dim) **Simon/Simon**'. See also **Fitzjohn**.

Flack Version of **Flagg** found by Bardsley in Kent in 1273.

Flagg L 'turf, sod, peat-cutting' ?ON; or 'flagstone' OE; or 'wild iris, flag-flower, reed, rush' ?ON; locality, or place in Derbys.

Flaherty F (for O F—) 'descendant of Bright Ruler' Irish.

Flanagan F (for O F—) 'descendant of Ruddy' Irish. The 69th commonest surname in Ireland in 1890.

Flanders L 'Flanders (= submerged land)' OF from Flemish; the ancient countship.

Flann(er) O 'flawn/pancake/custard-pie(-maker)' OF; a German surname Pfannkucher 'pancakemaker' exists. But **Flann** of Irish stock must be N 'red' Irish *flánn*.

Flash, Flask L 'pond, marsh' ME (from OF or Dutch). **Flasher, Flashman** L 'dweller/man at the pond'.

Flatman L 'man who lives on level ground' OE. An O origin 'sailor, pirate' OE *flotman* (as in the Norfolk village of Newton Flotman) is less likely. Chiefly a Suffolk surname.

Flaxman O 'dresser/seller of flax' OE.

Fleet L 'creek, estuary' OE; places in four counties. Or N 'swift' OE.

F: *first name*   L: *local name*   N: *nickname*   O: *occupational name*

Fleetwood The Lancs town was named from Sir Peter F— in 1836 – but an Elizabeth F— was living at nearby Rossall in 1624; L 'wood on a stream/creek' OE.

Fleming L 'Fleming, man from **Flanders**' OF normanized; various places (e.g. Canterbury, south Pemb) have evidence of these immigrants as weavers etc., but Guppy found the surname chiefly in Cumberland–Westmorland, and it was the 76th commonest surname in Scotland in 1958. Also spelt **Flemming**.

Flesher O 'butcher' OE; still the normal word for *butcher* on Scots facias; the English mincingly prefer *meat purveyor*. (Some early forms show that it can be a contraction of 'flesh-hewer' OE, with the same meaning.) And see **Fletcher**.

Fletcher O 'arrow-maker/-seller' OF; sometimes ?absorbing **Flesher**. Universal, especially in Derbys–Notts (which includes Sherwood Forest), but rarer in south-west.

Fletton L 'place on a river' (the Nene) OE; place in Hunts.

Flinn See **Flynn**.

Flint L 'rock' OE; the distribution of the surname is against the North Wales town. Sometimes ?N with meaning like '(hard as a) rock'.

Flintoff L 'house-site where flints are found' OE + ON (cf. **Toft**). The surname is found above all in the Yarm district of North Yorks, and in Yorks generally, along with **Flintoft**, **Flinton** ('flinty farm' OE, place in East Yorks), and **Flintham** ('flinty homestead' OE, place in Notts).

Flippance F '(son) of (dim.) **Philip**' (OF dim. *Phlipon*).

Flitton L '(on) the streams' OE dative plural after lost preposition; place in Beds.

Floater O 'mariner' OE *flota* 'boat, fleet' + suffix.

Flood L 'stream/gutter' OE (two cognate words). In Ireland, often a translation of **Tully**.

Flook A Glos surname, so that F 'matted, shaggy' ON *Flóki*, though possible, is less likely than in a Norse-influenced area.

Flower O 'arrow-maker' OE *flā* + –er. But also N 'flower' – used as a feminine F, ?with meanings of fragrance/delicacy/smooth skin. Or O '(maker of) flour'; *flower* and *flour* were once the same word, and OF. Chiefly a Wilts–Dorset–Somerset surname. Family name of the viscounts Ashbrook.

Flowerdew (rarer **Flowerday**) That this ?first appears as *Floure-dieu* in Norfolk in 1541, even as Ingledew is possibly the Latinized *Angel-Dei* (angel of God) in Lincs in 1273, is perhaps irrelevant, since 'flower of God' is not a known concept. Nor is modern French *à fleur d'eau* 'at water level' a likely L origin, although so much of Norfolk is nearly thus. And it certainly cannot be 'dew on flowers'.

Floyd N Perversion of **Lloyd**.

Fluck, Flux See **Flook**; and '(son) of **Fluck**'.

Flunder N 'flat-fish, flounder' ME; a ship was so named in 1319, but it is hard to see why a person should be.

Flynn F (for O F—) 'descendant of Ruddy' Irish. 41st commonest surname in Ireland in 1890. See **Flann**.

Foden L ?'colourful/variegated hollow' OE; fieldname in Fallibroome, Ches, and common in Ches as a place-name element and in Ches-Lancs as a surname.

Fogarty F (for O F—) 'descendant of ?Banished' Irish.

Fogg ?L 'rank tall grass' ME (probably as in ON). Found as a surname in Norfolk in 1500s, now chiefly Lancs.

Fold L 'fold, pen' OE. **Fold(e)s** 'of (i.e. at) the fold', or a plural.

Folder See **Falder**.

Foley F (for O F—) 'descendant of Plunderer' Irish. But the Worcs family has probably another origin, ?as **Folley**. 60th commonest surname in Ireland in 1890.

Foljambe N 'foolish/useless (i.e. maimed) leg' OF. Family name of the earls of Liverpool.

Folk F 'folk, people' Germanic. OF forms *Fulco* and *Fouques*, whence many surnames, including some with F— voiced to V— or mis-spelt ff—, and even the Welsh F *Ffwc*. **Folkes** '(son) of F—'.

Follenfant N 'silly child' OF.

Follet(t) N 'little fool' OF.

Folley L 'folly' (some capricious building or plantation) OF.

Folli(o)tt See **Follet**; cf. Becket's arch-enemy Gilbert Foliot, bishop of London (†1187).

Fook(e)s F '(son) of **Falk**'. **–ks** is chiefly a Dorset surname.

Foord See **Ford**.

Foot N 'foot' OE/ON, from some oddity.

Footman O 'servant on foot, pedestrian (who can't afford a horse), foot-soldier' OE.

Forbes L ?'field, district' Scots Gaelic + ?English plural; place in Aberdeens; until recently, pronounced with two syllables. 88th commonest surname in Scotland in 1958. Family name of the earls of Granard.

Ford(e), Forder L 'ford' OE; locality, or many place-names; –e is dative after a lost preposition. **Forder** is either this, with the neutral

---

F: *first name*   L: *local name*   N: *nickname*   O: *occupational name*

sound shown as **–er**, or 'dweller at the ford' – also places in Cornwall, Devon. Incidence of surname **Ford** is generally south of Ches–Derbys and of Suffolk.

Fordham L 'homestead by a ford' OE; places in Cambs, Essex, Norfolk.

Fordington L 'farm of the people at the ford' OE; places in Dorset, Lincs.

Fordyce L Johnston suggests 'land to the south' (cf. **Desmond**) or 'trim/fit land' Scots Gaelic; place in Banffs.

Foreman O 'pig-man, swineherd' OE; cf. **Forward**.

Forest O 'forest(-dweller/-worker/-official)' OF. Rare – only 3:100 **Forrest** in London TD.

Forest(i)er O 'forester, gamekeeper' OF, or an official in charge of a forest. Reaney cites the perquisites of one *forestarius* – Christmas log, wind-felled timber, and acorns/mast for his pigs. There must be some intermingling with **Foster**.

Formby L 'old farm' or ?'(Norseman called) Old's farm' both ON; place in Lancs.

Forrest(er) (rarely **Forrestor**) Normal forms of **Forest(er)**.

Forsdick, Forsdyke See **Fosdick**.

Forse See **Foss**; here, again, the distribution is against L 'waterfall' ON *fors/foss* (cf. **Frost**).

Forsett See **Fawcett**; none of this group means a 'tap', as *faucet* does to the Scots.

Forsey See **Fursey**.

Forster Could share the second and third origins of **Foster**. Mainly a north of England surname, especially Northd.

Forsyth F 'man of peace' Scots Gaelic. But there was also a place of approximately this name, evidenced by people called *de Forsith* in the 1400s. A surname of south of the Forth–Clyde.

Fortescue, Fortesquieu N 'strong shield' OF (cf. *escutcheon*).

Forth L 'ford' OE; the development in words from *–rd* to *–rth* is in general late ME and north-country. No likely connection with the Scots river.

Fortman N 'strong hands' OF.

Fortnam, Fortnum N 'strong young donkey' OF (*anon*, dim.).

Forty L 'projecting' (cf. *forth*) 'island, peninsula' OE, usually in marshy ground; places in Middx, Wilts, Worcs.

Forward (rarely **Forwood**) O 'pig-/hog-guard, swineherd' OE (cf. *farrow*). Disappointing, but comparable with **Foreman, Calvert**.

Fosbery, Fosbury L 'fort on a roof-like hill' OE though Ekwall prefers 'chieftain's fort' OE; two places (–u–) in Wilts.

Fosdick L 'ditch' OE 'of (a Norseman called) Foot' ON; place (Fosdyke) in Lincs.

Foss L 'ditch, Roman road called the Fosse Way' OE from Latin; locality, or places (mostly Fosse) in Norfolk (two), Warwicks (four), Wilts (two) (all near the road), and Lincs. Chiefly a surname of Devon–Somerset, at the south-west end of the road.

Fossett Probably a version (seen in Lancs) of **Fawcett**.

Foster Many origins: N 'foster-child/foster-parent' OE (cf. *food*). Or O '**Forester**'; 'shearer, cutler, scissors-maker' OF (form of *forceter*, **Forster**); '**Fewster**'. (Foster Lane, City, is none of these, but commemorates Saint Vedast/Vaast, bishop of Arras.) Very common in Notts, giving weight to a mainly woodland origin, and 38th commonest surname in USA in 1939.

Fothergill L 'ravine where fodder could be got' ON; place in West Yorks. Counted by Guppy in Durham–North/East Yorks.

Fotheringham L Place in Angus called *ffodryngay* in 1261, and named after Fotheringhay, Northants, which is probably 'island for foddering/grazing' OE. A Scots surname.

Foulk(e), Foulkes See **Folk**.

Fountain L 'fountain, spring' OF; locality, or from variously spelt places in France.

Fouracre, Foweraker L 'four-acre (holding)' OE.

Fournier O 'baker' OF.

Fouweather N 'dirty weather' OE, for similar reasons to **Fairweather**.

Fowden and **Foweraker** See **Foden** and **Fouracre**.

Fowke(s) See **Folk**.

Fowle N 'bird' OE, ?for a catcher; nearer the OE form is **Fuggle**.

Fowler O 'bird-catcher, fowler' OE (including the –er); *fowl* denoted a bird of any kind, not just the barnyard and game types. A surname more southern than otherwise.

Fox N 'fox' OE, from slyness or other attributes; no evidence for its being a L sign-name. Chiefly a north Midlands and northern surname.

Fox(h)all, Foxell L 'fox burrow' OE; place (Foxhall) in Suffolk.

Foxcroft L '**Croft** infested with foxes' OE; no place now recorded, but Bardsley shows the surname as first fixed on the Yorks border of north Lancs.

Foxeth L ?'fox-earth, group of burrows' OE+OE, and the compound exists in ME; locality, or place (Foxearth) in Essex.

F: *first name*　　L: *local name*　　N: *nickname*　　O: *occupational name*

Foxlee, Foxley L 'fox wood/clearing' OE; places (–ey) in Norfolk, Northants, Wilts.

Foxton L 'place infested with foxes' OE, or ?'fox hill' OE, places in Cambs, Leics, North Yorks; or 'fox valley' OE, places in Co. Durham, Northd both originally –den.

Foxwell L 'stream/spring with foxes' OE.

Frain L 'ash tree' OF.

Frampton L 'place on the (River) **Frome**' OW+OE, places in Dorset, Glos (three); but another Glos place, and one in Lincs, have as their first elements FS of owners.

Francis L 'Frenchman' OF. After the 1220s, it might be used as a F, after the Saint of Assisi, but the meaning is the same.

Francom(b), Francombe N 'free man' OF; the –b/be added mistakenly, to make it look like a place-name.

Frank L 'Frank, Frenchman' OF from Germanic. Or N 'free, freeborn' (not a serf), or 'liberal, generous' OF. Certainly not the dim. of **Francis**, which was *France*. **Franks** '(son) of **F**—'.

Frankham Despite its L look, same as **Francom**.

Franklen, Franklin(g), Franklyn O 'franklin, free citizen, gentleman' (of rank below the nobility but within striking distance of knights, esquires, and serjeants at law) OF; the classic example is Chaucer's prosperous and wholesome pilgrim.

Fraser Recorded in Scotland in mid-1100s as *de Frisselle, de Freseliere, de Fresel*, as if from a place in France, and Sir Simon **F**— (executed 1306) is referred to as *Simond Frysel*; first element ?'ash-tree' OF, the –er ?to make it 'strawberrier' – a pun on the three silver cinquefoils or *fraises* in their armorials. The 28th commonest surname in Scotland in 1958, and family name of the barons Lovat, and Saltoun, and Strathalmond.

Frater O '(in charge of the monastic) refectory' OF.

Frayn(e) See **Frain**.

Frazer Rarer and less Jacobite form of **Fraser**. In Ireland, –s– and –z– interchange in these surnames.

Freak(e) L See **Firth**. Or N 'man, warrior, hero' or adjective 'bold, brave, zealous' OE; the –e can be organic in the noun, and wake (after lost definite article) in the adjective.

Freane and **Frear** See **Frain** and **Frere**.

Frederick(s) F 'peace rule' Germanic. And '(son) of **F**—'.

Free N 'freeborn' or 'noble, generous' OE; cf. **Fry**.

Freebody O Same as **Freeman** in meaning, and likewise OE.

Freeborn N 'born free, not a serf' OE; early in use as a F.

Freegard F 'peace **Garth**/spear' Germanic; common in Wilts.

Freeland O or, rather, status: '(tenant of) land with no rental or service ties attached' OE.

Freelove F 'peace survivor' OE (cf. verb *leave*); but elements seen in **Free** and **Leaf** are perhaps involved sometimes.

Freeman O (or, rather, status) 'freeborn man, freeman' OE. Occurs chiefly south of Leics–Warwicks.

Freer See **Frere**. Chiefly a Leics–Rutland, North and East Yorks surname.

Fre(e)mantle L 'cold cloak' OF – a wood seen as a poor man's only covering; place (–ee–) in Hants. **Fremantle** is the family name of the barons Cottesloe.

French L 'French' OE, an early immigrant. Some Irish bearers assert that it is L 'ash-tree(s)' OF. Family name of the earls of Ypres and the barons De Freyne.

Frere O 'friar' OF; for this irregular behaviour, cf. **Abbott**.

Freshwater O '(seller of) fresh water' OE, rather than L from dwelling in F—, IoW, or some similar place.

Freston L 'place of the Frisians' (immigrants, not cows) OE; place in Suffolk.

Frewen, Frewin(g) F 'generous friend' OE. A 17th-century archbishop of York bore the nice name Accepted **Frewen**.

Friend N 'friend' OE.

Fright See **Firth**.

Frisby L ON version of **Freston**; two places in Leics.

Friskney L 'at the fresh-water river' OE (the –n– showing the dative of the adjective in the 'weak' position after the lost preposition and definite article); place in Lincs.

Friston L Same as **Freston**; place in Suffolk; but Sussex place may be 'furze hill' OE, or named from an AS owner.

Frith L 'woodland' OE, better spelt **Firth**.

Frizzell, Frizzle L From a French locality in Fris–/Fres– (see **Fraser**), with perhaps the belief that it meant 'strawberries'.

Frobisher O 'furbisher/polisher/burnisher of armour/swords, etc.' OF.

Frome and pronunciation-spelling **Froom(e)** L ?'brisk, fine' or some vaguer meaning like 'water' OW; five English rivers and places on their banks, especially the Somerset town.

Frost N ?'white-haired, white-bearded, cold in demeanour, born during a notoriously cold spell' – or for some other reason related

---

F: *first name*   L: *local name*   N: *nickname*   O: *occupational name*

to 'frost' OE. Common from Derbys to Somerset (so that L 'force, waterfall' – an ON word – is unlikely).

Froud(e) N 'wise, prudent' OE, or an early F based on this.

Frowen, Frowing and **Frude** See **Frewen** and **Froude**.

Fry(e) N 'freeborn' or 'noble, generous' OE (a form with –*ī*–, as opposed to the –*ēo*– giving **Free**); –e could show weak adjective after lost definite article. Sometimes ?'little person, child, offspring' ON, as in the *fry* of fish (Noah has *fry* in a Wakefield play). Chiefly a Wilts–Somerset–Dorset–Devon surname.

Fryd Probably one of the contortions of **Firth**.

Fryer Version of **Frere** found in Leics–Rutland–Notts–Yorks–Ches.

Fudge F dim. 'Foucher (= people army)' OF from Germanic. Mostly a surname of Hants–Dorset–Somerset–Glos–Wilts. The rare **Fuge** is chiefly of Devon–Cornwall, and TD shows **Fuidge** only in Devon, Sussex–Surrey, London.

Fuggle N See **Fowle** (which is the ME and modern form). **Fuggles** '(son) of **F—**', or a plural 'birds'.

Fulbrook L 'filthy/muddy brook' OE; places in Bucks, Oxon, Warwicks.

Fulford L 'filthy/muddy ford' OE; places in four counties.

Fullalove N 'full of love' (*amour* rather than *agape*) OE.

Fuller O 'fuller, bleacher' OE (entirely, as **Walker**), though the OF word is similar. Chiefly a south-east, and east Midlands, surname; cf. **Voller**.

Fullerton L 'bird-catchers' place' OE; place in Hants.

Fulleylove See **Fullalove**.

Fullshawe L 'filthy/muddy **Shaw**' OE; locality, or places (Fulshaw) in Ches, West Yorks.

Fulthrope L 'dirty/muddy **Thorp**' OE; no village now answers to this name.

Fulton L 'filthy/muddy place' OE.

Fulwell L 'dirty/muddy stream' OE; places in Co. Durham, Oxon.

Ful(l)wood L 'filthy/muddy wood' OE; places in Lancs, Notts.

Furber O Same as **Frobisher** (which has the OF –*iss*– infix). Chiefly a Ches surname.

Furfy N ?'complete, perfect' Irish.

Furlong L 'furrow-long' OE, eventually meaning 'furlong, eighth of a mile, square furlong (about ten acres), race-track' – the surname may even show speed at foot-racing.

Furmenger, Furminger O 'cheese-maker/-seller' OF (cf. Modern French *fromage*).

Furnace, Furnass, Furneaux, Furness, Furnish, Furniss L 'furnaces' OF, or from various places in France called Fourneaux. But also 'headland (cf. **Ness**) near the island called Rump' ON, now the Furness district of Lancs.

Furnell L 'furnace' OF (**Fourneaux** shows the plural); locality, or places called Fournel, Fournal, in Normandy.

Furnival(l) L 'Fournival (= ?well-wooded/richly cropped valley)' OF; places in Oise, Orne.

Fursdon L 'furzy hill' OE; place in Cornwall.

Furse(man), Furze(man) L 'one who lives in furzy land' OE. **Furse** and **Furze** found early and currently in Devon.

Fursey L 'furzy enclosure (see **Hay**)' OE. Found early in Dorset, just as **Forsey** is now.

Fusedale L 'cattle-shed ('fee-house') valley' ON; place in Westmorland.

Fyfe L The county-kingdom of Fife is probably named after Fib, one of the seven sons of Cruithne (legendary father of the Picts).

F: *first name*   L: *local name*   N: *nickname*   O: *occupational name*

G

Gabb N 'lie, mockery, deceit' OF.

Gabriel F 'God is a strong man' Hebrew; the Archangel of the Annunciation.

Gadd N 'goad, sting' ON, though Bardsley's earliest examples are from Somerset.

Gadsby L '(Viking settler called) Sting/Goad's farm' ON; place (–ddes–) in Leics. Guppy counted it in Hunts, Derbys.

Gadsden, Gadsdon L '(AS called) Goat/Kid's valley' OE; place in Herts (now Gaddesden), and surnames of Bucks–Beds.

Gaffikin For *Gavaghan*, a family of Crossmolina, Co. Mayo, from Irish Ó *Gaibhtheacháin*, meaning ?

Gail and **Gaillard** See **Gale** and **Gaylord**.

Gailor(d) –or can = **Gayler**, but a USA branch came from a 1630 Huguenot settler called **Gailord** (see **Gaylord**).

Gain(e) N 'trickery' OF; cf. the N meaning of **Ingham**. **Gain(e)s** '(son) of **G—**'.

Gainford L 'direct ford' OE (first element scandinavianized); place in Co. Durham.

Gaitskell, Gaitskill L 'shelter for goats' ON; place (Gatesgill) in Cumberland.

Galbraith L 'stranger Briton' Scots Gaelic, for a Welshman who had settled among Scots Gaels. Family name of the barons Strathclyde.

Gale L 'gaol' OF (Norman); we retain this spelling for *gaol*, but the OF pronunciation *jail*. Or N 'gay, jolly' OF; or 'merry, wanton, licentious' OE. Or F, the OF form of Germanic **Wale**. Found from Devon to Northants.

Gallacher, Galla(g)her F (for O **G—**) 'descendant of Foreign Help' Irish; –gher is easily the commonest spelling – 14th commonest surname in Ireland in 1890; –cher the 59th in Scotland in 1958 (by Irish immigration).

Galley, Gallie O 'galley, vessel with sails and oars, big rowing-boat (as on the Thames)' OF, from service on one. Or L 'galilee' OF, a porch/chapel at the entrance of a great church, the finest being that perched over the Wear at Durham.

Galloway L 'stranger/foreigner Gael' OW, which Johnston ascribes to this south-western part of Scotland's having been so long a province of English Northumbria. Guppy counted the surname in North and East Yorks.

Galpin O 'galloper, errand-boy' but also 'turnspit, scullion' OF. Guppy counted it only in Dorset.

Galsworthy L ' ?bog-myrtle/sweet-gale slope' OE; place in Devon.

Galton L ' ?taxed/rented farm' OF, rather than 'bog-myrtle/sweet-gale farm' OE; place in Dorset.

Galvin F (for O **G—**) 'descendant of ?Bright White' Irish.

Gamage L 'Gamaches' OF from Gaulish (first element *gam* is ?'winding', second is 'water'); place in Eure.

Gambell, Gamble N 'old' ON. Latter is chiefly a Norfolk surname.

Gambleton L Whereas this looks like 'Old's farm' ON+OE (see **Gamble**), no place is recorded, and the form could well arise, by metathesis, from one of the two places Galmpton in Devon, or from Galhampton and Galmington in Somerset – all 'farm of the gavelmen (rent-paying peasants)' OE.

Gamblin(g) is **Gamlin** with a *b*-glide.

Gambrill N 'crooked stick' OF (first element ?Keltic *cam*).

Game, Games(on) N 'game' OE, for an athlete; but other meanings are possible – 'joke, jest', 'sport of the chase', 'prize', or (from Welsh or Scots Gaelic) 'crooked, lame, strabismic, gammy'. And '(son)/son of **G—**'.

Gamlin N 'little old man' (dim. of **Gamble**) ON+OF suffix. Yet Gamelyn was the lusty and agreeable young hero of a medieval tale and (via Lodge's *Rosalynde*) the precursor of Orlando in *As You Like It*.

Gammon N dim. 'leg' OF (Norman); cf. a *gammon* of bacon. Chiefly a Devon surname.

Gant See **Gaunt**.

Gape N 'weak, feeble' OF.

Garbett F From a corruption of one of the three FS 'spear bold/bright (cf. names in –*bert*)/herald (cf. *bode*)' OE.

Gard O 'watchman, warder, guard' OF.

Garden, Gardyne L or O, from living/working at a 'garden' OF (Norman dialect); cf. **Jardine**, which is French of Paris.

Gardener O 'gardener' OF (Norman). For its rarity, see **Gardner**.

Gardham L '(at) the fences/enclosures' ON dative plural after lost preposition; place in East Yorks.

Gard(i)ner (rarely **Gardinor**) See **Gardener**; –dn– is easily the commonest of all: London TD has 432 –dn–, 181 –in–, 37 –en–.

Garfitt L A Yorks surname presumably from Garforth in West Yorks, 'ford of (an A S called) ?Spear' OE.

Garland O 'garland, chaplet' OF, a metonym for a maker/seller of

---

F: *first name*　　L: *local name*　　N: *nickname*　　O: *occupational name*

them in metal. Or L, as a sign – the 'bush' of an inn; or 'triangular piece (cf. the *gore* in dress-making) of land' OE. Or N – Chaucer mentions a dog called **G—**, ?'barking, croaking', from *grailler* OF.

Garlic(k), **Garlicke** O '(seller of) garlic' OE. –**ck** common in Wilts.

Garman North Wales version of **German**.

Garmon(d)sway L 'Spear Protector's road' OE; place (–d–) in Co. Durham.

Garmston L 'Spear Protector's farm' OE; place in Salop.

Garner See **Gardener**. Or L 'garner, granary' OF.

Garnet(t) O 'hinge' or 'pomegranate' OF, for suppliers of these. Or F dim. '**Warin**'. Common in Cumberland–Westmorland–Lancs–Ches.

Garnham Corruption of **Garnon**. Common in Suffolk.

Garnon(s) N 'moustache(s)' OF, an oddity among the clean-shaven Normans; cf. F *Algernon*, 'with a moustache'.

Garra(r)d, **Garratt**, **Garred**, **Garrett**, **Garritt**, **Garrod** F dim. '**Gerald/Gerard**'. **Garretts** '(son) of **G—**'. **Garret(t)son** 'son of **G—**'.

Garraway L '(church of St) Guoruoe' OW; place (Garway) in Herefords; the F recurs in the *Book of Llandaf*. But Reaney also instances early forms without *de* and far from Wales, which are F 'spear war' OE *Gārwīg*.

Garth L 'enclosure, garden, paddock' ON.

Garton L 'fenced farm' ON; two places in East Yorks.

Gartside L 'hill-slope with a **Garth**' ON+OE; place in Lancs.

Garve L 'rough (place)' Scots Gaelic; place in Ross.

Gascoign(e), **Gascoin(e)**, **Gascoyne** L 'Gascon' (same as *Basque*) OF from Latin.

Gask L 'point of land running out from a plateau (literally tail)' Scots Gaelic; place in Perths.

Gaskell, **Gaskill** See **Gaitskell**; –**ell** is a Ches–Lancs surname.

Gaskin See **Gascoign**.

Gatacre L ' ?gate/?goat field' OE; places in Lancs (Gateacre), Salop.

Gatcomb(e), **Gatcum** L 'goat valley' OE; places in Somerset, Wilts.

Gate L 'gates' OE – if 'correctly' from the OE plural; but also a later formation 'gate'; see **Yate**. In areas of Danish or Norwegian settlement, 'road, street' ON. **Gates** plural or 'of (i.e. at)' form of **G—**, in either meaning. Guppy counted **Gates** only in Sussex.

Gatehouse L 'gate-house' OE, house at the entrance of a castle, monastery, etc.; cf. **Gate**. Guppy found it countable only in Dorset.

Gateley L 'clearing with goats' OE; place in Norfolk.

Gatley L ' ?pass, gap (cf. *gate*)/?goat clearing' OE, place in Herefords; but place in Ches is 'goats' cliff' OE.

Gatward (Bardsley found it in Essex), **Gatwood** O 'goat-/gate-keeper (cf. **Ward**)' OE+OE; though if the name is early, *gate* is less likely (see **Gate**).

Gaukro(d)ger See **Gawkroger**.

Gauld L 'Lowlander' Scots Gaelic.

Gaunt L 'Ghent' (French **Gand**; Latin *Gandavum Castrum* from Keltic); the Belgian city. Or N 'gaunt, lean, haggard' ME from ?OF 'yellowish'; Shakespeare's John of G— puns on the L and N meanings. Or O 'glove(-maker)' OF. Chiefly a Lincs surname.

Gavin F Scots version of OF and ME *Gawain*, ultimately from OW *Gwalchmai* ?'hawk of the plain'; King Arthur's nephew, and in earlier romances the foremost of his knights.

Gawkro(d)ger N 'stupid/clumsy **Roger**'; first element northern dialect.

Gawn(e) Form of F *Gawain*; see **Gavin**. Also O 'son of the smith' Manx.

Gay N 'gay, cheerful' OF. Rarely ?L from 'Gaye' (named after owner Wado = **Wade**); place in Marne. Found chiefly from Hants to Cornwall.

Gaydon L 'hill of (an A S called) ?Gǣga' OE – his F ?related to the OE verb *forgǣgan* 'transgress, prevaricate', OE adjective *gāgol* 'lascivious, proud', and the Modern Icelandic verb *geiga* 'wander, take a wrong direction'; place in Warwicks.

Gayler, Gaylor O 'gaoler' OF (Norman); cf. **Gale.**

Gaylord N 'brisk, high-spirited' OF. Sometimes F 'lofty hard' Germanic. Both have been respelt **–lord** by folk-etymology, and **Gaylard** is rarer.

Gayton L 'goat farm' OE (first element scandinavianized), places in Ches, Lincs (two); but places in Norfolk, Northants, Staffs may be this or 'Gǣga's farm' (see **Gaydon**).

Gazeley L 'Gǣgi's clearing' OE; place in Suffolk; his name is ?related to *Gǣga*, as in **Gaydon**.

Gear N 'trick, fad, fit, impulse' ON. **Geary** is an adjective from this, 'giddy, capricious, fickle'; but can also be F *Geri* OF from Germanic *Geric* (first element 'spear'). Guppy counted **Geary** in Leics – Rutland.

Gearing N 'lecher, ?glutton, villain' ME *geering* from Germanic.

Geddes L ?'patch, ridge' Scots Gaelic; place in Nairns.

Geddie See **Giddy.**

F: *first name*   L: *local name*   N: *nickname*   O: *occupational name*

Gedge Form of **Gigg** found in Norfolk.

Gedye See **Giddy**; the –e may show a 'weak' adjective after *the*.

Geen is '**Jean**' if so pronounced, but some of the family pronounce the *g* as in *gig*, which sounds more like Guisnes in north-eastern France, an unlikely place of origin.

Geering See **Gearing**.

Geldard, Geldart, Gelder O 'man who tended the sterile cattle (literally geld-herd)' O N + O E. West Yorks surnames.

Gelding N 'gelding, eunuch' O N.

Gell Probably F dim. '**Gillian**'.

Genn See **Jean**.

Gent(le) N 'well-born, noble, courteous' O F. Gent was also 'neat, shapely'. It is found chiefly in Derbys.

Gentleman N or status 'man of gentle birth' O F + O E.

Geoffrey F O F version of two (or even three) Germanic names. Second element is 'peace' (as in F *Wilfrid*); first is variously 'district' (as with Hitler's *Gauleiters*), 'traveller', 'pledge' (cf. **Gilbert**). This basic form of the F is very rare as a surname, and most of its derivatives begin with **Jeff–**.

George F 'farmer' Greek. The ?mythical patron saint of England for some reason didn't much inspire the use of his F in surname-forming times; the Hanoverian kings began its long vogue; for Roman Catholics it has now declined again, since Pope John XXIII demoted Saint George (at the same time declaring that Saint Philomena never existed at all). A southern (especially South Wales) surname. **Georgeson** 'son of G—'. (See also **Gorge**.)

Gerald F 'spear ruler' Germanic, introduced by the Normans; whence (or from **Gerard**) many surnames in **Ger–, Garr–, Jarr–, Jerr–**.

Gerard F 'spear brave' Germanic, introduced by the Normans; whence the set of surnames tied in with **Gerald**.

German L 'German', also used as a F. No more their own name for themselves than **Welsh** is of *that* race, but one given to them by the Gauls – Keltic words meaning either 'neighbour' or 'battle-cry' have been proposed. The great Saint G—, bishop of Auxerre in the fourth and fifth centuries, was popular in Wales in the form *Garmon*. Guppy counted **German** only in Devon.

Gerra(r)d, Gerratt, Gerred, Gerrett F dim. '**Gerald/Gerard**'.

Gerrish N 'changeable, giddy, wayward' M E; cf. **Geary**.

Gervase, Gervis F 'spear servant' Germanic + Keltic (cf. **Vassall**); 1st-century martyr.

Gethin(g) F ?'dusky, swarthy' O W (–n).

Gibb F dim. **'Gilbert'**. In ME, a familiar term for a cat, especially a tom; whence one's surprise at the firm of **Gibbs Mew**, Melksham (= 'meadow good for milk' OE). **Gibbs** '(son) of G—', but much commoner, especially in west Midlands; family name of the barons Aldenham and the barons Wraxall. **Gibson** 'son of G—'; commonest surname of the **Gilbert** group, but rare in the south; 65th commonest surname in Scotland in 1958; family name of the barons Ashbourne.

Gibbard (counted by Guppy in Northants), **Gibberd** Variations of **Gilbert**.

Gibben(s) F Either the same as **Gibbon(s)**; or −en may be an archaic west Midlands retention of OE −an, the mark of the genitive singular of a weak noun, making **Gibben** '(son) of **Gibb**'.

Gibbes Older but much rarer form of **Gibbs**.

Gibbin F Either the same as **Gibbon**; or 'gift friend' Germanic (second element that of **Baldwin**); or second meaning of **Gibben**. **Gibbin(g)s** '(son) of G—', counted by Guppy in Beds, Devon.

Gibbon F dim. **'Gibb'**. **Gibbons** '(son) of G—'. The London TD has 202 −ons, 55 −ins, 15 −ens, 8 −ings.

Gibby F dim. **'Gibb'**, found chiefly in South Wales (but not connected with Llangibby, Mon).

Gibson See **Gibb**.

Giddy N 'insane, crazy' OE (originally 'possessed by a *god*').

Giffard, **Gifford** N 'bloated, puffy-cheeked' OF. The Conqueror granted this Norman family (−a−) over a hundred manors in England, whence its wide spread. Or ?F 'gift hardy' Germanic. Or L, place (−o−) in East Lothian, but this takes its name ?from the family, not vice versa. **Giffard** is the family name of the earls of Halsbury. Guppy counted −ord in Somerset–Dorset, Hunts–Cambs.

Gigg N 'loose/flighty girl, wench; bloke' OF.

Gilasbey See **Gillespey**.

Gilbert F 'pledge/hostage bright' Germanic. Brought by the Normans, and spread somewhat by Saint G— of Sempringham, founder of the only English monastic order. In Scotland it absorbed **Gilbride**. Source of many surnames in **Gib-**. **Gilbertson** 'son of G—'.

Gilbride F 'devotee of (Saint) Bridget' Scots Gaelic; the Saint's F means 'high one' Irish, from the F of a Keltic fire-goddess.

Gilchrist F 'devotee of Christ' Irish and Scots Gaelic; cf. **Gill**, *gillie*.

Gildea F 'devotee of God' Irish.

Gilder O 'gilder' OE.

F: *first name*   L: *local name*   N: *nickname*   O: *occupational name*

Gildersle(e)ve N 'golden sleeve' OE. (Any resemblance to angling/fowling terms *gilder* 'snare, trap' and *sleeve* 'fish net' is coincidental.)

Giles F 'kid', originally Latin *Aegidius* from Greek, whence OF Gide, Gire, Gile. Miracle-working 6th-century saint who modestly escaped publicity by moving from Athens to France; associated with cripples, beggars, hunted creatures. Common in south-west; there must be involvement with some of the **Gilbert** group.

Gilford L Still the pronunciation of Guildford, Surrey, 'ford where (golden) marsh marigolds grow' OE.

Gilfoyle and **Gilhespy** See **Guilfoyle** and **Gillespey**.

Gilkes F '(son) of (dim). **William**'. Chiefly a Cotswold and Oxon–Warwicks surname.

Gill (with G– as in *gag*) O 'servant, devotee' Scots Gaelic and ON (cf. Scots *gillie*). Or L 'ravine' ON. No evidence for F dim. '**Gilbert**'. This is a northern surname. Also (with G– as in *gem*) F dim. '**Gillian**'; no evidence for F dim. '**Giles**'. And see **Gillian**.

Gillam F English respelling of OF *Guillaume* '**William**'.

Gillanders F 'devotee of (Saint) **Andrew**' Scots Gaelic.

Gillard (with G– as in *gag*) F ?OF form of Norman **Willard**; (with G– as in *gem*) dim. '**Giles**'. Or involved with **Gaylord**, or with the **Gillet** complex. The **–ard** is an OF dim. suffix. Chiefly a Devon surname.

Gillem See **Gillam**.

Giller L 'one who lives at a ravine' ON + suffix.

Gillespey, Gillespie O 'bishop's servant' Scots Gaelic.

Gillet, Gillett(e) (with G– as in *gag*) L 'gill-head (i.e. top of the ravine)' ON + OE. Just possibly F double dim. '**William**', in OF form. But (with G– as in *gem*) F dim. '**Gill/Giles**'. The **–tte** is fanciful.

Gillham, Gilliam See **Gillam**.

Gillian F dim. '**Julian** (female and, rarely, male)/Juliana'; whence a **Gill** 'flirt', and *to jilt*.

Gilliard, Gilliart, Gilliat(t) See **Gillard** and **Gillet**. **–art** and **–att** chiefly Lincs.

Gillibrand F 'hostage sword' Germanic (cf. **Gilbert**).

Gillingham L 'homestead of Gylla's followers' OE (his name goes back to an element 'war'); places in Dorset, Norfolk (as in *got*), Kent (as in *jot*).

Gilli(e)s F 'devotee of Jesus' Scots Gaelic.

Gillman F From an OF dim. (in *–in*) of *Guillaume* '**William**'; from another dim. comes *guillotine*. Chiefly a Staffs–Derbys surname.

Gillow L 'retreat at the pool' OW (initial *c*– mutated to **G**–); place in Herefords.

Gillum and **Gilman** See **Gillam** and **Gillman**.

Gilmartin F (for McG—) 'son of the devotee' Scots Gaelic 'of (Saint) **Martin**'.

Gilmer, Gilmor(e), Gilmour F 'devotee of (Saint) Mary' Scots Gaelic. Non-Scots bearers may ?derive from L Gillamoor, place in North Yorks, 'moor belonging to the village of Gilling (= family/folk of an AS whose F is connected with the Gēats, as in **Elliot**)' OE.

Gilpatrick F 'devotee of (Saint) **Patrick**' Irish.

Gilpin A surname of south Westmorland since the 1200s, and a river-name there recorded since the 1600s; if the latter came first it might be an OE word related to 'gulp', but if the river is named after the family then some N meaning like 'bloated' may be intended.

Gilroy O 'servant of the red-haired lad' Irish and Scots Gaelic.

Ginger O 'ginger' OE (from the East via Latin), for a seller of it. No proof of its use as a N for hair-colour. Chiefly of Bucks origin.

Ginn L 'trap, snare.' OF; cf. **Ingham**.

Ginnifer See **Jennifer**.

Gipp F dim. '**Gilbert**'. **Gipps** '(son) of G—'.

Girard(et), Girardot See **Gerard**; and dim. '**Gerard**' with OF suffixes. Huguenot surnames.

Girdler O 'belt-/girdle-maker' OE.

Girle N 'girl, youth, young person' ME *girle/gurle/gerle*, so (east Midland and northern/south-western/south-eastern) probably from a lost OE form with *y*. The **-e** is not swank, but organic.

Girton L 'gravelly farm' OE (cf. **grit**); places in Cambs, Notts.

Gitsham L '(AS called) Gyddi's homestead (cf. **Giddy**)' OE; place (Gittisham) in Devon.

Gittin(g)s See **Gethin**; and '(son) of **Gethin**'. Guppy counted **Gittins** in Salop and North Wales.

Gladden, Glad(d)ing F dim. 'glad, cheerful' OE.

Gladman F 'cheerful man' OE.

Gladwin F 'glad friend' OE.

Glaisher O 'glazier, glass-maker' OE. Also **Glaister**, probably not feminine, as this form might imply.

Glanvill(e) L 'domain of a Norman called Gland (meaning ?)' Germanic+OF; place (–e) in Calvados.

Glas(s)cock, Glas(s)cote L ?'cottage/hut where glass is made' OE; place (Glascote) in Warwicks.

Glascoe L 'green hollow' OW, the Lanarks city of Glasgow.

F: *first name*   L: *local name*   N: *nickname*   O: *occupational name*

Glass O 'glass' OE, a metonym for a glazier. Guppy counted it in Wilts, Devon.

Glasson L ?'green place' Cornish *glasen*. Guppy's only count was in Cornwall. G—, Lancs, is ?'bright/shining spot' OE, and G—, Cumberland, is ?'green/blue river' Keltic.

Glastonbury L 'fort/mound of the people of the place where ?woad grows' Keltic+OE; place in Somerset.

Glaysher, Glayzer, Glazer, Glazier See **Glaisher**.

Glazebrook L 'blue/green brook' OW+OE; place in Lancs.

Gleave N 'lance, bill, sword' OF, including the winning-post lance set up as the prize.

Gleed N 'kite (the bird of prey)' OE.

Glen(n) L 'glen' Keltic; locality, or place in Leics.

Glendale L 'valley of the River Glen (= clean, holy)' Keltic+OE; area in Northd.

Glew N 'sensible, sagacious' OE.

Glossop L 'valley of (an A S called) Starer' OE; place in Derbys.

Gloster L 'bright/splendid Roman site' Keltic+OE, the city of Gloucester, Glos.

Glover O 'glove-maker/-seller' OE. Chiefly a Staffs–Warwicks–Ches–Lancs–Leics surname.

Glow See **Glew**.

Glyn(n), Glynne L 'valley, glen' Keltic.

Goacher N 'good/nice/happy face' OE+OF (cf. *cheer*). Chiefly a Sussex surname.

Goatman O 'man who tends goats' OE+OE.

Gobbett (a North Country surname) F dim. '**Godbert/Godbold**'.

Godbear, Godbe(e)r, Godbehere N 'God be here!' OE, from the ancestor's favourite exclamation; mingled with 'good beer' OE. **Godber** is a Notts–Derbys surname.

Godbert F 'god bright' OE.

Godbold F 'god bold' OE.

Goddard F '(pagan) god hard' OF from Germanic.

Godfray, Godfree Forms of **Godfrey**.

Godfrey (also **Godfery**) F 'god peace' Germanic – the god certainly pre-Christian. East Midlands, especially Cambs, and Somerset–Glos.

Godley L 'wood/clearing of (an A S called) **Good**' OE or just 'good clearing' OE; places in Ches, Devon, Surrey, Sussex, West Yorks.

Godman F 'good man' OE. Or O 'householder' OE.

Godney L 'island of (an A S called) **Good**' OE; place in Somerset.

Godrich, Godridge F 'God/good ruler' OE. Normans used *Godric* as a N for an Englishman, calling Henry I and his wife *Godric* and *Godiva* for his alleged English sympathies and her English lineage.

Godsafe, Godsa(l)ve N '(for) God's sake!' OE (cf. *behalf*); cf. **Godbear.**

Godsal(l) N 'good soul, decent chap' OE. But see **Godsell.**

Godsell L 'God's hill' OE, places (Ga/odshill, Godsell) in Hants, IoW, Kent, Wilts. Or from **Godsall**; the two are found in Herefords.

Godsmark N 'plague-spot' (called 'God's mark') OE.

Godwin F 'God friend/protector' OE, sometimes ?'good friend/protector'. Meanings illustrated neither by William **G**— the atheist nor by **G**—, Harold II's father, who blinded Prince Alfred between Guildford and Ely. Commonest in Wilts–Hants–Berks–Oxon.

Goff(e) O '**Smith**' OW, Breton, Irish; cf. **Angove.** There may also be some absorption of **Gough.** Guppy found **Goff** chiefly in Northants.

Gogarty Cognate with **Fogarty.**

Golborn(e), Golbourn(e) L 'marsh marigold stream' OE; places in Ches, Lancs.

Gold F of a N type 'golden-haired, precious, rich' OE – used as an AS male and female F; also a later N.

Golden N 'having golden hair' OE.

Golding F 'son of **Gold**' or dim. '**Gold**'. Guppy counted it in Wilts, Norfolk.

Goldsb(o)rough L '**Gold**'s fort' OE, place (–or–) in North Yorks; or 'Good Helmet's fort' OE, place (–or–) in West Yorks.

Goldsmith O 'goldsmith' OE; now reinforced by Jewish immigrant surname. Guppy counted it in Sussex, Suffolk.

Goldstone F 'gold stone' OE. Or L '**Gold**'s stone' OE, place in Salop; or '**Goldstone**'s farm' OE, place in Kent.

Goldthorpe L '**Gold**'s **Thorp**' OE; place in West Yorks.

Goldworthy L '**Gold**'s enclosure' OE; place in Parkham, Devon.

Golightly N 'go quickly' OE, for a runner/messenger.

Golley See **Gully.**

Gomer F 'good/battle famous' OE; cf. **Gummer.**

Gomersall L '**Gomer**'s nook' OE; place (–al) in West Yorks.

Gomm(e) N 'man' OE, found (with an intrusive –r–) in *bridegroom*. Chiefly of Bucks origin.

Gooch N (like **Goodge, Gough, Gudge, Gutch**) 'red(-headed/-faced)' Welsh *coch* mutated when used attributively with a proper name.

Good(e) N 'good' OE. Sometimes a F meaning 'good/god', or first element of a double name beginning thus; –e can show weak adjec-

F: *first name* L: *local name* N: *nickname* O: *occupational name*

tive after lost definite article. **Good** is commonest in Northants.

Goodale, Goodall N '(brewer/seller of) good ale' OE. **Goodall** is common in Derbys–Notts–Ches–Staffs–Salop.

Gooday See **Goodday**. Guppy counted it in Essex.

Goodbairn, Goodban(d), Goodborn, Goodbourn, Goodburn, Goodbun N 'good child' OE; typical of the counties where *bairn* remains in use.

Goodbody N 'good person; Good Sir (?a favourite greeting); handsome' OE.

Goodch(e)ap N 'good price, bargain' OE; cf. **Chapman**.

Goodchild N 'good **Child**' OE; perhaps sometimes for 'godchild' OE – but not a very distinguishing name in days of universal baptism.

Goodday N 'good day!' OE; an exclamation, like **Godbear**. But 'good **Day** (servant)' is possible.

Goodell Respelling of **Goodale**, found in USA.

Goodenough, Goodenow N 'very good' OE, or perhaps 'all right' (our usual meaning), or a favourite exclamation of somebody easily satisfied; but sometimes absorbing N *Goodknave* 'good boy/servant' OE. Form in –**ow** shows archaic and dialectal word *enow*.

Gooderick, Gooderidge See **Godrich**.

Goodeve F Better known for Lady *Godiva* 'God gift' OE.

Goodfellow N 'good companion/associate, popular man' OE+ON.

Goodge and **Goodger** See **Gooch** and **Goodyear**.

Goodhard See **Goodhart** or **Goddard**.

Goodh(e)art N 'good heart' OE.

Goodhew F 'good heart/mind (cf. **Hugh**)' OE. Reaney also supposes N 'good servant, good member of a household (cf. **Hewish**)' OE.

Gooding F 'son of **Good**' or dim. '**Good**'. Guppy counted it in Suffolk, Somerset.

Goodison F 'son of God/Good Battle' OE feminine.

Goodlad N 'good lad/servant' OE. Surname chiefly found in Scotland and the north. Also **Goodlet**.

Goodley L '**Good**'s wood/clearing' OE, parish (Goodleigh) in Devon; but place (Goodleigh) in Uffculme, Devon, is this or 'good clearing' OE.

Goodliff(e) F 'good/God dear, sweetheart' OE; cf. **Leaf**.

Goodman See **Godman** (which is the 'better' spelling, the *ō* being 'correctly' shortened before the consonant combination *dm*). Guppy counted it in Bucks–Beds–Northants–Leics, Cornwall.

Goodnough, Goodnow See **Goodenough**.

Goodrich, Goodrick(e), Goodridge Forms of **Godrich**. But perhaps sometimes L – place Goodrich in Herefords was *Castellum*

Godrici 'Godric's Castle' in the 1100s, which may account for Guppy's high count of **–ridge** in South Wales.

Goodrum F 'battle dragon/snake (cf. **Orme**, *worm*)' ON; King Alfred's great enemy is now usually styled *Guthrum*.

Goodsall See **Godsall**.

Goodson F 'son of **Good**' or 'son of (the pet-form of a F beginning) **Good**' or 'good son' OE; but not *godson* – every boy was a godson in our Middle Ages. Guppy counted it in Leics, Somerset.

Goodspeed N '(May) God prosper (you)!' OE, *speed* being here subjunctive and having no sense of quickness (cf. *more haste, less speed*); a N from a favourite valediction.

Goodwin F 'good friend/protector' OE (cf. the ?sarcastic name G— Sands). Commonest in Staffs–Derbys, Kent.

Goodwright Probably the same as **Godrich**, but made by folk-etymology to look like 'good craftsman'; cf. **Wright**.

Goodyear N 'good year!' OE, a New Year's greeting; cf. **Godbear**. Guppy counted it in Lincs.

Gook N 'cuckoo' ON, perhaps for promiscuity.

Gool L 'watercourse, sluice' ?OE (?affected by French *goule* 'throat'); locality, or place (–e) in West Yorks.

Goold Form of **Gold**; often Scots.

Goord See **Gourd**.

Goosey L 'goose island' OE; place in Berks.

Gordon L But ?'great hill' Scots Gaelic, places in Berwicks and Kincardines, is not the only origin; Gourdon (see **Gurden**) is also involved, and the ultimate source remains mysterious. 52nd commonest surname in Scotland in 1958. Family name of the dukes of Richmond and of the marquesses of Aberdeen and of Huntly.

Gore L 'triangular (originally spear-shaped; cf. *garlick*) plot of ground' (left after oblong plots had been allocated) OE – the shape of the dress-maker's *gore*; locality, or places in Kent, Wilts. (Or 'dirt/dung' OE may be involved; cf. **Gorton**.) Family name of the earls of Arran.

Gorge L 'gorge' OF; locality, or places in France. Whence one family of **George**, who bore a *gurge* 'whirlpool' as their armorials.

Gorham L ?'dirty/triangular homestead/river-meadow' OE; the family have long given their name to Gorhambury, Herts.

Gorman F (for McG—, rarely O G—) 'son/descendant of (dim.) Blue' Irish.

Gorton L 'dirt/dung place' OE; place in Lancs.

Gosden L 'goose valley' OE; a Surrey surname as early as 1364, whence

F: *first name*   L: *local name*   N: *nickname*   O: *occupational name*

G— House in Bramley, but the origin may be G— Hill in Send-with-Ripley in the same county.

Gosford L 'goose ford' OE; places in Devon, Oxon, Warwicks.

Goslin(g) N 'gosling' ME from OE *gōs*. Or sometimes by confusion with F 'good/god/Goth' Germanic+OF suffix *–lin*, as in **Jocelyn**. Guppy counted *–ing* in Hants–Berks, Suffolk, Lincs.

Goss(e) F Reduced form of one of the names under **Jocelyn**, **Joyce**, and **Gosling**. Guppy counted **Goss** in Bucks, Devon.

Gossard O 'goose-herd' OE – a pretty simple task.

Gostelow L 'gorsy mound' or 'mound at a gorse-hill' OE; place (now Gorstella) in Lower Kinnerton, Ches.

Gotelee L 'clearing with goats' OE; for instance, Gotleigh, in Clay-hidon, Devon, was *Goteleye* in 1274.

Gotham L 'homestead with goats' OE; place in Notts.

Gotliffe See **Goodliff**.

Gotobed N 'go to bed' OE; given probably on account of laziness.

Gough N 'red(-headed/-faced)' Welsh *goch*, but with the *–kh* sound made into *–ff*. Now found chiefly in Border counties Salop–Here-fords, and in Wilts. See **Gooch**.

Goulborn L 'stream with (*golden*) marsh marigolds' OE; places (Gol-borne) in Ches, Lancs.

Gould Commoner form of **Gold**. Found chiefly in west Midlands and the south-west.

Goulding See **Golding**. Guppy counted it only in Glos.

Goundry See **Gundry**.

Gourd N 'coarse, dull, lumpish' OF. Or perhaps O 'bottle-/flask-(maker)' OF, with reference to the dried shell of the gourd.

Gow O 'Smith' Scots Gaelic.

Gowan(s), **Gowen** Forms of **McGowan**.

Gowran L 'goat place' Irish; place in Co. Kilkenny.

Grace(y), **Gracie** F Latinized version (under influence of *gratia*) of feminine F meaning ?'grey' Germanic and OF. (No sign that it is ever N 'fat' OF *gras*, or F after the Cornish Saint Grace, co-patron with Saint Probus of Probus Church.) *–ie* chiefly Scots.

Gradidge L 'big ditch' OE; place (Graddage) in Devon.

Grady F (for O G—) 'descendant of Noble' Irish.

Grafham L 'homestead by a **Grove**' OE; places in Hunts and (–ff–) Sussex.

Grafton L 'farm by a **Grove**' OE; places in ten counties.

Graham L 'homestead of Granta' (an AS whose F meant ?'grinner, snarler, grumbler') OE or 'gravelly homestead' OE; place (Gran-tham) in Lincs; taken to Scotland early in 1100s by William de G—,

and now mainly Scots. Use as a F is recent. 32nd commonest surname in Scotland in 1958, 82nd in Ireland in 1890. Family name of
the dukes of Montrose.

Grainge(r) See **Grange(r)**. A North and East Yorks surname.

Granard L 'high shrubbery' Irish; place in Co. Longford.

Grand N 'big, tall; elder, senior' OF (**–d** or **–t**).

Grandfield See **Granville**, despite the English-looking 'field'.

Grange L 'grange, granary, barn' OF. **Granger** O 'one who works at
(or superintends) a grange, a farm bailiff'; chiefly of Worcs origin.

Grant Commoner form of **Grand**. Or ?F 'Granta' OE; see **Graham**.
44th commonest surname in Scotland in 1958 (dropping eight
places in a hundred years). Family name of the barons de Longueuil
and the barons Strathspey. Counted by Guppy in Warwicks, Dorset–Devon, Lincs.

Granville L 'Granville (= big place)' OF; place in Manche.

Grason, Gration See **Graveson**; the second oddly latinized.

Gratrix See **Greatrakes**.

Gratton L 'big hill' OE; places in Devon and Derbys (the latter may
be 'big farm' OE), and a Derbys surname.

Grave O 'steward, manager of property' ON; an ON F *Greifi* 'count,
earl' is sometimes also involved. But there may be late confusion
with **Greve**, **Greaves**. (No evidence for connection with L 'sandy/
pebbly soil' OF; and none with *grave* in sense of 'tomb'.) **Graves** O
'(son) of the steward' ON. Or F '(son) of G—'; but cf. **Greaves**.
Graves(t)on O 'son of the steward'. **Graveson** and its eight variants (see **Grason**, **Grayshan**) are largely Yorks–Lancs surnames,
but **Graves** was of Cambs–Lincs–Notts in 1890.

Gravell(e) L 'gravelly place' OF.

Gravener See **Gravenor**.

Graveney L 'stream of the ditch/trench' OE; place in Kent on a
stream; **–en–** is ?from OE *–an*, genitive singular of weak noun.

Gravenor O 'great hunter' OF (first element OF *grand*).

Gray Same as **Grey**, and everywhere commoner; 30th commonest
surname in Scotland in 1958. But those who were *de Gray* were L
from Graye in Calvados (= Latin F *Gratus* (cf. *grace*)) + a lost suffix.

Grayham See **Graham**.

Grayrigge L 'grey ridge' ON; place in Westmorland.

Grayshan, Grays(h)on, Grayston(e) Same as **Graveson**. But
–ston(e) can be L 'grey stone' OE, or place such as Greystones,
West Yorks.

Greagg See **Greg**.

F: *first name*   L: *local name*   N: *nickname*   O: *occupational name*

Grealey N 'pock-marked, pitted (literally hailstone-marked)' OF. But in Ireland for a Mc— F 'son of Raghallach' Irish (meaning ?).

Greasley L 'gravel/pebble clearing' OE; place in Notts.

Greathead N 'big head' OE.

Greathouse L 'big house' OE.

Greatrakes may be nearest to the original form of the group that follows; probably L 'long/wide hill-paths' OE *hraca*. Wherever the place was, Guppy counted **Greatorex** in Derbys–Staffs; **Greatrix** in Staffs, Lancs; **Gratrix** in Lancs (G— Lane, in Ashton on Mersey, Ches, is named after the family); **Greatrex** he did not count. He derived them all from Great Rocks, in Wormhill, Derbys.

Greave Usually L 'grove' OE; but also involved with **Grave** and **Grieve**.

Greaves L 'of (i.e. at) the **Grove**', or a plural; locality, or place in Preston, Lancs; but cf. **Graves** and **Grieves**. Family name of the earls of Dysart.

Grebby L 'stony/gravelly farm' ON; place in Lincs.

Greedy N 'greedy, gluttonous' OE.

Greeff See **Grieve**.

Greel(e)y See **Grealey**.

Green(e) L '(village) green' OE; the –e is justified – the OE word had it, or it could show a dative after a lost preposition. (Or ?N on analogy of French names, 'young, fresh, immature' – slang 'green'.) –n was the 17th commonest surname in England and Wales in 1853, 21st in USA in 1939.

Greenacre L 'green field' OE. Guppy counted it in Norfolk.

Greenfield L 'green **Field**' OE, locality, or places in six counties. Or the Englishing of a Jewish surname or (earlier) of **Grenville** (see **Grenfell**), from Grainville-la-Teinturière, Seine-Maritime, '**War-in**'s domain' OF.

Greenford L 'green ford' or 'ford at a green' OE; place in Middx.

Greengrass L 'green sward' OE+ON. Reaney's earliest examples are from Suffolk.

Greenhalf, Greenhalge, Greenhalgh, Greenhall L 'green **Haugh** (*halh*)' OE; place (–lgh) in Lancs now pronounced '*Greena*', so the surname is more conservative.

Greenham L 'green river-meadow' OE; place in Berks, but first element of place in Somerset may be a river-name from verb *grind* OE, ?'mill-stream'.

Greenhead L 'green top/hill' OE; place in Northd.

Greenhill L 'green hill' OE, locality, or places in a dozen counties; but place in Worcs is 'hill of the spectre/goblin' OE.

Greenhow(e), Greenough, Greenhoff L 'green mound/hill' OE (or ON, if second element be from *haug*–); places (–how) in North and West Yorks.

Greenidge L Though so like the modern 'Grinnidge' pronunciation of *Greenwich*, the surname is probably 'green hedge' OE, as at Greenhedge, Notts, or 'green escarpment' OE (cf. **Edge**).

Greening F 'son of Green' in its N sense, or dim. '**Green**'.

Greenleaf L Bardsley's John *de Grenelef* (Yorks, 1379) proves this to be a place-name, though no *Greencliff* OE is recorded. **Greenleaves** is equally obscure, unless it be '(of, i.e.) at the green cliff'.

Greenslade L 'green valley' or 'green glade between woodlands' OE; place in North Tawton, Devon, and a surname of Devon–Somerset.

Greensmith O 'worker in copper' OE, from the colour of its patination. (No connection with *grynsmiđ* 'evildoer' in the OE poem *Andreas*.)

Greenstreet L 'green highroad' OE.

Greenwell L 'grassy spring/stream' OE; places in Cumberland and Co. Durham, and a Co. Durham surname.

Greenwood L 'green wood' OE; sometimes ?absorbing **Grimwood**. Guppy found a huge incidence in West Yorks.

Greer F Scots form of dim. '**Gregory**'.

Greet L 'gravel' OE (cf. *grit*); places in Glos, Salop, Worcs. Or N 'big, fat' OE (cf. *great*). Or ?F dim. '**Margaret**' (cf. **Maggs**).

Greetham L 'gravelly homestead/river-meadow' OE; places in Lincs, Rutland.

Greeves See **Greaves**.

Greg(g), Gregor F dim. '**Gregory**' (–gg being commoner). **Greggs** '(son) of G—'. **Gregson** 'son of G—'. In general, –e– marks the northern dim., –i– (see **Grigg**) the southern.

Gregory F 'watchful' Greek; F of at least three great saints – G— Nazianzen and G— of Nyssa, among the Fathers of the Eastern Church, and Pope G— the Great, who sent Saint Augustine to Britain. A Midland and Somerset–Wilts surname; from the F derive surnames in **Greg–, Grig–**.

Greif See **Grieve**.

Greig F Scots form of dim. '**Gregory**'.

Grendon L 'green hill/valley' OE; places in Berks, Northants, Warwicks/Herefords (two), but Guppy counted it only in Devon.

Grenfell Despite its appearance of being 'green fell/hill' OE, = **Grenville** L '**Warin**'s domain' OF; half-a-dozen places (Grainville) in Normandy.

F: *first name*   L: *local name*   N: *nickname*   O: *occupational name*

Gresham L 'grass/grazing homestead' OE; place in Norfolk.

Gresley L Same as **Greasley**; two places in Derbys.

Gresty L 'badger-run' OE (cf. *grey*, **Anstey**); place in Ches.

Gretton L 'stony/gravelly place' OE; places in Glos, Salop.

Greve L '**Grove**'; **Greves** See **Greaves**.

Grew N 'crane, long-legs' OF.

Grey N 'grey-haired' (or ?'pale-faced') OE. Occurs with **Gray**. Family name of the earls of Stamford. Guppy counted it in Northd–Co. Durham.

Greygoose N 'grey/wild goose' OE (where the compound existed entire).

Greystoke L '**Stock** on the (renamed River) Cray (= clean, fresh)' OW+OE; place in Cumberland.

Gribbin F 'son (*Mac*) of Robin (see **Robins**)' Irish+Germanic+OF suffix.

Gribble L 'blackthorn, crab-apple tree' 16th-century Dorset–Devon–Cornwall dialect, probably related to *crab*; Devon places include G—Lane in Rockbeare, G— Inn in Little Torrington, G—ford Bridge in Hatherleigh, *Grybbelparke* on Dartmoor (1386), and a man Walter *atte Gribbele* in Crediton (1330).

Grice N 'pig' ON or 'grey' OF, a poor choice.

Gricks and **Grief(f)** See **Griggs** and **Grieve**.

Grier F dim. '**Gregory**'. **Grierson** 'son of G—'. Both Scots surnames.

Grieve O 'governor of a province' (originally), 'overseer, manager, bailiff' OE (Northumbrian). **Grieves** '(son) of G—'. A northern and Scots surname; involved with **Graves** and ?**Greaves**.

Griffin(g) F dim. '**Griffith**', though Guppy found it chiefly in Bucks; Welsh, Border, and Devon families must derive from Wales and Cornwall; those in East Anglia from the Conqueror's Bretons, who settled numerously there; and –n was the 75th commonest surname in Ireland in 1890. (No *atte Griffin* recorded to suggest the sign of the heraldic beast.)

Griffis Form of **Griffiths**.

Griffith F Middle Welsh *Gruffudd*, where –*udd* is 'lord'; supposed connection with Latin *Rufus* 'red-haired' not proven. **Griffiths** '(son) of G—'; 49th commonest surname in England and Wales in 1853, and Guppy found nearly three per cent of the people of North Wales bearing it.

Grig(g) F dim. '**Gregory**'; cf. **Greg**. But could be N 'dwarf' ME (?from Germanic). **Griggs** '(son) of G—'. **Grigson** 'son of G—'. **Grigg** is chiefly of Cornish origin.

Grill N 'fierce, cruel' (originally ?'tooth-gnashing') OE from verb.
Grills '(son) of G—'; counted by Guppy in Cornwall–Devon.

Grime F 'mask, helmet' ON. But sometimes absorbing N **Grimm**,
adjective 'grim' OE or noun 'spectre, goblin' OE. **Grimes** '(son) of
G—'; counted by Guppy in Warwicks. And see **Grimsditch** for
further horrors.

Grimley L 'spectre/goblin wood/clearing' OE; place in Worcs.

Grimm(e) Involved with **Grime**.

Grimmond Perths perversion of **McCrimmon**.

Grimsditch There were several earthworks of this name in AS
England – in south Wilts (still so called), Herts, Middx, and (the
origin of this Ches surname) in the Hundred of Bucklow, Ches: L
'the Name-Concealer's/Masked One's dyke' OE, referring to the
shape-changing god Woden (see **Othen, Grime**).

Grimshaw L '**Grimm**'s wood' OE; place in Blackburn, Lancs, and
a Lancs surname.

Grimsley L '**Grimm**'s wood/clearing' OE. Mainly a Leics surname,
and probably a lost place in Leics.

Grimstead, Grimsteed L 'green homestead' OE; place (–ea–) in
Wilts.

Grimston(e) L '**Grime/Grimm**'s place' second element OE; places
in six counties. **Grimston** is the family name of the earls of Veru-
lam.

Grimwade, Grimward, Grimwood F Second spelling is the nearest
to the original 'mask/helmet/grim (cf. **Grime**) guardian' Germanic; but cf. **Greenwood**. **Grimwood** is chiefly of Suffolk origin.

Grindal, Grindell, Grindle L 'green valley/hill' OE; places in Salop
(–dle), East Yorks (–dale).

Grindley L 'green wood/clearing' OE; place in Staffs.

Grinham See **Greenham**.

Grinnell Despite family tradition of Huguenot ancestry, same as
Greenhill.

Grinstead, Grinsteed L 'green place/site' OE; two places (–ead) in
Sussex.

Grinton L 'green place' OE; place in North Yorks.

Grisdale L 'valley with pigs' ON; place in West Yorks and two places
(Grizedale) in Lancs.

Grisenthwaite L 'pigs' clearing' ON.

Grisewood L 'wood with pigs' ON+OE.

Grissom, Grisson N 'greyish' OF.

Griswold L 'gravelly/pebbly woodland' OE; place in Warwicks.

F: *first name*　　L: *local name*　　N: *nickname*　　O: *occupational name*

Grix Form of **Gricks** (two of each in London TD).

Gronow is an anglicized version of the Welsh F 'Goronwy', OW *Guorgonui*.

Groocock N 'crane-cock' OF+OE, perhaps for someone with long legs.

Groom O 'servant, attendant, farm worker' ME. Guppy found it in Northants, Salop, Suffolk.

Groombridge L 'grooms'/servants' bridge' ME+OE; place in Kent.

Grose See **Gross**. Common in Cornwall.

Groser O 'wholesaler' OF (cf. *grocer*).

Grosmont L 'big hill' OF; places in Mon and (after a French monastic mother-house) North Yorks.

Gross N 'fat, big' OF; but many in (especially) London are recent European immigrants with German surnames of similar meaning.

Grosvenor O 'great/chief huntsman' OF. Descent claimed from an uncle of Rollo, founder of Normandy; first settler in England, Gilbert le **G—**, kinsman of the Conqueror. Family name of the dukes of Westminster and the barons Ebury.

Groundwater L 'shallow lake' ON; farm in Orphir, Orkney, on the Loch of Kirbister, and an Orcadian surname.

Grout N 'groats, porridge' OE (Reaney points out that there was a N of the same meaning in ON).

Grove L 'grove, copse, thicket' OE. **Grover** and genitive **Groves** will mean 'dweller in the grove, etc.', or –es could be a plural. Commonest in Dorset and Salop.

Growcott Version of **Groocock**. Guppy counted it in Salop.

Grubb N 'insect, dwarf'. Or O 'digger, grubber' ME from Germanic.

Grundy See, perhaps, **Gundry**; a surname made famous by the hypothetical prude Mrs **G—**. **Grundry** may still exist.

Grunsell O 'timber used as a foundation for a superstructure (cf. *ground*, *sill*), foundation' ME; perhaps for an expert at this work. Certainly no connection with the canary's groundsel.

Guard O 'watchman, guard' OF.

Gudge See **Gooch**.

Guest N 'guest, stranger, traveller' ON. Family name of the viscounts Wimborne. Guppy counted it in Worcs, Kent.

Guiatt See **Guyat**.

Guild O 'fraternity, trade/craft g(u)ild' OE and ON, probably from membership or from duties at the guildhall.

Guilfoyle F (for McG—) 'son of the devotee of (Saint) **Paul**' Irish.

Guin(n)ess Forms (–nn– much commoner) of **McGenis**. **Guinness** is the family name of the earls of Iveagh and the barons Moyne.

Guise Probably most often a respelling of **Guys**, with no reference to the French dukedom.

Gullett L 'water-channel, ravine, gully' ME from OF *goulet* (dim. 'throat'; cf. the *gullet* of a fowl). A south Devon surname originating in Gullet Farm and thereabouts, on Southpool Creek (I am grateful to Mr John R. Lyall of Ivanhoe, Australia, for his splendid documentation of all this). A Cardiff lane, once leading damply to the River Taff, is now called Golate, with a fatuous yarn about sailors' using it as a short cut when tardy.

Gullick F 'battle sport (cf. **Laker**)' OE; yet one famous Guthlac was a hermit saint in the Fens.

Gulliford, Gulliver N 'glutton' OF; latter chiefly a Northants surname.

Gully N 'giant, Goliath (= ?exile)' Hebrew ?from Arabic; no doubt confused with a word for 'glutton' (cf. *gullet*, **Gulliford**). Family name of the viscounts Selby.

Gumbold F 'battle bold' Germanic. Bardsley had heard of a grotesque version **Gumboil**, but couldn't track it down.

Gummer(son) F A fuller version of **Gomer**. And 'son of G—'.

Gundry F 'battle rule' Germanic. Bardsley saw it as the origin of **Grundy**, by metathesis, but this is not proven; in Co. Durham he found its derivative **Goundry** and its –son form **Gunderson**, and he quotes what he considers a transitional form **Grundry** at Plymouth (1873).

Gunn F 'war, battle' ON; but sometimes an abbreviation of the appalling female F *Gunnhildr* 'battle battle' ON – as is our *gun*.
. Chiefly a Notts surname.

Gunning F A derivative of some Germanic name with first element 'war' (cf. **Gunn**)+the dim. or patronymic –ing. Or a reduction of *Gundwin* 'battle friend' Germanic.

Gunnison F 'son of Gunnhildr' (see **Gunn**).

Gunson F 'son of **Gunn**'. **Gunsum** may be a version of this.

Gunter F 'battle army' Germanic. Counted by Guppy only in Berks–Glos.

Gunthorpe L '**Gunn**'s **Thorp**' ON; places in five counties; but place in Notts is 'Gunnhildr's **Thorp**' (see **Gunn**).

Gunton L '**Gunn**'s place' ON+OE; places in Norfolk, Suffolk.

Guppy L 'Guppa's enclosure (his name is a shortening of ?"Battle Bright")' OE; place in Dorset. The resonance of its origin is well worthy of the diligent counter of surnames.

Gurden N dim. '**Gourd**' in its boorish sense. But some bearers origi-

---

F: *first name*   L: *local name*   N: *nickname*   O: *occupational name*

nate in Gourdon, Saône-et-Loire, 'mountain' Gaulish+Latin suffix, and some may be **Gordon** misspelt.

Gurney L From one of several places called Gournai/Gournay in Normandy, based on a Gallo-Roman F *Gordinus* + suffix.

Gutch See **Gooch**.

Guthrie L 'windy' Scots Gaelic; place in Angus.

Guy F Germanic *Wido* (?noun 'wood, forest', ?adjective 'wide'), introduced by Normans in forms beginning W— and from the French of Paris in forms beginning G—; see **Wyatt**, **Whyatt**. Rarely, and without derivatives, it may be O 'guide' OF *gui*. F made unpopular by Fawkes. **Guys** '(son) of G—'.

Guyat(t), **Guyon**, **Guyot(t)** F dim. '**Guy**'; **Guye** is Guy.

Gwatkins Version of **Watkins** based on Welsh *Gwallter* for **Walter**.

Gwilli(a)m Representations of Welsh *Gwilym* for **William**.

Gwin, **Gwinn** Forms of **Gwyn**.

Gwyn(n), **Gwynne** N 'white(-haired/-faced)' O W, but common in Ireland.

Gwyther F 'victor' O W from Latin.

Gyatt See **Guyat**; here possibly belongs the Derbys surname **Gyte**.

Gye See **Guy**.

H

Hack F 'hook, crook' ON. Sometimes ?L 'grating, gate, hatch' OE, in dialect form with –**ck** by ON influence.

Hacker O '(?wood-)cutter, maker of hacks/hoes/mattocks/picks/bills' ME from Germanic. Or L 'dweller at the **Hack**' OE.

Hackett F dim. '**Hack**' ON; surname of the scandinavianized east coast.

Hackwood L 'haw wood' OE (cf. dialect *hag*); place in Hants; but place in Northants is ?'hacked/cut wood' ME+OE.

Haddon L 'heathery hill' OE; places in Derbys, Dorset, Northants.

Hadfield L 'heathery **Field**' OE; place in Derbys.

Hadley L 'heathery clearing/field' OE; places (also –leigh) in Essex, Middx, Suffolk, Sussex.

Hagan F (for O **H**—) 'descendant of ?Young/?(dim.) **Hugh**' Irish. But English bearers will be F 'thornbush, fence, protector' Germanic, and Germanic word for 'tomcat', to denote virility, has also been suggested (Kemp Malone).

Hagley L 'haw wood/clearing' OE (cf. dialect *hag*); places in four counties.

Hague See **Haig(h)**.

Haig(h) L 'enclosure' OE/ON, places (–gh) in Lancs, West Yorks; but in the case of the earls **Haig** 'La Hague (= enclosure, paddock)' Normanno-Picard from Germanic, place in Manche.

Haighton L 'place in a **Haugh** (*halh*)' OE; place in Lancs.

Hailey L 'hay clearing/field' OE; places in Bucks, Herts, Oxon.

Haim(e) F 'home' Germanic, usually normanized as *Hamo* (nominative) or **Hamon** (oblique case). **Haim(e)s** '(son) of **H**—'. 8/3/2/1/1 of these in London T D (but a couple look like recent European).

Hain(e) L 'fences' OE (see first meaning of **Hay**); **Hain** is the weak plural (cf. *oxen*) of **Hay**, just as **Hayes** is the strong one (in –s); **Hayne/Hayes** often figure in Devon place-names. Or N 'humble, mean, niggardly' OE, with –**e** for weak adjective after lost definite article. Or a Germanic F of **Hagan** type.

Hair See **O Haire** and **Ayer**.

Hake Cognate with **Hack**.

Hakewill L '**Hack**'s spring' ON+OE; see **Equ(e)all**.

Haldane, Halden, Haldin N 'half Dane' OE.

Hale L '(at) the **Haugh** (*halh*)'; form with –**e**, losing –*h*, is dative after lost preposition; places in various other counties, but the surname

---

F: *first name*   L: *local name*   N: *nickname*   O: *occupational name*

is found chiefly in Mon–Glos–Wilts. **Hales** 'of(i.e. at) the **H—**', or a plural; places in Norfolk, Salop, Staffs, Worcs.

Halford L 'ford in a **Haugh** (*halh*)' OE; places in Devon, Salop, Warwicks.

Halfpenny N ' ½d.' OE, from a lost joke or the rent of a holding.

Halifax L 'holy (i.e. church-owned) flax(-field)' OE, with loss of –*l*–; or 'holy rough grass' OE (cf. **Fairfax**), the West Yorks town with the punning 'holy head (of hair)' of Saint John Baptist on its shield.

Haliwell L 'holy well/spring' OE; place in Middx.

Hall L 'hall, manor-house' OE, from residence or employment; high incidence in Northd–Durham also suggests L 'boulder, slope' ON. 16th commonest surname in England and Wales in 1853, 20th in USA in 1939.

Hallam L '(at) the rocks/slopes' ON, place in West Yorks; or '(at) the **Haughs**', place in Derbys; OE dative plural –*um*, after lost preposition, retained as –**am**. Mostly a Derbys–Notts surname.

Hallawell See **Haliwell**.

Hallet(t) F A Dorset–Somerset–Devon surname, not related to **Henry** (since *Hal* cannot easily be proved an abbreviation in surnames) and not found with *de/atte* to suggest anything like 'hall-head'. Reaney assigns it as a dim. to **Adlard**.

Halliday, Hallidie Forms of **Holiday**; latter Scots.

Hallifax Form of **Halifax**.

Halliwell L Same as **Haliwell**; place in Lancs.

Hallmark N 'half-mark' OE, i.e. 6s. 8d., one third of a pound.

Hallowell See **Haliwell**.

Hallow(e)s L 'of (i.e. at) the **Haugh** (*halh*)', or a plural. A Lancs surname.

Halse L 'neck' (of land) OE; locality, or places in Devon, Somerset; but place in Northants was originally 'neck-like spur' (of land) OE. Sometimes ? N, from a peculiar neck.

Halste(a)d L '(strong)hold/shelter site' OE, places in Essex, Kent, Leics, and (Hawstead) Suffolk; or 'hall site' OE, places in Lancs, Lincs.

Halton L 'place in a **Haugh** (*halh*)'; places in six counties; but place in Northd was ?'lookout-hill place' OE.

Ham L See **Hamm**; locality, or places in seven southern counties.

Hamblen See **Hamblin**.

Hambleton See **Hamilton**.

Hamblett See **Hamlet(t)**.

Hamblin(g) See **Hamlin**; –**b**– added to ease pronunciation.

Hambrook L 'rocky/stony brook' OE; place in Glos.

Hamerton L Same as **Hammerton**; place in Hunts.

Hamilton L Most commonly from the Lanarks town, a name brought in the 1200s by an Englishman from H—, Leics, which (like **Hambleton**, Lancs, Rutland, North Yorks; Hambledon, Hants, Surrey, Dorset; Hambleden, Bucks; Hameldon, Lancs) has first element once meaning 'maimed, crooked, cut off, bent, scarred' + 'hill' (cf. **Down**), though the final element of some may have been 'place/ farm' OE *tūn*. 34th commonest surname in Scotland in 1958. Family name of the dukes of Abercorn and of five other peers.

Hamlen See **Hamlin**.

Hamlet(t) F dim. '**Haim**'. (No connection with a small village or the Prince of Denmark.)

Hamlin(e), **Hamlyn** F dim. '**Haim**'; –**lyn** found around Dartmoor.

Hamm L 'river-meadow' OE (original spelling).

Hammer L 'dweller in a **Hamm**'; or possibly '(hammer-shaped) crag, cliff' ON (and ?OE). Or O, a metonym for one who made/ wielded hammers.

Hammerton L Second element 'place/farm' OE; first element could be '(hammer-shaped) crag' or 'hammer(-smithy)' or plant-name 'hammer-sedge/-wort' ON/OE; three places in West Yorks.

Hammond F Form of **Hamon**, already found in OF with excrescent –*d*; or form of *Haimund*, with second element 'protector' Germanic.

Hamnet(t) F dim. '**Haim**'; –*t* was the F of Shakespeare's son (after a godfather).

Hamon See **Haim**.

Hampden L 'homestead valley' OE; place in Bucks.

Hampshire L 'shire/county of Southampton' OE (see **Hampton**); also for **Hallam**shire, district in West Yorks of which the cricketer John **Hampshire** is a native.

Hampton L 'homestead farm, chief manor', or 'place in a river-meadow' or '(at) the high place' (with –**m**–, from –*n*–, showing dative as in **Hanbury**), all OE; places in nine contiguous southern and Midland counties.

Hanbury L '(at) the high fort/mound/manor' OE, with –**n**– showing weak dative of adjective after lost preposition and definite article; places in Staffs, Worcs.

Hancock, **Hancox** F dim. '**Hann**' + **Cock/Cox**. But a joke on OE *hana* 'cock'/*henn* 'hen'/*henna* 'fowl' may have helped. West Midland and south-western surname.

F: *first name*   L: *local name*   N: *nickname*   O: *occupational name*

Hand N 'hand' OE, for some deformity or legerdemain.

Handcock See **Hancock**.

Handford L 'ford where there were cocks' OE, or 'ford of an AS called Cock'; places in Staffs (–anf–), Ches (–rth). **Hanford**, Devon, may be 'stone/rock ford' OE. The various places called **Hannaford** in Devon are likeliest to be 'cocks' ford'.

Handley L Same as **Hanley**, with parasitic **–d–**; places in four counties.

Hanford L See **Handford**.

Hankin(g) F dim. '**Hann/Hand/Hamon**'; the **–kin** suffix from Flemish. **Hankins** '(son) of H—'.

Hanks F Either a reduced form of **Hankins** or (on evidence of early spelling *Anke*) an ON F containing dim. 'Eagle' (*Arn*–); Glos surname.

Hanley L '(at) the high wood/clearing' OE (cf. **Hanbury**); places in Staffs, Worcs (three).

Hanly F (for O H—) 'descendant of Beautiful' Irish.

Hann F Most often dim. '**John**' (reduced from *Johan*); sometimes demonstrably dim. '**Henry**'; and even ?dim. '**Randolph**'.

Hannaford See **Handford**. A thoroughly Devon surname.

Hannah L 'island full of (wild) cocks' OE; or '(AS called) Cock's island' OE; place in Lincs.

Hannibal F (but not Carthaginian!) See **Hunnable**.

Hansard O 'cutlass, dagger' OF, metonym for a maker/seller.

Hanson F 'son of **Hann/Hand**' – so a wide choice of meanings.

Harberer, Harbisher O 'shelterer (i.e. lodginghouse-keeper)' OE and (from Germanic) OF; **–ar–** from the **–er–** of **Herbage** (cf. **Clark**).

Harborn(e) L 'dirty stream' OE; places in Staffs, Warwicks.

Harbottle L 'hirelings' dwelling' OE; place in Northd.

Harbourn(e), Harburn See **Harborn**.

Harbutt Form of **Herbert**, with **–ar–** for **–er–** as in **Clark**.

Harcourt L 'hawker's/falconer's cottage' OE, place in Salop near Cleobury Mortimer; but place in Salop near Wem is ?'harper's cottage' or ?'cottage at a salt-harp' (for sifting salt) OE; or 'Harcourt' – second element 'court, manor' OF from Latin, places in Calvados, Eure.

Hardcastle L 'cheerless dwelling' OE+OF (Norman); place in West Yorks.

Harden L 'grey/grey-stone (i.e. boundary)/hare valley' OE, place in West Yorks; but place in Staffs is ?'high enclosure' OE.

Hardie Much rarer form of **Hardy**.

Harding F 'brave man, warrior, hero' OE (also ?absorbing *Hardwin* 'bold friend' Germanic, brought by the Normans).

Hardwick L 'herd (dairy-)farm, sheep farm' OE; places (including a few in –e) in over fifteen counties; –**ar**– for –*er*– as in **Clark**.

Hardy N 'bold, tough, daring' OF (and originally Germanic).

Harewood L 'grey/hares'/stoneheap wood' OE; places in Hants, Herefords, West Yorks.

Harfoot N 'harefoot' ON/OE, for a fast runner.

Harford L 'stags' ford' OE (cf. **Hart**), place in Glos; or 'army ford' OE (as in Hereford), place in Devon.

Hargr(e)ave L '**Grove** with hares' OE or 'grey **Grove**' OE; places in Ches, Northants, Suffolk. **Hargre(a)ves** 'of (i.e. at) **H**—'.

Harlan Corruption of **Harland**. USA H— descends from George **Harland**, Durham Quaker.

Harland L 'cairn/rock/tumulus land' OE; place in North Yorks where there are some tumuli, and mostly a North and East Yorks surname.

Harley L 'wood/clearing with hares' OE (places in Salop, West Yorks), though 'grey wood' OE is possible.

Harlock N 'grey lock/hair' OE.

Harlow L 'army/people mound (hundred meeting-place)' OE; place in Essex.

Harman, **Harmon** F 'army man, warrior' OF from Germanic.

Harmsworth L '(AS called) Army Courage's **Worth**' OE (cf. **Harford**, **Moody**); place (–monds–) in Middx. Family name of the viscounts Rothermere.

Harold F 'army power' ON (and a similar F in OE).

Harper O 'harp-maker/-player' OE; cf. **Harpour**. Common and scattered.

Harp(o)ur O '**Harper**' but from OF, and much rarer.

Harrad, **Harral(d)**, **Harrall**, **Harrel(l)** See **Harold**.

Harrap See **Harrop**.

Harrie(s) Forms of **Harry**, **Harris**; –**is** vastly outnumbers –**ies** everywhere save in South Wales, where –**ies** slightly predominates.

Harriman O 'servant of **Harry**' second element OE.

Harrington L 'place/farm of the family/folk of (an AS called) He-Goat' OE, place in Cumberland; but place in Northants is of the same origin as **Hetherington**; and place in Lincs has a mysterious first element. (In Ireland, used for anglicizing three different Irish names.)

Harris F '(son) of **Harry**'; over 11,000 in the TD (and only 100 –**iss**);

cf. **Harries**. 26th commonest surname in England and Wales in 1853, 17th in USA in 1939. Family name of the earls of Malmesbury. **Harrison** F 'son of Harry'. 29th commonest surname in England and Wales in 1853, but it is rarish in the south-west and South Wales.

Harrismith Perversion of **Arrowsmith**.

Harriss(on), **Harrissmith** Rare forms of **Harris(on)**, **Harrismith**.

Harro(l)d See **Harold**.

Harrop L 'hares' valley' OE; place in West Yorks.

Harrow L Pre-Christian cult site such as 'heathen temple, sacred grove' OE; places in Middx and (Peper H—) Surrey.

Harry F Not so much a dim. of **Henry** as its regular ME pronunciation; but far rarer than its derivatives **Harris(on)**.

Hart N 'hart, stag' OE, with –ar– from ME *hert* as in **Clark**; from resemblance or association. The west Midlands and south-west dialect area should show **Hurt** for this, or **Hort**. (Popular idea of a sign-name is not borne out by early forms.) But Irish bearers have F (for O H—) 'descendant of **Arthur**'.

Hartfield L '**Field** with stags' OE; place in Sussex.

Hartford L 'stag ford' OE, places in Ches, Herts, Northd; but place in Hunts is 'army ford' OE (as in **Harford**).

Hartigan F (for O H—) 'descendant' Irish 'of ?(dim.) **Arthur**'.

Hartill L 'hill with stags' OE; places (–th–) in Ches, Derbys, West Yorks.

Hartland L 'island (i.e. peninsula) with stags' OE; place in Devon.

Hartley L 'stag wood/clearing' OE, places in eight counties; but place in Northd is 'stag hill' OE; and place in Westmorland is 'wood claw' (latter in sense 'tongue of land between streams') OE. The surname is found chiefly in West Yorks–Lancs.

Harton L 'hill with stags' OE, place in Co. Durham; or ?'stony/ stoneheap farm' OE, place in North Yorks.

Hartshorn(e) L 'headland with stags' OE; place in Derbys. Or a mysterious N 'stag's antler' OE.

Hartwell L 'stags' spring/stream' OE; places in Bucks, Northants, Staffs.

Harvey, **Harvie** F 'battle/carnage worthy' Breton, normanized as *Hervé*; introduced by Bretons after 1066. Spelling **Hervey** is older, much rarer, and no longer representative of the sound. **Harvie** is Scots.

Harwell L 'stream from the grey (hill)' OE; place in Berks.

Harwich L 'army camp' OE; place in Essex.

Harwood L Same as **Harewood**, of several origins; places in Lancs, Northd, North Yorks.

Hasel– For all surnames beginning thus, see **Hazel**–.

Haslam L '(at) the hazels' OE dative plural after lost preposition; place in Lancs.

Hasle–For all surnames beginning thus, see **Hazel**–.

Hasler L 'hazel slope' OE; places (Haselo(u)r) in Staffs, Warwicks.

Haslip, Haslop, Haslup L 'hazel valley' OE (cf. **Hope**).

Haswell L 'spring/stream in the hazels' OE; places in Co. Durham, Somerset.

Hatch L 'gate, forest-gate, floodgate, sluice' OE; locality, or places in Beds, Hants, Somerset, Wilts. Counted by Guppy only in Surrey, Somerset.

Hatcher L 'dweller by the **Hatch**'.

Hatfield, Hatfull L '**Field** overgrown with heather' OE; places in six counties, and chiefly a Notts–Derbys surname. Two examples of the bizarre **Hatfull** in the London TD.

Hatherleigh, Hatherley L 'hawthorn wood/clearing' OE; places in Devon, Glos (two).

Hathersage, Hathersich L 'he-goat's edge/ridge' OE; place (–age) in Derbys.

Hatherton L 'place in the hawthorns/?heather' OE, place in Ches; or 'hawthorn hill' OE, place in Staffs.

Hatry See **Hawtrey**.

Hatton L 'place on a heath' OE; places in seven counties.

Hattrick See **Arkwright**.

Hauff L Version of **Haugh**, with original –gh shifted from throat to bottom lip and top teeth (cf. *laugh*).

Haugh L 'nook, side-valley, retreat, alluvial land' OE *halh*; or 'hedge, enclosure' OE *haga*. Cf. **Hauff, Hallows, Hale**, and (from OE West Saxon form *healh*) **Heal, Heale, Hele**; also many compounds.

Haughton L 'place in a **Haugh** (*halh*)' OE, places in six counties; but place in Notts is 'place on a **Hough**' OE.

Hauxwell L 'spring/stream with hawks' OE (or first element may be an A S owner called '**Hawk**'); place in North Yorks.

Havelock F 'sea play/sport' ON. (But the Canute-like hero of the medieval romance *H— the Dane* is ?a mixture of OW *Abloc* and ON *Olaf*; cf. **Umpleby**.)

Havercroft L 'oat **Croft**' ON+OE; place in West Yorks.

Haverfield L 'oat **Field**' ON+OE.

Haw F Same as **Haugh** (*haga*). Or F dim. '**Hawk**', as in **Hawkett, Hawkin**.

F: *first name*   L: *local name*   N: *nickname*   O: *occupational name*

Hawes L 'of (i.e. at) the **Haugh**'; or a plural; or 'neck of land, col, defile' OE (Anglian) or ON *hals*, as in H—, North Yorks. Or F '(son) of **Haw**' in its second meaning; or 'battle wide' Germanic, a female F occurring as *Hawis, Haweis*.

Hawk(e) N 'hawk' OE; from rapacity, or keeping hawks, or paying them as rent. But those once preceded by *de/atte* are L '**Haugh**' (*halh*; ME *halke*, with the *-l-* vocalized). **Hawk(e)s** F '(son) of H—'; or L 'of (i.e. at) the **H**—'; or a plural.

Hawkett N dim. '**Hawk**'.

Hawkin(g) F ?dim. '**Hal**' (itself a diminutive of **Henry**); but cf. **Hallett**; and an early spelling is *Havekin*, which must be a diminutive looking back to **Hawk**. **Hawkin(g)s** '(son) of H—'. The commonest of the group is easily **–ins**, especially in Somerset–Glos–Wilts–Devon.

Hawkridge L 'ridge with hawks' OE; places in Berks, Somerset.

Hawksworth L '**Worth** of (an AS called) **Hawk**' OE, place in West Yorks; but place in Notts could be either this (scandinavianized) or '**Worth** of (an AS called) Hōc (= ?hook, hunchback)' OE.

Hawthorn(e) L 'hawthorn' OE; the **-e** could show dative after lost preposition; locality, or places in eight counties.

Hawton L 'place in a hole (i.e. hollow)' OE; place in Notts.

Hawtrey L 'Hauterive (= high bank)' OF; place in Orne.

Hay L 'fence, enclosure, hedge' OE; locality, or places in Herefords, Westmorland. Or N 'high, tall' OE. Or a F of which 'high, tall' is the remaining first element. But in Ireland it represents **O Hea**. 82nd commonest surname in Scotland in 1958, and the family name of the marquesses of Tweeddale and the earls of Erroll and of Kinnoull.

Haydock L 'barley/corn place' OW; place in Lancs.

Haydon L 'heather(-grown) hill' OE, place in Kent; or 'hay/**Hay** hill' OE, places in Dorset, Somerset, Wilts; or 'hay ?valley' OE, place in Northd; and there are other places in Glos, Herts, Surrey.

Hayes L 'of (i.e. at) the **Hay**'; or 'brushwood' OE; or a plural; common in Devon place-names; cf. **Hain**. But in Ireland it represents **O Hea**, and was the 52nd commonest surname there in 1890.

Hayho(e), Hayhow L 'high hillspur' OE (cf. **Hough**).

Hayne Can share any of the meanings of **Hain**. **Haynes** '(son) of H—' (N or F meaning only).

Haythornthwaite, Haythornwhite L '**Thwaite** with hawthorns' ON; place (Haw–) in Lancs.

Hayton L 'hay/**Hay** farm' OE; places in four counties.

Hayward O 'fence/hedge/enclosure guardian' OE; an official who supervised the Lammas lands enclosed for corn and controlled straying cattle; a bailiff. Cf. **Howard**. Found from Devon to Salop, Suffolk.

Haywood L 'fenced/enclosed wood' OE; places in five counties.

Hazel(l) L 'hazel tree' OE.

Hazeldeane, Hazelden(e), Hazeldine, Hazeldon L 'valley of hazels' OE; places (Hasel–, Hesel–, Hesle–, Hasling–+–den, –don) in four counties; and confused with **Hazelton**.

Hazelgrove L 'hazel **Grove**' OE; places in Ches, Notts.

Hazelhurst L 'hazel **Hirst**' OE; three places in Lancs.

Hazelrigg L 'ridge covered with hazels' ON; places in Cumberland, Lancs, Northd.

Hazeltine Form of **Hazelton** L 'place in the hazels' OE; places in Essex, Glos, Herts (?all originally 'hazel valley' OE; cf. **Hazelden**).

Hazelwood L 'hazel wood' OE; places (also Hazle–) in four counties.

Hazle– For all surnames beginning thus, see **Hazel–**.

Head L 'top of a valley, hilltop' OE. Or N from some peculiarity of the 'head' (the same OE word).

Headlam L '(at) the heathery clearings' OE dative plural after lost preposition; place in Co. Durham.

Headley L 'heathery clearing' OE; places in four counties.

Heal(e), Hele L '**Haugh** (*halh*)' and '(at) the **Haugh**'; form with –ea– is from OE West Saxon, and the –e is dative as in **Hale**; places in Somerset, Devon, and Somerset–Devon surnames.

Healy F (for O H—) 'descendant of Claimant/?Ingenious' Irish; names of two septs falling together. 48th commonest surname in Ireland in 1890.

Heard See **Herd**.

Hearn(e) See **Hern**. But Irish bearers may be from O **Aherne**.

Heath L 'heath' OE; locality, or places in ten counties.

Heathcote L 'cottage on a heath' OE; places in Derbys, Warwicks. Chiefly a Derbys surname, and pronounced *Hethket* in Yorks.

Heathfield L '**Field** with heather' OE; locality, or places in Somerset, Sussex.

Heatley L 'heathery clearing' OE; places in Ches, Staffs. Chiefly a Salop surname.

Heaton L 'high place' OE; places in five northern counties (three in Northd, four in Lancs, five in West Yorks).

Heaven F From Welsh F *Evan* (see **Evans**) by folk-etymology.

F: *first name*   L: *local name*   N: *nickname*   O: *occupational name*

Heavens '(son) of **H**—'. 14 –n: 1 –ns in Bristol TD, but 8:13 in London.

Hebble(th)waite, Hebblewhite L 'Thwaite by a plank-bridge' first element North Country dialect; place (–thwaite) in West Yorks.

Hebborn, Hebb(o)urn L 'high burial-mound/tumulus' OE; place (–burn) in Co. Durham.

Hebden L 'valley where hips grow' OE; place in West Yorks.

Heck L Northern version of **Hatch**; locality, or place in West Yorks.

Hector F ?'holding fast' Greek; the great Trojan hero's F was spread by medieval romances, and took root in Scotland (as a convenient rendering of Scots Gaelic FS *Eachdonn* 'brown horse' and *Eachann*).

Hedgecock, Hedgecoe Forms of **Hitchcock**, given an ornithological look by folk-etymology.

Hedges L 'of (i.e. at) the hedge' OE; or a plural. Found mainly in the counties around Bucks.

Hedley L Same as **Headley**; places in Co. Durham, Northd.

Hegarty F (for O H—) 'descendant of Unjust' Irish.

Hele L See **Heale**; various places in Cornwall, Devon, Somerset.

Helliar, Hellier O 'roofer, tiler, slater' OE; variants in **Hill**– are commoner, but **Hellier** is typical of Cornwall–Devon–Dorset–Somerset.

Hempstead L 'homestead' OE, places in Essex, Herts, Norfolk; but place in Glos is a contraction of 'high homestead' OE; and place in Norfolk near Holt is 'place where hemp grows' OE.

Henderson F 'son of **Henry**', with –d– as in **Hendry**. Northern and Scots surname; 29th commonest surname in Scotland in 1958. Family name of the barons Faringdon.

Hendon L '(at) the high hill' OE, with **Hen**– the weak dative adjective after lost preposition and definite article, place in Middx; but place in Co. Durham is 'valley with hinds (female deer)' OE.

Hendra L 'old farm/village' Cornish; various places in Cornwall.

Hendr(e)y, Hendrie Same as **Henry**, with parasitic glide –d–; yb far the commonest is **Hendry**.

Hendy N 'courteous, courtly, kind' ME (with OE cognate).

Henfrey F 'home peace' Germanic normanized.

Henham L '(at) the high homestead' OE, with **Hen**– as in **Hendon**; places in Essex, Suffolk.

Henley L '(at) the high wood/clearing' OE, with **Hen**– as in **Hendon**, places in five counties; but place in Salop is 'bird wood' OE (cf. *hen*).

Henness(e)y, Hennesy F (for O H—) 'descendant of **Angus**' Irish. **Hennessy** is the family name of the barons Windlesham.

Henry F 'home rule' (with no political implications) Germanic normanized. Occurs as a surname from Shetland to Cornwall, and is the source of many other surnames in **Han–**, **Hen–**, **Harr–**, Herr– (but not, apparently, **Hal–**, unless **Hawkins** belongs).

Hensman O 'groom, squire, carrier (literally stallion-man)' OE; cf. **Henstridge**.

Henstridge L 'ridge with stallions' OE (first element as in the virile name of Hengist, who began the expulsion of the Britons from England); place in Somerset.

Henthorn(e) L 'thorn-bush/-spinney with birds' OE; place in Lancs.

Henton L '(at) the high place' OE, with **Hen–** as in **Hendon**, place in Oxon; or ' ?hen farm' OE, place in Somerset.

Henwick L 'monks' **Wick**' OE (first element the genitive plural of the word for 'household, community' seen in **Hewish**); places in Northants, Worcs.

Henwood L 'nuns' wood' OE (cf. **Henwick**), place in Warwicks; but place in Cornwall is 'bird wood' OE.

Hepburn L Probably the same as **Hebburn**; place in Northd.

Hepple L '**Haugh** (*halh*) where hips grow' OE; place in Northd.

Heptonstall L '**Tunstall** where hips grow' OE; place in West Yorks.

Hepworth L '**Worth** where hips grow' OE; places in Suffolk, West Yorks.

Herapath L 'military road, highway (literally army path)' OE; cf. *harry*, **Harford**. A resounding old surname, which must have been applied early, before the *word* itself left our vocabulary.

Herbage L 'hostel, inn' OF (cf. **Harbisher**).

Herbert F 'army bright' Germanic, brought by Normans. Family name of the earls of Carnarvon, Pembroke and Montgomery, and Powis, and two barons.

Herculeson F 'son of Hercules' Latin version of Greek Hēraklēs, meaning unknown. Shetland corruption of 'son of Hakon' (= dim. 'handy, useful') ON.

Herd O 'herdsman' OE.

Hern(e) L 'nook, bend, corner, spit of land, curving valley' OE, with south-east –e– for OE –y– (and –e can be dative after lost preposition), places in Kent, etc.; but place in Beds is ?'(at) the stoneheaps' OE dative plural after lost preposition.

Herrick F 'Eric (first element?; second 'powerful', as in **Richard**)' ON; the **H—** is parasitic.

Herring O 'herring(-fisher/-seller)' OE (OF word was similar). Or N

F: *first name*   L: *local name*   N: *nickname*   O: *occupational name*

for something of little value (as in phrase of *c.* 1250, 'not worth a herring').

Herst See **Hirst**; easily the rarest of the group.

Hervey See **Harvey**. For the allegedly 'superior' pronunciation of –er– as –ar–, see **Clark**; it goes with calling the *stern* 'starn'. Family name of the marquesses of Bristol.

Hesel– For all surnames beginning thus, see **Hazel–**.

Hesketh, Heskett L 'horse-track, race-course' ON (cf. OE first element of **Henstridge**), places in Cumberland, Lancs, North Yorks; but Hesketh Newmarket, Cumberland, is 'ash-tree hill' ON+OE, with a wrongly acquired H–.

Heslop See **Haslip**.

Hessel– For all surnames beginning thus, see **Hazel–**.

Heston L 'place in the brushwood' OE (first element ?showing a young wood where pigs found acorns and mast); place in Middx.

Hetherington L ?'place of the heath-dwellers' OE; place in Northd.

Hett L 'hat(-shaped hill)' ON (or ?OE); place in Co. Durham.

Heugh L Same as **Hough**; place in Co. Durham.

Hever L 'high edge' OE; place in Kent.

Hewat F dim. 'Hugh'; common in Scotland; see **Hewet, Hewit**.

Hewer O 'stone-/wood-cutter' OE. Chiefly a Glos surname.

Hewet(t) F dim. 'Hugh' with OF suffix. But the second meaning of **Hewit** is also possible. Commonest of the group is –itt, then –ett. **Hewetson** 'son of H—'.

Hewick L 'high Wick' OE; place in West Yorks.

Hewish L '(measure of land to support a) family/household, hide of land' OE; two places in Somerset; more or less = **Hyde**.

Hewit(t), Hewitson See **Hewet**. But **Hewit(t)** could also be L 'cutting, cleared place' OE (cf. verb *hew*); there are two places Hewitts in Kent. **Hewitt** is the family name of the viscounts Lifford.

Hewlett, Hewlitt F double dim. 'Hugh', with OF suffixes –el and –ot run together.

Hewson See **Hughson**.

Hext N 'highest, tallest' OE.

Heydon L 'hay valley/hill' OE; places in Cambs/Norfolk.

Heysham L 'homestead in the brushwood' OE (cf. **Heston**); place in Lancs.

Heywood L 'high/enclosed wood' OE; places in Lancs/Wilts; or for **Haywood**.

Hick F dim. 'Richard'; cf. **Dick**. **Hicks(on)** '(son) of H—'.

Hickey F (for O H—) 'descendant of Healer/Physician' Irish.

Hickinbotham L 'valley with oaks' OE; place (Oakenbottom) in Lancs, affected by local dialect *hickin/higgin* 'rowan tree'.

Hidden L 'valley with a landing-place' OE (cf. **Hythe**); place in Berks.

Higgin F (for O H—) 'descendant of the Viking' Irish. Often anglicized to **Higgins**.

Higginbotham, Higginbottam, Higginbottom See **Hickinbotham**.

Higgins(on) F '(son) of (double dim.) *Richard*', where *Higg* is the voiced form of **Hick**. Guppy found –**ins** chiefly in North Wales, and it was the 83rd commonest surname in Ireland in 1890; see **Higgin**.

Higgs Form of **Hicks**; cf. **Higgins**. Chiefly a Wilts–Somerset surname.

Higham L 'high homestead' OE; places in eleven counties.

Higson F 'son of (dim). *Richard*'; see **Higgins**.

Hilary F 'cheerful' Latin (cf. *hilarious*); Saint H— of Poitiers (†368) made it popular as a *male* F. But also a perversion of *Eulalia* 'sweetly speaking' Greek, which early acquired an –*r*– for the second –*l*–; female patron saint of Barcelona. Each of these was also used for the other sex.

Hildebrand F 'battle sword' Germanic, the appropriate F of the most militant of all popes.

Hilder L 'dweller at the slope' OE+–**er**; cf. **Forder**.

Hill L 'hill' OE. (Very rarely, F – pet form of some Germanic F beginning *Hild*– 'battle' or of **Hilary**.) Occurs from Yorks to Cornwall, especially in Glos–Somerset–Devon. 25th commonest surname in England and Wales in 1853. Family name of the marquesses of Downshire and the barons Sandys. **Hills** L 'of (i.e. at) the hill' OE; or a plural; or F '(son) of **H**—'.

Hillam L '(at) the hills' OE dative plural after lost preposition; place in West Yorks.

Hilliar, Hillier See **Helliar**; **Hillier** the commonest of the group, especially in Wilts–Hants.

Hillyer See **Hillier**.

Hilton L 'place/farm on a hill' OE, places in Derbys, Hunts, Staffs, North Yorks; but place in Westmorland may have first element 'shed' ON; and place in Dorset may have first element '?slope/ ?tansy' OE.

Hind N 'hind (female deer)' OE, from ?timidity. Or O for **Hine**. **Hind(e)s** '(son) of **H**—'.

F: *first name*   L: *local name*   N: *nickname*   O: *occupational name*

Hindley L 'wood/clearing with hinds (female deer)' OE; places in Lancs, Northd.

Hine O 'servant' (later *hind*, with parasitic *–d*) OE; cf. **Hyde. Hines** '(son) of **H—**'.

Hingston L 'stallion farm' OE (or first element an owner's N, cf. **Henstridge**); place in Cambs.

Hinton L '(at) the high place/farm' OE, with **Hin–** as **Hen–** in **Hendon**, places in seven counties (four in Somerset); or 'monks'/nuns' farm' OE (cf. **Henwick**), places in nine counties (where no monastic ownership can be proved, first element may mean 'domestics'/household's').

Hird See **Herd**.

Hirst L 'copse, hill, wooded hill' OE West Saxon *hyrst*, which appears in ME as **Hirst** in east Midlands and north, **Herst** in south-east, **Hurst** in west Midlands and south; there are also places called **Hirst** in Northd, West Yorks.

Hiscock(s), Hiscoke, Hiscott, Hiscox, Hiscutt, Hiskett See **Hitchcock** etc. **–cock** is mainly a Dorset–Wilts–Somerset surname. But **–kett** may sometimes be for **Heskett**.

Hislop See **Haslop**.

Hitch F dim. '**Richard**'.

Hitchcock, Hitchcoe, Hitchcott, Hitchcox F '**Hitch**'+familiar **Cock. –cox** is for *–cocks* '(son) of' the same. **–cock** common in Suffolk.

Hitchmough F '**Hitch**'s in-law' second element ON (or some vaguer relationship OE).

Hix, Hix(s)on Forms of **Hicks(on)**. But sometimes ?L 'hill (cf. **Down**) of (an A S called) Joy' OE; place (Hixon) in Staffs.

Hoad, Hoadl(e)y, Hoath L 'heath' OE, places in Kent, Sussex; and 'heathery clearing' OE, places (also Hoathley) in Sussex.

Hoar(e) N 'grey, hoary' OE.

Hobart Form of **Hubert**; a Norfolk surname, like **Hubbard**.

Hobb F dim. '**Robert**'. **Hobbins, Hobbis(s), Hobb(e)s** '(son) of **H—**', **–bs** is a common south Midland surname. **Hobson** 'son of **H—**'; chiefly a West Yorks surname.

Hobday O '**Hobb**'s servant' or 'the servant **Hobb**'; see **Day**.

Hobson See **Hobb**.

Hockaday F From birth/baptism on 'the second Tuesday after Easter' ME; a rent-day/term-day as important as Michaelmas, and eventually a popular festival.

Hockham L 'homestead where hocks/mallows grow' OE (cf. *holly-*

hock) – unless first element be an AS owner; place in Norfolk.

Hockold L 'Wald where mallows grow' OE (cf. **Hockham**); place (Hockwold) in Norfolk.

Hodge F dim. 'Roger'. **Hodges** '(son) of H—'; a west Midland surname. **Hodgson** 'son of H—'; the concatenation of consonants sometimes reduces this to **Hodson**.

Hodgkin F dim. 'Hodge', with Flemish –kin. **Hodgkins, Hodgkiss** '(son) of H—'; –kiss is fanciful, but less suggestive than **Hotchkiss**. **Hodgki(n)son** 'son of H—'.

Hodgson See **Hodge**.

Hodnett L 'tranquil valley/stream' OW; place (–et) in Salop, and a Salop–Worcs surname.

Hodson F Usually a form of **Hodgson**, but sometimes 'son of Odo (= riches)' Germanic; cf. the **Ed–** in **Edward, Edmund**.

Hogarth See **Hoggard**.

Hogg N 'hog, pig' OE.

Hoggard, Hoggart(h), Hoggett O 'hog-herd' OE.

Hoghton L Same as **Houghton**; place in Lancs.

Hogsflesh O '(seller of) hog's flesh' OE; mispronounced *Hooflay*.

Holbech(e) L 'brook in a ravine' OE (cf. *hole, hollow*); places (–beche, –beach) in Staffs, Lincs.

Holbeck L Same as **Holbeche**, but ON (or OE scandinavianized); places in Lincs, Norfolk, North and West Yorks.

Holbert, Holbird F 'gracious bright' Germanic (?OE).

Holborn, Holbourn(e) L Same as **Holbrook** (with 'burn' OE for 'brook') or **Holbeche**; places (also –burn) in London, Derbys, Co. Durham, Northd.

Holbrook L 'brook in a ravine' OE; places in Derbys, Dorset, Glos, Suffolk, Sussex, Warwicks, yet counted by Guppy only in Notts.

Holcomb(e) L 'hollow/deep valley' OE; places in six counties (three in Devon). A West Country surname, and a good old one at Dorchester, Oxon.

Hol(d)croft L 'Croft in a hollow' OE; place in Lancs.

Holden L 'hollow/deep valley' OE (cf. **Dean**); locality, or places in Lancs, West Yorks, and chiefly a Lancs–West Yorks surname.

Holder See **Driver**.

Holderness L '(high-ranking) yeoman's land' ON (–er– from ON genitive singular –ar–); district in East Yorks; however high the rank, and *pace* Sherlock Holmes, it never had a duke.

Holeman See **Holman**.

F: *first name*   L: *local name*   N: *nickname*   O: *occupational name*

Holford L 'ford in a hollow (i.e. ravine)' OE; places in Somerset (three), Sussex.

Holgate L 'road in a hollow' OE/ON+ON; place in West Yorks.

Holiday F From birth/baptism on a 'holy day, religious festival' OE; the long *o* of *holy* is shortened as the first syllable of a trisyllable, and northern forms should keep the *a* of OE and not change it to *o*, as in the northern **Halliday**; but –o– forms occur even in Yorks.

Holker L 'marsh with hollows' OE/ON+ON; place in Lancs.

Holladay Form of **Holiday**, found in Suffolk 1674.

Holland L 'land at a **Hough**' OE, places in Essex, Lincs, and (Uph–, Downh–) Lancs; but place in Hunts is 'enclosed (?and sacred) grove' ON.

Holliday See **Holiday**; a Yorks and Cumberland form, and found in Ireland and USA.

Hollier O 'whoremonger' OF. Or ?L 'dweller in the hollies' OE.

Hollington L 'place in the hollies' OE; places in four counties.

Hollingworth L '**Worth** in the hollies' OE; places in Ches, Lancs.

Hollister O 'female brothel-keeper, debauchee' OF (+OE suffix) – the feminine of **Hollier**. (There is no evidence to save the face of this surname by relating it to O 'female haulier', or L 'hiding-place' OE *heolstor*, or N 'big, awkward man' northern dialect *hulster*, or some Norse-settled village in –*ster*.)

Holloway L 'hollow/sunk/artificially cut road' OE; locality, or places in a few counties. Chiefly a Worcs–Glos–Wilts–Dorset surname.

Hollowbread N 'holy bread' OE; for a baker or carrier of it.

Hollyer See, alas! **Hollier**.

Holm(e) L 'river flat, island in a fen' ON; but the poet Lawman's hunted fox flees to a *holm*, and this may be 'hill, mound' ?OE; the first (and usual) meaning is the source of many place-names, especially in the Danelaw, called Holm(e) or **Holmes**; a third meaning, 'holly, holm-oak' OE (source of Holme, Dorset, West Yorks, and Holne, Devon) is possible. **Holmes** L 'of (i.e. at) the **H**—'; or a plural. The ON meaning is likeliest, as the surname is so very common from Co. Durham to Derbys.

Holman L 'dweller in a hollow' OE, occurring as **Holeman** and perhaps involved with **Holyman**. Guppy counted it only in Sussex, Cornwall.

Holmer L 'pool in a hollow' OE; places in Bucks, Herefords, and (Homer) Devon; or 'dweller at the **Holm**' in any of its senses.

Holmwood L 'holly wood' OE, locality, or place (Holmewood, first element? **Holm**) in Derbys; but place in Surrey is 'wood in a river-meadow' OE.

Holohan F (for O H—) 'descendant of ? ?Proud/Gay' Irish.

Holt L 'wood' OE; locality, or places in several counties.

Holton L 'place at a **Hough/Haugh** (*halh*)/hollow' OE, places in Lincs (three)/Oxon, Somerset/Dorset; two places in Suffolk perhaps have an A S owner's F as first element.

Holyman N Literally 'holy man' OE, but no doubt often sarcastic, or used for 'humbug, hypocrite'.

Holyoak(e), Holyoke L 'holy oak, gospel-oak' (where the Gospel for the day was read at the parish boundary during the Rogation Days' beating of the bounds) OE; place Holy Oakes, Leics, was once singular, and must be a source.

Home L 'holly, holm-oak' OE, a corruption of **Holm** in its third meaning; distribution of the surname does not suggest an ON origin. But Scots **H—** or **Hume** (in the latter the original ð is fronted and raised) is from the barony of **Home**, Berwicks, which is the ON **Holm**.

Homer O 'helmet-maker' OF. But sometimes L = **Holmer**. Chiefly a Dorset surname.

Homfray See **Humfrey**.

Honeyball See **Hunnable**.

Honeybone, Honeybourne, Honeybu(r)n L 'stream on whose banks honey could be got' OE; places (–bourne) in Glos, Worcs; the delicious **Honeybun** comes from a folk-recipe, but approximates to the local pronunciation.

Honley L 'stony clearing' OE; place in West Yorks.

Hook(e) L '**Hough**'; locality, or places in six counties. Or N 'crook-backed, hook-nosed' OE, also used as a F. **Hooke(s)** 'at/of the **H—**', dative and genitive.

Hoole L 'hut, shed' OE (cf. *hull, hulk*), places in Ches, Lancs; but another place in Ches is '(in) the hollow' OE dative after lost preposition.

Hoon L '(at) the hillocks/burial-mounds' ON (cf. **Howe**) dative plural after lost preposition.

Hooper O 'hooper, one who makes/fits hoops on casks or barrels' OE +–**er** (so almost = **Cooper**). Common in Glos–Somerset–Devon.

Hooton L Same as **Hutton**; places in Ches, West Yorks (three).

Hope L 'enclosed valley, little blind valley opening out of the main dale' OE; locality, or places in eight counties; also 'piece of enclosed land rising from a fen' OE. Family name of the marquesses of Linlithgow and the barons Rankeillour.

F: *first name*   L: *local name*   N: *nickname*   O: *occupational name*

Hopkin F dim. 'Hobb'. **Hopkins(on)** '(son) of H—'; **–ns** is very common in South Wales, despite its 'Flemish' suffix. **Hopkinson** is the family name of the barons Colyton.

Hoppen L '(in) the valleys' OE (cf. **Hope**) dative plural after lost preposition; place in Northd.

Hopper O 'leaper, dancer' OE+ **–er.**

Hopton L 'place in a valley' (cf. **Hope**) OE, places in six counties (six in Salop); but place in fen-country of east Suffolk has the last meaning given under **Hope**.

Hopwood L 'wood in a valley' (cf. **Hope**) OE; places in Lancs, Worcs (but if OE *hopu* could be trusted Ekwall would prefer 'privet wood' for the Worcs place). Family name of the barons Southborough.

Horden L 'dirty valley' OE; place in Co. Durham.

Horder O 'treasurer' (and sometimes 'cellarer') OE; a *hoarder* did not then mean one who keeps tins of peaches under a mattress in time of war.

Hordern L 'store-house' (cf. *hoard*, **Arne**) OE; place in Lancs.

Horley L 'wood/clearing in a **Horne**' OE, place in Oxon; but the place in Surrey is ?'wood/clearing belonging to the village of **Horne**' OE.

Horlick, Horlock See **Harlock.**

Hornblow(er) O 'horn-blower' OE; among this dignitary's duties was the summoning of workmen by the equivalent of our factory hooter.

Horncastle L 'Roman site in a **Horne** (between two rivers)' OE; place in Lincs.

Horne L Two OE words meaning variously 'horn-shaped hill, gable, pinnacle, corner, land in a river-bend, peninsula'; places in Rutland and Surrey are by suitable river and hill respectively.

Horner O 'maker of horn objects' (combs, spoons, and even window 'glass') OE+ **–er**; only later a maker/blower of musical horns. Mainly a Yorks surname, though Little Jack H— was a real Somerset resident.

Hornsby L 'Orm's (= Dragon) farm' ON; place in Cumberland.

Horrell L 'felon hill, hill where felons were hanged' OE, place in Cumberland; but Horrel in Devon is 'dirty hollow' OE.

Horrocks L 'piles of rubbish/stones' North Country dialect *hurrock* (from ON); either locality or three other places in Lancs.

Horsenail, Horsenell O 'horseshoenail(-maker), shoer of horses' OE.

Horsey L 'horse island' OE; places in Norfolk, Somerset.

Horsford L 'ford that can be crossed on horseback' OE; places in Norfolk and (–rth) West Yorks.

Horsham L 'horse homestead/river-meadow' OE; places in Norfolk, Sussex.

Horsley L 'horse-pasture' OE; places in five counties.

Horsmanden L 'horse-stream pasture' OE (but *burn* has become **man** by folk-etymology); place (Horsmonden) in Kent; taken to USA by an emigrant from Purleigh, Essex, the next county.

Horsnail(l), Horsnall, Horsnell See **Horsenail**.

Horste(a)d L 'horse farm' OE; places in Kent, Norfolk, Sussex.

Hort See **Hart**

Horton L 'muddy place' OE, places in over fourteen counties; or ?'stag hill' OE, place in Glos.

Horwich L 'grey wych (elm)' OE; place in Lancs.

Horwood L 'muddy wood' OE; places in Bucks and (?meaning 'grey wood') Devon.

Hos(e)good Illiterate version of **Osgood**.

Hosmer F '(pagan) god fame' OE; with added **H—**; cf. **Osgood**.

Hotchkin(s), Hotchkiss Forms of **Hodgkin** etc.

Hotham L '(at) the shelters' OE (cf. *hood*) dative plural after lost preposition; place in East Yorks.

Hott(er) O 'basket(-maker)' OF (cf. *hod*).

Hough L 'hill-spur, steep/slight rise' OE, locality, or places in Ches, Derbys; or 'enclosure' OE, place in Lincs.

Houghton L 'place on a **Hough**' OE, at least three dozen places, mostly down east England from Northd to Hants; or 'place in an enclosure' (the last meaning of **Hough**) OE, places in Lancs, West Yorks; or 'place where ale-hoof (ground-ivy) grows' OE, place in East Yorks – though perhaps the first element is the F of an AS owner *Hofa*.

Houlihan See **Holohan**. Probable origin of *hooligan*, from a rowdy London Irish family.

Houneen F (for O **H—**) 'descendant of Green' Irish.

Hounslow L 'burial-mound of (an AS called) Dog' OE; place in Middx.

House L 'house, religious establishment' OE. Sometimes? = **Howes**.

Housto(u)n L '**Hugh**'s place' second element OE; place in Renfrews called *Villa Hugonis* c. 1200; **–oun** is characteristically Scots.

Hove L 'hood' OE – ?from the shape of a hill, or to mean 'shelter'; place in Sussex.

How See the more frequent **Howe**.

Howard F 'heart/mind (cf. **Hugh**) brave/hardy' Germanic, or 'high/chief warden' Germanic. But absorbing also O **Hayward** and even

---

F: *first name*   L: *local name*   N: *nickname*   O: *occupational name*

'ewe-herd' OE; 'hog-ward' OE may (very rarely) be a source, but the theory that the premier duke and earl stems from one is just a pretty paradox. Family name of the earls of Carlisle, Effingham, and Suffolk and Berkshire.

Howe L 'hill, hillock, burial-mound' ON; places in Norfolk, North Yorks, and a common place-name element in the Danelaw; –e can show dative after lost preposition. But sometimes confused with **Hough**. **Howes** 'of (i.e. at) the H—'; or plural; or for **House**, **Hughes**.

Howel(l) F 'eminent' Welsh *Hywel*, F of a great lawgiving Welsh king. **Howel(l)s** '(son) of H—'. –ell and –ells are very common in South Wales; Norfolk –ell is due to Breton settlers after 1066.

Howgrave L 'Grove on a Hough'; place in North Yorks.

Howick L 'dairy-farm on a Hough' OE; place in Lancs.

Hoyland L 'land on a Hough' OE; four places in West Yorks.

Hoyle L 'hole, hollow' OE in modern Yorks dialect. **Hoyles** 'of (i.e. at) the H—', or a plural.

Hubbard, Hubbart, Hubbert Forms of **Hubert**. **Hubbard** is especially common in East Anglia, and family name of the barons Addington.

Hubert F 'heart/mind (cf. **Hugh**) bright' Germanic; popularized by Saint H—, bishop of Liège, patron of hunters (†727).

Hucker O 'haggler, bargainer, petty trader, huckster' ME from Germanic.

Hudd F dim. 'Hugh/Richard'. **Hudson** F 'son of H—'; common throughout Midlands and north.

Huggin F dim. 'Hugh'. **Huggins** '(son) of H—'; a Norfolk surname and family name of the viscounts Malvern.

Hugh F 'heart/mind' Germanic; popularized by Saint H— of Avalon, prior of Witham and bishop of Lincoln (†1200), and by the 'martyred' child H— of Lincoln, hero of an anti-Semitic yarn. **Hughes** '(son) of H—'; one of the commonest surnames of North Wales, and 19th commonest in England and Wales in 1853, 85th in Scotland in 1958, 34th in Ireland in 1890. **Hughson** 'son of H—'.

Huish L Same as **Hewish**; places in Dorset, Devon (three), Somerset (four), Wilts.

Hulbert, Hulburd See **Holbert** or **Hurlbatt**; –bert common in Wilts.

Hull L 'hill' OE (with west Midland and southern vowel –u– for OE –y–); locality, or places in Ches, Somerset, Worcs; rarely, perhaps, the East Yorks town, properly Kingston upon Hull (latter a Keltic river-name meaning ?'water, muddy river'). Probably more often

F dim. '**Hugh**' (from dims. *Hulin*, *Hulot*; cf. **Hewlett**). Counted by Guppy only in Co. Durham and in Hants–Dorset–Wilts.

Hullyer See **Hollier**.

Hulme L 'river-island' (cf. **Holm**) ON; places in Ches (three), Lancs (three), Staffs.

Hulse L 'hollows' OE; place in Ches.

Hulton L 'place on a hill' (cf. **Hull**) OE; places in Lancs, Staffs.

Hume See **Home** and **Hulme**.

Humfrey F ' ?giant peace' (second element as in **Geoffrey**) Germanic normanized.

Humpherson, Humpherus, Humphery, Humphrey(s), Humph(e)ries, Humphris(s), Humphry(es), Humphrys See **Humfrey**; and '(son) of **Humfrey**'; newer forms with –ph– are much commoner than –f–. –phreys is easily the commonest of the group.

Hungerford L 'ford near unproductive land' OE; place in Berks.

Hunnable, Hunneyball, Hunneybell, Hunnibal, Hunnibell F 'lovable' Latin (cf. *amiable*, *Annabel*, *Mabel*); further corruptions include **Honeyball** and the heroic **Hannibal**.

Hunt(e) O 'huntsman, hunter' (which are later derivatives) OE; –t is found everywhere (just as hunting country was), but is commoner in the south and Midlands; the rare –e could recall the –a of OE.

Hunter O 'huntsman' OE (the –er added); younger and rarer surname than **Hunt**, and much more northern. 36th commonest surname in Scotland in 1958.

Huntingdon L 'huntsman's hill' OE; place in Hunts.

Huntingford L 'huntsmen's ford' OE; places in Dorset, Glos.

Huntington L 'huntsmen's farm' OE, places in Herefords, Salop; or 'huntsmen's hill' OE, places in Ches, Staffs, North Yorks; or mistakenly for **Huntingdon**.

Huntley L 'huntsman's wood/clearing' OE; places in Glos, Aberdeens.

Hunton L 'place with hounds' OE; place in Hants.

Hurl A thorough illiteracy for **Earl**.

Hurlbatt, Hurlbert, Hurlbut(t) N From a game of throwing short iron-spiked bats ME (from Germanic)+OF. Even a USA **Hulbert** claimed this origin.

Hurley L 'wood/clearing in a **Hurn**' OE; places in Berks, Warwicks; but Guppy counted it only in Somerset. The Irish family is from O Herlihy.

Hurn Same as **Hern**, with west Midland and southern –u– for southeastern –e– (OE West Saxon –*y*–).

F: *first name*   L: *local name*   N: *nickname*   O: *occupational name*

Hurr(e)y F 'wolf powerful' OE *Wulfric* ironed out by the Normans; its most accurate form is **Woolrich**.

Hurst See **Hirst**. Easily the commonest of the group.

Hurt See **Hart**. Its incidence in Notts is not in line with its dialect.

Husband O 'householder, farmer, husbandman' OE.

Huss(e)y O 'housewife' OE (a less reduced form is seen in the soldier's sewing-compendium or *hussive*); insulting only if applied to a man. Or N 'trunk-hosed, booted' OF.

Huston L 'place with a house' OE.

Hustwayte, Hustwitt L '**Thwaite** with a house' ON; place (–thwaite) in North Yorks.

Hutchence, Hutchens, Hutcheon, Hutche(r)son, Hutchin(s), Hutchings(on), Hutchi(n)son F double dim. 'Hugh' and '(son) of Hugh', based on OF form *Huchon* (to which **Hutcheon** is near); **–ings** is common in the south-west, **–inson** in the north and Scotland.

Huthwaite L '**Thwaite** on a **Hough**' OE+ON; places in Notts, West Yorks.

Hutton L Same as **Houghton** (*hut*, apparently, does not figure); over thirty places, almost all in Yorks but also in Cumberland, Co. Durham, Lancs, Westmorland, yet found by Guppy chiefly in Lincs.

Huxley L Second element 'clearing' OE, first element either an A S owner or 'ignominy, mockery' OE, perhaps in allusion to inhospitable ground; place in Ches.

Huxtable L 'post on a spur of land' OE; place (*Hokestaple* 1330) in East Buckland, Devon.

Huyton L 'landing-place (cf. **Hythe**) farm' OE; place in Lancs.

Hyde L 'hide of land' OE (*c.* 120 acres); from the same stem as *hind* ('farm-servant') and **Hewish**.

Hynd, Hynde(s) See **Hind**.

Hyne(s) See **Hine**.

Hyslop See **Haslip**.

Hythe L 'landing-place' OE; locality, or place in Kent.

I

I'Anson Same as **Janson**, with elegant muddle over the fact that capital I and J had once the same form.

Ibbett, Ibbitt, Ibbott, Ibell, Ible F *Ib* is dim. '**Isabell**', so forms with –t(t) and –ll are double dims. **Ibbs** '(son) of (dim.) **Isabell**'. **Ibbetson, Ibbitson, Ibbotson, Ibson** 'son of (dim.) **Isabell**'.

Icemonger O 'ironmonger' OE; first element south-east dialect.

Ick(e) F dim. '**Richard**' – *Hick* losing its aspirate. Also **Ickes** '(son) of I—'.

Ide(son) F 'labour' Germanic *Ida* (masculine). And '(son) of I—'.

Iden L 'woodland pasture (?the same as our *den* "lair") in the yews' OE; places in Kent, Sussex.

Idle N 'empty, vain, lazy' OE. Or L 'uncultivated/profitless (land)' from same word, place in West Yorks; or 'island' Norman dialect of OF. Or F (usually Welsh *Ithel*) 'lord bountiful' OW.

Ifield L '**Field** with yews' OE; places in Kent, Sussex.

Ifo(u)ld L 'fold in river-land' OE; place (–old) in Sussex.

Iggulden L 'pasture of the people of (an A S called) ?Ig/?Igil (= hedge-hog)/?Ing (cf. **Ingham**) Wolf' OE; place (Ingleden) in Kent.

Iles L 'of (i.e. at) the island' OF. Chiefly a Glos surname.

Illingworth L 'enclosure of Illa's people' OE; place in West Yorks, and a West Yorks–Lancs surname.

Ilsley L 'Hild (female name meaning "war/battle")'s clearing' OE; places (East and West I—) in Berks.

Imm(s) F '**Emma**' (see **Emmet**). And '(son) of I—'.

Imp(e)y L 'enclosure for saplings/orchard-trees/grafted trees' OE.

Ince L 'island, river-meadow' OW; places in Ches, Cornwall, Lancs.

Ingall See **Ingle**.

Inger F '**Ingvar**' ON (the first element as in **Ingham**).

Ingersoll See **Inkersall**.

Ingham L 'Ing's homestead' OE; places in Lincs, Norfolk, Suffolk; the F of the god Ing (Yngvi-Freyr, descendant of Odin) has been connected with Latin *anguis* 'serpent', Greek *enkhos* 'lance/pole', Latin *inguen* 'groin/phallus' – all fertility symbols. Rarely ? N 'trickery' OF (cf. *ingenuity, engine, gin-trap*).

Ingle L 'Ing (see **Ingham**)'s valley' OE, place (Ingol) in Lancs; or ?'Ing's hill' OE; or ?'Englishman' ON – a possible meaning in a Norse-settled area like Lincs, where the name is commonest. Sometimes possibly F 'Ing wolf/rule/tribute-money' OE.

F: *first name*   L: *local name*   N: *nickname*   O: *occupational name*

Inglebright F 'angel bright' Germanic, normally *Engelbert*.

Ingleby L 'Englishmen's farm' ON; places in Derbys, Lincs, North Yorks (three).

Inglis(h) L Scots form of **English**, with Scots disregard of any English sensibility about the initial; a far better spelling, since *eng* had by surname times turned into *ing* (as in *string* for earlier *streng*); –*is* is frequent for unaccented –*ish* in Scots.

Ingpen See **Inkpen**.

Ingram L 'pastureland homestead/river-meadow' OE; place in Northd. But often F for *Angilramn–*/*Ingilramn–* Germanic (adopted in OE, and in OF *Enguerran*), second element 'raven', first element 'angel' or *Ingil* (a derivative of *Ing*; see **Ingham**).

Inker See **Inger** (no *inker* = 'inkmaker' is recorded in ME).

Inkersall L '(A S called) ?Limper's hill' OE (cf. dialect *hink* 'to limp'); place in Derbys.

Inkpen, Inkpin L ?'hill hill' OE+Keltic, tautologically; place (–e–) in Berks.

Inman O 'inn/lodginghouse-keeper' OE.

Inskip(p) L 'island (cf. **Ince**) with a ?kipe (basket for catching fish)' OW+OE; place in Lancs. Also occurs as **Inskeep**.

Insole, Insoll, Insull L 'Iron Hard's hill' OF (from Germanic)+OE; lost place in Elmley Lovett, Worcs, called Insoll in 1642; this *Isnard* (c. 1135) also leaves his F at Innerstone, Redmarley, Worcs.

Inward, Inwood L A fusing of an 'in-wood' (near the manor) OE, and Inworth in Essex, 'Ina (masculine)'s **Worth**' OE.

Iorwerth F 'lord value' Welsh.

Irby L 'Irishmen's farm' ON; places in Ches, Lincs, North Yorks.

Iredale, Iredell L 'Irishmen's valley' ON; farm in Cumberland, between Loweswater and Fangs Brow; people called **Iredale** have been here from the 16th century, and it is largely a Cumberland surname.

Ireland L 'Ireland' (OE and) ON, derived from Irish *Eriu*; cf. **Irish**.

Iremonger O 'ironmonger' OE.

Ireton L 'Irishmen's farm' OE; three places in Derbys.

Irish L 'Irish' OF ultimately from Irish *Eriu*; applied in the Middle Ages indiscriminately to Scots and Irish Gaels.

Irmithyge Forms of **Armitage** found in Kent.

Ironside N 'armoured warrior', or one as doughty as if he had 'iron flanks' OE.

Irvin(e), Irving L '?green/fresh river' British; places in Ayrs, Dumfs. Common in Cumberland–Northd and Scots Border.

Irwin F 'boar friend' OE.

Isaac F 'He (God) may laugh (i.e. smile favourably upon)' Hebrew, the son of Abraham; used even by non-Jews in the Middle Ages. **Isaacs(on)** '(son)/son of I—'. Isaacs is the family name of the marquesses of Reading.

Isabell F Spanish and southern French form of *Elizabeth* 'my God (is) satisfaction' Hebrew. Popular through Saint John Baptist's mother rather than through Aaron's wife. Only one in London TD.

Isard F 'ice battle' Germanic (but a Keltic origin is just possible); latinized as *Isolda*, OF *Iseut/Isaut*. Her behaviour with **Tristram** in the romance makes the F a rather risky choice.

Isbister L 'estuary/more-easterly/outermost farm-settlement' ON; four places in Orkney (also found in Shetland), and a typical Orkney and Shetland surname, including that of the first civilian casualty of the Second World War.

Isgar F 'iron spear' OE; chiefly a Somerset surname.

Isham L 'homestead on the (River) Ise (meaning no more than "water")' OW+OE; place in Northants.

Islip L 'slippery place on the (River) Ise (see **Isham**)' OW+OE, place in Northants; but place in Oxon may be 'slipway/portage' OE 'on the (River) Ight' (meaning ?).

Issard, Issatt, Issett, Issit(t), Issolt, Issott Forms of **Isard**.

Ive F ?'yew' Germanic, a common F among Normans and Bretons. (The saints of Cornwall and Hunts are respectively local and legendary.) **Ives** F '(son) of I—'; counted by Guppy only in Middx, Norfolk.

Ivers(on) F '(son)/son of **Ivor**'.

Ivor F 'yew/bow army' ON, early used by Irish, Scots, and Welsh; cf. Saint Patrick's contemporary Saint Ivor.

Iz(z)ard, Izant, Izatt, Izod, Izzet(t) Forms of **Isard**; of all the Isolda family, **Izzard** is the commonest, especially in Berks (says Guppy); and cf. with **Izod** Chapelizod, place in Dublin.

F: *first name*   L: *local name*   N: *nickname*   O: *occupational name*

J

Jack F dim. 'John' or (cf. French *Jacques*) 'James'; both uses are certainly medieval. **Jacks(on)** '(son)/son of J—'; –s counted by Guppy only in Salop. –**son** occurs throughout England – 24th commonest surname in England and Wales in 1853, 16th in USA in 1939. **Jackson** is the family name of the barons Allerton.

Jacklin F double dim. 'Jack' with two OF suffixes.

Jackman O 'servant of **Jack**', second element OE. Guppy counted it only in Devon.

Jacob(y) F ?'he supplanted' Hebrew (with reference to his treatment of his elder brother Esau); the Hebrew F became Latin *Jacobus* (whence **Jacob, Jacques, Jago**) and later also *Jacomus* (whence **James** and pet forms *Jim/Jem*); an ancient Bristol church is of Saints Philip and Jacob (i.e. James the Less). –**y** preserves the –*i* of the Latin genitive. **Jacobs(on)** '(son)/son of J—'.

Jacques F Either a frenchifying of **Jakes**, or a late (Huguenot etc.) introduction of French F meaning **James**.

Jaggard F dim. 'Jack' with OF suffix.

Jagger O 'carter, hawker' ME, Yorks dialect. But sometimes ?a corruption of **Jaggard**. **Jaggers** '(son) of J—'.

Jago(e) F Welsh and Cornish form of **James**; see **Jacob**.

Jakeman O 'servant of **Jack**', second element OE.

Jakes F '(son) of **Jack**' in either of its two meanings. Not a popular surname, in view of its also meaning 'privy'.

James Form of **Jacob** popularized by the two Apostles. Very common in South Wales and along the Border. 35th commonest surname in England and Wales in 1853, 40th in USA in 1939. Family name of the barons Northbourne. **Jameson, Jami(e)son** F 'son of J—'; common forms in Scotland and north England, sometimes with pronunciation almost *Jimmy-son*. –**ieson** was the 95th commonest surname in Scotland in 1958.

Jane(s) Form of **John(s)** based on an OF version *Jan*; **Jane** is common only in Cornwall.

Janson F 'son of **John**'; cf. **Jayne**.

January L 'Genoese, man from Genoa (= ?"re-entrant, recess, bay" Pre-Roman)' in ME (via OF) *Janaway*. (The city is probably not from the god *Janus* or Latin *janua* 'door/gate' – these would take us back to cognates of our month-name.) A Somerset–Devon surname.

Jaques See **Jacques**.

Jardine L 'garden' OF.

Jarman See **German**; with **–ar–** for **–er–** as in **Clark**.

Jarra(r)d, Jarratt, Jarraud, Jarred, Jarrett, Jarritt, Jarro(l)d, Jarrott F dim. 'Gerald/Gerard' – though **–old** will be from **Gerald** alone, and **–ard** from **Gerard**. Guppy found **–ett** countable only in Kent.

Jarvis See **Jervis**.

Jasper F 'Gaspar/Caspar' of unknown origin, perhaps Eastern, perhaps fanciful; the supposed name of one of the Three Kings (the Bible makes them neither kings nor three); the surname further popularized by its resemblance to the precious stone 'jasper' Greek from ?Arabic. Mainly a Cornish surname.

Jay(e) N 'jay' OF. The bird is beautiful, chattering, and (from man's point of view) wicked; the second is the likeliest cause of the N, though a Middle English poet said his girl friend was as pretty as a jay. **Jay(e)s** '(son) of **J—**'.

Jayne(s) Form of **John(s)**, based on version *Jan*.

Jaze N '(son) of **Jay**'.

Jeacock F 'Jack'+the familiar **Cock**.

Jean F 'John' OF. **Jean(e)s** '(son) of **J—**'.

Jebb F dim. 'Geoffrey'.

Jeeves F '(son) of Genevieve' (first element 'race') OF from Gaulish; the female patron saint of Paris.

Jeff, Jeffares, Jefferis(s), Jeffers(on), Jeffer(e)y, Jeffery(e)s, Jeffray, Jeffree, Jeffress, Jeffrey(s), Jeff(e)ries, Jeffry(es), Jeff(e)s F dim. 'Geoffrey' and 'Geoffrey', and '(son)/son of' these forms; **–erson** is a northern surname, but most of the rest are from further south, with **–reys** the commonest of the whole family.

Jeffcock, Jeffcoat(e), Jeffcote, Jeffcott F dim. 'Geoffrey'+the familiar **Cock**. Chiefly Warwicks surnames.

Jefford See **Gifford**.

Jehu F 'Yahweh (God) is he' Hebrew; rare and late (Puritan) surname.

Jekyll See **Joel**. The fictional unreliability of Dr **J—** is happily balanced by the real worth of the great gardener Miss Gertrude **J—**.

Jenckes Form of **Jenks**, with the older **–es** genitive.

Jenkin(g) F double dim. 'John', the **–g** being intrusive. **Jenkin(g)s** '(son) of **J—**'. Although **–ins** is so thoroughly a Welsh surname, its form, especially the **J—** (see **Jones**) and the **–kin** (Flemish in origin, but soon acclimatized), is not at all so. It was the 42nd commonest surname in USA in 1939. **Jenki(n)son** 'son of **J—**'.

Jenks A contraction, and **Jenkyns** a swankification, of **Jenkins** – unless the **–y–** was for manuscript clearness next to a minim letter.

F: *first name*   L: *local name*   N: *nickname*   O: *occupational name*

Jennaway See **January**.

Jenner O 'engineer, military engineer, architect' OF; common in Kent–Sussex and Glos–Wilts (the vaccinator was of Berkeley, Glos).

Jennett F dim. '**John**' (cf. **Jenkin**).

Jennifer F 'white smooth' OW, a version of *Guinevere*, the beautiful but peccant wife of King Arthur.

Jennin(g)s F '(son) of (dim.) **John**', based on OF dim. *Jeanin*; the –g– is intrusive, but –ings is by far the commoner form.

Jephcott See **Jeffcock**.

Jepson F 'son of (dim). **Geoffrey**'. Chiefly a Ches–Yorks–Notts surname.

Jeremiah, Jeremy, Jermine, Jermyn F 'may Yahweh (God) exalt' Hebrew, the lugubrious prophet.

Jerningham F ?'iron famous' Breton (–*an*/–*on* corrupted into the appearance of an English place-name). East Anglian surname brought by Bretons after 1066.

Jerome F 'sacred name' Greek *Hieronumos*, reduced in OF; but the surname has sometimes absorbed such a F as *Gerram* 'spear raven' Germanic.

Jerratt, Jerreat(t), Jerred, Jerrett, Jerrold F dim. '**Gerald/Gerard**'.

Jervis, Jervois(e) Forms of **Gervase**. But those descended from the Yorks family of *de Gervaux* are L, from 'Jervaulx' in North Yorks, OF version of 'Ure dale' OE, Ure being Keltic ?'strong river'. Often pronounced **Jarvis** (cf. **Clark**). **Jervis** is the family name of the viscounts St Vincent.

Jesper See **Jasper**.

Jesshop(e) Rare forms of **Jessop**.

Jessop(e), Jessopp, Jessup Frequent ME forms of **Joseph** (?brought by Italian Jews familiar with *Giuseppe*).

Jevon F 'Ieuan', one of the Welsh forms of **John**. Or N 'young' OF from Latin *juvenis*. **Jevons** '(son) of **J—**'.

Jewel(l), Jewels See **Joel(s)**, a Breton origin supported by **Jewell's** being chiefly a Cornwall–Devon surname. But perhaps sometimes O 'jewel' OF, a metonym for a seller of them.

Jewett, Jewitt See **Jowett**.

Jewsbury L Mispronunciation of the place Dewsbury, West Yorks; second element 'fort/manor' OE, first element ?'water, stream (literally dew)' OE, or 'Dewi (i.e. **David**)'s' Welsh, or an OE F.

Jex F '(son) of **Jack**'. Or N '(son) of the geck/simpleton' ME.

Jinkin(s), Jinkinson, Jinks Later forms of **Jenkin**, etc.

Job F 'persecuted, hated' Hebrew; but cf. **Jubb**. **Jobson** 'son of **J—**'.

Jobbins F '(son) of (dim.) **Job**'.

Jocelyn F 'little Goth' Germanic normanized. Family name of the earls of Roden.

Joel F (not the minor prophet 'Yahweh is God' Hebrew, but) 'lord/ chief generous' Breton *Iudhael, Iudicael*, saint and hermit of Ponthieu. **Joels(on)** '(son)/son of J—'.

John F 'Yahweh (God) has favoured' Hebrew (the –**h**– is a relic of Hebrew via Latin); not even the worst English king could unpopularize the F, which (probably through the Baptist more often than the Evangelist) remained almost the favourite name at the font. (But the feminine form *Joan/Johanna* has contributed to the surname, too.) Whence many surnames from the pet forms *Jan, Jen, Jon, Han, Jack*. **John(e)s, Johnson, Johnston(e)** F '(son)/son of J—'; –**ns** frequent in south-west, and South Wales; –**nson** universal; the –**t**– forms, common in Scotland and north England, may sometimes be L from places in Staffs and Dumfs 'J—'s farm' (second element OE) or even from Perth, formerly Saint Johnston (cf. the football team). –**nson** was the tenth commonest surname in England and Wales in 1853, and the second in USA in 1939; –**ston** was the tenth in Scotland in 1958, the 33rd in Ireland in 1890, and the 47th in USA in 1939.

Johncock F '**John**'+the familiar **Cock**.

Joiner O 'joiner' OF.

Jolley, Jollie, Jolliff(e), Jolly N 'cheerful, lively, pretty' OF –*i* and –*if*. **Jolliffe**, a Hants surname, is the family name of the barons Hylton.

Jolson F 'son of **Joel**'.

Joly See **Jolley**.

Jones F '(son) of **John**', based on *Ioan* (one of the Welsh forms of the F. The others are *Evan*, whence **Evans**; and *Ieuan*, one source of **Jevon** and very doubtfully of **Ewan, Owen**). Anomalously, there is no *J* in the excellent Welsh alphabet! – but **Jones** is notoriously the commonest surname in Wales (perhaps of ten per cent of the rural population in 1890); it is the second (after **Smith**) in England and Wales, and was the sixth in USA in 1939. It was *not* the name of Paul Jones, born John **Paul** in Scotland.

Jope, Jopp See **Jubb**.

Joplin F double dim. '**Job**' with two OF suffixes.

Jordan F (essentially a font-name, after the river) 'flowing down' Hebrew; Crusaders often brought back J— water for their children's baptism. 44th commonest surname in USA in 1939.

F: *first name*   L: *local name*   N: *nickname*   O: *occupational name*

Jose F Mainly Cornish version of **Joyce**.

Joseph F 'may Yahweh (God) add' Hebrew. **Josephs(on)** '(son)/son of J—'. Many, but not all, medieval bearers of the F were Jews.

Joshua F 'Yahweh (God) is generous' Hebrew; a variant of this F is *Jesus*.

Joslin(g), Joslyn, Josolyne, Josselyn See **Jocelyn**.

Joule(s) F See **Joel(s)**. The electrical unit *joule* is from the English physicist (†1889).

Jouxson F 'son of **Juck**'.

Jowett, Jowitt F dim. '**Jull**', itself a diminutive of **Julian**.

Jowle See **Joel**.

Joy F 'joy' OF, male or female.

Joyce F 'Josse' Breton, from *Iodoc*, Breton prince and saint, son of Iudicael (see **Joel**), with his hermitage at what is now St Josse–sur–Mer; or a feminine version of this, mixed with 'joy' and 'joke' OF. But Burton J— in Notts is named after a Norman family from Jort in Calvados (originally *Diodurum* 'divine citadel' Gaulish). Commonest in Beds, but occurs also in Essex and Somerset.

Joyner See **Joiner**.

Joynes, Joynson Forms of **Johnes, Johnson**; **Joynson** is a Ches surname.

Jubb This and **Jupe, Jupp** are part of the inextricable mixture of N OF *jupe* 'man's long woollen garment', ME *jubb* 'four-gallon liquor vessel' (both these could be O, metonyms for makers), OF *joppe* 'fool', and F **Job**.

Juck(es) F 'Iudicael' (see **Joel**). And '(son) of J—'.

Jucker N 'trickster' ME; in Sussex as early as the 1200s. Scots *jewkery-pawkery* (recorded 1686) is the origin of our *jiggery-pokery*.

Judd F dim. '**Jordan**', but perhaps sometimes absorbing **Jude**, or a diminutive form of it. Guppy found it chiefly in Hants, and from Norfolk to Wilts. **Judson** 'son of J—'; a Yorks surname; also corrupted to **Jutson, Jutsum**.

Jude F Jude the Apostle, Judas (Iscariot and Maccabaeus cancelling each other out in popularity), and Judah the fourth son of Jacob and Leah are the same name, 'Yahweh (God) leads' or 'He will be confessed' Hebrew. Involved with **Judd**.

Judge O 'judge' OF. Counted by Guppy only in Bucks and Kent.

Judson and **Juell** See **Judd** and **Joel**.

Juggins F '(son) of (dim.) **Juck**'.

Juke(s) See **Juck(es)**.

Julian, Julien F 'of the Julius family' Latin (said without evidence to be from Greek *ioulos* 'downy'); used in the Middle Ages as both

male and female F, though *Juliana* also existed. Male saint was J—
the Hospitaller, patron of wayfarers; Saint Juliana was martyred in
Nicomedia, but her bones were just over the Channel, so that her F
was popular here. **Julians** '(son) of **J**—'.

Juliffe See **Jolley**. Found in South Wales.

Jull F dim. '**Julian**'.

Juniper See **Jennifer**; no connection with the tree.

Junkin F dim. '**John**'.

Jupe, Jupp See **Jubb**.

Jury L 'Jewry, ghetto' OF; our medieval cities had these quarters
before the expulsion of the Jews.

Justice An O 'judge, officer of justice' OF is likelier than a N of abstract
type 'justice'.

Jutson, Jutsum See **Judd**.

Juxon F 'son of **Juck**'.

F: *first name*   L: *local name*   N: *nickname*   O: *occupational name*

K

Kane See **Cain(e)**. 72nd commonest surname in Ireland in 1890.

Karslake See **Carslake**.

Kavanagh F 'associated with (Saint) Caomhán (= ?gentle/tender)' Irish. 53rd commonest surname in Ireland in 1890.

Kay(e) F Welsh or Breton (cf. Sir Kay of the Arthur story) from Latin *Caius*, properly *Gaius* 'rejoicing'. Or L 'quay, wharf' OF. Or O 'key (-maker/-bearer)' OE, a metonym. Or N 'jackdaw' ON – with *ā* retained in northern dialect (as opposed to **Coe** further south); or 'left-handed/-footed' ON. And the Manx surname is for **McKay**. Thus the meaning of this delightfully ambiguous surname will depend partly on ultimate place of origin – F the Welsh Border or Breton-settled East Anglia, N the north.

Keal L 'ridge' ON (cf. *keel*); places in Lincs.

Kearn(e)y F (for O K—) 'descendant of Victorious' Irish (there are other origins).

Kearslake See **Carslake**.

Keat(e) N 'kite (from greed or rapacity)' OE. **Keat(e)s** '(son) of K—'. Rarely ?L 'shed, outhouse for beasts' OE, and **-s** 'of (i.e. at)' the same, or a plural.

Keay See **Kay**.

Kedge N 'lively, brisk' ME from ?ON.

Keech O 'butcher (really, a lump of animal fat)' ME from an unknown source; Shakespeare calls Wolsey this, with reference to his parentage.

Keegan F Irish corruption of McEgan, 'son of **Egan**'.

Keele L 'cows' hill' OE; place in Staffs; cf. Scots plural *kye*.

Keeling F Tribal name, or dim., based on A S name 'Keel, Ship' OE.

Keen(e) N 'brave, astute' OE; or first element of an originally double F, with same meaning. **Keen(e)s** '(son) of K—'.

Keep L '(castle) keep, strongest and innermost tower of a castle' ME from OE verb; perhaps from having the job of turnkey.

Keetch See **Keech**.

Keevil L ?'clearing in a hollow (lit. "tub")' OE; or ?'wood where timber for tubs was got' OE; or ?'wood of (an A S called) Cufa' OE; place in Wilts, and a Wilts surname.

Keeworth L 'enclosure made with ?poles' OE; place (Keyworth) in Notts.

Keigwin L 'white hedge' Cornish; Welsh *cae* and its Cornish and Breton versions are the ultimate source of our *quay* OF.

Kelby L ?'ridge farm' (cf. **Keal**) ON; place in Lincs.

Kelham L 'at the ridges' ON dative plural after lost preposition; place in Notts.

Kellaway See **Callaway**.

Kellet(t) L 'slope with a spring' ON; places (–et) in Lancs, and a Lancs surname.

Kelleway See **Callaway**.

Kelley Form of **Kelly**.

Kellogg N 'kill hog' ME+OE, for a slaughterman. An Essex surname.

Kelly F (for O K—) 'descendant of War' Irish; high incidence in Ireland (second commonest surname there in 1890), Man, Scotland (42nd there in 1958, by Irish immigration). But some Scots bearers will be of L origin – K—, Angus, or Kellie, Fifes, 'woods' Scots Gaelic; and the common Cornwall–Devon surname is L 'wood, grove' Cornish; locality, or place in Devon.

Kelton L 'calf farm' OE; place in Cumberland.

Kember O 'comber' (of flax/wool) OE.

Kemble F 'chief war' OW *Cynbel* (cf. *Cymbeline*); or 'family (cf. *kin*) bold' OE. Or L 'royal (cf. *king*) (bell-shaped) hill' OE; places (Kimble) in Bucks; no evidence for origin from place Kemble, Glos, a ?British place-name, though the surname occurs in nearby Wilts.

Kemp(e) O 'warrior, **Champion**' OE (later 'athlete'); the –e could reproduce OE –a. A resounding *old* name, since the word soon passed out of the vocabulary and must therefore have been applied and fixed early. Mainly a surname of East Anglia and the south; –e is of Devon–Cornwall. **Kemp** is the family name of the barons Rochdale. **Kempson** 'son of K—'.

Kempster O Female 'comber' (of flax/wool) OE; cf. *spinster*.

Kendal(l), Kendell, Kendle L 'valley of the (River) Kent (= ?high, exalted, holy)' Keltic+OE; place in Westmorland.

Kendrick Same as **Kenrick**, but with a –d– glide.

Kennard L 'yard with cows' OE; place in Somerset; cf. archaic plural *kine*. Or F for **Kenward**.

Kennedy N 'ugly head' Irish and Scots Gaelic. 16th commonest surname in Ireland in 1890, and among the first dozen by the 1950s; 53rd in Scotland in 1958, partly by Irish immigration. Family name of the marquesses of Ailsa.

Kennet(t) L A Keltic ?hill-name that has been applied to the River Kennet and to places East and West K–, Wilts, on its banks.

Kennington L 'royal farm' OE, place in Kent; or 'farm of the family/ folk of (an A S called) **Keen**' OE, places in Berks, Surrey.

F: *first name*   L: *local name*   N: *nickname*   O: *occupational name*

Kennish F 'son of **Angus**' Manx contraction of a *Mc*– name.

Kenrick F 'chief man/hero' OW.

Kent L ? ?'rim, border' or ? ?'host, party' Keltic, the county. A surname now scattered in the south.

Kentish L 'from **Kent**' Keltic+OF suffix.

Kenton Offers a choice of L origins – 'place on the (River) Kenn (meaning ?)' Keltic+OE, place in Devon; or 'royal manor' OE, places in Northd, Suffolk; or '**Kemp**'s place' OE, place in Middx.

Kenward F 'brave (cf. **Keen**)/royal (cf. **King**) guardian' OE.

Kenway F 'brave/royal (cf. **Kenward**) war' OE.

Kenyon L ?From OW *cruc Enion* '**Ennion**'s mound' (a Bronze Age barrow once stood there); place in Lancs, and a Lancs surname.

Ker See **Kerr**.

Kermode Manx and Connacht version of **McDermot**.

Kernan See **Kiernan**.

Kerr Scots form of **Carr**. 35th commonest surname in Scotland in 1958, and family name of the marquesses of Lothian and the barons Teviot.

Kersey L 'watercress island' OE; the lovely Suffolk village that perhaps gave its name to the coarse woollen cloth.

Kershaw L 'church **Shaw**' ON+OE; place in Lancs.

Kerslake See **Carslake**; place in Cornwall, and a Devon surname.

Kerswell L 'watercress spring' OE; places in Devon.

Keswick L 'cheese dairy-farm' OE (but scandinavianized; cf. **Chiswick**); places in Cumberland, Norfolk, West Yorks.

Ketteringham L 'homestead of the followers of (an AS called) ?Famous Peace' OE; place in Norfolk.

Kettle (also **Kettel(l)**) F '(sacrificial) cauldron' (cf. *kettle*) ON.

Kew O 'cook' OF (cf. **Lequeux**). But Reaney shows it to be sometimes L, from 'Caieu', Pas–de–Calais.

Kewish F 'son of the noble' Manx contraction of a *Mc*– name.

Key(e) See **Kay**. **Keyes** '(son) of **K**—'.

Keymer L 'cow pool' OE; place in Sussex.

Keynes See **Cains**.

Keyte See **Keat**. Chiefly a Warwicks surname.

Kid(d), **Kidde** N 'kid, young goat' ME (?from ON). But sometimes ?F for **Kitt**. Or ?O, metonym for **Kidder**. **Kidson** F 'son of **K**—' (from **Kitt**).

Kiddell, **Kiddle** L 'weir, dam, fish-trap' OF. Both are found in Somerset and Norfolk.

Kidder Reaney favours an O 'woodman, faggot-seller', from ME *kidde* 'faggot, bundle of twigs'.

Kiernan As **Tiernan**, but from *Mc*– form with aspirated *Th*–.

Kilborn, Kilbourn(e), Kilburn(e) L 'stream by a kiln' OE; places in Derbys, Middx, North Yorks.

Kilby L 'farm of the young nobles/gentlemen' (cf. **Child**) ON, with ON K– replacing the OE sound *ch*–; place in Leics.

Kilham L '(at) the kilns' OE dative plural after lost preposition; places in Northd, East Yorks.

Killip F 'son of **Philip**' Manx contraction of a *Mc*– name.

Killmister, Kilmi(n)ster L 'Kidderminster' (see **Kittermaster**) in Worcs; it once had an –*l*– in it. Chiefly surnames of Glos.

Kilmartin See **Gilmartin**.

Kilner O 'worker at a kiln, lime-burner' OE.

Kilpatrick L 'church of (Saint) **Patrick**' Irish and Scots Gaelic; places in Dunbartons, Dumfs, and in five Irish counties. But also F (for Mc**Gilpatrick**).

Kilpin L 'calf pen' OE; place in East Yorks.

Kilroy Corruption of Mc**Gilroy**.

Kilsby L 'farm of the **Child**' ON (first element adapted from OE); place in Northants.

Kimball, Kimbell See **Kemble**.

Kimber L 'warrior's grave' OE (cf. **Kemp**), place in Devon. But the surname is chiefly of Berks, and F 'royal fortress' OE, a female name, may sometimes be the origin.

Kimberl(e)y L 'wood/clearing of (an AS woman called) Royal Burgh', place in Norfolk; or 'of (an AS called) Royal Famous', place in Notts; or 'of (an AS called) Royal Bold', place in Warwicks; all OE, and all places –ley.

Kimble See **Kemble**.

King N 'king' OE, from swagger, or appearance, or service in the royal household, or playing the king in a pageant, or being 'king' of some festivity. A L sign-name is just possible. Very common everywhere save in the north – 36th commonest surname in England and Wales in 1853, 92nd in Scotland in 1958, 24th in USA in 1939. Family name of the earls of Lovelace.

Kingsbury L 'king's fort/manor' OE, places in Middx, Somerset; but place in Warwicks is '(AS called) Royal's fort' OE.

Kingsford L 'king's ford' OE, place in Warwicks; but place in Worcs is '(AS called) Bold's ford' OE (cf. **Keen**).

Kingsley L 'king's wood/clearing' OE; places in Ches, Hants, Staffs.

F: *first name*   L: *local name*   N: *nickname*   O: *occupational name*

Kingston L 'king's farm/manor' OE; places in over a dozen counties, including K– on Thames, Surrey, and the official name of Hull.

Kingswood L 'royal chase' OE; places in Glos (two), Surrey, Warwicks.

Kington L 'royal farm/manor' OE; places in five counties.

Kininmonth L 'head of the white hill' Scots Gaelic (last element from British, cf. Welsh *mynydd* 'mountain'); places in Aberdeens and Fifes.

Kinnersley L '(AS called) Royal Hardy's wood/clearing', places in Herefords, Worcs; or '(AS called) Royal Guardian's wood/clearing', place in Surrey; or '(AS called) Royal Hardy's island' (with intrusive –l–), place in Salop; all OE.

Kinsey F 'royal victory' OE. Chiefly a Ches surname.

Kinsley L '(AS called) Royal's wood/clearing' OE; place in West Yorks.

Kippen N 'fatty' OE *Cypping*.

Kipps N '(son) of ?fatty' OE.

Kirby Simplification of **Kirkby**; many places in the Danelaw.

Kirk L 'church' ON. Common as surname in Notts–Lincs–Yorks, and all over the Danelaw, also south Scotland. **Kirke** '(at) the church' ON dative after lost preposition.

Kirkbride L 'church' ON 'of (Saint) Bridget' (see **McBride**); place in Cumberland.

Kirkby L 'church farm/village' ON; many places in the Danelaw.

Kirkdale L 'church valley' ON; places in Lancs, North Yorks.

Kirkham L 'church homestead/village' OE scandinavianized; places in Lancs, East Yorks.

Kirkland L 'church land' ON, places in Cumberland, Ayrs, Dumfs, Lanarks; or 'church wood' ON (cf. **Lund**), place in Lancs.

Kirkley L 'hill hill' (cf. **Creech** and **Low**); place in Northd.

Kirkpatrick L 'church' ON 'of (Saint) **Patrick**'; several places in Scotland.

Kirkup L 'church valley' ON+OE (cf. **Hope**); locality, or places in Peebles, Selkirks. Counted by Guppy only in Co. Durham.

Kirkus L 'church house' ON+OE/ON.

Kirkwood L 'church wood' ON+OE; locality, or place in Oxspring, West Yorks.

Kirtland Corruption of **Kirkland**.

Kirton L 'church farm/village' OE scandinavianized; places in Lincs, Notts, Suffolk; but chiefly a surname of Co. Durham.

Kislingbury L 'fort of the followers of (an AS called) Cysela' OE –

his name is a dim. of *Cusa*, of unknown meaning; place in Northants.

Kiss(er) O '(maker of) thigh-armour' OF *cuisse*.

Kissack F 'son of **Isaac**' Manx contraction of a *Mc*– name.

Kitchen, Kitchener, Kitchenor, Kitchiner, Kitchin(g) O 'kitchen-worker' OE.

Kite See **Keat**.

Kitley L 'wood with kites' OE; place in Devon.

Kitson F 'son of **Kitt**'.

Kitt F dim. '**Christopher**' or dim. 'Katherine' (cf. **Catlin**). **Kitts** '(son) of K—'.

Kittermaster L 'church of (an AS called) *Cydela*/*Cydda* (?related to *chide*)' OE; place (Kidderminster) in Worcs.

Knape O 'servant, lad' OE (cf. *knave* in a pack of cards).

Knapman L 'man at a hillock' OE (see **Knapp**).

Knapp L 'top, hilltop' OE; locality, or places in Devon, Hants, Sussex; and a Wilts surname.

Knapper L 'man at a hillock' OE (see **Knapp**).

Knapthorpe L 'boy's/youth's/servant's **Thorp**' OE, or '**Thorp** of (an AS called) Boy' OE (cf. **Knapton**); place in Notts.

Knapton L 'farm of (an AS called) Boy' or 'boy's farm' or 'farm on a hill' (cf. **Knapp**) – all OE; places with confusion of these possible meanings in Norfolk, East and West Yorks.

Knatchbull N 'knock out the bull' ME (as in a 'knacker's yard')+OE, for a butcher. Family name of the barons Brabourne.

Kneebone L 'kneecap' OE, probably a topographical feature resembling a kneebone. A Cornish surname.

Knell L Same as **Knoll**; a south-east dialect form. **Kneller** 'dweller at the **Knoll**'.

Knevet(t) Norman mispronunciation of **Knight**.

Knife O 'knife' OE, from making them.

Knight O 'youth, servant, soldier, feudal tenant bound to serve as a mounted warrior, knight' OE. (Or, of course, N from service in a knight's household.) Common Midland and south surname. **Knights** O '(son) of the K—'; or L '(at the) K—'s (house)'.

Knighton L 'farm of the knights/retainers/youths' OE; places in ten counties (four in Dorset).

Knightsbridge L 'bridge of the knights' OE; place in Middx.

Knill L 'knoll, hillock' OE; place in Herefords.

Knipe L 'steep beetling rock' ON *gnipa*; place in Westmorland; or possibly 'narrow place' ON (cf. Norwegian *knip*) or 'hillock' Welsh *cnipell*.

F: *first name*   L: *local name*   N: *nickname*   O: *occupational name*

Knock L 'hillock, hump' Irish and Scots Gaelic, but also Germanic (later sometimes meaning 'sandbank'); locality, or places in Scotland and Westmorland.

Knoll L 'hilltop' OE; locality, or places (Knole, Knowle) in six counties. **Knollys** 'of (i.e. at) the K—', or a plural; a monosyllable.

Knott F 'thickset' (cf. *knot*) OE or (as with the great king whom we now call *Canute*) ON. Rarely L 'hill' ME.

Know(e)lden L From the Kent place **Knowlton**.

Knowles See **Knollys**.

Knowlton L 'place by a **Knoll**' OE; places in Dorset, Kent.

Knox L 'of (i.e. at) the **Knock**', or a plural. Family name of the earls of Ranfurly.

Knoyle L 'knuckle' OE, from the shape of the ridge near East and West K–, Wilts.

Kynaston L '(A S called) Royal Peace's farm' OE; two places in Herefords.

L

Labbett O 'the' OF '**Abbot**'.

Lac(e)y L 'Lassy' in Calvados, from Gaulish F *Lascius*+suffix. Chiefly a name (–**ey**) of Leics. The earls of Lincoln bore the name **Lacy** and a shield with a purple rampant lion on gold.

Lachlan L 'lake/fjord land (i.e. Scandinavia)' Scots Gaelic – applied at first to a Viking.

Lackford L 'ford where leeks are grown' OE; place in Suffolk.

Lacock L ?'streamlet' OE; place in Wilts.

Lacon L '(at) the streams' OE dative plural after lost preposition; place in Salop.

Ladd O 'lad, servant, lowborn man' (?meaning someone *led*) ME.

Ladel(l) O 'ladle(-maker)' OE.

Laimbeer and **Linebear** have the appearance of a Devon place-name ending in **Bear/Beer**, though none is recorded; they may be forms of **Langabeer**.

Laing, **Laird** Scots forms of **Long**, **Lord**, with –**ai**– showing the former long –*ā*–.

Lake L 'stream' OE (very rarely ?'lake' from Latin and OF); locality, or place in Wilts.

Lakeman L 'one who lives by a stream' OE+OE.

Laker L 'dweller at the stream' (cf. **Lake**). Or O 'player, actor, sportsman' ON; the grave, industrious peasants of the English Lake District referred to early holiday-makers there as *Lakers*.

Lalonde L Four places in Normandy are called La Londe, from OF 'the' and ON *lund* 'grove, wood'.

Lalor F (for O **L**—) 'descendant of Half-Leper' Irish.

Lamb(e) N 'lamb' OE, from tending lambs, or from docility (but it was sarcasm, and their badge, that labelled Col Kirke's brutal soldiery 'Kirke's Lambs' after Sedgemoor). Also L, a sign-name, the Paschal Lamb being a common sign. Or F dim. '**Lambert**'. Found throughout England, but chiefly in the north. Family name of the barons Rochester.

Lambern See **Lamborn**.

Lambert F 'land bright' Germanic, popularized by Flemings after Saint L—, 7th-century bishop of Maestricht. Sometimes ?O 'lamb-herd' OE.

Lamberton L More nearly original form of **Lamerton**.

F: *first name*   L: *local name*   N: *nickname*   O: *occupational name*

Lambeth L 'Hythe' for shipping lambs' OE; place on Surrey side of the Thames in London.

Lambley L 'lambs' pasture' OE; places in Northd, Notts.

Lamborn(e), **Lambourn(e)** L 'loamy/clayey stream' OE (?rather than 'stream for washing lambs' OE); places in Berks, Essex, and surnames of Bucks–Oxon–Berks.

Lambrick L ?'ridge with lambs' OE, place (–rigg) in Westmorland; or 'land (i.e. boundary) brook' OE, place (–rook) in Somerset. Or see **Lambright**.

Lambright Version of **Lambert** closer to OE *Landbeorht*.

Lambton L 'lamb farm' OE; place in Co. Durham, and the family name of the earls of Durham.

Lamburn(e) See **Lamborn**.

Lamerton L 'farm on a lamb(-washing) stream' OE (the stream is still called Lumburn); place in Devon.

Lamond, **Lamont** O 'lawman, lawgiver' Scots Gaelic from ON (occurring *c.* 1200 in Worcs as the F of the great epic poet **Lawman** son of Leovenath).

Lampitt, **Lamputt** L or O 'living/working at a claypit (cf. *loam*)' OE.

Lampl(o)ugh L 'church of the parish' OW (cf. Welsh *Llan*– and Latin *plebs*); place (–lugh) in Cumberland, and a Yorks surname.

Lamport L 'long market-place' OE; places (also –angp–) in five counties.

Lampshire Despite its occurrence in Cornwall, this may be a slovenly version of **Lancashire**.

Lampson N 'son of **Lamb**'. Family name of the barons Killearn.

Lancashire L 'shire/county' OE 'of **Lancaster**'.

Lancaster L 'Roman site' OE 'on the (River) Lune (= ??health-giving)' Keltic, the Lancs town.

Lancastle See **Lancaster**; Chaucer puns on John of Gaunt, Duke thereof, by mention of a 'long castel' in *The Book of the Duchess*.

Lance F A Norman version of Germanic *Lanzo*, which contains the element 'land'.

Lanchester L 'long Roman site' OE; place in Co. Durham.

Land L Either 'glade' OF (now *lawn*, but cognate with OE *land*) or – if from OE *land* – a 'selion, arable strip between two furrows when an open field is divided, a basic unit of ploughing'. Chiefly a Norfolk surname.

Landcastle See **Lancastle**.

Lander Form of **Lavender**. **Landers** '(son) of **L—**'.

Landreth L ?'court of justice' Cornish; place (Lanreath, pronounced –*reth*) in Cornwall.

Landseer L 'landmark, boundary' OE.

Lane L 'lane' OE; south and Midlands surname, especially found in Glos–Herefords–Worcs. (In Ireland, sometimes for Lehane, from two different sources, meaning ?.)

Lang See **Long**, of which this is the northern and Scots form, though rarer in Scotland than **Laing**; an odd outlier in Devon.

Langabeer L 'long grove/pasture' OE; place in Sampford Courtenay, Devon.

Langbain N 'long bone (i.e. long leg)' ON.

Langcake O ?'long cake' OE+ON, from baking them. A surname seen recently at Horsham, Sussex.

Langdale L 'long valley' OE/ON; place in Westmorland.

Langdon L 'long hill' OE (cf. **Down**); places in five counties, and a Somerset–Devon–Cornwall surname.

Langebeer See **Langabeer**.

Langford L 'long ford' OE; places in seven counties (three in Somerset).

Langham L 'long homestead' OE, places in four counties; but place in Essex is 'homestead of the family/folk of (an AS with a name like) Lāwa'; and place in Lincs is 'long river-island' OE.

Langley L 'long wood/clearing' OE; places in sixteen counties from Northd to Wilts.

Langmaid, Langmead L 'long meadow' OE. –aid a Devon surname.

Langridge L 'long ridge' OE; locality, or place in Somerset. Mainly a Kent surname.

Langrish L 'long rush-bed' OE; place in Hants.

Langston(e) L 'long (standing-)stone, menhir' OE; places in Devon, Hants, and (Llangstone) Mon; but counted by Guppy only in Bucks.

Langthorne L 'tall thornbush' OE; place in North Yorks.

Langton L 'long place/farm' OE, a dozen places in six counties; but place in Co. Durham is 'long hill' OE.

Langtree L 'tall tree' OE; place in Devon.

Langwith, Langworth L 'long ford' ON; places in Derbys, Lincs, Notts, East Yorks; confused with ON for 'wood' and OE **Worth**.

Lank N 'lanky, skinny' OE.

Lankester Form of **Lancaster**.

Lankshear Form of **Lancashire**.

F: *first name*   L: *local name*   N: *nickname*   O: *occupational name*

Lansdell See **Lonsdale**; for the –a–, cf. **Lancaster**.

Lanyon L 'church of (St) John' Cornish; cf. Lannion in Brittany.

Lapham L 'homestead/river-meadow of (an AS called) ?Læppa (= ?skirt) or ?Hlappa (?cognate with *leap*)' OE; such owners' names occur in villages Lapford, Lapley, Lapworth. Surname nowhere common, but mainly of the south-coast counties and Wilts–Glos.

Lappin(g) N 'rabbit' OF. Or O, a metonym for a dealer in them.

Lapthorne L 'lopped/polled thorn' OE; places (–e) in Modbury and Dittisham, Devon.

Larbalestier See **Ballester**.

L'Archer (or one word) O 'the archer' OF.

Larcombe L 'wild iris valley' OE, place in Diptford, Devon; or 'lark valley' OE, place in Blackawton, Devon – a pretty choice.

Lardner O 'official in charge of pig food (acorns, mast) in the forest, official in charge of the larder' OF.

Large N 'generous' OF. Guppy found it common in Wilts.

Lark N 'lark' OE; from ?singing, ?early rising, ?catching and selling them to eat.

Larkcombe See **Larcombe**.

Larkin(g) F double dim. '**Laurence**'. **Larkins** '(son) of **L—**'. Larkin is chiefly a Kent surname.

Larnach L 'man from Lorne' (the district of Argylls named after Loarn, = 'fox', first king of the Dalriadic Scots, *c.* 500) Scots Gaelic. **L—** Nevill is the family name of the marquesses of Abergavenny.

Larner Formally, O 'pupil, student; scholar; teacher, instructor' ME *lerner* from OE, changing to *larner* (as with *clerk* and **Clark**, and *I'll larn 'im*), is attractive, but no form *larner* is extant in ME.

Larry F dim. '**Laurence**'.

Larter ?N 'deceiver, trickster, cheat' OE verb stem *lyrt–*, through south-eastern ME *lert–* to *lart–* (as in **Clark**), and still a surname of Kent–Essex–Suffolk–Norfolk.

Lascelles L 'Lacelle (= the cell/hermitage)' OF; place in Orne. Family name of the earls of Harewood.

Lashford See **Latchford**.

Last Probably O 'maker of shoemakers' lasts' OE, rather than N 'last' OE, for the Benjamin of a big family. Chiefly a Suffolk surname.

Latch L 'wet place, stream' OE; locality, or places in Ches (Lach, Lache), Glos (–leach).

Latcham L 'homestead/river-meadow at a stream' OE, as at **L—** in Wedmore, Somerset.

Latchford L 'stream ford' OE; places in Ches, Oxon.

Latchmore A tangle of place-names with Latch–/Letch–/Lech– and –more/–moor/–mere in Devon (two), Essex, Hants, Herts, London, and Sussex; the dominant meaning may be 'stream'+'moor/pool' OE.

Latham, Lathom L '(at) the barns' ON dative plural after lost preposition; places in West Yorks, Lancs.

Latimer O 'interpreter' or *Latin–er* OF. Or L, the Bucks place named from the family after 1330.

Laton Probably for **Layton**.

Latter O 'lathe-maker/-worker' OE.

Lattimer, Lattimore See **Latimer**.

Latton L 'leek plot, herb garden, (later) kitchen-garden' OE; places in Essex, Wilts.

Lauder L 'grey water' Scots Gaelic, says Johnston; place in Berwicks.

Laughlan(d), Laughlin Forms of **Lachlan**.

Laughton L Same as **Latton**; places in Leics, Lincs, Sussex, West Yorks; but another place in Lincs is 'enclosed farm' OE.

Launder Form of **Lavender**.

Laurence (rarely **Laurance**) F 'of Laurentum' (an Italian town named from its bay trees; cf. *laurel*) Latin; saint and deacon, horribly martyred on a gridiron at Rome, A.D. 258. Whence a number of surnames in Lau–, Law–, Low–.

Laurenson See **Lawrenson**.

Laurie F dim. 'Laurence'; still the normal Scots pet-form of the F (whereas Larry/Lanty are Irish). A Scots and Northd surname.

Lavacraft L A '–croft' surname of Devon, probably from the mysterious **Lovecraft**.

Lavender O 'washer–(wo)man, launderer' OF; no connection with the fragrant herb.

Laventure N 'the adventure' OF, for a daring or much-travelled person; this abstract-noun surname, of a type commoner in French than in English, is a Huguenot or later importation.

Laverack, Laverick, Laverock See **Lark**.

Laverton L 'place with larks' OE or 'place in the irises/rushes' OE; places in Glos, Somerset; but place in West Yorks is 'place on the (River) Laver (= talkative, babbling)' Keltic+OE.

Laverty Ulster corruption of **Flaherty**.

Law F dim. 'Laurence'. But those whose names were preceded by *de/atte* are L 'hill, (burial–)mound' OE – especially in the north,

---

F: *first name*　　L: *local name*　　N: *nickname*　　O: *occupational name*

since the Old English word became **Low** in the south. Family name of the barons Coleraine and barons Ellenborough. **Lawson** 'son of L—'. A firmly established northern surname – Yorks–Lancs–Cumberland–Westmorland–Northd–Co. Durham, and south Scotland; family name of the barons Burnham. **Law(e)s** '(son) of **Law**', or 'at the hill' or 'hills'.

Lawday N 'Loveday', or a typically French abstract N 'loyalty' OF *leaute* (see **Leuty**).

Lawler See **Lalor**.

Lawless N 'law-breaking, licentious' ON (and late OE)+OE.

Lawlor See **Lalor**.

Lawman O 'lawman, lawgiver' ON; cf. **Lamond**.

Lawrance, Lawrence F Forms of **Laurence**. **Lawrence** is the commonest surname derived from the F, especially in the south; family name of the barons Oaksey and barons Trevethin.

Lawrenson 'son of **Laurence**'; found in the north, as far as Shetland; a rarer variant is **Laurenson**.

Lawrey, Lawrie, Lawry See the commoner **Laurie**.

Lawton L 'place on a hill' OE (cf. **Law** in its second meaning); places in Ches, Herefords, and a common surname in Ches.

Lax N 'salmon' ON.

Lay L From OE *lēah*; see **Legh**. But the later dative singular (used after prepositions like *at/in*) was *lēage*, which yields diphthongized forms lay, ley, lye. (Sometimes perhaps L from one of the places in France called Laye, originally *La Haie* 'the hedge' OF.)

Laycock L ?Same as **Lacock**; place in West Yorks.

Layer L A Keltic river-name, of unknown meaning but cognate with the *Loire* and with **Leicester**, gives rise to Leire, Leics, and to the group of villages in Essex called **Layer**. But Reaney also makes it N 'the heir' OF, and O 'layer (of masoned stones)' OE.

Layland See **Leyland**.

Layton L Same as **Latton**; two places in North Yorks; but place in Lancs is 'place on a waterway' OE.

Lazar N 'leper' ME (through Low Latin *Lazarus*) from Greek version of *Eleazar* 'God helped' Hebrew; the brother of Martha and Mary, and the dying beggar of the parable.

Lazenby L 'freedman's farm' ON, or first element the Old Norse F *Leysing* (= 'freedman'); places in North Yorks (two) and (–on–) Cumberland.

Lea L From OE *lēah*; see **Legh**. But the old dative singular (used after prepositions like *at/in*) was *lēa*, and this is the origin of such forms without *–gh*; locality, or places in many counties.

Leabrook L ?'brook in a clearing' OE; cf. Leabrooks, Derbys, and **Leebrook**.

Leach Much commoner version of **Leech**; groups in Ches–Lancs–Yorks and Cornwall–Devon.

Leadbeat(t)er, **Leadbetter**, **Leadbitter** O 'lead-beater/-worker' OE.

Leader O 'driver, carter' OE; sometimes perhaps 'lead-worker' OE.

Leaf(e) N 'dear, loved' OE (cf. *as lief*).

Leagrave L 'bright/light-coloured **Grove**' OE, perhaps with trees well apart; place in Beds.

Leah, a Ches surname, is **Lear** made to look biblical (though the lady's name unfortunately meant 'cow' in Hebrew); but, if pronounced as **Lee**, then it may be a version of **Legh**.

Leahy F (for O L—) 'descendant of ? ?Poetical' Irish.

Leak(e) L 'stream' OE (cf. **Latch**, *leak*); locality, or places (also Leek, Staffs) in three counties. Or O 'leek' OE, a metonym for a seller of them. Both forms occur chiefly in East and North Yorks.

Leaker O 'grower/seller of leeks' OE+suffix.

Leal N 'loyal' OF.

Leaman See **Loveman**.

Lean(e) N 'lean, thin' OE; the **-e** existed in the Old English adjective. Or a reduction of **McLean**.

Leaper O 'runner, jumper, dancer' OE; or ?'basket-maker' OE.

Lear, a Devon surname, is L from some 'clearing' Germanic (normanized) in Normandy, or from Leire, Leics (see **Layer**). Anyway, nothing to do with a mythical King of Britain.

Learmouth L 'mouth of the (River) Lever (= iris/rush)' OE; place in Northd.

Leary F (for O L—) 'descendant of Calf-Keeper' Irish. 62nd commonest surname in Ireland in 1890.

Leasam L 'river-meadow of (an AS called) Dear' OE; place in Sussex.

Lease L 'pasture' OE.

Leat L 'watercourse, pipe, conduit' OE; locality, or place in Devon.

Leather O 'leather-worker/-seller' OE. Chiefly a Ches surname.

Leatherbarrow, **Leatherberry**, **Leatherbury** L Probably 'hill with an animal's lair' ON *látr*+OE *beorg*; two places (Latterbarrow) in Crook and Witherslack, Westmorland.

Leatherhead L 'people's/public bridle-path' OE; place in Surrey.

Leaver See **Lever**.

Leaves F '(son) of Dear' OE (see **Leaf**).

F: *first name*　　L: *local name*　　N: *nickname*　　O: *occupational name*

Leavins F '(son) of (dim.) Dear' OE (see **Leaf**).

Lebeau N 'the handsome (man)' OF.

Lecomber O 'the comb-maker' OF+OE.

Le Cue Probably a respelling of the common **Lequeux**.

Ledbury L 'fort/manor on the (River) Leadon (= ?broad)' Keltic+
OE; place in Herefords.

Ledger F 'people spear' Germanic; popular through the excruciating
martyrdom of Saint Léger, bishop of Autun (†678). A surname of
Kent–Surrey, at times perhaps disguising **Letcher**.

Lediard See **Lydiard**.

Ledsham L 'homestead belonging to **Leeds**' Keltic+OE, place in
West Yorks; or 'homestead' of an AS whose first element is 'dear'
and second uncertain, place in Ches.

Lee See **Lea**. A late spelling, yet the commonest of the *lēah* family;
locality, or places in five counties (three in Salop). 47th commonest
surname in England and Wales in 1853. But Irish bearers may be F
(for O L—) 'descendant of ?Poetical' Irish.

Leebrook L ?'brook in a clearing' OE, as at Brampton Bierlow, West
Yorks; and cf. **Leabrook**.

Leech O 'doctor, physician' OE; the bloodsucking insect got its name
from the doctor, not *vice versa*. Both this and the commoner **Leach**
may sometimes be the same as **Latch**.

Leecomber Strange form of the strange **Lecomber**.

Leed(h)am, **Leedom** Versions of **Latham**, **Lathom**.

Leeds L The West Yorks city has a Keltic ?river-name once applied
to the whole district; Kent place is ?'loud (stream)' OE.

Leeford L 'ford at a shelter' OE; place in Devon.

Leek(e) See **Leak**.

Leeming Probably a form of **Leaman**, ME *leman*, 'sweetheart, lover'
from OE. Chiefly a West Yorks–Lancs surname.

Leese L 'pasture' OE. **Lees** is the same, rather than the plural of **Legh**.

Leewood L 'wood with a clearing' OE is probably, with spellings in
Lee–/Lea–/Leigh–, a common feature, as in Leigh Woods, Somerset.

Le Fanu (it rhymes with *deafen you*). A Huguenot refugee family from
the Caen area; a family history makes it N 'red-headed' from a Latin
word *fenutio* which is not in my vocabulary.

Le Fever, **Le Fevre** (or one word) see **Feaver**; Huguenot surnames.

Legat(t), **Legate** O 'legate, ambassador, deputy' OF. It must often be
a N from having appeared as a foreign legate in a pageant.

Legg(e) N 'leg' ON. **Legge** is the family name of the earls of Dart-
mouth.

Leggat(t), Leggate, Legget(t), Leggitt, Leggott See **Legat**. The commonest of the whole group is –**ett**. Chiefly Lincs surnames.

Legh L 'wood, glade, clearing, field, pasture' OE; of a numerous family of surnames, this (though now rare: 8 in London TD, 276 **Leigh**, 1,104 **Lee**, 105 **Lea**) is the nearest to the original Old English *lēah*, which here appears with –**gh** for –*h* and with the diphthong simplified. Either a locality name, or from one of the numerous places now called Lea, Lee, Leigh(s). Family name of the barons Newton.

Le Good (or one word) N 'the good' OF+OE, a hybrid more illiterate than elegant.

Le Grand (or one word) N 'the big' (See **Grand**) OF.

Le Gros (or one word) N 'the fat' (See **Gross**) OF.

Leicester L 'Roman site' OE 'belonging to the dwellers on the River Leire' Keltic (see **Layer**), the Leics city.

Leigh Form of **Legh**, with a new diphthong caused by a glide vowel –i– before –**gh**; but the whole *lēah* family are now pronounced alike; locality, or places in quite sixteen counties.

Leighfield L 'grassland, pastureland' OE; places in Rutland and (Leyfield) Notts, or a locality.

Leighton L Same as **Latton** (oddly, there seems to be no evidence for 'place in a **Leigh**'); a dozen places from North Yorks to Somerset; but place in Northd is 'bright/light-coloured hill' OE.

Leitch Scots form of **Leech/Leach**.

Lejeune N 'the young' OF.

Leleu N 'the wolf' OF (cf. **Low**).

Le Mare O 'the mayor' OF, respelt and looking like a female horse with the wrong gender for *the*.

Lemmer F 'dear/people famous' OE.

Lemon See **Loveman**.

Lempriere N 'the emperor' OF; a Huguenot surname.

Lench L ?'hill' OE; five places in Worcs.

Lenfestey N 'the playful/wanton' OF.

Leng N 'taller' OE, comparative of *long*.

Lennard Later spelling of **Leonard**.

Lennox L 'people of the district round the (River) Leven (= elm-water)' Scots Gaelic (including an English plural –s); place in Dunbartons.

Lenthall L '**Haugh** (*halh*) on the (River) Lent (= torrent, stream)' Keltic+OE; two places (–ein–) in Herefords.

Leonard F 'lion hardy' Germanic, the patron saint of prisoners.

F: *first name*   L: *local name*   N: *nickname*   O: *occupational name*

Leopard N from a 'leopard' OF in a sign or in a coat of arms (*not*, probably, from having spots such as acne).

Le Patourel O 'the (dim). shepherd' OF (Norman). Channel Islands surname.

Leppard Chiefly a Sussex form of **Leopard** or **Lepper**.

Lepper N 'leper' OF; ultimately from Greek meaning 'scaly'; cf. **Lazar**. Doubtless other skin diseases in medieval England were wrongly diagnosed as leprosy also.

Lequeux O 'the cook' OF; this downright yet elegant surname could also indicate 'cooked-meat seller, eatinghouse-keeper'.

Lesley See **Leslie**. This form has strangely become a girl's F.

Leslie L First element 'court/garden' British or Scots Gaelic; second 'by the pool' (Johnston, 1892) or 'of hollies' (Johnston, 1934) Scots Gaelic; place (earlier *Lesslyn*) in Aberdeens (and Fifes place named after it). Use as a male F is very recent. Family name of the earls of Rothes.

Lessiter, Lester See **Leicester**.

Le Sueur O 'the shoemaker' OF. Channel Islands surname.

Letcher N 'lecher, profligate' OF. Sometimes L 'one who lives at a Latch' OE.

Lethaby, Lethebee, Letherby L In field-names, 'leather' OE means 'hard, stubborn soil'; these place-names may thus be 'tough-soiled farm' OE+ON.

Leth(e)ren ?N 'rogue, thief' ME *led(e)ron* from OF. A Devon surname.

Lett See **Lettice**.

Lettice F feminine 'joy, gladness' Latin *laetitia*, whence dim. **Lett**; **Letts** and **Letson**, '(son)' and 'son of **Lett**'; and double dim. **Lett(e)y**.

Letton L Same as **Latton**; two places in Herefords; but place in Norfolk is ?'farm on a stream (**Latch**)' OE.

Leuty N 'loyalty' OF; a surname of rare abstract type.

Lever L 'reeds, rushes, wild iris' OE; locality, or place in Lancs. Or N 'hare' and, if shortened from *Leverer*, 'harrier' OF. Chiefly a Lancs surname.

Leveridge F 'dear/loved ruler' OE (surviving as F *Leofric*).

Leveson N 'dear/loved son' OE.

Levick F dim. 'dear' OE Lēofeca, pet-name of the poet Lawman's father Leovenath. Or O 'the bishop' OF. See also **Luke**.

Levy F 'beloved warrior' OE; but, if the family is of Jewish descent, the name is Hebrew *Levi* 'pledged'.

Lew L 'hill, mound' OE; place in Oxon.

Lewell L 'spring/stream at a shelter' (perhaps 'sheltered/sunny spring') OE; place in Dorset.

Lewellin(g) English and USA corruptions of **Llewelyn**.

Lewes L 'hills, mounds' OE; place in Sussex.

Lewin F 'dear/loved friend' OE. Or 'devotee of (Saint) **John**' Manx contraction of a *Gil*– name.

Lewis F 'renowned/famous (cf. *loud*) battle' Germanic normanized (it was also the name of King *Clovis*). Early a popular F in Wales (as a sort of translation of **Llewelyn**), and mainly a Welsh surname. 21st commonest surname in England and Wales in 1853, 18th in USA in 1939. Family name of the barons Merthyr.

Leworthy L 'enclosure of (an AS called) Love' OE; three places in Devon (at Bratton Fleming, Clawton, and Woolfardisworthy).

Lewt(e)y and **Lewton** See **Leuty** and **Luton**.

Ley For meaning, see **Legh**; for form, see **Lay**.

Leyland L 'untilled/fallow land' OE; place in Lancs.

Leyshon F 'son of **Lewis**', a non-Welsh spelling of a non-Welsh name, but of Welsh provenance.

Leyton L 'place on the (River) Lea (= light; or a deity-name)' Keltic +OE; place in Essex.

Libby F dim. '**Isabell**'.

Lichfield L 'grey wood (cf. **Lloyd, Chetwode**) Field' Keltic+OE; place in Staffs (no connection with corpses as in *lychgate*).

Lickerish, Lickorish N 'lecherous, wanton' OF (Norman).

Liddel(l), Liddle L 'valley of the loud (river)' OE; place (–el) in Cumberland. **Liddell** is the family name of the barons Ravensworth.

Liddiard See **Lydiard**.

Liddiment The nearest thing in any language is OE *lidmann* 'sailor, pirate', with parasitic –t as in *varmint*.

Liddington L 'farm on the torrent (*loud* stream)' OE; places in Rutland and Wilts.

Lidgate, Lidgett L 'swing-gate' OE (cf. *lid*); places (also Lyd–) in four counties, including Derbys–West Yorks–Lancs.

Lidiard See **Lydiard**.

Light N 'swift, gentle, bright' OE; or confused with **Lyte**. Reaney assigns early *de/atte* forms to L 'light place, glade' OE. Chiefly a Hants surname.

Lightbody N 'little/nimble person' OE.

Lightborn(e), Lightbourn(e), Lightbown(e), Lightbound L Vari-

F: *first name*   L: *local name*   N: *nickname*   O: *occupational name*

ants of a stream-name such as Lightburne in Ulverston, Lancs, 'bright stream' OE, and still mainly Lancs surnames.

Lightfoot N 'nimble/quick foot' OE.

Lilley L 'flax field' OE; place in Herts. Or ?F dim. 'Elizabeth' (see Isabell). A rarer form is **Lilly**.

Lillicrap(p), Lilliecrap, Lillicrop, Lillycrap, Lillycrop N 'white hair, head like a lily' OE; Peter Liliecrop, recorded 1330, probably left his name at Lillicrapp in Sourton, Devon, and they are still Devon–Cornwall surnames. But they look oddly L, a derogatory field-name 'little crop/yield/profit' OE.

Lillywhite N 'as white as a lily' OE (of skin rather than hair).

Limbrick L ?'**Lingen**-brook' OW+OE; place in Heath Charnock, Lancs. But the surname is chiefly of Glos, where the lost *Lymerykes* in Cranham, and *Limericks* changed to Limbrick's in Bisley, suggest that the holder's name came from Limerick in Ireland, as does the five-line rhyme.

Limer O 'limeburner, whitewasher' OE; chiefly a Staffs surname.

Linacre L 'flax field' OE; locality, or places in Kent, Lancs.

Linch L 'hill' OE; locality, or place in Sussex.

Lincoln L '(Roman) colony at the pool/water' Keltic+Latin, the Lincs city.

Lind L 'lime-tree' OE (the linden, not the citrus-fruit tree).

Lindall, Lindell L 'lime-tree valley' OE; two places (–dal, –dale) in Lancs.

Lindfield L 'lime-tree Field' OE; place in Sussex.

Lindley L 'flax field' OE; places in Leics, West Yorks (two), though the Leics place may be 'lime-tree clearing/wood' OE.

Lindridge L 'lime-tree ridge' OE; place in Worcs.

Lindsay See **Lindsey**; the great Scots family (which includes the earls of Crawford) was of English origin. 89th commonest surname in Scotland in 1958.

Lindsell L 'huts among the lime-trees' OE; place in Essex.

Lindsey L '**Lincoln** island' second element OE, the administrative county within Lincs; but the Suffolk place was 'Lelli's island' OE.

Linebear See **Laimbeer**; but Limebar Hill in Minskip, West Yorks, was OE *lim beorg* 'limestone hill'.

Lineker See **Linacre**.

Ling L 'ling, heather' ON or 'ridge, bank' OE; locality, or places (also **Lyng**) in several counties.

Lingen L ?'clear water' Welsh *llyn-gain*, probably the former stream-name; place in Herefords. **Lingham** (since no 'homestead in the ling/heather' ON+OE is recorded) may well be a version of it, and Bardsley notes a Richard Lingam, or **Lingen**, of Stoke Edith, Herefords, in 1542.

Linklater, Linkletter L 'heath-covered rocks' ON plural, farm-names on the Orkneys, and still an Orcadian surname.

Linthwaite L '**Thwaite** where flax is grown' OE+ON; places in West Yorks and (Linethwaite) Cumberland.

Linton L 'flax/lime-tree/torrent/hill place' OE, according to whether they come from OE *līn/lind/hlynn/hlinc*; places in six counties. But place in Northd is 'place on the (River) Lyne (= flowing, stream)' Keltic+OE; and place in Kent is 'place of Lilla's family/folk' OE; and places in East Lothian, Peebles, Roxbs have first element 'pool' Scots Gaelic. **Lynton**, Devon, is (aptly) 'place on the torrent' OE, and must often be the source of the surname.

Linwood L 'lime-tree wood' OE; places in Hants, Lincs (two).

Lipp N for some oddity of the 'lip' OE.

Lippiatt, Lippiett L 'leap-gate (one that deer and horses can leap, but not sheep)' OE; places (Lypiatt, Lypiate, Lipyeate, Leapgate) in Glos, Somerset, Wilts, Worcs.

Lipton L A locality in East Allington, Devon; a *lip* is usually a 'leap, chasm, sudden drop, place where you can cross water by jumping' OE, but the name is not recorded early enough for certainty.

Liscombe L 'pigsty valley' OE, place in Somerset near Winsford; or 'valley with an enclosure' OE, place in Bucks.

Lisemore Probably from **Loosemore** (even as **Liscombe** = **Luscombe**).

Lisle L 'the island' OF; locality in England or Normandy.

Liss L 'court, hall' Keltic; place in Hants.

Lister O 'dyer' OE+–**er**.

Litchfield See **Lichfield**. Chiefly a Derbys surname.

Litham L 'at the slopes' OE dative plural; place (Lytham) in Lancs.

Lithgow L 'wet hollow' Scots Gaelic from British; place (now Linlithgow) in West Lothian.

Lithman N 'gentle man' OE or 'little man' OE (see **Lythe, Lyte**).

Littell Form of **Little**, and reproduces better the Old English *–el*.

Litten L A Somerset surname, so probably from the Somerset place **Litton**.

Little N 'little' OE. Chiefly a Cumberland–Westmorland–Northd surname, but found all over England.

Littleboy N 'little boy' OE+ME.

F: *first name* L: *local name* N: *nickname* O: *occupational name*

Littlebury L 'little fort' OE; place in Essex.

Littlechild N 'little youth' OE (cf. **Child**). Chiefly an Essex surname.

Littlefield L 'little **Field**' OE.

Littlejohn N 'little **John**' OE+Hebrew; a valid joke, whether applied to Titch or Lofty.

Littler L 'little (place on a) slope/ridge' OE; place in Derbys, and a Ches surname.

Littleton L 'little place/farm' OE; places in a well-defined area of the south-west – three in Somerset, two in Glos–Wilts, one in Dorset, then two in Hants, and one in Middx, Worcs. Family name of the barons Hatherton.

Littlewood L 'little wood' OE; locality, or places in Dorset, Lancs, etc. Chiefly a surname of Derbys–West Yorks–Staffs–Ches.

Littlewort(h) L 'little **Worth**' OE, place in Berks; or '**Worth** of the family/folk of (an AS called) Little' OE, place in Bucks; both places –th.

Littley L 'little **Hay**' OE; place (L— Green) in Essex. But Reaney has also found a N of the 1100s 'little eye' OE for someone with piggy eyes.

Litton L 'place on the loud (stream)/torrent' OE; places in four counties; though the Somerset place may be 'gate (cf. *lid*) farm' OE.

Livermore L 'clotted/coagulated lake' OE, place (–mere) in Suffolk; the first element may be that of *Liverpool* also.

Liversedge, Liversidge L 'edge/ridge of (an AS called) Dear Army' OE; place (–e–) in West Yorks.

Liverton L 'farm on a stream with thick/clotted water' OE (cf. **Livermore**, *Liverpool*); place in North Yorks.

Livesey L 'island with a shelter' OE; place in Lancs. Also **Livsey.**

Livings F '(son) of (dim.) Dear' OE.

Livingston(e) L '(AS called) Dear Friend's place' OE (if the *Levin* of 1250 is from OE *Lēofwine*); place in West Lothian.

Llewellin, Llewel(l)yn, Llewhel(l)in F Only –elyn fairly represents the Welsh original; first element is Welsh *llyw* 'leader', the rest ?; F of the last reigning Prince of Wales, and still firmly a South Wales surname. Initial **Ll**– (which counts as one letter in the admirable Welsh alphabet) is very easy to pronounce (see **Lloyd**), but Shakespeare could manage only *Fluellen*.

Lloyd N 'grey, hoary' Welsh. Mainly a Welsh surname, but sometimes grossly anglicized to **Loyd, Floyd**; the best rule for saying *Ll*– is the advice of the bilingual 19th-century dean of Saint David's to the new English-speaking bishop, that he should press the tip of his episcopal tongue against the roof of his apostolic mouth and hiss like a goose.

Loader O 'carrier, ferryman' OE+suffix. Or L 'one who lives at a ferry/drainage-channel/?ford/?track' OE+suffix.

Load(e)s L '(of, i.e.) at the ferry, etc.' (see **Loader**; a *load/lode* is that which 'leads' anywhere) OE.

Loan L 'lane' OE, here in West Midland dialect with –o– for the OE *an/on* alternation.

Loasby L 'farm on a slope' ON; place (Lowesby) in Lancs.

Lobb L ?'steep hill' (apparently the sense is of a heavy, clumsy mass) OE; places in Devon, Oxon. Or N 'spider' OE.

Lochhead or **Lockhead** L 'top of the loch' Scots Gaelic+OE; former name (Lochead) of Campbeltown, Argylls.

Lochore L 'grey loch' Scots Gaelic; place in Fifes.

Lock(e) L 'fold, enclosure (that can be *locked*), lock (river-barrier), bridge' OE (there were no canals to have locks in *our* sense); –e could show dative after lost preposition, or reproduce the –a of OE *loca*. Or N 'lock (of hair), curly' OE. Guppy counted –k only in Devon–Somerset–Dorset–Hants and Norfolk–Suffolk, assigning –ke mainly to Hants.

Lockett F dim. '**Luke**' rather than a form of **Lockhart**. Chiefly a Staffs–Salop surname.

Lockhead See **Lochhead** and possibly **Lockhart**.

Lockh(e)art O 'sheep/cattle-fold herdsman' OE+OE. Or F 'enclosure / stronghold' (the same first element) 'hardy' Germanic.

Lockley L 'clearing with an enclosure/fold' OE; no place now recorded, but Lockerley, Hants, is 'folder's/shepherd's clearing' OE.

Locksmith O 'locksmith' OE.

Lockton L 'place in an enclosure' OE (see **Lock**); place in North Yorks.

Lockwood L 'enclosed wood' OE; place in West Yorks.

Lockye(a)r O 'lock-maker, **Locksmith**' OE. Mainly a Somerset–Dorset–Hants surname.

Locock F '**Love**'+the familiar **Cock**.

Lodder O 'beggar' (if this can be called an occupation) OE; or 'loader, carrier' OE. Or L 'dweller at the lode/path/drain' OE. But it is mainly a Dorset surname, and the two Dorset places Loders and Uploders (once *Lodre*, ?a stream-name of Keltic origin) may be involved.

Loder See **Loader** and **Lodder**. Chiefly a Dorset surname, so the place-names may be involved in it. Family name of the barons Wakehurst.

F: *first name*   L: *local name*   N: *nickname*   O: *occupational name*

Lodge L 'hut, cottage, masons' lodge' OF. Mainly a West Yorks surname.

Loft L 'upper-room, attic' ON.

Lofthouse, Loftus L 'house with an upper floor' ON; places in West and North Yorks. **Loftus** is the family name of the marquesses of Ely.

Logan L 'little hollow' Scots Gaelic; places in four Scottish counties.

Loman See **Lowman**.

Lomas, Lomax L 'Haughs (*halh*) by the pool' OE (cf. **Lumb**); place (–x) in Lancs. Guppy counted **Lomas** in Derbys–Ches–Staffs–Lancs.

Lombard L 'Lombard, native of Lombardy in Italy'; literally 'Long-Beard' Germanic, supposed to be the great-grandson of Japhet (this is unlikely) and founder of the Lombards; the race practised usury, and the surname could be O 'moneylender, banker'. Or F = **Lambert**.

London L pre-Roman (and of course pre-AS) British name perhaps based originally on a personal name (cf. Old Irish *lond* 'wild'). Rarish example of a big town as a surname.

Long N 'long, tall' OE. Midland and southern form (whereas **Lang/Laing** is northern).

Longbotham, Longbottom L 'long valley' OE.

Longden, Longdon L 'long hill' OE; places in Salop (two), Staffs, Worcs (two); and possibly confused with **Langdon**.

Longfellow N 'tall chap' OE+ON.

Longfield L 'long **Field**' OE; locality, or place in Kent.

Longhirst, Longhurst L 'long **Hirst**'; place (–hirst) in Northd.

Longland L 'long piece of ground' OE.

Longley L 'long wood/clearing' OE; locality, or places in Salop, Worcs, West Yorks; and possibly confused with **Langley**.

Longman N 'tall man' OE; counted by Guppy only in Dorset–Somerset.

Longmire L 'long bog' OE+ON; place in Westmorland and a Westmorland surname.

Longmoor, Longmore, Longmuir L 'long moor' OE, but confused also with 'long mere/pool' OE.

Longsdon L ?'hill of the long (ridge)' OE; place in Staffs.

Longstaff N 'long staff' OE, for personal use or to indicate the function of a tipstaff/bailiff/constable/catchpole. Found chiefly in Co. Durham and East and North Yorks.

Longton L 'long farm' OE; places (some –town) in four counties; and possibly confused with **Langton**.

Longville L Same as **Longfield**, given a French look; two places in Salop.

Longworth L 'long **Worth**' OE; places in Berks, Lancs; but place in Herefords is 'long ford' OE.

Lonsdale L 'valley of the (River) Lune' (see **Lancaster**) Keltic+OE; places in Lancs, Westmorland.

Look(s) See **Luck(es)**. Guppy counted –**k** only in Somerset.

Looney F (for O **L**—) 'descendant of Armed' Irish.

Loos(e) L 'pigsty' OE; place (–e) in Kent.

Loosel(e)y, **Loosley** L 'wood/clearing with a pigsty' OE; places in Bucks and (Loseley) Surrey.

Loosemor(e), **Loosmoor** L 'pigsty moor' OE; place (Loosmoor) in Oakford, Devon.

Lord O (or, rather, status) 'lord, master, landowner' OE (originally 'loaf-ward, breadwinner'). Or N from uppish behaviour.

Lorimer, **Loriner** O 'bit-/spur-maker, spurrier' OF.

Loring L 'man from Lorraine' OF from Germanic, the province having been named from its King Lothar (†869) 'renowned/famous (cf. *loud*) army' Germanic.

Lorraine See **Loring**.

Louch N 'cross-eyed, squinting' OF. Chiefly an Oxon surname.

Loud N 'loud-mouthed, noisy' OE. Or L, a stream-name (cf. **Ludwell**), or for **Louth**.

Lougher L 'muddy place' OW; place (–or) in Glam, and a South Wales surname.

Loughlin See **McL**—.

Lound, **Lount** L Same as **Lund**; places in Lincs, Notts, Suffolk.

Louth L 'loud/babbling (stream)' OE; places in Lincs (though the stream is now called Lud), and a surname of Yorks–Lincs.

Lovat(t) L 'rotting/putrefying place' Scots Gaelic (says Watson); 'muddy place, swamp' Pictish (says Johnston, 1934); place in Inverness. But for the old Staffs surname –**att** see **Lovett**.

Love N or male/female F 'love' OE. Or N 'she-wolf' OF.

Lovecraft and (an Oxon–Bucks name) **Lovegrove** must be L 'croft/wood of (an AS called) **Love**' OE, but they are no longer on the map.

Loveday N 'loveday' OE, a day set apart for reconciliation and concord between litigants and feuders, the day of the court leet, settlement-day; the surname perhaps indicates an arbitrator. Also a female F 'dear day' OE.

Lovegood F 'dear good/god' OE. Or ?N 'one who loves good' OE.

F: *first name*   L: *local name*   N: *nickname*   O: *occupational name*

Lovejoy N 'joy in love' OE+OF; disturbingly, however, there are French surnames Lobjoie, Lobjois, Lobjoit, said by Dauzat to mean *l'objet* (this is unconvincing).

Lovel N 'wolfcub, little wolf' OF; Reaney quotes William called *Lupellus* because his father had acquired the name *Lupus* through violent temper – so a sort of 'Wolf Junior'; cf. **Low**.

Lovelace, Loveless N 'loveless, heart-whole' OE, or 'love lass, love the girls' OE; but the temptress in *Sir Gawain and the Green Knight* gave Gawain her girdle as a *luf-lace*, and the meaning may sometimes be 'keepsake, love-token', in the form of a belt.

Loveland L '**Land** of (an AS called) **Love**', places in Hartland and Langtree, Devon; cf. **Lovecraft** and **Lovegrove**. The existence of **Lovemore** L '**Love**'s moor/mere' OE, and of places Loveclough (Lancs) and Lovedean (Hants), further suggests how popular the F was – unless these last two were 'ravine/dell for love-making'.

Lovell Much commoner (east Midlands, Sussex–Hants, Somerset) form of **Lovel**.

Lovelock, Loveluck N 'artificial curl, lovelock' OE, for a dandy who wore them.

Loveman F 'dear person' OE. And from same stems N 'sweetheart, lover', commonly *leman*.

Loveridge See **Leveridge**. A surname of Glos, Dorset–Devon.

Lovering F dim. 'dear army' OE. Chiefly a Devon surname.

Lovett, Lovitt N 'wolfcub' OF. An east Midlands surname (and cf. Staffs surname **Lovatt**).

Loveybond, Lovibond N 'bond/chain of love' OE; Bardsley records a Nicholas Loveband in Norfolk at the end of the 1200s.

Low F dim. '**Laurence**'. Or L 'hill, (burial-)mound' OE – in Midland or south dialect areas (cf. **Law**). Or N 'low, short' ON; or 'wolf' OF. **Lowe** L Usually '(at) the hill, (burial-)mound' OE, with -e of dative after lost preposition; but another meaning of **Low** is possible. **Lowes** F '(son) of L—' (probably in its first meaning from **Laurence**); but perhaps L 'of (i.e. at) the **Low**', or a plural. **Lowson** 'son of L—' (in its first meaning from **Laurence**).

Lowcock See **Locock**.

Lowder See **Lowther**, rather than **Loader**.

Lowell Form of **Lovel**; cf. **Low**.

Lowless See **Loveless**.

Lowman O 'dim. **Laurence**'s servant'. But **Lowman** and **Loman** both occur in Devon, so that places (Uplowman, Craze Loman, Chieflowman) on the River Loman ('elm river' Keltic) in Devon may be origins.

Lowndes L 'groves, woods' ON; a Staffs–Ches surname.

Lowrie, Lowr(e)y F dim. '**Laurence**'. **Lowries, Lowri(e)son** '(son)/ son of (dim.) **Laurence**'. Chiefly Scots forms, also Northd–Co. Durham.

Lowther L Ekwall offers 'bath' British (whence some vaguer meaning 'water') and 'froth' ON; place in Westmorland on River L—. Family name of the earls of Lonsdale and the viscounts Ullswater.

Lowton L 'hill farm' OE, place in Lancs; but place in Devon is ?'warm/sunny hill' OE.

Loxley L 'clearing of (an AS called) Lock of Hair' OE; places in Staffs, Warwicks, and (two) West Yorks,

Loyd Perversion of **Lloyd**.

Lubbock L 'Lübeck' (superseding the Wendish village of *Liubice* 'lovely'), the north German town that headed the Hanseatic League. Family name of the barons Avebury.

Lucas See **Luke**. Midlands and south-west surname.

Luce F Female *Lucia* rather than male *Lucius*, both derived from Latin *luc*– 'light'; Lucia was a virgin martyred at Syracuse (with a silly later story of her having deoculated herself), Lucius a less spectacular saint and pope (†254).

Luck See **Luke**. Chiefly a Kent surname. **Luckes** '(son) of **L**—'.

Luckett F dim. '**Luke**'. Chiefly an Oxon surname.

Luckham L Probably 'valley for courting' OE; places Luccombe ('love-**Combe**') in Somerset, Wilts.

Luckhurst L from an owner's F 'dear spear' OE, *Lucker's* being made to look like a **Hirst** place-name; place in Mayfield, Sussex, and a surname of adjoining Kent.

Luckin(g) F dim. '**Luke**' or dim. '**Love**'. –**ing** is chiefly an Essex surname.

Luckman O '**Luke**'s servant' second element OE.

Lucksford See **Luxford**.

Ludbrook L 'loud/babbling brook' OE; place in Devon.

Ludford L 'ford over the loud/babbling (river – the Teme)' OE, place in Salop near **Ludlow**; but place in Lincs is 'ford on the way to **Louth**' OE.

Ludlow L 'hill by the loud/babbling (river – the Teme)' OE; place in Salop; cf. **Ludford**.

Ludwell L 'loud/babbling stream' OE; places in five counties including Somerset, Wilts; and a surname of the Bristol region.

Luen F 'dear/loved friend' OE (= Lewin).

F: *first name*　　L: *local name*　　N: *nickname*　　O: *occupational name*

Luff N 'dear' OE (cf. **Leaf**). Or male F (see **Love**). Guppy found it scattered in Mon, Sussex, Somerset.

Lugg N 'stick, staff, pole' ME. Now chiefly a Cornish surname.

Lugton L 'place on the (River) Lugg (= bright)' Keltic + OE, former spelling of Lucton, Herefords.

Luke F 'man from Lucania' Greek (and Lucania is ?'marsh' Keltic, ?'light' Latin, ?'white' Greek), better represented by **Lucas**; the third Evangelist, beloved physician, and reputed limner of the Blessed Virgin. But also L, from Lucca, Italy ?'marshy place' Keltic; or from Luick (Liège), Belgium, another Keltic name, ?'people's place'. It may sometimes have absorbed **Levick**.

Lukeman Rarer but original form of **Luckman**.

Lumb L 'pool' OE; places in Lancs, West Yorks; and a West Yorks surname.

Lumbard, Lumber See **Lombard**.

Lumby L 'wood/grove farm' ON (cf. **Lund**); place in West Yorks.

Lumley L 'wood/clearing by the pool' OE (cf. **Lumb**), place in Co. Durham; but place in West Yorks is 'long wood/clearing' OE, and it is mainly a Yorks surname. Family name of the earls of Scarbrough.

Lumsden L ?'valley of the pool' OE; place in Coldingham, Berwicks; chiefly a Northd and Aberdeens surname.

Lund (inferior spelling **Lunt**) L 'wood, (sacred) grove' ON; five places in Lancs, Yorks. Any religious association will have been with pagan gods and the right of sanctuary. The two surnames are found mainly in Yorks–Lancs–Ches.

Luscombe L 'pigsty valley' OE; five places in Devon.

Lusher O 'the usher' OF.

Lutey L 'calf-house' Cornish; and a Cornish surname.

Luther O 'lute-player' OF.

Lutley L 'little wood/clearing' OE; places in Staffs, Worcs.

Luton L 'farm on the River Lea (British river-name meaning "light" or the god "Lugus")', place in Beds; or 'Dear Gift (a female)'s farm' and 'Dear's farm', two places in Devon; or 'Dear's farm', place in Kent; all OE.

Lutton L 'pool farm' OW+OE, place in Lincs; or 'farm of (an AS whose name began) Lud-/Lund-' OE, place in Northants; or 'farm on the loud river' OE, place in East Yorks.

Luttrell N dim. 'otter' OF; a family famous for its tenure of Dunster Castle, Somerset, since early in the 1400s, and of the manor of nearby East Quantoxhead since the 1200s.

Luxford L 'ford of (dim.) **Love**' OE. A Sussex–Kent surname also found in Kent as **Lucksford**.

Luxon, Luxton L 'Lugg's farm' ME+OE; places in Winkleigh (*Luggeston* in 1346) and Upottery, Devon. A north Devon family in the 1500s, spreading thence into Cornwall and Somerset.

Lyal(l) F dim. '**Lyon**'.

Lydbury L 'fort/manor on the slopes' OE; place in Salop.

Lydford L 'ford over the loud/babbling (stream)' OE; places in Devon, Somerset (two).

Lydiard L First element obscure, second 'hill' OW *garth*; places in Wilts and (Lydeard) Somerset.

Lydiate, Lydiatt L Same as **Lidgate**; places (–te) in Lancs, Worcs.

Lye For meaning, see **Legh**; for form, see **Lay**; locality, or places in Herefords, Worcs.

Lyford L 'ford where flax grows' OE (cf. *linen*); place in Berks, and a Berks surname.

Lyle See **Lyal, Lisle**.

Lymburner O 'limeburner' (who made lime by burning limestone) OE.

Lynch L Same as **Linch**; locality, or place in Somerset. Or, if Irish, F 'son of Sailor' Irish. The family boasts Charles **L—** (†1796), who invented lynching. 17th commonest surname in Ireland in 1890.

Lyncroft L '**Croft** where flax grows' OE; there is a Lincroft House in Armley, West Yorks.

Lyndhurst L 'lime-tree **Hirst**' OE; place in Hants.

Lyndon L 'lime-tree hill' OE; place in Rutland.

Lyn(h)am L 'homestead/river-meadow where flax grows' OE; places (Lyneham) in Devon, Oxon, Wilts. Or, if Irish, F (for O **L—**) 'descendant of Snow Birth' Irish. Counted by Guppy only in Derbys.

Lyng L 'ridge, bank, hill' OE; places in Norfolk, Somerset (cf. **Linch, Lynch**).

Lynn L 'lake, pool' Keltic; place in Norfolk, now King's **L—**, on the Wash.

Lynton See **Linton**.

Lyon F 'lion' Latin; *Leon/Lyon* is a fairly common F in the English Middle Ages, especially for Jews; and *Leo* was the name of thirteen popes. Of course, it could be a N of similar meaning. Or, if *atte/ de* forms were found, a L sign-name. **Lyons** '(son) of **L—**'; or (since *de L—* forms exist) L, from Lyons-la-Forêt, Eure; the city *we* call Lyons (French Lyon) is ?'raven/crow hill/fort' OF from Gaulish. 80th commonest surname in Ireland in 1890.

Lyte N 'little' OE; or confused with **Light**. The family gave their

---

F: *first name*　　L: *local name*　　N: *nickname*　　O: *occupational name*

name to Lytes Cary, Somerset, and one of them wrote *Abide with Me*.

Lyth(e) L 'slope' ON, places in Westmorland, North Yorks; or place in Surrey of same meaning, from OE; the –e may show dative after lost preposition. Or N 'gentle' OE, where the –e is historically right.

Lythgo(e) See **Lithgow**; Scots, but counted by Guppy only in Lancs.

Lyttelton See **Littleton**. Family name of the viscounts Chandos and Cobham.

M

Mabb F dim. 'Mabel', itself a dim. of *Amabel* 'lovable' Latin.

Mabbett, Mabbitt, Mabbott, Mabbutt F dim. 'Mabb'. **Mabbs** '(son) of M—'. **Mabson** 'son of M—'.

Mabl(e)y F dim. 'Mabel' (see **Mabb**); –ly chiefly a Cornwall surname.

Mac– See **Mc–**.

Mace(y) F dim. '**Thomas**' or dim. '**Matthew**' (cf. **Massey**).

Machen(t), Machin, Machon. See **Mason**, of which this is a Norman spelling; –in a Midland surname, –on Lincs. –ent has a parasitic –t, as in *varmint*; the –ch– is pronounced –*tch*–, whereas the author Arthur **Machen Jones** used his second F (his mother's Scots surname), pronounced –*kh*–, by coincidence the name of a Mon village near his birthplace at Caerleon.

Macin See **Machin, Mason**.

Mack F Version of '**Magnus**' Irish (cf. **Maxwell**), though Guppy found many in Norfolk.

Macy See **Macey, Massey**.

Madden F (for O M—) 'descendant of ?Dog' Irish.

Maddicks F '(son) of **Maddock**'.

Maddison F Normally 'son of **Maud/Matthew**'; hardly 'son of Magdalen' (see **Maudling**). Counted by Guppy in Co. Durham, Lincs.

Maddock F 'fortunate, goodly' O W *Madoc*. **Maddocks, Maddox** '(son) of M—'. South Wales and Welsh Border surnames.

Maddy F dim. '**Maud**'. Chiefly a Herefords surname.

Madeley L '(A S called) ?Mad's wood/clearing' O E; places in Salop, Staffs; and a Salop surname.

Madge F dim. '**Margaret**' (see **Maggs**) or dim. '**Margery**'. A Devon surname.

Madgett F dim. '**Madge**'.

Madle See **Male**.

Madley L 'good place' O W, place in Herefords; but place in Worcs is 'maidens' wood/clearing' O E – though whether from ownership, or use as a trysting place, or what, is now unknown.

Maffey N 'ill-omened, devil' O F *malfé*.

Magee See **McGee**. 93rd commonest surname in Ireland in 1890.

Magennis See **McGenis**.

Maggs F '(son) of (dim.) Margaret (=pearl)' Greek. Saint Margaret of Antioch, said to have been martyred in the third century after

F: *first name*   L: *local name*   N: *nickname*   O: *occupational name*

quelling a dragon, was invoked in childbirth and as one of the fourteen Holy Helpers, with added lustre to the F through the sainted queen of Scotland (†1093).

Maginnis See **McGenis**.

Magnus F 'great' Latin, borrowed from the much-admired Charlemagne, *Carolus Magnus*, as the F of M— I, king of Norway and Denmark (†1047); thence taken to Norse parts of Ireland and Scotland, where it survives vigorously in Shetland; the cathedrals of Orkney and Faeroe are dedicated to Saint M— the Martyr, earl of Orkney. **Magnuson** 'son of M—'. **Magness** might be from **McGuinness**.

Magson F 'son of Magg' (see **Maggs**).

Maguire See **McGuire**.

Maher See **Meagher**. 87th commonest surname in Ireland in 1890.

Mahon F 'bear' Irish.

Mahon(e)y F (for O M—) 'descendant of Bear' Irish. 46th commonest surname in Ireland in 1890, with its chief home in south-west Cork. **O –ny** is the best spelling, but there are only nineteen in the London TD, with 15 **O –ney**, 26 **M –ny**, and 102 **M –ney**. The real name of 'Father Prout', the lapsed Jesuit who heard the bells of Shandon, was **Mahony**.

Mahood See **Maud**.

Maiden N 'maiden' OE, for a cissy.

Maidment O 'maidens' (?nuns') servant/man' OE, with parasitic –t as in **Machent**. Thus the better but rarer form is **Maidman**.

Maidwell L 'maidens' spring/stream' OE (cf. **Madley**); place in Northants.

Maile(s) Presumably for **Male**; and – a Herefords name – '(son) of M—'.

Main(e) See **Mayne**.

Mainprice, Mainprise, Mainprize N 'surety, mainpernor, one who gives security for the appearance in court of a bailed prisoner at the specified time' OF (the Modern French words involved are *main*, *prendre*).

Mainstone L 'big rock' OE, place in Salop; or '**Matthew**'s farm' OF *Mahieu*+OE, place in Hants; or '**Mayne**'s farm' OF+OE, place in Herefords.

Mainwaring L '**Warin**'s manor' OF; pronounced as **Mannering**, and said to have nearly a gross of recorded spellings.

Maisey L 'Maisy' OF, from Latin F *Masius*+suffix; place in Calvados. The family left their name at Meysey Hampton, Glos.

Maitland L ?'inhospitable/unproductive (soil)' OF; place (Mautalant) in Manche. Chiefly a Scots surname, but the English surname is usually N 'discourteous, rude' (the same word in another sense). Family name of the earls of Lauderdale.

Major See **Mauger. Majors** '(son) of **M—**'.

Makepeace N 'peacemaker, arbiter' OE+OF. Counted by Guppy only in Co. Durham. Also misspelt **Makepiece**.

Maker L 'wall, ?ruin' Cornish (from Latin *maceries*); place in Cornwall (yet the church is oddly of Saints Julian, Mary, and *Macra*).

Makin N or F dim. '**May/Maiden**'. **Makins** '(son) of **M—**'; a Norfolk surname.

Malco(l)m F 'devotee of (Saint) Columba' (*Colm* the Irish form of Latin *Columba* 'dove') Scots Gaelic; the spelling **—om** is inferior. **Malco(l)mson** 'son of **M—**'.

Malden, Maldon L 'hill with a sign/monument/cross' OE; places in Surrey, Essex.

Male N 'male, manly' OF. **Males** '(son) of **M—**'.

Malham, Mallam L 'at the stony/gravelly place' ON dative plural; place (–h–) in West Yorks. Guppy counted –ll– in Derbys.

Malin F dim. 'Mall' (see **Malleson**). An Oxon–Warwicks–Derbys surname. **Malins** '(son) of **M—**'.

Maliphant N 'bad/naughty child' OF (cf. *infant*).

Malise F 'tonsured servant/devotee of Jesus' Scots Gaelic (and the Name of Jesus meant – like Joshua – 'Yahweh is generous' or 'Yahweh is a help' Hebrew).

Malkin F dim. 'Mall' (see **Malleson**); the F was also used to mean 'slattern, slut'. Counted by Guppy only in Staffs.

Mallalieu L ?'Malleloy (= place with medlar trees)' OF; place in Meurthe–et–Moselle. A Huguenot surname.

Mallard N 'drake of the wild duck' OF.

Mallary, Mallery Inferior spellings of **Mallory**.

Mallender or malander is 'a dry, scabby eruption behind a horse's knee' OF; *malandrin* was a 'highwayman' OF; *malantari* was a 'leper hospital' Low Latin. None of these is satisfactory as a surname, but N 'malandre, a medicinal plant of the lychnis species' ME from OF is feasible, for one who concocted herbs and simples.

Malleson F 'son of (dim.) Mary' (see **Marriott**), and cf. *Molly*; Chaucer gives the old widow in the 'Nun's Priest's Tale' a sheep called *Malle*.

Mallet(t) F dim. 'Mall' (see **Malleson**). But Reaney shows how various OF names may have met in this spelling – N 'cursed', N dim.

F: *first name*   L: *local name*   N: *nickname*   O: *occupational name*

'hammer' (cf. *mallet*), and a F dim. 'Malo/Maclou' from a 6th-century Welsh monk *Maclovius* (meaning ?).

Mallinson F 'son of (dim.) Mary (see **Marriott**)' Hebrew+OF suffix+OE. Chiefly a West Yorks name.

Mallory N 'unlucky, unfortunate' OF *maloret* from the Latin stem in 'ill-*augur*ed'.

Malone F (for O **M—**) 'descendant of the devotee of (Saint) **John**' Irish.

Malory See **Mallory**.

Malpas(s) L 'bad passage/crossing' OF; places in Ches, Cornwall, Mon.

Maltby L 'Malti's (= ?sharp, bitter) farm' ON; places in Lincs, North and West Yorks; and a Notts–Lincs–Derbys–West Yorks surname.

Malter O 'maltster' OE. Or L 'bad/unproductive ground' OF.

Malthouse, **Malthus** L 'malt-house' OE; so Thomas **Malthus** only *sounds* Low Latin.

Malton L 'middle place' OE scandinavianized; place in North Yorks.

Maltravers ?L 'bad passage/crossing' OF (cf. **Malpas**) – but no place in France is known, and *de* forms are lacking, so it may be a N in the sense of 'obstacle, trouble-maker'.

Malvern L 'bare hill' OW; place in Worcs.

Malyn See **Malin**.

Man OE and ON 'man' used early as a F, and also as an O for 'servant, vassal, bondman'; the much commoner form is **Mann** (especially East Anglia and west Midlands), retaining the double *n* of OE and ON. **Manson** 'son of **M—**' or (in Scotland) 'son of **Magnus**'.

Manby L '**Man**'s farm' ON, two places in Lincs; or '*Magni*'s farm' ON, place (Maunby) in North Yorks.

Manchester L 'Roman site called Mamucio' British+OE, the Lancs city; the British name is based on *mammā* 'breast hill'.

Mander L 'huts, stables' OF, places (Mandres) in Eure, Seine-et-Oise, etc. Traditional connections with 'basket, Maundy, commander, beggar' are unlikely.

Mandeville L Various stocks that ultimately resorted to this spelling came from an assortment of places called Manneville and Mandeville (in Calvados, Eure, Seine-Inférieure, etc.) 'site belonging to various Frankish or Scandinavian settlers beginning *Man*-' OF, and Magneville (Manche) 'big site' OF. Where the great topographical writer Sir John **M—** comes in is hard to say, since his every other statement is false.

Manfield L ?'common/communally-owned **Field**' OE; place in North Yorks.

Mang(n)all, **Mangold** O '(operator of a) mangonel/catapult/siege-engine' OF.

Manley (rarely **Manly**) N 'manly' ME (only OE *adverb* is extant), 'brave, independent, upright'. (A L origin, from 'communal wood/clearing' OE, place in Ches, is mostly ruled out by Guppy's count only in Devon.)

Mann and **Mannering** See **Man** and **Mainwaring**.

Manners L 'Mesnières (= ?domestics, servants, inhabitants/tenants of a demesne or manor)' OF; place in Seine-Maritime. Family name of the dukes of Rutland.

Manning F Based on 'man' OE. Scattered between Essex, Devon, Ches.

Mannington L 'farm of **Man**'s people' OE; places in Norfolk (two), Dorset, though Guppy counted it only in Sussex.

Mannix Anglicized form of an Irish O name derived from 'monk'.

Mansell L 'from Le Mans (originally the capital of the Gaulish tribe of *Cenomanni*)' or 'from Maine (the province)' OF. Reaney takes it further than Dauzat, pointing out that an OF *mansel* lived in a *manse* (enough land to keep a family) as a feudal tenant. Guppy counted it in Salop.

Manser Readers of Kingsley's *Hereward* should note that *mamzer* 'bastard' (Low Latin from Hebrew) is not extant in ME, and cannot figure here; nor does the (southern) distribution allow L '**Man**'s shieling' ON, place (Mansergh) in Westmorland. The name is surprisingly F from 'Manasseh (= he who causes to forget)' Hebrew, or sometimes O *mansier* 'tenant of a *manse*' OF (see **Mansell**).

Mansfield L '**Field** by the hill called Mam (= mother, breast)' Keltic + OE; place in Notts. Family name of the barons Sandhurst.

Manton L 'farm held in common' OE, places in Notts, Rutland, Wilts; or 'farm with sandy soil' OE, place in Lincs.

Manwood L 'communally-owned wood' OE; locality, or place in Wilts.

Mapledoram L 'maple-tree homestead' OE; places (–durham) in Hants, Oxon.

Mapleton L 'place in the maples' OE; places in Derbys, Kent.

Mapp See **Mabb**.

Mapperley L 'maple wood/clearing' OE; places in Derbys, Notts.

Mappin F dim. '**Mapp**'.

Mapplebeck L 'brook in the maples' OE + ON; place (–apl–) in Notts.

Mapplethorp(e) L '**Malbert**'s (= ?Work Bright) **Thorp**' OF (from Germanic) + ON; place (Mablethorpe) in Lincs.

F: *first name*   L: *local name*   N: *nickname*   O: *occupational name*

Mapson F 'son of **Mapp**'.

Mapstone L 'Mætta's (his name is related to "degree, honour, state")
pan-stone (the big haystack-like granite block that the road has to
bend round)' OE, place in Newton Abbot, Devon, called *Mattepan-
ston* in 1249. Chiefly a Somerset surname.

Marb(l)er O 'marble-quarrier/-carver' OF.

Marcell F dim. '**Mark**' OF from Latin, the Roman family name *Mar-
cellus* popularized by a 4th-century pope and a 5th-century bishop
of Paris.

March L 'boundary' OE, but more probably from OF cognate (cf. the
Marches between England and Wales); place in Cambs may be from
the OE locative case.

Marcham L 'homestead where smallage (wild celery) grows' OE; place
in Berks.

Marchant O '**Merchant**, trader' OF. Guppy counted it in Kent–
Sussex.

Marchbank(s) See **Marjoribanks**.

Marchmont L 'horse hill' British; place in Berwicks (and lost name
in Roxbs).

Marden, Mardon L 'mare pasture' OE, 'boundary hill' OE, 'boundary valley' OE, '?plain/?stone valley' OW+OE, places (–e–) in
Kent, Sussex, Wilts, Herefords; or 'boundary hill' OE, place (–o–)
in Hennock, Devon. Dauzat also produces a F *Mardon*, oblique case
of *Mard*, form of *Médard* 'strength hard' Germanic.

Marfleet L 'fen/marsh stream' ON+OE; place in East Yorks.

Margary F 'Marjorie, (dim.) Margaret'; cf. **Margery**, with its
different *g*-sound.

Marger(i)son F 'son of **Margery**'. Counted by Guppy only in Lancs.

Margery F 'Marjorie, (dim.) Margaret' (see **Maggs**) in OF forms; but
early dissociated from the saint's F and fancifully connected with
the herb *marjoram*.

Margesson, Margetson, Margetts F '(son)/son of **Margery**'.

Margrie See Margary.

Marian, Marion F dim. 'Mary' (see **Marriott**).

Marjoram N 'marjoram' OF, the herb, from Low Latin *majorana* of
uncertain meaning; bestowed as a surname in tribute to sweetness
and aroma, and no doubt wrongly linked with **Margery** and Margaret.

Marjoribanks L 'banks/hillsides' OE granted by King Robert Bruce
in 1316 to his daughter Marjorie (see **Margery**) when she married
Walter the Steward, ancestor of the royal Stewarts; the estates, in
the barony of Ratho, Midlothian, were eventually owned by one

Johnson, who changed his name to **M—** (now pronounced **March-banks**).

Mark(e) F The second Evangelist, Latin *Marcus*, ultimately from *Mars* the god of war (where *mar–* meant 'gleam'); never a popular medieval F, and the surname (especially **–e**, ?showing dative after lost preposition) could well be L 'boundary' OE, as in Somerset place Mark (and **–e** is a Somerset surname), or place Marck in Pas-de-Calais. **Marks** F '(son) of **M—**'; original surname common only in Devon–Cornwall – it is now chiefly Jewish.

Markby L 'farm of (a Norseman called) Marki' ON; place in Lincs.

Marker O 'embroiderer' OE+**–er**; the castaway Emare taught her hosts to 'sew and mark All manner of silky work' (but OE *mearcere* itself meant 'scribe, notary'). Reaney explains an obvious F *Markere* (1168) as ?'boundary army' Germanic.

Markham L 'homestead on the boundary' OE; place in Notts.

Markland L 'boundary lane' OE; place in Lancs.

Markley is ?a version of **Martley**.

Marland L 'land on a mere/lake' OE, place in Devon; but place in Sussex is 'land fertilized with marl' OF+OE.

Marlborough L '?gentian/?marsh-marigold hill' OE; place in Wilts.

Marler O 'worker in marl' OF from ?Gaulish.

Marley L First element 'boundary/pleasant (cf. *merry*)/martens' (or weasels')', and second element 'wood/clearing' all OE; places (according to first element) in Devon/Kent/West Yorks – there are others in Ches, Co. Durham, Sussex.

Marlow L 'at the leavings of a mere' OE – that is, 'at what is left after draining a pond'; place in Bucks.

Marmaduke F 'servant of Madoc' (see **Maddock**) Irish, *Maelm–* being normalized to **Marm–**. Chiefly a Yorks F, and rare as a surname.

Marment, Marmont L 'black/bad hill' OF; place (**–o–**) in Lot-et-Garonne.

Marmion N dim. 'brat, monkey, grotesque' OF; an ancient Norman family.

Marner O 'mariner, sailor' OF.

Marple L 'hill by the valley (Mersey) that forms the (county) boundary' OE; place in Ches.

Marquand Channel Islands form of **Marchant**.

Marr L 'marsh, pool' ON, locality, or places in East and West Yorks;

F: *first name*   L: *local name*   N: *nickname*   O: *occupational name*

or Mar, Aberdeens, ?a British tribal name cognate with the *Marsi* of Italy and the *Marsigni* of Bohemia.

Marrable F 'Mirabel (= wonderful)' Latin, feminine.

Marrick L ' ?horse (cf. *mare*) ridge' ON; place in North Yorks.

Marries, Marris L 'marsh' OF (cf. the church of St Saviour in the Marishes, York); locality, or places (Marais) in Calvados, Eure.

Marriott F dim. 'Mary (= ?wished-for child)' Hebrew. An east Midlands surname.

Marrow N 'mate, chum' (as in Cumberland dialect), 'spouse, sweetheart' ME.

Marroway L 'morning-gift' OE (much corrupted from *morgengifu*), a piece of land given by a husband to his wife on the morning after their wedding, as was customary in A S times in some more southerly counties; place (Marraway) in Warwicks.

Marsden L 'boundary valley' OE, places in Glos, West Yorks; or 'boundary mark valley' OE, two places in Lancs.

Marsh L 'marsh' OE (which had –*er*–; cf. **Clark**). Guppy counted it only south of Ches–Derbys; it may have trespassed on **March** and **Marks**.

Marshall O 'horse(cf. *mare*)-servant' Germanic normanized. A word that extended to a wide range of functions, rising in status to a high officer such as the Earl Marshal and remaining also as 'farrier, shoeing-smith, groom, horse-doctor'. Widespread, and the 49th commonest surname in Scotland in 1958.

Marsham L 'homestead by a marsh' OE; place in Norfolk. Family name of the earls of Romney.

Marshfield L '**Field** by a marsh' OE; locality, or places in Ches, Glos, Mon.

Marshman L 'man who lives at a marsh' OE.

Marson Form of **Marston**. (The tempting guess F 'Mary's son' is virtually impossible – Mary was a very rare name in medieval England, as if too good for mere mortal girls.)

Marston L 'place by a marsh' OE; places in many counties.

Martel(l) F double dim. '**Martin**' with OF suffix. Or O/N for a 'hammer (-maker/-user)' OF.

Marten(s) See **Martin(s)**, even though the beast *marten* has no linguistic kinship with the bird *martin*, or with the F.

Martin F dim. 'Mars' (cf. **Mark**) – a pagan god of war giving his Latin name to one of the greatest apostles of the West, Saint M— of Tours. But may sometimes be L, places in six counties, with same meaning as **Marton**. It is found all over England (including one

237

per cent of the people of Cornwall on Guppy's count). 31st commonest surname in England and Wales in 1853, 40th in Scotland in 1958, 38th in Ireland in 1890, 14th in USA in 1939. **Martins(on)** '(son)/son of **M**—'.

Martindale L '**Martin**'s valley' Latin+OE; place in Westmorland.

Martineau (western French), **Martinet** (the commonest derivative) F dim. '**Martin**'; *martinet* for a pernickety disciplinarian comes from a general who was one of Louis XIV's drill-masters.

Martland A Lancs variation of **Markland**.

Martley L 'marten (?weasel) wood/clearing' OE; places in Suffolk, Worcs.

Marton L 'place by a mere/lake' OE; places in seven counties (nine in Yorks); first element may sometimes be 'boundary' OE.

Martyn(s) See **Martin(s)**. The F is nowadays often spelt affectedly with a –y–, which is to be deplored. As a surname, found mainly in Cornwall.

Martyr N 'weasel' OF *martre* (cf. *marten*), affected by the nobler word.

Marvin See **Mervin** (and cf. **Clark**, clerk).

Marwick L 'seamew bay' ON; place in Orkney, and an Orcadian surname.

Marwood L 'bigger wood' OE (cf. *more*, Scots *mair*), place in Co. Durham; but place in Devon is ?'boundary wood' OE.

Mascall, Maskall, Maskell See **Marshall. Maskell** is an Essex surname.

Maskery, Maskrey O 'butcher' OF; cf. *massacre*.

Maslen (a Berks surname), **Maslin** F dim. '**Matthew**/Matilda (see **Maud**)/Mazo (Germanic)/? ?**Thomas**' with OF suffix. Or perhaps O 'mazer, maplewood bowl' OF, for a maker of them.

Mason O '(stone-)mason' OF (Norman version was more like **Machen**); found everywhere, though rarer in the north. Family name of the barons Blackford.

Massacrier O (and not as horrid as it looks) 'butcher' OF. There is only one in the London TD.

Massey, Massie F dim. '**Matthew**'. But often L, from various places in France: Massy ?'hill, range' OF *massif*, Seine-Maritime; La Ferté-Macé (= **Matthew**), Orne; Marcy (?connected with *marciage*, the seigniorial right to take every three years the produce of natural crops – grass, timber OF), Manche; Macey, Manche; Macé-sur-Orne, Orne. Hamo de Masci, who in 1086 held Dunham Massey, Ches, was from one of these Normandy places. –**ey** is a surname of Ches-Lancs-Derbys-Staffs-Salop.

F: *first name*   L: *local name*   N: *nickname*   O: *occupational name*

Massinger O 'messenger' OF (the **–n–** is a slovenly adenoidal English insertion, as in *passenger*).

Massingham L 'homestead of the gang of (an AS called) Mæssa' OE; places (Great and Little M—) in Norfolk.

Masson See **Mason**.

Masters O '(son)/at the house of the master' OF (?school-, ?task-, etc.). Common in Somerset.

Matchett See **Madgett**.

Mather O 'mower' OE (cf. *aftermath*). Guppy counted it only in Lancs, Northd, Derbys.

Matherson Form of **Matheson**, and used for **McMathan**.

Matheson F 'son of (dim.) **Matthew**'; mainly Scots.

Mathew(son), **Mathew(e)s**, **Mathieson** Rarer (and historically less accurate) forms of **Matthew**, etc. **–ieson** is Scots.

Mathias Commoner form of **Matthias** in South Wales.

Matkin F double dim. '**Matthew**'.

Matlock L 'moot-oak, oak where meetings are held' OE; place in Derbys.

Maton F double dim. '**Matthew**' (cf. **Mattin**).

Matravers See **Maltravers**.

Matte(r)son, **Matson** See **Matthewson**.

Matthew, **Matthias** F 'gift of God' Hebrew, from the Apostle. The Authorized Version of the Bible uses **–ew** for the publican and the Greek/Latin **–ias** for the 13th Apostle. **Matthews(on)** '(son)/son of M—'; **–s** is very common in South Wales, Welsh Border, Cornwall.

Mattin(son), **Matti(ng)son** Forms of double dim. '**Matthew**', etc.

Mattock(s) See **Maddock(s)**.

Maud(e) F dim. 'Matilda (= Strength Battle)' OF from Germanic, feminine; cf. Henry I's daughter, the near-queen 'Matilda or Maud'. **Maude** is the family name of the viscounts Hawarden.

Maudesley See **Mawdesley**.

Maudling F 'Magdalen, woman from Magdala (= tower)' Hebrew, feminine; hence, from Saint Mary Magdalen's tears, the adjective *maudlin* (the pronunciation as in the Oxford and Cambridge colleges). Sometimes ?L, from a Magdalen hospital for fallen women (named in the unscriptural belief that *she* was such).

Maufe N 'in-law', etc. (see **Maw**).

Mauger F 'council spear' Germanic (with **–alg–** vocalized in OF); origin of the deceptive **Major**.

Maugham Version (found by Guppy in Co. Durham) of **Maughan** (frequent in Northumberland) L '?river plain' Scots Gaelic; place (once Machan, now Dalserf) in Lanarks.

Maul(e) F 'Mall' (see **Malleson**).

Mauleverer N 'poor harrier' OF. Also L from Maulévrier, place in Seine-Maritime. A family prominent in the Civil War, but never ennobled as was the fictional Lord M— of *The Magnet*.

Maull See **Maule**.

Mault See **Maud**. Or O 'malt' OE, for a maltster.

Maund L 'plain' or 'rocks' OW; place in Herefords.

Maunder Common Devon version of **Mander**.

Maundrell, Maundrill These cannot be a *mandrel, maundrel* 'miner's pick' or the superb baboon *mandrill* or a lost –*hill* place-name or even a mysterious ME measure of capacity *mandrel*. But *maunder* 'beggar' OF (or Romany), though first instanced late (1609), may have had a dim. form+OF suffix –*el*. Bardsley's first instances are in Yorks (1379) and Wilts (1605), and the name –**ell** is still commonest in Wilts.

Maunsell See **Mansell**.

Maurice F 'Moorish, swarthy' Latin; saint said to have been martyred in Switzerland, A.D. 286. Still the usual form of the F, but the normal surname is **Morris**.

Maw A complicated surname. A few will be L 'meadow, mow' OE. Or N 'seamew' OE (this is hard to believe). Or F (?with one of these two origins) Germanic. But Reaney's first choice is N female 'relative, in-law' ON or OE (cf. **Hitchmough**).

Mawby L For **Maltby** or for Mautby, Norfolk (which means the same).

Mawditt N 'badly educated' OF from Latin.

Mawd(e)sley L 'Maud's wood/clearing' second element OE; place in Lancs; and see **Moseley**.

Mawle Guppy counted this form of **Maule** in Northants.

Maxey L 'Maccus (Irish-ON form of **Magnus**)'s island' second element OE; place in Northants.

Maxted L 'dungy/filthy site' OE; place in Kent, and a Kent surname.

Maxton L 'Maccus (= **Magnus**)'s farm' Scots Gaelic+OE; place in Roxbs.

Maxwell L 'Maccus (= **Magnus**)'s spring/stream' Scots Gaelic+OE; place in Roxbs.

May N 'youth, girl, virgin, demure young man' OE. Or F dim. '**Mayhew**', itself a form of **Matthew**; 'May' OF, from birth/baptism in time of flowers, is just possible, though month surnames are rare.

Maybank N First element 'ill, badly' OF, second unknown. A Norman

F: *first name*   L: *local name*   N: *nickname*   O: *occupational name*

family *Malbedeng, Malbeenc, Melbanc* (1084, 1086), which held Clifton M—, Dorset, and Nantwich, Ches.

Maycock F dim. 'Matthew'+familiar **Cock**.

Mayer O 'physician' (see **Myer**) OF, or rarely 'mayor' OF; now much reinforced by 'bailiff, farmer' German, brought by Germans and Jews. **Mayers** '(son) of **M**—'.

Mayes F '(son) of **May**'. A 1611 emigrant to USA also called himself **Mease**.

Mayfield L '**Field** with mayweed/madder' OE; places in Sussex/Staffs.

Mayhew OF version of **Matthew**. Counted by Guppy only in Beds, Suffolk.

Maykin See **Makin**.

Mayland L '(at) the island' OE, where the *–m* of the dative of the definite article after a lost preposition has got wrongly attached; place in Essex.

Maynard F 'strength hardy' Germanic; cf. **Mayne**. Chiefly a Cornwall–Devon surname.

Mayne F 'strength' Germanic (cf. *might and main*). Or N 'big' OE from Latin *magnus*; or 'hands' OF. Or L, from the French districts Maine or Mayenne; or some 'dwelling, manor, village' OF *maine*. Or F (usually spelt **Main**), a reduction in Scotland of **Magnus**.

Maynell F 'strength battle' Germanic, feminine. Or = **Meynell**.

Mayo Same as **Mayhew**, but perhaps influenced by the name ('yew plain' Irish) of the Irish county. Guppy found it chiefly in Dorset.

McAdam F 'son' Scots Gaelic 'of **Adam**'.

McAlaster F 'son of **Alexander**' in its Scots Gaelic form *Alasdair*.

McAleese F 'son of the servant of Jesus' Irish (see **Malise**).

McAlery See **McChlery**.

McAlevy F 'son of **Donlevy**' Irish.

McAllaster, McAllister Forms of **McAlaster**; –i– the commonest of the group.

McAlonie F 'son of the servant of Storm' Scots Gaelic.

McAlpin(e) F 'son of Alpin' Scots Gaelic, a F of unknown meaning (apparently not connected with *Alb*–; cf. **Alban**) akin to *Elphin*.

McAndrew F 'son' Scots Gaelic 'of **Andrew**'.

McAra F 'son of Charioteer' Scots Gaelic. A Perths surname.

McArdle F 'son of Super-Valour' Scots Gaelic.

McArthur, McArtney F 'son' Scots Gaelic 'of **Arthur**, (dim.) **Arthur**'.

McAsgill, McAskie F 'son' Scots Gaelic 'of **Askell**, (dim.) **Askell**'.

McAteer See **McIntyre**.

McAulay, McAuley, McAuliffe F 'son of Olaf (= relic of the gods)' ON, in its Irish and Scots Gaelic forms. A Hebridean and Irish group.

McAuslan(d), McAuslane F 'son' Scots Gaelic 'of **Absalom**'.

McAvaddy F 'son of ?Dog' Irish.

McAvoy F 'son of Golden-Haired Lad' Scots Gaelic.

McBain, McBean F 'son of **Bean**' Scots Gaelic; and cf. **McBeath**.

McBe(a)th F 'son of Life' Scots Gaelic; cf. **Bean** in its Scots Gaelic sense.

McBradden F 'son of Salmon' Scots Gaelic.

McBrayne O 'son of the judge' Scots Gaelic.

McBride F 'son of the devotee of (Saint) Bridget' Irish; see **Gilbride**.

McCabe F 'son of Cap/Hood' Irish (Hebrideans who reached Ireland c. 1350).

McCafferky, McCafferty F 'son of Steed Rider' Irish.

McCaffray, McCaffrey Forms of **McGaffrey**, sometimes absorbing **McCafferky**.

McCaig O 'son of Poet/Philosopher' Scots Gaelic.

McCall F 'son of War Wielder' Scots Gaelic.

McCallum F 'son of the devotee of (Saint) Columba' (see **Coleman**) Scots Gaelic. 98th commonest surname in Scotland in 1958.

McCambridge F 'son' Scots Gaelic 'of **Ambrose**', fatuously respelt.

McCann F 'son of Wolfhound' Irish.

McCarlish F 'son' Scots Gaelic 'of **Charles**'.

McCarter Misspelling of **McArthur**.

McCarthy F 'son of **Craddock**' in its Irish form. 13th commonest surname in Ireland in 1890, and the commonest Mc– name there.

McCartney See **McArtney**.

McCaskie See **McAskie**.

McCausland See **McAuslan**.

McCaw F 'son of **Adam**' in its Irish and Scots Gaelic form.

MccGwire This strange aberration for **McGuire** occurs in Dorset.

McChlery O 'son of the clerk' Irish; cf. **Clery** and **Clark**. This is claimed as the oldest hereditary surname in Europe.

McClacher O 'son of the mason' Scots Gaelic; cf. **Clachar**.

McClan(n)achan, McClanaghan F 'son of the devotee of (the Irish Saint) Onchu (= Wolfhound)' Scots Gaelic.

McCleary, McCleery Forms of **McChlery**.

McCleish Form of **McLeish**.

F: *first name*   L: *local name*   N: *nickname*   O: *occupational name*

McClellan(d) F 'son of the devotee of (Saint) Fillan (= Wolf)' Scots Gaelic.

McClements Corruption of **McLamont**; an excellent example of folk-etymology (though Saint Clement was known and venerated in Scotland – cf. the great Hebridean church dedicated to him at Rodel, Harris).

McClintock F 'son of the devotee of (Saint) Findan (= dim. *Finn* "white")' Scots Gaelic.

McCloy F 'son of (dim.) **Lewis**' Scots Gaelic.

McClumpha F 'son of the devotee of (Saint) Imchad' Scots Gaelic.

McClung F 'son of Ship' Scots Gaelic.

McComb(e), McCombie, McComie F 'son of (dim.) **Thomas**' – the first two from the one Scots Gaelic diminutive, the second two from another.

McConachie, McConachy, McConagh(e)y Forms of **McDonaugh**.

McConnal, McConnel(l) F 'son of Conall (= high mighty)' Irish and Scots Gaelic; but often a variant of **McDonald**.

McCorkill, McCorkle F 'son of Torquil'; see **McCorquodale**.

McCormack F 'son of Chariot Lad' Irish and Scots Gaelic.

McCorquodale F 'son' Irish and Scots Gaelic 'of **Thurkettle** (Thorketill, Torquil)' ON; cf. **McCorkill**.

McCosh O 'son of the footman/courier' Scots Gaelic. An Ayrs surname.

McCoy Irish variant of **McKay**. The 'rale McCoy' commemorates either the dandy pugilist Kid **M—** or heroin from Macao.

McCrimmon F 'son of Famed Protector' Scots Gaelic from ON.

McCrindell, McCrindle Misspellings of **McRanald**.

McCrossan O 'son of the rhymer' Irish and Scots Gaelic.

McCruddan F 'son of (dim.) Spirited' Irish.

McCrum N 'son of the bent one' Scots Gaelic.

McCrystal F 'son of (dim.) **Christopher**' in its Scots Gaelic form.

McCulloch F 'son of ?Boar' Scots Gaelic.

McCurtin N 'son of the hunchback' Scots Gaelic.

McCusker F 'son of Oscar/Champion' Irish.

McCutcheon F 'son of **Hutcheon**' in its Scots Gaelic form.

McDaid F 'son of **David**' Irish + Hebrew.

McDa(i)rmid, McDearmid, McDermaid, McDerment, McDermid, McDermit, McDermot(t) F 'son of Freeman' or 'son of Unenvious' Irish and Scots Gaelic. **McDermott** was the 96th commonest surname in Ireland in 1890.

McDevitt F 'son of **David**' Irish + Hebrew.

McDonald F 'son of **Donald**' Scots Gaelic. 'Properly speaking there is no such surname as Macdonald', says Black in a sixty-line essay; be that as it may, it was the second commonest surname (after **Smith**) in Scotland in 1858, dropping to third (after **Smith** and **Brown**) by 1958; and the 95th in Ireland in 1890.

McDonaugh F 'son of **Duncan**' Scots Gaelic.

McDonnell Same as **McDonald**. Irish family, but principally of Argylls origin. 63rd commonest surname in Ireland in 1890. Family name of the earls of Antrim.

McDonogh See **McDonaugh**.

McDougal(l), McDowall, McDowell F 'son' Irish and Scots Gaelic 'of **Dougal**'.

McDuff(ie) F 'son' Scots Gaelic 'of **Duff(ie)**'; latter also corrupted to **McFee**.

McEachan F 'son of Horse Lord' Scots Gaelic.

McElder(r)y – the double **r** is preferable, as suggesting the correct stress on the second **e** – N 'son of the dark youth' Irish *MacGiolla Dorcha*. A Co. Tyrone surname common also in Co. Antrim.

McElfrish F 'son of the devotee of (Saint) **Brice**' in its Scots Gaelic form.

McElligott F 'son' Irish 'of (double dim.) **William**'.

McEllistrim Rare form of **McEllistrum** F 'son' Irish 'of **Alexander**'. A Co. Kerry family.

McElroy See **McIlroy**.

McEvilly See **Stenton**.

McEwan, McEwen, McEwing F 'son of **Ewan**' Scots Gaelic.

McFadden, McFadye(a)n, McFadze(a)n F 'son' Scots Gaelic 'of (dim.) **Patrick**'; for the –z– cf. **Menzies**.

McFail, McFall See **McPhail**.

McFarlan(d), McFarlane F 'son of Parlan (Old Irish *Partholon* = ?"sea waves", who seized Ireland 278 years after the Flood; often "anglicized" as **Bartholomew**)' Scots Gaelic. –ne was the 54th commonest surname in Scotland in 1958.

McFarquhar F 'son of **Farquhar**' Scots Gaelic.

McFate, McFeat F 'son of **Pate**' Scots Gaelic.

McFee See **McDuffie**. Black praises its tremendous antiquity.

McFetridge (corrupted to **McFrederick**) F 'son' Scots Gaelic 'of **Peter**'.

McGachan, McGachen See **McEachan**.

McGaffrey F 'son' Irish 'of **Godfrey**'.

McGarrigle F 'son of Super-Valour' Irish.

McGee F 'son of Aodh' Irish (rendering **Hugh**); cf. **McKay**.

F: *first name*   L: *local name*   N: *nickname*   O: *occupational name*

McGeorge See **McIndeor**; cf. **McJarrow**; sometimes F ? ?'son of George'.

McGenis F 'son of **Angus**' Irish; cf. Scots **McInnes**.

McGhee, McGhie Forms of **McGee** found in Scotland.

McGibbon F 'son' Scots Gaelic 'of **Gibbon**'.

McGilchrist F 'son' Scots Gaelic 'of **Gilchrist**'.

McGill L 'son of the stranger/Lowlander' Scots Gaelic. Or O 'son of the servant' Irish and Scots Gaelic.

McGillivray F 'son of the devotee of knowledge/judgement' Scots Gaelic.

McGilp See **McKillop**.

McGlashan N 'son of the (dim.) grey/sallow lad' Irish and Scots Gaelic.

McGoldrick F 'son of High Temper' Irish.

McGorman F 'son of **Gorman**'. Rare, and chiefly of Co. Monaghan.

McGovern F 'son of Samhradhan (his name is connected with "summer")' Irish, a surname of Cos. Cavan–Leitrim–Fermanagh.

McGowan, McGowing, McGown O 'son of the **Smith**' Irish and Scots Gaelic.

McGrath, McGraw See **McRaith**. Irish equivalents of Scots **McRae**. **McGrath** was the 55th commonest surname in Ireland in 1890.

McGregor F 'son of **Gregory**' in its Scots Gaelic form. 51st commonest surname in Scotland in 1958 (dropping nine places in 100 years).

McGuinness F 'son of **Angus**' Irish.

McGuire F 'son of Dun-Coloured' Irish. With **Maguire** the 39th commonest surname in Ireland in 1890.

McHardie, McHardy F 'son of Sloe' Scots Gaelic.

McHendrie, McHenry F 'son' Scots Gaelic 'of **Henry**'.

McHugh F 'son of Aodh' Irish (rendering **Hugh**); cf. **McKay, McGee**.

McHutchin F 'son' Scots Gaelic 'of **Hutchin**'.

McIlraith N 'son of the brindled lad' Scots Gaelic.

McIlroy N 'son of the red-haired lad' Scots Gaelic and Irish.

McIlvain(e), McIlwain(e) N 'son of the white/fair lad' Scots Gaelic; or 'son of the devotee of (Saint) Beathan' (see **Bean**) Scots Gaelic.

McIlvany, McIlvenna N 'son of the small youth' Irish (north-east Ulster, and rare) and **McIlveen** N 'son of the servant of the gentle one' Irish (Co. Down) have been intermingled by misspelling.

McIlwraith, McIlwrick See **McIlraith**.

McIndeor N 'son of the pilgrim/stranger' Scots Gaelic, with –in– representing *an* 'the'; cf. **Dewar**.

McInerny O 'son of the erenagh (steward of church lands)' Irish.

McInnes F 'son of **Angus**' Scots Gaelic.

McIntosh O 'son of the chieftain' Scots Gaelic, with –in– representing *an* 'the'; cf. **Toshack** and Welsh *tywysog* 'prince'. 69th commonest surname in Scotland in 1958. The serviceable *mac* is named after Charles **M—** (†1843).

McIntyre O 'son of the carpenter/**Wright**' Irish and Scots Gaelic, with –in– representing *an* 'the'. 70th commonest surname in Scotland in 1958.

McIvor F 'son' Scots Gaelic 'of **Ivor**'. Also **McIver**.

McJarrow, McJerrow Perversions of **McIndeor**, lacking the –in–.

McKail See **McCall**.

McKay F 'son of Aodh (= ?"fire")' Irish and Scots Gaelic (rendering **Hugh** or even Germanic *Odo*). 19th commonest surname in Scotland in 1958 (dropping nine places in 100 years). Family name of the earls of Inchcape and the barons Reay.

McKechnie F 'son of Eachann/Eachdonn' Scots Gaelic; see **Hector**.

McKee F 'son of Aodh (see **McKay**)' Irish; but some called Mac an Chaoich, 'son of the blind one' Irish, changed their name to **McKee**.

McKeith F 'son of Wolf' Scots Gaelic.

McKellar F 'son of **Hilary**' in its Scots Gaelic form.

McKelvey, McKelvie Some state that this is the same as McElwee, N 'son of the yellow youth' Irish. An Ulster name, with –ey ten times as common as –ie.

McKendrick See **Enright**; anglicized to **Henderson**.

McKenna F 'son of Cionaodh' Irish. 88th commonest surname in Ireland in 1890.

McKenzie N 'son of Comely' Scots Gaelic. 16th commonest surname in Scotland in 1958 (dropping five places in 100 years). Family name of the earls of Cromartie and the barons Amulree.

McKeone F 'son of **John/Owen**' Irish + Hebrew/Keltic from Greek.

McKeown See **McOwen**.

McKibbin, McKibbon See **McGibbon**.

McKie Form of **McKay**. 99th commonest surname in Scotland in 1958.

McKillop F 'son' Scots Gaelic 'of **Philip**'.

McKim(mie) F 'son of (dim.) **Simon**' in two Scots Gaelic forms.

McKinder, McKindewer See **McIndeor**.

McKinlay, McKinley F 'son of **Finlay**' Scots Gaelic.

McKinnawe F 'son of ?Swimming Hound' Irish.

F: *first name*　　L: *local name*　　N: *nickname*　　O: *occupational name*

McKinness See **McGuinness**.

McKinnon F 'son of ?Fair-born' Scots Gaelic.

McKintosh See **McIntosh**.

McKissack, **McKissock** F 'son of Isaac' in its Scots Gaelic form.

McLachlan F 'son of **Lachlan**' Scots Gaelic.

McLaine See **McLean**.

McLamon(t) O 'son of **Lamond/nt**' Scots Gaelic.

McLane See **McLean**.

McLaren F 'son of **Laurence**' in its Scots Gaelic form. Family name of the barons Aberconway.

McLarty F 'son of Wealthy Prince' Irish.

McLaughlin L 'son of **Laughlin**' Irish. 21st commonest surname in Ireland in 1890, and by 1958 78th in Scotland (by Irish immigration).

McLay F 'son of Brown of the Hill' Scots Gaelic (though popular etymology makes it 'son of the surgeon' Scots Gaelic).

McLean F 'son of the devotee of (Saint) **John**' Scots Gaelic, the –l– being the remains of *gille* 'servant, lad, etc.' 20th commonest surname in Scotland in 1958.

McLeay See **McLay**.

McLehose F 'son of the devotee of (Saint) **Thomas**' in its Scots Gaelic form.

McLeish F 'son of the devotee of Jesus' Scots Gaelic; cf. **Malise**.

McLennan F 'son of the devotee of (Saint) Finnan' Scots Gaelic.

McLeod N 'son of Ugly' Scots Gaelic, second element from O N. 27th commonest surname in Scotland in 1958.

McLoughlin Irish version of **McLachlan**; but also (for a name formerly spelt *O Melaghlin*) 'descendant of the devotee of (Saint) Secundinus' Irish.

McMahon F 'son of Bear' Irish. 64th commonest surname in Ireland in 1890.

McManus F 'son' Irish 'of **Magnus**'.

McMarquis F 'son' Scots Gaelic 'of **Mark**'. A rare Argylls surname.

McMartin F 'son' Scots Gaelic 'of **Martin**'.

McMaster O 'son of the master' Scots Gaelic approximated to the English form, itself from Old French; in Scotland, *master* was a courtesy title of barons' eldest sons and lords' uncles, or for 'schoolmaster'.

McMathan F 'son of Bear' Irish.

McMichael F 'son of the devotee of (Saint) **Michael**' in its Scots Gaelic form; reduced to look like 'son of **Michael**'.

McMillan N 'son of the shaveling/bald-head/tonsured (servant)/ tonsured (religious)' Scots Gaelic. 50th commonest surname in Scotland in 1958.

McMinn L 'son of **Menzies**' Scots Gaelic.

McMorran F 'son of Seal's Slave' Scots Gaelic (were not seals humans under a curse?).

McMullan Irish form of **McMillan**.

McMurchie F 'son of **Murdoch**' Scots Gaelic.

McMyn(n) See **McMinn**.

McNab O 'son of the abbot' Scots Gaelic; a somewhat irregular beginning excusable by making the early chiefs *lay* abbots of Glendochart; the –N– remains from *an* 'the'.

McNaboe N 'son of Premature' Irish.

McNaghten F 'son of Nechtan (= "pure")' Scots Gaelic, though the name has been linked with that of the Roman sea-god Neptune; Hartland Church, Devon, and a chapel in Cheddar Church, Somerset, are dedicated to St Nectan.

McNair Various stocks, with as many interpretations – N 'son of the sallow/tanned one', or ? ?'son of the heir/**Smith**/stranger' all Scots Gaelic.

McNally F 'son of the ? ?wreathed one' Irish.

McNamara F 'son of Hound of the Sea' Irish. 94th commonest surname in Ireland in 1890.

McNaughton See **McNaghten**.

McNeice Ulster variant of **McGenis**.

McNevin N 'son of the little saint' Irish; see **Neven**.

McNic(h)ol F 'son of (dim.) **Nicolas**' in its Scots Gaelic form.

McNid(d)er O 'son of the weaver' Scots Gaelic.

McNiven See **McNevin**.

McNulty L 'son of the Ulsterman' Irish.

McOmie See **McComie**.

McOmish F 'son of **Thomas**' in its Scots Gaelic form.

McOwen F 'son of **Ewan/Owen**' Irish and Scots Gaelic.

McPartland See **McFarlan**.

McPhail F 'son of **Paul**' in its Scots Gaelic form.

McPhee See **McDuffie**.

McPheeters F 'son of the devotee of (Saint) **Peter**' in its Scots Gaelic form.

McPherson O 'son of the parson' Scots Gaelic; cf. **Parsons**. 86th commonest surname in Scotland in 1958. Family name of the barons Strathcarron.

F: *first name*   L: *local name*   N: *nickname*   O: *occupational name*

McPhie See **McDuffie.**

McQuarrie F 'son of Proud /Noble/ ?**Godfrey**' Scots Gaelic.

McQueen F from two sources: 'son of Good-/Well-going' Scots Gaelic, and in Skye 'son' Scots Gaelic 'of Sveinn (see **Swain**)' ON.

McQuillan, McQuillen Probably F 'son' Irish 'of **Hugh**'.

McQuilly N 'son of Cock' Irish and Scots Gaelic.

McQuistan, McQuisten, McQuistin, McQuiston F 'son of **Hutchin**' in its Scots Gaelic form.

McRae Form of **McRaith.**

McRaith F 'son of grace/prosperity' Irish and Scots Gaelic; whence also **McRaw** and forms mistakenly in *McCr–*.

McRanald F 'son of **Ranald/Ronald**' Scots Gaelic; rare.

McRaw See **McRaith.**

McRobb F 'son' Scots Gaelic 'of (dim.) **Robert**'.

McRory F 'son of Red King' Irish and Scots Gaelic; *Rory* often used as an equivalent of **Roderick**.

McRuer O ?'son of the brewer' Scots Gaelic.

McSorley F 'son of **Summerlad**' Scots Gaelic.

McSporran N 'son of the purse' Scots Gaelic.

McTaggart, McTaggert O 'son of the priest' Scots Gaelic; though marriage within priests' orders was illegal and invalid after the 12th century.

McTague O 'son of **Teague**' Irish.

McTavish F 'son of Tammas (Lowlands Scots for **Thomas**)' Scots Gaelic.

McTeague, McTigue See **McTague.**

McTurk F 'son of Boar' Scots Gaelic.

McVarish F 'son of **Maurice**' in its Scots Gaelic form.

McVicar O 'son' Scots Gaelic 'of the vicar' Latin; cf. **McTaggart.**

McWatters F 'son' Scots Gaelic 'of **Walter**'.

McWhirter O 'son of the harper' (often an hereditary office) Scots Gaelic. An Ayrs surname.

McWilliam(s) F 'son' Scots Gaelic 'of **William(s)**'.

Meacham, Meachem, Meachim, Meachin, and (west Midlands and New Zealand variant) **Meacheam** Unless these are sometimes L from **Measham/Mitcham**, they are a late development of **Machin**. The TD reveals 55 –am, 28 –em, 8 –im, 2 –eam, mostly in the west Midlands.

Mead(e) L 'meadow' (originally kept for *mow*ing) OE; –e could show dative after lost preposition. Or O '(seller of) mead' OE, a metonym.
Meade is the family name of the earls of Clanwilliam.

Meaden L First element 'mead(ow)' OE; second ?an OE dative plural

–um (so 'in the meadows') or 'end' OE or 'dene, valley' OE. Guppy counted it only in Dorset.

Meadow L 'meadow' OE. **Meadows** 'of (i.e. at) the meadow'.

Meager N 'lean, skinny' OF (cf. *meagre*).

Meagher F (for O M—) 'descendant of Hospitable' Irish.

Meake See **Meek**.

Meaken, Meakin See **Makin**.

Mear(e) L 'pool/boundary' OE; locality, or places (Meare, Mere) in four counties, all meaning 'pool, lake'. **Mear(e)s** 'of (i.e. at) the pool, etc.'.

Mearns L ?'stewartry, district ruled by a steward' Scots Gaelic from British; probably the place in Renfrews rather than the old name of Kincardines.

Mease Probably a form of **Mayes**. Or see **Meese**.

Measham L 'homestead on the River Mease (cf. *moss*)' OE; place in Leics.

Measures L 'hovels, tumbledown dwellings' OF *masure*; so says Weekley, but the French surname *Mesureur* 'surveyor' suggests that something more elegant is possible. Guppy counted it in Northants.

Meazey, Mecock and **Medcalf(e)** See **Maisey, Maycock** and **Metcalf(e)**.

Meddon L 'meadow hill' OE; place in Devon.

Medley L 'middle island' OE; place in Oxon.

Medlicott L 'middle cottage(s)' OE; locality, or place in Salop, and a Salop–Herefords surname.

Medwin F First element 'reward/meadow/mead (the drink)' OE, second 'friend' OE.

Mee Probably a version of **May**, though differing from it by being so frequent in Lancs.

Meecham, Meechem See **Meacham**.

Meehan F (for O M—) 'descendant of Honourable' Irish.

Meek(e) N 'meek, humble, gentle' ON; *–e* could show weak adjective after lost definite article.

Meekins F '(son) of **Meakin/Makin**'.

Meese L 'moss' OE; locality, or place (*–ce*) in Staffs.

Meg(gi)son F 'son of (dim.) Margaret' (see **Maggs**).

Meggett, Meggitt F double dim. 'Margaret' (see **Maggs**).

Meikle N 'big' OE. Scots dialect.

Meiklejohn N 'big' (see **Meikle**) 'John'.

Melbourn(e), Melburn L Second element 'stream' OE; first element

---

F: *first name*   L: *local name*   N: *nickname*   O: *occupational name*

'mill' OE/'middle' OE scandinavianized/'milds' OE (the plant variously known as *Atriplex, Chenopodium*, fat-hen, wild spinach, orach); places in Derbys/East Yorks/Cambs.

Meldon L 'multicoloured hill' OE, place in Devon; but place in Northd is the same as **Maldon**.

Meldrum L 'bare, bulging ridge' Scots Gaelic; place in Aberdeens.

Melford L 'ford by the hill' OE; place in Suffolk.

Melhuish L 'multicoloured hide of land' OE; place in Devon, and a Devon surname.

Melk N or O 'milk' OE *meolc* (unless there are beares originating in Melk in Austria); cf. **Milk**, which might have reference to an albino.

Mellanby L 'farm of the devotee of (St) Mary' Irish *Maelmuire* +ON; places (Melmerby) in Cumberland and North Yorks, though A. H. Smith suggests 'farm with sandy soil' ON for the second.

Melledew Version of **Merridew** (with an obvious attempt to make it mean 'honeydew', from Latin *mel*).

Mellersh L 'multicoloured ploughland/stubble-field' OE; place (M—'s Farm) in Surrey, and still a Surrey surname.

Mellican See **Millican**.

Mellis Same as **Malise**. Or L 'mills' OE; place in Suffolk.

Mellish See **Melhuish** (rather than **Mellis**).

Melloney, Mellonie F 'black' Greek feminine, from a Greek St Melania who occasioned Cornish girls' names of this shape.

Mellor L 'bare hill' British; places in Ches, Derbys. Lancs; Welsh version would be Moelfre.

Mells L 'mills' OE; locality, or places in Somerset, Suffolk.

Melrose L 'bare moor' British; places in Roxbs, Aberdeens.

Melton L 'middle farm' OE scandinavianized, places in Leics, Lincs, Norfolk, Yorks (three); but place in Suffolk and M— Constable, Norfolk, may be 'mill farm' OE or have the same first element as **Maldon**.

Meluish See **Melhuish**.

Melville L Place in Midlothian named by a man from Émalleville, Eure, 'Amalo's (a doubtful Germanic F) site' OF. Another version is **Melvin**.

Membry, Memory See **Mowbray**.

Mendham L 'Mynda's homestead (his F is from *mund* "protector")' OE; place in Suffolk.

Mendoza L 'mountain' Basque + Spanish suffix; place in Alava province, north-western Spain. Two bearers have earned their way into the *DNB*: Joseph de M—, a Spanish naval officer who settled in

England and won the F.R.S. for work in navigation and nautical astronomy; and Daniel M—, the pugilist, who wrote *The Art of Boxing*.

Menheneott, Menhenet(t), Menhenitt, Menhennett L First element 'stone' Cornish; second an owner whose F is found in ow as *Huniat*; place (–iot) in Cornwall.

Menmuir L Second element 'moor' OE, first doubtful – Johnston suggests 'stone' Welsh and 'little' Scots Gaelic; place in Angus.

Menzies L Scots form of **Manners**; the –z– represents the obsolete letter *yogh* (shaped like a 3 and sounding like *gh*), and the name is correctly pronounced *Mingis*.

Mepham L 'homestead of (an AS called) Mēapa' OE (Ekwall relates his F to our *mope*); place (Meopham, pronounced *mep*–) in Kent.

Mercer O 'merchant, (especially) dealer in luxury fabrics' OF.

Merch See **Murch**.

Merchant O More nearly original form of **Marchant**; cf. **Clark**.

Mercy N 'mercy, compassion' OF. Abstract names are rare and suspect, but ME *merci* 'fine, amercement', from OF *amercie*, is no more satisfactory.

Mere See **Mear**.

Meredith F Last element 'lord' ow; accent on second syllable. Common in Wales and its Border.

Merivale L 'pleasant valley' OE (cf. *merry*)+OF, but first element was once Latin *mira* 'wonderful'; places (Mere–, Merry–) in Herefords, Leics, Warwicks.

Merrall, Merrell F See **Muriel. Merralls, Merrells** '(son) of M—'.

Merrett See **Merri(o)tt**.

Merrick(s) See **Meyrick**; and '(son) of M—'. Guppy counted –ick in Herefords–Salop, Middx.

Merridan L 'pleasant valley' OE (cf. *merry*, **Dean**); place (Meriden) in Warwicks.

Merriday, Merridew English versions of **Meredith** which have also found their way to Ireland.

Merrifield L 'pleasant **Field**' OE; two places in Devon.

Merrill(s) See **Merrall(s). Merrills** counted by Guppy only in Notts.

Merriman N 'cheerful/amusing/pleasant man' OE.

Merri(o)tt L ?'boundary gate' OE; place in Somerset. Or F 'famous Gēat' OE (the Gēats were a southern Swedish tribe, to which Beowulf belonged; the Greeks called them *Gautoi*, some have tried to

---

F: *first name*　　L: *local name*　　N: *nickname*　　O: *occupational name*

say they were Jutes, and the king of Sweden is still king also *Gothorum* – see **Woollatt**).

Merrison N Formally, this is 'son of **Merry**'.

Merry N 'cheerful, amusing, pleasant' OE; really, a south-east dialect form – cf. **Murry**.

Merrygold N 'marigold, golden flower of St Mary' ME.

Merryman See **Merriman**.

Merryweather N 'nice weather' OE – ?from a favourite exclamation, or ?from sunny personality.

Merton L Normally 'place by a lake' OE, places in Devon, Norfolk, Oxon; but place in Surrey (from which the founder of Oxford's oldest college got his name) is ?'(AS called) Famous's place/farm' OE or ? ?'mare farm' OE.

Mervin F 'famous friend' OE; any connection with Welsh F Myrddin (the Merlin of the Arthur story) is doubtful.

Messenger, Messinger O 'messenger' OF (cf. **Massinger**). East Midland surnames.

Messum See **Measham**.

Metcalf(e) N ?'meat-calf' (i.e. 'calf fattened up for food') OE, for a fat man.

Metford L ?'convenient/excellent (cf. archaic adjective *meet*) ford' OE (or ON)+OE; or first element 'mediocre' OE or 'meadow' OE. Chiefly a Somerset surname.

Methley L 'middle wood/clearing' OE scandinavianized; place in West Yorks.

Methuen, Methven L Watson, and Johnston 1934, give this as 'mead (the drink) stone' British, others as 'river-plain' and 'middle' Scots Gaelic; place (–v–) in Perths.

Meux L 'sandbank lake'; place Meaux in East Yorks, Old Norse re-modelled on French place Meaux.

Mew O 'mew, hawks' cage' (for when they were 'mewing' – moulting) OF, for the man who looked after it. On the site where the royal hawks were kept at Charing Cross were built the royal stables called *mews*.

Meyer(s) See **Mayer(s)**.

Meynell L 'abode, (nobleman's) domain' OF *mesnil* (cf. *mansion*, of which this is a dim.); various places in France. Or = **Maynell**.

Meyrick F Welsh form (*Meuric*) of **Maurice**. Preceded by Welsh *Ap* 'son of', it is the probable origin of the name *America*, since, when John Cabot returned to Bristol after his second transatlantic voyage in 1498, the king's pension of £20 was handed to him by the two collectors of customs for Bristol, the senior being Richard Ameryk (also appearing in the Customs Roll as *Amerik* and *Ap Meryke*), who was 'probably the heaviest investor' in the expedition. He lived at Lower Court, Long Ashton, Somerset, from 1491, and his daughter Joan Brook is buried beneath a brass in St Mary Redcliffe, Bristol. (See especially B. Dunning in *Country Life*, 20 June 1963, pages 1507–9.) His title to be the eponym of the continent is surely stronger than the frivolous claim of the Italian Amerigo Vespucci.

Meystre O 'master' OF *maistre* – but whether school-, task-, etc., is not clear (in one poem, it is the master-blacksmith).

Miall Form of **Michael**.

Michael F 'Who is like God?' Hebrew; the Archangel, Captain of the Heavenly Host. **Michaels(on)** '(son)/son of M—'. But the popular forms from OF, in **Mitch-/Mial-/Miel-/Mil-**, are much commoner as surnames.

Micham and **Michell** See **Mitcham** and **Mitchell**.

Michie F Scots dim. of **Michael**.

Micklem L 'big homestead/river-meadow' OE; place (–leham) in Surrey.

Micklethwait(e), **Micklewhite** L 'big **Thwaite**' ON; places in Cumberland, West Yorks.

Mickley L 'big wood/clearing' OE; places in five counties.

Middle L 'middle' (of the village) OE. Or N (same word) for one 'of middle height'.

Middlebrook, **Middleburgh**, **Middlecoat/Middlecott**, **Middledi(t)ch**, **Middlehurst** L 'middle brook, fort/manor, cottage, ditch (but also 'dike'), **Hirst**' OE; localities, or three places (–cott) in Devon, and original form of the town of Middlesbrough, North Yorks.

Middlemas(s), **Middlemiss**, **Middlemist**, **Middlemost** L 'middlemost (part of Kelso, Scotland)' OE. (A seasonal surname 'Michaelmas' is not supported by early forms.) Guppy counted **–miss** in Northumberland.

Middlemore L 'moor set in the middle' OE, as with Middlemoor in Tavistock, Devon, and two places in West Yorks.

Middleton L 'middle place/farm' OE A common surname, and the name of dozens of places from Northd to Devon. The meaning given applies to all save M— on the Hill, Herefords, 'big (cf. *mickle*) farm' OE, and M— Baggot and M— Priors, Salop, 'confluence field farm' OE.

F: *first name*　　L: *local name*　　N: *nickname*　　O: *occupational name*

Middleweek, Middlewich, Middlewick L 'middle **Wick**' OE; localities, or places in Ches, Essex.

Middlewood L 'middle wood' OE; localities, or places in Cornwall, Devon, Herefords.

Midgley L 'wood/clearing infested by midges (gnats)' OE; two places in West Yorks.

Midwinter N From birth/baptism at 'Christmas, midwinter' OE.

Miell See **Michael**.

Miggles F '(son) of **Michael**'.

Mighty N 'mighty, strong, important' OE.

Milborrow, Milbour F 'mild/gentle fortress' OE feminine, in honour of Saint Mildburh, 7th/8th-century princess, abbess of Much Wenlock.

Milbourn(e), Milburn L 'mill stream' OE; places in five counties.

Mildmay N 'gentle maiden' OE; a mocking surname like **Maiden**.

Mileham L 'homestead with a mill' OE; place in Norfolk.

Miles F The Germanic *Milo*, ?connected with Old Slavonic *milu* 'merciful', was brought here by the Normans as *Miles* (nominative) and *Milon* (oblique case). Also involved is *Mihel*, a popular form of **Michael**, making this surname '(son) of **Michael**'. (An O meaning 'soldier' Latin is sometimes possible.) Guppy found it only from Norfolk to Dorset.

Milford L 'ford by a mill' OE; places in ten counties.

Milk N or O 'milk' OE; by Reaney's supposition, the N would be for a looked-down-on milk-drinker or for someone with white hair (and he quotes a 12th-century name meaning 'Milkhead'). Guppy counted it only in Norfolk.

Milkins ?N '(son) of (dim.) **Milk**'.

Mill L Altered from **Miln** (see **Milner**). Or, when not preceded by *de/at*, etc., F dim. '**Miles**' or even dim. '**Millicent**'. **Mills** L 'of (i.e. at) the mill', rather than a plural. Also sometimes F '(son) of M—'. Very common, but less so in the north; **Mill** is far rarer. **Mills** is the family name of the barons Hillingdon.

Millar O Scots form of **Miller**.

Millard Form of **Millward**, common in Glos–Somerset.

Millbourn(e) See **Milbourn**.

Millbrook L 'mill brook' OE; places in six counties.

Millburn See **Milbourn**.

Millen See **Miln**.

Millenste(a)d L 'site with a mill' OE.

Miller Altered from **Milner**, but now much commoner; Guppy found one per cent of the people of Dorset with it in 1890. Eleventh commonest surname in Scotland in 1958, fifth in USA in 1939.

Millerchip, Millership See **Millichap**.

Millers(on) O '(son)/son of the miller' OE.

Millett F dim. '**Miles**'.

Millham L 'river-meadow/homestead with a mill' OE.

Millican, Milligan, Milliken, Millikin See **Mulligan**. But the incidence of **Millican, Millikin** in Cumberland–Northd is (for an Irish name) surprising.

Millicent F 'work strong' Germanic, feminine (once beginning *Amal*–). Charlemagne had a daughter Melisenda. F brought to England after 1066.

Millicha(m)p, Millicheap, Millichip, Millichope L 'valley by the mill hill' OE (in fact, **Mill–Linch–Hope**); place (–hope) in Salop.

Millier See **Miller** (though OE *mylier* meant 'mill-weir/-dam').

Millington L 'mill farm' OE (cf. **Miln**); places in Ches, East Yorks.

Millinship See **Millichap**.

Millman O Still in *OED* for a man who has charge of, or works in, a mill; both elements OE. Counted by Guppy only in Devon.

Milln(s) See **Miln(s)**.

Millward, Millwood O 'mill-keeper' OE – an older word than **Miller**; –**wood** is almost certainly a corruption (there is a place Millwood in West Yorks, but the surname is mainly of the south and west).

Miln L 'mill' OE. **Milne** '(at) the mill' (if –e shows dative after lost preposition). For the –n, see **Milner**. –e (71st commonest surname in Scotland in 1958) is far commoner than –n; **Millen** (found with them in Kent) belongs here, with a glide vowel to ease pronunciation. **Miln(e)s** L 'of (i.e. at) the mill' OE; rarer than –e.

Milner O 'miller' OE; the Old and early Middle English words for 'mill(er)' had this –n–, so that **Miller** (despite its distinction of having its own specific N *Dusty*, from the flour) is an altered later form. Common only in Yorks–Lancs–Derbys–Notts.

Milnthorp(e) L '**Thorp** with a mill' OE+ON; places in Notts, Westmorland, East Yorks.

Milsom Version of **Milson** F 'son of **Miles**' or 'son of Milde (= "mild")' OE feminine.

Milste(a)d L 'middle place' OE; place in Kent.

Milston L 'centre (literally middlest) farm' OE; place in Wilts.

Milton L 'middle farm' OE, in a dozen counties south of Derbys (including five in Somerset); but 'mill farm' OE in a few northern counties and two places in Kent.

F: *first name*　　L: *local name*　　N: *nickname*　　O: *occupational name*

Milverton L 'mill-ford farm' OE; places in Somerset, Warwicks.

Milward and **Mimpriss** See **Millward** and **Mainprice**.

Minchin N 'nun' OE (feminine of *monk*); some disreputable joke lurks.

Minchin(g)ton L 'nuns' farm' OE; place (–g–) in Dorset; a place in Devon is now respelt Minchendown.

Miner O 'miner' OF (a Somerset surname, from the early coal-workings and the lead-mines of Mendip) or '(military) sapper'. **Miners** '(son) of M—'.

Minet(t) N 'dainty, delightful' OF. Reaney also detects a 13th-century female F *Minnota*, dim. of a woman's pet-name *Minna*.

Mingay, Mingey F 'stone dog' Breton *men-ki*, Menguy; found early in Essex, where many Bretons were settled after the Conquest.

Minnie F dim. 'Minna' (see **Minnis**).

Minnis, Minns F '(son) of Minna' ME, a pet-form of some Norman female name (Reaney gives three possibles); cf. **Minett**. Guppy counted **Minns** only in Norfolk.

Minnitt See **Minett**; this dainty name was Daisy Ashford's unerring choice for the flunkey Francis M— in *The Young Visiters*.

Minor(s) See **Miner**; no connection with **Major**, though these terms must have been familiar from pairs of village names.

Minshall L 'Man's shelf/ledge of land' OE; two places (Minshull) on either side of the River Weaver in Ches, and a Ches surname.

Minskip L 'community, common land' OE (cf. *mean, –ship*) scandinavianized; place in West Yorks.

Minster L 'church, monastery, collegiate church, cathedral' OE; locality, or places in Kent, Oxon.

Minter O 'moneyer, coiner' OE. Counted by Guppy only in Kent.

Mintern L 'house where mint grows' OE; place (–ne) in Dorset.

Minto L First element 'hill' British (cf. Welsh *mynydd*), second (–o) as in **Heugh** or **Hough** or **How**; place in Roxbs.

Minton L 'mountain farm' British (cf. **Minto**)+OE; place in Salop (the hill above is still called Longmynd), and a Salop surname.

Minturn See **Mintern**.

Minty L 'island with mint' OE; place (Minety) in Wilts, and a Wilts surname.

Mirfield L 'pleasant **Field**' OE (cf. *merry*); place in West Yorks.

Mirfin Form of **Mervin** found in Yorks.

Miskin N 'paltry, stingy; young man, junior' OF. Mainly a Kent surname.

Missenden L ?'water-lily valley' OE; two places (on the Misbourne) in Bucks.

Misson L ' ?water-lilies' OE; place in Notts.

Mitcham L 'big homestead' OE; place in Surrey. Also **Mitchem** and **Mitchum**.

Mitchel(l) Two certain origins: F popular form of **Michael**; and N 'big' OE (cf. *much* and dialect *mickle*). **Mitchell** was the 24th commonest surname in Scotland in 1958. **Mitchel(l)son** 'son of M—'.

Mitchenson, Mitchinson Versions of **Mitchelson**.

Mitford L 'ford at the confluence' OE; places in Norfolk Northd.

Mitton L 'farm at the confluence' OE; places in Lancs, Staffs, Worcs, West Yorks. **Mitten** is a version of this, not a garment.

Mizen Perhaps for **Misson**, since the place is thus pronounced; but there have been people of this name in Bradford-on-Avon, Wilts, for at least 200 years.

Mobbs See **Mabbs**.

Moberley L 'moot-/assembly-mound clearing' OE; places (–bb–) in Ches, Staffs.

Mobl(e)y L Form of **Moberley**; or 'maple-tree clearing' OE; place (Mobley) in Hamfallow, Glos.

Mockler N 'bad scholar/cleric' OF *mauclerc*.

Mockridge See **Mogridge**.

Moffat(t), Moffett, Moffitt L ?'long plain' Scots Gaelic; place in Dumfs; the surname is found in south Scotland and Cumberland–Northd.

Mogford L Presumably 'Mogga's ford' OE (cf. **Mogridge** – both are Devon surnames).

Mogg F dim. 'Margaret' (see **Maggs**); or the AS male name 'Mogga' of **Mogford, Mogridge**.

Mog(g)ridge L 'Mogga's ridge' OE; place (–ogr–) in Devon, and a Devon surname. There was a family called *Mogg(e)* in Devon in the 1200s and 1300s.

Moignard N 'one-armed' OF.

Moir N 'big' Scots Gaelic.

Mold See **Maud**.

Mole See **Maud**; but a N for a distinguishing 'mole' OE is possible, and Bardsley found two men *de Mol(e)* in Glos in the late 1200s, so it was L too (but 'mole' = 'jetty, causeway, embankment' OF is probably too late a word).

Molesworth L 'enclosure of (an AS called) Mūl (?"muzzle" or ??"mule")' OE; place in Hunts. But there is bound to have been absorption by/of **Mouldsworth**.

Molineux See **Molyneux**.

F: *first name*   L: *local name*   N: *nickname*   O: *occupational name*

Moll F 'Mall' (see **Mallet**). **Mollet(t)**, **Mollitt** dim. '**M—**'. **Mollison** 'son of **M—**'.

Molland L 'land by a bare hill' Welsh *moel*+OE; place in Devon.

Molloy F (for O **M—**) 'descendant of Venerable Chieftain', but also 'descendant of the devotee of (Saint) Aedh' Irish.

Molon(e)y F (for O **M—**) 'descendant of the servant of the church' Irish. 97th commonest surname in Ireland in 1890.

Molseed L Probably from Mole's Head, in Longwood, West Yorks, 'Malle (dim. Mary/Matilda)'s slope' OE (see **Mallett/Maud**).

Molton L 'farm by a bare hill' Welsh *moel*+OE; places (North and South **M—**) in Devon; or for **Moulton**.

Molyne(a)ux O 'miller' OF. Also L 'little mills' OF; two places (Moulineaux) in Seine and Seine-Maritime. **Molyneux** is the family name of the earls of Sefton.

Mompesson L 'Montpinçon (= ?finch/chaffinch hill; though Norman *pinçon* = pincers)' OF; places in Calvados, Manche. A surname grown great from one man, Revd William **M—** (†1709), who heroically confined the plague to Eyam, Derbys, in 1665.

Mona(g)han O (for O **M—**) 'descendant of the monk' Irish.

Monckton See **Monkton**.

Moncrieff(e) L 'hill of the ?tribal tree' British+Scots Gaelic; place (–ff) in Perths.

Monday N '(born on a) Monday' OE; the first element is the genitive singular, *mōnan*, of the word for 'moon'. Reaney suggests also O 'holder of Mondayland' (you worked for your lord on Mondays). The commoner **Munday**, **Mundy**, must sometimes be versions of this.

Money Bardsley's choice of L 'Monnai (Latin F *Modinnus*+suffix)' OF, place in Orne, and O 'monk' OF *moigne*, etc., with *de* and *le* forms to support it, seems reasonable.

Moneypenny N 'many a penny' OE, for a rich man.

Monger O 'seller, trader' OE.

Monk O 'monk' OE, in scandalous jest, or from service at a monastery.

Monkhouse L 'monks' house' OE; locality, or place in Staffs.

Monksfield L '**Field** belonging to monks' OE.

Monkton L 'monks' place/farm' OE; a dozen places in eight counties.

Monro(e) See **Munro**.

Montacute L Latinized version of **Montagu**; place in Somerset with a conical hill above it.

Montagu(e) L 'pointed hill' OF; many places (–a– and –ai–) in France; the principal family derives from a place in Manche. **Montagu** is the family name of the dukes of Manchester and earls of Sandwich.

Montgomerie, Montgomery L 'hill' OF 'of (a Norman called) Man Powerful' OF from Germanic (cf. bride*groom*, *Rich*ard); two places in Calvados.

Montrose L 'moor on the cape' Scots Gaelic; place in Angus.

Monument If Bardsley is right in supposing this to be a corruption of *Monemute* (1191) or of some other early spelling of *Monmouth*, it is 'mouth of the little Wye' Welsh *Mynwy* (now styled in English *Monnow*)+OE.

Mood(e)y, Moodie N 'bold, proud, passionate' OE.

Moon L 'Moyon (Latin F *Modius*+suffix)' OF, place in Manche. Or N 'monk' OF (Norman dialect) *moun*, from some joke now lost. Guppy counted the name in Sussex, Somerset, and Lancs–Yorks.

Mooney N (for O M—) 'descendant of Dumb' Irish.

Moor North and East Yorks form of **Moore**.

Moorby L 'moor/fen farm' ON; place in Lincs.

Moorcock Probably F dim. '**Maurice**'+familiar **Cock**, but the existence of **Morehen** suggests that a N 'moorcock' OE must sometimes be intended – it is hard to see why.

Moorcraft, Moorcroft L '**Croft** in a moor/fen' OE.

Moore F 'the Moor' OF *Maur* from Latin *Maurus*, name of a 6th-century saint. Or N of like meaning, 'darkie'. But those once preceded by *at/de*, etc., are L 'moor, fen' OE, with –e of dative after lost preposition, or from places in Ches and (More) Salop. 39th commonest surname in England and Wales in 1853, 12th in USA in 1939. (In Ireland, often an anglicized form of **O More**, and the 20th commonest surname in Ireland in 1890.) Family name of the earls of Drogheda.

Moor(e)head L 'top/edge of the moor/marsh' OE; locality, or places (Moorhead) in Northd and West Yorks.

Moor(e)house L 'house in a moor/fen' OE; locality, or places (–rh–) in Cumberland, Notts, West Yorks – chiefly a Yorks surname.

Moorman L 'moor-/fen-dweller' OE.

Moorton L Same as **Morton**; places in Glos, Oxon.

Moorwood L 'wood on a moor' OE; locality, or two places in Derbys.

Moraillon, Morellon N 'little darkie' OF (see **Moore**).

Moralee L 'swampy clearing' OE; place (–rr–) in Northd.

Moran N (for O M—) 'descendant of ?Big' Irish (but there are other origins). 56th commonest surname in Ireland in 1890.

Morby See **Moorby**.

Morda(u)nt N 'biting, vehement, sarcastic' OF present participle.

F: *first name*   L: *local name*   N: *nickname*   O: *occupational name*

Mordecai F 'devotee of Marduk' (the Babylonian supreme god) Babylonian, respelt by Jews; despite his pagan name, he shows up well in *Esther*, and the surname is fairly common in South Wales.

Morden L 'hill in a moor/fen' OE; places in Cambs, Dorset, Surrey.

More See **Moore**.

Moreby See **Moorby**; place in East Yorks.

Morecombe L (Not Morecambe, Lancs, which is later than 1771, but) 'valley in a moor' OE; place in Woodleigh, Devon (though Morecombelake, Dorset, has as its first element ?*mort*, late ME for 'young salmon').

Morehen N 'moorhen' OE (cf. **Moorcock**) – but the point of this surname is lost.

Moreland See **Morland**.

Moresby L 'Maurice's farm' second element ON; place in Cumberland.

Moreton L Same as **Morton**, but the place-name is found more south and west. Family name of the earls of Ducie.

Morfee, Morfey N 'ill-omened, devil' OF; more correct would be *Mauf–*.

Morgan F 'sea ?bright' Keltic, still found abundantly as surname and first-name in South Wales. 37th commonest surname in England and Wales in 1853. **Morgans** '(son) of M—', rare. A Morgan, graecized as *Pelagius*, founded our first Christian heresy.

Moriar(i)ty O (for O M—) 'descendant of Mariner' Irish.

Morice, Morison See **Morris(on)**.

Morland L 'moor-/fen-land' OE; or 'grove by a moor' ON; place in Westmorland (cf. **Lund**).

Morley L 'fen/moor clearing' OE; places in Ches, Derbys, Co. Durham, Norfolk, West Yorks, and the surname more widely distributed.

Morpeth L 'murder path' OE; place in Northd; the police station there is an Ancient Monument.

Morphew, Morph(e)y See **Morfee**.

Morrant N 'darkish' OF *Morant* (cf. **Moore**), or Reaney's OF *(de)-morant*, a 'visitor who stays on'.

Morrell N 'little darkie' OF (cf. **Moore**). A Yorks surname.

Morris(h), Morriss F See **Maurice**, or N of like meaning, 'darkie'. **Morrison** 'son of M—'. **Morrish** (especially Somerset–Devon) is as vulgar as saying *liquorish*; –**is** is frequent in Wales, its Border, and the south – 34th commonest surname in England and Wales in 1853; –**ison** is found quite elsewhere (north England, Scotland) – 26th commonest surname in Scotland in 1958 (rising five places in

100 years). **Morris** is the family name of the barons Killanin, **Morrison** of the viscounts Dunrossil.

Morrissey Usually F (for O **M—**) 'descendant of Muiris' Irish. But the Norman family *De Marisco*, L 'of the marsh' Low Latin, became MacMuiris and later **Morrissey**, and this is the bigger stock. Mostly of Cos. Waterford–Limerick–Cork, but almost as plentiful as **Morris** in Ireland.

Morrow L 'row of houses on a moor' OE; locality, or places in Cumberland (two), Somerset.

Morse (a Wilts name), **Morss** Reductions of **Morris**.

Mort N 'stumpy' ME dialect *murt* from Germanic (cf. **Murch**); or the late ME *mort* 'young salmon'. Or F 'Morta' OE. Guppy counted it in Salop, Lancs.

Mortimer, Mortimore L 'dead sea (in the sense of stagnant lake)' OF; place in Seine-Maritime. Both spellings typical of Devon.

Mortlock L 'young salmon stream' late ME *mort*+OE; places Mortlake in Surrey, the former *Mortelake* in Herts, and Mortlocks in Essex.

Morton L 'moor/fen farm' OE; dozens of places in most English counties; in northern places, first element could be originally ON.

Mosedale L 'moss/bog valley' ON; place in Cumberland.

Moseley L Second element 'wood/clearing'; first element either 'marsh/bog', places in Bucks, Notts, West Yorks; or 'field-mouse', place in Worcs; or '(AS called) Moll's (= ?crazy)', place in Staffs; all OE. Some USA bearers are from 17th-century John **Maudesley**. (There are also localities called Moseley in Glos, Herefords, Warwicks.) A West Midlands surname.

Moses F Of unknown meaning – possibly Egyptian rather than Hebrew; the name of the great Jewish leader was sometimes used by medieval Christians, and among Puritans and in Wales after the Reformation. Occurs as a surname chiefly in Mon.

Mosley See **Moseley**; but Guppy found it only further east, in Derbys–West Yorks.

Moss F dim. '**Moses**'. Or L 'marsh, swamp' OE and ON; locality, or place in West Yorks. Mainly a surname of Worcs–Staffs–Ches–Lancs.

Mosscrop L ?'hill in a bog' OE, two places in West Yorks; but it is also an archaic word for the 'tufted clubrush', which must be regarded as just coincidental.

Mossman N or O, a dim. or 'servant of' form of **Moses**. Guppy counted it only in Beds, and this weighs against any supposed northern word meaning 'man who lives in a swamp' OE/ON.

F: *first name*   L: *local name*   N: *nickname*   O: *occupational name*

Mostyn L 'field of the fortress' Welsh *maes-ddin*; place in Whitford, Flints.

Mothersill, Mothersole Reaney gives a choice of: N, the oath 'by my mother's soul' OE+OE; N 'proud soul' OE+OE (cf. **Moody**); and, less credibly, L 'Heart/Spirit Counsel's **Haugh** (*halh*)' OE, place (Moddershall) in Staffs.

Motley L There is a place in Kent, but Bardsley found the name chiefly in Lincs, and his first occurrence of it is Thomas de Motlawe ('moot/assembly hill' OE) in Yorks in 1379; the Kent place means 'moot/assembly field' OE. (No connection with the motley – i.e. mottled – garb of the jester.)

Mottram L '(at) the pig farms' Welsh (*mochdre*) given an OE dative plural after lost preposition; two places in Ches.

Mouat(t) See **Mowat**; when I was last in Unst, the furthest north innkeeper in Britain was a Mouat.

Mould, Moult F 'Maud' in other OF forms; or N 'top of the head' OE *molda*. **Moulds** '(son) of M—'. **Moulson** 'son of M—'.

Mouldsworth L 'enclosure by a hill-top' OE *molda* 'top of the head'; place in Ches. But there is bound to have been absorption by/of **Molesworth**.

Moule (a Worçs name), **Moull** Forms of '**Maud**'. Or N 'top of the head' (see **Mould**).

Moulton L Usually 'Mūl's farm (his F meant ?"muzzle" or ??"mule")' OE or 'farm with mules' OE or (near Yarmouth, Norfolk) 'Proud's farm' OE; places in Ches, North Yorks, Northants–Lincs–Norfolk–Suffolk.

Mouncey, Mounsey L 'little hills' OF; places Monceaux in Calvados and Monchaux in Seine-Inférieure. Guppy counted –s– in Cumberland–Westmorland.

Mount L 'hill' OF.

Mountain Probably L 'mountain' OF, but very rare save in Oxon, Lincs – after all, most of England's real mountains are called by the locals 'fells'; the name could perhaps be for Mounton, localities in Lancs, Mon, and Pembs, but there are three places called Mountain in West Yorks.

Mountjoy L 'Montjoie'; place in Manche. A *montjoie* OF was a cairn set up to mark a victory – especially the spiritual one won by Saint Denis at the site of his martyrdom; the *Montjoie Saint-Denis* was the old war-cry of the French (even in Charlemagne's time, according to the *Song of Roland*).

Moverley L Last element 'clearing' OE; place just over the Lancs border from Todmorden, West Yorks; or for **Moberley**.

Mowat(t) L 'Montaut (= high hill)' OF; several places in France.

Mowbray L 'Montbrai' (first element 'hill' OF; second ?'mud, slime' OF from Gaulish); place in Manche. Counted by Guppy only in Lincs.

Mowle(s) See **Moull** or **Maud**; and '(son) of **M—**'.

Moxham gives **Moxon** a place-name look.

Moxon F 'son of Mog' (a dim. of Margaret; cf. **Maggs**).

Moyes, Moyse The usual medieval spellings of **Moses** (as in Moyse's Hall, Bury St Edmunds).

Moyle N 'bald' Cornish.

Moyne O 'monk' OF, for the same reasons as **Monk**.

Moynihan L (for O M—) 'descendant of Munsterman' Irish.

Mozley See **Moseley**.

Muat Rare version of **Mowat**.

Much N 'big' OE, as in place-names like Much Wenlock.

Mucklestone L 'farm of (an AS called) Mucel' OE; place in Staffs.

Muckridge See **Mogridge**.

Mudd Probably F, either from '**Maud**' or from an AS male name beginning *Mōd*– 'heart, courage', the word which gives us the shiftier *mood*. The topographical word *mud* ME could be a possible L origin.

Mudford L 'muddy ford' OE; place in Somerset; M— Sock, in the parish, is a further refinement.

Mudge A Devon name that could be N 'midge, gnat' in south-western dialect from OE West Saxon *mycg*.

Mugford and **Mugg(e)ridge, Mugridge** See **Mogford** and **Mogridge**. Guppy counted **Muggeridge** in great numbers (0·5 per cent of the yeomen) in Surrey and (0·25 per cent) in Sussex.

Muir L 'moor' OE, with ō fronted and raised to the French *u*/German *ü* sound in Scots dialect. 57th commonest surname in Scotland in 1958.

Muirhead L 'top of the moor' OE, Scots dialect (cf. **Muir**).

Mulcahy F (for O M—) 'descendant of the servant of Warlike' Irish.

Mulcaster See **Muncaster**.

Mule(s) N 'mule' OE, with vowel raised by influence of OF; and '(son) of M—'. Or see **Moull**.

Mulhearn F (for O M—) 'descendant of the devotee of (Saint) Ciaran (of Clonmacnois)' Irish.

Mulholland F (for O M—) 'descendant of the devotee of (Saint) Callan' Irish. An Ulster surname.

F: *first name*   L: *local name*   N: *nickname*   O: *occupational name*

Mullan N (for O **M—**, **McM—**) 'descendant/son of the shaveling/ bald-head/tonsured (servant)/tonsured (religious)' Irish. 70th commonest surname in Ireland in 1890. Also **Mullane** in Co. Cork.

Mullarkey F (for O **M—**) 'descendant of the devotee of (Saint) Erc' Irish.

Mullen(s) See **Mullin(s)**.

Mulligan N (for O **M—**) 'descendant of the (dim.) shaveling, etc.' (see **Mullan**).

Mullinar, Mullin(d)er, Mullinger O 'Miller' OF.

Mullin(s) L 'mill(s)' OF; locality, or one of the many places Moulin(s) in France. Guppy counted **Mullins** in Dorset–Somerset.

Mulrenan F (for O **M—**) 'descendant of the devotee of (Saint) Brendan (see **Brandon**)' Irish.

Mulvihil F (for O **M—**) 'descendant of the devotee of (Saint) **Michael**' Irish.

Mumford L 'strong hill' OF, from various places in Normandy called Montfort; or 'ford of (an AS called) Protector' OE, place (Mundford) in Norfolk. Guppy found it scattered in Bucks, Warwicks, Cornwall, Essex.

Mummery See **Mowbray**.

Muncaster L 'Mūla's (perhaps see **Molesworth**, **Moulton**) Roman fort' OE; place in Cumberland.

Muncey See **Mouncey**.

Mund(a)y Sometimes F 'Protector' ON *Mundi*, including the –*i* inflexion. But the surnames occur chiefly in Hants–Wilts–Oxon– Bucks–Berks, which were not Norse areas, and there must have been absorption of **Monday**.

Munn See **Moon**.

Munro(e), Munrow L 'mouth of the (River) Roe' (in Co. Londonderry) Irish; *Bun*– has become **Mun**– after a preposition; thence to the north of Scotland, especially Ross. **Munro** and its variants, including **Mon–**, were the 68th commonest surname in Scotland in 1958 (dropping 21 places in 100 years).

Munsey See **Mounsey**.

Munton, still found in Essex, is perhaps L for Mundon, Essex, 'hill with a ?palisade/protection' OE.

Murch N 'dwarf' ME.

Murchie, Murchison See **McMurchie**; the **–son** is repetitive.

Murcott L 'moor/fen cottage(s)' OE; places (–ott and –ot) in Northants, Oxon, Wilts, Worcs.

Murdoch, Murdock O 'mariner' Scots Gaelic; cf. **Moriarty**.

Murfin Derbys–Yorks form of **Mervin**.

Murgatroyd L 'Margaret's (see **Maggs**) clearing' OE; lost place in ?Yorks; see **Royds**.

Muriel F 'sea-bright' Keltic; now a rare surname, but the prolific ancestress of **Merr–ll**, **Murr–ll**. All may sometimes be L 'pretty/ pleasant hill' OE (cf. **merry**).

Murph(e)y F (for O M—) 'descendant of Sea Warrior' Irish. The –ey spelling is much rarer than **Murphy**, which is easily the commonest surname in Ireland and was by 1958 the 72nd in Scotland (by Irish immigration).

Murray L The County of Moray, Scotland, 'seaboard settlement' Scots Gaelic from British. 12th commonest surname in Scotland in 1958 (rising seven places in 100 years), and common in Northd– Durham; 18th in Ireland (especially north Ireland) in 1890. Family name of the dukes of Atholl.

Murrell F See **Muriel**. **Murrells** '(son) of M—'.

Murrey, Murrie Forms of **Murray**; but in south-western use may be dialect forms of **Merry**.

Murrill See **Muriel**.

Murrow L 'row (of dwellings) in a moor/fen' OE; place in Cambs.

Murry See **Merry** and **Murrey**.

Murshed ?L 'head/top of the moor' OE.

Murton L Same as **Morton**; places in four northern counties, yet Guppy found it countable only in Kent.

Muscat See **Muskett**.

Muscroft L '**Croft** infested with mice' OE.

Musgrave, Musgrove L '**Grove** full of mice' OE; places in Westmorland, Somerset.

Muskett N 'male sparrowhawk' OF. It was proper for a holy-water clerk when hawking.

Musson Bardsley supposes corruptions of **Muston** or **Misson**.

Mustard O 'mustard(-dealer)' OF, though Reaney would like to add a N meaning, for one with a 'biting tongue'.

Mustell, Mustill N 'weasel' OF. An old Cambs surname.

Musters L 'churches' OF (cf. *monastery*); place Les Moutiers (*Mostiers*, 1155)–Hubert in Calvados.

Musto(e), Mustow L 'hundred meeting-place (literally moot-stow)' OE.

Muston L 'mouse-infested farm' OE or ?'muddy farm' OE, place in Leics; the place in East Yorks may be similar, or had an owner with the ON name *Músi*.

F: *first name*   L: *local name*   N: *nickname*   O: *occupational name*

Mutch Commoner form of **Much**.

Mutlow L 'moot/assembly mound' OE; place in Ches.

Mutter O 'one who speaks at the moot, public-speaker' OE; a good example of the danger of guessing at etymologies.

Mutton N 'sheep' OF. Or O, for a shepherd. Or L, for **Mitton** or **Mytton**.

Muxworthy L 'dungy enclosure' OE (cf. **Oldmixon**); place in High Bray, Devon.

Myall See **Michael**.

Myer(s) L 'marsh' ON, and 'of (i.e. at)' the same, or a plural (cf. *mire*). Or O 'physician' OF, and '(son) of **M—**'.

Myerscough L 'marshy/boggy wood' ON (cf. **Shaw** from OE); place in Lancs.

Mylchreest F 'son of the devotee of Christ' Manx (with contraction of *Mc–* and *Gill*).

Myles See **Miles**.

Mynett, Mynott See **Minett**. John Mynot held Carlton Miniott in North Yorks in 1346; of this family was the savage and jingoistic 14th-century poet Laurence Minot.

Myt(t)on L Same as **Mitton**; places in Salop, Warwicks, Yorks.

N

Nabb F dim. 'Robert'. **Nabbs** '(son) of N—'.

Nairn(e) L The Scots town and county (–n) take their name from the River Nairn, a Keltic word ?related to Latin *no* 'swim'.

Naisbett, Naisbitt See **Nesbit**.

Naish L Form of **Nash**; cf. **Aish**. But there may sometimes be confusion with the N 'nesh, soft, timid, delicate' OE.

Naismith O 'knifesmith, cutler' OE.

Nancarrow L 'stag valley' Cornish.

Nance L 'valley' Cornish; locality, or place in Illogan, Cornwall.

Nancekevill, Nancekivell, Nankevill, Nankivell L 'horse valley' Cornish; place (–nki–) in Cornwall.

Napier, Napper O 'naperer (i.e. table-linen-keeper)' at a great household OF; cf. *apron* (it has lost its first *n*– to the indefinite article), *napkin*. A family motto, *N'a pier* 'has no equal' OF, is a mere pun. **Napper** is common in Berks.

Napton L 'place on a bowl(-shaped hill)' OE; place in Warwicks.

Nares N '(son) of Black' OF (cf. Modern French *noir*).

Narracott, Narramore, Narraway L 'northern cottage(s)', 'north of the moor', 'north of the road' OE; places in Devon (including ten Narracott).

Nash L '(at) the ash tree' OE; early ME *at them* (preposition+masculine dative singular of the definite article) became *atten* and so *'n* – the noun had been of masculine gender in OE. Guppy found a lot in Herts–Bucks–Surrey.

Nathan F 'gift' Hebrew; the Prophet. Post-Reformation or immigrant surname.

Naunton See **Newton**; places in Glos, Worcs.

Nayland L '(at) the island' OE (cf. **Nash**); place in Suffolk.

Nayler, Naylor O 'nail-maker' OE.

Nayshe Form of **Naish**; –e could show dative after lost preposition.

Neal(e), Neall F 'champion' Irish, brought here by Scandinavian settlers from Ireland, and by the Normans; a Latin form was made for it (whence we derive F *Nigel*) as if it were connected with Latin *niger* 'black, dark'. Of the many spellings in this group, **Neale** is the commonest.

Neam(e) N 'dwarf' OF *nain* or 'uncle' OE *ēam*, according to Reaney; and though in the latter he gives no early forms to account for 'mis-

---

division of syllable', the use of *mine eme* and *thine eme* in ME must have occasioned it. Guppy found **Neame** countable in Kent.

Neap See **Neep**.

Nears N Possibly '(son) of Black' OF *neir*.

Neat(e) O 'ox-/cow-(herd)' OE, a metonym; cf. *neat's-foot-oil*.

Neave N 'nephew' OE. Counted by Guppy only in Norfolk–Suffolk, Kent. **Neaves** '(son) of N—'.

Nebbs N Possibly '(son) of Bill/Beak/Nose/Face' OE.

Neck N 'neck' OE, for some oddity of it.

Needham L 'need/poverty homestead, misery farm' OE; places in Derbys, Norfolk, Suffolk (three). Found by Guppy most commonly in Lincs–Leics–Derbys–Staffs. Family name of the earls of Kilmorey.

Needle(r) O 'needle(-maker)' OE.

Neep N 'turnip' OE (as in modern Scots), ?from growing them.

Neeve(s) See **Neave(s)**. Guppy assigns **Neeve** to Suffolk.

Negus ?L Forms in the 1500s and 1600s end in –ose, –oose, –us, –house; it may be a –house name like **Loftus**, and 'neighbouring house' OE *nēah + hūs* is feasible. Guppy counted it only in Beds; it was also known around Norwich.

Neighbour N 'neighbour' OE (one whose **Bower** was *nigh*).

Neil(d), Neill, Nell F Forms of **Neal** (one with parasitic –d). **Neilson** 'son of N—'.

Nelm(e)s L '(at) the elms' OE, where N— remembers the –m of the dative plural of the definite article after the lost preposition; cf. **Elm(e)s**.

Nelson F 'son of **Nell**' (and so back to **Neal**). 25th commonest surname in USA in 1939, and counted by Guppy most thickly from Cumberland to Norfolk.

Nepean L 'little valley' Cornish.

Nesbit(t) L 'bend like a nose (literally nose bight)' OE; places in Co. Durham, Northd, Berwicks.

Nesfield L 'open land for cattle' (cf. **Neat**) OE; place in West Yorks.

Nesmith See **Naismith**.

Ness L 'headland, projecting ridge' OE/ON; locality, or places in Ches, Salop, North Yorks. But sometimes a corruption of **Nash**.

Nethercoat, Nethercot(e), Nethercott L 'lower cottage' OE; places in adjacent Devon, Somerset, Glos, Oxon, Warwicks, Leics.

Netherton L 'lower place' OE; places in thirteen counties (more than one in several of them).

Netherwood L 'lower wood' OE.

Netley L 'deserted/desolate/let-alone clearing' OE, place in Hants (originally more like *Letley*); but place in Salop is 'clearing with nettles' OE; and N— Marsh, Hants, is 'wet clearing' OE.

Nettleship L ' ?**Hope** with nettles' OE. A Yorks surname.

Nettleton L 'place in the nettles' OE; places in Lincs, Wilts.

Neve See **Neave**. Ethel Le Neve, who eloped, disguised as a youth, with Dr Crippen, represents a Gallic refinement of this.

Neven N 'little saint' Irish.

Nevett A really defeatist Norman spelling of **Knight** (the French shy away from consonant-clusters).

Neville L 'Neuville (= new place)' OF; 150 places in France, including Calvados; but the great Durham family were from Néville in Seine-Maritime. Family name of the barons Braybrooke.

Nevin F See **Neven**. **Nevins** '(son) of N—'.

New N 'new(-comer)' OE. Or L '(at) the yew-tree' OE (cf. **Nash**). A Glos surname. **Newson** 'son of N—', or corrupted from **Newsom**.

Newall L 'new hall/manor-house' OE (see **Newhall**). Chiefly a Ches surname.

Newark L 'new building' OE (cf. *clerk of works*); places in Northants, Notts (these were forts), and Surrey (a priory).

Newbald L See **Newbold**; two places in East Yorks.

Newbegin See **Newbiggin**.

Newber(r)y L See **Newbury**. Guppy found it only in Warwicks, Devon, Beds.

Newbiggin L 'new building' OE+ME (from ON); places in five northern counties.

Newbo(u)ld, Newbolt L 'new building' OE; places in eight contiguous Midland and northern counties, and a surname of these counties.

Newbrough L 'new market-town/borough' OE, place in Northd; or 'new fort', cf. **Newbury**; or from places Newburgh, Lancs, North Yorks, or one of the places (e.g. in Staffs) called Newborough.

Newbury L 'new market-town' OE (if referring to N—, Berks, founded in twelfth century) or 'new fort' (see **Bury**); also places in Essex, Somerset, Wilts.

Newby L 'new farm' OE+ON; places in Cumberland, Westmorland, Yorks (six).

Newcomb(e), Newcombes, Newcome N 'newly arrived' OE; only **Newcome** is a reasonable spelling. Guppy found **Newcombe** common in Devon.

Newcomen L 'recent arrival' OE, from the past participle *cumen*

F: *first name*   L: *local name*   N: *nickname*   O: *occupational name*

'having come'. The inventor of the atmospheric steam-engine was from Devon.

Newell, Newill L 'newly-cultivated/-acquired hill/**Haugh**' OE; or for **Newall** or **Neville** or **Noel**/**Nowell**.

Newhall L 'new hall/manor-house' OE; places in Ches, Derbys, Herts, Warwicks, West Yorks.

Newham L 'new homestead' OE; places in Northd, North Yorks; cf. **Newnham**.

Newhouse L 'new house' OE.

Newill See **Newell**.

Newington L See **Newton**. Guppy found it countable only in Sussex.

Newiss See **Newhouse**.

Newland L 'newly acquired/cultivated land' OE; locality, or places in Glos, Lancs, Worcs.

Newman N 'new man/settler, newcomer' OE (from another form of the OE word for 'new' comes **Nyman**). Widespread, especially west Midlands. (No proof that it may have sometimes absorbed **Newnham**.)

Newnham L '(at) the new (newly acquired/cleared/built) homestead' OE, with –n– a relic of the weak dative adjective needed after the lost preposition and definite article; places in many counties (and Nuneham Courtenay, Oxon).

Newport L 'new town' (especially one with market rights) OE+OE from Latin ; places in many counties.

News(h)am, Newsholme, Newsom(e) L '(at) the new houses' OE dative plural after lost preposition; places in five northern counties, especially Yorks, and mainly West Yorks surnames.

Newstead L 'new site/farmstead' OE; places in Northd, North Yorks, and (with meaning 'new monastery') Lincs, Notts.

Newsum See **News(h)am**.

Newton L 'new place/homestead/farm/village' OE – probably the commonest English place-name, found in over 100 villages from Northd to Cornwall and even in Wales; but Ekwall shows how in a few southern counties its place is taken by forms keeping the OE weak adjective in –n after a lost definite article – **Naunton, Newington**, Newnton – and by Niton. Guppy found the name countable from Northd to Cornwall.

Niall A version of **Neal** impaired by speculation on what he did with his Nine Hostages.

Nibbs F '(son) of (dim.) **Isabell**'; cf. **Ibbs. Niblett** is a double dim., found in Glos.

Nichol(ds), Nicholas(s), Nichole(tt)s, Nicholl(s), Nichols(on) F Forms (with added –**h**–) of **Nicolas**, its dims., and ‘(son)/son of N—’. –**lass** very rare; –**letts** from double dim;. –**olls** is easily the commonest English surname from the F, but –**ols** was the 50th commonest surname in U S A in 1939; –**lson** is typically north and Scots.

Nickal(ls), Nickel(s), Nickell(s), Nicklas(s), Nickle(ss), Nickol(ds), Nickol(l)s, Nickson F Forms of **Nicol**, **Nichol**, etc. Guppy counted only –**less**, in Worcs.

Nicol F dim. ‘**Nicolas**’. 80th commonest surname in Scotland in 1958. Rarely L, from a Norman mishandling of **Lincoln**.

Nicolas F ‘victory people’ Greek. The patron saint of children, mariners, pawnbrokers, wolves, and Russians naturally had a great vogue. Spelling –**c**– is original, the –**h**– an intrusion but far commoner. Hence many surnames in Nic-/Nich-/Nick-/Nix-.

Nicole, Nicoll(e) F Forms of **Nicol**. **Nicol(l)s** ‘(son) of N—’. **Nicolson** ‘son of N—’. Some of these are rarities, but **Nicolson** holds the field with **Nicholson** in the north and Scots Lowlands, and is the family name of the barons Carnock.

Nightingale N ‘nightingale (literally “night-singer”)’ OE, from a sweet voice.

Niker N ‘water-sprite’ OE (often found as first, i.e. owner’s, element of field-names).

Ninham L Same as **Newnham**; place in IoW.

Ninnim L ‘at the enclosed/in-taken field’ ME *at then innom* from OE/ON.

Nisbet(t), Nisbit L See **Nesbit**; but Nisbet in Jedburgh, Roxbs, is said to be ‘ness/nose+bit/mouthful’ ON, a projecting site. The surname is found chiefly in south Scotland.

Niven Commoner form of **Neven**.

Nixon F ‘son of (dim.) **Nicolas**’. A northern surname.

Noad L ‘(at) the pyre/ash-heap/pile’ OE; see **Oade**, and N– of **Nash**.

Noake(s) See **Noke(s)**. Guppy counted **Noakes** only in Sussex–Kent.

Noar L ‘(at) the bank/slope’ OE; see **Over**, and N– of **Nash**.

Nobbs, Nobes F ‘(son) of (dim.) **Robert**’.

Noble N ‘notable, noble’ OF. Counted by Guppy only in West Yorks.

Noblet(t) N dim. ‘**Noble**’. Or F, double dim. (*Nob-el-ot*) of *Nob*, itself a dim. of **Robert** (cf. **Nobbs**).

Noel F ‘Christmas’ OF, from birth or baptism then. Family name of the earls of Gainsborough.

Noke(s) L ‘(at) the oak(s)’ OE; see N– of **Nash**.

Nolan F (for O N—) ‘descendant of (dim.) **Noble**’ Irish.

F: *first name*   L: *local name*   N: *nickname*   O: *occupational name*

Norburn L 'northern stream' OE.

Norbury L 'northern fort/manor-house.' OE; places in five counties, including Ches, and a Ches surname.

Norcott L Same as **Northcott**; places in Glos, Herts.

Norgate L 'north gate' (of a walled town, or of a castle) OE.

Norgrove L 'northern **Grove**' OE. A Herefords–Salop surname.

Norman(d) L 'Northman, Viking' OE (used also as a F by 1066) or 'Norman' (which meant the same thing originally) OF – but only the latter meaning will carry the alternative **–d**. The present vogue of the F is recent and apparently non-U; the surname in **–n** is widespread, and obviously of many stocks.

Norris(h) L 'northerner' OF, naturally commonest in Midlands and south. But also O 'nurse' OF. With **Norrish** cf. **Morrish**; it is a Devon version.

North L 'newcomer from the north, dweller to the north of the village' OE. Family name of the earls of Guilford.

Northam L 'northern river-meadow' OE; places in Devon, Hants, and a Devon surname.

Northcliffe L 'northern cliff' OE; locality, or place in East Yorks.

Northcote, Northcott L 'northern cottage' OE; about ten places in Devon, and others in Cornwall, Middx, and **–cott** is a Devon–Cornwall surname. **Northcote** is the family name of the earls of Iddesleigh.

Northcroft L 'northern **Croft**' OE.

Northern L 'from the north' OE.

Northfield L 'northern **Field**' OE; locality, or places in seven counties.

Northmore L 'northern moor/fen' OE; places (–moor) in Lancs, Oxon, Somerset, but counted by Guppy only in Devon.

Northolt L Originally '(at) the northern **Haugh**s (*halh*)' OE dative plural; place in Middx.

Northorpe L 'northern **Thorp**' OE; place in Lincs.

Northover L 'northern river-bank' (of the Yeo) OE; place in Somerset.

Northwood L 'northern wood' or 'north of the wood' OE; locality, or places in a dozen counties from Salop to IoW.

Norton L 'northern/north-facing place/farm/village' or 'north of the village' OE; places in most English counties, but counted as a surname by Guppy only in Dorset–Somerset and Norfolk–Suffolk. Family name of the barons Grantley and barons Rathcreedan.

Norwell L 'northern spring/stream' OE; place in Notts.

Norwich L 'northern town' (a developed meaning of **Wick**) OE, the Norfolk city.

Norwood L Same as **Northwood**; places in nine counties.

Notley L 'nut wood' OE; places in Bucks, Essex, Herts.

Nott N 'bald, cropped' OE. Counted by Guppy only in Worcs–Herefords, Herts–Essex, Devon. **Notts** '(son) of N—'.

Nottingham L 'homestead of the family/folk of (an AS called) Snot (connected with *snot* = "nasal mucus", and *snout*)' OE; place in Notts.

Notton L 'wether-sheep/cattle farm' OE; places in West Yorks, Dorset, Wilts.

Nourse See **Nurse**.

Nowell F See **Noel** (though this English version of the OF word even meant 'Hurrah!' – as when Henry V was welcomed back to London after Agincourt – or 'news', French *nouvelles*).

Noy F 'Noah (= long-lived)' Hebrew, sometimes from acting the part in a play (cf. **Virgin**). **Noyce**, **Noyes** '(son) of N—'.

Noyle Probably for **Knoyle**.

Nunn O 'nun' OE; either recording some scandal, or describing a demure and prissy man. Guppy found many in Suffolk, some in nearby Essex.

Nunney L 'nuns' island' OE (but first element may be an owner's F); place in Somerset.

Nurse O 'nurse' OF. Mentioned by Guppy only in Norfolk.

Nutbeam, Nutbeem L 'nut-tree' OE; locality, or place (–bane) in Hants.

Nutcombe L 'valley with nuts' OE; four places in Devon, so that it is not surprising to find a memorial in Exeter Cathedral to the Revd Nutcombe **Nutcombe**.

Nutley L 'wood/clearing with nuts' OE; places in Hants, Sussex.

Nuttall (rarely **Nuthall**) L '**Haugh** (*halh*) where nuts are found' OE; place in Lancs also called Nuthalgh; or Nuthall, Notts; a Lancs–Derbys surname.

Nye L '(at) the island' OE; see **Eye**, and N– of **Nash**; locality, or place in Somerset.

Nyland L '(at) the island' OE (cf. **Nayland**); locality, or places in Dorset, Somerset. Our –s– in *island* is an incorrect borrowing from OF.

Nyman See **Newman**.

F: *first name*   L: *local name*   N: *nickname*   O: *occupational name*

O

Oade L 'pyre/ash-heap/pile' OE, with **–e** ?for dative after lost preposition. Or F *Odo* 'riches' OF from Germanic.

Oak L 'oak tree' OE. **Oake** '(at) the oak(s)' OE, the **–e** for dative (singular or plural) after lost preposition; locality, or place in Somerset. **Oakes** 'of (i.e. at) the oak' OE, or a plural; counted by Guppy only in Ches.

Oakden L 'oak valley' OE; two places (now Ogden) in Lancs.

Oakeley L 'oak wood/clearing' OE.

Oakey L 'oak copse' OE (cf. **Hay**).

Oakford L 'ford at the oak(s)' OE; places in Devon, Dorset (three Oke–).

Oakhill L 'hill with oaks' OE; places in Somerset, Staffs, Sussex.

Oakley L 'oak wood/clearing' OE; places (also –leigh) in twelve Midland and southern counties. Counted by Guppy only in Staffs–Warwicks.

Oaten F 'riches' Germanic *Odo/Otto*, in an OF version *Oton*.

Oates F Same meaning as **Oaten**, but in an OF version *Otes*.

Oatley L 'clearing/field where oats are grown' OE; locality, or place (Ote–) in Salop.

Oatten See **Oaten**.

Oborne L 'winding stream' OE; place in Dorset.

O Brien F 'descendant of **Brian**' Irish. Sixth commonest surname in Ireland in 1890. Family name of the barons Inchiquin, legitimist kings of Ireland.

O Buhilly F 'descendant of Boy' Irish.

O Connell See **Connell**.

O Con(n)or See **Connor**.

Odam N 'son/brother-in-law' OE. **Odams** '(son) of O—'.

Oddie, Oddy F Same meaning as **Oaten**, but in an OE or ON version.

Odell L 'hill where woad grows' OE (it was prized as a blue dye); place in Beds, and a Beds–Herts–Bucks surname.

Odger F 'wealth spear' OF from Germanic. **Odgers** '(son) of O—'. Despite their non-Keltic background, Guppy found them only in Cornwall. **Odges** must be a variant of **Odgers**.

Odiam L 'wooded homestead' OE; place (Odiham) in Hants.

O Donnell F 'descendant of **Donald**' Irish. 44th commonest surname in Ireland in 1890.

O Donovan N 'descendant of Dark Brown' Irish.

Offer O 'goldsmith' OF (cf. Modern French *or*, and **Feaver**).

Offord L 'upper ford' OE; two places in Hunts.

Ogborn(e), Ogbourn(e), Ogburn L 'stream of (an A S called) Occa' OE; places (Ogbourne St George and O— St Andrew) in Wilts, on a stream now misnamed the Og.

Ogden L See **Oakden**; but a third place in Lancs is the valley of an A S owner whose name was related to 'ugly'.

Ogg N 'young' Scots Gaelic.

Ogilvie, Ogilvy L Johnson suggests Welsh *uchel* + Gaelic *bheinn*, 'high hill'; place (–ie) in Angus. The second spelling is the family name of the earls of Airlie.

O Hagan F 'descendant of Young' Irish.

O Haire, O Hare, O Hear F 'descendant of Sharp/Angry' Irish.

O Hea F 'descendant of **Hugh**' Irish.

O Kane F 'descendant of Warrior' Irish.

Oke See **Oake**.

O Keef(f)e N 'descendant of ?Gentle/Tender/Beautiful' Irish. These, and forms without **O**, were the 92nd commonest surname in Ireland in 1890.

Old N 'old, senior' OF. Counted by Guppy only in Cornwall.

Oldacre, Oldaker L 'old ploughland' OE (cf. **Acker**).

Oldbury L 'old fort (a pre-A S camp)' OE; places in five counties.

Older See **Alder**; it acknowledges the rounding of **Al–** in southern speech.

Oldfield L 'long-/formerly-cultivated **Field**' OE; locality, or places in six counties.

Oldham L 'long-/formerly-cultivated river flat' OE + ON (once –Holm); place in Lancs.

Oldland L Probably 'neglected arable land' OE; place in Glos.

Oldmixon L 'old dunghill' OE; place in Somerset near Weston-super-Mare.

Oldreave, Oldreive O 'old official/steward/sheriff' OE. Chiefly Devon surnames.

Oldridge L 'dairy-farm among alders' OE; places (Aldridge) in Staffs and elsewhere. Or F, a version of **Aldrich**.

Oldroyd L 'old clearing' OE, Yorks dialect (cf. **Royds**).

O Leary See **Leary**.

Oliphant Reaney allows this to be 'elephant' ME only as a late sign-name; the earlier occurrences are from a choice of F sources. But the clumsy adversary of Chaucer's Sir Thopas was Sir Olifaunt.

Olive F 'olive' Latin feminine, the name of two saints. Or = **Olliff**.

F: *first name*   L: *local name*   N: *nickname*   O: *occupational name*

Oliv(i)er F Charlemagne's peer, Roland's friend Oliver, must have borne a Germanic name, but Germanic *Alfihar* 'elf army' (cf. **Harford**) would need to be much changed, and ON *Olaf* (see **Olliff**) is even less likely; anyway, in the popular mind the shaping influence was OF *oliv(i)er* 'olive branch'. Naturally, the F lost face at the Restoration, but it now has some currency again.

Ollerenshaw, Ollerearnshaw L 'Shaw with alders' OE; place (–en–) in Derbys, and a Ches–Derbys surname.

Olliff(e) F 'Olaf (= relic of the gods)' ON. Or = **Olive**.

O Lynn Ulster form of **O Flynn**.

Oman(d), Omond F 'great-grandfather protector' ON, or (losing an *H*–) 'high protector' OE. Chiefly Orkney and Shetland surnames.

O More N 'descendant of Stately' Irish.

On This extraordinary surname, instanced in South Wales, is ?for **Onn**.

O Neil(l) (Rarely **O Neal(e)**, **O Neall**) F 'descendant of **Neal**' Irish. Tenth commonest surname in Ireland in 1890.

Onions (or, as if Irish) **O Nions** F '(son) of **Ennion**'. Rarely, O '(seller of)onions' OF. Counted by Guppy only in Salop.

Onley L 'lonely glade' OE; place in Northants.

Onn L ?'kiln' Welsh, place in Staffs; or ? ?'ash-trees' Welsh.

Openshaw L 'unenclosed **Shaw**' OE; place in Lancs.

Oram F Same as **Orme**; but it is a Somerset name, and the Norse did not penetrate Somerset, so it may be a concealed place-name in –ham.

Orchard L 'orchard' (the two stems survive in *wort* and *yard*) OE, locality, or places in Devon, Somerset; but place in Dorset is 'edge of the wood' Welsh.

Ord(e) L 'spear, point (i.e. spit, projecting ridge)' OE; locality, or place in Northd, and **Ord** is a Northd–Co. Durham surname.

Ore L 'slope, hillside; shore, bank' OE, locality, or places (also Oare) in four southern counties; but Oare, Somerset, is a British river-name meaning?.

Orford L 'upper/Irishmen's/seashore ford' OE; places in Lancs/Lincs/Suffolk, though the second may be named from an owner in its first element; the surname is mainly of Norfolk–Suffolk, so the Suffolk place is the likeliest origin.

Orgill N 'pride' OF.

Oriel F 'fire strife' Germanic feminine, and unconnected with the overhanging window or the Oxford college.

Orlebar L '?pasture/?grove/?burial-mound/?hill of the family/folk of (an A S whose pet-name was based on) Spear/Sword-point (cf. **Ord**)' OE; place (Orlingbury) in Northants.

Orledge, Orlich O 'clock(-maker)' OF, a metonym.

Orme F 'snake, dragon' ON *Orm* (Great Ormes Head, Caern, is the ON equivalent to OE Worms Head, Glam). **Ormes** '(son) of O—'.

Orm(e)rod L 'Orm's clearing' ON+OE (cf. **Orme, Roads**); place in Lancs, and Lancs–West Yorks surnames. The owner's F may have been a compound of *Orm*.

Ormiston L 'Orm's farm' ON+OE (see **Orme**); places in East Lothian and Roxbs.

Ormond(e) L 'east Munster' Irish (cf. **Desmond**). The surname has a foothold in South Wales.

Ormsby L 'Orm's (or a compound of this) farm' ON (cf. **Orme**); places (also –mes–) in Lincs, Norfolk, North Yorks.

Ormside L 'Orm's hill (literally head)' ON (cf. **Orme**)+OE; place in Westmorland.

Orpet(t) N 'valiant, vigorous' OE *orped*; also made to look like a L **Orpwood**.

Orrell L 'hill where ore is found' OE; two places in Lancs.

Orton L Same as **Overton**; places in five counties (including Leics, Warwicks); but place in Cumberland is 'Orri's (= Black Cock) farm' ON+OE. Chiefly a Leics–Warwicks surname.

Orwin F 'boar friend' OE.

Osbaldeston, Osbaldiston, Osbaldstone L '(AS called) (pagan) God Bold's farm' OE; place in Lancs.

Osborn(e), Osbourn(e), Osburn F '(pagan) god man/warrior' OE; but the F is perhaps always from ON, with second element meaning 'bear' (the animal); also reintroduced (with this latter origin) by the Normans. **–orne** easily the commonest form, and the family name of the dukes of Leeds. (The place on IoW isn't connected – so neither is the biscuit.)

Oscroft L '**Croft** with oxen' OE; place in Ches.

Osgathorp(e) L '**Osgood's Thorp**' ON; place in Leics.

Osgerby L '**Osgood's** farm' ON; places (Osgodby) in Lincs (three), East and North Yorks, and (Osgoodby) North Yorks.

Osgood F '(pagan) god god' OE; or, if from Old Norse F *Ásgautr*, the second element is a name of Odin cognate with OE *gēotan* 'pour, sacrifice'.

Osler O 'bird-catcher, poulterer' OF (cf. Modern French *oiseau*).

Osman(t), Osmon(d), Osmont See **Osmund**.

F: *first name*   L: *local name*   N: *nickname*   O: *occupational name*

Osmaston L 'Osmund's farm' OE/ON+OE; two places in Derbys.

Osmotherley L 'Osmund's mound/clearing' ON+OE; places in Lancs/North Yorks.

Osmund F '(pagan) god protector' OE or ON.

Ostler O 'innkeeper, keeper of lodgings' OF.

Ostridge O 'hawk(er), falcon(er)' OF (ultimately from Latin word meaning 'of Asturias', Spain); no connection with *ostrich*.

Oswald F '(pagan) god ruler' OE or ON. Its popularity was established by the sainted king of Northumbria (†642).

Otes See **Oates**.

Othen F 'Odin, Woden' OE; for the sense of 'divine frenzy, prophecy' in this alarming pagan name, cf. **Wood**.

Ott F Same meaning as **Oaten, Oates,** but without the OF inflexion.

Ottaway See **Ottoway**.

Otter O 'otter(-hunter)' OE. Or F 'dread army' ON.

Ottewell, Ottewill F 'Otuel' OF dim. of *Odo* 'riches' Germanic (see **Oaten**).

Ottoway F 'Otois' OF dim. of *Odo* 'riches' Germanic (see **Oaten**).

Oughtred F 'dawn/dusk counsel' OE.

Outlaw N 'outlaw' ON, a surname happily settled in USA.

Outridge F 'dawn powerful' OE (cf. **Woolrich**).

Ovens L 'of (i.e. at) the oven/furnace' OE, or a plural.

Over L 'river-bank/hill-slope' OE; locality, or places in Cambs/Ches, Derbys, Glos (Littleover, Mickleover, several just Over).

Overal(l) L 'upper hall' OE.

Overbeck L 'across the stream' OE+ON.

Overblow L 'of the smelters' OE, the second element of Kirkby O—, West Yorks, and a Yorks surname.

Overbury L 'upper earthwork' OE; place in Worcs.

Overend L 'upper end' (of a place) OE or 'end of the slope' OE (cf. **Over**).

Overton L 'river-bank/hill-slope/upper farm' OE (*ōfer/ofer/ufera*); places in nine counties, of which those in Lancs, North Yorks are on river-banks. Counted by Guppy only in Lincs.

Overy L 'beyond the river/island' OE; locality, or place (over the Thame from Dorchester) in Oxon.

Owen F See **Ewan**, with which it is certainly connected – cf. the entangled Saints Owen (of churches in Bromham, Beds, and Hereford) and Ewan (Bristol). **Owen** is the commonest of the whole group, especially in Wales. **Owens** '(son) of O—'; much rarer in Britain, but 51st commonest surname in USA in 1939.

Ox This tiny surname at least doesn't look like a preposition, as do

By and **On**; it must either be N 'ox' OE (?from tending them) or =
Oakes.

Oxberry, Oxborough, Oxborrow, Oxbrow, Oxburgh, Oxbury L
'fort/manor where oxen are kept' OE; place (–borough) in Norfolk.

Oxby L 'ox farm' OE+ON.

Oxenham L 'water-meadow/island with oxen' OE+ON; place
(–holme) in Westmorland.

Oxford L 'ford for oxen' OE, the Oxon city.

Oxlade L 'oak **Slade**' OE. (No early forms exist of Oxlode, Cambs,
which is ?'ox-track' OE, second element as in our verb *lead*.)

Oxley L 'clearing/field for oxen' OE; place in Staffs.

Oxnard O 'herder of oxen' OE.

Oxton L 'place/farm where oxen are kept' OE; places in Ches, Notts,
West Yorks.

Oyler O 'dealer in oil' OF.

Ozanne F 'Hosanna! (= ?Save now ?Save, pray)' Hebrew feminine.
Or perhaps a N from birth/baptism on Palm Sunday, when it was
sung.

F: *first name*   L: *local name*   N: *nickname*   O: *occupational name*

P

Pace, Pack F 'Easter' (cf. **Patch**, and *pace-eggs* for 'Easter eggs') ME; or (in the case of **Pace**) 'peace, concord' OF.

Pac(e)y L 'Pacy' in Eure, OF from a Roman F *Paccius*+suffix.

Packer O '(?wool-)packer' ME from Germanic.

Packman Later form of **Pakeman**.

Packwood L 'Pacca (= ?Pack/Bundle)'s wood' OE; place in Warwicks.

Padbury L 'Padda's fort' OE or 'fort with toads/frogs (to which Padda's name may be related)' OE; place in Bucks, and an Oxon surname.

Paddison See **Pattison**.

Paddock N 'toad/frog' OE. Sometimes ?L 'paddock, enclosure' OE – variant of **Parrock**. Counted by Guppy only in Salop.

Paddon L 'Peatta's farm (his name is ? ?connected with **Peat**)' OE; place in Devon, and a Devon surname.

Padfield L '**Field** with toads/frogs' OE; place in Derbys (or first element may be F of AS owner), but chiefly a Somerset surname.

Padget(t) See **Paget**.

Padley L 'clearing with toads/frogs' OE; place in Derbys (or as in **Padfield**).

Pagan F Nearer to the original Latin than **Pain/Payn**, but rarer.

Page O 'page' OF; an even smaller pageboy was **Paget**. **Page** is not in general a northern surname.

Paget(t) O 'little page' OF; cf. **Page**. This immature surname was no bar to promotion; it is the family name of the marquesses of Anglesey. Guppy counted it only in Leics–Rutland.

Paige Form of **Page** found by Guppy in Devon, Sussex.

Pailthorp(e) L '**Thorp** with toads/frogs' OE or '**Thorp** of an AS called Toad/Frog' OE; place (Pallathorpe) in Bolton Percy, West Yorks, called Pailthorpe in 1591.

Pain(e) F 'villager, country-dweller', but later 'pagan', OF from Latin. Theories that the F was given to children baptized late, or to backsliding Christians, may occasionally be right, but it was early a F with no intended meaning. **Paine** is fairly common. **Paines** '(son) of **P**—'; rare.

Painter O 'painter' OF. A Midland and south-western surname.

Paish See **Pash**.

Paisley L 'church, cemetery' British or Scots Gaelic, from Latin

281

basilica (cf. Bassaleg, Mon). (So Watson; but Johnston makes it ?'pasture slope' British.)

Pakeman O 'packman, hawker, pedlar' ME.

Pakenham L 'Pacca's homestead (cf. **Packwood**)' OE; place in Suffolk.

Palairet L 'farmyard, strawrick' OF. Huguenot surname.

Palethorp(e) See **Pailthorp**. Chiefly a Lincs surname.

Palfrey O 'palfrey, (lady's) saddle-horse' OF, for the man who looked after them. Mostly a Devon surname, whereas **Palfreyman**, **Palframan**, **Palfreman** are Derbys–Yorks.

Pallant L 'palace, palatinate' OE, a Sussex name from the charming district (now Georgian) south-east of the Cross at Chichester, owned as a 'peculiar', with palatine rights, by the archbishop of Canterbury.

Pallis(t)er O 'paling-/fence-maker' OF. A Co. Durham surname.

Palmer N 'pilgrim' OF – one who had brought back a palm-branch from the Holy Land; fairly common throughout England. Family name of the earls of Selborne.

Palser and **Pane(s)** See **Palliser** and **Paine(s)**.

Paniers O 'maker/user of panniers' OF. This and **Panniers** are Herefords surnames.

Pankhurst F Form of **Pentecost**, despite its L look. A Sussex surname.

Pannell F dim. '**Pain**', as with the two Normans who left their names at Littleton P—, Wilts, and Newport Pagnell, Bucks. Mainly an Essex surname.

Panniers See **Paniers**.

Pant(h)er O 'official in charge of the pantry/bread (including its distribution to the needy)' OF (cf. Modern French *pain*); **Panther** by wrong association with the beast (a kindly creature, it was said, that symbolized Christ). Counted by Guppy only in Northants.

Panton L ' ?hill farm' OE; place in Lincs.

Pape OF version of **Pope**, given for the same reasons.

Papigay N 'popinjay, parrot' OF; sometimes a wooden one (to be shot at) decided the winner at the sports.

Papworth L 'Papa's (= ?priest) **Worth**' OE; two places in Cambs. Cambs–Hunts surname.

Paradice, Paradise L 'garden, pleasure-ground' OF ultimately from an Avestic (ancient Persian) word meaning 'formed around (cf. *dough*, *peri*–)' and so 'enclosure'.

Paramor(e), Paramour N 'sweetheart, lover (literally "with love")'

F: *first name*   L: *local name*   N: *nickname*   O: *occupational name*

282

OF; not an opprobrious term in Middle English, or necessarily the third party of a triangle.

Pardew, Pardey N 'By God!' OF, from a favourite oath; whence the other surnames in **–oe** (easily the commonest), **–ow**, **–ue**, **–y**.

Pardner O 'pardoner, (licensed) seller of indulgences' (i.e. remissions of punishment due for sins) OF; for instance, the vilest character among Chaucer's Canterbury pilgrims.

Pardoe (chiefly a Worcs–Salop name), **Pardow, Pardue, Pardy** See **Pardew.**

Pardon A metonym for **Pardner.**

Parfett, Parfit(t) N 'perfect, complete, highly trained' OF.

Parget(t)er, Pargiter O 'plasterer' OF (cf. **Dauber**); late in the English Middle Ages his work became highly decorative, as on house fronts in Essex, Suffolk.

Parham L 'homestead where pears grow' OE; places in Suffolk, Sussex.

Paris(h) L 'Paris (= the tribe *Parisii*)' OF from Gaulish, the French city; the illiterate **–sh** is like the common pronunciation of *liquorice* as *liquorish* (and cf. the eminent misprint, 'The Vicar appeals for helpers to distribute Paris Magazines'). Most common in Essex.

Park(e) L 'park, enclosure, thinly wooded land kept for beasts of the chase' OF from Germanic; showing residence or, more probably, work therein; the **–e** ?for a dative after a lost preposition. (Sometimes ?a contraction of **Parrock**, with like meaning.) **Parkes** L 'of (i.e. at)' the same. Guppy counted it only in Warwicks–Worcs; **Parks** is a later form, losing the inflexional **–e–**.

Parker O '**Park**-keeper/-ranger' OF. 40th commonest surname in England and Wales in 1853. Family name of the earls of Macclesfield and of Morley.

Parkhouse L 'house in the **Park**' OE; locality, or places in Derbys, Surrey, but counted by Guppy only in Devon.

Parkin, Parkyn F See **Perkin**, with **–ar–** as in **Clark. Parkins(on)** '(son)/son of P—'. **–in** and **–inson** very common in the north; **–yn** found in Cornwall.

Parkman O '**Park**-keeper/-ranger' OF+OE.

Parlabean N 'speak well' OF.

Parley L 'clearing/field where pears grow' OE; places in Dorset, Hants.

Parme(n)ter, Parmi(n)ter O 'tailor' OF, ultimately from Latin *paro* 'prepare'; cf. the church of St Peter Parmentergate, Norwich; *potage Parmentier* is from an 18th-century French potato-grower of that name.

Parnall, Parn(w)ell F Latin feminine *Petronilla*, from Roman clan *Petronius* (?from Greek for 'stone'), and mythically said to be Saint Peter's daughter. In England, usually abbreviated to *Pernel*, thence *Parnel*; for some reason, it came to mean 'priest's concubine' or even 'prostitute'. Chiefly south-west surnames. **Parnell** is the family name of the barons Congleton.

Paroissien O or status 'parishioner' OF.

Parr F dim. 'Piers (= **Peter**)'; cf. **Parkin**. But more often L 'enclosure (sometimes for animals)' OE (cf. German *Pfarr*); place in Lancs. Guppy's count, Notts–Lincs, Lancs, invalidates Par in Cornwall. The claim of Thomas P— (†1635) to have lived to be 152 is not now accepted.

Parratt, Parrett, Parritt See **Parrot(t)**.

Parrell F dim. 'Peter' (see **Parr**). Or O, an aphetic form of 'apparel' OF, for a maker of it.

Parrock L 'paddock, enclosure' OE (of same ultimate Germanic origin as **Park**, to which form the surname is sometimes contracted).

Parrot(t) F Form of **Perrot(t)**; cf. spelling **Parkin**. Even if this is N 'parrot', the bird is still ultimately named after **Peter**. Found in Bucks–Oxon.

Parry F 'son' (from Welsh *Ap-*) 'of **Harry**'. Common in Wales and its Border.

Parsley, Parsloe, Parslow N 'cross the water' OF (*pass-* and *l'eau*); cf. **Passmore**. Guppy counted –low only in Glos.

Parsons O 'of the parson' OF (with the same Latin origin as *person*, and –ar– as in **Clark**); much less likely to be '(son) of' than '(servant) of', since the former would show a notorious bastardy. Or it could be L '(at) the parson's/parsonage'. Common south of Norfolk. Family name of the earls of Rosse.

Partridge N 'partridge' OF. Or O, from catching them.

Pascall, Pasco(e) F 'connected with Easter' Latin (cf. **Patch**), from 9th-century sainted pope Paschal. –oe is a Cornwall version.

Pash(e), Pask(e) See **Patch**; OF forms, and Breton F *Pasc*.

Pashley L 'clearing of (an AS called) Pæcc' OE; but Reaney also associates it with **Parsley**. Pashley Green is in West Yorks.

Paskin F 'feeding, feasting' OW from Latin *Pascentius*. **Paskins** '(son) of P—'.

Passmore N 'cross (the) sea' OF (*pass-* and *mer*); cf. **Parsley**. Guppy counted it in Devon, Hants.

Patch F 'Easter' ME (*pasch, pask*) from church Latin from Greek from Hebrew (= 'passover'). Reaney's four early instances (1177–1327,

---

F: *first name*   L: *local name*   N: *nickname*   O: *occupational name*

from Sussex, Oxon, Dorset, Suffolk) have no *de*/*at*, so that L 'patch of ground' ME is out of the question; but there was an obscure AS personal name *Pæcc–*, left at places Patcham, Patching, Patchway, in Sussex (and cf. **Pashley**).

Pate F dim. '**Patrick**'. Or N 'pate, skull; baldy' ME. **Pates** '(son) of P—'. But another important source is **Peat(e)**.

Pateman F dim. '**Pate**'. Or O '**Pate**'s servant'.

Paternoster N 'Our Father' Latin, used for a 'rosary(-bead)'. Reaney shows how it could be applied not only to dealers in them but to those who held land by the service of repeating the Lord's Prayer for the souls of benefactors.

Pat(t)erson F 'son of **Patrick**'; –t– commoner than –tt– in Scotland, but not in north England. Together the 17th commonest surname in Scotland in 1958.

Pat(e)y F dim. '**Pate**'; but the great 18th-century Bristol family of house-decorators were spelt **Paty** or **Patty**, which would suggest a short –a–.

Paton F double dim. '**Patrick**', with OF suffix.

Patrick F 'patrician, aristocratic' Latin, thence Irish; Welsh- (or Scots-)born saint (originally named *Sucat* 'good at war' Keltic), the Apostle of Ireland. The F was chiefly north and Scots, and so with the surname.

Patte(r)n O 'patten-/clog-maker' OF. Or from **Patton**.

Patterson See **Paterson**.

Pattison Especially a Cumberland–Westmorland form of **Paterson**.

Patton and **Pattrick** See **Paton** and **Patrick**.

Paul(e), **Paull** F 'small' Latin, the name taken by Saul of Tarsus on his conversion; not a common F in medieval England, and oddly unpopular for the dedication of churches (save with Peter). Usual pronunciation was **Pole** or **Pool** (spelt *Poul*), and it is even one of the origins of **Powell**. In Cornwall, **Paul(l)** may sometimes be L, from Paul near Mousehole (Saint Paul Aurelian or Pol de Léon). –le very rare. **Paulson** 'son of P—'; mainly Notts.

Pauncefoot, Pauncefort, Pauncefote N 'arched/round stomach' OF (cf. *paunch*, *vault*). Sometimes ?L 'dingle ford' OW+OE; place (Ponsford) in Devon.

Pav(i)er, Pavio(u)r O 'paviour, pavement-layer' OF.

Pawle See **Paul**. **Pawley, Pawlin(g)** dim. '**Paul**'.

Pawlett L 'stream with poles/stakes (? to tie up at)' OE; place in Somerset.

Paybody See **Peabody**.

Payn(e), Paynes F Same as **Pain** etc. But **Payne** is perhaps twice as common even as the common **Paine**.

Paynter See **Painter**. Guppy assigned it to Cornwall.

Payton See **Peyton**.

Peabody N '?having the body of a gnat' OE *pēo*; this makes a kind of sense, but doesn't satisfactorily explain **Paybody** (which looks equally like 'peacock-body' OE) or Bardsley's *Pyebody* in the early 1600s (which looks like 'magpie-body' OF+OE) – unless *Pyebody* was from OE *pīe*, the alternative form of *pēo*. But see **Peasebody**.

Peace See **Pace**.

Peach The fruit and its OF name (from the '*Persian* apple') had arrived by Chaucer's time, and must sometimes be the O origin, from growing/selling them. But ?normally N 'sin' OF *peche*, made to look like the fruit. Chiefly a Dorset surname.

Peachey N 'sinful' (see **Peach**). Mainly a Suffolk and Sussex surname.

Peacock(e) N 'peacock' OE, early used as a F, but also for ?arrogance, for winning the peacock-prize in athletics, or as a L (sign) name.

Peagram, Peagrim N See **Pilgrim** (and nearer than it to Latin *peregrin*–).

Peak(e) L 'hill' OE; –e may show dative after lost preposition, is the family name of the viscounts Ingleby, and was counted by Guppy in Staffs, Norfolk.

Pear N 'peer, equal, companion' OF.

Pearce F Same as **Piers**. Strongly south-west and Midlands.

Peareth Local pronunciation of **Penrith**.

Pearl O or N 'pearl' OF, from trade or personal adornment.

Pearman O 'pear-grower/-seller' OE. Guppy counted it in Herts, Worcs–Warwicks.

Pears(e) F Same as **Piers**. **Pearson(s)** 'son of P—'; –son is very common in north and Midlands; the odd form –sons '(son) of the son of **Piers**' is authentic. **Pearson** is the family name of the viscounts Cowdray.

Peart N 'beautiful, smart, intelligent, adroit, cheeky, lively' OF.

Peascod, Peas(e)good N 'pea pod' OE, ?for a pea-seller, or suggestive of little worth.

Pease O 'pea' OE, from growing/selling them. Chiefly a surname of Co. Durham, and the family name of the barons Daryngton, Gainford, Wardington.

Peasebody N 'body the size of a pea' OE – if this is the origin of the **Peabody** series, our doubts there are at an end.

F: *first name*   L: *local name*   N: *nickname*   O: *occupational name*

Peasley L 'clearing/field where peas grow' OE.

Peat(e) Probably N 'pet, darling, pampered person' ME, northern and Scots in origin; the related *peat* 'spoiled girl, poppet' is also northern. A L origin 'peat' ME *pete* is feasible, but Bardsley's only *de* name was from Somerset in the 1300s, whereas the surname was counted by Guppy only in Derbys, and was common in Yorks and Scotland. From Yorks it reached Montgomerys in and before the 1600s, and thence Brecknocks, changing to **Pate**; Maurice **Pate**, Director of UNICEF, had a Welsh grandfather Morris **Peat**.

Peay N 'peacock' OE.

Peckham L 'homestead by a hill' OE (cf. *peak*); places in Kent, London.

Peddar, Pedder, Pedlar, Pedler L 'pedlar, hawker' OF. But –lar and –ler may sometimes be 'foot of hare' OF, for a fast runner.

Peden F dim. '**Patrick**' Scots Gaelic.

Pee N 'peacock' OE. A surname of the west Midlands.

Peebles L 'tents, shielings' British, with English plural –s; place in Peebles.

Peek(e) See **Peak**; –e (Devon surname) may show dative after lost preposition.

Peel L '(stake; stockade, palisade) castle' OF; especially the massive towers and fortified houses of the Scots Border; and a northern surname.

Peers Same as **Piers**.

Peet Guppy counted this form of **Peat** in Lancs and Notts.

Peever O 'pepper(-seller), pepperer' OF. Or L for **Peover**, which is so pronounced.

Pegg F dim. '**Margaret**' (see **Maggs**). Or O 'peg(-maker/-seller)' ME from Germanic. **Pegge** is found in Derbys.

Pegler O 'peggler, rough mender, patcher, clumsy workman' west Midland dialect, and chiefly a Glos surname. Also **Peglar**.

Pegram, Pegrum See **Peagram**. Guppy counted **Pegrum** only in Essex.

Peirce, Peirs(e) Forms of **Piers**.

Pell F dim. '**Peter**'. Or O 'skin, hide' OF, for a fellmonger. Or (in the south-east) L 'creek, stream' (see **Pill**).

Peller L 'one who lives at a **Pill**' OE, in south-eastern dialect. Or O 'maker of rich (especially purple) cloth' OE (cf. *pall*).

Pellew N 'wolf-skin' OF. Family name of the viscounts Exmouth. Also **Pellow(e)**.

Pelly N 'bald' OF. Or ?dim. of F **Pell**.

Pelter, Peltor O 'skinner, fellmonger' OF.

Pember ?L 'mound/grave/pasture with a pen/enclosure' OE; place (Pamber) in Hants, formerly *Penbere*.

Pemberton L '**Barton** by a hill' OW+OE; two places in Lancs.

Pembridge L 'bridge at the pens/enclosures' OE or 'bridge by a hill' OW+OE; place in Herefords.

Pender See **Pinder**; but Guppy counted it only in Cornwall.

Pendergast, Pendergrest See **Prendergast**.

Pendle L 'hill hill' OW+OE, tautologically, hill in Lancs. **Pendlebury** adds 'fort/manor' OE; place in Lancs. **Pendleton** adds 'place/farm' OE; two places in Lancs.

Pendock, Penduck L 'barley hill' or 'top of the barley field' OW; place (–o–) in Worcs.

Pendrell, Pendrill N 'hang-ear' OE.

Pendry is **Penry** with a **d**-glide.

Penfold See **Pinfold**.

Pengell(e)y, Pengill(e)y L 'top of the wood, chief wood' Cornish; place (–elly) in Cornwall, and Cornwall surnames.

Penketh L 'top/end of the wood' OW (there are places in Wales called Pencoed); place in Lancs.

Penn L 'pen, enclosure, fold' OE or 'hill' OW; locality, or places in Bucks, Staffs. But sometimes ?F, dim. of **Parnell**.

Pennant L 'top of the valley, high valley' Welsh; seven places in five Welsh counties.

Pennefather See **Pennyfather**.

Pennell L 'Pennel' in Renfrews, first element 'hill' OW *pen*, or one of the various places called repetitively Penhill 'hill hill' OW+OE. Or (as Reaney shows for 1580) F, a form alternating with *Pernell* (= **Parnell**).

Penney See **Penny**.

Pennington L 'farm paying a penny rent' OE (or the owner may have had a N '**Penny**'), places in Hants, Lancs; but another Lancs place was 'farm of (an AS with a N meaning) Pin/Peg' OE. A surname of Lancs–Ches.

Penny N 'penny' OE, early used as a F. Counted by Guppy only in Somerset, Hants. Family name of the viscounts Marchwood.

Pennycuick L 'hill of the cuckoo' OW; place (Penicuick) in Midlothian.

Pennyf(e)ather N 'miser (literally penny-father)' OE. A weird pronunciation exists with the stress on the **y**.

Penrith L 'chief ford' OW; place in Cumberland.

Penrose L 'top/end of the heath' Cornish; places in Cornwall, Devon.

F: *first name*   L: *local name*   N: *nickname*   O: *occupational name*

Penruddock L 'head/top of the ? ?ford' OW; place in Cumberland.

Penry F 'son' (from Welsh *Ap*–) 'of **Henry**'.

Pentecost F 'Pentecost, Whitsun' OF, ultimately from Greek '50th (day after Easter Sunday inclusive)'; from birth/baptism then. Also **Penticost**.

Pentland L 'land of the Picts' ON; the surname will be from the P—Hills in the Lowlands rather than from the P—Firth.

Penton L 'farm paying a penny rent' OE; group of villages in Hants, and still a Hants surname (cf. **Pennington**).

Pentreath L 'head of the ferry/beach' Cornish. Dolly **Jeffery** née P–(†1777) is always (wrongly) claimed to have been the last speaker of Cornish (before its fortunate recent revival).

Pentycross Perversion of **Pentecost**.

Peover L 'bright' British, a Ches river on which are two places called Nether and Over P—; pronounced as **Peever**.

Peploe, Peplow L ?'pebble hill' OE; place (–ow) in Salop.

Pepper O 'pepperer, dealer in pepper/spice' based on OE; an east Midland and East Anglian surname.

Peppercorn O 'peppercorn(-seller), spicer' OE. Or N for a tiny man, or for one who paid a nominal 'peppercorn' rent, or for one with a violent temper.

Pepperell N dim. 'pepper' Latin, for a man tiny or black-haired or bad-tempered, early used as a F.

Peppett, Peppiatt, Peppiett F dim. '**Peppin**'.

Peppin, Pepys F 'Pepin' Germanic, from verb meaning 'tremble'; name of several early Frankish kings, including Charlemagne's father; a nominative form was *Pepis* (whence **Pepys**, the family name of the earls of Cottenham, pronounced *peeps*). Rarely ? ?N 'fruit-seed, pip' OF, for a fruit-grower.

Perceval, Perciful, Percival (the commonest) N 'pierce valley, rush through the valley' OF, ?invented by the 12th-century poet Crestien de Troyes as the name of his hero, who became bound up with the Grail legend. But sometimes L, from Perc(h)eval, Calvados. **Perceval** is the family name of the earls of Egmont.

Percy L Not an abbreviation of **Percival**, though often taken as such: the Percies, dukes of Northumberland, descend from the Conqueror's companion William de Perci, who took his name from place Perci-en-Auge, Calvados; there are other places Perci/Percy in Calvados and Manche, from a Latin F *Persius*.

Perdue N Rare (four in London TD; twenty-eight **Pardoe**) form of **Pardew**, respelt as if meaning 'lost' OF.

Peregrine N (and occasional F) '**Pilgrim**' Latin; cf. **Peagrim**.

Perfect Pedantic latinized respelling of **Parfett**.

Perrement sounds like a version of **Palfreyman**.

Perkin F double dim. 'Piers'. **Perkins** '(son) of P—'; a surname of the south Midlands, south, and South Wales. For suffix **–kin** see **Jenkins**.

Perks is to **Perkins** as **Jenks** is to **Jenkins**. A Warwicks–Worcs surname.

Perowne F double dim. 'Piers' OF. A Huguenot surname anglicized.

Perret(t) F double dim. 'Piers', OF *–ot/–et* both forming pet-forms. But it occurs in Somerset, so see also second meaning of **Perrot(t)**.

Perrier O 'quarryman' OF (cf. *pierre*, **Peter**). Or L 'man at a pear-tree' OE + suffix, as are **Perriman**, **Perriment** and **Perryman**.

Perrin(g) F double dim. 'Piers' with yet another OF suffix. **Perrins** '(son) of P—'. Guppy counted **Perrin** only in Devon.

Perriton L 'pear tree farm' OE; places (Peri–, Piri–, Puri–, Pyri–) in seven counties in the triangle Essex, Worcs, Somerset.

Perrot(t) F double dim. 'Piers'; cf. **Perret(t)**. But in Somerset and adjacent counties the places North (Somerset) and South (Dorset) Perrott (from the River Parret – origin ?) must be involved.

Perry L 'pear tree' OE. Probably no connection with **Peter**, despite its OF dim. *Perre*. But sometimes F 'son' (from Welsh *Ap–*) 'of (dim.) **Henry**'; cf. **Parry**, **Penry**. Fairly common in Midlands and the south-west.

Person O 'parson, priest' OF (cf. *clerk*, **Clark**).

Pertuce, Pertwee L 'ravine, pass, cave' OF *pertuis*; places (-uis, –us, –uy, –huis) in France.

Pestell O '(one who uses a) pestle (and mortar); druggist, spicer' OF.

Pester O 'baker' OF.

Petcher O 'fisherman' OF.

Petch(ey) N 'sin(ful)' OF, like **Peach(ey)**.

Peter F 'stone, rock' Greek, the Greek version of the Aramaic name *Cephas* bestowed by Our Lord on Simon the brother of Andrew. **Peters(on)** '(son)/son of P—'. This learned form of the F was rare compared with OF forms *Piers*, etc.; so is the surname **Peter**. –s is late and mainly from Cornwall and Wales (but cf. **Piers** and its numerous progeny). Whatever setbacks the F received from the unpopular Peter's Pence and the Reformation, it was brought back to tiresome popularity by *Peter Pan* in 1904.

Pether(s) F South and south-west forms of **Peter(s)**.

F: *first name*   L: *local name*   N: *nickname*   O: *occupational name*

Petherbridge, Pethybridge L 'bridge of (an A S called) Pidda/ Pudda' O E; place (–y–) in Lustleigh, Devon, and Devon surnames.

Peto L 'Poitevin' (see **Portwaine**) O F; literally 'Poitou'.

Petre Same as **Peter**, and a fitting surname for a family that so obstinately adhered to the Papacy after the Reformation.

Petrie, Petry F dim. 'Peter/Patrick' Scots Gaelic forms.

Pett L South-east form of **Pitt** (–e– where Old English West Saxon had –y–); also places in Kent, Sussex.

Pettengale, Pettengell, Pettengill See **Pettingale**.

Pettet(t) See **Pettit(t)**.

Petticrew, Petticrow N 'little growth' O F, for a dwarf.

Pettifer, Pettifor(d) N 'foot of iron' O F, for a man with a false limb, or a tireless walker.

Pettigrew Much commoner form of **Petticrew**.

Pettingale, Pettingall, Pettingell, Pettingill L 'Portugal (= port of Cale – a city of old Lusitania, west of Oporto)' Portuguese from Latin.

Pettipher Oxon version of **Pettifer**.

Pettit(t) N 'little' O F. Guppy counted it only in the south-east from Suffolk to Sussex.

Petty N 'little' O F, with no suggestion of meanness. Guppy counted it only in West Yorks.

Peutherer O 'pewterer' O F.

Peverall, Peverell, Peverill O F versions of **Pepperell**.

Peyton L '**Hough** of (an A S called) Pack/Bundle' O E, place in Essex; or 'farm of (an A S called) Pǣga' O E, place in Suffolk.

Pharaoh, Pharo(ah) Same as **Farrar**. No connection with the Egyptian king, though the absurd F was in use by Pharaoh **Dyer** in Cardiff *c.* 1900 – and *he* was a farrier!

Phasey See **Facey**.

Phelp(s) Contracted forms of **Philip(s)**. –s common in Somerset– Glos–Worcs.

Phemister and **Phibbs** See **Femister** and **Phipps**.

Philcox F dim. 'Philip'+**Cox**.

Philip F 'fond of horses' Greek; from the Apostle. The F lost face in England when P— II was King Consort of Bloody Mary and national enemy of Good Bess; the present Consort has revived its popularity. Whence many surnames with –ll– or –pp–, and beginning **Philp**–, **Phelp**–, **Phip**–, **Pip**–. **Philip(p)s, Phillips** '(son) of P—'. **Phil(l)ipson** 'son of P—'. **Phillips** is easily the commonest surname based on the F – 44th in England and Wales in 1853, 28th in

PHILL

USA in 1939. **Philipps** is the family name of the viscounts St Davids, the barons Milford, and the barons Strange of Knockin.

Phill F dim. '**Philip**'.

Phillpot(s), Phillpott(s) Same as **Philpot(s)**.

Philp(s) Contracted from **Philip(s)**. Guppy counted **Philp** only in Cornwall.

Philpot(s) F double dim. '**Philip(s)**'; and cf. **Phillpot**; this sub-group (to which a recent licensee of the Mitre, Llandaff, misleadingly belonged) was found by Guppy especially in the west Midlands and south. In the same group are **Philpin** and **Philpott**.

Phimister See **Femister**.

Phipp F dim. '**Philip**'. **Phipps** '(son) of P—', but far commoner; mainly a Glos–Worcs–Warwicks surname. Family name of the marquesses of Normanby.

Phippen, Phippin F double dim. '**Philip**', forms found mainly in Somerset.

Phizacklea See **Fazackerley**.

Phyfe A version, established in USA, of **Fyfe**.

Physick O 'physic, medicine' OF from Latin from Greek, a metonym for a doctor; surname seen recently over a chemist's in Adelaide, South Australia.

Phythian See **Vivian**.

Pick Short-vowelled form of one of the **Pike** names. Mainly a Lincs surname.

Pickard L 'Picard' OF, from the province of Picardy. A surname scattered in Wilts, Devon, and West Yorks.

Pickavance N 'prick/spur forward' OF.

Pickbourne, Pickburn L 'pike stream' OE; place (–burn) in West Yorks.

Pickering L ?'people of the hill-edge' OE $p\bar{\imath}c+\bar{o}ra$; place in North Yorks, and surname of the northern counties and Leics.

Pickersgill L 'footpad's ravine' ME+ON; place in Killinghall, West Yorks, and a Yorks surname.

Pickett A dim., with OF suffix –et, of the mysterious pair **Pick/Pike**; OF *picot* = 'point, pointed object', but can hardly figure here. Chiefly a Wilts surname.

Pickles L '(of, i.e.) at the pightle, little enclosed field' ME; a surname of Lancs–West Yorks.

Pickup L 'hill with a peak' OE; place in Lancs, and a Lancs surname. Despite its saucy sound, ten people answer to it in the London TD.

F: *first name*   L: *local name*   N: *nickname*   O: *occupational name*

292

Pickwell L 'spring/stream by the peak(s)' OE; place in Leics, and a Lincs surname.

Picton L 'place by a ?pointed hill' (or first element could be an AS owner ?'Skinny') OE; places in Ches, Pemb.

Piddell L 'marsh, fen' OE (cf. *puddle, poodle*); one of the places called Piddle in Dorset and Worcs.

Piddock, Pidduck Kent surnames, like **Pittock,** and of the same N origin.

Pidge(o)n N 'pigeon' OF, especially for someone easily plucked/swindled. But Reaney shows how in 12th-/13th-century Sussex it could be 'little (OF *petit*) **John**'. Or the bearer looked after pigeons – they were a useful article of diet.

Pierce Form of **Piers,** much rarer than **Pearce.**

Pierpo(i)nt, Pierrepoint L 'Pierrepont (= stone bridge)' OF; places in Calvados, Manche, Seine-Maritime.

Piers (also **Pierse**) F Old French form of **Peter,** and the usual form of the F in medieval England; whence many surnames in **Pear–/Peir–/Pier–/Peer–,** and dims. in **Par–/Per–/Pir–. Pierson** 'son of **P—**'.

Pigg N 'pig' OE. Or O, from keeping them. Counted by Guppy only in Herts, Northd. A more elegant form is **Pigge.**

Piggott (Beds–Berks–Herts–Cambs), **Pigott** (chiefly Cambs) See **Pickett.**

Pike L 'peak, point, hilltop' OE. Or O 'pike, pick-axe' (in sense of 'pikeman') OE; or 'pike' (the fish) OF, as a metonym for a fishmonger. Or N 'woodpecker' OF *pic*; or a known Old Norse N *Pík* 'tall/lanky man'. Mainly a surname of the close group Wilts–Dorset–Devon–Somerset.

Pilcher O 'maker of pilches' OE+–er; the *pilch* was at first an outer garment of skin with the hair (cf. *pelt*), later of leather or wool (and only eventually a baby's wrapper worn over the nappy). Counted by Guppy only in Kent.

Pile L 'post, stake' OE (cf. *pile*). A surname of Devon–Dorset–Wilts.

Pilgrim N 'pilgrim' (to the Holy Land or Rome) OF. An Essex surname.

Pilkington L 'farm of the followers of (an AS called) Pileca' OE (his name can hardly be connected with OE *pilece* 'robe, pilch'); place in Lancs, and a Lancs surname.

Pill L 'creek, stream' OE.

Pillar L 'pillar' OF; but the English townscape doesn't go in for isolated pillars to any extent, and N 'robber, plunderer, pillager' OF may be the commoner origin.

Pilley L 'stake/shaft/pile wood/clearing' OE; places in Hants, West Yorks – but whether the wood was good for gathering them, or the clearing stockaded or landmarked with them, cannot be guessed.

Pilling L ?'little pill/creek' or 'creek water' OW); river and place in Lancs, and mainly a Lancs surname.

Pillinger O 'baker' OF (it began with *b* – see **Bullinger**); but see also **Pollinger**.

Pilton L 'place by a pill/creek' OE (first element from OW, places in Devon, Rutland, Somerset; but first element of place in Northants is F of an AS owner.

Pimblett (mainly a Lancs surname), **Pimblott** are **Pimlett**, **Pimlott** with a **b**-glide, as in *shamble* for OE *sceamol*.

Pimlett, Pimlott (mainly a Ches surname) F double dim. '**Pim**'+OF suffixes *–el–* and *–et/–ot*.

Pim(m) F Reaney finds an OE *Pymma*, but the meaning is unknown.

Pinch See **Pink**.

Pinchbeck L 'minnow/? ?finch stream' OE (second element scandinavianized); place in Lincs. Alas, Christopher **P**— (†1732) invented a nasty alloy that looked like gold, and debased the name to the meaning *spurious*.

Pincher ?N 'grumbler, fault-finder, haggler' ME from OF. But it must often be F from **Pinchard**, a name ?connected with **Punchard**.

Pindar (rare), **Pinder** O 'impounder (of stray animals)' OE. Mainly a Notts–Lincs surname.

Pine L 'pine-tree' OE/OF; perhaps from a Normandy place with this feature. A hyphenation **Pine-Coffin** is reported.

Pinfold L 'pinfold, pound' (cf. **Pinder**) OE, for the man in charge of it. But Reaney quotes a surname *Pynfoul* 'pen (the) bird' OE, 1322 and 1327, which may have been absorbed here.

Pingree ?N 'game of knucklebones' OF *pingre* or (post-medieval) 'miser'.

Pink N 'chaffinch' OE (cf. **Finch**, **Spink**). (The name of the colour, from the flower – carnation/pink – is ?as late as the 18th century.)

Pinker N 'chaffinch' OE *pinca*; or see **Pincher**.

Pinkney L 'Picquigny' in Somme, from Germanic F *Pinc–* (variant of *Banc–*)+double suffix.

Pinn O 'pin(-maker)' OE.

Pinney (Devon surname), **Pinnie** L 'enclosure with a pound/pond/?dam' OE, place (Pinhay) in Axmouth, Devon; or 'enclosure with a pen/fold' OE, place (Penhay) in Poughill, Devon.

Pinnock N 'hedge-sparrow' ME. But sometimes ?L, from place in

F: *first name*   L: *local name*   N: *nickname*   O: *occupational name*

Glos 'little hill' (?OE from) OW; place in Cornwall is from a Keltic saint.

Pipe F ?The same Germanic stem as **Peppin**. Or O, a metonym for **Piper**. Or L 'water-pipe, conduit, stream' OE; locality, or places in Herefords (with a stream) and Staffs (Pipehill, with its pipe to Lichfield).

Piper O 'piper, player on the pipe/fife' OE. But sometimes absorbing **Pepper**, since Peter **P**— in the jingle was surely a pepperer.

Pippin(g) and **Pirie** See **Peppin** and **Perry**.

Pitcairn L '**Croft**/field of the cairn' Scots Gaelic; place in Perths. The south Pacific island is named after Robert **P**—, the midshipman who sighted it in 1767.

Pitcaithl(e)y, **Pitke(a)thly**, and (wrongly) **Pitt-Kethley** L 'share belonging to (dim.) Cathal (= war-wielder)' Pictish + Scots Gaelic; place (Pitkeathly) in Perths.

Pitcher L A version of **Pickard**; or O – the utensil doesn't figure, but the bearer used 'pitch' OE. Chiefly a Bucks and Sussex surname.

Pitchford L 'ford near a source of pitch' OE (it was a bituminous well); place in Salop, and a Salop surname.

Pither(s) South and south-west forms of **Peter(s)**.

Pitman L 'man living at the pit/hollow/excavation' OE; meaning 'miner' came only later, but it is strange that the name is so common in Somerset, where coal was early dug; also Dorset–Wilts.

Pitney L 'island of (an A S called) Pytta/Pēota' OE; place in Somerset.

Pitt L 'pit/hollow/excavation' OE (east Midland and north –i– = Old English West Saxon –y–); locality, or place in Hants. **Pitts** 'of (i.e. at) the **P**—'. Despite the dialect, Guppy found **Pitt** mainly in Herefords–Worcs–Glos.

Pittaway L 'Poitevin' OF *Pitouais* (?more derogatory than **Portwine**); or for Pitway, Somerset, ?'track in a hollow' OE.

Pitter, **Pittman** L 'dweller at the **Pitt**' OE.

Pittock (a Kent surname), **Pittuck** See **Puttock**.

Pizar, **Pizer** See **Poyser**.

Piz(z)ey, **Pizzie** See **Pusey**.

Place, **Plaice** L 'town square, market-place; manor-house' OF; or (cf. *pleach*) 'quickset hedge' OF.

Plain L 'open tract, flat meadow' OF. Or N 'candid, frank' OF.

Plaisted L 'sports-ground (literally play-place)' OE (cf. *stead* in *instead, bedstead*).

Plaistow(e) L 'sports-ground (literally play-place)' OE; the one in West Ham has now lost the atmosphere of the village green, but there are other places in seven counties (some with –ay–/–ey–). Chiefly a Bucks surname.

Plampin See **Blamphin**.

Plant L 'enclosure, plantation' OF. Or O 'plant' OF, a metonym for a gardener. Or (from the same origin) N 'sprig/cudgel, young offspring'. Two big stocks certainly, Staffs–Salop and Suffolk.

Plaster L For **Plaisted, Plaistow**, as in Chapel P—, Wilts. Or O 'plasterer' OF.

Plater O 'pleader, advocate' OF, or 'plate-armour-maker' OF.

Platt L 'plot, patch' OE, or 'level ground, footbridge' OF – as in P— Bridge, Lancs. The surname is chiefly of Ches–Lancs–Derbys. **Platts** is '(of, i.e.) at the P—', and is found in Derbys–Notts.

Player O 'athlete' OE; but *to play* was to take one's pleasure/leisure, and there may be N senses or reference to a musician.

Playford L 'ford where sports are held' OE; place in Suffolk.

Pleace, Please, Pleass, Pleece L 'quickset hedge' OF (cf. *pleach*, **Place**).

Pleasa(u)nce F 'pleasant' OF feminine. Or L 'Piacenza' Italian from Latin *Placentia* (again with meaning 'pleasing'); place in Italy. (The word is found in the early 15th century for the fine linen or gauze made there, but the use as a 'pleasure garden' not until the late 16th century.)

Plenderleith, Plenderneath L The lost 12th-century name *Prenteineth* in Loudoun, Ayrs; *Pren–* is 'tree' OW.

Plew(e)s, Plewis L '(of, i.e.) at the plough(land)' OE; a *plough(land)* was the northern and eastern word for the area able to be tilled by one ploughteam of eight oxen in a year (southern and south-western *hide*), and the surnames are chiefly of Yorks, Northd, and south-east Scotland.

Plimpton L 'plum-tree farm' OE; place (Plympton) in Devon.

Plomer and **Plomley** See **Plumer** and **Plumley**.

Plott L 'plot (of ground)' OE.

Plowden L 'valley where sports are held' OE (cf. **Playford**); place in Salop.

Plowman O 'ploughman' OE.

Plowright O 'plough-maker' OE (cf. **Wright**). Chiefly a Notts–Lincs surname.

Pluckrose N 'pick/pluck a rose' OE+OE; Reaney lets it be a rose paid for land tenure, in lieu of rent.

Plum(b), Plumbe O '(worker in) lead' OF, a metonym for **Plummer**.

Plumbl(e)y L Same as **Plumley**, with parasitic –b–; place in Derbys.

F: *first name*   L: *local name*   N: *nickname*   O: *occupational name*

Plumer O 'dealer in plumes/feathers' OF, sometimes meaning (or absorbed by) **Plummer**.

Plumley L 'clearing/field where plums grow' OE; places in Ches, Hants.

Plummer O 'plumber, worker in lead' OF; but cf. **Plumer**. Guppy counted it in Wilts–Berks, Norfolk.

Plumpton L 'plum-tree farm' OE; places in five counties.

Plum(p)tre, Plum(p)tree L 'plum-tree' OE; locality, or two places in Notts, and a Notts surname. **Plumptre** is the family name of the barons Fitzwalter.

Plush L 'pool' OE (cf. *plash* and its derivative *splash*); place in Dorset.

Poad, Poat(e) N 'toad' OE.

Pobgee and **Pobjoy** See **Papigay**.

Pocket N dim. 'pouch', so a kind of 'handbag' OF, like Lucy Locket's.

Pocklington L 'farm of the gang of (an AS called dim.) Pocket/Bag/Pouch' OE; place in East Yorks, and a Lincs surname.

Pocock See **Peacock** A Wilts surname.

Podmore L 'toad moor' OE; place in Staffs, and chiefly a Salop surname; other places named from AS owners of moorland.

Poe N 'peacock' ON.

Poggs F '(son) of (dim.) Margaret' (see **Maggs**). Or L 'man from (Le) Puy (= hillock)' OF; common place-name in France; such an immigrant gave his name to Stoke Poges. **Pogson** 'son of (dim.) Margaret'.

Poindexter N 'right fist' OF (adjective second).

Points, Poyntz F 'Pontius', Pilate's forename (see **Punchard**), used by Shakespeare for his shady character Poins. But there are also L origins from places in Normandy called Ponts 'bridges' OF.

Pole L '(at) the **Pool**', –e for dative after lost preposition. Or F See **Paul**. **Poles** 'of (i.e. at) the **Pool**', or '(son) of **Paul**'. Cardinal P—'s family had the L origin.

Polglase, Polglaze L 'blue/green/grey pool' (adjective second) Cornish; place in Cornwall.

Polkinhorn(e), Polkinghorn(e) L 'pool in a corner' Cornish.

Poll(ard), Polle F See **Paul**, of which **Pollard** may be dim. with OF suffix. Or **Poll(e)** may be L, see **Pool**. And **Pollard** may be N 'crop-head, big-head' (as with pollarded trees/animals) ME from Germanic.

Pollinger See **Bullinger**; but this is less acceptable than L 'pollarded tree' late ME *pollenger* (from *polling*).

Pollit(t) F dim. 'Hippolytus (= letting horses loose)' Greek; in Greek legend the son of the Amazon Queen (Hippolyta), but the use of the

F stems from a Roman saint, martyred A.D.252. Counted by Guppy only in Lancs.

Pollock L ?'pool in a field' Scots Gaelic; place (–ock, –ok) in Renfrews. Family name of the viscounts Hanworth.

Polmear, Polmeer L 'big pool' Cornish; place (–ea–) near St Austell, Cornwall.

Polson F 'son of **Paul**'.

Polyblank N 'white hair' (adjective second) OF.

Pomeroy (rarely **Pomery**) L 'apple-orchard' OF; locality, or from various places in France (all denoting apple-growing) called La Pommeraie/–raye. Guppy counted it only in Dorset. Family name of the viscounts Harberton.

Pomfret, Pomphrett L 'broken bridge' (adjective second) Latin; place (Pontefract) in West Yorks. –fret was counted by Guppy only in Lancs.

Pond L 'pond' ?OE (?variant of *pound*; see **Pound**).

Ponsford L See second meaning of **Pauncefoot**.

Ponson F 'son of ?Pontius' (see **Points, Punchard**).

Ponsonby L 'Puncheon/Awl/Bodkin's farm' OF N+ON; place in Cumberland. Family name of the earls of Bessborough and three barons.

Pont L 'bridge' OF.

Pontifex, Pontyfix N 'pontiff, bishop, pope' Latin, for same reasons as **Pope**; the original Roman meaning was 'bridge-/?path-maker'.

Ponton L 'hill farm' OE (same origin as **Panton**); place in Lincs.

Pook N 'goblin, water-sprite, elf, Puck' OE.

Pool(e) L 'pool, tidal stream' OE; –e could show dative after lost preposition; places in Devon and Dorset must sometimes be involved, as the surname is found in Somerset–Dorset; also places in Ches, Glos, and the surname is common in Glos. Or F See **Paul**.

Poolman L 'one who lives at a pool' OE+OE.

Poor(e) N 'poor' OF. But often L 'man from Poix (in Picardy), a Picard' OF *Pohier*. Or O 'herald' OF (one em*power*ed to do something). These often occur as **Power**.

Pope N 'pope' OE, ?for an austere man, a killjoy, one who had played the part in a pageant, one who had even been abroad in the pope's service. Common in Worcs–Glos and Hants–Dorset–Devon.

Popejoy See **Papigay**.

Popham L Earliest spelling of place (document of 903) is the same; ?'pebbly homestead' OE; place in Hants.

Popkin F 'son' (from Welsh *Ap*–) 'of **Hopkin**'. **Popkins, Popkiss**

F: *first name*   L: *local name*   N: *nickname*   O: *occupational name*

'(son) of **P**—'. **Popkiss** has naturally been the victim of misinter-
pretation. Bardsley quotes a grotesque Elizabethan name 'Hopkyn
ap Popkyn'.

Pople (a Somerset surname) See **Popple**.

Popley L 'clearing with poplars' or 'clearing with cockle, etc.' (see
Popple) or 'pebbly clearing' OE; there is a place Popeley in Spen-
borough, West Yorks.

Poppinger ?a form of **Pottinger**.

Popple L 'poplar-tree' late OE; in late ME a word of unknown etymology means 'cockle, darnel, tares, charlock', but this and OE
popel 'pebble' are far less likely as surnames.

Popplewell L 'pebbly spring/stream' OE; place in West Yorks.

Poppleton L 'pebbly farm' OE; place in West Yorks.

Popplestone N 'pebble' OE *popelstān*.

Porch L 'porch' OF, perhaps as door-keeper; an early instance
(Somerset, late 1200s) is *atte Porche*.

Porcher O 'pig-keeper' OF (cf. *pork*).

Porchmouth An unflattering version of **Portsmouth**.

Port L 'gate' OF; the earliest instances are *de la Port(e)*, but 'port,
harbour' is unlikely. A name early eminent in Herefords and Derbys,
where the family founded Repton School (with the punning *porta*
in its motto).

Portal L 'town-gate' OF. A Huguenot surname.

Porter O 'gate-keeper, door-keeper' OF or 'carrier, porter' OF; it
depends on descent from OF *portier* or *porteour*; the former office
was slightly superior. The real surname of 'O. Henry'.

Portly N 'stately, dignified' OF+suffix.

Portman O 'townsman, burgess' OE.

Portsmouth L 'mouth of the harbour' OE; place in Hants, and a
Hants–Berks surname.

Portwaine, Portwin(e) L 'Poitevin, man from Poitou' (Gaulish tribe
Pictavi, ?connected with *Pict*, of unknown meaning – 'painted/
tattooed men' being a Latinism; ?a hybrid Keltic and pre-Keltic
tribe). **Portwine** must be a late misspelling, since the stuff isn't
mentioned in England until *c.* 1700.

Posnett was the local way of saying **Postlethwaite**, and **Posshe-
white** is a bad spelling.

Postan(ce), Poston L or O 'one who lived at or kept the postern-gate'
OF; –*ce* is for '*s* – '(of, i.e.) at the postern'.

Postle N 'apostle' OF, perhaps from taking the part in a play, or from
excessive piety (one OF meaning is 'pope'). A Norfolk surname.

Postlethwaite L ' ? ?apostle's **Thwaite**' ON, but this field in Millom,

Cumberland, has no known religious associations. A Lancs surname.

Potbury A Devon surname, but perhaps from 'Portbury' in Somerset, 'fort/manor by the harbour' OE.

Pothecary O 'spice-/drug-store keeper, druggist, apothecary' OF, ultimately from Greek word for a place where one 'puts things away'.

Potipher See **Pettifer**; confused with Potiphar, the Egyptian with the wicked wife.

Potkin F dim. 'Pott', itself a kind of treble dim. of **Philip**. The suffix is originally Flemish. **Potkins** '(son) of P—'.

Pott F dim. 'Philpot', already a double dim. of **Philip**. Or O 'potter' OE, a metonym. Or L 'hole, pit, pothole' OE. **Potts** F '(son) of P—'; or O '(maker of) pots'; or L 'potholes' or 'of (i.e. at) the pothole'; common in Northd–Co. Durham.

Pottell F dim. 'Pott', so as dim. as **Potkin**; the suffix is OF.

Pottenger (a Somerset surname) See **Pottinger**.

Potter O 'potter' (who made crockery, metal pots, and even bells) OE. Guppy found it most commonly in Derbys.

Potterell, Potterill N 'colt' OF (cf. **Pullan**).

Potterton L 'potters' place' OE; place in West Yorks.

Pottinger O 'soup-/broth-maker' OF; the –n– has found its way into *pottage* as into **Massinger**.

Pottle See **Pottell**.

Poulter O 'poulterer' OF.

Poulton L 'place at a **Pool**' OE; places in Ches (three), Glos, Kent, Lancs (three).

Pound L 'pound, pinfold, enclosure for stray cattle' OE. Rarely O '(maker of) pound(s)/weight(s)' OE, a metonym. **Pounds** '(of, i.e.) at the pound'.

Pountney L 'island of (an AS called) ?Pulta' OE, place (Poultney) in Leics; but there has been confusion (as in St Laurence Pountney church, London) with Pontigny in Yonne, topical in England as the refuge of the exiles Saint Thomas Becket and Saint Edmund Rich, and spelt by us *Pountney* or the like.

Poupard, Poupart N 'chubby child, baby doll' OF.

Povey N 'barn-owl, puffy (from its appearance)' Herefords–Glos–Wilts dialect, though Guppy counted it only in Berks.

Pow (a Somerset surname), **Powe** N 'peacock' OE.

Powderham L 'homestead in marshland (especially reclaimed from the sea)' OE (cf. the *polder* in Dutch place-names); place in Devon.

F: *first name*   L: *local name*   N: *nickname*   O: *occupational name*

Powdrell, Powdrill N 'colt' OF.

Powel (rare), **Powell** Usually F 'son' (from Welsh *Ap*–) 'of **Howel**'; common in Wales and its Border; or see **Paul**. Sometimes L, see **Pool** (which is now the U pronunciation of **Powell**); or some –well ('spring, stream') place-name.

Power See **Poor**. Largely Irish – 54th commonest surname in Ireland in 1890. **Powers** '(son) of P—'.

Powle F Usually = **Paul**. **Powles** '(son) of P—'.

Powley, Powling F dim. '**Paul**'.

Pownall L 'nook of (an AS called) Pocket/Bag/Pouch' OE; place in Ches, and a Ches surname.

Poxon F 'son of (dim.) Margaret' (see **Poggs, Maggs, Pogson**).

Poyner O 'boxer, fighter' OF.

Poyntz See **Points**.

Poyser, Poyzer O 'weigher, scale-maker, superintendent of a public weighing-machine' OF. **Poyser** fairly common in Staffs–Derbys.

Prall L 'look-out hill (cf. *pry*)' OE; place (Prawle) in Devon.

Pratlett looks like **Pratt**+two OF dim. suffixes –*el* and –*et*.

Pratt N 'trick, craft' OE, developing to ME adjective 'smart, cunning, astute', cognate with much later meaning 'pretty'. Slang meaning 'buttocks' (*OED*'s first instance is 1567) may sometimes be the source. A surname of eastern England, from Yorks to Sussex, and family name of the marquesses Camden.

Pray L 'meadow' OF (cf. *prairie*).

Preastley Odd spelling of **Priestley**.

Preater See **Pretor**.

Precious F 'precious, valuable' Latin feminine. Counted by Guppy only in Yorks.

Preece, Prees(e) F 'son' (from Welsh *Ap*–) 'of **Rhys**'. Or L 'brushwood, covert' OW; places in Lancs, Salop (Preese, Prees).

Preen L Probably '(hill shaped like a) brooch' OE; places (Church P—, Holt P—) in Salop.

Prendergast (Misspelt as **Prendergrass, Prendergrast, Prenderguest**) L It looks something like a corruption of 'castle village' OW, place near Haverfordwest, Pemb; but early forms are lacking, and the linguistic map of this part of Pemb is ON/OE rather than Welsh. There is a (later) Prenderguest Farm in Berwicks.

Prentice, Prentis(s) O (but a N that stuck as the lad grew up) 'apprentice' OF. Counted by Guppy only in Suffolk.

Presbrey, Presbury Forms of **Prestbury**.

Prescot(e), Prescott (rarely **Prescod**) L 'priests' cottage/manor'

OE; places in Glos, Lancs, Oxon. In Devon there are three places Prescott and four Priesta–/two Presta–/one Prista–, but **Prescott** (the usual form) is mainly a Lancs–Ches surname.

Press See **Priest**, and for short vowel cf. **Prescot, Preston**.

Presswood L 'priests' wood' OE; locality, or places (–st–) in Bucks, Salop, Staffs.

Prestbury L 'priests' manor' OE; places in Ches, Glos.

Prested L 'place where pears grow (literally pear place)' OE; place in Essex.

Prestige Corruption of **Prestwich**, as if to make it *very* superior.

Preston L 'priests' place/farm' OE; places in two dozen counties, including the Lancs town – and surname is found mainly in Lancs. Sometimes ?N, 'priest's son' OE, formed by assimilation of –stess– to –st–. Family name of the viscounts Gormanston.

Prestwich L 'priests' farm, parsonage' OE; place in Lancs.

Pretor O Learned translation (Latin *praetor*) of **Reeve**.

Pretty N 'smart, crafty' OE. Counted by Guppy only in Leics, Suffolk.

Prettyjohn F 'Prester **John**' (first element *prestre* 'priest' OF), the mythical Christian priest-king who ruled over an incredible area, at the fringe of the known world, for an incredible time. His fame began in the 12th century, and even in the 14th century Mandeville claimed to have found him emperor of India. Counted by Guppy only in Devon.

Prevost See **Provost**.

Prew N 'valiant, doughty' OF, related to **Prowse**. **Prewett** dim. 'P—'.

Price F 'son' (from Welsh **Ap**–) 'of **Rhys**'. Very common throughout Wales, its Border, and the south-west; 43rd commonest surname in England and Wales in 1853. Reaney supposes an occasional O 'price' OF, a metonym for a fixer of prices.

Prichard More 'correct', but much rarer, form of **Pritchard**; found by Guppy chiefly in North Wales.

Prickett N 'stag in his second year (having straight and unbranched horns)' OE + Latin suffix (cf. *prick, prickle*).

Priddy L 'earth house' OW; the Somerset hilltop village where the boy Christ is said to have walked.

Pride N 'pride' OE, of the rare abstract type.

Prideaux L 'near the waters' OF; place in Cornwall.

Pridham See **Prudhomme**.

Priest O 'priest' OE, going back to *presbyter*, the Greek word for 'elder' that occurs in the epigram 'New Presbyter is but old Priest

---

F: *first name*   L: *local name*   N: *nickname*   O: *occupational name*

writ large'. Priests were celibate; the surname is thus either a little scandalous or (for a rake and rogue) sarcastic. Chiefly a Bucks–Middx surname.

Priestley L 'priests' wood/clearing' OE; locality, or places in Beds, Herts, West Yorks – and surname found chiefly in West Yorks–Lincs–Derbys.

Prime N 'first', also 'fine, delicate' OF; cf. **Prin**.

Primrose L 'tree of the moor' OW; places in Berwicks, Midlothian, Fifes, and a Scots surname. Family name of the earls of Rosebery.

Prin N 'first', also 'slender' OF; cf. **Prime**, but the short vowel is as in Modern French *printemps*.

Prince N 'prince' OF (ultimately from Latin *princeps* 'first, chief'), ?from lordly manners, or playing the part in a pageant, or service in a prince's household. The surname is grouped chiefly in Staffs–Derbys–Ches.

Pring, Prinn See **Prin**. –ng was counted by Guppy only in Devon.

Pringle L 'ravine (**Gill**) of (a Norseman called) ?Brooch/Pin' ON; place in Selkirks, and a surname of south Scotland and Northumberland.

Prior O 'prior' OE/OF, from Latin. The head of a monastic family should not also be the head of an ordinary family, and the surname must often be a N based on service in a prior's household. A surname of East Anglia, south Midlands, Hants, Cornwall.

Priscott See **Prescot**.

Priston L 'place in the copse/brushwood' OW + OE; place in Somerset.

Pritchard (corrupted to **Pritchett**) F 'son' (from Welsh *Ap–*) 'of **Richard**'. Common in Wales and its Border.

Pritt See **Pratt**, though the change from OE *prætt* is mysterious.

Privett L 'privet (copse)' OE; places in Hants, Wilts.

Probert, Probin, Probyn F 'son' (from Welsh *Ap–*) 'of **Robert**/Robin' (cf. **Robins**).

Prockter is an eccentric spelling of **Proctor**.

Procter, but normally **Proctor** O 'steward, agent, tithe-collector, attorney in a spiritual court, one licensed to collect alms for lepers or enclosed anchorites' Latin (contracted from *procurator*, ultimate origin also of *procurer*). Found from Glos to Northd.

Proffitt, Profit N 'prophet' OF, either for a fortune-teller or for one who had acted as an Old Testament prophet in a mystery play.

Proger F 'son' (from Welsh *Ap–*) 'of **Roger**'.

Prosser F 'son' (from Welsh *Ap–*) 'of **Rosser**'. Common in Wales and its Border.

Prothero(e), Protherough Forms of **Prydderch**.

Proud(e) N 'proud' OE *prūd* or *prūt* (cf. **Prout**); **–e** could show weak adjective after lost definite article. **–d** is chiefly a Co. Durham–Yorks surname.

Proudfoot N 'proud foot/gait' OE.

Prouse (a Devon surname) See **Prowse**.

Prout See **Proud**. Chiefly a Cornwall, Glos surname.

Provins L 'Provence', the large area of the south of France once called *Provincia* 'the province' Latin.

Provost O 'provost, steward, head of various kinds of body' OF; it may sometimes have absorbed Huguenot **Prevost**, of the same meaning. **Provis** is another form.

Prowse, Pruse N 'valiant' OF; related to **Prew**. **Prowse** is mainly south-western.

Prudham See **Prudhomme**.

Prudhoe L '(AS called) **Proud**'s **Hough**' OE; place in Northd.

Prudhomme N 'wise/honest man, expert' OF.

Pruett, Pruitt See **Prewett**.

Pryce See **Price**; **–y–** is not an affectation, but near the original.

Prydderch F 'son' (from Welsh *Ap–*) 'of **Rhydderch**'.

Pryde See **Pride**.

Pryer An unpleasant Norfolk form of **Prior**; and **Pryor** is found in Cornwall.

Pryke N 'point, prick, lance' OE.

Puckle N 'little puck/elf/goblin' OE *pucel*.

Puckridge L 'goblin's/water-sprite's stream' OE; place (–ker–) in Herts.

Puddephat(t), Puddefoot, Puddifoot N 'bulgy barrel' OE (cf. *pudding*, which is ?something swollen up, and *vat*), for a man with a fat stomach. A Bucks–Beds–Herts group.

Pudsey L 'island/river-meadow of (an AS called) ?**Wart**' OE; place in West Yorks.

Pugh F 'son' (from Welsh *Ap–*) 'of **Hugh**'. Common in Wales (especially North) and its Border.

Pugsley L 'clearing of (an AS called) Pocg' OE, farms (East and West P—) in Satterleigh and Warkleigh, Devon, spelt *Poghlegh* 1303, *Poggeslegh* 1330 (though not related to the Norman *le Pugeis* family who held Broughton Poggs, Oxon). A north Devon surname.

Pulford L 'pool ford, ford by a pool' OE; place in Ches.

Pulham L 'homestead/river-meadow by a pool' OE; places in Dorset, Norfolk.

F: *first name*   L: *local name*   N: *nickname*   O: *occupational name*

Pullan, Pullen, Pullin N 'colt' OF; for someone wild, frisky, or lascivious. In frequency they occur –e–, –i–, –a–; Guppy found them in the groups Mon–Glos–Oxon–Wilts–Berks–Bucks, and West Yorks (with –a– in the latter).

Pullman, Pulman L 'dweller by the pool' OE.

Pulteney See **Pountney**.

Pumfrey, Pumphrey F 'son' (from Welsh *Ap*–) 'of **Humfrey**'. But sometimes L, for **Pomfret**.

Pummery Corruption of **Pomeroy**.

Punchard, Puncher F Old French (Norman dialect) dim. of *Pontius* 'man from Pontus' (the Asia Minor province at the east end of the Black Sea, meaning 'sea' Greek) Latin; name of two 3rd-century saints.

Punshon F dim. 'Pontius' OF (see **Punchard**).

Punter O 'man at the bridge, bridge-keeper' OF (cf. Modern French *pont*).

Purbrook L 'goblin's/water-sprite's (our *Puck*) brook' OE; place in Hants.

Purcell N 'piglet' OF.

Purchas(e) N 'pursuit, chase, hunting, pillage' OF, but eventually used for couriers.

Purcifer Yorks corruption of **Perceval**.

Purday, Purdey, Purdie, Purdue, Purdy N 'by (literally for) God!' OF; from a favourite exclamation.

Purdham From **Prudham**, by metathesis.

Purefoy N 'by (my) faith' OF; from a favourite exclamation; **Pure–** is a high-sounding alteration from *Par–*.

Purkess, Purkis(s) See **Purchase**. Guppy counted –**kis** in Cambs only.

Purley L 'pear-tree clearing/field' OE; place in Surrey.

Purnell See **Parnell**.

Purseglove, Purs(g)love N ?'glove with a purse in it' OE+OE (but none is mentioned in any dictionary). Chiefly a Derbys surname.

Purser O 'purse-/pouch-maker' OE; by the 15th century, ship's officer in charge of accounts and provisions.

Pursey See **Percy**.

Purves, Purvis O 'purveyor, caterer' (in a religious house, etc.) OF; both should have two syllables; Guppy found –**is** only in Northd–Co. Durham.

Puscat N 'pussy-cat' second element OE, first imitative and no doubt native. Reaney noted one in the London TD in 1949 – it had gone by 1962.

Pusey L 'island where peas grow' OE (or, rather, the original singular *pease* as in *pease pudding*); place in Berks. Also spelt **Pussey**.

Putley L 'kite wood' OE (or the AS owner of the wood/clearing may have been nicknamed 'Kite' for voracity); place in Herefords.

Putman is **Pitman** with west Midland and south-western –**u**– from OE West Saxon –*y*–.

Putnam L 'Putta's homestead' OE; places (Puttenham) in Herts, Surrey.

Putt West Midland and south-western form of **Pitt**, with –**u**– for OE West Saxon –*y*–.

Puttack, Puttick, Puttock, Puttuck N 'kite' OE, denoting a greedy eater. Guppy counted **Puttock** only in Surrey.

Pyatt N dim. 'magpie' OF. Chiefly a Staffs surname.

Pye N 'magpie' OF. Or L, from living at the sign. Or O 'pie(-baker/seller)' ME from ?, a metonym.

Pym(m) (Devon surnames) See **Pim(m)**.

Pymont L ?'foot of the hill' OF; places (Pimont) in Manche and Seine-Inférieure.

F: *first name*   L: *local name*   N: *nickname*   O: *occupational name*

Q

Quaif(e) O 'skullcap(-maker/-seller)' OF (cf. *coif*). Or N for a wearer of one.

Quail(e) F 'son of **Paul**' in its Manx Gaelic form, the **Q**– being the remains of *Mc*–. On the other hand, when of English stock the sur-name is a N, from the 'quail' OF, a bird with a reputation for timi-dity and lasciviousness (not an attractive combination).

Quaintance N 'acquaintance, companion' OF (cf. **Friend, Neighbour**).

Quainton L 'queen's manor' OE; place in Bucks.

Qualtrough F 'son of **Walter**' in its Manx form; see **Quail**.

Quant N 'clever, smart, crafty' OF (ultimately from Latin *cognit*–, with sense of 'knowing'); cf. *quaint*.

Quantick, Quantock L From the Quantock Hills in Somerset (see **Cannington**).

Quantrell, Quantrill N 'fop, dandy' OF.

Quarendon L 'quern hill (i.e. hill where millstones are got)' OE; place in Bucks.

Quarless L '(?stone) circles' OE; place (–es) in Norfolk.

Quarrell O 'crossbow bolt/arrow' OF (like most of the nastier sophis-ticated words of medieval warfare), for a maker/shooter.

Quarrie, Quarry O 'quarry(man)' OF. Or N 'square-built, stocky' OF.

Quarrington L The place in Co. Durham is the same as **Quarendon**, but place in Lincs is ? more like 'millers' place' OE.

Quartermain(e), Quarterman N 'four hands' OF – the extra pair being mailed.

Quayle See the Manx **Quail**.

Queen N 'queen' OE, from acting the part (all medieval theatricals were performed by males) or from service with the Queen.

Queenborough L 'queen's borough' OE; place in Kent raised to borough status in 1367 and named after Queen Philippa (and having the dubious distinction of being the last place in England to be captured and occupied by foreigners – the Dutch 300 years later).

Quenby L 'queen's manor' OE scandinavianized; place in Leics; but first element may be from 'woman' or a personal F of like meaning.

Quen(n)ell F 'woman/queen war' OE feminine.

Quested L Probably Wherstead in Suffolk, 'place by a wharf' OE, spelt *Querstede* in 1283.

Quick N 'brisk, lively' OE. Or L 'quickset hedge' or 'quitch, couch-grass' OE, places in Lancs, West Yorks; or from Cowick 'cow farm'

OE, places in Devon, West Yorks, But the surname is found chiefly in Cornwall–Devon. Also spelt **Quicke**; for the **-e**, see **Goode**.

Quickfall L 'Wigg's place where trees have been felled' (or the first element may be 'horse' or 'beetle') OE; place (Wigfield, formerly Wigfall) in West Yorks.

Quickson F 'son of **Quick**'.

Quiddington L Probably from Quidhampton in Hants, Wilts, and (lost) IoW, 'dirty/dungy **Hampton**' OE. Bardsley found it in Surrey.

Quigley N (for O Q—) 'descendant of ? ?Untidy' Irish.

Quilliam F 'son of **William**' in its Manx Gaelic form; cf. **Quail**.

Quilter O 'maker of quilted mattresses/coverlets' OF. An Essex surname.

Quin(n) F (for O Q—) 'descendant of ?Counsel' Irish. **Quin** is more Protestant than the Roman Catholic **Quinn**, which was the 19th commonest surname in Ireland in 1890.

Quinc(e)y L Whether from the earliest settlers from Cuinchy (Pas-de-Calais), or later from one of the six places Quincy in France, the origin is a F from Latin *Quintus* 'fifth' + Gaulish place-name suffix *-acos*.

Quine F 'son of Counsel' Manx; for the **Q–** see **Quail**.

Quinney N 'son of Crafty' Manx; for the **Q–** see **Quail**.

Quinton L 'queen's manor' OE; places in Glos, Northants, Worcs. Or F 'fifth' Latin; popularized by Saint Quentin, martyred in north France in the 3rd century – whence also L, from places Saint-Quentin, Manche and Somme. Or N for someone who tilted at the 'quintain' OF.

Quirk F 'son of Heart' Irish or Manx; cf. **Quail**.

Quixley L 'clearing of (an AS called) Brisk Helmet' OE; place (Whixley) in West Yorks.

Quorn L Same as **Quarendon**; place in Leics.

Quy L 'cow island' OE; place in Cambs.

F: *first name*   L: *local name*   N: *nickname*   O: *occupational name*

R

Rabbatts, Rabbetts, Rabbit(t)s F '(son) of (dim.) **Robert**' or '(son) of Counsel Messenger' Germanic (cf. **Alfred, Beade**). **Rabson** 'son of (dim.) **Robert**'. Guppy counted **Rabbetts** in Dorset.

Raby L 'landmark/boundary farm' ON; places in Ches, Cumberland, Co. Durham.

Rackcliffe is an ill-spelt version of **Radcliff**.

Rackham L 'homestead by (a hill resembling) a hayrick' OE; place in Sussex under R— Hill, but a Norfolk–Suffolk surname.

Rackstraw, Rakestraw N Doubtfully combining with 'straw' OE the words *rake* 'go over with a rake', *rack* 'manger', or *rack* 'fill up with' OE, the most likely reference being to stinginess, for one who rakes up every scrap even of straw; but a place Rakestraws in Longwood, West Yorks, spelt *Rake Straw* in 1771, is hard to interpret. Surnames of Lancs–Yorks.

Radbourne, Radburn L 'reedy stream' OE; places in Derbys (–ourne), Warwicks (–ourn).

Radcliff(e), Radclyffe L Same as **Redcliffe**; places in five counties. Chiefly West Yorks surnames.

Raddon L 'red hill' OE; three places in Devon.

Radford, Radforth L 'red (from the colour of the nearby soil)/road/ riding (one that can be passed through on horseback)/?reedy ford' OE; places of any of these four meanings in five counties. Guppy found **–d** to be very common in Derbys, with fewer in Oxon, Notts, Essex.

Radge L 'red stubble-field' OE *ersc*; place (Radersh in 1238) in Tavistock, Devon.

Radley L 'red clearing' OE; place in Berks.

Radnage, Radnedge L '(at) the red oak' OE, with **–n–** for weak dative singular after lost preposition and definite article, and the original *k* sound palatalized in the dative; place in Bucks.

Radstone L 'rood-stone (i.e. stone cross)' OE; place in Northants.

Radway L 'way /road fit to ride on' OE; place in Warwicks, and a Glos surname.

Radwell L 'red spring/stream' OE; places in Beds, Herts.

Rae Scots form of **Roe**.

Rafe, Raff See **Ralf**.

Rafferty F (for O R—) 'descendant of ?Floodtide/?Prosperity-Wielder' Irish.

Raggett F dim. 'counsel' OF *Ragot/Raguet* from Germanic. Sometimes perhaps L 'gate for roe-deer' OE, place (Rogate, but Ragat in 1229) in Sussex. Bardsley supposes it to be N 'ragged, shaggy' ME.

Raikes L 'of (i.e. at) the **Rake**', or a plural; locality, or places in Surrey, West Yorks.

Rain(e), Rain(e)s Mainly north-eastern surnames, especially of Co. Durham, with a daunting choice of origins: F 'power' Germanic; L 'strip of land, boundary' Co. Durham dialect *rain*, or 'Rennes/ Reims' (from Gaulish tribes *Redones/Remi*); N 'queen' OF or 'frog' OF. And '(son) of' the preceding.

Rainbird F 'power bright' OF from Germanic.

Rainbow F 'power bold' OF from Germanic, respelt to look like a phenomenon; the *–d* is still seen in **Raybould**. Frequent in Warwicks.

Rainey F dim. **Reynold**, here in its Scots dim. form; or the remains of an Irish Mac/O form.

Rainford L 'ford of (an AS called) Power' OE; place in Lancs, and a Lancs surname.

Rake L 'narrow valley, defile, pass' OE (originally 'throat'); locality, or places in Lancs, Staffs, Sussex.

Rakestraw See **Rackstraw**.

Raleigh L ?'red clearing' OE; place in Pilton, Devon, but first element may be 'roe (deer)' OE; and place in Northam, Devon, was ?'clearing where rye grows' OE.

Ralf(e) F 'advice wolf' Germanic; *Radulf/Raulf* in its Norman form, *Raoul* in the French of Paris – whence surnames such as **Rawle**. The *–ph* spelling is now much commoner for both F and surname; the old vernacular pronunciation **Rafe** has become superior, and the spelling-pronunciation vulgar. The numerous progeny are (sometimes hopelessly) intertwined with those of **Rolf**. **Ralfs** '(son) of R—'.

Ralling(s), Rallis(on) Forms of **Rawlin(s), Rawlinson**.

Ralph(s) Commoner version of **Ralf(s)**.

Rama(d)ge N 'living in the branches' a hawking term; so, 'wild' OF.

Ramm N 'ram' OE, for sexual aggressiveness, or winning the ram-prize at wrestling, or living 'at the sign of' this zodiacal beast.

Rampton L 'ram farm' OE; places in Cambs, Notts.

Ramsay Scots form of **Ramsey**, the Scots family being descended from a 12th-century settler from Hunts. Family name of the earls of Dalhousie.

Ramsbotham, Ramsbottom, Ramsdale, Ramsden L All 'wild-garlic valley' OE (more probably than 'ram's/rams' valley' OE);

F: *first name*   L: *local name*   N: *nickname*   O: *occupational name*

places in seven counties. **–bottom** is a Lancs surname, **–den** West Yorks. **Ramsbotham** is the family name of the viscounts Soulbury.

Ramsey L 'wild-garlic island' OE; places in Essex, Hunts.

Ramshaw L 'Shaw with rams' OE; place in Co. Durham; or from **Ravenshaw**.

Ramson Possibly N 'wild garlic' OE *hramsan* plural, later taken as a singular (with plural *ramsons*). Or 'son of **Ramm**'.

Ranald Scots Gaelic (*Raonull*) form of **Ronald**.

Rand Usually F dim. '**Randolph**'. Or L 'border, untilled margin of a field, strip of land on a river-bank' OE; locality, or places in Lincs, North Yorks. Guppy counted the surname only in Bucks, Northd.

Randall, Randell, Randle, Randoll F dim. '**Rand**', with OF suffix *–el*. **Randles** '(son) of R—'. **–a–** is commonest, **–o–** rarest; the group are found in Dorset, east and west Midlands, East Anglia.

Randolph F 'shield wolf' Germanic normanized; probably absorbing 'raven wolf' Germanic also. Whence **Rand** and its offspring.

Rank N 'strong, exultant, proud' OE.

Rankin(e), Ranking F dim. '**Randolph**'.

Ransford L ?'ford for rams' or 'ford at wild garlic' OE.

Ransom F 'son of **Rand**', with *–son* becoming **–som** by folketymology. Guppy counted it only in Suffolk.

Raper O 'rope-maker' OE (northern dialect form retaining *ā*). One bearer had an unfortunate address in **Sabine** Road, London SW11.

Rapkins F '(son) of (double dim.) **Robert**'; see **Rapson**, **Rabson**.

Rapson F 'son of (dim.) **Robert**' (cf. **Rabson**). Chiefly a Cornish surname.

Rasch Form of **Rash**.

Rasen L 'plank(?-bridge)' OE; three places in Lincs.

Rash L '(at) the **Ash**', early ME *at ther* (preposition + feminine dative singular of definite article) becoming *atter* and so *'r*; here wrongly used before an OE masculine noun.

Rasmussen F Scandinavian version of 'son of Erasmus (= "beloved")' Greek, the saint whose bowels were wound out on a windlass in Diocletian's persecution. (This exotic surname is included because the saint doesn't get a look-in in British nomenclature.)

Raspberry, Raspery L 'red (land with) brushwood' OE (cf. *spray*); place (Ratsbury) in Devon. No connection with the fruit.

Rastel(l) O 'dealer in, or user of, rakes' OF *rastel*.

Rastrick L 'stream/ditch at a resting-place' ON, place in West Yorks; Ekwall prefers 'stream with a plank-bridge' OE.

Ratcliff(e) L Same as **Redcliffe**; places in Devon, Leics, Notts,

London (Stepney). Guppy found it most commonly in Staffs, Glos.

Ratford L Same as **Radford**; farm in Sussex.

Rathbone All other suggestions for what Reaney calls a 'difficult name' having failed, is it possible that this is N 'quick killer' OE *hrathe+bana*?

Ratley L 'wood/clearing of (an AS called) Cheerful' OE (or the place may have been for some reason 'jolly/sportive'); place in Warwicks.

Ratliff(e) See **Ratcliff**.

Rattenbury L 'rat-infested fort/hill/mound' OE.

Ratter O 'rat-catcher' OF. But in north Scotland, Orkney, Shetland, ?L from Rattar Brough, Dunnet, Caithness, 'red headland' ON.

Rattray L 'circular fort' Scots Gaelic or British (the antiquarian's *rath*)+'dwelling/village' British (cf. Welsh *tref*); places in Aberdeens, Perths.

Raven N 'raven' OE or ON, also used as a F. Or L, a sign-name. Counted by Guppy only in Essex.

Ravenhill L 'hill with ravens' OE; place in North Yorks.

Ravenscroft L 'Croft of (an AS called) Raven' OE; place in Ches, and Ches surname.

Ravensdale L 'valley of (an AS/Dane called) Raven' OE or ON; places in Derbys, Notts, Staffs.

Ravenshaw L 'Shaw with ravens' OE; places in Co. Durham, Warwicks, and (Renishaw) Derbys, but Guppy counted it only in Salop.

Raw See **Rowe**. Counted by Guppy only in North and East Yorks.

Rawbone N 'bone (i.e. leg) like a roe (deer)' OE, for a runner.

Rawcliff(e) L 'red cliff' OE scandinavianized, places (also Rockcliffe, Roecliffe) in Cumberland, Lancs, North and West Yorks; but Rowcliffe, Devon, is 'rough hillside' OE. A Lancs surname.

Rawdon L 'rough hill' OE; place in West Yorks; or first element ?'row' (cf. **Rowe**).

Rawle(nce), **Rawles** Forms of **Ralf**, **Rawlins**, **Ralfs**. **Rawle** is a Somerset–Devon surname.

Rawley L 'rough/heron/red/rye/roe-deer clearing' OE; places Raleigh/Rayleigh in Devon/Essex, and perhaps lost places Rawley elsewhere.

Rawlin(g) F dim. '*Raoul*' (see **Ralf**). **Rawlings(on)**, **Rawlins(on)**, **Rawlison** '(son) of **R**—'. But Bardsley observed that some of the many **Rawlinson**s in Cumberland and Furness, Lancs, must be the same as **Rowlandson**, which is there pronounced *Raw*–; **–in(g)s** are Wilts–Somerset surnames. **Rawnson** is a corruption.

F: *first name*   L: *local name*   N: *nickname*   O: *occupational name*

Rawnsley L 'clearing of (an A S called) Raven' O E; lost place in ?West Yorks.

Rawson F 'son of **Ralf**'.

Rawsthorn(e), **Rawstorn(e)**, **Rawstron** L '(Norseman called) Red's thornbush' O N; place (now Rostherne) in Ches.

Ray N 'king' O F, for the same reasons as **King** was used; or 'female roe (deer)' O E, or Scots **Rae**. Or L, same as **Rea** or **Rye**.

Raybould See **Rainbow**.

Raydon L 'hill where rye grows' O E; place in Suffolk.

Rayleigh L 'clearing/field where rye grows' O E, or ?'roes' clearing' (cf. **Raleigh**) O E; place in Essex.

Rayment, **Raymond**, **Raymo(u)nt** F 'might/counsel protector' Germanic normanized. The surnames in **–t** are chiefly from Devon.

Rayne(s) See **Raine(s)**.

Rayner, **Raynor** F 'might/counsel army' Germanic normanized. East Anglia and Notts surname, with **–or** found in Notts.

Rea L '(at) the stream/river' O E (with **R–** as in **Rock**); or = **Rye**.

Reace Rare form of **Rhys** (two in London T D).

Read(e) Usually N 'red(-faced/-haired)' O E; the **–e** for weak adjective after lost definite article. But some of this group (**–ea–/–ee–/–ei–**) are from places Read, Lancs, 'roe headland'; Rede, Suffolk, 'reed-bed'; Reed, Herts, ?'rough place'; or from a 'clearing' (cf. **Ride**) – all O E. **Read** is very common in Midlands, East Anglia, south, south-west.

Reader O 'thatcher (with reed)' O E; a medieval craft commonest in Norwich itself and in Norfolk.

Reading L 'clearing' O E (cf. verb *rid*); sometimes ?the Berks town, 'family/folk of (an A S called) Red' O E.

Ready N 'prompt, quick, opportunist' O E.

Reakes L '(of, i.e.) at the narrow/rough path' or 'at the narrow valley' O E, or a plural (cf. **Rake**). Mainly a Somerset surname.

Realf(f) See **Relf**.

Rearden, **Reardon** See **Riordan**.

Reaveley L 'the Reeve's wood/clearing' O E (or ?'rough clearing' O E); place in Northd.

Reaves See **Reeves**.

Redb(o)urn, **Redbourne** L Same as **Radbourne**; places in Herts, Lincs.

Redcliffe, **Redclift** L 'red cliff' O E, locality, or the Bristol area with Britain's finest parish church.

Redding See **Reading**.

Reddish L 'reedy ditch' OE; places in Ches, Lancs and (Redditch) Worcs.

Redfe(a)rn L 'red bracken' OE, a surname common in Rochdale, Lancs, *c.* 1600 and counted by Guppy in Derbys–Staffs.

Redford L 'red/reedy ford' OE (cf. **Radford**); place in Sussex.

Redgewell L Though looking like a lost place-name 'ridge spring' OE south-eastern dialect, this is Ridgewell, Essex, still pronounced with an *–e–* and meaning 'reedy spring/stream' OE.

Redgrave L 'reedy ditch/digging' OE (cf. *engrave*); place in Suffolk.

Redland L 'cleared (literally ridded) land' OE; but the place in Bristol is 'third (?part of an estate) land' OE.

Redman (and early version **Redmayne**) L Bardsley's examples are *de R—*, so the likeliest origin is place Redmain in Cumberland, for which Ekwall suggests 'red cairn' OE, rejecting 'ford of stone' OW since the place is on no stream. But O 'reed man' (a cutter or thatcher) OE is possible. Or F, corruption of **Redmond**. Two common stocks – in Wilts and West Yorks; and *–ayne* occurs in the latter.

Redmile L 'red earth' (cf. *mould*) OE; place in Leics.

Redmond Irish version of **Raymond**.

Redwood N Literally 'red-mad' (cf. second meaning of **Wood**) OE, 'blazingly angry, crazy'. The tree has too late a name to figure here, and no place R— survives, but a L name 'cleared (cf. **Redland**) wood' OE is possible.

Ree and **Reece** See **Rea/Rye** and **Rees**.

Reed (mainly in Cornwall–Devon, Northd–Co. Durham) See **Read**.

Reeder See **Reader**.

Reeman L 'man living at a stream' OE+OE (see **Rea**).

Rees(e) Commonest spelling of **Rhys**, found by Guppy to be the surname of over three per cent of the people of South Wales; *–e* rare; often spelt **Reece**.

Reeve O 'reeve, chief magistrate, bailiff, overseer' OE (cf. *portreeve*, **Sheriff**). **Reeves** 'servant/?son/(dweller at the house) of **R—**'; but Reaney adds one L origin for **Reeves**: a man living in Worcs in 1327 *atte Reuese*, which is ME *atter evese* 'at the edge' (?of woodland), from OE singular *efes* (cf. *eaves*).

Regan F (for O **R—**) 'descendant of Little King' Irish. 66th commonest surname in Ireland in 1890.

Reid Scots form of **Read**, probably in its N meaning. 14th commonest surname in Scotland in 1958, 81st in Ireland in 1890, and found in Northd–Co. Durham.

F: *first name*   L: *local name*   N: *nickname*   O: *occupational name*

Reilly F (for O **R—**) 'descendant of Valiant' Irish. Eleventh commonest surname in Ireland in 1890.

Relf(e) F 'power wolf' Germanic (if from OF *Riulf*). A Sussex surname.

Rem(m)ington See **Rimington**, which was spelt *Remington* in 1303.

Rendall, Rendell, Rendle, Rendoll F dim. '**Randolph**', or dim. '**Reynold**' in its **Rennell** form +a *d*-glide. Surnames of Dorset-Somerset-Devon.

Renfrew L 'point of current' OW, the Renfrews town.

Rennell(s) and **Rennick** See **Reynold(s)** and **Renwick**.

Renner O 'runner, messenger' ON + suffix.

Rennie F dim. '**Reynold**' (see **Rainey**).

Rennison (a Yorks surname) See **Reynoldson**.

Renowden F dim. '**Reynold**' OF *Renaudon*.

Renshall, Renshaw See **Ravenshaw**. –aw is a Derbys surname.

Renton L 'farm of (an AS the first element of whose name is) Power' OE; place in Berwicks, and a Northd surname.

Renwick L 'dairy-farm of (an AS called) Raven' OE; place in Cumberland, and a Northd–Cumberland surname.

Restler O 'wrestler' OE (when the *w*– was correct in both spelling and pronunciation); it was not a gentlemanly sport – Chaucer's Miller was good at it (but then, so was his absurd Sir Thopas).

Retallack L ' ?high heath' Cornish, place in Cornwall; also **Retallick**.

Retford L See **Redford**; places in Notts.

Retter O 'net-maker' OF. Counted by Guppy only in Devon.

Revel(l), Revill(e) F 'rebel' Latin or 'sport, revelry, rebellion, insolence' OF (from same Latin source). Chiefly Derbys surnames.

Reveley See **Reaveley**.

Revere L '(at) the slope' OE (in south-eastern dialect), with **R–** as in **Rock**. Or N 'reaver, robber, pirate' OE. But Paul **R—**'s family are said to have been Huguenots, via Guernsey, with French surname *de Revoire*, from some place-name meaning 'view' OF.

Rew L 'row (of houses/cottages), ?hedgerow' OE; locality, or places (also Rewe) in Dorset, Devon, IoW, and a Devon surname.

Rex Remains obscure, since neither N 'king' Latin, nor F = **Rix**, nor L 'rush(es)' Dorset–Somerset–Devon dialect *rix/rex*, is wholly convincing.

Rextrew See **Rackstraw**.

Reynold F 'might/counsel power' Germanic. Hence other surnames in **Ren–**; F *Reginald* is cognate. **Reynolds(on)** '(son)/son of **R—**'. –s is the commonest of the whole group, especially south of Lancs-Notts–Norfolk.

Rhoad(e)s, Rhodes L Same as **Roads**; **Rhodes** (with meaning 'clearings') is the name of two estates in Lancs, and a surname of West Yorks–Lancs–Notts–Derbys; the **–h–** is intrusive, based on the well-known island or its Knights.

Rhydderch Welsh F used as equivalent of **Roderick**, but for probable meaning see **McRory**.

Rhyder An inaccurate version of **Ryder**.

Rhys F ?'ardour' OW; origin of the much commoner **Rees/Price**. Family name of the barons Dynevor.

Ribton L 'place where ribwort/hound's-tongue grows' OE; place in Cumberland.

Rice Form of **Rhys**; and see the much commoner **Price**.

Rich N 'rich' OE. Or F dim. '**Richard**'. Or L; those who were *atte riche* lived by the 'stream' OE. Found by Guppy only in Somerset–Wilts–Devon–Cornwall. **Riches** usually '(son) of **Rich**'.

Richard F 'powerful brave' Germanic (both elements exist in OE), popularized by the Normans. **Richard(e)s** '(son) of **R—**'. **Richar(d)son** 'son of **R—**'. Hence many surnames in **Rich-/Rick-**, of which **Richards** (especially Cornwall, South Wales, Midlands) and **Richardson** (everywhere save south-west; and especially north) are by far the commonest; also many in **Di-/Hi-**, from petforms. **Richards** is the family name of the barons Milverton.

Richey, Richie F dim. '**Richard**'.

Richmond L 'splendid hill' OF; various places in France called Richemont; this name was borrowed for **R—**, North Yorks, of which Henry VII was earl before his accession (1485); after this event, it was given also to the former Sheen, Surrey.

Rick F dim. '**Richard**'. **Ricks(on)** F '(son)/son of **R—**'; or L 'rush, rushes' OE (West Saxon *rix-*), in which case **–on** goes back to a dative plural (in *–um*) after a lost preposition.

Rickard, Rickard(e)s Forms of **Richard(s)**, of which **–ard** is very common in Cornwall.

Rickerby L '**Richard**'s farm' second element ON; place in Cumberland.

Ricket(t) F Either forms of **Rickard**, or dim. (*Ricot* OF) of **Richard**. **Ricket(t)s** '(son) of **R—**'. **Ricketson** 'son of **R—**'. **–tt** and **–tts** found in Essex/Glos.

Rickman O 'servant of (dim.) **Richard**'.

Rickward, Rickwood F 'powerful guardian' Germanic.

Riddett L 'clearing with reeds' OE.

Ridding, Ride Both L 'clearing' OE (cf. **Reading**).

F: *first name*   L: *local name*   N: *nickname*   O: *occupational name*

Rideout N 'ride out' OE, from some lost joke.

Rider O 'rider, knight, cavalryman' OE. Or L 'man at the **Ride**'; now much rarer than its derivative **Ryder**, and found mainly in Yorks.

Ridge L 'ridge, long hill' OE, in east Midlands dialect form (cf. **Rudge**). **Ridges** '(of, i.e.) at the ridge', or a plural; or for **Riches**.

Ridg(e)way L 'ridge road' OE; locality, or places in a dozen counties. Counted by Guppy only in Bucks, Ches.

Ridg(e)well L 'reedy stream' OE; place (–e–) in Essex.

Riding L Same as **Ridding**; locality, or places in Berks, Northd, Warwicks; but the surname was counted by Guppy only in Lancs.

Ridler O 'sieve-maker' OE, or one who riddled or sifted corn or (for making mortar) sand and lime. A Somerset–Devon surname.

Ridley L 'cleared (literally ridded, by burning or cutting) wood/ clearing' OE; places in Ches, Northd, and chiefly a Northd–Co. Durham surname (the martyred bishop was of a Border family); some bearers in the south-east may be from places 'reedy clearing' OE in Essex and Kent, but the Suffolk family descend from that of Northd.

Ridout See **Rideout**. Guppy found it common in Dorset.

Rigby L 'ridge farm' ON. Chiefly a Lancs–Ches surname.

Rigden F dim. '**Rickard**' with OF suffix (despite the L look). Counted by Guppy only in Kent.

Rigg L 'ridge' ON. **Riggs** 'of (i.e. at) the ridge', or a plural.

Riggulsford L 'ford at the ?thicket' OE; place (now Woodlesford) in West Yorks.

Rigmaiden L 'maiden's ridge' ON+OE, the possessive put second in the Keltic manner; farm (Rigmaden) in Westmorland.

Riley See **Reilly**. Or L 'clearing with rye' OE; places in Devon, Lancs.

Rimell F 'border battle' OE feminine (cf. *rim, Hilda*); a Glos–Worcs surname.

Rimer See **Rymer**.

Rimin(g)ton L 'place on a river-bank/ridge/boundary' OE (cf. *rim*); place in West Yorks on the Lancs border.

Rimmer O 'rhymer, poet' OE/OF. Chiefly a Lancs surname.

Ring N 'ring' OE, from wearing one. Or O, for a jeweller or bell-ringer. Or L, for a '(stone) circle' or some ring-shaped topographical feature.

Ringer O '(bell-)ringer' OE; Reaney suggests also a 'wringer (of ?cheese)' OE. Or F 'ring army' OE (cf. **Herapath**).

Ringstead L 'site with a salt-pan' OE, place in Dorset; or 'site with a ?stone circle or circular earthwork' OE, places in Norfolk, North-ants.

Ringwood L 'border/boundary wood' OE, place in Hants; but place in Essex is ?'marsh in a curve' OE (cf. *ring*).

Riordan F (for O **R**—) 'descendant of Royal Bard' Irish.

Ripley L 'wood/clearing shaped like a strip' OE; places in Derbys, Hants, Surrey, West Yorks (but the last is near Ripon, and Ekwall suggests that it may be 'wood/clearing of the people of Ripon' – a tribal name meaning ?).

Ripper O 'basket-maker/-seller' ON.

Rippingale L 'the **Haugh** (OE *halh*) of the followers of (an AS called) Active' OE; place in Lincs.

Rippon L 'at the (Anglian tribe called the) Hrype' OE dative plural *–um* after lost preposition; place (Ripon) in West Yorks. The tribe recurs at Repton and **Ripley**, but the meaning of their name is obscure. Chiefly a surname of Lincs.

Risborough L 'hill(s)/mound(s) overgrown with brushwood' OE; two places in Bucks.

Risby L 'farm at a clearing' ON, places in Suffolk, East Yorks; but two places in Lincs are ?'farm in the brushwood' ON.

Riseley L 'brushwood clearing' OE; places in Beds, Berks.

Rishton L 'place where rushes grow' OE; place in Lancs.

Risley L Same as **Riseley**; places in Derbys, Lancs.

Ritchie F dim. '**Richard**', or for Mc**Ritchie** 'son of **Richard**'. 75th commonest surname in Scotland in 1958.

Ritson is a Cumberland–Westmorland–Durham contraction of **Richardson**.

Rivers L One of many places in France called Rivière(s) 'river-bank(s)' OF; or Rievaulx in North Yorks, a frenchified version of *Ryedale* 'valley of the ?hill-stream' OW+OE.

Rix(on) See **Ricks(on)**.

Roach See **Roch**. Guppy counted it in Cornwall and Glos.

Roadnight O 'mounted servant' OE (cf. **Knight**).

Roads L 'clearings' OE (cf. **Ridding, Ride**), much more probable than '(cross-)roads' OE. Road/Roade 'clearing' are places in Somerset/Northants; and cf. **Royds**. Counted by Guppy only in Bucks.

Roan L 'Rouen' OF from Latin *Rotomagus*, second element 'field' Gaulish; city in Seine-Maritime.

Roantree and **Robarts** See **Rowntree** and **Roberts**.

Robb F dim. '**Robert**'. **Robbins** '(son) of (double dim.) **Robert**'.

Robens See **Robins**.

Robert F 'fame bright' Germanic, a favourite Norman F. Whence many surnames in **Rob–** and its pet-forms **Hob–/Dob–/Nob–**

F: *first name*   L: *local name*   N: *nickname*   O: *occupational name*

(*Bob* is a later dim.). **Roberts(on)** F '(son)/son of **R—**'. **-s** widespread, very common in North Wales, rare in the north; ninth commonest surname in England and Wales in 1853, 27th in USA in 1939. **-son** chiefly Scots – eighth commonest surname in Scotland in 1958 (dropping from fifth in 100 years). **Roberts** is the family name of the barons Clwyd.

Robeson Form of **Robson/Robertson/Robinson**.

Robey L Same as **Raby**; place in Derbys. But Scots bearers are F dim. '**Robert**'.

Robins(on) F '(son)/son of (double dim.) **Robert**'. **-son** is the commonest surname based on the F – 12th in England and Wales in 1853, 73rd in Ireland in 1890, 22nd in USA in 1939; two per cent of Guppy's Co. Durham yeomen were called it in 1890.

Robjohn F double dim. '**Robert**'+two OF suffixes; or from dim. '**Robert**' OF *Robion*.

Roblett, Roblin F double dim. '**Robert**', with OF suffixes *–el–* and *–ot/–in*.

Robson F 'son of (dim.) **Robert**'. Huge incidence in Northd–Co. Durham.

Roby L or F Same as **Robey**; place in Lancs.

Roch(e) L 'rock' OF, locality, or places in Cornwall, West Yorks; sometimes from plural Les Roches, place in Seine-Maritime. Rarely ?F from Saint Roch 'rest, repose' Germanic, the healer of plague (†1337). Form **Roach** is much commoner. **Roche** is the family name of the barons Fermoy.

Rochester L ('town at the bridges' British, much changed in form and thence wrongly associated with) 'roof' OE+'Roman site' OE from Latin; place in Kent.

Rochford L 'hunting dog's ford' OE; places in Essex, Worcs.

Rock L '(at) the oak' OE, with **-r** (ME from OE *–re*) of dative of feminine definite article, after lost preposition, carried over into the noun; locality, or place in Worcs. But 'rock' OE or OF is sometimes possible; locality, or places in Devon, Northd. Other places of either derivation in Cornwall, Somerset. Sussex, IoW.

Rockcliffe L Same as **Rawcliffe**; place in Cumberland.

Rocker L 'dweller at the rock' OE or OF. Or O 'distaff-maker, spinner' ON.

Rockley L 'rook wood/clearing' OE; place in Wilts.

Rodbourn(e) L 'reedy stream' OE; two places in Wilts.

Rodd L 'clearing' OE (cf. **Ridding**); place in Herefords. **Roddam** '(at) the clearings' OE dative plural after lost preposition; place in Northd, and a Northd surname. **Rodd** is the family name of the barons Rennell.

Rodden L 'roe bucks' valley' OE; place in Somerset.

Roderick F 'fame powerful' Germanic.

Rodger, Rodgers(on) Rarer forms of **Roger, Rogers(on)**.

Rodway L Same as **Radway**; place in Somerset.

Roe N 'roe (deer)' OE *rā*, which in the north and Scotland remained **Rae**. The N might be given for speed, shyness, hunting. There may be confusion with **Rowe**.

Roebuck N 'roe buck' OE, from some odd resemblance to the handsome animal. Counted by Guppy only in West Yorks.

Rofe, Roff See **Rolf**.

Roffey L 'deer fence' OF (cf. *roe, hedge*), place in Sussex; sometimes ?'rough enclosure' OE, locality, or place (Roffy) in Essex.

Roger F 'fame spear' Germanic (the rarely used modern F *Hrothgar*); one of the many Germanic Fs popularized by the Normans. **Rogers-(on)** '(son)/son of R—'. -s is very common in Midlands, south, South Wales, and was the 31st commonest surname in USA in 1939. Pet-forms include **Hodge** and **Dodge**.

Roget(t) F dim. '**Roger**'.

Roke L '(at) the oak' OE (see **Rock**).

Roland F 'fame land' Germanic, popular as the F of Charlemagne's most famous peer; spelling *–ow–* became commoner than *–o–*. **Rolands** '(son) of R—'.

Roles F '(son) of **Rolf**'.

Roley See **Rowley**.

Rolf(e) F 'fame wolf' Germanic, especially in ON form *Hrólf–*. Reaney lists its family of over two dozen surnames, admitting the alternative origins of some of them, and especially the involvement with **Ralf**. The form with –e is found in Norfolk–Suffolk–Essex–Kent and Bucks–Herts; Pocahontas's husband John **Rolfe** (†1623) of Heacham, Norfolk, must take pride of place here; **Rolfe** was the real name of 'Baron Corvo'. **Rolfs** '(son) of R—'.

Roll(e), Rollo, Rolph F Forms of **Rolf**. **Roll(e)s** '(son) of R—'.

Rolland(s) See **Roland(s)**.

Roller O 'dealer in rolls/scrolls (of parchment or vellum)' OF.

Rollin(s), Rolling(s), Rollinson F dim. '**Rolf/Roland**' or for **Rawlin**; and '(son)/son of R—'.

Rollo, Rolph See **Roll**.

Roman(s) F 'Roman' OF, with the slender chance (as Reaney points out) that one of three saints Romanus may be intended; and '(son) of **Roman**'.

Rome L The Italian city, from ? a pre-Roman river-name for the

---

F: *first name*   L: *local name*   N: *nickname*   O: *occupational name*

Tiber, or ? an Etruscan family name, or ? Latin *ruma* 'breast' (the Palatine Hill); *not* from Greek *rhōmē* 'force, might'. or from the legendary Romulus. For a pilgrim who had been there, rather than an immigrant.

Romilly L 'Remilly, Romilly, Rumilly' OF from male F *Romilius*+ suffix, over a dozen places in France; sometimes perhaps 'roomy/spacious clearing' OE, place (Romiley) in Ches.

Ronald F Scots form of **Reynold**, but through ON form *Rognvald*–. **Ronalds(on)** '(son)/son of **R**—'.

Ronicle L 'rye field' OE *rygen*+*æcer*.

Ronson Lancs version of **Rowlandson**.

Rook(e) N 'rook' OE (?from black hair). Or L, see **Roke**. Chiefly a surname of Cumberland and Yorks. **Rook(e)s** '(son) of **R**—'.

Room(e) L The old pronunciation of **Rome**, giving point to Shakespeare's pun 'Rome indeed, and room enough' in *Julius Caesar*.

Roope O 'rope(-maker)' OE.

Roos(e) See **Rose**.

Root N 'cheerful, bright' OE. Or O '(player on the) psaltery/rote' OF.

Roper O 'rope-maker' OE; counted by Guppy only in the scattered counties Dorset, Worcs, Suffolk (whereas **Raper** belongs to the north).

Rosaman Form of **Rosamond**.

Rosamond F 'horse protection' Germanic, mistaken in the Middle Ages for Latin *rosa munda* 'rose undefiled'.

Roscoe L 'roe-buck wood' ON; place in Lancs.

Rose L 'promontory, cape' Scots Gaelic, 'wood' Irish and Scots Gaelic, 'moor' Cornish and Welsh; also a sign-name, 'at the Sign of the Rose' OF. But although the Clan **R**— of Kilravock, the barons de Ros (from Roos in East Yorks), and place Roose in Lancs have a Gaelic or Welsh beginning, the usual origin is a Germanic feminine F 'fame kind' (cf. **Robert**, –*hood*) occurring as *Rohesia* and giving rise to **Royce**. (Many of the 900 in the London TD must be Jewish, with abbreviated surnames based on the flower.) Guppy found it in contiguous counties from Lincs to Dorset.

Roseberry L 'Newton-under-*Ouesbergh*', North Yorks, changed to *Roseberry* by metanalysis; *Ouesbergh* may well have been 'Woden's hill' ON, and a centre of pagan worship – it is now called Roseberry Topping.

Rosedale L 'valley of horses' ON; two places in North Yorks.

Roseman See **Rosamond**.

Rosevear(e) L 'big moor' (adjective second) Cornish; place in Cornwall.

Rosewall L 'heath with a wall' (says T. F. G. Dexter, unconvincingly) Cornish; place (R— Hill) in St Ives, Cornwall.

Rosewarne L 'alder-tree heath' Cornish; two places in Cornwall.

Rosier Still found in South Wales, and presumably an early form of **Rosser**.

Rosomon See **Rosamond**.

Ross L See **Rose**; places in Herefords, Northd, and some families from places Roos(e), and some from Rots, place in Calvados. Also F meaning 'fame' Germanic (cf. **Robert**). 22nd commonest surname in Scotland in 1958 (dropping six places in 100 years), ?mainly denoting the county = 'promontory, isthmus' Scots Gaelic. In England, Guppy counted it only in Dorset.

Rosser F A Welsh F of unknown origin, though **Roger** may have become *Rhosiêr*; the *Ap*– form **Prosser** is much commoner, especially in Mon.

Rossiter See **Rochester**. But counted by Guppy only in Dorset.

Rost(r)on See **Rawsthorn**.

Rotherham L 'homestead/river-meadow on the ?chief river' British +OE; place in West Yorks on the River Rother.

Rothwell L 'spring/stream in a clearing' OE; places in Lincs, Northants, West Yorks.

Roughead N 'rough head (of hair)' OE.

Round N 'rotund, plump' OF.

Rounsivell L 'Roncesvalles' (once Basque *Rozabal*, second element *zabal* 'extensive'; wrongly associated with 'dewy/spear/sorrel/ nags'+'valley' Latin), place in Navarre, north Spain, where traditionally Charlemagne's rearguard was attacked by Saracens and Roland was killed; its priory had as a cell a hospital at Charing Cross (dedicated to Our Lady of Rouncevale). Also N 'monstrous, gigantic; a loose/raucous woman' (origin unknown).

Rountree See **Rowntree**.

Rous(e) N 'red (hair/face)' OF. **Rous** is the family name of the earls of Stradbroke.

Rover O 'roofer' OE.

Rowan L 'rowan, mountain-ash' ON.

Rowberry, Rowbory See **Rowbury**.

Rowbotham, Rowbottom L 'rough valley' OE. Chiefly a Derbys– Staffs surname.

Rowbrey, Rowbury L 'rough hill' OE; these surnames, and others like them, are from a group of places with first element Ro–/Row–/

F: *first name*　　L: *local name*　　N: *nickname*　　O: *occupational name*

Ru– and second element –berrow/–borough in Devon, Somerset, Wilts.

Rowcliffe See **Rawcliffe**.

Rowden, Rowdon L 'rough hill' OE (cf. **Down**); places (–e–) in Herefords, Devon, Wilts.

Rowe L 'row (of houses/cottages), hedgerow' OE, with –e for dative after lost preposition. Or N 'rough' OE, with –e of weak adjective after lost definite article. Or ?F See **Rolf, Ralf**.

Rowell L 'rough hill' OE, place in Devon; or 'roe bucks' hill' OE, places in Glos (also Roel), Westmorland – second element perhaps 'spring/stream' OE; or even a simplification of **Rothwell**. Guppy shows it as oddly scattered – Northd, Devon, Hunts.

Rower O 'wheelwright' OF (cf. *roulette* 'little wheel', and a spur-*rowel*).

Rowhay L 'rough enclosure/hedge' OE (like Rowhedge, Essex).

Rowland F Common form of **Roland**. But also possibly L, from place in Derbys 'roe wood' ON (especially as the surname occurs in Derbys–Ches). **Rowlands(on)** '(son)/son of **R—**'. **Rowlands** is chiefly a surname of Wales.

Rowles F '(son) of **Rolf**'. Chiefly an Oxon surname.

Rowley L 'rough wood/clearing' OE; five places from Co. Durham to Devon.

Rowney L '(at) the rough enclosure' OE, with –n for weak dative singular after lost preposition and definite article; places in Beds, Essex, Herts, Worcs.

Rowntree L 'rowan/mountain-ash tree' ON+OE. A Yorks surname.

Rowsell N 'little red-head/-face' OF (cf. **Russell**).

Rowthorn L 'rough thorn-bush' OE; place in Derbys.

Rowton L 'rough(-soiled) place' OE; places in Salop, East Yorks (others in Ches, Salop are more doubtful).

Roxburgh L Johnston makes the place in Roxburghs 'castle on a rock' OF+OE or 'castle of a man called **Roch/Rock**'.

Roxby L '(Norseman called) Red's farm' ON, two places in North Yorks; or '(Norseman called) Rook's farm' ON, places in Lincs, North Yorks.

Roy N 'king' OF, from ?royal service, or ?swagger, or ?acting in a play; and early used as a F. (But the present F is really 'red' Scots Gaelic, and has not given rise to a surname.)

Royal and **Royce** See **Royle** and **Rose**.

Royden L 'hill where rye grows' OE; places (–don) in Essex, Norfolk, Suffolk.

Royds L Yorks dialect version of **Roads** 'clearings' (cf. Yorks *'oil* for *hole*); –royd/–rod is also a common element in place-names – cf. **Murgatroyd, Ormerod.**

Roylance See **Rylands.**

Royle L 'hill with rye' OE; place in Lancs, and a Ches–Lancs surname.

Royston L Originally 'Rohesia's (see **Rose**) cross' Germanic+OF, but changed to her 'place/?stone (cross)' OE; place in Herts but place in West Yorks is 'farm of (an AS called) Vigorous/Strong' OE (now curiously in vogue as a F, as if a full form of F Roy!).

Rubery See **Rowbury.**

Ruck See **Rook,** in its N sense.

Ruckley L 'rook wood' OE; two places in Salop.

Rudd N 'red-haired, ruddy' OE. Counted by Guppy only in Norfolk, Salop.

Rudderham See **Rotherham.**

Ruddick, Ruddock, Rudduck N 'robin red-breast' OE.

Rudge L West Midlands dialect form of **Ridge**; locality, or places in Glos, Salop. Or N 'red (hair/face)' OF (cf. *rouge*). A surname of Herefords–Worcs–Glos.

Rudgewick L 'Wick on a ridge' OE; place (Rudgwick) in Sussex.

Rudkin N dim. 'red-haired, ruddy' OE+Flemish suffix.

Rudrum Further reduction of **Rudderham.**

Ruff F See **Rolf.** Or L 'rough (ground)' OE. Or N 'rough, hairy, violent' OE. Anyway, nothing to do with the fish, the bird, or the linen collar.

Rufford L 'rough ford' OE; places in Lancs, Notts, West Yorks.

Rugby L 'fort of (an AS called) Rook' OE, but with 'fort' changed to 'farm' ON; place in Warwicks which gave its name to the game after William Webb Ellis cheated there and picked the ball up.

Rugman L 'dweller on a ridge' OE *hrycg,* here in its south-west Midland form with –u–. Chiefly a Glos surname.

Rumball, Rumbell, Rumble, Rumbold F 'glory bold' Germanic; popular through the precocious Saint Rumbald, or Rumwald, who at birth confessed himself a Christian, demanded baptism, preached a sermon, and died aged three days. But Rumbold Farm, Sussex, is 'roomy fold' OE. Guppy counted the surname only in Hants.

Rumbelow L '(at) three hills/barrows' OE; initial *th–* of *three* has dropped, but the –**m** of its dative after lost preposition remains. Reaney nicely shows that the resemblance to a sailors' heave-ho song is coincidental.

Rumens ?Form of **Romans,** seen in Glos.

F: *first name*   L: *local name*   N: *nickname*   O: *occupational name*

Rumford L The correct pronunciation of Romford, Essex, 'roomy/ wide ford' OE; also **Rumfitt**.

Rump N 'buttocks' ME from ?ON, sometimes also used for an 'ugly creature' in dialect.

Rumsey L The correct pronunciation of Romsey, Hants, 'island of (an AS called) Noble/Liberal/Ample (cf. *roomy*)' OE.

Rumsum L '*Rūm*'s homestead (the same F as at **Rumsey**)' OE; place (Rumsam) in Barnstaple, Devon.

Runciman O 'man who looks after the nags/rouncies' OF (+ *man* OE) – ?ultimately connected with German *Ross*, English *horse*, and Don Quixote's jade *Rocinante*.

Runcorn L 'wide bay' OE (cf. *roomy*, *cove*); place in Ches.

Rundall, Rundle N 'plumpish, somewhat rotund' OF *rondel*; or L '(stone) circle' OF – the surnames are chiefly Cornish, and there is a Rundle Stone off the Cornish coast. But south-eastern bearers may be from Rundale in Shoreham, Kent, the second element of which is 'valley' and the first 'fallen tree' or 'council' or an AS owner called 'Counsellor' all OE.

Runnacles, Runnicles L 'rye fields' OE *rygen* + *æcer*.

Runton L 'farm of (an AS called) Counsellor (his name is connected with mystery/secret and the *runic* alphabet)' OE; places (East and West R—) in Norfolk.

Rush L 'rush(-bed), rushes' OE. Counted by Guppy only in Suffolk–Norfolk.

Rushbrook(e) L 'brook in the rushes' OE; place in Suffolk.

Rushforth L 'ford in the rushes' OE; places (–rd) in Lancs, Norfolk, Suffolk.

Rushmer, Rushmore L 'mere/lake with rushes' OE; places (–mere, –more) in four counties.

Rushton L 'place/farm in the rushes' OE; places in Ches, Dorset, Northants, Salop, Staffs, but surname counted by Guppy only in Staffs, Lancs.

Ruskin F dim. '**Ross**' in its F sense.

Russ N See **Rous**; an old Wilts surname. But one USA family at least had changed it from **Rust**.

Russel(l), Russill N dim. 'red (hair/face)' OF (cf. **Rous**). **Russell**, the family name of the dukes of Bedford and four other peers, occurs all over England and was the 48th commonest surname in Scotland in 1958.

Rust N 'rust' OE; ?for red hair/face – but this is unconvincing.

Ruston L 'farm in brushwood' OE, two places in Norfolk; or 'farm with ?roosts/perches/rafters' OE, place in North Yorks; or 'farm of (an A S called) Vigorous/Strong' OE, place in East Yorks. But Guppy counted it only in Cambs. Also spelt **Rustan**.

Ruth N 'pity' ME, from OE or ON; an abstract surname of rare type (but the Moabite woman's F is first recorded in use in Britain *after* the Reformation). The TD shows a thin line of the name from Devon, Wilts–Hants, Essex, Northants, Staffs, Notts–Yorks, Glasgow. None in *DNB*, and not even Babe in *DAB*.

Rutherford L 'ford for oxen' OE, place in North Yorks; place in Roxbs probably means the same, though Johnston says 'red ford' ON+OE. Guppy counted it in Northumberland, Warwicks.

Ruthven L 'red place (one with red stone/earth)' Scots Gaelic; place in Perths.

Rutley L 'red cliff' OE; place in Northlew, Devon.

Rutter O 'rote-player' OF (see **Root**). Or N 'highwayman, ruffian' OF. Occurs north of Ches–Yorks–Lincs.

Ryal(l) L 'hill where rye grows' OE, places in Northd, East and West Yorks; or '**Haugh** (*halh*) where rye grows' OE, places in Worcs, Rutland, variously Ryal(l), Ryhall, Ryhill, Ryle. But N 'royal' OF is possible. So is F dim. 'Riulf (= power wolf)' OF.

Ryan (for O R—) Irish name of quite uncertain meaning; but eighth commonest surname in Ireland in 1890, and one of the 200 commonest in USA. ? the name of a pre-Christian sea or river deity (cf. *Rhine*).

Rycott L 'cottage in the rye' OE; place (–cote) in Oxon. The surname was also warped into **Ryecart**.

Rycraft, Rycroft L '**Croft** where rye grows' OE; five places (all –o–) in Derbys, Staffs, West Yorks.

Ryde L Same as **Ride**; rarely perhaps from places in Surrey, IoW, 'stream' OE.

Rydell L 'valley where rye grows' OE; place (Rydal) in Westmorland.

Ryder Commoner but affected spelling of **Rider**. Family name of the earls of Harrowby. Guppy counted it only in North Wales – not good cavalry country, which made Weekley think it came from **Rhydderch**.

Rydout See **Rideout**.

Rye L '(at) the island, (at) the low-lying land' OE (with **R–** as in **Rock**); locality, or 'the little brown city' in Sussex, and elsewhere. But sometimes '(at) the stream' OE (see **Rea**).

Ryecart See **Rycott**.

Ryland L 'land where rye grows' OE; places in Cambs, Lincs.

F: *first name*   L: *local name*   N: *nickname*   O: *occupational name*

Rylands L 'fields of rye' OE; places in Deane, Lancs, in Wilmslow, Ches, and in Beeston, Notts.

Ryle See **Ryal**.

Ryman L 'man living at the island/low-lying land' OE+OE (see **Rye**).

Rymell, Rymill See **Rimell**.

Rymer O 'rhymer, poet' (especially in the vernacular) OE/OF. Counted by Guppy only in Glos.

S

Saban, Saben, Sabin(e) F 'Sabine' Latin (one of an ancient race of central Italy, ?'descendants of the god Sabus'). There were several saints Sabinus, and a martyred Roman matron Sabina, an unfortunate F in view of the alarming experience of the Sabine women.

Sacheverell L 'kid's leap' OF; place (Sault-Chevreuil) in Manche.

Sacker O 'sack-/sackcloth-maker' OE; 'sacques' (loose dresses/coats) are too late to figure.

Sadd N 'settled, serious, firm' OE (originally 'sated').

Saddington L 'farm of the folk of (an AS called) S . . . d/t' OE (the forms are too late and wavering for certainty); place in Leics.

Saddler, Sadle(i)r O 'saddle-maker' OE; **–dd–** now rarer than **–d–**.

Saer See **Sayer**.

Saffron N 'saffron' OF (?from yellow hair). Or O, from cultivating the plant.

Sagar F 'sea spear' OE. A Lancs surname.

Sage N 'wise' OF. Guppy counted it only in Devon–Somerset.

Sager Rare form of **Sagar**.

Sailer O 'dancer' OF.

Sainsbury L 'Sea Friend's fort' OE; place (Saintbury, in 1186 *Seinesberia*) in Glos.

Saint N 'saint' OF, for excessive or exiguous piety.

Saint Clair, etc. See **St Clair**, etc.

Salaman, Salamon F Typical medieval forms (especially **–mon**) of *Solomon*, a Hebrew F based on a word meaning 'peace'. **Salamons** '(son) of S—'.

Salathiel F 'the god is my ?' Babylonian, sometimes hebraized to mean 'requested of God'; the father of Zerubbabel. Found chiefly in South Wales.

Salcombe L 'salt valley' OE; two places in Devon (one a tidal creek, one where salt was ?processed/?stored).

Sale L 'sallow/willow' OE; locality, or place in Ches. But it could also be O from service at a 'hall' OE. In both cases, **–e** could be for dative after lost preposition.

Salesbury See **Salisbury**.

Salford L 'ford at the sallows/willows' OE, places in Beds, Lancs, Worcs; or 'ford where salt was transported' OE, places in Oxon, Warwicks.

F: *first name*   L: *local name*   N: *nickname*   O: *occupational name*

Salingar, Salinger L 'Saint Léger' (see **Ledger**); places in Manche, Seine-Maritime.

Salisbury, Salisberry L Second element is 'fort' OE; first was Keltic *Sorvio–* (meaning ?), changed by A Ss to *Searo–* (?imitating OE word for 'armour'), as in Latin *Sarum*; then by Normans the *r . . . r* were 'dissimilated' to **l . . . r**; the Wilts city. But surname is mainly found in Lancs–Derbys, so Lancs place Salesbury 'fort by the sallow/willow (pool)' OE may be the usual origin.

Salkeld L 'sallow-/willow-wood' OE; two places in Cumberland.

Salley L 'sallow (loosely "willow") clearing' OE, two places (Sawley) in West Yorks; or 'sallow/willow hill' OE *salh + hlāw*, place (Sawley) in Derbys.

Sallows L 'of (i.e. at) the sallow/willow' OE, or a plural.

Salman, Salmen, Salmon(d), Salmons, Salomon(s) F See **Salamon(s)**; **Salmon** is the commonest of the whole Solomon group, and has no connection with the fish.

Salt L 'salt works/pit' OE; locality, or place in Staffs. A very common Staffs surname, also Derbys–West Yorks.

Salter O 'salt-worker/-seller' OE; but sometimes 'player on the (stringed) psaltery' OF. Counted by Guppy only in Devon, Suffolk.

Salthouse L 'salt-store' OE; locality, or places in Lancs, Norfolk, Salop, and a Lancs surname.

Saltmarsh L 'salt marsh' OE; locality, or places in four counties.

Salton L 'place in the sallows/willows' OE; place in North Yorks.

Saltonstall L 'homestead in the sallows/willows' OE (cf. **Tunstall**); place in West Yorks.

Saltram L 'salt-workers' homestead' OE; place in Devon.

Salusbury See **Salisbury**.

Salway Reaney postulates a F *Sǣlwīg* 'prosperity war' OE.

Sam F dim. '**Samson**' (for F *Samuel* was rare among medieval Christians). **Sams** '(son) of **S—**', rarely **Sames**.

Sambourne L 'sandy stream' OE; places in Warwicks and (–n) Wilts.

Sambrook L 'sandy brook' OE; place in Salop. Also **Sambruck**.

Samman, Sammon(d)s, Sammons See **Salman**.

Sampford L Same as **Sandford**; places in Dorset, Devon (three), Essex (two), Somerset (two).

Sample See **Semple**.

Sampson Much commoner form (found in Cornwall–Devon, Derbys, Kent) of **Samson**.

Samson F of a Welsh bishop (*c.* 550) who crossed to Brittany and was greatly venerated; it is either Keltic, or the Biblical hero 'son of

Shamash (the sun-god)' Hebrew – though the 'son' has nothing to do with the –**son**. A L origin, from one of the places Saint-Samson in France, is sometimes possible.

Samuel F 'name of God' Hebrew. **Samuels** '(son) of S—'. Cf. **Sam**. Samuel is the family name of the viscounts Bearsted.

Samways N 'stupid' OE (cf. *semi-*, *wise*). Mainly a Dorset surname.

Sanctuary L 'sanctuary, shrine' OF; sometimes for one who had taken refuge in a church/monastery.

Sandal(l) L 'sandy **Haugh** (*halh*)' OE; three places in West Yorks. Or F 'sand wolf' ON (it is not suggested that this was an existing species).

Sandbach L 'sandy stream/valley' OE; place in Ches.

Sandbrook L 'sandy brook' OE.

Sandell L 'sand hill/slope' OE; the second elements in OE West Saxon were *hyll/hylde*, and the –**e**– from –*y*– is a south-eastern feature. Or see **Sandal**.

Sandeman O 'servant of (dim.) **Alexander**' (see **Sanders**).

Sander, Sanders(on) F dim. 'Alexander' and '(son)/son of S—'. Sanders and **Saunders**, where the –**u**– imitates a French nasal, are abundant south of Humber–Dee, especially in Devon. –**son** common in Co. Durham–Northd–Yorks–Lancs–Lincs.

Sandford L 'sandy ford' OE; places in eleven counties.

Sandhurst L 'sandy **Hirst**' OE; places in Berks, Glos, Kent.

Sandifer, Sandiford, Sandiforth L 'sandy ford' OE; there are places Sandy Ford (two), Sandyford, Sandyforth in West Yorks, a Sandy Ford in Devon, and no doubt others elsewhere.

Sandison See **Sanderson**.

Sandon L 'sandy hill' OE; places in Berks, Essex, Herts, Staffs.

Sands L 'sands' OE; locality, or places in Bucks, Cumberland, Sussex, but mainly a Norfolk surname.

Sandwith L 'sandy ford' ON; places in Cumberland, West Yorks.

Sandy L 'sandy island' OE; place in Beds. Or F 'sand' ON (cf. the first element of F **Sandal**).

Sandys Form of **Sands** retaining the inflexional vowel of Middle English.

Sanford See **Sandford**.

Sang(st)er O 'singer, chorister' OE; –**st**– at first denotes females (as in *spinster*), but can later be male as well.

Sanigar L 'herdsman's wooden slope' OE *swān+hangra* or 'wooded slope with swans' OE (there is a pool, and the Severn not far); place (Saniger Farm) in Hinton, Glos.

F: *first name*   L: *local name*   N: *nickname*   O: *occupational name*

Sankey L British river-name, from ?'holy'; two places in Lancs, but the surname settled in Salop, where it was *Zanchey* as late as the 1670s.

Sansam, Sansom(e), Sanson, Sansum, Sansun See **Samson**.

Sant See **Saint**.

Sapcote L 'sheep-shelter' OE; place in Leics.

Sapper O 'soap-maker/-seller' OE (since what we now call a 'sapper' was called a *miner*).

Sapperton L 'soap-makers' place' OE; places in four counties.

Sargant, Sarge(a)nt, Sarjant, Sarje(a)nt O 'servant, officer of the courts, tenant by military service below the rank of a knight' OF (cf. *sergeant*); *–er–* becomes *–ar–* as in **Clark**. **Sarge(a)ntson, Sarj(e)antson** 'son of S—'.

Satterlee, Satterl(e)y L 'robbers' wood/clearing' OE; place (–leigh) in Devon.

Satterthwaite L '**Thwaite** by a shieling/hill-pasture' ON; place in Lancs.

Saturley Form of **Satterley**, with spelling ?influenced by *Saturday*.

Saul F 'asked for' Hebrew; rare among medieval Christians. Or L 'sallow/willow wood' OE, place in Glos; or 'room, chamber' OF *salle*.

Sault See **Salt**.

Saulter See **Salter** (probably in its second meaning).

Saun(d)by L 'farm with sandy soil' ON; place (–d–) in Notts.

Saunders(on) See **Sanders(on)**. –s is common, but –son rare.

Saut(t)er See **Salter** (in its second meaning).

Savage N 'wild, savage' OF (originally 'of the woods'; cf. *sylvan*). Occurs from west Midlands to Norfolk.

Savagar, Savager, Savaker, Saveker, Savigar L 'Saint Vigor (= "vigour" Latin)' OF, a 6th-century bishop of Bayeux who has a rare dedication of the church at Stratton-on-the-Fosse, Somerset; five places (Saint-Vigor) in Normandy.

Savin(s) See **Sabine**; and '(son) of S—'. **Savin** and **Sabin** are Oxon surnames.

Sawbridge L 'bridge by the sallows/willows' OE; place in Warwicks. But sometimes F 'sea/victory bright' OE, e.g. the owner of Sawbridgeworth, Herts.

Sawdon L 'sallow/willow valley' OE; place in North Yorks.

Sawer O 'sower' OE, though this seasonal job leaves the rest of his working year unaccounted for.

Sawford is probably for one of the places called **Salford**.

Sawyer O 'sawer (of wood)' OE. Counted by Guppy only in Suffolk.

Saxby (ill-spelt **Saxbee**) L 'farm of (a Norseman called) Short Sword (cf. **Saxon**, **Sex**)' ON; places in Leics and (two) Lincs. Reaney also supposes N 'draw-sword' OF.

Saxon L 'Saxon' (the race being the 'people of the *seax*/dagger/ short-sword') Germanic latinized.

Saxton L '**Saxons**' farm' OE; places in Cambs, West Yorks.

Say L 'Sai' in Orne, OF from Gaulish F *Saius*+suffix. Guppy counted it only in Somerset.

Sayce L '**Saxon**, Englishman' OW; what the Scots call *Sassenach*.

Sayer O '**Sawyer**'; or '**Sewer**'; or 'assayer (of metals), food-taster' OF; or 'serge-(literally *say-*)maker' OF; or ?'sayer' OE in sense of 'reciter, professional story-teller'. Or F ?'victory army' OF from Germanic. **Sayers** '(son) of S—'. **Sayer** counted by Guppy only in Norfolk, Yorks; **Sayers** only in Sussex.

Saysell See **Cecil**. Still a South Wales surname.

Saywell See **Sewell**.

Scaife N 'awkward, crooked, wild' ON.

Scale(s) L 'hut(s)' ON; locality, or places (–s) in Cumberland, Lancs; but an old Norfolk surname.

Scammell N 'lean, scraggy' late ME (?from ON; cf. Scots *skemmel* and Milton's *scrannel pipes*). Or L, a northern variant of *shamble*, so 'bench, stall, slaughterhouse, meat-/fish-market' OE; modern slang 'shambles' (for a mess) is an extension of meaning.

Scandrett Is it conceivably dim. '**Alexander**'? The TD shows very few save in Glam and Herefords–Salop.

Scarborough L '(Norseman called) Hare-Lip's fort' ON+OE; we find in saga that Thorgils Skarthi started the North Yorks town *c.* 965. A Lincs surname.

Scarf(e), **Scarff(e)** N 'cormorant' ON, a North Country surname, and the Orkney and Shetland dialect word for the bird.

Scargill L 'valley/ravine with mergansers' ON; place in North Yorks. Macaulay in *A Jacobite's Epitaph* gives it 'whispering trees'.

Scarisbrick L '(Norseman called) Skar's hill-slope' ON; place in Lancs.

Scarlet(t) N 'scarlet' OF, from favourite wear, or from cloth made or sold. **Scarlett** is the family name of the barons Abinger.

Scarth L 'gap, pass, cleft' ON, places in Lancs (S— Hill), North Yorks (Ayton S—), and compounds with this element. Guppy counted it only in North and East Yorks.

Scatliff L 'slate cliff' OF+OE; two places (Scaitcliffe) in Lancs.

F: *first name*　　L: *local name*　　N: *nickname*　　O: *occupational name*

Scattergood N 'scatter goods/property' ME+OE, for ?a prodigal or ?a philanthropist. Mainly a north Midlands surname.

Schofield L See **Scholfield**. Common in West Yorks–Lancs.

Scholar(d) L 'shieling with a hut' ON. O 'scholar' ME from Low Latin cannot be proved.

Scholes L 'huts' ON; locality, or six places in West Yorks and one in Lancs; a form of **Scales** with the vowel rounded. A Lancs surname.

Scholfield L '**Field** with a hut' ON+OE (cf. **Scholes**). A Lancs surname.

Schoolcraft L '**Croft** with a hut' ON+OE (cf. **Scholes**), despite its educational look.

Scobie, Scobbie L From ancient possession of land of this name in Perths, meaning unknown; but the **Scoby** family of Yorks must derive from an ON '-farm' name.

Scoots ?O '(son) of the scout/spy' OF.

Scorer L '?one who lives on a steep projection' OE; a Devon surname – and there is such a place, Score, in Ilfracombe.

Scothorne L 'Scots' thorn' OE; place (also spelt –hern) in Lincs.

Scotland L The country (for meaning, see **Scott**; second element OE; rare, and sometimes for Scotlandwell, Kinross, an important spring; nicely instanced in the Scots rugby full-back Ken **S—**.

Scott L or 'nationality' name. The Scots came from Ireland, and are represented by the Highlanders and Hebrideans of Scotland (the Lowlanders being mostly of English stock, and the Orcadians and Shetlanders Norse); their name is mysterious – Sir John Rhys linked it with Welsh *ysgwthr* 'cutting/carving' and made it mean 'tattooed' (as if the Picts were the 'pictured/tattooed' people; but see **Portwaine**). In south Scotland the emphasis may be on Gaelic origin; in north England it will just mean 'from over the Border' – it is very common on both sides. 13th commonest surname in Scotland in 1958, 90th in Ireland in 1890. The frequent **S—** of east England and Devon (and **Scutt** in Dorset) may be settlers, or derived from a personal name of N type. Family name of the earls of Eldon.

Scottorn See **Scothorne**.

Scotton L 'Scots' place/farm' OE; places in Lincs, North and West Yorks, though counted by Guppy only in Leics.

Scoular, Scouler See **Scholar**. But it must often be O 'scholar, school-master' Scots from OF and Low Latin.

Scrafield L '**Field** near a landslide/scree' ON+OE; place in Lincs.

Scragg N 'someone lean/scraggy' late ME of unknown origin.

Scrimgeo(u)r, Scrimger, Scrimshaw, Scrimshire O 'fencing-master' OF (cf. *skirmisher*), classed with rogues and vagabonds such as actors, and forbidden to keep schools in the City of London.

Scrine L 'shrine' OE *scrīn*.

Scriven(er), **Scrivenor** O 'writer, copier, scribe, clerk' OF. Guppy counted –en only in Northants, –ener only in Beds.

Scrut(t)on L '(Norseman called) Scurfy's farm' ON+OE; place (–t-) in North Yorks, but –tt– is far commoner as a surname.

Scrymgeour See **Scrimgeor**. **Scrymgeour-Wedderburn** is the family name of the earls of Dundee.

Scudamore See **Skidmore**. It is *not* 'shield of love' OF *escu d'amour*! – despite the family motto SCUTO AMORIS DIVINI.

Scull ?F ON *Skúli* 'protector', even 'king', as in place Sculcoates, East Yorks. But surname is common in Bristol, which does not suggest ON origin.

Scullion O 'menial kitchen servant' OF; it is not derived from *scullery*, though it imitates the spelling.

Sculthorp(e) L 'Skúli's **Thorp**' ON (cf. **Scull**); place (–e) in Norfolk.

Scutt O 'scout, spy' OF. Or N 'scut/tail of the hare' ME. Or L = **Scott**. Guppy counted it only in Dorset.

Seaborn(e), **Seabourn(e)** F 'sea warrior' OE.

Seabright (ill-spelt **Seabridge**) F 'sea/victory bright' OE.

Seacombe L 'valley by the sea' OE; place in Ches.

Seaford L 'ford by the sea' OE; place in Sussex.

Seager See **Sagar**.

Seagrave, **Seagrief**, **Seagrove** L '**Grove**/ditch at the sheepfold/pit' OE – thus four possible meanings; place (–ave) in Leics.

Seagrim F 'sea guardian' ON.

Seal(e) L 'hall' OE, place (–l) in Kent; but two places (–l) in Derbys are 'little **Shaw**' OE; and place (–le) in Surrey is 'hall' or '(at) the sallow/willow' OE, with –e for dative after lost preposition. Mainly a Derbys surname. It might sometimes be N 'seal' OE, the mammal.

Seales L '(of, i.e.) at the hall/sallow' OE, or a plural.

Sealey, **Seal(l)y** N 'happy, blessed' OE (whence, later, by the belittling ways of speech, 'innocent, simple', and at length 'silly').

Seaman O 'seaman' OE (though the word could mean also 'Viking, pirate'). Used also as a F. Common in Norfolk–Suffolk with their famous old ports. **Seamens**, **Seamons** '(son) of **S**—'.

Seamer L 'lake lake' OE, tautologically; places (also Semer) in Norfolk, Suffolk, North Yorks. Or F 'sea famous' OE. Or O 'seamer, tailor' OE.

Sear(s), **Seare(s)** See **Sayer(s)**. –rs a Herts surname, –r Bucks.

F: *first name*　　L: *local name*　　N: *nickname*　　O: *occupational name*

Searl(e), Searl(e)s F Containing meaning 'armour' Germanic (cf. **Salisbury**), normanized as *Serlo*. **–le** counted by Guppy only in Cornwall–Devon and Cambs. **–(e)s** '(son) of **S—**'.

Seath L 'pit, well, pool' OE. Counted by Guppy only in Kent.

Seaton L 'place by the sea' OE, places in four northern counties and Devon; but two places in East Yorks are 'place by a lake'; place in Kent is ?'plantation'; and place in Rutland is ?stream/?owner's name + 'place' all OE.

Seavers and **Seaward** See **Severs** and **Seward**.

Sebastian F 'man from Sebastia (= venerable)' Greek, city in Pontus; Roman soldier martyred with arrows; the dim. forms lose the **Se–**.

Secker O 'sack/sackcloth-maker' ON, cognate with **Sacker**.

Sec(c)ombe See **Seacombe**. Counted by Guppy only in Cornwall.

Secrett N 'discreet' OF.

Secular N 'wordly' OF.

Seddon L Second element probably 'hill' OE; first could be 'house, dwelling, seat' OE or 'shieling, hill pasture' ON. Mainly a Lancs surname.

Sedgebeer L 'grove of (an AS called) Warrior' OE; place (Sedge-barrow) in Worcs.

Sedg(e)field L 'open country belonging to (an AS called) Warrior (Secg)/Cedd (see **Chadwick**)' OE; place in Co. Durham.

Sedgemoor, Sedgemore L 'moor with sedge' OE; area (–oo–) in Somerset.

Sedgewick(e) L 'dairy-farm of (a Norseman whose F *Siggi* is ?related to Germanic *Sig*–) Victory' ON+OE; place in Westmorland. A North Country surname, so 'dairy-farm in the sedge/reeds/rushes' OE, place in Sussex, is less likely. The **–e** could be for dative after lost preposition, or an adornment.

Sedgley L 'wood/clearing of (an AS called) Man/Warrior' OE (rather than 'clearing with rushes' OE); place in Staffs.

Sedgman O 'sedge man (i.e. thatcher with reeds)' OE.

Sedgwick See **Sedgewick**. Chiefly a West Yorks surname.

Seear See **Sear**.

Seedall L ?'wide **Haugh** (*halh*)' OE; as in Siddal (Lancs, West Yorks), Siddells (Notts).

Seeds O Rarely, from dealing in 'seeds' OE; but normally F, a short form of a *Sidu*– name ('custom, morality, purity' OE)+patronymic –s.

Seel See **Seal**.

Seeley, Seely(e) Versions of **Sealey** (–ye a USA spelling). **Seely** is the family name of the barons Mottistone and barons Sherwood.

Sefton L 'place in the sedge/rushes' ON+OE; place in Lancs, and a Lancs surname.

Segrave See **Seagrave**.

Selbourne L 'stream in the sallows/willows' OE; place (Gilbert White's Selborne) in Hants. Also occurs as **Selborne**.

Selby L 'sallow/willow farm' ON; place in West Yorks. Surname mainly of nearby Notts.

Selden, Seldon L 'house/hall hill' OE; place (–don) in Devon; Weekley prefers 'at the booths/shops' ME, with –**en**/–**on** for dative plural (OE –*um*) after lost preposition. –**on** was counted by Guppy only in Devon.

Sell L 'shelter/hut (for animals or for the man who tended them)' OE or ON.

Sellar, Seller O 'cellarer, storeman, purveyor' OF, with initial S– for *c*–; or 'saddler' OF; or 'dealer, hawker' OE (cf. *sell*). **Sellars, Sellers** '(son) of S—'. Guppy counted –**ars** and –**ers** only in Yorks.

Selley See **Sealey**.

Sellick (or **Selleck**) L There are Devon places Sellick and Sellake (second element 'stream' OE, first element ?'sluggish' OE), and Guppy counted the form **Sellek** only in Devon; there were people called **Sellick**, Sellecke, Sellak, in Somerset *c*. 1600. Thus Sellack in Herefords ('Saint Tysilio' Welsh) is unlikely to be the place of origin.

Sel(l)man N 'blessed/happy person' OE.

Sel(l)wood L 'sallow (loosely "willow") wood' OE; wood and parish (–elw–) in Somerset, in OW *Coit Maur* 'big wood'.

Selth N 'prosperity, happiness' OE.

Selway See **Salway**.

Selwin F 'sylvan, of the woods' Latin, the name of a woodland deity and later of a saint (*Silvanus*). Or N 'wild, savage' OF from same source. Rarely ?F 'hall friend' OE. Or even F 'ardour/zeal fair' OW.

Selwood See **Sellwood**.

Selwyn See **Selwin**. Chiefly a Glos surname.

Semens F Either '(son) of **Seaman**', or see **Simmance**.

Semken, Semkin See **Simkin**.

Semmence, Semmens, Semmons See **Simmance**, though they may be '(son) of **Seaman**'.

Semper L 'Saint-Pierre (= Saint **Peter**)' OF; various places in France (and one, keeping the French form, in Mon).

Semple L 'Saint-**Paul**' or 'Saint-Pol (i.e. Saint Paul Aurelian)' OF;

F: *first name*   L: *local name*   N: *nickname*   O: *occupational name*

many places in north France. But the Scots **S—** is the same as **Simple**.

Senchal, Senchel(l), Senec(h)al, Seneschal(l), Seneshall O 'seneschal' OF from Germanic (literally 'old servant'), the administrator of a great (even royal) household, a major-domo.

Sendal(l) O or N 'silken cloth' OF, for a producer or wearer of it.

Senhouse L 'seven hills' OE+ON (cf. **Howe**); a Cumberland surname, from Cumberland place Hallsenna, formerly *Sevenhowes*.

Senior O 'lord (of the manor, etc.)' OF from Latin (literally 'older'). Or N of same origin, 'senior' (as opposed to 'junior'), or from swagger.

Senneck, Sennick L 'seven oaks' OE, contracted forms of **Sevenoaks**.

Sennett, Sennitt See **Sinnatt**.

Sennington L 'farm on the River (once called) Semnet' Keltic+OE (*Sem–* is related to the Somme and to a Sanskrit word for 'drink'); place (Semington) in Wilts.

Sensicall, Sensicle See **Senchal**.

Sentry See **Sanctuary**.

Sergeant(son), Sergent(son), Serjeant(son), Serjent See **Sargeant**.

Serle See **Searl**.

Serrell (with a glide-vowel between –r– and –l–) See **Searl**.

Service O 'ale(-seller)' OF (cf. Modern French *cervoise*).

Sessions L 'Soissons' OF from Gaulish tribe *Suessiones*; city in Aisne.

Setchfield L 'dry domain' OF; place (Secqueville-en-Bassin) in Calvados. There may be some falling-together with **Sedgefield**.

Seton See **Seaton**.

Settatree L 'planted tree' OE+OE.

Settle L 'seat, abode; eminence' OE; place in West Yorks.

Sevenoaks L 'seven oaks' OE; locality, or place in Kent; the number seven must have folk-lore significance.

Sever(s) F 'sea voyage (cf. *fare*)' OE feminine; and '(son) of **S—**'.

Sevier O 'sieve-maker' OE.

Sewall F 'sea ruler' OE; occurring in Middle English as *Sewal*, but now largely absorbed by **Sewell**.

Seward, Sewart F 'sea (OE *sǣ*)/victory (OE *sige*) guard' OE. But occasionally it may be O 'sow-herd' OE. **Sewards** '(son) of **S—**'. **Seward** was counted by Guppy only in Devon.

Sewell F 'sea/victory (cf. **Seward**) ruler' OE. But those originally *de Sewell* are L, from **S—**, Bucks; Seawell, Sywell, Northants; Sowell, Devon; all meaning 'seven springs' OE (cf. **Sevenoaks**). The proverb 'Say well is good, but Do well is better' suggests an occasional

N. The surname is chiefly of East Anglia and Cumberland–Westmorland.

Sewer O 'shoemaker' OF, or 'seater' (who had tables laid, allotted guests to places, and superintended the service) OF, or 'sawyer' OF, or 'sewer (i.e. tailor)' OE.

Sex ?N 'knife, dagger, (and later) tool for chopping slates' OE *seax*, *sæx*, or *sex*. A Winchester blacksmith of this name changed it to **Southern** in 1969.

Sexton O 'sacristan' much corrupted from OF; his demotion to grave-digger is comparatively modern.

Seyler O See **Sailer**.

Seymour, Seymo(u)re L 'Saint-Maur' OF (cf. **Moore**); several places in France. –**mour** was counted by Guppy only in Bucks–Berks. **Seymour** is the family name of the dukes of Somerset and the marquesses of Hertford.

Shackleton L 'farm on a tongue of land' OE; place (Scackleton) in North Yorks, the surname going back to the OE form before it was scandinavianized.

Shadbolt See **Shotbolt**.

Shade (since its cognate **Shadow** also exists in USA) may be N 'shadow' OE, for ?grubbiness or ?wispiness; but Reaney found also a *de la Schade* in Devon, and this will be L 'boundary (cf. *watershed*)' OE.

Shadwell L 'boundary stream' OE; places in six counties (but a couple may be 'shady stream' OE); place in Middx is 'shallow stream' OE.

Shafto(e) L '**Hough** with a boundary-post' OE (cf. *shaft*); place in Northd.

Shakesby See **Saxby** in its second meaning; the OF *sac*- has been changed to the *shake*- of **Shakeshaft, Shakespear**.

Shakeshaft N 'brandish lance/spear' OE. Found in Salop–Ches and Bucks.

Shakespear(e) N 'brandish spear' OE, still a Stratford surname; Robert Greene (†1592), wishing to be nasty at a greater playwright's expense, parodied the name as *Shake-scene*.

Shallcross L 'cross with a shackle/fetter attached' OE; place in Derbys (in which county a place Shacklecross also occurs).

Shallish See **Challis**.

Shank(s) N 'leg(s)' OE. –**s** common in Northd and the Scots Lowlands. **Shankson** 'son of **Shank**'.

Shanklin L 'hill with a waterfall' OE (the first element is *scenc* 'cup, drink'); place in IoW.

F: *first name*   L: *local name*   N: *nickname*   O: *occupational name*

Shanly F (for McS—) 'son of ?Old Hero' Irish.

Shannon L 'old (river)' Irish; the longest river in the British Isles.

Shap L 'heap' (a nearby stone circle) OE; place in Westmorland.

Shapcott L 'sheep shed' OE.

Shapeley N 'well-formed, of elegant shape' OE. Sometimes perhaps L for Shapley 'sheep clearing' OE; two places in Devon.

Shapland See **Shopland**.

Shardlow L 'cleft/notched mound' OE; place in Derbys.

Sharman O 'shearman' (cutter of superfluous nap off woollen cloth) OE. An east Midland and Norfolk surname.

Sharp(e) N 'sharp, keen, smart, quick' OE; –p is very much commoner than –pe, where the –e could show a weak adjective after a lost definite article. Widespread, but rare in the south-west.

Sharples(s) L Probably 'steep pasture' OE; place (–es) near Bolton, Lancs; there are still residents there named **Sharples**.

Sharrad See **Sherrard**.

Sharwood is **Sherwood** pronounced in the 'correct' ME way (cf. **Clark**).

Shatwell See **Shadwell**.

Shave L 'at the **Shaw**' OE dative singular; places in Dorset and Somerset, but Guppy counted it only in Essex.

Shaw L 'copse, thicket, small wood' OE. Very common in Yorks–Ches–Derbys–Notts–Staffs–Lancs and Midlands, but rarer in south. 45th commonest surname in England and Wales in 1853, 87th in Scotland in 1958. Family name of the barons Craigmyle.

Shawcross L Either for **Shallcross** or 'cross in/at a copse' OE; place in Dewsbury, West Yorks.

Shea F (for O S—) 'descendant of ?Hawk-like/?Dauntless/?Stately' Irish. 49th commonest surname in Ireland in 1890.

Shean See **Sheen** or (for an Irish family) **Sheehan**.

Sheard L 'gap, cutting, cleft' OE. Chiefly a West Yorks surname.

Shearman See **Sharman**. And **Shearer** means the same.

Shearn ?L 'mud, filth, dung' OE *scearn*, common as the first element of place-names.

Shears ?N '(son) of bright/beautiful (cf. *sheer*)' OE. Or ?O 'shears-/scissor-(maker)' OE. Or L '(of, i.e.) at the division/boundary (cf. *share*)' OE or even '(of, i.e.) in the shire' OE. Guppy counted it (or them!) only in Devon and Surrey.

Sheather O 'maker of sword-sheaths' OE+–**er**.

Shebbeare L 'grove good for getting poles/shafts' OE; place (–r) in Devon.

Shedder L 'one who lives at a shelter (cf. *shed*)/boundary (cf. *watershed*)' OE+-**er**.

Sheddon L Lost hall-name in Mistley, Essex, now Old Hall, called in Domesday Book *Sciddinchou* 'hill-spur/rise of the shed-dwellers' OE Kentish *scedd*.

Shee (for O S—) See **Shea**.

Sheehan F (for O S—) 'descendant of ? ?Peaceful' Irish. 77th commonest surname in Ireland in 1890, especially Limerick–Cork–Kerry.

Sheehy F (for McS—) 'son of ? ?Peaceful' Irish.

Sheen L 'huts, sheds' OE (a 'weak' plural in –**n**, like oxen); places in Surrey, Staffs. Sometimes ?N 'beautiful' OE. Counted by Guppy only in Ches.

Sheepshanks N 'legs like a sheep' OE, a bit of Yorks humour.

Sheepwash L 'place for washing/dipping sheep' OE; places in Devon, Northd, Sussex.

Sheer(e) N 'bright, lovely' OE (now applied mainly to silk stockings). **Sheer(e)s** '(son) of **S**—'.

Sheffield L Second element '**Field**'; first element ?'hut/shed' OE, place in Berks; or 'sheep' OE, place in Sussex; or '(River) Sheaf (= boundary)' OE, the West Yorks city.

Shefford L 'sheep ford' OE; places in Beds, Berks.

Sheldon L ?'steep-sided valley' OE, place in Devon; or ?'flat-topped hill' OE, place in Warwicks (cf. *shelf*); but place in Derbys was once 'heathery hill with a shed' OE. The surname occurs in Derbys–Staffs–Ches and Oxon.

Sheldrake, **Sheldrick** N 'sheldrake' OE (the first element means 'parti-coloured'), a duck noted for its bright, pied plumage. Guppy found both forms in Suffolk.

Shelford L 'ford in the shallows' (it seems a good place to have one) OE; places in Cambs, Notts; first element may mean 'with a shelter' OE or even ?'in the shield-shaped/round pond' OE.

Shellabear See **Shillabeer**.

Shelley L 'wood/clearing on a ledge/bank/plateau' OE (cf. *shelf*), places in Essex, Suffolk, West Yorks; but place in Northd is 'clearing/field with a shieling' OE.

Shelton L 'place on a ledge/bank/plateau' OE (cf. *shelf*); places in six counties; from the Notts place derives the surname in Notts–Leics–Hunts.

Shenfield L 'beautiful/bright **Field**' OE; place in Essex.

Shep(e)ard, **Shep(h)erd**, **Sheph(e)ard**, **Sheppard**, **Shepperd** O

F: *first name*　　L: *local name*　　N: *nickname*　　O: *occupational name*

'sheep-herd, shepherd' OE. **–pherd** still far commoner than any of its derivatives (of which **–ppard** is the commonest), and spread (as were shepherds) from Cumberland to Cornwall. (It may sometimes have absorbed the ?lost *Shipward* 'sheep-ward' OE or 'ship-master' OE.) **Shep(h)erdson, Sheppardson, Shepper(d)son** 'son of S—'. Guppy found **Shepperson** very numerous in Cambs.

Sheppey L 'island with sheep' OE; place in Kent.

Sher A form, seen recently in Glasgow, of ?**Sheer.**

Sheraton L Originally ?same as **Scruton**; place in Co. Durham. The style of furniture is named after Thomas S— (†1806).

Sherborn(e), Sherb(o)urne, Sherburn L 'bright stream' OE; places in eight counties, the biggest being in Dorset.

Sherd See **Sheard.**

Shere N See **Sheer.** Or L, also meaning 'bright' (?from a stream) OE; place in Surrey.

Shergold N 'bright gold' OE.

Sheriff O 'sheriff' OE (originally 'shire-**Reeve**'). **Sheriffs** '(son/servant) of S—'.

Sherlock N 'bright/fair hair' OE (Holmes's was black, with that unerring inaccuracy of detail for which Watson's wandering wound prepares us).

Sherman See **Sharman.** But often a respelt German–Jewish surname.

Sherra(r)d, Sherratt F 'bright hardy' OE or 'bright' OE+OF suffix –*ard*. Chiefly Staffs names.

Sherriff(s) See **Sheriff(s).**

Sherwin Bardsley's early forms end in –*wyne* (?'friend' OE), but from 1273 to 1379 his eight forms end in –*wynd*; the –*d* he takes as '*excrescent*', but Reaney finds 12th-century forms in –*d*, and it becomes clear that N 'shear/cut the wind' OE, for a fast runner, is intended. Guppy counted the name only in Derbys.

Sherwood L 'wood belonging to the shire' OE, forest in Notts; two places in Yarnscombe and Feniton, Devon, are 'bright wood' OE and 'clear ford' OE, but the surname is found mainly in Yorks and Worcs, nearer to Notts.

Shewell N 'scarecrow' OE *scīewels*. A Glos surname, found in the county as a place-name element at S– Hill, Shewel Wood, Shewhill Barn/Coppice.

Shields L 'of (i.e. at) the shed/shallows' OE, or plural; locality, or places North and South S—, Northd and Co. Durham (with first meaning of 'sheds, shelters'). Or ?O 'shields' OE, for a maker of them. Also spelt **Shiels.**

Shillabe(e)r, Shillibeer L ?'grove on a ledge/bank' OE; lost place in Meavy, Devon. Whence the early names for a London omnibus and a funeral coach, from their pioneer George **Shillibeer** (†1866); an apt spelling **Shillibier** exists.

Shilling N 'shilling' OE; from rent, or from some lost joke.

Shillington L 'farm of the folk of (an AS whose name is related to) ?Shuttle' OE; place in Beds.

Shilston(e) L 'cromlech (literally shelf-stone)' OE; two places (–e) in Devon.

Shilton L Probably the same as **Shelton**; places in Berks, Leics, Oxon, Warwicks.

Shingler O 'roofer (with wooden tiles)' ME (ultimately from Latin).

Shinn N Various OE words for 'shin/skin/spectre' (*scinu*, *scinn*, *scinna*) suggest themselves. Or an O '(worker/dealer in) skin, skinner'.

Ship O 'ship' OE, a metonym for a sailor. Or ?L, a sign-name.

Shipley L 'sheep pasture' OE; places in eight counties. Guppy counted it only in Yorks, Staffs.

Shipman O 'sailor' OE (like Chaucer's pilgrim); but also (remembering **Shipley**, **Shipton**) 'shepherd' (as if 'sheep-man') OE – it is a common surname in inland Leics–Notts.

Shipp See **Ship**.

Shippam L 'sheep farm' OE; locality, or place (–pham) in Somerset.

Shippard See **Shepherd**.

Shippen L 'cattle-shed, byre' OE; locality, or places in Berks (–on), Devon, West Yorks. Early settler in USA was from Methley, West Yorks.

Shipperbottom L 'valley of the sheep-wash (literally -stream)' OE; place in Lancs. Also spelt **Shipperbotham**.

Shipperdson See **Shepherdson**.

Shipperley L 'pasture with sheep/?**Shippen**' OE.

Shipston L 'place at a sheep-wash' OE; place in Warwicks.

Shipton L 'sheep farm' OE, places in five counties; but others in North and East Yorks are 'place in the hips/dog-roses' OE; and S— Lee, Bucks, is 'hill with sheep' OE. Counted by Guppy only in Worcs, Derbys.

Shipwright O 'shipwright, shipbuilder' OE.

Shirland L 'grove of the shire (?meeting-place of the shire-court)' OE+ON (cf. **Lund**); place in Derbys.

Shirley L 'bright (?thinly grown) wood/clearing' OE (though first element may sometimes be 'shire' OE as in **Shirland**); places in

---

F: *first name* L: *local name* N: *nickname* O: *occupational name*

five counties. (Use as a female F, dreadfully abbreviated to *Shir*, is very recent.) Family name of the earls Ferrers.

Shirt L 'skirt, detached (*shortened*) piece of land' OE. A Derbys surname.

Shitler See **Shutler**.

Shobbrook, Shobrooke L 'goblin brook' OE; place (Shobrooke) in Devon.

Shoebotham, Shoebottom See **Shipperbottom**. Guppy counted them only in Staffs.

Shoemake(r), Shoemark O 'shoemaker' OE + OE.

Shoesmith O 'shoeing-smith, horseshoe-maker' OE.

Shooter O 'shooter' OE + –**er**, for a good archer (the –**er** might derive from –*a* in the OE noun *scytta*; see **Shutt**).

Shopland L 'island with a shed/shop' OE; place in Essex (but the surname was counted by Guppy only in faraway Devon).

Shopper O 'shop-keeper' OE (*shop* is cognate with **Shippen**).

Shore L 'shore' OE; the most famous bearer was Edward IV's mistress Jane **S—**, who did *not* give her name to Shoreditch. Family name of the barons Teignmouth.

Short N 'short' OE. A surname scattered from Northd to the southwest.

Shorthose N 'short boot/stockings' OE; or 'short neck' OE (cf. **Halse**).

Shortman N 'short man' OE.

Shortt Rare form of **Short**.

Shotbolt N 'shoot-arrow' OE, for an archer.

Shotton L 'hill of the Scots' OE, place in Northd; or 'place/farm of the Scots' OE, places in Co. Durham (three), Northd – but some of these may be 'place on a slope' or 'steep hill' OE. Mainly a Co. Durham surname, so the place in Flints is an unlikely origin.

Shoulder N 'shoulder' (?hunched or ?broad) OE.

Shovel(l), Shoveller, Shouler O 'maker/user of shovels' ME.

Showell See **Shewell** or **Shovell**; **Showler** is from **Shoveller**.

Shrapnel N 'little dusky man' OF *charbon* + dim. suffix –**el**, corrupted via *Sharpnel*. Not all would agree with what *DNB* says of Henry **S—** (†1842), the inventor of shrapnel: '... his great invention ... steady and triumphant ... more highly thought of, if possible, in the present day than ever ... (deserving of) fame and honour'.

Shrawley L 'clearing by a hill-recess' OE; place in Worcs.

Shreeve(s), Shrive(s) See **Sheriff**. Guppy counted –**eeve** only in Norfolk.

Shrimp N 'a puny, undersized person' ME from Germanic, with original sense of 'shrunken' – not from the little crustacean.

Shuck N 'devil, fiend, goblin' OE (cf. **Shuker**).

Shuckburgh L 'goblin/demon hill' OE; place in Warwicks.

Shufflebot(h)am, **Shufflebottom** Perversions of **Shipperbottom**, found in Staffs/Ches.

Shuker ?N 'devil, fiend, goblin' OE *scucca*, with –**er** for –*a*. Guppy counted it only in Salop.

Shumack and **Shurn** See **Shoemake** and **Shearn**.

Shute L 'strip/nook of land' OE, locality, or places in Devon (also Shewte); but S— Shelve, Somerset, has for its first element 'steep slope' (as in a 'mill-shoot') OE. Guppy counted it only in Dorset.

Shuter See **Shooter**.

Shutler O 'maker/user of shuttles (for weaving)' OE+–**er**.

Shutt Probably O 'shooter' OE *scytta*, for a good archer.

Shuttle O 'maker/user of shuttles' OE; but Reaney shows that the swiftly alternating shuttle could be used as a N for 'variable, flighty'.

Shuttleworth L 'gated (with a bolt/bar or *shuttle*) enclosure' OE; places in Derbys, Lancs, West Yorks, and still a Lancs–West Yorks surname.

Sibl(e)y F (for all its L look) 'Sibyl' Greek, one of the females acting as mouthpieces for the gods; later accepted as blessed with divine revelations, and admitted to the Christian heaven along with the Prophets (as on the Sistine Chapel ceiling). The Conqueror's son Robert married a *Sibylla*, and the F took root in England; quite properly, the Reformation hated it.

Sibson F 'son of (dim.) Sibyl' (see **Sibly**).

Sibthorp(e) L '**Thorp** of (an AS/Norseman called) Sibba/Sibbi' OE/ON (his name is related to *sibling*); place (–e) in Notts.

Sice See **Sayce**.

Sich L 'stream, ditch, etc.' (see **Sykes**).

Siddall, **Siddel(l)**, **Siddle** L 'broad/hill-slope' OE *sīd/sīde*+'**Haugh** (*halh*)/hall/rock (*hallr* ON)'; places in West Yorks and Lancs, and Yorks–Derbys surnames.

Siddorn ?F 'linen shroud' Greek *sindon*, whence girl's name Sidony (in honour of Christ's winding-sheet) and metronymic **Siddons**. Guppy counted **Siddorn** in Ches.

Sidebotham, **Sidebottom** L 'wide valley' OE; mispronunciations such as *siddibottARM* and *siddibottOME* shouldn't deceive *anybody*. Derbys surnames.

Sidg(e)wick See **Sedgewick**. Chiefly West Yorks forms.

Sidney L '(at the) wide island' or '(at the) wide well-watered land' OE, with –**n**– as in **Hendon**; places in Alfold, Surrey (whence Sir

---

F: *first name*   L: *local name*   N: *nickname*   O: *occupational name*

Philip S— and the family of the barons De L'Isle and Dudley
derived their names), Lincs, Ches (Sydney); but place in Sussex is
'south of the water' (River Ouse) OE. The Australian city is named
after a Secretary of State, Viscount Sydney (†1800). The popular F
stems from Whig idolization of Algernon S—, the republican
'martyr' (†1683). The surname is probably never from a place
Saint-Denis in Normandy.

Siev(e)wright O 'sieve-maker' OE.

Siggers F '(son) of Victory Spear' OE.

Siggins F '(son) of (dim). Victory' OE.

Silberry L '?dwelling/hall fort' OE; place (Silbury) in Wilts – though
archaeologists would be cautious about thus interpreting Silbury
Hill.

Silburn N 'blessed/happy child' OE.

Silcock(s), Silcox F Forms of **Sill** + familiar **Cock(s), Cox.**

Silk O 'silk(-weaver/-dealer)' OE.

Sill F dim. '**Silvester**'. **Sills** '(son) of S—'.

Sillars and **Sillman** See **Sellars** and **Sellman.**

Silver O 'silver(smith)' OE. Or L 'silvery stream', as in places such as
Monksilver, Somerset.

Silverley L 'clearing with some silvery/whitish plant' OE; place in
Cambs.

Silverstone L 'Sea/Victory Wolf's farm' OE; place in Northants.

Silverthorn(e) L 'silvery/whitish thorn-bush' OE.

Silvester F 'forest-dweller' Latin, the name of three popes. Guppy
found it only in Hants, Herts.

Sim F dim. '**Simon**', an old abbreviation; it is found with **Simm** in
the Lake District, whereas Guppy found its –s form only in Derbys–
Ches and Glos–Somerset–Wilts. But cf. **Sime. Sims(on)** '(son)/
son of S—'; **Simson** is older but rarer than **Simpson.**

Simco(e), Simcock(s), Simcox F Forms of **Sim** + familiar **Cock(s),
Cox.**

Sime F dim. '**Simon**' – whereas **Sim** might sometimes be rather
from F *Simmond* (see **Simond**). **Simes** '(son) of S—'.

Simeon F of the Old Testament is later usually spelt as **Simon.**

Simington L '**Simon**'s farm' Hebrew + OE; places (Symington)
in Ayrs, Lanarks, Midlothian.

Simister O 'sempstress' OE; but sometimes male like **Seamer.**

Simkin F double dim. '**Simon**'. **Simkins** '(son) of S—', also turned
into **Simkiss**. Cf. **Simpkin.**

Simm See **Sim. Simms** '(son) of S—'.

Simmen F Form of **Simon**; but cf. **Simond. Simmance, Sim-**

mans, **Simmens**, **Simmins**, **Simmon(d)s** '(son) of **S—**'. Of the whole **Simon** group, the second commonest (after **Simpson**) is **Simmons**, essentially a southern surname.

Simmer(s) Scots forms of **Summer(s)**.

Simmonite F dim. '**Simon**' with OF suffix –*et*.

Simon F 'hearkening' or perhaps 'little hyena' Hebrew *Shimeon* ?influenced by Greek word meaning 'snub-nosed'; a pretty poor choice. A very popular medieval F, less because of the Apostle Saint Simon Zelotes than as the first name of the nicknamed Saint Peter. Whence many surnames in **Sim(p)–/Sym–/Simm–/Symm–**; but cf. **Simond** – two stocks are inextricably mixed in this group.

Simond F Form of **Simon**. The excrescent **–d** is as in *sound* (from OF *son*); or it may be the sign of a totally different F 'victory protector' ON (*Sigmund–*) and also later Norman. **Simon(d)s** '(son) of **S—**'. **Simonson** 'son of **S—**'.

Simper See **Semper**.

Simpkin F double dim. '**Simon**', with glide consonant between **–m–** and **–k–**. **Simpkins**, **Simpkiss** '(son) of **S—**'. **Simpkinson** 'son of **S—**'. With **–kiss** cf. **Hotchkiss**. The **p**-glide recurs in **Simpson**. **–kin** is a Leics surname, **–kins** Wilts.

Simple N 'simple' OF, in a good sense – 'guileless, honest'.

Simpson F 'son of (dim.) **Simon**', with parasitic glide consonant **–p–** (cf. **Simpkin**). Easily the commonest of the **Simon** group; with variant spellings, the 39th commonest surname in Scotland in 1958, and much more northerly than most of the **Simon** derivatives.

Sinclair(e), **Sinclar** L Forms of **St Clair**. **Sinclair** was the 64th commonest surname in Scotland in 1958 (apparently dropping sixteen places in 100 years!), and is the family name of the earls of Caithness and four other peers.

Sinderby L 'southern farm' ON; place in North Yorks.

Singer O 'singer' OE. Counted by Guppy only in Somerset.

Singleton L 'farm in a burnt clearing' OE (cf. *singe*), place in Sussex; but place in Lancs is 'farm on shingle' or 'farm roofed with shingles' OE – and the surname is found mainly in Lancs.

Sinisbury See **Sainsbury**.

Sinkin(s), **Sinkinson** See **Simkin(s)** and **Simpkinson**; the original **–m–** here becomes **–n–** before **–k–** for ease of pronunciation.

Sinnatt, **Sinnett**, **Sinnott** F 'victory bold' OE *Sigenōth*.

Sinnex See **Sevenoaks**.

F: *first name*   L: *local name*   N: *nickname*   O: *occupational name*

Sirett F 'victory counsel' OE.

Sisley F Feminine form of Latin *Caecilius* (see **Cecil**); Saint Cecilia, martyred with her equally chaste husband Valerian, is the patron saint of music.

Sisson F 'son of (dim.) Cecilia' (see **Sisley**).

Sitch Commoner than **Sich**.

Sittingbourne L 'stream of the dwellers on the slope' OE; place in Kent.

Sixsmith O 'scythe-smith' OE (or ?for **Sucksmith**).

Sizeland L 'land of (an AS called) Victory (or some name beginning "Victory")' OE; place (Sisland, pronounced *size*–) in Norfolk.

Sizer O 'juryman, sworn witness in an assize court' OF.

Skeat(e) N (also early found as a F) 'swift' ON. **Skeat(e)s** '(son) of S—'; another version is **Skates**.

Skeffington L 'place/farm of the family/folk of (an AS called) Spear' OE scandinavianized (cf. *shaft*); place in Leics. Family name (usually combined with **Clotworthy** as F) of the viscounts Massereene and Ferrard.

Skegg N 'beard' ON. **Skeggs** '(son) of S—'.

Skelhorn L 'horn(-shaped land) at a shieling' ON+ON/OE, a surname which has given itself to Skellorn Green, Ches.

Skelton L 'place on a bank/hill' OE scandinavianized (cf. *shelf*), places in Cumberland, Yorks (six), and a Notts–Lincs–Yorks surname; it was even the surname of the first real Poet Laureate.

Skene L 'bush' Scots Gaelic; place in Aberdeens.

Skerton L 'place by the reefs/sandbanks (in the River Lune)' ON+ OE; place in Lancs.

Skevington See **Skeffington**.

Skidmore L 'muddy moor' OE *scite* scandinavianized. Guppy counted it only in Derbys – the distribution of its offshoot **Scudamore** is much more western.

Skinner O 'skinner' ON+–er; part of the great tanning industry. The surname is not common north of Worcs–Lincs.

Skipp N 'leap, jump' ME from Germanic. Or O 'basket(-maker)' ON.

Skipper N 'jumper, dancer' ME. Or O 'shipmaster, skipper' ME from Dutch.

Skippon Form of **Shippen** scandinavianized.

Skipsey L 'pool/harbour for ships' ON+OE; place (–sea) in East Yorks.

Skipwith L 'sheep **Wick**' OE scandinavianized and second element falsified to 'wood' ON; place in East Yorks.

Skirton See **Skerton**.

Skrimshaw, Skrimshire See **Scrimgeor**.

Slack L 'hollow; little shallow valley' ON. Or N 'slack, lazy, careless' OE. Counted by Guppy only in Notts–Derbys–Staffs–Ches and Cumberland–Westmorland.

Slade L 'valley, dell, strip of greensward between woods' OE; –e could show dative after lost preposition; locality, or place in Lancs – but the surname is chiefly of Somerset–Devon.

Sladen L 'mud valley' OE (cf. *slaver*); place in Lancs.

Slader L 'one who lives in a **Slade**', or (a Devon habit – and this is a Devon name) the –er may be a retention of the dative –e of the noun after a preposition.

Slafter Form of **Slaughter**, with the spirant misspelt.

Slape L 'slippery place' OE or 'slipway/portage' OE (cf. **Islip**).

Slate See **Sleight**.

Slater O 'slater' OF+–er. North Midlands surname, especially Derbys.

Slatter Form of **Slater**, counted by Guppy only in Oxon–Glos.

Slaughter L 'slough, muddy place' OE, places in Glos; or 'sloe-tree, blackthorn' OE, an element found in several Sussex place-names. Or O 'slaughterer' ME, for a butcher. Counted by Guppy only in Surrey.

Slaymaker O 'maker of slays' (used 'in weaving to beat up the weft', *OED*) ME.

Sledmere L 'mere/pool in a **Slade**' OE; place in East Yorks.

Slee L 'grassy slope' OE. Or N '**Sleigh**'. Guppy counted it only in Devon.

Sleeman N 'clever person' OE+OE. Or L 'one who lives at a **Slee**'; a surname of Cornwall–Devon.

Sleeper N 'sleeper, lazybones' OE+–er.

Sleigh N 'smart, cunning, clever' ME from ON (cf. *sly*), yet more Midland and southern than northern.

Sleight L 'sheep-pasture' OE *slæget*; locality, field-name, or place in Dorset.

Sleightholme L 'level (field) island' ON; place in North Yorks, and a Yorks–Lincs surname.

Slingsby L 'farm of (a Norseman called) ?Idler' ON; place in North Yorks.

Slipper O 'polisher, sharpener (of blades)' ME from OE adjective *slipor*. Guppy counted it only in Norfolk.

F: *first name*   L: *local name*   N: *nickname*   O: *occupational name*

Slocomb(e), Slocum L 'valley where sloes grow' OE; locality, or place (–um) in IoW; **–omb(e)** a Somerset family in the 1600s.

Sloley L 'wood/clearing where sloes grow' OE; places in Norfolk, Warwicks.

Sloman L 'man at the **Slough**' OE. Counted by Guppy only in Devon, Kent.

Sloper O 'maker of slops' (loose clothes – tunics, smocks, trousers; still used by old engine drivers of their overalls) ME.

Slough L 'slough, mire' OE; locality, or places in several counties.

Slowley and **Slowman** and **Sly** See **Sloley** and **Sloman** and **Sleigh**.

Smail L ?'burrow' OE. **Smail(e)s** 'of (i.e. at) the burrow', or a plural. But in north England and Scotland, same as **Smale(s)**.

Smalbridge See **Smallbridge**.

Smale N See **Small**. **Smales** '(son) of **S**—'; or L 'narrow (stream)' OE, place in Northd. But **Smale** is mainly a Devon surname.

Small N 'thin, slender' and less often 'small' OE. Guppy counted it only in Somerset, Worcs, Notts. **Smalls** '(son) of **S**—'.

Smallbone(s) N 'small/skinny bone(s)' OE – second element meaning especially 'leg(s)'.

Smallbridge L A Devon surname perhaps misrepresenting **Smallridge**, or ?'narrow bridge' OE.

Smallcombe L 'narrow valley' OE, probably a spot in Devon.

Smalldridge is **Smallridge** with a parasitic –d–.

Smalley L 'narrow wood/clearing/field' OE; place in Derbys.

Smallpage Despite the appearance of being 'little **Page**', *small* in ME usually means 'slender, narrow', and an equivalence with **Smallpiece** is as likely.

Smallpeace, Smallpeice, Smallpiece L 'narrow allotment of land' OE+OF, a common field-name.

Smallridge L 'narrow ridge' OE; two Devon hamlets, in Axminster and Langtree. **Smaridge** is another Devon surname based on this.

Smallwood L Any 'narrow wood' OE; or places in Ches, Lancs, Suffolk.

Smart N 'smart, brisk, prompt' OE.

Smartman N 'smart/brisk man' OE+OE.

Smeardon The rarer original of **Smerdon**.

Smeaton L 'place/farm of the smiths' OE; places in Cornwall, Yorks (four).

Smedley L 'smooth/level clearing' OE; place in Lancs, and a common Derbys surname.

Smee L 'smooth/level place' OE. Or N 'smooth, polite, suave'. The

OE word was closer to **Smeeth**, of which **Smeed** is a version.

Smeeth L 'smithy' OE, place in Kent; sometimes ?'smooth (place), level' OE. Or N 'smooth, suave' OE. See **Smee**.

Smeeton L Same as **Smeaton**; place in Leics.

Smele N 'small, slender, thin' OE; the –e can be the weak adjective form after a definite article.

Smerdon L 'hill with rich pasturage (literally butter hill)' OE (cf. *smear*); place –ear– in Devon, and a Devon surname.

Smethurst L ' ?level **Hirst**' OE.

Smith O 'metal-worker, blacksmith, farrier' OE. The primate and patriarch of our surnames, its form unchanged for over 1,000 years; forms with medial –y– and final –e are usually both ignorant and affected, though the first may sometimes have been used for clarity next to the minim letter **m**, and –e may rarely represent L 'smithy' OE. Easily the commonest surname in England and Wales (though **Jones** is far ahead in Wales alone), Scotland, and USA, and the fifth in Ireland in 1890; the family name of five peers. It is thus a frequent victim of hyphenation, either in a sincere effort to avoid ambiguity or in an insincere one to sound distingué; and it has recently gathered to itself many changed foreign surnames. Yet it remains primitive: a smith *smites*, and his honoured name rings down the ages like an anvil. **Smithson** 'son of the **S**—'; a Lincs–Yorks surname.

Smither O 'smith, hammerman' OE. **Smithers** '(son) of **S**—'. Guppy counted it in Surrey only.

Smithwhite See **Smorthwaite**.

Smollett N 'small/narrow head' OE.

Smorthwaite, Smorthit, Smurthwaite, Smurfit L 'small clearing' ON; a former *Smerthwayt* in Guiseley, West Yorks, or two called Smaithwaite and two called Smallthwaite in Cumberland.

Smyth(e) See **Smith**. Of these normally 'wrong' and ostentatious forms, **Smythe** is everywhere uncommon, but **Smyth** (which must occur about once to every 100 **Smiths**) astonishingly runs well ahead of its true source in Northern Ireland (420 –y–:230 –i– in the TD).

Snaith L 'piece, detached land' ON; locality, or place in West Yorks. Chiefly a Northd–Co. Durham surname.

Snape L 'boggy patch' OE, places in Devon, Suffolk, Sussex, Wilts; but places in Lancs, Notts, North and West Yorks are ?'poor pasture, place where sheep snuffle for grass' ON.

F: *first name*　　L: *local name*　　N: *nickname*　　O: *occupational name*

Snare N 'swift' OE or ON. Or L '(animal) snare, trap' OE.

Snawdon See **Snowden**.

Snead L ?'detached piece of ground' OE (cf. **Snaith**); locality, or place in Worcs.

Sneath L Same as **Snaith** (and cf. **Snead**). Mainly a Lincs surname.

Snedden L '**Snead** valley' OE, though no place is now recorded.

Snelgrove See **Snellgrove**.

Snell N 'bold, brisk' OE. Counted by Guppy only in Cornwall–Devon and Suffolk.

Snellgrove L ?'**Snell**'s copse' OE or ?'copse full of snails' OE.

Snelling F 'relative/son/dependant of **Snell**' OE.

Snelson F 'son of **Snell**' OE. Or usually L '**Snell**'s farm' OE; place in Ches, and a Ches surname.

Sneyd L Same as **Snead**; place in Staffs.

Snider O 'cutter, tailor' OE. **Sniders** '(son) of the tailor'.

Snook L 'point, projection' OE. Or the same word, as a N 'nose'; or ?'snake' OE.

Snow N 'snow' (?for snow-white hair) OE; or ?for birth/baptism in time of great snow. Guppy found it scattered – Devon, Essex, Staffs.

Snowball N 'snowy patch, bald spot' OE. Chiefly a Co. Durham–Northd surname.

Snowden, Snowdon L 'snow hill, hill where snow lies long' OE; places in West Yorks and Devon, but the surnames are of Northd–Co. Durham–Yorks–Lincs.

Snuggs N '(son) of snug, neat, trim, (and eventually) cosy, comfortably-off' ME of unknown origin. Snug the Joiner in *Midsummer Night's Dream* had a name appropriate to his skill.

Soame L 'homestead on a lake' OE (cf. *sea*); places (Soham) in Cambs, Suffolk, and a surname of nearby Norfolk. **Soames** must be 'of Soham'.

Soan(e) N 'son' OE, often to mean 'junior'. **Soan(e)s** '(son) of the son'!

Softley L 'soft/spongy clearing' OE, place in Northd; but place in Co. Durham has second element 'hill' OE.

Solomon(s) See **Salaman, Salamons**. Now normally Jewish surnames.

Somer(s) Forms of **Summer(s)**. –s is found chiefly in Somerset.

Somerby L 'farm used in summer' ON; places in Lincs (four), Leics.

Somerfield and **Somerford** See **Summerfield** and **Summerford**.

Somerset L 'dwellers at **Somerton**' all elements OE.

Somerton L 'farm/settlement used in summer' OE; places in four counties – the men of the Somerset place gave their name to the county.

Somervell, Somerville See **Sommerville**.

Sommers See **Summers**.

Sommerville L When this is not an 'improvement' of **Summerfield**, it is from Sommeville, 'place on the Somme' (a Keltic river-name like the Sem – see **Sennington** – and meaning 'drink, water'). A Walter de Somerville 'came over with the Conqueror' and was lord of places in Staffs and Glos. Graveron-Sémerville in Nord may also be involved.

Soper O 'soap-maker/-seller' OE. Counted by Guppy only in Devon.

Sopwith L The second element is 'wood' ON; the first is obscure, but can hardly be the AS settler's name Soppa of Sopworth (Wilts), Sopwell (Herts), Sodbury (Glos): 'Until my grandfather's time no Sopwith ever came south of Durham that I know of', wrote a correspondent in the 1970s.

Sorrel(l) N 'chestnutty, reddish-brown' OF. An old Essex surname. Also spelt **Sorrill**.

Sotheby L 'south in the village' ON.

Sotheran, Sotheron See **Southern**; here with a trilled –r– (shown by the added glide-vowel) characteristic of the North Country. It is lacking in **Sothern**.

Soutar, Souter, Soutter O 'shoemaker, cobbler' OE.

South L 'newcomer from the south, dweller to the south of the village' OE.

Southall L 'southern **Haugh** (*halh*)' OE, place in Middx; but it may sometimes be 'southern hall' OE.

Southam L 'homestead to the south' OE; places in Glos, Warwicks.

Southcombe L 'south valley' OE; four places in Devon.

Southcott L 'southern cottage' OE; a dozen places in Devon alone, and others (–tt, –t, –te) in Berks, Bucks, Wilts.

Southerland See **Sutherland**.

Southern L 'southerner' OE.

Southey L 'southern island'/'south of the river'/'southern enclosure' all OE; places in Somerset, West Yorks/Devon/Devon.

Southgate L 'south gate' of some old town OE; also places in Middx, Norfolk. A Suffolk surname.

Southwell L 'southern spring/stream' OE; places in Dorset, Notts, but the surname counted by Guppy only in Hants.

Southwick L 'southern **Wick**' OE; locality, or places in six counties.

F: *first name*   L: *local name*   N: *nickname*   O: *occupational name*

Southwold L 'southern **Wald**' OE; place in Suffolk.

Southwood L 'wood to the south' (or ?'south of the wood') OE; places in Devon (seven), Kent, Norfolk, Somerset, Sussex, Worcs; and see **Southworth**.

Southworth L 'southern enclosure' OE; place in Lancs, and surname in use by 1281. There has been some absorption by **Southwood**, now the name of a farm at Walton-on-Thames once called Southworth.

Sowden L 'south hill, south of the hill' OE; places in Devon. Or N 'sultan' OF, from arrogance or from being Head Saracen in a play. Also spelt **Sowdon**.

Sowerbutts L 'former end-pieces of the common field' ME from Low Latin *butta* 'with (in John Field's phrase) coarse, worked-out or acid soil' OE; fields (Sour Butts) in Derbys and Westmorland, and no doubt elsewhere, but anyroad a northern surname.

Sowerby L 'farm in the mud/marsh' ON; places in four northern counties (five in Yorks), and a Cumberland–Co. Durham–Yorks–Lincs surname.

Sowman L 'man from the south' or 'man living to the south' OE+ OE.

Sowton L 'southern farm' OE; place in Devon.

Spackman See **Speakman**.

Spaight See **Speight**.

Spain L In view of surnames like **Pettingale** (Portugal), this will normally be the country 'Spain' Latin *Hispania*, with which medieval England had a lively trade. Even Épaignes, in Eure, the origin of a Domesday Book bearer, refers to a colony of Spaniards.

Spalding L 'family/folk of (an AS pioneer whose F is) ?connected with the verb *to cleave*' OE; place in Lincs; this tribe are found at Spaldington and Spalding Moor, East Yorks; Spaldwick, Hunts; Spalford, Notts.

Spanyol L 'Spanish' OF.

Spark(e) N 'sprightly, lively' ON. **Spark(e)s** '(son) of **S**—'; Guppy counted –ks in Somerset–Devon, –kes in Sussex.

Sparrow N 'sparrow' OE. Counted by Guppy only in Glos, Essex–Suffolk.

Sparrowhawk N 'sparrowhawk' OE+OE, the bird of prey; the surname is now also found newly hyphenated as **Sparrow-Hawk**.

Speak(e), **Speck** N 'woodpecker' OF (cf. **Speight**).

Speakman N 'spokesman' OE+OE. Guppy found it in Essex, Lancs.

Spear(e) N 'spear' OE, for a notable wielder of one.

Speed N 'prosperity, success' OE (as in *more haste, less speed*).

Speer See **Spear**. Or possibly O 'watchman (*spier*)' OF.

Speight N 'woodpecker' OE (cf. OF **Speak**) – from noise, or gay apparel.

Speirs See **Spiers**.

Speke N See **Speak**. Or L ' ?brushwood, twigs' OE; place in Lancs.

Spellar, Speller, Spel(l)man O 'speaker, discourser, (professional) narrator' OE.

Spence O '(worker in/controller of) larder or buttery' OF, a metonym; cf. **Spencer**. Counted by Guppy only in Yorks.

Spencer O 'house steward, butler, dispenser of provisions, one who looked after the **Spence**' OF *desp–*, Anglo-Norman *esp–*. Mainly a Midland and Yorks surname, but particularly common in Warwicks. **Spencer-Churchill** is the family name of the dukes of Marlborough.

Spender O 'steward' OF (cf. **Spencer**). If a N, it could be 'waster, squanderer' OE (cf. *spend*).

Spendlove N 'spend/lavish/squander love' OE. Counted by Guppy only in Derbys, Northants.

Spens(er) See **Spence(r)**.

Spice O 'spice' OF, a metonym for **Spicer**.

Spicer O 'spice-seller, grocer, druggist' OF. Counted by Guppy only in Dorset, but also an old Devon surname.

Spick(er)nell O 'sealer of the King's writs in Chancery' ME *spigurnel* from Anglo-Latin.

Spier O 'watchman' OF (cf. *spy*). **Spiers** '(son) of S—'; Guppy found it common only in Worcs.

Spiller N 'waster, parasite, jester' OE. Guppy found it in Somerset–Devon.

Spilsbury L ' ?look-out fort' OE or ' ?(AS called) Watchful's fort' OE; place (Spelsbury) in Oxon.

Spindler O 'spindle-maker' OE.

Spink(e) N 'finch, chaffinch' ME. **Spinks** '(son) of S—'. The reason for bestowing this N is hard to see, but cf. **Finch**. –**k** and –**ks** were Norwich surnames in Guppy's time.

Spital, Spittal(l), Spittle L 'hospital' ME, having lost the (*h*)*o*– of OF; locality, or from the unhygienically named place Spital in the Street, Lincs (which is on Ermine Street). **Spittles** '(of, i.e.) at the hospital'.

Spittlehouse L 'hospital house' OF+OE.

Spode L ' ?spade(-shaped field)' OE *spadu*, place (Spoad) in Salop;

F: *first name*   L: *local name*   N: *nickname*   O: *occupational name*

there was a family Spoade in Biddulph, Staffs, in 1550, and Josiah **Spode** the potter moved to Stoke *c.* 1695.

Spofforth L 'ford at a spot/plot of land' OE, place in West Yorks; the surname also occurs as **Spofford**.

Spong L 'long narrow strip of ground' ME, later East Anglia–Leics–Northants dialect.

Spooner O, and much likelier to be 'maker of roofing-shingles' or 'shingle-roofer' than 'spoon-maker' OE *spōn*, in two senses, +–**er**. Mainly a northern surname. *Spoonerisms* take their name from the Rev. W. A. S— (†1930), something of whose spirit was upon me just now when I nearly invented the melancholy trade of 'roofer with shingles'.

Sprackling N dim. 'sprightly, lively' ON (cf. **Sprake**).

Spragg(e), **Sprague**, **Sprake** Same as **Spark**, but with metathesis of –**r**– and voicing of –**k**– to –**g**–.

Sprat(t) N 'sprat (presumably from small stature)' OE *sprott*. But **Spratling** is less likely to be a dim. of this than a version of **Sprackling**. **Spratt** was counted by Guppy only in Somerset.

Spray N 'twig; lanky person (like **Sprigg**)' ME from Germanic. Or, an extension of this, L 'brushwood', as in the first element of Sprytown, Devon.

Spreckley L 'clearing with shoots, twigs' OE, place (Spreakley) in Surrey, its pronunciation perhaps influenced by ME *spreckle* (from Germanic), a 'freckle, speckle'.

Spriddell ?N dim. 'sprout, twig, peg, chip' OE.

Sprigg(s) N 'twig/skinny' ME from Germanic; and '(son) of S—'.

Spring N The season 'spring' ME from the OE verb; hence 'a nimble and lusty youth'.

Springall N 'youth, stripling' ME *springold*, *springald*, *springal(l)* from the verb *spring* 'leap, burgeon' OE. But Reaney also calls in O *springalde* 'catapult, ballistic engine' OF (Norman dialect).

Springer N 'jumper, leaper' OE+–**er**.

Springett N dim. '**Spring**', or a form of '**Springall**'.

Springthorpe L '**Thorp** by a copse/spring' OE; places in Cambs/Lincs.

Sproat N 'shoot, twig, sprout, (?youngster)' OE *sprota* becoming *sprote* in ME and then 'correctly' *sproat*; or 'freckle' ME *sprote* from Germanic.

Sprot(t), and possibly **Sprod(d)**, are forms of **Sproat** or (from OE *sprott*) **Sprat**; and **Sprudd** could be from **Sprodd**.

Sprunt N 'trim, smart, nimble' ME from Germanic.

Sprutt Perhaps from **Sprott**.

Spuffard See **Spofforth**.

Spurrier O 'spur-maker' OE (cf. the street called Spurriergate, York).

Spurstow L 'assembly-place (**Stow**) for inquiries (A. H. Smith's ingenious use of our *spoor*, 'track')' OE; place in Ches.

Squarey N The word *squary* (based on *square*, ultimately from OF) occurs as early as 1602 to mean 'squarish, square-built', and might be the origin. The name is now found in Wilts–Dorset.

Squibb N The word *squib* (probably imitative in origin) occurs early in the 16th century for the familiar firework, a lampoon, and 'a paltry, despicable fellow'.

Squier O 'young gentleman attending a knight, shield–bearer, squire' OF; this form in –ier is older but rarer than –ire. **Squiers** '(son) of **S**—'.

Squire(s) See **Squier**; **Squire** is the commonest of the group, and Guppy gave it a high count in Devon.

Squirrel(l) N 'squirrel' OF, ultimately from Greek 'shadow-tail', as if the creature used it for a parasol; applied to ?a good climber or ?a hoarder. Guppy counted it only in Suffolk. A hyphenation **Squirrel**-Badger exists.

Srawley and **Sreeve(s)** These exceptional (for no dictionary word begins with *sr*–) and strangely attractive spellings are versions of **Shrawley** and **Shreeve(s)**.

Stable L 'stable' OF. Or N 'reliable, steady, stable' OF. Both ultimately from same Latin stem *sta*– 'stand'. **Stables** 'of (i.e. at) the stable', or a plural.

Stack L 'pile, heap, isolated column of rock, haystack' ON. But the only early forms quoted by Reaney support his decision that O 'haystacker' or N 'hefty as a haystack' are more likely.

Stackhouse L 'house at/for ricks' OE; locality, or place in Giggleswick, West Yorks, where the meaning was 'at the rick-houses'.

Stac(e)y F dim. '**Eustace**'. Guppy found **Stacey** only in Cornwall–Devon–Somerset and the Home Counties.

Staddon L 'bullock (cf. **Stott**)/stud (cf. **Stoddart**) hill' OE; places in Devon (six), Somerset.

Stafford L 'ford by a staithe/landing-place' OE; place in Staffs; the surname is chiefly found in Derbys–Leics, so this is the usual origin. The places in Dorset/Sussex are 'stony/steers' (bullocks') ford' both OE.

Stagg N 'stag' OE; various reasons suggest themselves.

Stainburn L 'stony stream' OE scandinavianized or ON; places in Cumberland, West Yorks.

F: *first name*   L: *local name*   N: *nickname*   O: *occupational name*

Stainer O 'painter' OF.

Staines L ' ?of (i.e. at) the stone' OE (originally without –s), place in Middx; but place in Surrey is more like 'stony places' OE. An Essex surname.

Stainfield L 'stony **Field**' OE scandinavianized, place in Lincs near Lincoln; but place in Lincs near Haconby is 'stony **Thwaite**' ON.

Stainforth L 'stony ford' OE scandinavianized; two places in West Yorks.

Stainton L Same as **Stanton**, scandinavianized, places in six northern counties (five in Yorks); but Great and Little S—, Co. Durham, may be 'place/farm on a **Stanway**' OE.

Stallabrass, Stallebrass, Stallybrass The place-name Stalybridge, Ches, is too late (first recorded 1687) to be the origin of a surname which was already *Stallowbrace* in 1652 (at Waltham, Essex), and the epicentre of the group was Suffolk–Cambs–Hunts. N 'stalwart arm' ME *stalworth*+OF *bras* is attractive but shaky.

Stallard N 'stalwart, study, brave' OE. A Somerset surname.

Stallion (more rarely **Stallan**) N 'stallion' OF, for virility or lasciviousness.

Stallwood, Stallworthy N 'stalwart, robust, brave' OE.

Stamford L Same as **Stanford**, places in Lincs–Northants, Northd, East Yorks; but place in Middx was once the same as **Sandford**.

Stamp L 'Étampes' OF *Estampes* (ultimately Stampae, a pre-Roman name of unknown meaning); place in Seine-et-Oise.

Stamper Forms exist in ME (from Germanic) meaning a 'pestle or rammer' or 'one who stamps his feet or treads (grapes)'.

Stanbridge L 'stone bridge' OE; places in Beds, Hants and (Stam–) Essex, and still a Beds surname.

Stanbury L 'stone fort' OE; places (also –borough) in Devon, Herts, West Yorks. Reaney also supposes a female F, of the same tough meaning.

Standage See **Standish**.

Standaloft N 'stand erect' OE+ON.

Standen L 'stony valley' OE; places in Berks, Kent, Lancs, Wilts. The surname is chiefly of Kent–Sussex – its variant –**ding** is found in Lancs, Sussex.

Standerwick L '**Wick** on stony ground' OE; place in Somerset.

Standeven N 'stand straight' OE.

Standfast N 'stand firm' OE, for a resolute character.

Standfield, Standidge and **Standing** See **Stanfield, Standish** and **Standen**.

Standish L 'stony enclosure/pasture' OE; places in Glos, Lancs Myles **S**— was of Lancs stock.

Standley See **Stanley**.

Standon L 'stony hill' OE; places in Hants, Herts, Staffs.

Stanfield L 'stony **Field**' OE; places in Norfolk, Staffs.

Stanford L 'stony ford' OE; places in nine counties, which do not click at all with Guppy's count in only Sussex, Dorset, Suffolk. Or see **Stamford**.

Stanhope L 'stony valley' OE; place in Co. Durham. Family name of the earls of Harrington.

Staniford, Staniforth L 'stony ford' OE. Mainly Derbys–Yorks surnames.

Stanistreet L 'paved (Roman) road' OE compound *stānstræt*.

Stanley (rarely **Stanly**) L 'stony clearing/field' OE; places in twelve counties (three in Glos), but chiefly a Glos–Warwicks surname. The strange use as a F dates from the fame of the explorer H. M. **S**— (†1904), whose real name was **Rowlands**! **Stanley** is the family name of the earls of Derby and barons Sheffield.

Stannard F 'stone hard' OE. Counted by Guppy only in Suffolk.

Stanney L 'stony island' OE; place in Ches.

Stansfield L 'stony/(AS called) Stone's **Field**' OE; places in Norfolk, Suffolk, West Yorks, and a West Yorks surname.

Stanton L 'stony place/farm' OE, places in at least fifteen counties; but **S**— Harcourt, Oxon, and **S**— Drew, Somerset, are named from prominent prehistoric stone monuments. Guppy counted the surname only in Beds. But see **Stenton**.

Stanway L 'stone (i.e. paved) road' OE; places in Essex and the contiguous Glos–Herefords–Salop; the reference will normally be to a Roman road.

Stanwell L 'stony spring/stream' OE; place in Middx.

Stanwix L 'stone walls' ON + English plural –*s*; place in Cumberland on Hadrian's Wall.

Staple L 'pillar, post' OE; locality, or places in Devon, Kent, Somerset. **Staples** 'of (i.e. at) the **S**—', or a plural; counted by Guppy only in Notts.

Stapleford L 'ford marked by a post' (or 'by posts') OE; places in eight counties.

Staplehurst L '**Hirst** where posts could be cut' OE; place in Kent.

Stapleton L 'place/farm with a (?prominent) pillar/post' OE, places in seven counties; though the first element of the Herefords place may be 'steeple' OE.

F: *first name*　　L: *local name*　　N: *nickname*　　O: *occupational name*

Starbuck L 'stream in sedge/bent-grass' ON; place (Starbeck) in West Yorks.

Stark(e) N 'firm, tough, stiff, harsh' OE; no connection with *stark naked* (see **Stert**).

Starkey, Starkie N dim. '**Stark**'. Guppy counted –ie only in Lancs.

Starling N 'starling' OE; it is hard to see *why*.

Starr N 'star' OE, for no obvious reason. Or L, as a sign-name.

Start L Same as **Stert**; locality, or places in Cornwall, Devon.

Startifant N 'start/leap forward' ME (from Germanic)+OF.

Startup N 'jump up' ME (from Germanic)+OE.

Statham L '(at) the staithes/landing-places' OE dative plural after lost preposition; place in Ches.

Stather L or O 'one who lives/works at a staithe (landing-place, wharf, embankment)' OE.

Staughton L Same as **Stockton**; places in Beds, Hunts.

Staunton L Same as **Stanton**, places in Glos, Herefords, Somerset, Worcs, and Leics, Notts; but S— on Wye, Herefords, is 'stony hill' OE. And see **Stenton**.

Stav(e)acre L Probably from a plot of 'stavesacre' ME from Latin reproducing Greek *staphisagria* 'wild raisin', the seeds of which were used against vermin and as an emetic.

Staveley L 'wood/clearing where staves can be got' OE; places in Derbys, Lancs, Westmorland, West Yorks, and a Yorks surname.

Stavordale L ' ?stony ford valley' OE; place (priory) in Somerset.

St Clair L Two places in Calvados and Manche, named after a 7th-century Norman saint and a 3rd-century bishop of Nantes, from Latin *clarus* 'bright, shining' (cf. **Clare**). Families originating therefrom reached as far as Orkney (in the form **Sinclair**).

Stead L 'place, estate, farm' OE; locality, or place in West Yorks – it is mainly a Yorks surname. Or N 'steed, stallion, stud-horse' OE; or perhaps O, from tending them.

Steadman O 'farm-man' or 'groom/cavalryman (literally steed-man)' OE (see **Stead**).

Stear See **Steer**.

Stearman O 'man who looked after steers/bullocks' OE+OE, or 'steersman, skipper' OE compound.

Stearn(s) See **Stern**; and '(son) of S—'.

Stebbing(s), Stebbins L The place Stebbing in Essex means 'the folk of (an AS called) Stub' OE; but the surnames may sometimes relate to OE *stybbing* 'clearing', with Kent–Essex –e– for the –*y*–. Chiefly surnames of Essex, Norfolk.

Stedham L 'homestead with horses' OE (cf. **Stead**); place in Sussex.

Steed, Ste(e)dman Forms of **Stead, Steadman**. Guppy counted **Stedman** only in Kent, Suffolk.

Steel(e) O 'steel(-worker)' OE, a metonym. Or N, for firmness and reliability. Common in south Scotland, Lake District, Staffs–Ches– West Yorks.

Steen L Places called Steen, Stean(e), for instance in Northants, mean 'at the stone' OE locative of *stān* by *i*-mutation. The meaning 'stone' applies even if the family origin is Dutch or German.

Steeples L '(of, i.e.) at the steeple' OE.

Steer N 'steer, young ox' OE. Or O, from tending them.

Steggall, Steggal(l)s, Steggell, Steggle(s) See **Stile(s)**.

Stell ?L 'salmon-trap, nets spread across a river' OE (probably cognate with *stall* 'place').

Stenson L 'Stein's farm' ON (his name is cognate with *stone*)+OE; place (*Steineston* in 1206) in Derbys.

Stenton L Of the same meaning as **Stanton, Stainton, Staunton**; place in East Lothian. There is a large pocket of the group (mainly **Staunton**) in Co. Mayo, alternating with **McEvilly** 'son of the knight' Irish.

Stephen F 'crown, wreath, garland' Greek. The protomartyr – a F popular with the Normans; –ph– is more in line with the original spelling, but the form with –v– is more faithful to our pronunciation. **Stephens(on)** '(son)/son of S—'; both commoner as surnames than the simple F. –s is very common in Cornwall, and common in Wales, Midlands, south, south-east, but in south and south-east **Stevens** prevails, as it does in USA; whereas –ph– is usual in Cornwall, Wales, and its Border. **Stephenson** is largely a northern surname, mingling with **Stevenson** and replaced by it in Midlands and Sussex, and in Scotland, where –v– was the 62nd commonest surname in 1958.

Sterling See **Starling** (?influenced by Scots town **Stirling**).

Stern N 'stern, austere' OE (cf. **Sterne**). Recently reinforced by many German–Jewish immigrants (= 'star'). Family name of the barons Michelham.

Sterndale L 'valley with stony ground' OE; places in Derbys.

Sterne An acceptable form of **Stern**, since the OE adjective bore an –e; and it could show a weak adjective after a lost definite article.

Stert L 'promontory, hill-spur (literally tail)' OE; locality, or places in Dorset (–te), Somerset, Wilts. Also rewritten **Sturt** in the south; and changed to **Start** (cf. **Clark**), and corrupted in *stark naked*.

Steuart Rare spelling of **Steward, Stewart**.

F: *first name*   L: *local name*   N: *nickname*   O: *occupational name*

Steven, Stevens(on) See **Stephen, Stephens(on)**.

Steward, Stewart O 'steward, keeper of a household (only very doubtfully is the first element *sty* as in *pigsty*), seneschal' OE; so to the Lord High Steward of Scotland, and on to a dynasty; unvoicing of final –d to –t is typically Scots. **Stewardson, Stewartson** 'son of the steward'. **Stewart** and its variants formed the sixth commonest surname in Scotland in 1958, and the 58th in Ireland in 1890; family name of the earls of Galloway. **–d** common in East Anglia.

Stickells, Stickles and **Stigell, Stiggles** Forms of **Stile(s)**.

Stickland L 'at the steep lane' OE; place now leaving its name in Winterborne S—, Dorset.

Stickler L 'one who lives at a steep place or declivity' OE+–er. The meaning 'moderator, umpire, mediator between combatants' ME (from Germanic) is first instanced in *OED* in 1538, but may have existed in surname-forming days.

Stickley L Bardsley's *William atte Sticlegh* in Somerset, 1327–8, proves it a 'clearing' OE place-name; the first element could be 'steep' OE (which remained a West Country word) or conceivably 'stick, branch' OE *sticca*.

Stiff N 'tough, obstinate' OE.

Stile L 'stile/ascent' OE *stigol* (whereafter, the –g– is vocalized). Forms in **Steg-/Stig–** retain –g–, which is unvoiced to –k– in forms in **Stick-**. **Stiles** 'of (i.e. at) the **S—**', or a plural.

Still N 'quiet' OE. Or L 'fishing enclosure, fish-weir' OE, or short-vowelled form of **Stile**.

Stilton L 'place at a stile/ascent' OE; place in Hunts, which also gives its name to the cheese.

Stilwater sounds L 'quiet water' OE. But there may be an O reference to 'distilling water' ME (from Latin)+OE. (Nautical term meaning 'slack-water' is too late to be the origin.)

Stilwell L 'quiet spring/stream' OE.

Stim(p)son F 'son of (dim.) **Stephen**'. **–mpson** counted by Guppy only in Norfolk. **Stinson** also occurs.

Stinchcombe L 'sandpiper/dunlin valley' OE; place in Glos, and a Glos surname.

Stirk N 'bullock/heifer' OE.

Stirling L The Scots town was *Strivelin* in 1147, and *ystref Felyn* 'dwelling of Melyn' OW has been suggested (Johnston even put 'perh. the same man' (i.e. Melyn) at Dunfermline).

Stirton L 'farm on a Roman road (cf. **Stratton**)' OE; place in West Yorks.

Stith N 'tough, stiff, strong' OE.

St John, St Leger, St Maur L Various places in France called Saint-Jean (see **John**), Saint-Léger (see **Ledger**), Saint-Maur (see **Moore**). There are fancy slurrings of these available (though not obligatory) – *singe-on,* **Salinger, Seymour**; all uglier than their originals, but none so distasteful as calling a training college, dedicated to the Blessed Virgin *Simmeries.*

Stock L 'tree-trunk, tree-stump, foot-bridge' OE; sometimes perhaps from OE *stoc* – see **Stokes**. The surname reached its greatest eminence with Saint Simon **S—** (†1265), the ?centenarian who became head of the Carmelites. Guppy counted it only in Essex. **Stocks** '(of, i.e.) at the **Stock**', or a plural.

Stockbridge L 'tree-trunk/log bridge' OE; locality, or places in four counties (seven in Yorks).

Stockdale L Counted by Guppy only in Cambs, yet eight times a place-name of the northern counties: 'tree-stump valley' OE, in Westmorland (two), Cumberland (three), West Yorks (in Salterforth); 'pillar valley' ON, in Cumberland (Uldale); '?outlying cattle-farm valley' OE, in West Yorks (near Settle, above the treeline).

Stocker O A West Country word for 'one who fells or grubs up tree-stumps' OE *stocc.* Or L, from living near a **Stock**.

Stockfield L 'open country with tree-stumps' OE; or, later, an enclosed field with such stumps – but the sense '(live) stock' is probably too late to form a surname.

Stockfish O '(seller of) stockfish, dried cod' ME from Dutch.

Stockford L 'ford at a tree-stump' OE.

Stocking L 'ground cleared of tree-stumps' OE; locality, or many places in several counties (six each in Herts and Yorks). **Stockings** 'of (i.e. at)' the same, or a plural, as at the Derbys and Northants places; also spelt **Stockins**.

Stockland L 'land belonging to a religious house' (cf. **Stokes**) or 'land having a **Stock**/*stoc*' (see **Stokes**) OE; places in four counties.

Stockley L First element as in **Stockland**, second 'wood/clearing' OE; places (also –leigh) in six counties. (Meanings like 'wood where logs are got' and 'clearing with tree-stumps' are likeliest.)

Stockton L 'place in/with a **Stock**' OE; locality, or places in eight counties, and the Co. Durham town; some of these could be 'log-built farm' OE. Counted by Guppy only in Ches, where there are two places so called.

F: *first name*　　L: *local name*　　N: *nickname*　　O: *occupational name*

Stockwell L 'tree-stump spring/stream, plank-bridge stream' OE; place in London.

Stockwood L 'wood belonging to a religious house' (cf. **Stokes**) or 'wood in/with a **Stock**' or 'tree-stump wood' OE; places in Devon, Dorset, Somerset.

Stod(d)art, Stoddard, Stoddert, Stodhart O 'stud-herd, keeper of a stud' OE. **–ard** counted by Guppy only in Staffs.

Stoker L 'one who lives at a **Stock**' OE + **–er**.

Stokes L Plural or 'of (i.e. at)' form of OE *stoc* 'place, religious site, secondary (outlying) settlement', of which a correct ME plural could also be *stoke* (which could also be a dative singular after a lost preposition); from these, variously, the Staffs town of Stoke and many villages. A Midland surname.

Stokoe L ?'tree-stump **Howe**' OE + ON; place (Stockhow) in Cumberland.

Stone(s) L 'stone(s)' OE; from dwelling near a prominent rock or stone (such as a hundred-stone) or (**–e**) at one of the places called Stone in seven counties. **–e** counted by Guppy only in south-west, south-east, Derbys; **–es** only in West Yorks–Lincs.

Stoneham L 'stony homestead' OE; two places in Hants.

Stonehill L 'stony hill' OE; there are, for instance, two places Stone Hill in West Yorks.

Stonehouse L 'stone house' OE – perhaps a marvel alongside wooden huts; places in Devon, Glos, but a Yorks surname.

Stonelake L 'stony stream' OE, as at Stanlake, Devon.

Stonham See **Stoneham**; place of same meaning in Suffolk.

Stonor L 'stony slope/edge' OE; place in Oxon. Family name of the barons Camoys.

Stoodley L 'horse clearing/pasture' OE (cf. *stud*); place (**–leigh**) in Devon.

Stopford, Stopforth, Stoppard (the last counted by Guppy only in Derbys) L 'market at a hamlet' OE *stoc* + *port*; place (Stockport) in Ches.

Storer O 'one who stocks/furnishes/caters/stores' OF.

Storey F Old Norse personal name *Stóri*, probably 'big'. A northern surname – Co. Durham – Northd – Cumberland – Westmorland – Yorks – Lincs – Norfolk. Also **Storie**.

Stork L 'dried-out/drained land' ON; place (now Storkhill) in Beverley, East Yorks.

Storr N 'big' ON. **Storrs** '(son) of **S—**'; or could be L 'young trees, plantation' ON, as in places in Lancs, Yorks.

Story Form of the commoner **Storey**.

Stothard, **Stotherd**, **Stothert** See **Stoddart.**

Stott N (or O, a metonym) 'bullock, steer, heifer, horse, nag' OE. Guppy found a Somerset group and a Lancs–Yorks–Northd group.

Stoughton L Same as **Stockton**; places in Leics, Surrey, Sussex.

Stourton L 'place on the (River) Stour' OE (the river-name meaning ?'strong, fierce'); places in five counties. Family name of the barons Mowbray, Segrave, and Stourton (premier barony of England).

Stout N 'bold, stately, stout' OF (the Middle English poet will praise his lady for being stout, presumably the second meaning); or 'gnat' OE; or 'bullock' ON. Or L 'hillock, tump' OE. The commonest surname on Fair Isle, between Shetland and Orkney.

Stove L 'room, house' ON; five farms in Orkney, and an Orkney and Shetland surname.

Stow(e) L 'place, assembly-place, religious site' OE; locality, or many places (both spellings) in eleven counties, and –e mainly a Lincs surname. Harriet Beecher **Stowe**'s husband added *his* –e after graduation!

Stowell L 'stony spring/stream' OE; places in Berks, Glos, Somerset, Wilts.

Strachan L 'little valley' Scots Gaelic; place in Kincardines.

Straffan L 'streams' Irish; place in Co. Kildare.

Strahan See **Strachan.**

Straight N 'upright in posture' OE (literally 'stretched').

Strang Northern form of **Strong.**

Strange N 'newcomer, foreigner, man from a distance (literally foreign)' OF. Counted by Guppy only in Dorset, Berks.

Stranger L 'foreigner, newcomer, stranger' OF.

Strangeways L 'strong wash/flow/current' OE; place in Lancs.

Stratford L 'ford on a Roman road' OE (cf. **Street**); places in eight counties, with three in Bucks (it is chiefly a Bucks surname).

Stratton L 'place on a Roman road' OE (cf. **Street**), places in nine southern and East Anglian counties; but place in Cornwall has as first element 'valley, stream' Cornish. Chiefly a Norfolk, Wilts surname.

Strawbridge L 'market/assembly-place bridge' OE; place in Hatherleigh, Devon, called *Stowbridge* in 1532.

Streat, **Street** L 'Roman road' OE from Latin (cf. *street*); locality, or places in six counties; a later meaning was 'hamlet'. Guppy counted **Street** only in Wilts–Hants–Surrey, Beds.

Streeter L 'one who lives on a **Street**'.

Streetly, **Strelley** L 'wood/clearing on a Roman road' OE (cf.

F: *first name*   L: *local name*   N: *nickname*   O: *occupational name*

Street); places (also Streat– and –ly) in six counties, not all with a proven Roman road.

Stretch N 'firm, severe, vehement, violent' OE *strec*.

Stretton L Same as **Stratton**; sixteen places in eight Midland counties. Counted by Guppy only in Derbys–Leics.

Strib(b)ling See **Stripling**.

Strickland L 'land for bullocks/heifers' OE (cf. **Stirk**); several places in Westmorland, and a Lancs–Yorks–Westmorland surname.

Stringer O 'bowstring-maker' OE.

Stringfellow N ' ?strong friend/chap' OE+ON.

Stripling N 'youth' (?one as slim as a strip) ME from Germanic+ –ling (dim.).

Strong N 'strong' OE. A Midland and southern surname.

Strongitharm N 'strong in the arm' OE.

Strood and **Stroud** L 'marshland overgrown with brushwood' OE; places in Kent, Glos, Middx.

Stroulger, Strow(l)ger N 'astrologer, fortune-teller' Latin from Greek.

Strudwick L 'dairy-farm in bushy marshland (cf. **Strood**)' OE; place (now Strudgwick) in Sussex.

Struthers L 'streams' Scots Gaelic; place in Fifes.

Stuart O Respelling (?frenchified) of **Stewart**; common in Scotland and north of England. Family name of the earls Castle Stewart and the earls of Moray.

Stubbing, Stubbs L 'clearing, place of tree-stumps' OE (and **Stubbs** is 'tree-stumps'). **Stubbin(g)s** 'of (i.e. at) the clearing'; locality, or places in four counties. Guppy counted **Stubbs** only in Staffs–Ches–Yorks–Lincs, Hants; and **Stubbins** in Notts. Or N 'stub, stumpy man' OE, and dims. of this.

Studd L or O, from living/working at a 'stud' OE (cf. **Stoddart**). But Tengvik makes it N 'gnat' OE *stūt* normanized.

Studley L Same as **Stoodley**; places in four counties, and mainly a Dorset surname.

Stumbles L '(of, i.e.) at the tree-stump' OE; or a plural.

Sturdee, Sturdy N 'brave, ferocious' OF. Counted by Guppy only in East and North Yorks.

Sturge, Sturges(s), Sturgis F 'Thor's hostage' ON *Thorgils* (cf. **Thorburn, Gilbert**).

Sturgeon N 'sturgeon' OF, the fish – but why? Guppy counted it only in Suffolk.

Sturmer L 'mere/lake formed by the (River) Stour' OE (see **Stourton**); places in Essex, Suffolk.

Sturt L Same as **Stert**; locality, or place in Worcs, but Guppy counted it only in Sussex.

Sturtevant, Sturtivant See **Startifant**.

Sturton L Same as **Stratton**; places in Lincs, Northd, Notts, West Yorks.

Stuttard See **Stoddart**.

Stutter N 'stutterer' ME.

Stych(e) L 'bit/piece/allotment of ploughland' OE, frequent in Cambs–Essex field-names; locality, or place (–e) in Salop.

Style(s) See **Stile(s)**.

Such L 'tree-stump' OF, from some French place; the surname long remained near Stavordale Priory, Somerset, among the founder **Zouch**'s kin.

Suckley L 'wood/clearing with sparrows' OE; place in Worcs.

Suckling N 'suckling, unweaned infant' OE.

Sucksmith O 'ploughshare-smith' OF+OE.

Sudbury L 'southern fort/manor' OE; places in Derbys, Middx, Suffolk.

Suddaby See **Sotheby**. Guppy counted it in North and East Yorks.

Suddell L 'southern valley' OE (cf. **Dell**).

Sudden N 'impetuous, importunate, quick to act' OF. Or L 'southern valley' OE (cf. **Dean**); place in Rochdale, Lancs.

Suffield L 'southern **Field**' OE; places in Norfolk, North Yorks.

Suffolk L 'southern folk/people' (of East Anglia) OE, the county.

Sugarwhite N 'white as sugar' OF+OE.

Sugden L 'swampy (cf. *suck*) hill/valley' OE; places in Salop and West Yorks, and a West Yorks surname. Family name of the barons St Leonards.

Suggate and (North and East Yorks forms) **Suggett, Suggitt** See **Southgate**.

Sullivan N (for O **S—**) 'descendant of ?Black-/?One-/?Hawk-Eyed' Irish. Third commonest surname in Ireland in 1890.

Summer O Despite the existence of **Winter**, Reaney rejects **S—** as a season-name, and makes it '**Sumpter**, packhorse-man, muleteer' OF. **Summers(on)** '(son)/son of **S—**'; –s is chiefly a Devon–Somerset–Glos surname, but Guppy counted it also in Northd.

Summerbee See **Somerby**.

Summerell L 'summer hill' OE – that is, 'hill facing south'; the –ell could best be explained as south-eastern dialect (OE West Saxon *hyll*), and there is a place Summerhill in Kent (and others from Aberdeens to Co. Clare).

F: *first name*   L: *local name*   N: *nickname*   O: *occupational name*

Summerfield, Summerford, Summerhay(e)s, Summer(h)ill L 'Field/ford/Hayes/hill used in summer' OE, though the first element may sometimes mean 'sunny, facing south' ; locality, or places (also spelt Somer–) widely scattered (e.g. –field in Kent, Norfolk, Warwicks, Worcs, West Yorks, though the surname is chiefly of Ches); **–hayes** is a Somerset–Devon surname.

Summerla(n)d, Summerlat F 'summer rover, Viking' ON (still in occasional use as F *Somerlad*); a Scots Gaelic version leads to the corruption **McSorley.**

Summerscale(s) L 'hut(s) used in summer' .ON; locality, or place (–s) in West Yorks.

Sumner O 'summoner, an officer citing and warning people to appear in court' OF; not all can have been as nasty as Chaucer's in the *Canterbury Tales.* Chiefly a Lancs–Ches surname.

Sum(p)ter O See **Summer**, which is from *somier* OF, whereas **–ter** is from *sometier* OF.

Sumption, Sumsion N From birth or baptism on 15 August, the Feast of the 'Assumption' Latin of the Blessed Virgin Mary into Heaven – dogma in the Orthodox East and Roman West.

Sunderland L 'separate land' OE (?private or ?away from the main estate); places in Cumberland, Lancs, and the Co. Durham town; but North S—, Northd, was originally 'southern land' OE. Chiefly a West Yorks surname.

Sundridge L 'separate (cf. *asunder*) ploughland' OE *ersc*; place in Kent.

Sunter See **Sumpter.** Counted by Guppy in North and East Yorks.

Supple N 'nimble, lithe; compliant, adaptable' OF.

Surgeon O 'surgeon' OF (ultimately from Greek *cheirourgia* 'handling, operating', applied even to crafts such as carpentry).

Surrey L 'southern district' OE, the county.

Surridge L 'southern' OF (cf. **Norrish**); also 'southern ridge' OE, place in Morebath, Devon.

Surtees L 'on' OF '(the River) Tees (= ?"boiling, fervent" – as it *is* in its great waterfalls)' Keltic; naturally, a Co. Durham surname.

Susan F 'lily' Hebrew; the embarrassing story of Susannah and the Elders in the Apocrypha has been no bar to the popularity of the F since the 17th century, but it was uncommon in the Middle Ages.

Sussams F '(son) of **Susan**'.

Sussex L 'south **Saxons**' OE, the county.

Sutch See **Such.**

Sutcliff(e) L 'southern cliff' OE; the **–e** could be for dative after lost preposition; three places in West Yorks, and chiefly a Yorks–Lancs surname.

Suter See **Soutar**.

Sutherland L The Scots county, 'south land' ON – it was south to the Vikings compared with Orkney and Shetland. 58th commonest surname in Scotland in 1958 (dropping nine places in 100 years).

Suttill, Suttle L 'soot hill (i.e. ?hill with black soil, ?hill where charcoal is burnt)' OE; place (Soothill) in West Yorks. Or N 'subtle, smart, crafty, insidious' OF.

Sutton L 'southern/south-facing farm' or 'to the south of the farm/village' OE; often a settlement lying to the south of the main one, like S— Montis, Somerset, nestling at the southern foot of the conspicuous Cadbury Castle; almost every English county has a place, but Guppy found the surname plentiful only in Ches–Lancs–Derbys, Midlands, Lincs–Norfolk, Kent, Wilts.

Swaddle ?L 'dale with a track/pathway (cf. *swathe*)' OE; place (Swaddale) in Derbys.

Swaffer L 'track/pathway ford (cf. *swathe*)' OE; place (now Swatfield) in Kent, and a Kent surname.

Swaffield L Swafield in Norfolk is 'open country with a track (cf. *swathe*)' OE, but Guppy counted the surname only in Dorset.

Swain(e) F 'boy, servant' ON *Sveinn*. Or the word used as an O name (sometimes of a swineherd, peasant). It occurs even in non-Danish Devon, Surrey.

Swainson F 'son of **Swain/Swan**'. Or L, for **Swainston**.

Swainston L '**Swain**'s place' ON+OE; places in Co. Durham, IoW.

Swaithes L 'paths, tracks (cf. *swathe*)' OE.

Swallow L 'whirlpool, rushing water' OE; place in Lincs. Or N 'swallow' (the bird) OE, for some lost reason.

Swan(n) Falls into all four classes of origin: F See **Swain**, which was anglicized to *Swan* in Old English; L '(at the Sign of the) Swan' OE; O 'herdsman, swineherd, peasant' OE *swān*; N 'swan' (the bird) OE, for some forgotten reason. Found together in Northd–Co. Durham; –nn is mainly from Essex. **Swanson** 'son of **S**—'.

Swansborough, Swansbury L '**Swan**'s/**Swain**'s fort/manor' OE, though there is now no place in the Gazetteer. In the legend of King Havelock the Dane, his little sister is called Swanborough.

Swanton L 'swineherds' place' OE; places in Kent, Norfolk (three), but a Somerset surname.

Swanwich L This looks like 'swineherds' dairy-farm' OE, but no such mixed-stock place is recorded, and it is probably for **Swanwick**.

F: *first name*   L: *local name*   N: *nickname*   O: *occupational name*

Swanwick L 'swineherds' **Wick**' OE; places in Derbys, Hants.

Swart N 'swart, swarthy' OE/ON.

Swatridge F 'sweet power' OE, made to look like a place-name.

Swayne Surrey form of **Swain**.

Sweatman F 'sweet creature' OE.

Sweet N 'sweet, pleasant' OE; it might, of course, be over-polite and sarcastic in its application. Guppy found it chiefly in Somerset.

Sweetapple N 'sweet apple' OE.

Sweeting N 'darling, sweetheart' OE, early in use as a F.

Sweetland L 'fertile/productive field' OE; locality, or found in plural Sweetlands, Devon, and S— Corner, Kent.

Sweetlove F 'sweet love' OE feminine.

Sweetman F 'sweet creature' OE.

Swetenham L 'homestead of (an AS called) Sweet' OE (the –n– being a sign of the possessive case); place (Swettenham) in Ches, and a Staffs surname.

Swetman and **Swetnam** See **Sweatman** and **Swetenham**.

Swift N 'swift, quick' OE. Mainly a north Midlands surname.

Swinburn(e) L 'pig brook' OE; place (–n) in Northd. Lake District and Co. Durham surnames.

Swindell(s), **Swindler** may be modern jests misrepresenting *swingle(s)*, **Swingler**. Guppy counted –ell in Derbys–Staffs, –ells in Ches– Staffs.

Swinden, Swindin L 'pig valley' OE; place (–en) in West Yorks.

Swindon L 'pig hill' OE; places in Glos, Staffs, Wilts.

Swinebank L 'hill with pigs' OE.

Swinfen L 'pig marsh' OE; place in Staffs.

Swinford L 'pig ford' OE; places (also Swineford) in seven counties. John of Gaunt's mistress Katherine S— (her married name) was ancestress of Henry VII and of the ducal house of Beaufort.

Swingler O 'one who uses a scourge/rod/swingle (for beating flax)/ flail' OE *swingell*.

Swinnerton L 'farm by the pig ford' OE; place in Staffs.

Swinscoe, Swinscow L 'pig wood' OE/ON+ON; place in Staffs.

Swinstead L 'homestead with pigs' OE; place in Lincs.

Swinton L 'pig farm' OE; places in Lancs, North Yorks (two), West Yorks; an odd name for an earldom. Guppy counted the surname only in Ches.

Swinyard L 'pig enclosure' OE.

Swire See **Swyer**.

Swithenbank L 'hillside cleared by burning' OE.

Sworder O 'sword-maker' OE. A Herts–Essex surname.

Swyer L 'neck, col, hollow on a ridge' OE; locality, or place (Swyre) in Dorset. But normally O, northern version of **Squier/Squire**.

Sycamore L 'sycamore' OF, ultimately from Greek (where it means 'fig-mulberry').

Sydenham L 'wide river-meadow' OE, places in Devon, Oxon, Somerset (the Kent place-name is of later formation; but Sydenhams Farm, Bisley, Glos, had no –s in 1830).

Sydney See **Sidney**.

Sykes L 'of (i.e. at) the stream/ditch/gully/boundary-stream (or the meadow alongside it)' OE or ON, or plural; –k– forms are northern, whereas –ch– forms like **Si(t)ch** are Midlands and south, and from OE only. A very common surname of West Yorks, found also in Lincs.

Sylvester See **Silvester**.

Sym(m), Syme(s), Symm(e)s, Symmons See **Sim**, etc.

Symon(d) Forms of **Simon**; but cf. also **Simond**. **Symon(d)s** '(son) of S—'. **Symon(d)son** 'son of S—'. These –y– forms are typical of the south-west.

Syrop N 'syrup' OF, ultimately from Arabic and related to *sherbet* and the drink *shrub*.

Syzling L '(AS called) Victory's (or some two-element F of which this was the first element) land' OE; place in Norfolk, and a Norfolk surname.

F: *first name*   L: *local name*   N: *nickname*   O: *occupational name*

T

Tabard N 'sleeveless coat, tabard' OF, of a shape now associated with heralds but not restricted to them in the Middle Ages. Or L, as a sign-name (Chaucer's pilgrims assembled at 'The Tabard' in Southwark).

Tabbe(r)ner O 'drummer' OF; or a version of **Taverner**.

Tabberer, Taber(er) O 'drummer, tabor-player' OF (cf. *tambourine*), **Taber** being a metonym, found, with **Tabor**, in Essex.

Ta'bois The one bearer in the London TD must derive from the same source as **Talboys**.

Tabor O 'drum, tabor' OF, a metonym (see **Taber**).

Tackley L 'pasture for tegs (i.e. young sheep)' OE; place in Oxon.

Tad(d) ?N 'toad' OE *tadde*.

Taffinder Version of **Taverner**, said to be north-country.

Taft Form of **Toft**, with –o– unrounded.

Taggart See **McTaggart**.

Tailor, Tailyour O Forms of **Taylor**. **Tailorson** 'son of the tailor'. All very rare.

Tainton L 'farm on the River Teign (= stream)' OW+OE, places (Bishops/Drews/Kings-teignton) in Devon, also Taynton (on a stream once called Teign) in Oxon; but place Taynton in Glos is 'Tæta's (his F may be related to **Tate**) people's farm' OE.

Tait N 'jolly, cheerful' ON, but sometimes perhaps confused with **Tate**. Chiefly a Northd–Co. Durham surname.

Talbot(t) F From a Germanic name like ?*Dalabod* (? ? = dale/valley +offer/command), through OF. (No proof that it is ever a L sign-name from the breed of hunting-dog named ?after the family. And the idea that it is N *taille-botte* 'cut-faggot' OF is fanciful.) Guppy counted –ot only in Somerset–Dorset, Notts, Lancs. Chetwynd-**Talbot** is the family name of the earls of Shrewsbury.

Talboys, Tallboy(s) O 'woodcutter (literally cut-wood)' OF. Or rarely L 'Taillebois (= copse wood)' OF; place in Orne.

Tall is only doubtfully N 'tall' ME from OE, as this is a late (16th-century) sense – earlier 'decent, handsome, valiant, prompt'.

Tallemach N 'knapsack' OF.

Tallentire L 'end of the land' OW, –en– representing 'the'; place in Cumberland.

Tallmadge USA alteration of **Talma(d)ge**. See **Tallemach**.

Tallon F 'Talon' OF, the oblique case of a F like the *Tal*– of **Talbot**.

Tambling, Tamlin, Tam(b)lyn, Tamplin(g) F double dim.

'**Thomas**'; the simple form is **Tamlin**, and the others have labial glides –**b**/–**p** before the –**l**–. Although *Tam* seems an essentially Scots pet-form, –**blyn** is found mainly in Cornwall.

Tancock F dim. '**Andrew**'+familiar **Cock**. A Devon name.

Tancred F 'thought counsel' Germanic (for first element cf. *think*). It must have acquired some currency through being the F of a great Crusader.

Tandy F dim. '**Andrew**'. Guppy counted it in Worcs.

Tang L 'tongue/spit of land' ON or OE; locality, or places in North and (several) West Yorks.

Tanguy, Tangye F 'fire ? ?dog' Breton. Saint Tanguy was an associate of Saint Pol de Léon; F brought by Bretons after 1066, especially to east England.

Tank ?L, perhaps a west Midland version of **Tang** (certainly nothing to do with *tank*, which is an Indian word).

Tanner O 'tanner' OE (OF form also existed). Common in Hants–Wilts–Glos–Oxon.

Tanton L 'place on the (River) Tame (= "dark"; related to the South Wales Taff)' Keltic+OE; place in North Yorks.

Taper O 'taper-/candle-/lamp-wick-(maker or seller)' OE.

Taplin F dim. '**Tapp**'.

Taplow L 'Tæppa's (see **Tapp**) burial-mound' OE, which yielded the excavators a good hoard at T—, Bucks, in 1883.

Tapp F 'Tæppa' OE, of unknown meaning, and counted by Guppy in Somerset–Devon. **Tapps** could be either F '(son) of T—', or L 'at the aspen' OE; place in Oakford, Devon.

Tapper O 'tapper (of casks), ale-seller, inn-keeper' OE, including the –**er**.

Tappin(g) F dim. '**Tapp**' or 'son of **Tapp**'. –**ing** is a Bucks name.

Tappington L '**Tapp**'s farm' OE; place in Kent.

Tapscote, Tapscott L '**Tapp**'s cottage' OE, not now on the map.

Tapsfield L '**Tapp**'s open country' OE.

Tapson F 'son of **Tapp**' OE.

Tapton L '**Tapp**'s farm' OE; place in Derbys.

Tarbox, Tarbuck L '(of) brook in the thorns' OE; place (–**bock**) in Lancs; the –**x** represents genitive –**ck's**. (The medieval shepherd carried a tarbox full of tar as a salve for his sheep, but this is probably unconnected.)

Tardew, Tardieu, Tardif N 'sluggish, tardy, lazy' OF and Huguenot (cf. Modern French *tardif*).

Targett N or O 'little round shield' OF, for a user or maker of them.

| F: *first name* | L: *local name* | N: *nickname* | O: *occupational name* |

Tarl(e)ton L '(Norseman called) Thor Ruler's place' ON+OE; place (-e-) in Lancs. (The surname is mainly northern, so the place in Glos, = **Thornton**, need not be considered.)

Tarn L 'tarn, mountain pool' ON. A North Country surname.

Tarr Ekwall's F *Teorra*, as a short form of a *Tīr*– ('fame, glory, honour' OE) compound, would give rise to *Terr* and thence **Tarr**; but hardly in Somerset, where the name is commonest – there, and in Devon, it is a mysterious place-name element.

Tarrant L British river-name, same as Trent, of unknown meaning (Ekwall supposes 'trespasser, flooder'); whence eight places in Dorset, and one in Hants, on its banks – all now with distinguishing suffixes.

Tarry See **Terry** (and cf. **Clark**, *clerk*).

Tarvin L 'boundary' Welsh *terfyn*, from Latin *terminus* with –er– becoming –ar– as in **Clark**; place in Ches on a river of that name.

Tas(c)h L 'at the ash tree' OE, with **T**– a reduced form of ME *atte* 'at the'.

Tasker O 'task-worker, piece-worker' (as opposed to a day-labourer) OF (Norman dialect); or ?'task-master; assessor or regulator of rates and prices'.

Tatam and **Tatchell** See **Tatham** and **Tattershall**.

Tate F (OE ?*Tāt*, form of) OE *Tāta*, for which Tengvik offers a choice of meanings 'dear, glad, hilltop, dice, lock of hair, daddy, teat'! A Co. Durham–Northd surname (as is **Tait**).

Tatem See **Tatham**.

Tatham L '**Tate**'s homestead' OE; place in Lancs. Chiefly a West Yorks surname.

Tatlow L Somebody's 'mound' OE – perhaps for **Taplow**, by assimilation.

Tattam Version of **Tatham** counted by Guppy in Bucks.

Tatters(h)all, **Tattershaw** L 'Haugh (*halh*) of (an AS called) **Tate**'s Army' OE; place (-shall) in Lincs.

Tatton L '**Tate**'s farm' OE; places in Ches, Dorset.

Taunton L 'place on the (River) Tone (= ?"thunderer/roarer" – but the little river roars like a sucking-dove; or "beacon" as in Welsh *tân* "fire")' ?Keltic+OE; place in Somerset. Common in nearby Wilts.

Taven(d)er, **Taverner**, **Tav(i)ner** O 'taverner, inn-keeper' OF. Guppy counted the commonest (**Taverner**) only in Devon.

Tayler The commonest variant (but only 1:100) of **Taylor**, its chief home being the Glos–Bristol area. **Taylerson** 'son of **T**—'.

Taylor O 'tailor' OF (originally meaning a 'cutter'; cf. **Talboys**). A good example of how the possession of a French surname does not make one necessarily superior or exclusive, for T— was the fourth commonest surname in England and Wales in 1853, 18th in Scotland in 1958 (rising eight places in 100 years), and tenth in USA in 1939; it must still be among the first five in Britain, and nearly 25,000 are telephonigerous; and it vastly outnumbers its variants.

Taylour Second commonest variant (but less than 1:1,000) of **Taylor**. Family name of the marquesses of Headfort.

Tazewell N 'tease/toze well' OE, for an efficient teaser of cloth with a teasel. Mainly a Somerset surname. (It has a L look, but no place is known resembling it.)

Teacher O 'teacher' OE+**-er**.

Teague O 'poet, philosopher' Irish.

Teal(e), Teall N 'teal' ME; but why anyone should be nicknamed from a waterfowl is hard to say. Guppy counted **Teal(e)** in West Yorks only.

Teape might be a version of **Tapp**, if John *Tepe* (Devon, 1273) were of the same linguistic origin as the *Tæppa* who left his name at Tapeley, in Westerleigh, Devon.

Tear(e) Manx version of **McIntyre**.

Teasdale, Teasdall L 'valley of the (River) Tees' Keltic+OE (cf. **Surtees**). Not surprisingly, a northern surname. **Teasdall** is rare.

Tebb(oth), Tebbet(t), Tebbit(t), Tebbut(t) F dim. 'Theobald'; **-oth**, because in OF *th* was pronounced *t*. A Cambs–Northants–Leics–Warwicks group.

Tector O 'plasterer, pargeter, stuccoer' Latin; the family claims to be of Lancs origin.

Tedbury L 'manor of (an AS lady called) Tette (perhaps King Ine's sister, an abbess)' OE; place (Tetbury) in Glos.

Tee L 'at the river/stream' OE (cf. **Tash**).

Teesdale Original, but far rarer, form of **Teasdale**.

Tegg L 'teg, young sheep' OE, for one who herded them.

Telfair, Telfer, Telford O 'cleave/cut iron' OF *taille-fer*, for one who could pierce his enemy's armour; a skill which Thomas **Telford** the engineer (†1834) put to better use. **-fer** common in Northd and Lowlands, **-ford** a rather rarer Northd surname.

Tempest N 'storm; agitation, fuss' OF.

Templar, Temple(r) Of these, **-lar** and **-ler** are O 'Knight Templar' OF (Norman), a member of the military and religious order founded to protect pilgrims to the Holy Land and taking its name

F: *first name*   L: *local name*   N: *nickname*   O: *occupational name*

from Solomon's Temple, but suppressed in 1312 for alleged vice and heresy. **Temple** (which Guppy counted only in Lincs) should show residence at/near one of their houses, but many 18th-century foundlings were given the surname at their baptism in Temple Church, London. **Templeman** (chiefly a Notts surname) 'servant/tenant of the Templars' second element OE. **Templeton** L 'Templars' place' OF+OE; places in Berks, Devon.

Tench N 'tench' OF, the fish well described by Reaney as 'fat and sleek'.

Tennant, Tennent O 'tenant' (originally a present participle 'holding') OF – the holder of a *tenement* (which in those days wasn't a tall block of slummy apartments). –ant is a Yorks surname, and is also found in south Scotland. Family name of the barons Glenconner. **Tennents** '(son) of T—'.

Tennison, Tennyson See **Dennison**. Guppy counted –i– in North and East Yorks, but the famous family were of Lincs.

Terris F '(son) of **Terry**'.

Terry F dim. 'people rule' Germanic (best known as F *Theodoric*). An old Kent surname, also found in the 1300s in Yorks, Bucks–Oxon–Northants–Hunts.

Tesche, Tesh Forms of **Tash**; cf. **Esh**; –e for dative after lost preposition.

Tes(s)ler O 'teaseler (of cloth)', who raised a nap on the surface, OE.

Tester N 'big-head' OF *testard*, an opprobrious derivative of *teste* (Modern French *tête*), ultimately from Latin *testa* 'pot'. A Sussex surname.

Tetley and **Tetlow** are Ches surnames, and place-name Tetton, Ches, is '**Tate**'s farm', so they are likely to be '**Tate**'s clearing' and his 'mound' OE.

Tew L '?meeting-place, court' OE; places (Great/Little/Duns Tew) in Oxon. Or N 'plump' Welsh *tew* – but Guppy's count in Northants and Hants is against this.

Thacher, Thacker Same as **Thatcher**, but form with –k– may be based on ON.

Thacker(a)y, Thacra(h), Thack(w)ray L 'nook with thatching (-reed)' ON, places (Thackray) in West Yorks (now under Fewston Reservoir), Cumberland. Mainly West Yorks surnames.

Thackham L 'thatched homestead' or 'homestead where good thatching (such as reeds) is got' OE; places in Berks (–tch–), Sussex (–akeh–).

Thackway L '**Thwaite** with thatching (-reed)' ON; places (Thackthwaite) in Cumberland (two), North Yorks.

Thackwell L ' ?spring/stream with thatching (-reed)' OE.

Thain(e), Thane O 'thane, tenant by military service (and in Scotland, eventually, clan chieftain and king's baron)' OE.

Tharp See **Thorp**.

Thatcher O 'thatcher' OE. Chiefly a Berks–Hants–Wilts–Somerset surname.

Thaxter O Female, but later also male 'thatcher' OE.

Theadom N 'prosperity' (cf. the archaic verb *thee* 'prosper') OE; the rare type of abstract surname.

Theaker O 'roofer' ON (cf. **Thatcher**, **Thacker**).

Thelwall, Thelwell L 'pool by a plank (-bridge)' (cf. north and Scots dialect *weel* 'deep pool') OE; place in Ches.

Theobald F 'people bold' Germanic, with the original *Theud–* misrepresented as Greek *Theo–* 'God'. From the vernacular *Tebald/ Tibald* come a number of surnames in **Teb–/Tib–/Dib–**. **Theobalds** '(son) of T—'.

Theodore F 'God's gift' Greek; the F was respected in England chiefly for T— of Tarsus (†690), the great reorganizing Archbishop of Canterbury.

Theophilus F 'dear to God' Greek, the friend of Saint Luke.

Thetford L 'people's (i.e. public) ford' OE (cf. **Theobald**); places in Cambs, Lincs, and especially Norfolk.

Thew O 'serf, slave, thrall' OE.

Thewles(s), Thewliss N 'ill-mannered, immoral, void of good qualities' OE (though *thews* are now 'muscles', not 'virtues').

Thick N 'stocky, thick-set' OE.

Thickbroom L 'thick broom (-brushes)' OE; place in Staffs.

Thimpson F 'son of **Timm**'.

Thirkell, Thirkettle See **Thurkettle**. Guppy counted –kell in Kent, –kettle in Norfolk, Suffolk, but **Thirkell** and **Thirkle** in Cumberland–Yorks and the north-east are from **Threlkeld**.

Thirlby L 'thralls'/serfs' farm' ON; place in North Yorks.

Thirlwall, Thirlwell L 'holed wall' OE (cf. *nostril* 'nose-hole' and *thrill* 'pierce, transfix') – a gap in Hadrian's Wall; place (–a–) in Northd.

Thirsk L 'fen, lake' ON; place in North Yorks.

Thistlethwaite, Thistlethwayte L '**Thwaite** with thistles' OE+ON; lost place in Cumberland.

Thistleton L 'place in the thistles' OE; places in Lancs, Rutland, East Yorks.

Thoburn See **Thorburn**.

F: *first name*   L: *local name*   N: *nickname*   O: *occupational name*

Thoday L 'people's way, highway' OE. Guppy counted it only in Cambs.

Thom F dim. '**Thomas**'. An essentially Scots surname. **Thoms(on)** same meanings as **Toms(on)**; and see **Thompson**. With variant spellings **–son** formed the fourth commonest surname in Scotland in 1958 (as it had done 100 years before).

Thomas F 'twin' Aramaic (the Greek version being *Didymus*); the N of the Apostle, whose F (says Eusebius) was Judah. Unpopular as a F at first, as he was the Doubter, but swept to a foremost position by the murder of Thomas Becket in 1170, until it became even a generic term for males in *tomcat*, *tomboy*. The origin of many surnames in **Tom(p)-/Thom(p)-**, **Thomas** itself is far commoner than any of its numerous family – seventh in England and Wales in 1853, 11th in USA in 1939; it is the pre-eminent surname of South Wales – seven per cent of Guppy's yeomen there were so named – and in 1938 there were eighteen **Thomas**es in the 200-odd boys at Cowbridge Grammar School, so that with the traditional numeration one of them was **Thomas** Duodevicesimus. **Thomas(s)on** 'son of T—'.

Thomassin, Thomazin F dim. '**Thomas**'.

Thomerson F 'son of **Thomas**'.

Thomes F '(son) of **Thom**'.

Thomline See **Tomlin**.

Thomlinson See **Tomlinson**. A Cumberland–Westmorland surname.

Thompkins See **Tompkins**. There is only one in the London TD.

Thompsett See **Thomsett**; a glide-consonant –p– has developed.

Thompson F 'son of (dim.) **Thomas**', with glide-consonant –p–. Huge incidence (along with the rarer **Thomson**) in Northd, and common everywhere save in the south-west. 15th commonest surname in England and Wales in 1853, 42nd in Ireland in 1890, 15th in USA in 1939.

Thomsett F dim. '**Thomas**', from the pet-form *Thomaset*, with French suffix.

Thorburn F 'Thor (whose name is connected with *thunder*) bear' ON; but anglicized to 'Thor warrior' OE (*beorn*).

Thorley L 'thorn wood/clearing' OE; places in Herts, IoW. But counted by Guppy only in Ches–Staffs.

Thorn(e) L 'thorn, hawthorn' OE; the –e (dative) form is commoner, and sometimes derives from places Thorne in four counties. Both are found as surnames in Devon–Somerset–Dorset–Wilts–Berks–

Bucks, Kent. (*Thorn* is also the name of the OE letter for *th*.)

Thornborough, Thornburrow, Thornbury L A complex of 'hill/ mound covered with thorns' and 'fort/manor protected by thorns' all OE; places in seven counties. A USA form is **Thornberry**.

Thornby L Same as **Thornborough**, but scandinavianized, place in Northants; but place in Cumberland is 'old farm' (once Fornby) ON.

Thorncroft L '**Croft** in the thorns' OE; locality, or place in Staverton, Devon.

Thorndike L 'embankment/ditch covered with thorns' OE, though the second element could be ON.

Thorndycraft and **Thornely** See **Thorneycroft** and **Thornley**.

Thorner L 'thorn slope' OE; place in West Yorks. Or simply L 'dweller in the thorns' OE + suffix.

Thorney L 'island with thorn-bushes' OE, places in Cambs, Middx, Somerset, Suffolk, Sussex; or 'enclosure made by thorn-bushes' OE, place in Notts.

Thorneycroft, Thornicroft L 'thorny **Croft**' OE.

Thornfield L '**Field** with thorns' OE.

Thornhill L 'hill covered with thorns' OE; locality, or places in many counties. Counted by Guppy only in Ches. Also **Thornill**.

Thornley L 'clearing with thorns' OE, places in Co. Durham (two), Lancs (two), IoW; but place in Kelloe, Co. Durham, is 'mound/hill covered with thorns' OE. Mainly a surname of Ches-Derbys.

Thornthwaite L '**Thwaite** with thorns' ON; places in Cumberland, Westmorland, West Yorks, and a northern surname.

Thornton L 'place in the thorns' OE; of the thirty-odd places in Ekwall, there are groups of sixteen in Yorks, four in Lincs, three in Ches, two in Lancs, and it is a surname of Northd-Co. Durham– West Yorks–Lancs, Leics.

Thornwell L 'spring/stream in the thorns' OE.

Thornycroft L 'thorny **Croft**' OE.

Thorogood Now commoner than **Thurgood**.

Thorold F 'Thor ruler' ON (cf. **Thorburn**).

Thoroughgood, Thorowgood F See **Thurgood** (rather than N 'thoroughly good' or 'good throughout' OE).

Thorp(e) L 'farm (especially "outlying dairy-farm"), village' OE or ON; –e could show dative after lost preposition, and is twice as common as –p as a surname. Common place-names in the Danish-settled counties of Midlands and north-east, but rarer in purely English areas; versions with Thr– are also common. The surname

---

F: *first name*   L: *local name*   N: *nickname*   O: *occupational name*

pattern is similar (mainly Derbys–Ches–West Yorks–Lincs–Leics–Norfolk) but with outliers in Kent, Hants; and cf. forms in **Thr–**.

Thorrington L 'place in the thorns/thornbushes' OE; place in Essex.

Thouless and **Thow** See **Thewless** and **Thew**.

Thrale, Thrall O 'serf, villein' OE from ON.

Thrasher See **Thresher**.

Threader O 'maker/user of thread' OE+–**er**.

Threadgall, Threadgill, Threadgo(u)ld O 'thread gold' OE, for an embroiderer.

Threepland L 'disputed/debatable (literally quarrel) land' OE; places (–eap–) in Cumberland, West Yorks.

Threlfall L 'thrall's/serf's/slave's clearing' ON (cf. *felling*). There were T—s living at T— in the Fylde, Lancs, from Edward IV to James I, and it is still chiefly a Lancs surname.

Threlkeld L 'thrall's/serf's/slave's spring' ON; place in Cumberland.

Thresher O 'thresher' OE. What did he do for the rest of the year?

Thrift See **Firth**. Sometimes perhaps an abstract N 'thrift' ME from ON.

Thring L 'slope with trees (literally 'tree-hanger')' OE; place (Tring) in Herts.

Thripp See **Thorp** and **Throop**.

Throckmorton, Throgmorton L 'place on a pool with a ?drain (or a ?trestle bridge for washing from)' OE; place (–ck–) in Worcs.

Throop(e), Thro(u)p, Thrupp See **Thorp(e)**; all these forms, like **Thripp**, show metathesis of the –**r**–; locality, or places in six southern counties.

Thrower O A 'thrower' (OE+–**er**) of material at his work, like a 'potter'; but Reaney also identifies it as a 'thread-thrower' in the silk trade. Guppy counted it in Norfolk.

Thrush N 'thrush' OE, perhaps from a good voice or whistle.

Thrussell N 'throstle, song-thush' OE.

Thulbo(u)rn is likely to be from **Thurborn**.

Thum N 'thumb' OE (the –*b* is an excrescence), for some deformity.

Thundercliff L A. H. Smith's nine places containing the name of the pagan god *Thunor* make it clear that his worship was confined to the Saxons – in Essex (three). Surrey (two), Herts, Sussex–Hants–Wilts. But this place was in Anglian territory, West Yorks, and was a grange of Kirkstead Abbey, with the monks' iron-workings; so the first element is 'thunder', from the noise of the forges, or (some strange spellings suggest) 'cinder'+'cliff' all OE. It does *not* mean 'th' under-cliff'.

Thurban, Thurbin, Thurbon, Thurborn See **Thorburn**.

Thurgar F 'Thor spear' ON (cf. **Thorburn**).

Thurgood F 'Thor Gēat' ON (see **Thorburn** and **Merrett**). Guppy counted it in Essex–Herts; a popular corruption was to **Thorough-good**.

Thurkettle F 'Thor's (sacrificial) cauldron' OE from ON (cf. **Thor-burn** and *kettle*). This ferocious surname, common in the Danelaw and Normandy as a F, also descended by marriage to the gentle novelist Angela **Thirkell**, whose grandfather Burne-Jones was admittedly the uncle of Kipling and Baldwin. **Thurkle** is an East Anglian version.

Thurley L If from place Thurleigh, Beds, this is '(at) the wood/ clearing' OE, with **Thur–** reproducing the feminine dative singular of the definite article after a lost preposition.

Thurlow L ?'warriors' burial-mound' OE; two places in Suffolk. Surname is chiefly of Suffolk–Norfolk, so place in Cambs, 'gapped hill' OE (cf. **Thirlwall**), is perhaps not involved.

Thursby L 'Thori's farm' ON (cf. **Thurston**); place in Cumberland.

Thurstan(s), **Thursting**, **Thurston** F 'Thor stone' OE from ON (cf. **Thorburn**). But **–ston** must often be L 'Thori's (F related to *Thor*) farm' ON+OE; place in Suffolk – and the surname is common in Suffolk–Norfolk (and Worcs).

Thwaite L 'clearing, meadow, enclosed land' ON; locality, or places in Norfolk, Suffolk. **Thwait(e)s**, **Thwaytes** 'of (i.e. at)' the same, or plural. Chiefly Yorks surnames.

Thwing L Probably 'shoelace, thong' ON, descriptive of a long ridge; place in East Yorks.

Thynne N 'thin, slender' OE. Family name of the marquesses of Bath.

Tibb F dim. '**Theobald/Isabell**' male/female. **Tibbs** '(son) of T—'.

Tibbenham Commoner form of **Tibenham** L 'homestead of (an AS called) Tibba' OE; place (–b–) in Norfolk.

Tibbett, **Tibbit(t)**, **Tibble**, **Tibbott** F dim. '**Tibb**', so male or female. **Tibble** is most likely to be the remains of **Theobald**. **Tibbal(l)s**, **Tibbatts**, **Tibbet(t)s**, **Tibbins**, **Tibbit(t)s**, **Tibbles**, **Tibbotts** '(son) of (dim.) **Tibb**'. Guppy counted **–ett** and **–it** in Cambs, **–etts** and **–itts** in Warwicks. **Tibby** also exists.

Ticehurst L '**Hirst** with kids' OE; place in Sussex.

Tichbon, **Tichbo(u)rne** L 'stream near where kids are kept' OE; place (–borne) in Hants.

Tichener, **Tichenor** Forms of **Titchener**.

F: *first name*   L: *local name*   N: *nickname*   O: *occupational name*

Tickle L 'hill of (an AS called) Tica' OE; place (Tickhill) in West Yorks.

Ticknell L 'Haugh (*halh*) with kids' OE; place (–nall) in Derbys.

Tickner (Kent form), **Ticknor** See **Titchener**.

Ticktum L Corruption of **Titcomb** or **Tidcombe** (all three are Bristol surnames) or **Tickenham**, Somerset, 'homestead of (an AS called) Tica' OE (cf. **Tickle**).

Tidbald, Tidball See **Theobald**.

Tidcombe L 'valley with tits' OE or 'valley of (an AS whose name is a pet-form of a F beginning) Time (cf. *tide*)' OE; places in Wilts, Devon.

Tidd L 'shrubs, brushwood' OE (Ekwall supposed *teat* in the sense of 'slight hill'); places (–y–) in Cambs, Lincs.

Tiddeman, Tid(i)man O 'tithingman, head of a frankpledge/tithing (of ten householders), headborough' (though by the time that Verges was assisting Dogberry, the headborough was a petty constable) OE.

Tideswell L 'spring of (an AS called) Tīdi' OE; place in Derbys.

Tidmarsh L 'marsh of (an AS called) Tid–/Tyd– (or some other member of the group in **Tidcombe, Tideswell**)' OE; place in Berks.

Tidwell L 'spring/stream with tits' OE (or it may have belonged to an AS of the type seen in **Tidmarsh**); but the two places in Devon are said to be 'Tudda's spring' OE or 'the Tiddy Brook' (a Keltic stream-name).

Tid(e)y N 'of good appearance, worthy' ME from Germanic. Or F, of the type appearing in **Tidcombe, Tideswell, Tidmarsh**. Guppy counted it in Warwicks.

Tiernan F (for McT—) 'son of Lord' Irish.

Tierney F (for O T—) 'descendant of Lord' Irish. Commoner in Ireland than **Tiernan**.

Tiffany, Tiffen, Tiffin F 'the manifestation of God' Latin *Theophania* from Greek, occurring as French *Tiphaine* for girls born on the Feast of the Epiphany.

Tigar F 'people spear' Germanic.

Tighe and **Tiler** See **Teague** and **Tyler**.

Tilford L 'convenient ford' OE, place in Surrey; or first element may be from an AS owner *Tila*, whose F means 'good' OE.

Till F dim. 'Matilda' (see **Maud**). Found by Guppy only in Glos. **Tillett** double dim. 'Matilda'.

Tiller O 'tiller (of the soil)' OE + –er.

Tillett F double dim. 'Matilda' (see **Till**).

Tilley, Tillie F double dim. 'Matilda' (see **Till**). Or L 'clearing with branches/boughs' OE, place (–ey) in Salop; or places (Tilly) in Calvados and Eure (from a Latin F *Tilius*) and Seine-et-Oise (from a Latin F *Attilius*). Guppy counted **Tilley** only in Somerset.

Tilling(s) F The dim. of an AS male F Till–/Tyll– (see ?**Tilford**), or double dim. 'Matilda' (see **Till**). And '(son) of' the same.

Tillman O 'tile maker' OE or 'tiller, farmer' OE.

Tillott F See **Till(ett)**. **Tillotson, Tilson** 'son of **Tillott/Till**'.

Tillyard may sometimes be L 'place with linden-trees' OF *tillard*; it can hardly be 'tournament-ground, lists' late ME *tiltyard* from OE+OE.

Tilton L 'Tila's farm' OE (cf. **Tilford**); place in Leics.

Timberlake L 'wooded stream' OE; a lost place-name in Bayton, Worcs.

Timberman O 'dealer/worker in timber' OE+OE.

Timblin F dim. '**Timm**'+*b*-glide+OF suffix –*lin*.

Times is probably for **Timms**.

Timm F An OE name of unknown meaning. **Timmis** (chiefly Staffs–Salop–Ches), **Timms, Tims** (both chiefly Oxon–Warwicks) '(son) of **Timm**'; **Timkiss** '(son) of (dim.) **Timm**'.

Timothy F 'honouring God' Greek; a late arrival in England as a F, and perhaps never the ancestor of any of the **Tim**– series.

Timperon L ?'hillock/menhir' Irish+'thicket' ON; place (–y–) in Cumberland.

Timpson F 'son of **Timm**'.

Tindal(l), Tindell, Tindill, Tind(a)le See **Tyndale**.

Tindsley See **Tinsley**.

Tingay, Tingey See **Tanguy**.

Tingle ?L 'little farm, small estate' OE *tȳnincel*, as at Tincleton, Dorset. A Devon surname. Reaney's early forms are not place-names, but suggest makers of a 'kind of small nail' ME of uncertain origin.

Tink(l)er O 'tinker, (itinerant) mender of pots and pans, metal-worker' ME; –l– is distinctly a northern form, from Lancs–Yorks to Scotland (where James **Tinkler** held land in Perth *c*. 1175).

Tinknell L 'hill of (an AS called) Tint (meaning ?)' OE; place (Tintinhull) so pronounced near Yeovil, Somerset; the –hull is for –*hill* in south-western dialect.

Tinniswood L 'Tynni's wood' OE (cf. **Tinsley**). A Yorks–Lancs surname.

F: *first name*　　L: *local name*　　N: *nickname*　　O: *occupational name*

Tinsley L 'Tynni's mound' OE (cf. **Tinniswood**); place in West Yorks. A Lancs and Lincs surname.

Tipp Form of **Tibb**. **Tippell, Tippett, Tipple** dim. '**Tibb**'. Guppy counted –ett in Cornwall. **Tippetts, Tipples** '(son) of (dim.) **Tibb**'.

Tipper ?F An AS probably called *Tippa* owned Tiptree, Essex. But normally O 'maker of tips/ferrules/pendants/arrowheads' ME from Germanic.

Tipping F dim. '**Tibb**'. Guppy counted it in Worcs.

Tippins F '(son) of **Tipping**'.

Tippling F dim. '**Tipple**' – that is, double dim. '**Tibb**'.

Tipson F 'son of **Tibb**'.

Tipton L 'Tibba's farm' OE (cf. **Tibbenham**), place in Staffs; T— St. Johns Devon, is named from the slightly different Tippa, but the surname is chiefly found in Salop, and comes from the Staffs place.

Tisser(and) O 'weaver' OF and Huguenot.

Titball Perversion of **Theobald**.

Titchener (and rarely **Titchner**) L 'dweller at the cross-roads' (see **Twitchen**) OE. (Yet the Chichester origin of one family tempts us to associate the surname with *at Itchenor* nearby – 'Ycca's landing-place' OE.)

Titcomb(e) L 'valley with tits' OE; place (–b) in Berks. Chiefly a Wilts surname.

Tite N ' ?swift, eager' ME from ON, found only in northern texts and now obsolete.

Titler N 'tittle-tattler, gossip' ME (imitative of whispering); but Reaney cautiously adds *titlere* 'hound' ME.

Titley L ?'wood/clearing with tits (or other small birds)' ME; place in Herefords.

Titmas, Titmus(s) N 'titmouse' ME+OE (the word is not related to *mouse*), for smallness or insignificance. Found in Beds–Herts.

Titt N 'tit' ME from Germanic, used not only for the bird but for a small horse, or a girl.

Tixerant See **Tisserand**.

Tobias, Tob(e)y F 'Yahweh (God) is good' Hebrew *Tobiah*, with –ias as the Greek and Latin version, and –y in familiar use.

Tobin F dim. '**Tobias**'+OF suffix –*in*.

Tod(d) N '(bush, whence the bushy-tailed) fox' ME from ON. This could be O 'foxhunter', a metonym. No evidence of its being L, a sign-name. **Todd** is the commoner, and mainly of Northd–Co. Durham–Cumberland and the north. **Todds** 'son of T—' is rare.

Todhunter O 'foxhunter' (especially one employed by the parish)
first element **Tod**, second OE. Still a surname of the John Peel
country.

Todman O 'foxhunter' ME+OE.

Toft L 'building-site, curtilage' ON and late OE (sometimes, as in
Piers Plowman, 'hillock in flat surroundings', though Miss Muffet's
tuffet is not related). **Tofts** 'of (i.e. at)' the same, or a plural.

Toll Found recently in Hants, and probably L 'copse, clump of trees'
southern and south-eastern dialect, of unknown origin. But Guppy
counted it only in Cornwall.

Tolland L 'land on the (River) Tone' ?Keltic+OE (see **Taunton**);
place in Somerset – really on a tributary.

Tollemache See **Tallemach**.

Toller O 'toll-collector, tax-gatherer' OE. Or L, from one of the places
called T— in Dorset, 'stream in a hollow' OW.

Tolliver, Tolver See **Telfer**.

Tolman O 'toll man/collector' OE.

Tombs See **Toms**; with parasitic –b– and no reference to a graveyard.
Counted by Guppy only in Worcs–Glos–Oxon.

Tome(s) Forms of **Thom(s)**. Guppy counted **Tomes** only in Bucks.

Tomison F One of the rarest forms of **Thompson**.

Tomkin F double dim. 'Thomas'. **Tomkins(on)** '(son)/son of T—'.
Guppy found –n only in Kent, –nson only in Staffs.

Tomlin F treble dim. 'Thomas'. **Tomlins(on)** '(son)/of' the same
pet form *Tom-el-in*. –n is mainly of Warwicks–Northants, but
–nson is common in Derbys–Notts–Lincs–Yorks–Lancs–Ches–
Staffs.

Tompkin, Tompkins(on) Same as **Tomkin, Tomkins(on)**, with
glide-consonant –p–. –kins is particularly a Bucks surname.

Tompsett, Tompson See **Tomsett, Tomson**, with glide-consonant
as in **Tompkin**. Guppy counted –sett only in Kent.

Toms(on) F '(son)/son of (dim.) Thomas'. –s a Devon surname.

Tomsett See **Thomsett**.

Toner L/O 'one who lives/works at a farm' OE *tūn*+–er.

Tong(e) L 'tongue (of land)/river-fork (literally tongs)' OE; places in
five counties. But there must also be confusion with N 'tongue,
chatterbox' OE.

Tongue See first and third meanings of **Tong**. Guppy counted it only
in Worcs.

Tonkin Cornish version of **Tomkin**.

Tonks F '(son) of (dim.) Thomas'.

F: *first name*　　L: *local name*　　N: *nickname*　　O: *occupational name*

Tonstall Rare variant of **Tunstall**.

Toogood N 'too good' OE, no doubt ironical. A Somerset surname.

Took, Tooke(y) F 'Tóki' ON (meaning ?, but perhaps sometimes used as a pet-form of *Thorkil*; see **Thurkettle**).

Toombs See **Tombs**.

Tootal, Tootell, Tootill See **Toothill**.

Tooth N 'tooth' OE; it must have protruded, or stood in ugly isolation.

Toothill (sometimes **Tootle**) L 'look-out hill' OE, locality, or places with various spellings in seven counties; but Northants place is 'Toft hill'.

Toozer See **Tozer**; but the –oo– from a presumed OE *ā* is difficult.

Top(p) F of a N type 'tuft, topknot, forelock' ON.

Topcliff(e) L 'hilltop cliff/**Toft** cliff' both OE; places (Topcliffe) in North/West Yorks.

Topham L 'water-meadow with rams' OE, place (now T— Road) in Conistone, West Yorks; or 'homestead with a look-out' OE, place (formerly Totham) in Sykehouse, West Yorks. Guppy found it chiefly in North and East Yorks, but also in Hunts.

Toplady, Toplass N 'tup the lady/girl' (*lady* OE; rest ME from Germanic). Obscene names for libertines, the former sadly inappropriate to the author of *Rock of Ages*.

Toplis(s) See **Toplass**.

Topper Perhaps for **Tupper**, or L for 'one who lives on a hilltop' OE (but the element is rare). Reaney confines it to O 'the one who put the *toppe* (the tuft of flax or tow) on the distaff' OE+–**er**.

Torr L 'hill, peak' OE. Or N 'bull' OF. A Staffs surname, which would fit with a *tor* in the hills of nearby Derbys.

Tor(e)y F 'Thor' ON, including the –*i*.

Toshach, Toshack N 'chief, leader' Scots Gaelic (even as the prime minister of Eire is the *Taoiseach*).

Tostdevine must be Dauzat's N *Tostivin* 'toast dunked in wine' OF.

Totham L 'look-out homestead' OE; two places in Essex by a hill.

Tot(h)ill See **Toothill**.

Totley L 'Tota's (his name is related to ?'pomp, parade') people's clearing' OE (an internal –*ing*– is now missing); place in Derbys.

Tott N 'simpleton' ME (? connected with ON word for 'dwarf').

Tottingham L 'Tota's homestead (cf. **Totley**)' OE; place (Tottenham) in Middx.

Tottle See **Toothill**.

Tough N 'tough, enduring, stubborn' OE.

Toussaint F 'All Saints' OF, from birth or baptism on 1 November. The surname is a late-comer.

Tout N 'buttocks' ME (used twice by Chaucer in the *Miller's Tale*). Sometimes ?L, for a hill so shaped.

Tovey F 'Tófi' (dim. of 'nation ruler') ON.

Towell cannot be a 'towel' or (since it is a surname chiefly of Yorks–Lancs–Co. Durham–Northd) a '**Toll**'; it looks L, but no place-name is extant. Reaney makes **Towle** F, a pet-form of *Thorleifr/Thorleikr* 'Thor relic/game' ON.

Tower L 'tower' OE and OF (the word is cognate with **Torr**). Or O 'tawer, leather-dresser' OE. **Towers** 'of (i.e. at) the tower', or a plural.

Towler See **Toller** in its O sense.

Town(e) L 'place, farm, village, town' OE; –e shows dative after lost preposition. **Town(e)s** 'of (i.e. at) the place, etc.'; **Towns** is the later form, losing the inflectional –e–. This is the same stem as in –ton place-names, and as in modern English *town*.

Towner L/O 'one who lives/works at a farm' OE *tūn*+–er. Reaney prefers to take it back to a Worcs name *le Tolnur*, 1221, 'toll-/tax-gatherer' OE.

Townl(e)y L 'clearing belonging to the town (of Burnley)' OE; place (Towneley) in Lancs.

Towns(h)end L 'end of the village/town, suburb' OE; we no longer make inanimates (like *town*) possessive by adding 's in this way, just as we do not make animates possessive by using 'of the'; so 'the mayor of the town', but 'the mayor's chain'. –send is a Midland surname.

Townsin Corruption of **Townsend** or **Tomlinson**.

Toy(e) N 'close-fitting cap' ME from ? ?Dutch; related to our word for 'plaything', and certainly Germanic.

Tozer O 'one who tozes/teases/combs/cards wool with teasels' OE. Common in the south-west (Devon and Bristol).

Trac(e)y L 'Tracy' OF, from an owner *Thracius* 'the Thracian' Latin; two places in Calvados.

Trafford L 'ford in a valley (literally trough)' or 'ford by a trap/snare' or 'ford on a street (i.e. Roman road)' all OE; places in Ches (three), Northants, and Lancs respectively. But Guppy counted the sur-name only in Lincs.

Traherne F 'Trahaearn' (first element superlative, second 'iron') Welsh; a Prince of North Wales, killed in 1081.

Trainer, Trainor O 'trapper, snare-layer' OF.

Tranent L 'place in the dells/brooks' British (cf. Welsh *tref* and *nant*); place in East Lothian.

F: *first name*   L: *local name*   N: *nickname*   O: *occupational name*

Tranmer L 'cranes'/herons' sandbank' ON; place (–re) in Ches.

Trant N 'cunning, trickery, stratagem' ME (northern dialect) from Germanic.

Tranter O 'carrier, waggoner' OF from Low Latin *travetarius* (cf. *trans–* and *vehicle*).

Trapnell N 'too quick' OF (cf. Modern French *trop*).

Trapp O '(animal) trap, snare' OE, for the man who set them.

Travers (reduced to **Travis(s)**) L 'crossing, tollgate, tollbridge' OF – perhaps the surname of the keeper and collector; **Travis** is a Lancs–Derbys–Lincs surname.

Trayhern(e), Trayhorn(e), Trayhurn See **Traherne**.

Trayler, Traylor O The only dictionary definitions are 'huntsman hunting by the trail, tracker' and 'one who travels on foot, footpad' OF or ?OE, from Latin.

Traynor F (for McT—) 'son of Strong-Man/Champion' Irish. Or if English, see **Trainer**.

Treadgold See **Threadgold**.

Treasure N 'treasure' OF, for ?a miser or ?a magnate. Or O, a metonym for 'treasurer'. Counted by Guppy only in Somerset.

Trebilcock L 'place/farm of ?Darling (the rude Pillicock in *King Lear* III. 4)' Cornish+OE; place in Cornwall. Even the rash Dexter puts a '?' against this.

Tredgett N 'juggling, trickery' OF, for a mountebank/juggler.

Tredgold See **T(h)readgold**.

Tredinnick L 'fortified place/farm' Cornish; place in Cornwall.

Tree L 'tree' OE; it must have been conspicuous, or a meeting-place.

Treeby L ?'dry curve/bend (in a river)' OE; place (Treby, pronounced *tree–*) in Devon.

Treeton L 'place in the trees' OE; place in West Yorks.

Treffgarne L 'place at the cairn/stone-heap' Welsh; two places in Pembs, one thus mis-spelt and the other correctly Trefgarn.

Trefusis L 'place/farm at the entrenchments' Cornish (cf. **Foss**) from Latin; place in Cornwall.

Tregear L 'place/farm at the fort' Cornish; place in Cornwall.

Tregellas, Tregelles, Tregilas L 'place/farm at the grove' Cornish (cf. **Kelly**); places in Cornwall.

Tregoning L 'place/farm on the ?little down' Cornish; place (Tregonning) in Cornwall.

Treharne See **Traherne**.

Trelawny L 'church village' Cornish; place in Cornwall.

Treleaven L 'level place/farm' Cornish; place in Cornwall.

Tremain(e), Tremayne L 'place/farm of the stone/monolith' Cornish; place (–aine) in Cornwall. But certain USA bearers had altered their surname from **Truman**.

Trembath, Trenberth L 'place of the grave' Cornish.

Tremelling L '?mill farm' Cornish; place (Tremellen) in Cornwall.

Tremenheere L 'place at the long standing-stone (cf. *menhir*)' Cornish; place in Cornwall.

Trench L 'cut track, hollow walk, ditch, military excavation' OF.

Trenchard O A noted 'cutter' of some kind, with sword or cleaver or carving-knife or trenching-spade.

Trenowath, Trenoweth L 'new place/farm' Cornish; place (–eth) in Cornwall.

Trent L See **Tarrant**; place in Dorset, on a stream formerly called Trent whose name is identical with that of the River T—.

Trentham L 'homestead on the (River) Trent' Keltic+OE (see **Tarrant**); place in Staffs.

Trerice, Trerise L '?Rhys's place/farm' Cornish; places in Cornwall.

Treseder, Tresidder L 'place/farm of the ?archer' Cornish; places in Cornwall.

Trethew(e)y L '**David**'s place/farm' Cornish (cf. **Dewsall**); place in Cornwall.

Trethowan L 'place/farm by the sandhill (locally *towan*)' Cornish.

Trett N 'shapely, handsome, neat' OF (ultimately from Latin *tract–*, 'drawn out, slender'), used of the features.

Trevellick L 'walled place/farm' Cornish; place (–ack) in Cornwall.

Trevelyan L 'mill farm' Cornish; place in Cornwall.

Trevor L 'big village' (adjective second) Welsh; places in Anglesey, Caern, Denb. Use as a F is fairly recent.

Trew See **True**.

Trewartha L 'upper house' Cornish; place in Cornwall.

Treweek L 'place in the creek' Cornish; place in Cornwall.

Trew(h)ella L 'farm at the ?beacon' Cornish, place (Trewolla) in Gorran which Guppy makes their heartland; for the place Trewhella itself, Dexter offers a second element 'best/in the fields/at the mines'!

Trewick L 'Wick in the trees' OE; place in Northd.

Trewin L 'white farm' Cornish; place in Cornwall.

Trible N The only ME meaning is 'treble (singer)' OF, from Latin and cognate with *triple*.

Tricker N 'trickster, cheat' OF (Norman dialect)+–er. Guppy counted it only in Suffolk.

F: *first name*   L: *local name*   N: *nickname*   O: *occupational name*

Trickett N 'trickster, cheat' OF (Norman dialect). Guppy counted it only in Ches.

Trickey L Second element 'enclosure' OE, first (*Trike-*, 1238) doubtful; place in Devon. Guppy counted it in Devon–Somerset.

Trig, Trigg(e) N 'faithful, trusty' ON, early used as a F. **Triggs** '(son) of T—'.

Trigger N 'trustworthy, honest' ON *tryggr* – it is thus possible that this name keeps the inflectional *-r* of ON.

Trimby L 'farm by a thorn-bush' ON; place (Thrimby) in Westmorland.

Trindell L 'circle (of trees, stones, earthworks)' OE.

Trinder O '?turner, ?wheelmaker, ?one who uses a spindle to braid or plait' OE.

Tripe O '(seller of) tripe' OF, a metonym.

Tripp(e) O Either the same as **Tripe**, or a metonym 'dance' for **Tripper**.

Tripper O 'dancer' OF or Germanic.

Trist O 'an appointed station (not for an assignation but) for a hunt' OF, so that this denotes a responsible huntsman.

Triston, Tristram F The original Keltic F *Drystan* (connected with 'tumult, din') was modified by French *triste* 'sad' into *Tristan*/*-tram* – and sad his story certainly was. His name lives on in the dolorous island of Tristan da Cunha, called after a Portuguese admiral; and cf. **Isard**.

Trivett ?N 'three-legged cooking-stand' ?OE, ultimately from Greek (cf. *tripod*); the family had the device of such a stand on their armorials.

Troake L 'at the oak' OE, with ME *at ther oake* (cf. **Rash**) becoming *atter oake*. This is probably more of a Devon surname, and **Troke** more Cornish.

Trott N From verb to 'trot' OF, or in sense of 'trotter, runner, messenger'; or 'hag, crone' OF *trote*. Counted by Guppy only in Devon. **Trotman** (chiefly a Glos name) means the same as the first sense.

Trotter See **Trott**. Found by Guppy only in Northd, Yorks.

Troubridge See **Trowbridge**.

Trounce(r) O 'cudgel-maker/-seller/-user' OF (cf. *truncheon*).

Troup(e) Corruption of **Throup**.

Troutbeck L 'trout stream' OE+ON; places in Cumberland, Westmorland.

Trow See **True**.

Trowbridge L 'wooden (cf. *tree*) bridge' OE; place in Wilts, and a Dorset surname.

Trowel(l) L 'spring/stream in the trees' OE; place (–ll) in Notts.

Trowse L 'wooden (cf. *tree*) house' OE; place in Norfolk.

Troy F (once an O name) 'descendant of Footsoldier' Irish. Or L 'Troyes' OF from Gaulish tribe *Tricasses*; place in Aube, which also ?gives its name to *troy weight*.

Trubshaw L I should like to think that this is 'truffle wood' OF+OE, but the dialect word *trub* is first instanced very late (1668).

Tru(e)body N 'faithful man' OE+OE.

True N 'trusty, faithful' OE (cf. **Trueman**). Or L 'tree' OE *trēow*; locality, or places in Devon called Trew/True.

Truelove N 'faithful love(r), sweetheart' OE. Common in Warwicks.

Trueman N 'trusty/faithful man' OE (cf. 'Be true to me', which doesn't just mean 'Don't tell me lies'). Counted by Guppy only in Ches.

Trull L 'ring, circle (of ?stones/trees/earth)' OE; place in Somerset – but rare as a surname even there, because of the later meaning 'concubine, trollop'.

Truman Commoner form of **Trueman**. Counted by Guppy only in Notts.

Trumble, Trumbull F 'firm/strong bold' OE.

Trumfitt L 'stream with a circuitous course' OE *trun*+*flēot*; place (Trumfleet) in West Yorks, . .

Trump(er) O 'trumpet(er)' OF, **Trump** being a metonym.

Truscott L 'cottages on (the stream once called) Trysull (= ?laborious, strong)' Keltic+OE; place (Trescott) in Staffs. Worryingly, Guppy counted it only in Cornwall.

Trustram Form of **Tristram**.

Try N 'choice, excellent' ME, probably from OF past participle (cf. *tried*).

Tubman O 'tub-maker, cooper' ME *tub* from Germanic+'man' OE.

Tuck F An ON name of doubtful origin, perhaps a pet-form of a 'Thor' name, doubtfully related to **Tooke(y)**, and certainly *not* related to **Tucker**; the fat Friar adds more mystery, since there weren't any friars in the reign of Richard I. Guppy counted it in Wilts and Norfolk – and Wilts isn't an ON area.

Tucker O 'fuller' OE, one who fulled, teased, and burled cloth (from a verb meaning 'maltreat'). A strongly south-western surname, especially Devon, commemorating a great medieval cloth industry. The form may sometimes have swallowed up N 'all heart, courage' OF (cf. Modern French *tout*, *cœur*).

Tuckerman Same meaning as **Tucker**.

F: *first name*   L: *local name*   N: *nickname*   O: *occupational name*

Tuckey and **Tudball** See **Tookey** and **Theobald.**

Tuddenham L 'homestead of (an AS called) Tudda' OE (the **–en–** is the sign of the genitive of a 'weak' noun); places in Norfolk and Suffolk.

Tudor F Welsh version of **Theodore**. This great dynastic name is now found chiefly in North Wales.

Tudway L 'people's way, highway' OE (cf. **Thoday**).

Tuesley L 'wood/clearing dedicated to (the pagan god) Tīw' OE (his name is cognate with Latin *deus* 'god', and he gives it to *Tuesday*); place in Surrey.

Tuff ?L 'tuft, clump of trees, grassy hillock' ME.

Tuffley L 'clearing of (an AS called) ?**Town** Peace' OE; place in Glos, and a Glos surname.

Tufts L 'of (i.e. at) the **Toft**' or 'of (i.e. at) the tuft/cluster of trees or bushes' ME (though OE form began with *th*-), or plural. A USA bearer (†1815) was insensitively named Cotton **T—**. **Tuft** is rarer.

Tugwood Corruption of **Toogood**.

Tulk N 'man' ON; the original O sense 'spokesman' does not occur in extant ME.

Tulloch L 'hill, knoll, mount' Scots Gaelic; places in Aberdeens, Ayrs, Perths, Ross.

Tully F (for McT—) 'son of ?Flood' Irish.

Tumman O 'Town-man (i.e. villager)' OE; or 'Tom's servant' (see **Thom**). A Yorks surname.

Tunbridge L 'bridge of (an AS called) Tunna (pet-form of 'Town/ Place/Farm')' OE, place (Tonbridge) in Kent; or locality 'town bridge' OE.

Tunks See **Tonks**.

Tunnah O 'tunner, maker/user of casks' OE+**–er**, slurred to **–ah**.

Tunnard O 'farm/village herd(sman)' OE+OE.

Tunnicliff(e) L 'cliff by the **Town** well/stream' OE; place (Tonacliffe) in Lancs, and still a Lancs surname, found also in Staffs.

Tunstall L 'farm-site, farmstead' OE+OE; a dozen places in Co. Durham–Yorks–Lancs, Staffs–Salop, Norfolk–Suffolk, Kent, but the surname is common only in the north and north Midlands. Rare and very rare variants are **Tunstill** and **Tunstell**.

Tupholme L 'Holm with rams' ME+ON; place in Lincs.

Tupper O 'rammer, a workman who beat and rammed with *tups*' ME from Germanic; or a weakening of *tup-herd*, who herded rams. But it may be a N as obscene as **Toplady**.

Turberfield, Turberville L 'Thouberville (= **Thorburn**'s place)' ON+OF from Latin *villa*; place in Eure.

Turk N 'Turk' OF from the Middle East (the national name is of unknown meaning). Or ?F, pet-form of *Thorkil* (cf. **Took**).

Turke(n)tine F Two OF dim. suffixes, *–et* and *–in*, added to dim. 'Thirkell' (cf. **Took, Turk**).

Turley L 'round clearing' OE; place in West Yorks.

Turnbull N Whether the bearer could 'turn a bull' OF/OE+OE in the course of his duties, or as an act of daring and strength, is not clear. A Border surname – very common in Northd, and found in Co. Durham, Roxbs.

Turner (rarely **Turno(u)r**) O 'turner, one who worked with a lathe' (making objects of wood, metal, bone, etc.) OF. But Reaney shows how other occupations may be meant – 'turnspit, translator, maker of wooden wine- and ale-measures, jouster (one who *tourneys*)' – and even N 'turn-hare' OF/OE+OE, for one who could outstrip a hare. 23rd commonest surname in England and Wales in 1853, 30th in USA in 1939. Family name of the barons Netherthorpe.

Turney L 'height, eminence' Gaulish (or a Gaulish F *Turnus*)+suffix; places (Tournai/Tournay/Tourny) in Normandy.

Turnpenn(e)y N 'profiteer, haggler' OF/OE+OE.

Turpin F 'Thor Finn' ON, the god and the race, normalized.

Turpitt L 'turf-/peat-pit' OE.

Turtle N 'turtle-dove' OE. Or F, contraction of **Thurkettle**.

Turtledove exists in USA (see the more ambiguous **Turtle**).

Turton L 'Thor's farm' ON+OE (the owner's name is really that of the pagan god of *thunder*); place in Lancs.

Turvey L 'turf island' OE; place in Beds.

Turvill(e) L 'dry **Field**' OE; places in Bucks, Glos.

Tut(h)ill See **Toothill**.

Tuttle See **Toothill, Turtle**.

Tuttlebee, Tuttleby L 'Thirkell's farm' ON; places (Thirkelby) in East and North Yorks.

Twatt L Orkney and Shetland form of **Thwaite**; places in Orkney and Shetland.

Tweddell, Tweddle, Tweedle Versions of **Tweed(d)ale** L 'Tweed (= ?swelling, strong) valley' Keltic+OE, on the English-Scots Border.

Twell(s) L 'at the spring(s)/stream(s)' OE (cf. **Attwell**).

Twelvetrees L 'group of twelve trees' OE, perhaps a round number for a clump.

Twemlow L '(by) two hills' OE, with *–m–* the relic of the dative of *two* after a lost preposition; place in Ches.

F: *first name*   L: *local name*   N: *nickname*   O: *occupational name*

Twichell See **Twitchell**.

Twinberrow L ?'between hills/burial-mounds' OE.

Twineham L 'between streams' OE, with –m for dative after the preposition; locality, or place in Sussex, and original name (Twinham) of Christchurch, Hants (but churches dedicated to the Holy Trinity are always getting popularly called Christchurch, a mysterious medieval habit).

Twinn N 'twin' OE.

Twiss L ' ?river-fork (related to *twin*)' OE; place in Lancs.

Twist(let)on L 'river-fork farm' OE; places in Lancs, West Yorks.

Twitchell L 'river-/stream-fork' OE; or ?'narrow passage' in modern dialect of Leics–Notts–Derbys, Beds.

Twitchen, Twitchin, Twiching(s) L 'road-fork, cross-roads' OE, the –s probably denoting 'of (i.e. at)'. Common Devon place-name element. But Guppy found –**chin** only in Hants.

Twite See **Thwaite**. (Whether it could also be N 'twite' ME, the linnet of our northern uplands, seems doubtful.)

Twopence N 'twopence' OE, from a rent paid or for some lost joke.

Twyford L 'double ford' OE; places in many counties (not northern). Would there be any need for two side by side? This is surely not an early one-way system, and the water must have forked, requiring two fords consecutively.

Twyn(h)am See **Twineham**.

Tyas L 'German' OF.

Tydeman See **Tiddeman**.

Tye L 'enclosure, common pasture' OE; locality, or places in Essex, Kent, Suffolk.

Tyldesley L 'clearing of (an AS called) ?Good Rule' OE; two places in Lancs.

Tyler O 'tiler, tile-maker' OE. Chiefly a Leics–Lincs surname.

Tyndale, Tyndall L 'valley' OE 'of the Tyne' Keltic (meaning ?no more than 'river'); or from Tindale, Cumberland, which may have the same meaning (though Ekwall suggested the two elements seen in the **Din–** of **Dinwiddie** and in **Yale**). Surnames mainly of Co. Durham–Yorks–Lincs, but the Bible translator and martyr was from Glos.

Tyrwhitt L 'resinous wood at the bends (in Wreigh Burn)' ON+OE; place (now Trewhitt) in Northd.

Tysoe L 'hill-spur dedicated to Tīw' OE (cf. **Tuesley**); place in Warwicks, though Guppy counted the surname only in Beds.

Tyson N 'firebrand' OF. But sometimes ?F = **Dyson**. Guppy found the surname abundant in Cumberland–Westmorland, and less so in Lancs.

Tyte See **Tite**.

Tytherleigh L 'fragile/young wood' OE; places in Devon, Hants (two –ley).

F: *first name*   L: *local name*   N: *nickname*   O: *occupational name*

U

Udall L 'yew valley' OE; place (Yewdale) in Lancs.

Ulman O 'oil-maker/-seller' OF+OE; –*nn* spellings will be recent German importations.

Ulph F 'wolf' ON.

Ulrich See **Woolrich**, and cf. **Urry**.

Umpleby L 'farm of (a Norseman called) Relic of the Gods/Ancestors' ON (see **Olliff**); place (Anlaby) in East Yorks.

Uncle F 'wolf cauldron' ON (cf. **Ulph**, *kettle*), much corrupted. **Uncles** '(son) of **U**—'. (Whence '**Uncles** and Sons, Ironfounders, Bradford-on-Avon'.)

Underdown, Underhill L 'foot of the hill' OE. –**hill** is a Devon surname.

Underwood L 'below (or ?in the shelter of) the wood' OE; locality, or places in Derbys, Notts. Guppy found it very common in Northants, less so in Bucks–Beds.

Unsworth L 'enclosure of (an AS called) Hound/Dog' OE; place in Lancs.

Unthank L From OE adverb meaning 'without leave, willy-nilly' – hence the place where a squatter settled; there are two in Cumberland, and others in Derbys, Leics, Northd.

Unwin F 'foe (literally "un-friend")' OE, or (after loss of an initial *H*-) 'bear-cub friend' OE. Counted by Guppy only in Derbys, Essex.

Upchurch L 'upper church' OE; place in Kent.

Upcott L 'upper cottage/hut' OE; places in Devon (four), Herefords, Somerset.

Upcraft L 'upper **Croft**' OE.

Uphill L Usually 'upper hill, on the hill' OE; but the place in Somerset is 'above the creek/pill' OE.

Upjohn F 'son' (from Welsh *Ap*—) 'of **John**'.

Upmaster L 'upper church' OE; place (Upminster) in Essex.

Uppington L 'up in the village' OE; but the place in Salop, originally Upton, was changed to 'place/farm of the **Upton** people' OE.

Uprichard F 'son' (from Welsh *Ap*—) 'of **Richard**'.

Upright N 'erect' OE (though *lying upright* meant 'flat on one's back'); the meaning 'just, honourable' ?comes too late to affect the surname.

Upsall L 'upper hall/dwelling' ON; two places in North Yorks.

Upton L 'upper place/farm' OE; places in nearly thirty counties from Cumberland to Kent, and counted by Guppy in two groups – Warwicks–Staffs–Derbys and Sussex–Kent. Family name of the viscounts Templetown.

Urban F 'citizen' Latin, popularized through seven popes.

Uren (also spelt **U'ren**) F ' ?town-born' OW, the Arthurian *Urien*. Mainly a Cornwall–Devon surname.

Urmston L '(Norseman called) Dragon's place' ON+OE; place in Lancs (cf. **Ormside**).

Urpeth L 'aurochs (wild ox) path' OE; place in Co. Durham.

Urquhart L 'on the wood, wood-side' British; places in Inverness, Moray, Ross and Crom; but places in Fifes contain Scots Gaelic element 'cast/shot', recording some event.

Urry See **Hurry**.

Ursell F 'little bear' Latin (the feminine form being *Ursula*).

Urwin F 'boar friend' OE.

Usher O 'door-keeper, chamberlain, usher' OF. Guppy counted it only in Northd.

Ussell, Uzzell N 'bird' OF (cf. Modern French *oiseau*).

Utteridge F 'dawn powerful' OE, with *–rich* made to look like a L *–ridge* name.

F: *first name*   L: *local name*   N: *nickname*   O: *occupational name*

V

Vacher O 'cowman' OF.

Vail(e) See **Vale**.

Vaisey, Vaizey N 'playful' OF.

Vale L 'valley' OF. Or confused with **Veal, Veil**. Common in Herefords.

Valence L Place in Drôme, from an owner with the same F as **Valentine**.

Valentine F dim. 'strong, healthy' Latin; through a clash of dates, a pagan festival when lots were drawn for lovers was transferred to the feast-day of a 3rd-century Roman martyr.

Val(l)ance See **Valence**; chiefly a Devon surname.

Vallis Occurs in Frome, Somerset, near which is Vallis (Vale) 'valley' OF, but is probably L Vallois 'valley' OF, the name of many places in France, or the province 'Valois'.

Vane Southern form of **Fane**, with F- voiced; an OE lexicon will reveal no initial *v*-, and any word or name in Modern English beginning with *v*-/V- will be either an importation (mostly from French and Latin) or a southern (including south-western and south-eastern) dialect form of this kind. Family name of the barons Barnard.

Vann Southern form of **Fann** (cf. **Vane**).

Vantage N 'profit, gain' OF (cf. the *van in* and *van out* of tennis).

Varah Late and southern form of **Farrow** (cf. **Vane**).

Varden, Vardon Forms of **Verden**, with -ar- as in **Clark**.

Varley Southern form of **Farleigh, Farley** (cf. **Vane**); or from places V- and Varleys (originally without -s) in Devon, of same meaning – but the surname is mainly of West Yorks.

Varney See **Verney**, with -ar- for -er as in **Clark**.

Varrow Southern form of **Farrow** (cf. **Vane**).

Varty Form of **Verity**, with -ar- as in **Clark**.

Vassall, Vassar O 'vassal, servant' OF from Keltic.

Vaughan N 'little' OW *fechan* (there is no *v* in the Welsh alphabet, but single *f* is so pronounced; here, too, the -ch- sound has gone silent, though recalled by the -gh- spelling). Common in Wales (especially the north) and its Border; in Ireland, can be for O Mahon (see **McMahon**). Family name of the earls of Lisburne.

Vaux L 'valleys' OF; many places in France. Or N 'false, lying' OF, in southern form (cf. **Vane**).

Vavasour, Vavasseur O 'feudal tenant next below a baron (literally vassal of vassals)' Latin from Keltic.

Veal(e) N 'calf' OF or 'old' OF. Or confused with **Vial, Veil, Vale.** Cornwall–Devon–Somerset surnames.

Vearncombe L 'bracken valley' OE, in southern form (cf. **Vane**).

Veck O 'bishop' OF *l'eveske* wrongly divided as *le vesk*, later *veck* and **Vick**; surname bestowed for the same reasons as **Bishop.**

Veil O 'watch(man)' OF. Or confused with **Veal, Vale.**

Vellacott L The locality in Combe Martin, Devon, was Velecote, Velacote in 1399, 1428; it can't contain 'veal' OF or 'many' OE *fela*, and F *Willa* OE is too unlike, but 'calf, calves' OF is possible. The second element is 'cottage(s)' OE.

Venables L 'Venables (= ?hunting area)' OF from Latin; place in Eure; chiefly a surname of Ches–Salop–North Wales.

Vender O 'seller, tradesman' OF.

Venn Southern form of **Fenn** (cf. **Vane**); locality, and name of thirty-three places in Devon, and chiefly a surname of Devon–Somerset.

Vennall, Vennell L 'alley, lane' OF.

Venner O 'hunter' OF. Reaney shows that a very few may be L 'dweller at the **Venn**'; like **Venn**, it is a Devon surname.

Vennicker L 'dweller at the **Fenwick**', in southern form (cf. **Vane**).

Venton L 'place/farm in a fen' OE (cf. **Venn**), six places in Devon, or southern pronunciation of Fenton, Devon; but in Cornwall 'fountain, spring' Cornish *fenten*, with initial *f*– voiced (cf. **Vane**).

Ventress, Ventris(s) N 'adventurous' OF, fit name for the decipherer of Mycenean Linear B Script, Michael **Ventris** (†1956). Mainly Yorks surnames.

Verden, Verd(u)in, Verdon, Verduyn L 'Verdun (from Gaulish *Virodun*–, second element "hill, fort")' OF; places in seven *départements.*

Verity N 'truth' OF. Counted by Guppy only in West Yorks.

Vernay, Verney L Several places in Normandy, OF from Gaulish word for 'alder-tree'. **Verney** is the family name of the barons Willoughby de Broke.

Vernon L Common place-name in France, OF from Gaulish word for 'alder-tree' (cf. **Vernay**); the Conqueror's companion Richard de V— came from V—, Eure. Guppy found the surname only in the group Ches–Staffs–Salop; use as a F is recent. Family name of the barons Lyveden.

Verrier O 'glass-worker, glazier' OF.

Vial(l) See **Vital. Vial(l)s** '(son) of V—'. Or confused with **Veal.**

F: *first name*　　L: *local name*　　N: *nickname*　　O: *occupational name*

Vicar O 'vicar, substitute parish priest for the rector or for the religious house to which the tithes are appropriated' OF (cf. *vicarious* pleasure). **Vicars** '(son/servant) of the V—' – who should have been sonless.

Vicarage Probably not 'vicarage' but **Vicary**'s, 'the **Vicar**'s son/servant'.

Vicary Nearer to the Latin origin of OF **Vicar**; chiefly a Devon surname.

Vick See **Veck**.

Vicker(age), Vickers, Vickery See **Vicar** etc. Guppy counted –s only in Co. Durham, Derbys, Lincs, but –y in Devon (like **Vicary**), Somerset.

Vidal(l) Late southern French form of **Vital**.

Vidler N 'face of (a) wolf' OF (cf. **Leleu**). Or O, southern form of **Fiddler** (cf. **Vane**). Counted by Guppy only in Berks.

Vig(g)ars, Vig(g)ers, Vigo(u)rs, Vigrass, Vigu(r)s N 'vigorous, lusty' OF. All of these forms are in the 1963 London TD. Guppy counted some of them in Somerset, so see **Savigar**.

Vile(s) See **Vial, Veal** (the meaning N 'vile' is quite impossible); and '(son) of V—'.

Villiers, Villis L 'part of an estate, farm, village' OF, from many places called Vil(i)er(s) in France.

Vimpany N 'win-penny' OE, perhaps from farming profitable land; whence Vimpennys Common in Redwick-and-Northwick, Glos; still a Glos surname.

Vince F dim. '**Vincent**'; chiefly an Essex–Suffolk surname.

Vincent, Vincett F 'conquering' Latin, 3rd-century Spanish martyr (*–ent*). Slovenly pronunciations result in **Vincett, Vinson** (with its pretended *–son* ending). Guppy counted –ent in the two groups Wilts–Somerset–Devon–Cornwall and Norfolk–Suffolk.

Vine L 'vine(yard)' OF, probably for a worker in one; **Viner** will be 'dweller at a vineyard' or 'vine-grower'. **Vines** 'of (i.e. at) the vineyard', or a plural. The vine was cultivated in medieval England, even as wine was in the last century produced at Castell Coch, Glam, by the medievalizing marquis of Bute.

Vin(n)icombe L 'fenny/marshy valley' OE; place (–nn–) in Crediton, Devon, spelt *Venycomb* in 1524.

Vinson Form of **Vincent**, found in Kent. Also **Vintcent**.

Vinter O 'vintner, wine-merchant' OF. Guppy counted it only in Lincs. Also spelt **Vintin(n)er**.

Vipont, Vip(p)ond L 'Vieuxpont (= old bridge)' OF; place in Calvados.

Virgin, Virgo(e) N 'virgin' Latin (*-o* nominative, *-in* oblique cases); if not some impudent joke, this records a man who had played the Blessed Virgin in a mystery play (there being no actresses).

Visick Southern form of **Physick** (cf. **Vane**).

Vital(1) F 'living, vital' Latin, F (*Vitalis*) of several early saints.

Vivash N 'lively' OF *vivace* (rejecting the traditional L interpretation 'five ash-trees' OE, with *f–* voiced to south-western V–). Common around Devizes in Wilts.

Vivian F Derivative of adjective 'living' Latin; a 5th-century martyr. Counted by Guppy only in Cornwall (though there is no evidence of a cult of the saint there). Family name of the barons Swansea.

Vizard See **Wishart**. (Respelt by association with *vizard* 'mask', from visor OF; but meanings of *vizard* – 'masked person, prostitute' – are fortunately too late to apply to the surname).

Voak, Voke(s) See **Volke(s)**.

Voce L 'valleys' OF *vaux*; numerous places in France. All the earliest occurrences of the surname are '*de* **Voce**'.

Vodrey L Dauzat interprets the original home of this family, Vaudry in Calvados, and Vaudrey in Jura, as 'Waldhar (our **Walter**)'s place' Germanic+Latin; but the Calvados place is locally thought to be *Val de Reuil* '**Ralph**'s valley' OF. A surname of the Staffs potteries.

Voice An *–i–* added to **Voce** to give 'meaning'. Chiefly a surname of Surrey.

Voisey See **Vaisey**.

Vokins F '(son) of (dim.) **Folk**', with southern voiced V–.

Volant N 'flying' OF present participle, so 'agile, speedy'.

Volk(e) Southern form of **Folk** (cf. **Vane**). **Volk(e)s** '(son) of V—'.

Voller O 'fuller, bleacher', southern form (especially Hants) of OF *foleur* (cf. **Vane**) rather than of equivalent **Fuller**. **Vollers** '(son) of V—'.

Voss Southern form of **Foss** (cf. **Vane**).

Vowell(s), Vowels, Vowles N 'bird(s)' OE; or *–s* could mean '(son) of V—'; cf. *fowl* and **Fowle, Fowler**; this is the voiced southern form (cf. **Vane**). **Vowles** is common in Somerset.

Voyce See **Voice**.

Voyle N 'bald' Welsh *foel*, mutated form of *moel* (both often figure in names of bald Welsh hills).

Vroome L Somerset dialect form of **Frome**.

Vyvyan An ostentatious form of **Vivian** that, before printing, had the excuse of greater legibility.

W

Wackrill F 'watchful war' OE feminine.

Waddell Perhaps (though often accented on the second syllable) L 'ward/watch/look-out hill' OE (cf. **Wardle**). Or F dim. 'Wade' with an OF suffix.

Waddilove, Waddilow F 'power thief' OE *Wealdthēof*, with metathesis of –l– and further corruption; or 'slaughter thief' OE *Wælthēof*, the source of **Walthew**.

Waddington L 'place of the men from (nearby) Waddow' (which may contain element 'ford' – as in **Wade** – since it is on the River Ribble, or be '**Wade**'s **Hough**') OE; place in West Yorks. The surname is found mainly in Lancs–Yorks, so place in Surrey, 'hill where wheat grows' OE, may not be concerned.

Waddle See **Waddell**.

Waddon L 'hill where woad grows' OE (woad continued in use as a blue dye among the English, long after the Britons stopped painting their bodies with it), places in Dorset, Surrey; but place in Worcs has first element 'wheat' OE.

Wade F Popularized by the legendary hero *Wada* OE/*Wade* ME (with his boat), from OE word for 'to go' (cf. *wade*). Or L '(at) the ford' OE, with –e for dative after lost preposition; also Suffolk place of same meaning. Counted by Guppy only in the north and Norfolk–Suffolk. **Wadeson** 'son of W—'.

Wadey Probably belongs in the numerous **Walthew** group beginning **Wald–, Wad–, Wat–**.

Wadley L '**Wade**'s wood/clearing' OE, place in Berks. Guppy counted it only in Glos. Also spelt **Wadleigh**.

Wadlow L 'watch/look-out hill' OE; place (Wadloo) in Cambs and lost place in Toddington, Beds.

Wadsworth L 'homestead of **Wade** (or a similar F)' OE; place in West Yorks, and still a West Yorks surname; it is also the origin of **Wordsworth** – though, as everyone realizes, the poet came from Cumberland.

Wafer O 'waferer (as was Activa-Vita, met by the dreamer in *Piers Plowman*), baker of sacramental bread and of thin, sweet cakes' OF (Norman dialect) from Germanic (cf. *waffle*).

Wager O ?'watchman' ME *wacher(e)*. Chiefly a surname of Derbys.

Waggoner O The noun *waggoner* 'waggon-/cart-driver' is no older than the 1500s, and probably from Dutch; the surname is likely to be a version of German *Wagner*, especially in USA, where **Waggonseller** has also arisen.

Waghorn(e) O (rather jocosely expressed) 'wield-horn' OE, for a hornblower/trumpeter.

Wagstaff(e) O (expressed somewhat as **Waghorn**, though a Middle English warrior is seriously described in verse as *wagging* a weapon) 'wield-staff' OE, for some functionary like a beadle. Counted by Guppy only in Notts–Derbys, Essex.

Waight(e), **Waights** See **Wait(e)**, **Waites**.

Wailes See **Wales**.

Wain(e) O 'wain, wagon, cart' OE, a metonym for a maker of them (or a carter). But Reaney cites a 1327 instance in Derbys of *Attewayne*, so that it may sometimes be a sign-name; **Wayne** is still found in Derbys. Guppy counted **Wain** only in Staffs–Ches–Derbys, putting **Waine** in Glos and Bucks.

Wainford L 'ford for a wagon/cart' (cf. **Wain**) OE; places in Norfolk, Suffolk.

Wainman O 'waggon-maker/-driver' OE+OE, found in Yorks in the 1200s and 1300s.

Wain(w)right O '**Wain**-maker' OE (the –w– is correct). Guppy counted –w– only in West Yorks–Derbys–Ches–Salop–Worcs and in Suffolk.

Waistcoat Perversion of **Westcott**

Wait(e) O 'watchman, watch' OF (Norman dialect). **Waites** '(son) of W—'; the *waits* were eventually a body of musicians also. The surname may sometimes have absorbed **Wheat**, and has taken bizarre forms in –aigh–, –eigh–, Wh–. Guppy counted –e only in Yorks–Lincs.

Wake N 'watchful, alert' OE/ON, the N of the patriot Hereward.

Wakefield L 'field for the (yearly) wake/festival' OE; locality, or places in Northants, West Yorks. Counted by Guppy only in Glos–Warwicks, Lincs.

Wakeford L 'Waca's ford' OE, lost place near Trotton, Sussex. His name may be akin to **Wake**; he, or his like, got around, grabbing also **Wakeham** and Wakehurst in Sussex.

Wakeham L 'river-meadow of (an AS called) **Wake**' OE; places in Devon, Sussex, and still a Devon surname.

Wakelin(g) F double dim. 'Walho' Germanic+two OF suffixes. A surname of Essex–Suffolk–Cambs.

Wakel(e)y L 'wood/clearing of (an AS called) **Wake**' OE; place (–ley) in Herts; but it might be 'field where the wake (annual festival) is

F: *first name*   L: *local name*   N: *nickname*   O: *occupational name*

held' OE. **–ly** is mainly a Dorset surname, which is against the Herts
derivation.

Wakeman O 'watchman' OE (cf. the motto on the exterior frieze of
Ripon town hall: 'Except Ye Lord Keep Ye Cittie, Ye Wakeman
Waketh In Vain'; and the Mayor there was Wakeman until 1604).

Wakley See **Wakely**.

Walbrook L 'brook of the **Welsh**/serfs' OE; place in London.

Walby L 'farm on the (Roman) wall' OE+ON, place in Cumberland;
or 'farm in/on the **Wald**' OE+ON, place (Wauldby) in East Yorks.
But counted by Guppy only in Herts.

Walcot(t) L 'hut(s) of the **Welsh**/serfs' OE; places (also –cote) in ten
Midland and neighbouring counties; but Walcot, Somerset, is
'hut(s) outside the (town) wall (of Bath)' OE.

Wald L 'forest, woodland; open upland; waste ground' (cf. Yorks and
Lincs *Wolds*; Kent and Sussex *Weald*; Cots*wold*; **Weld**; **Wold**) OE.

Walden L 'valley of the **Welsh**/serfs' OE; places in Essex, Herts,
North Yorks. But counted by Guppy only in Dorset.

Waldern(e) L 'house in a wood' OE (cf. **Wald**, **Arne**).

Waldman L 'dweller in the **Wald**' OE (Anglian dialect).

Waldo and **Waldram** and **Waldren** See **Walthew** and **Walraven**
and **Walderne**.

Waldron L Same as **Walderne**; place in Sussex, but surname found
in Berks–Hants–Wilts, Worcs.

Wale F ?'foreign' (cf. **Welsh**) Germanic. Or N 'choice, excellent,
noble' ME (cf. *will*, *would*, from OE). Or L 'ridge, bank' OE (cf. *weal*).

Wales L The offensive OE name for the country properly called
Cymru, and (with meaning 'Welshmen') that of a place in West
Yorks (cf. **Welsh**); also sometimes a variant of **Wallis**. Or F of
similar meaning, an OF nominative of **Wale**; or '(son) of **Wale**'.

Walford L 'stream ford' OE, places in Herefords, Salop; but place in
Dorset is 'unsteady ford' OE – or the first element is an owner; and
place in Herefords near Ross is ?'ford of the **Welsh**'. None of these
places in any way suits Guppy's count of the surname in only Essex.

Walkdene L 'valley of the (stream called) ?Roller' OE or 'valley of
(an AS called) Wealaca' OE; place (–den) in Lancs.

Walker O 'fuller' OE, one who trod on cloth in a trough in the fulling
process; the whole word is OE, unlike some which are not found
with **–er** until ME. Widespread, but mainly a northern and Midlands
surname, with high figures in Co. Durham–West Yorks–Derbys–
Notts. 18th commonest surname in England and Wales in 1853,
23rd in Scotland in 1958 (rising seven places in 100 years), 39th in
USA in 1939. If any of the Co. Durham–Northd bearers are from

a L origin, place in Northd, the derivation is 'marsh by the (Roman) wall' OE+ON.

Walklate F double dim. 'Walho' Germanic+two OF suffixes (cf. **Wakelin**).

Wall L 'wall' OE – from residence near a conspicuous one (town, ruined Roman, sea); but in west Midlands dialect area it could be 'spring/stream' OE. Numerous in Salop–Worcs–Herefords, and scattered in Derbys, Co. Durham. Somerset. **Walls** 'of (i.e. at) the wall', or a plural.

Wallace L Scots form of **Wallis**, and normally referring to Strathclyde Welshmen. Surname chiefly Scots and Northd–Co. Durham –Yorks. 47th commonest surname in Scotland in 1958.

Wallbank L 'bank of a stream' OE, in west Midland dialect form (cf. **Wall**). A Lancs surname (the dialect of medieval Lancs was west Midlands) from a Lancs place.

Waller L 'dweller at the wall' or 'dweller at the spring/stream' OE (cf. **Wall**). Or O 'salt-worker, salt-weller' OE or 'waller, wall-builder' OE. Or N 'good-tempered man, gay spark' OF (Norman dialect). The various possible origins are reflected in Guppy's scattered count in Suffolk, Cumberland, Herts, Devon.

Walley From **Whalley** in Lancs, a village locally pronounced without the *h*. Chiefly a surname of Ches–Salop, so Whaley, Ches, 'clearing on a road' OE, may be involved.

Wallinger F 'Warin spear' Germanic.

Wallington L The Berks and Surrey places are 'place of the Welsh' OE; the Norfolk place is 'place of the people at the wall (?river-embankment)' OE; the Northd and Herts places were held by the gangs of Wealh ('foreigner, stranger, Briton') and Wændel ('Vandal') respectively.

Wallis L 'Kelt, Welshman, Breton, foreigner' OF (Norman dialect) – according to which part of post-Conquest England mentioned these indigenous people. Scots form is **Wallace**; cf. **Wales**, **Walton**. The surname is scattered from Yorks to Kent and Cornwall.

Wallop L 'stream valley' (cf. **Wall**, **Hope**) OE; places in Hants.

Walmer L 'pool of the **Welsh**/serfs' OE, place in Kent; but place in Lancs is ?'mire/bog in a wood' (cf. **Wald**) OE+ON.

Walm(e)sley, Walmisley L Second element 'wood/clearing/field' OE; first element 'wood-lake' OE or 'wood-boundary' OE or ? ?F 'Wald/Welsh famous'+'s OE; place (Walmersley) in Lancs, also ?transferred by an owner to Walmesley, Lancs. **Walmsley** common in Lancs.

F: *first name*   L: *local name*   N: *nickname*   O: *occupational name*

Walpole L 'pool by a (Roman) wall' OE, place in Norfolk; or 'pool of the **Welsh**/serfs' OE, place in Suffolk; and still a Norfolk–Suffolk surname.

Walraven, **Walrond** F 'slaughter raven' OE from Germanic; the second form influenced by the OF form, and found in Somerset.

Walsh(e) Same as **Welsh**, but from OE form with different vowel. Now a distinctly Irish surname – fourth commonest in Ireland in 1890. Guppy counted it only in Lancs. Family name of the barons Ormathwaite. **-e** is rarer.

Walsingham L 'homestead of Wæls's people' OE; place in Norfolk; this pioneer's F is the OE version of the gloomy eponym of the Icelandic *Volsunga Saga*, father of Sigmund and Signy. Whether the surname ever means 'one who has been on pilgrimage to Our Lady of Walsingham' is doubtful.

Walter F 'rule army/people' Germanic normanized; origin of a number of surnames in **Walt-/Wat-** (and cf. **Bridgwater**). Its two most distinguished bearers bore the duke of Monmouth (and was possibly Charles II's lawful wife) and founded *The Times*. Guppy counted it in Sussex–Kent, Devon–Somerset, Lincs, Oxon. **Walters** F '(son) of W—'; far commoner than W—, especially in South Wales and its Border, and Devon.

Waltham L 'homestead in/on a **Wald**' OE; places in eight counties of the south and east.

Walthew See **Waddilove**. Sometimes perhaps F 'foreign servant/slave' OE *Wealhthēow*. Another version is **Waltho**.

Walton L There are places in twenty-three English counties, some with more than one; of three, and possibly four, distinct origins, though the second element is OE *tūn* (see **Town**) in each case, and each first element is also OE: (1) 'place/farm of the **Welsh**/slaves/serfs' (cf. Corn*wall* and the *wal*nut, the latter being 'foreign nut'; the AS invaders insolently called the autochthonous people 'foreigners'); place is often strikingly near the new AS settlement – as in Staffs near Eccleshall, Stafford, and Stone; (2) 'place/farm in a wood' or 'place/farm on a wold' (see **Wald**); (3) 'place/farm by a wall' or 'place/farm with a wall'; (4) 'place/farm by a spring/stream' (cf. **Wall**, *well*). Mainly a north Midland and northern surname, with its greatest numbers in Co. Durham–Cumberland–Northd.

Walwin F 'power friend' OE; or a *W*– form of *Gawain* (see **Gavin**).

Walwork L The two elements normally mean 'wall' or 'of the Welsh', and 'building' OE (as in *Clerk of Works*), but no place is now recorded.

Walworth L 'enclosure of the **Welsh**/serfs' OE; places in Co. Durham, Surrey.

Walwyn See **Walwin**.

Wanbon L Probably 'at the winding stream' OE; place (Wombourn) in Staffs.

Wanhill L ?'dark/lurid hill' OE (our *wan* has changed its meaning).

Wanklyn Possibly a form of **Wakelin** (OF *Walchelin*, but with –n– for the first *l*).

Wann N 'pale, wan' ME.

Want O 'mole(-catcher)' ME, or N 'mole'. Also L 'path, turning' (see **Went**), as in Four Wents or Four Wantz, Essex.

Wantling F 'fair-flaxen' (female) Welsh *Gwenllian*.

Waple N 'wag/wield pole' OE; *Wagepole* was found in Wilts in the 1100s, and **Waples** '(son) of W—' is still found there.

Warboys L Second element is 'bush(es), wood' OE/ON influenced by OF (cf. Modern French *bois*); first element has been interpreted as 'look-out, hill' (cf. *ward*) OE, or 'beacon, cairn' ON, or an AS owner with a F meaning 'protector, guardian' OE; place in Hunts. But the place-name may also have absorbed N 'guard (the) wood' OF, for a forester.

Warburton L 'place/farm of (an AS lady called) Faith Fortress' (cf. *borough*) OE; places in Ches, Lancs, West Yorks, and the surname very common in Ches (also Lancs, Notts); the F is now spelt *Werburgh* (the former patron saint of Chester Cathedral). Also spelt **Warbutton**.

Warcup L 'cairn/beacon hill' ON (cf. **Warboys**)+OE; place (–cop) in Westmorland.

Ward(e) O 'guard, watchman' OE. Or L 'guard-house, prison, fortifications of castle or town' OE (–e could show dative after lost preposition, '(at) the fort'); or rarely the Herts–Essex–Kent word for 'marsh' ME. But in Ireland O (for McW—) 'son of the bard' Irish. 30th commonest surname in England and Wales in 1853 (and still scattered from Northd to Cornwall), 78th in Ireland in 1890. Family name of the earls of Dudley and the viscounts Bangor.

Wardale L 'valley of the (River) Wear (= water/river)' Keltic+OE; district in Co. Durham (as the distribution of **Wardell** suggests).

Wardell Commoner form of **Wardale**, found in Northd–Co. Durham; sometimes for the less northerly **Wardle**.

Warden L 'watch/look-out hill' OE (cf. **Down**); places in four counties. None of these suits the high incidence of the surname in Warwicks, and O 'guard, warden, sentinel' OF (Norman dialect) is likelier.

Wardle L 'guard/look-out hill' OE (even as such a hill in Shetland would still be called Ward Hill); places in Ches, Lancs, and a surname of Ches–Staffs–Derbys; it is also involved with **Wardell**.

Wardlow L 'guard/look-out hill' OE; places in Derbys, Staffs.

Wardrobe, Wardrop(e) O '(official of the) wardrobe, man in charge of the robes and clothes of a household' OF (Norman dialect – whereas OF *garderobe* is now the antiquarian's word for a privy).

Ware N 'wary, cautious, prudent' OE. Or L 'weir, dam' OE; locality, or places in Herts, Dorset, Kent – and especially five in Devon, where the surname is mainly found.

Wareham L 'homestead at a weir' OE; place in Dorset, and a Dorset surname.

Wareing Form of **Warin**, found (with **Waring**) in Lancs.

Warfield L The place in Berks was originally something like 'Field of the wrens' stream' OE (rather than containing the element 'weir').

Warin(g) F Germanic name connected with verb 'shelter, protect' (from OF form we get *garage*); the –g is an excrescence, as is the odd –e– in **Wareing**. There is some confusion with **Warren**.

Wark L 'building' (as in *Clerk/Office of Works*) OE; locality, or two places in Northd.

Warleigh L 'wood/clearing by a river-bank' OE, place in Devon; or 'wood/clearing by a weir' OE, place in Somerset. Sometimes involved with **Warley**.

Warley L 'cattle clearing/pasture' OE, two places in Worcs; or 'treaty/compact field' OE, place in Essex; or 'oath-breaker's/traitor's/(AS called) Wērlāf's field' OE, place in West Yorks. See the similar **Warleigh**.

Warlock Form of **Werlock**, with –ar– as in **Clark**.

Warlow See **Wardlow** (though Warlow Pike in Saddleworth, West Yorks, was *Harelowe* 'grey/boundary hill' OE in 1468).

Warman O 'chapman, merchant (literally ware-/goods-man)' OE. Or F 'faith/bond protector' OE *Wǣrmund*.

Warme N 'eager, zealous' OE, with –e of weak adjective after lost definite article.

Warmington L 'place/farm of the family/folk of (an AS called) Dragon' (cf. *worm*, **Orm–**) OE, place in Northants; or 'place/farm of the family/folk of (an AS called) Faith Protector' (cf. **Warman**) OE, place in Warwicks.

Warne L 'alder trees' (or ?'swamp') Cornish; and a Cornwall–Devon surname.

Warner F 'Warin army' Germanic via OF (Norman dialect). Or contracted from **Warrener**.

Warnet(t) F dim. '**Warin**' (cf. **Garnet**).

Warr N 'war' OF (Norman dialect), for a warrior. Guppy found it common in Bucks. The title of the earls de la W— preserves an older form; from an early-17th-century member is named the USA state of Delaware.

Warren Form of **Warrenne**, very common in the south and in East Anglia. The surname has sometimes absorbed, or been absorbed by, **Warin** and its group.

Warren(d)er O 'warrener, (game-)park-keeper' OF; the –d– is parasitic. **Warrender** is the family name of the barons Bruntisfield.

Warrenne L From La Varenne, Maine-et-Loire, 'sandy soil; wasteland, game preserve' Gaulish. The great family of W—, still headed (albeit in France) by Reginald, comte de Warren, was of immense power in England from the 11th to the 14th centuries, with holdings in twelve counties, and their emphatic gold and blue check shield figures often in English civic heraldry. See the much commoner version **Warren**.

Warrington L 'place/farm at a weir' OE or 'place/farm of the family/folk of (an AS called) Wary' OE, the Lancs town; place in Bucks, 'place/farm of the family/folk of (an AS called) Wary Hard' OE, is unlikely, since the surname is found chiefly in Staffs–Derbys. Its most eminent bearer, Rev. Percy W— (†1961), founded nine public schools and a theological college.

Warsop L 'valley of (an AS called) Wary' OE; place in Notts.

Warter L 'gallows (literally felon tree)' OE; place in East Yorks.

Warth L 'shore, bank, land near a stream' OE; locality, or place in Glos.

Warthall L 'cairn/beacon (cf. **Warboys**) hill' ON; place in Cumberland.

Warton L 'guard/look-out place' OE, places in Lancs, Northd; but place in Warwicks may be 'farm at the ?shaking tree' or 'farm in ?spongy ground' OE.

Warwick L 'dairy-farm of Wary's gang' OE or 'dairy-farm at a weir/dam' OE, place in Warwicks; but northern and Scots bearers may mean 'dairy-farm on a river-bank (the Eden)' OE, place in Cumberland.

Washbourn(e) L 'stream for washing (clothes or sheep?)' OE, place (–e) in Devon; or 'swampy stream' OE, place (–e) in Glos; or ?'the **Walkers'** stream' OE, place (–burn) in West Yorks.

Washbrook L 'brook for washing' OE (cf. **Washbourn**); places in Lancs, Somerset, Suffolk, and a Lancs surname.

Washburn(e) See **Washbourn(e)**.

F: *first name*   L: *local name*   N: *nickname*   O: *occupational name*

Washer O 'washer, launderer' OE+**-er**.

Washington L 'place/farm of the family/folk of ?Wassa' (an AS whose F may be a pet-form with first element 'hunt') OE; place in Co. Durham (there is another in Sussex). The five **W**—s naturally take up a large amount of the *DAB*, but there are only 150 telephonigerous ones in all Britain.

Wasp(e) N 'wasp' OE (in which the commoner form was more like our colloquial *wopse*); no certain reason can be seen for the bestowal of this N.

Wass L 'fords' ON; place in North Yorks. But the surname counted by Guppy only in Lincs.

Wastall, more often **Wastell** O 'fine bread/cake' OF (Norman dialect; cf. Modern French *gâteau*), a metonym for a baker/seller of it. Reaney also shows evidence for L 'watch-tower' OE (cf. **Ward**, **Settle**); place (Wast Hills) in Worcs.

Watcher, **Watchman** O 'watchman' OE.

Watchorn, **Watchous** L 'watch-house, guard-house' OE (cf. **Arne**).

Water F It represents the medieval pronunciation of **Walter**, with abbreviation *Wat* (whereas *Wal*, *Wally*, *Walt* are now usual); cf. **Bridgwater**. But those who were *de/atte* are from L 'water, stream' OE. **Waters(on)** '(son)/son of W—' (in its F meaning). Guppy found –s scattered – common in Mon, then Norfolk, Wilts, Kent, Cornwall.

Waterer O 'water-seller' or 'one who waters land/beasts' OE.

Waterfall L 'the going-underground of a river' (the Hamps, which is from a Welsh word meaning 'dry in summer') OE; a Staffs place which has given a surname in nearby Derbys.

Waterfield L Sounds self-explanatory, but is probably 'Vatierville' OF, first element ?'of **Walter**', second element 'place'; place in Seine-Maritime.

Waterhouse L 'house by the water' OE; locality, or places in Co. Durham, Staffs (–es), the latter perhaps giving the Derbys surname.

Waterman O 'water-carrier/-seller, ?boatman' OE; or '**Walter**'s servant' second element OE. Guppy counted it only in Kent.

Wates See **Waites**.

Wath L 'ford' ON; locality, or places in Westmorland, North and West Yorks. **Wathen** '(at) the fords' dative plural after lost preposition.

Watkeys, **Watkies** Versions of **Watkins** found in South Wales.

Watkin(g) F dim. 'Watt'. **Watkins**, **Watkis(s)** '(son) of W—'. **Watkinson** 'son of W—'. **–ns** common in Wales and its Border (and Devon), **–nson** a Yorks surname.

Watling F 'of the family of (dim.) Bold, Vigorous' OE *hwæt*; not the origin of the main road Watling Street (which meant 'the road to St. Albans').

Watmore, Watmough, Watmuff F 'Watt's in-law' second element ON (or some vaguer relationship OE); cf. **Hitchmough.**

Watson F 'son of Watt'. Found everywhere, but especially in north England and south Scotland. 48th commonest surname in England and Wales in 1853, 25th in Scotland in 1958. Family name of the barons Manton.

Watt F dim. 'Walter', from its form **Water.** Now mostly Scots. 60th commonest surname in Scotland in 1958. The *watt* from James W— (†1819). **Watts** '(son) of W—' – but, unlike it, mainly a southern surname, especially Glos–Somerset–Wilts.

Watters(on) Rare forms of **Waters(on).**

Watthey F One of the **Walthew** derivatives.

Watton L 'place/farm where woad grows' OE, place in Herts; or 'Wade's place' OE, place in Norfolk; or 'wet hill' OE scandinavian-ized, place in East Yorks; or two places in Devon, one of them 'farm in a ?wood' OE.

Waudby L 'village on a hill/wold' OE+ON; place (Wauldby) in East Yorks.

Waugh L 'Welsh (?Briton of Strathclyde)' OE. A surname of Northd–Co. Durham and the Scots Lowlands.

Wavell L 'Vauville (= valley place)' OF; place in Manche.

Wax(man) O 'dealer in wax' OE, the first form being a metonym.

Way(e) L 'road, path' OE; locality, or seventeen places in Devon, and others elsewhere. Guppy counted it mainly in Devon, and in Hants, Kent, Oxon.

Waycott(s) L 'cottage(s) on the road' OE. –tt is a Devon surname.

Waylett, rarely **Waylatt** L 'way/road junction, cross-roads' OE; and see **Willet.**

Waymark and **Waymouth** and **Wayne** See **Wymark** and **Weymouth** and **Wain.**

Wayt(e), Waytes See **Wait(e), Waites.**

Wear L 'weir, dam, fishtrap' OE. **Weare** '(at) the weir', with –e for dative after lost preposition; locality, or places in Devon, Somerset; cf. **Ware.**

Wearing See **Waring.**

Weather O 'wether, neutered ram' OE, a metonym for one who tended them. Or a rude N. Or F 'valiant army' OE. **Weathers** '(son) of W—', or a plural.

F: *first name*   L: *local name*   N: *nickname*   O: *occupational name*

Weatherall, Weatherell, Weatherill L Same as **Wetherall**. Guppy counted –**all** only in Notts, –**ill** only in East and North Yorks.

Weatherby See **Wetherby**.

Weatherhead O 'herder of wethers' OE (cf. **Weather**).

Weatherhogg O 'male sheep (wether or ram) before its first shearing' ME (with *hog* in sense of 'young sheep'), from tending them. Chiefly a northern and Scots surname.

Weatherley L 'pasture for wethers' OE.

Weaver O 'weaver' OE with added suffix –**er**; cf. **Webb**. A very few may be L, from W— Hall, Ches, where the element means 'winding (river)' ?OE. A surname of Salop–Worcs–Herefords–Glos–Somerset, Essex.

Webb(e) O 'weaver' OE; form without –**e** is very common in Midlands and south, especially Wilts–Somerset (cf. **Weaver** in Somerset), but form with –**e** well reproduces the –*a* or –*e* (masculine or feminine) of the OE noun. **Webber** and **Weaver** are younger surnames, and **Webster** was originally feminine.

Webber O 'weaver' OE, but a later formation (with –**er**) than **Webb**; again, a surname from the medieval textiles area oft he south, especially Devon.

Webley L 'clearing of (an AS called) ?Beetle' OE *Wibba*, place (Weobley) in Herefords.

Webster O 'female weaver' OE (cf. **Webb** and *spinster*); but in Middle English used early, and more often, of men. Unlike the preceding surnames, this is found mainly in Lancs–Yorks and Midlands (especially Derbys).

Wedderburn L 'stream where there were wethers' OE (cf. **Weather**).

Wedlake (cf. **Widlake**) L 'wide stream' OE, place in Petertavy, Devon. **Wedlock** must often be a form of this, though Wedlock Farm in Gumfreston, Pemb, was *Wideloke* 'wide enclosure' OE in 1362.

Wedmore L 'hunting moor' OE; place in Somerset.

Weech See **Wich**.

Weedon L 'hill (cf. **Down**) with a heathen temple' (**Wee–** being cognate with the last element of Odense, Denmark, 'Odin's temple') OE; places in Bucks, Northants.

Week See **Wich**.

Weekes L Plural of **Wick**, retaining the inflectional –**e**–.

Weekl(e)y L 'wych-elm wood/clearing' OE; place (–ley) in Northants. All honour here to Professor Ernest **Weekley** of Nottingham, that engaging and popular writer on surnames, whose wife ran away with D. H. Lawrence.

Weeks Developed and much commoner form of **Weekes**, found especially in Kent and Glos–Somerset–Wilts–Hants–Devon.

Weeley L 'willow wood/clearing' OE; place in Essex.

Weem(y)s See **Wemyss**.

Weetch Later form of **Weech**.

Weevers O '(son) of the **Weaver**' or L 'at the **Weaver's**' OE.

Weigall, Weighell, Weighill L '**Haugh** (*halh*) with a **Wick**' OE; place (Wighill) in West Yorks, and a Yorks group of surnames.

Weight(s) See **Wait(es)**.

Weir See **Wear**. Black tries to associate it with places Vere in Calvados, Manche, Eure-et-Loir, and suggests also an anglicizing of *McAmhaoir* 'son of the officer' Scots Gaelic. 100th commonest surname in Scotland in 1958, and family name of the barons Inverforth.

Welbon, Welborn(e), Welbourn(e), Welburn L 'stream from a spring' OE; places in Norfolk, Lincs, North Yorks (two). Guppy counted –**urn** only in East and North Yorks.

Welby L 'farm by a spring' OE+ON, place in Lincs; but first element of place in Leics is name of ON owner Áli.

Welch is now commoner (especially in Bucks, Essex, Notts, Wilts–Somerset) than the better spelling **Welsh**.

Welchman and **Welcome** See **Welshman** and **Wellcome**.

Weld Southern form of **Wald**.

Weldon L 'hill with a spring/stream' OE; place in Northants.

Welfare N 'prosperous, faring well' OE.

Welford L 'ford at the willows' OE, place in Berks; or 'ford over the stream' OE, place in Northants; or 'ford at the springs/streams' OE, place in Glos. But Guppy counted the surname only in North Yorks, around Whitby.

Welham L '(at) the springs' OE dative plural after lost preposition, places in Notts, East Yorks; but place in Leics is 'homestead by the river' OE.

Wellaford See **Welford**.

Welland L 'land on the ?white river' OW+OE; place in Worcs.

Wellbelove(d), Wellbelow N 'well-beloved' OE.

Wellcome N 'welcome' OE, or 'well-combed/-kempt' OE. Or L 'spring/stream valley' OE; places (Welcombe) in Devon, Warwicks.

Weller L 'dweller at the spring/stream' OE. Or O '(salt-)boiler' OE. Guppy counted it only in Surrey–Bucks.

Welles See **Wells**.

Wellfare N 'getting on well' OE.

F: *first name*   L: *local name*   N: *nickname*   O: *occupational name*

Wellman L 'man at the spring/stream' OE. Or Norman version of OF **Gillman**.

Well(e)s L 'of (i.e. at) the well/spring/stream', or a plural; locality, or the places meaning 'springs' in Somerset, Norfolk. Found from Lancs–Yorks to the south, but commoner in south-east than in south-west. The **–es** form preserves the older form of inflection.

Wellstead L 'site with a spring/stream' OE.

Welsh L 'Keltic, Welsh, British, foreign' OE; needless to say, the Welsh called and call themselves no such thing, and **W—** shows the point of view of the A S invader. See **Walton**.

Welshman L 'Welshman' OE, probably in a more modern and restricted sense (a man from present-day Wales) than that of **Welsh**.

Welton L 'farm by a spring/stream' OE, places in Cumberland, Lincs (three), Northants, East Yorks; also places in Northd, Somerset of obscure meaning.

Wemyss L 'caves' Scots Gaelic with English –s plural and with Scots –is/–ys for original –es; places in Fifes, Ayrs.

Wenden, Wendon L 'winding (stream) valley' OE; places in Essex (now Wenden Lofts and the latinized Wendens Ambo 'both the Wendens'); and **–den/–don** are still Essex surnames.

Wenham L 'pasture homestead/river-meadow' OE; places in Suffolk, Sussex.

Wenlock L 'white/holy monastery' OW; places in Salop.

Wenn L 'wen, wart, tumour' OE; the early forms in Reaney do not suggest a N, and the use is topographical – 'mound, hillock' (no, not London).

Wensley L 'wood/clearing sacred to (the pagan god) Woden (cf. **Wood**)' OE, place in Derbys; or 'Vandal's wood/clearing' OE (the F is a reference to race, not to hooliganism), place in North Yorks from whose dale comes the cheese.

Went L 'path' OE. Counted by Guppy only in Herefords.

Wentworth L ?'**Worth** occupied in winter' or ?'**Worth** of (an A S called) **Winter**' OE; places in Cambs, West Yorks.

Were A Devon version of **Wear**.

Werlock N 'fiend, traitor, devil, monster, sorcerer, wizard' OE (and ?ON).

Wesbroom and **Wesley** and **Wesson** See **Westbroom** and **Westley** and **Weston**.

West L 'newcomer from the west, dweller to the west of the village' OE. Counted by Guppy from Yorks to Sussex, and in Warwicks–Worcs, Somerset, Cornwall.

Westacott See **Westcott**. Counted by Guppy only in Devon.

Westall L 'western hall/nook' OE; locality, or place (Westhall – from *halh*; see **Haugh**) in Suffolk.

Westborough L 'western fort' OE; places in Essex, Lincs, Surrey, West Yorks.

Westbrook L 'western brook' or 'west of the brook' OE; places in several counties, with two in Berks.

Westbroom L 'western place of broom/gorse/furze' OE; a now nameless spot in Woolpit, Suffolk.

Westbury L 'western fort/manor' OE; places in Bucks, Glos, Hants, Salop, Somerset, Wilts.

Westby L 'western farm' ON; places in Lancs, Lincs, West Yorks; or the second meaning of **Westerby**.

Westcott L 'western cottage(s)/hut(s)' OE; locality, or places (also –ot, –ote) in nine southern counties. Mainly a Devon surname.

Westerby L 'western farm' ON; place in Leics; but sometimes ?'west in/of the village' ON. A Lincs surname, rarer than **Westoby**.

Westerham L 'western homestead' OE; place in Kent.

Western L 'from the west' OE. Counted by Guppy only in Devon.

Westfall L 'western clearing/felling' OE. Or ?N 'waste-straw' OF (for a squanderer), the owner of Hartley Westpall, Hants.

Westfield L 'western **Field**' OE; places in several counties.

Westgarth L 'western enclosure' OE, as in a spot at Chapel Allerton, West Yorks.

Westgate L 'west gate' OE; places in five counties, and any such gate or (in the Danelaw) any 'west street' of a medieval town. Guppy found it only in Norfolk, Sussex.

Westhall L 'western **Haugh** (*halh*)' OE; place in Suffolk.

Westhead L 'western hill/promontory' OE; locality, or place in Lancs.

Westhorp(e), **Westhrop** L 'western **Thorp**' ON or OE; places in six counties.

Westlake L 'west of the stream/?lake' (cf. **Lake**) OE; locality, or place in Devon, and a Devon–Somerset surname.

Westley L 'western wood/clearing' OE; places in Cambs, Salop, Suffolk (and mainly a surname of Cambs–Suffolk–Northants); or from a place of same meaning called Westleigh, as in Devon, Lancs, Somerset.

Westma(n)cott L 'cottage(s)/hut(s) of the western men (?Welsh)' OE; place (–ancote) in Worcs.

Westmarland, **Westmor(e)land** L 'district of the men living west of the (Yorkshire) moors' OE; the county.

Westoby See **Westerby.**

Weston L 'western/west-facing farm' or 'to the west of the farm/ village' OE; places in most English counties – and Glos–Somerset and Salop–Staffs have half a dozen each. Guppy counted the surname only in Northants–Leics–Staffs–Worcs, Kent, Wilts.

Westover L 'western bank/slope' OE; places in Hants, Somerset, IoW.

Westren See **Western**; and, like it, a Devon surname.

Westrip, Westrop(e), Westrup L Same as **Westhorp**; places in Glos (–ip). Wilts (–op).

Westwood L 'western wood' OE, places in Warwicks, Wilts, Worcs, and small spots from West Yorks to Devon; but place in Kent is 'west of the wood (Blean Forest)' OE. Guppy counted the surname only in Essex-Herts.

Wetherald, Wetherall L 'Haugh (*halh*) with wethers' OE (cf. **Weather**); place (–al) in Cumberland, but a Yorks–Notts group of surnames.

Wetherbee, Wetherby L 'farm with wethers' ON; place (–by) in Yorks.

Wethered See **Weatherhead**. A West Yorks surname.

Wetherell, Wetherill See **Wetherall.**

Wetmore L 'mere by a bend' (cf. **White**) OE; place (–oor) in Staffs.

Wettenhall L '(at) the wet **Haugh** (*halh*)' OE, –n– showing weak dative of adjective after lost preposition and definite article; place in Ches.

Wetton L 'wet hill' OE; place in Staffs, and a surname of nearby Derbys.

Wexham L 'homestead where (bees-)wax is found' OE; place in Bucks.

Weyman, Weymont See **Wyman.**

Weymouth L 'mouth of the (River) Wey' Keltic (same as the River Wye, but meaning ?)+OE; place in Dorset.

Whackum See **Wakeham.**

Whait(e), Whait(e)s See **Waite, Waites.**

Whale N 'whale' OE, for girth or clumsiness.

Whalebelly N 'belly as fat as a whale's' OE. A Norfolk surname which I was pleased to see on a butcher's shop in that county.

Whaley L 'wood/clearing by a road' (cf. *way*) OE, with parasitic –h–; place in Ches; but place in Derbys is the same as **Whalley.**

Whalley L 'wood/clearing by a hill' OE; place in Lancs, and a Lancs– Ches surname.

Wharf(e) L 'wharf, embankment' OE, or 'bend, nook, corner' ON (place Wharfe in West Yorks is the latter).

Wharmby L 'farm with a quern/mill' ON; place (Quarmby) in West Yorks.

Wharrom L 'meadow in a basin (in a "feature shaped like a pot")' OE; two places (–am) in East Yorks, and a Yorks surname.

Wharton L 'place/farm on the (River) Weaver' ?OE/?Keltic+OE (see **Weaver**), place in Ches; or ?'brushwood farm' OE, place in Herefords; or '?look-out/?shore farm' OE, place in Lincs; or 'wharf/embankment farm' OE, place in Westmorland on the River Eden. Guppy's count of the surname in only Norfolk–Suffolk adds to the confusion.

Whatcott L 'cottage(s) where wheat grows' OE; place (–cote) in Warwicks.

Whatel(e)y, Whatley L Same as **Wheatley**; places in Warwicks, Somerset. **Whatley** is a surname of Wilts.

Whatman F 'brisk/brave man' OE.

Whatmore L 'damp moor' or 'moor in a bend' OE; place (–moor) in Salop. Or F 'Watmough'.

Whatton L 'wheat farm' OE; places in Leics, Notts.

Wheadon L 'wheat hill (**Down**)/valley (**Dean**)' OE; or for **Weedon**.

Wheal(e), Wheals See **Wheel(e), Wheels**.

Wheat N 'brisk, brave' OE. Sometimes perhaps O '(grower/seller of) wheat' OE, a metonym.

Wheatcroft L '**Croft** where wheat grows' OE; locality, or place in Devon.

Wheatfill L 'wheat field' or 'white **Field**' OE; locality, or places in Oxon (Wheatfield = 'white–') and Suffolk (Whatfield = 'wheat–'); or from **Whit(e)field**.

Wheatley L 'clearing/field where wheat grows' OE; places in eight counties including Co. Durham, Notts (Guppy counted it only in these two).

Wheddon L 'valley/hill where wheat grows' OE; place in Somerset (two spellings of 1253 give –den/–don; cf. **Dean, Down**).

Wheel(e) L '(water-)wheel' OE. **Wheels** 'of (i.e. at) the wheel'.

Wheeler O 'wheel-maker, wheelwright' OE, a surname of Bucks–Berks–Oxon–Wilts–Glos–Worcs.

Wheelwright O 'wheel-maker, wheelwright' OE.

Whenray and **Wherlock** See **Whinneray** and **Werlock**.

Whick(er) Same as **Wick(er)**, but with an erroneous and affected aspirate.

Whickham L 'homestead with a quickset hedge' OE; place in Co. Durham; or affectedly for **Wickham**.

F: *first name*   L: *local name*   N: *nickname*   O: *occupational name*

Whinneray, Whinnerah, Whin(e)ray L Place (–nneray) in Gosforth, Cumberland; the earliest record – *Wynwarrowe* 1599 – is late and unhelpful, but 'pasture nook' OE+ON (see **Wray**) is feasible.

Whisker See **Wishart**.

Whistlecraft, Whistlecroft L 'at the river-fork **Croft**' OE; *at tw–* (cf. **Twistleton**) has become *at w–*, and then an aspirate has been added in imitation of the word *whistle*.

Whistler O 'whistler, piper, flautist' OE.

Whitaker L 'white field' (cf. *acre*) OE, the whiteness being from chalk or liming (but see **Whitefield**), locality, or place in the parish of Whalley, Lancs, or place (Whitacre) in Warwicks; possibly 'wheat field' OE, locality, or places in Norfolk (Wheatacre) or Kent (Whiteacre). But the surname (and the commoner **Whittaker**) belongs to West Yorks–Lancs–Ches–Derbys–Staffs, so the Lancs place is the usual origin.

Whitbourn(e) L 'white stream' OE; places (–e) in Herefords, Wilts; but cf. second meaning of **Whitburn**. Or N 'fair-haired child' OE (cf. *bairn*).

Whitbread O 'white bread' OE or 'wheat(en) bread' OE, metonyms for a baker of these. Or N 'white beard' OE, with metathesis of *–r–*.

Whitburn L 'white stream' OE and '**White**'s ?barn/?tumulus' OE; several places in Co. Durham.

Whitby L 'white town' ON, place in North Yorks; also place in Ches, in sense 'white farm'.

Whitcher O 'maker of chests' OE. Or L – the suffix *–er* may indicate 'dweller at the dairy-farm/wych-elm' (**Wich**, wrongly aspirated) OE. Guppy counted the surname only in Hants.

Whitcomb(e) L 'wide valley' (perhaps sometimes 'withy valley') OE; places (–e) in Dorset, Wilts, IoW; in either case, an *–h–* has been wrongly added, as if to mean 'white'.

Whitcroft See **Wheatcroft**.

Whitcutt L 'white cottage(s)' OE; locality, or place (Whitcott) in Salop.

White Normally N 'white (of hair or complexion), fair' OE. But it must sometimes have absorbed **Wight**; also place in Hunts, Great Whyte, was once *wiht*, which may be 'curve, bend (of river/road)' OE; and place in Devon, White, was *Wayte* 'look-out, place to watch from' OF. Occurs everywhere in England, with large numbers in Devon–Dorset–Somerset–Wilts–Hants. 22nd commonest surname in England and Wales in 1853, 41st in Scotland in 1958, 50th in Ireland in 1890, 13th in USA in 1939. Family name of the barons Annaly. **Whites(on)** '(son)/son of W—'.

417

Whitefield L 'white **Field**' OE; locality, or places in seven counties; not all can mean 'chalky' or 'limed', and Smith cites the dialect meaning of 'dry open pasture'; Ekwall gives the place in Glos the meaning '**Field** by a bend (in a hill)' OE. The form **Whitfield** is much commoner as a surname.

Whitefoot N 'white foot' OE.

Whitehair Though an O origin similar to **Whittier** is usual, a N 'white hair' is possible, especially in USA, with its sensible coining of new literally true compounds.

Whitehead N 'white/fair head' OE (if it were ever 'white hood' OE, this spelling has not survived). Or L 'white top/eminence' OE, of the same derivation. Guppy found it scattered – Warwicks, Lancs–West Yorks, Kent.

Whitehill L 'white hill' OE, locality, or place in Co. Durham; or 'hill with a curved hollow' OE, place in Oxon.

Whitehorn(e) L 'white house' OE (cf. **Arne**). But earliest forms suggest rather N 'bright drinking-horn/trumpet' OE.

Whitehouse L 'white (whitewashed or stone) house' OE. Also N 'white neck' OE (cf. **Halse**). Found in the group Worcs–Warwicks–Staffs.

Whitehurst L 'white/bright **Hirst**' OE; place in Staffs, and a Staffs surname.

Whitelaw L 'white hill' OE; places near Kelso and Melrose on the Border, and elsewhere in Scotland.

Whitelegg N 'white leg' OE+ON. Mainly a Ches surname.

Whiteley L 'white clearing' (cf. **Whitefield**) OE; places in Ches, Co. Durham, West Yorks, and elsewhere, and a surname of West Yorks. Family name of the barons Marchamley.

Whitelock(e) See **Whitlock**.

Whiteman F An OE F *Hwītmann* 'white/fair man' existed. Or O 'servant of **White**' OE. Counted by Guppy only in Salop, Hunts.

Whitemore L 'white moor/mere' OE; locality, or places in Staffs (Whitmore, with first meaning) and Devon (Whitmoor). But surname **Whitmore** belongs to Suffolk.

Whiter O 'whitewasher' OE. He must have been much in demand – Reaney reminds us that many big buildings (e.g. the White Tower, or Keep, of the Tower of London, and Corfe Castle) were so coloured; and some of the many places Whitchurch may have had whitewashed churches.

Whitesmith O 'whitesmith, tinsmith' OE; Trevisa, in his 1387 translation of Higden, says that all Europe likes and wants the 'whyt metayl' of this land.

F: *first name*　　L: *local name*　　N: *nickname*　　O: *occupational name*

Whiteson F 'son of **White**'.

Whiteway L 'white road' OE; places in Devon–Dorset–Somerset–Glos, or some road with bright stones or on chalk or white clay. An old Devon surname.

Whitfield Commoner form of **Whitefield**; places in eight counties. Counted by Guppy in Northd–Co. Durham–Yorks–Lancs, Oxon–Berks–Wilts, Salop. Family name of the barons Kenswood.

Whitford L 'white ford' (?for the same reasons as **Whiteway**) OE; places in Devon, Worcs, Flints.

Whitgift L 'gift (?dowry) of (a Norseman called) **White**' second element OE or ON; place in West Yorks. A surname made famous by Elizabeth I's zealous Archbishop of Canterbury and his school at Croydon.

Whiting F 'son/descendant of **White**'. Counted by Guppy only in East and North Yorks, Bucks.

Whitley L Same as **Whiteley**; places (also –leigh) in nine counties including West Yorks (two), and chiefly a surname of West Yorks.

Whitlock N 'white lock/hair' OE. Sometimes ?F 'elf/creature (cf. *wight*) play' OE. Rarely ?L 'white stream' (cf. **Lake**) OE.

Whitman See **Whiteman**.

Whitmarsh L 'white (?chalky, ?shining) marsh' OE; locality, or places (Whitemarsh and Witmarsh) in Wilts.

Whitmer, Whitmore See **Whitemore**.

Whitney L '(at) the white island' OE (with –n– the sign of the dative of a weak adjective after a lost preposition and definite article) or '**White**'s island' OE (with –n– the sign of the genitive of a weak masculine noun); place in Herefords – but Guppy counted the surname only in Northants, and it may often be a mis-spelling of **Witney**, from the place in nearby Oxon.

Whitridge L 'white ridge' ON or OE; places in Cumberland (three –rigg), Northd (Wheatridge). Or F 'elf/sprite/creature (cf. *wight*) ruler' OE.

Whitson, Whitsun F 'son of **White/Whitt**'. Sometimes ? L 'white stone' OE; places in Cornwall (–stone), Worcs (–stones). No connection with Pentecost.

Whitt See **White** in its first meaning.

Whittaker See **Whitaker**.

Whittall L 'white hall/**Haugh**/hill' OE. See **Whittell, Whittle**.

Whittell L As **Whittall**, with 'white spring/stream (cf. **Wells**)' OE as another possibility; there are places called Whitwell in nine counties, some of them sounding like **Whittle**.

Whittelsey L 'island of (an AS called) Wittel (a dim. of *Witta*; see

Witney)' OE; place (–tle–) in Cambs where was once England's biggest lake.

Whittemore Devon version of **Whitemore**.

Whittenham and **Whitteridge** See **Whittingham** and **Whitridge**.

Whittier O 'whittawer, white-tawer, dresser of skins into white leather' OE.

Whittingham L 'homestead of the family/folk of (an AS called) **White**' OE; places in Lancs, Northd (the latter pronounced –*nj*–), East Lothian. Chiefly a Derbys surname, and probably from the Lancs place.

Whittingstall See **Whittonstall**.

Whittington L The dozen places in eight counties are variously 'white place', 'place/farm of (an AS called) **White**' and 'place/farm of the family/folk of **White**' all OE. Guppy counted the surname only in Middx, Sussex.

Whittle L 'white hill' OE; locality, or places in Lancs, Northd, and the surname occurs in Lancs – but it is commoner in Dorset–Somerset and Leics (or was in 1890). Sometimes ?for **Whitwell**.

Whitton L Same as the first two meanings of **Whittington**, places in six counties; but the place in Lincs was 'white/**White**'s island' OE. Guppy counted the surname only in Northants.

Whittonstall L 'farmstead (cf. **Tunstall**) with a quickset hedge' OE; place in Northd.

Whittredge and **Whitty** See **Whitridge** and **Witty**.

Whitwell L 'white spring/stream' OE; locality, or one of the dozen places from Westmorland to IoW. Guppy counted it only in East and North Yorks.

Whitwham L 'white corner/valley' OE or ON; place in Northd.

Whitwood L 'white wood' OE; place in West Yorks.

Whitworth L '(AS called) **White**'s **Worth**' OE; places in Co. Durham, Lancs. But Guppy found it chiefly in Lincs, Bucks.

Whomsley L Probably 'clearing of (an AS called) **Will Famous**' OE; place (Womersley, which was *Woomersley* in 1557) in West Yorks.

Why(e) F Variant of **Wy**– (see **Wyatt**, **Wye**), Norman form of OF **Guy**. –e is meaningless.

Whyatt F dim. '**Why**', much rarer than **Wyatt**.

Whybrew, Whybro(w) See **Wybar**, etc.

Whyman See **Wyman**.

Whysall L 'hill-spur with a (heathen) temple' OE (cf. **Weedon**, **Hough**); place (Wysall) in Notts.

Whyte Form of **White**, altered to no purpose (*y*, as opposed to *i*, *did*

F: *first name*   L: *local name*   N: *nickname*   O: *occupational name*

have a usefulness in manuscripts, for clarity's sake, when it was used next to the minim letters *n m u w*; but that does not apply here). The form is almost entirely Scots; it is common throughout Scotland, and in Dundee and the east central area, Aberdeens, Inverness, Orkney, and Shetland, it actually outnumbers **White** (or, at least, its telephonigerous members do).

Wiat(t) See **Wyatt** (but these are rare forms).

Wibrew, Wibroe, Wibrow See **Wybar**.

Wich L Palatalized form of **Wick**; or (perhaps oftener) 'wych(-elm)' OE; Ekwall allows the meaning 'salt-works' in the former case (but A. H. Smith does not).

Wicher L or O 'one who lives/works at a **Wich**'.

Wick(e) L 'abode, hamlet, (and eventually and normally) dairy-farm' OE; occurs as surname also in forms with **Wich/Wych/Wik–/Wyk–/Week–**. There are also places called **Wix** in Essex, **Wyke** in Dorset, Surrey, and (especially in Devon) **Week**. The –e could show dative after lost preposition. But in Scotland **Wick** could be 'creek, inlet, corner of land' ON (e.g. the Caithness town). **Wick(e)s** 'of (i.e. at) the W—', or a plural; –ks is the later and commoner form.

Wicken L '(at) the dairy-farms etc.' OE (see **Wick**), with –en for –*um* of OE dative plural after lost preposition; or even 'dairy-farms', a weak plural (like *oxen*) in –en extended to an OE strong noun (a southern habit); places (also Wyken, Wykin) in six counties from Salop to Essex.

Wicker L or O 'one who lives/works at a dairy-farm' OE.

Wickfield L '**Field** with/by a **Wick**' OE.

Wickham L 'homestead/river-meadow with a **Wick**' or just 'manor, dwelling-place' OE, places in eight south-eastern counties (several in some), with added titles or forming parts of compound names; but for the element in Childs W—, Glos, Ekwall suggests OW 'lodge in a plain/moor' or 'plain/meadow in a wood'. Guppy counted the surname only in Somerset, Sussex.

Wickwar L '**Wick** belonging to the (de) la Warre family (cf. **Warr**)' OE+OF; place in Glos.

Widdecombe, Widdicombe L Same as **Withycombe**; places in Devon, and Devon surnames.

Widdop, Widdup L 'wide valley' OE; area (–o–) in West Yorks.

Widdow(e)s N '(son) of the widow(er)' OE. Or a corruption of **Woodhouse**. Counted by Guppy only in Oxon. **Widdowson** N 'son of the widow(er)' OE; a Derbys–Notts surname.

Widger F 'elf/sprite/creature (cf. *wight*) spear' OE, or 'battle army'

Germanic; a family of the latter origin left their name at Broad-
woodwidger, Devon, in the 12th/13th century.

Widlake L 'wide stream' OE (there is a Willake in Meavy, Devon).

Widley L 'willow wood/clearing' OE (cf. **Withycombe**); place in
Hants.

Widmer L 'mere/pool in the willows' OE (cf. **Widley**); places in Bucks
and (Widmerpool) Notts.

Widnes L 'wide ness/promontory' OE; place in Lancs, though of late
stupidly put in Ches.

Wigg N ' ?beetle' OE (cf. *earwig*). **Wiggs** '(son) of W—'.

Wigglesworth L '**Worth** of (an AS called) Wincel (= Child)' OE;
place in West Yorks.

Wight N 'valiant, strong, nimble' ON (–t really the neuter inflection of
the adjective). Hardly N 'person, creature' (cf. *wight*) OE, which
would be pointless. And only rarely L, from the Isle of W—, ancient
Keltic name meaning ? ?'raised land, island'.

Wighton L Perhaps little more precise than 'dwelling-place' OE (cf.
Wick, Town); place in Norfolk.

Wigley L 'wood/clearing infested with beetles' (cf. *earwig*) OE, or
first element may be an AS owner with an insect N; place in Derbys,
and a Derbys surname (so the place in Hants may not figure).

Wigmore L Perhaps 'big wood/glade' (adjective second) OW; place
in Herefords.

Wignall L '**Haugh** of (an AS called) Beetle' OE; group of villages
(Wiggenhall) in Norfolk.

Wike Form of **Wicke**, with –i– lengthened.

Wilberforce, Wilberfosse L 'ditch of (an AS lady called) Will Fortress' OE+OE from Latin (cf. **Foss**); place (–foss) in East Yorks,
and East Yorks surnames.

Wilbourn L 'stream from a spring' OE (see **Welbourn**).

Wilbraham L 'homestead of (an AS lady called) Will Fortress' OE;
place in Cambs.

Wilby L An East Anglian surname, so that 'willow farm' OE+ON,
place in Norfolk, and 'willow circle/ring' OE, place in Suffolk, are
likelier sources than the Northants place, where the 'farm' ON was
owned by a man with a Norse name. See, however, **Willoughby**.

Wilcock(e) F Forms of **Willcock**. **Wilcocks, Wilcox** '(son) of W—'.
Wilcockson, Wilcoxson 'son of W—'. In a very interesting count,
Guppy shows how the whole group (–ll– included) is characteristic
of Cornwall–Devon–Somerset–Glos–Mon and Lancs–West Yorks–
Notts, with –ck especially in Lancs–West Yorks and –x in Somerset–

F: *first name*　　L: *local name*　　N: *nickname*　　O: *occupational name*

Glos, Notts, and all the six varieties (–l–/–ll– with –ck/–cks/–x) in Cornwall.

Wild(e) N 'wild, undisciplined' OE. Or L. the same word used as a noun 'wilderness, waste/uncultivated place'. A Midland surname, with offshoots in West Yorks, Sussex. **–e** is a good spelling (even if it is not for the weak adjective after a lost definite article), since the OE word ended in –*e*. **Wild(e)s** '(son) of W—'.

Wildblood N 'wild blood' (i.e. rake, hooligan) OE.

Wildbore N 'wild boar' OE; apart from his ferocity, he symbolized pride; nor was he extinct in the north of England until the close of the Middle Ages.

Wilder N 'wild animal' OE (as in *wilderness* and the 'mice, and rats, and such small deer' of *King Lear*). Guppy counted it only in Berks. **Wilders** '(son) of W—'.

Wildgoose N 'wild goose' OE.

Wilding N dim. 'wild' OE, early used as a F.

Wildman N 'wild/undisciplined man' OE.

Wildridge F 'will/resolve rule/powerful' OE, with –*rich* (from –*rīc*) made to look like a place-name.

Wildsmith O 'wheel-smith' (who made the iron parts of wheels) OE, as Reaney proves.

Wiles L '(of, i.e.) at the trap/device/machine/fish-trap' OE, or a plural. Or N for trickery or artifice. Chiefly a Kent surname.

Wiley L From one of the places called **Willey**; or Wylye Wilts, on the River Wylye (see **Wilton**); or '(heathen) temple clearing' OE, places (Whyly, Whiligh) in Sussex. Or possibly N 'wily, tricksy' ME.

Wilford L 'ford in the willows' OE; places in Notts, Suffolk, and a Leics surname.

Wilk(e) F dim. '**Wilkin**' (cf. **Jenks** from **Jenkin**); or contracted form of **Willock**. **Wilk(e)s** '(son) of W—'; –**ks** is the later form, losing the inflectional –**e**–. –**es** and the rarer –**s** are grouped in Salop–Worcs–Warwicks.

Wilkerson See **Wilkinson**.

Wilkie F Pet-form of **Wilk**, found mainly in Scotland.

Wilkin F double dim. '**William**', with Flemish suffix –**kin**. **Wilkin(g)s** '(son) of W—' (the –**g**– is intrusive). **Wilkinson** 'son of W—'. –**ns** is common in Somerset–Wilts (Guppy found it also in Norfolk, Berks), but –**nson** is very northern, with offshoots in Salop–Staffs, Bucks.

Wilkshire is just a bad spelling of **Wiltshire**, even as many people nowadays say 'ekcetera' for *etcetera*.

Will F dim. '**William**'; but second meaning of **Wille** is possible.

Wills '(son) of W—'; occasionally L 'of (i.e. at) the spring/stream' (cf. **well**) OE. Grouped in Cornwall–Devon–Somerset. Family name of the barons Dulverton.

Willard F 'will/resolve bold' OE; or Norman from Germanic *Widelard*; or even double dim. '**William**', with OF suffix. And see **Willet**.

Willats, Willatt(s) See **Willet(s)**.

Willbond sounds like **Wilbourn** with a parasitic –**d**.

Willcock(s), Willcox F dim. '**William**'+familiar **Cock(s), Cox**; these –**ll**– forms are rarer than **Wilcock**, etc. Guppy puts **Willcock(s)** in Devon.

Wille F dim. '**William**'. Or L '(at) the spring/stream' OE (cf. *well*), with –**e** for dative after lost preposition.

Willen L '(at) the willows' OE dative plural after lost preposition; place in Bucks.

Willet(t) F double dim. '**William**', with OF suffix –*et*. **Willet(t)s** '(son) of W—'. But all this group (–**att**/–**ett**/–**itt**/–**ott**) may be reduced forms of **Willard**, or even L, for **Waylatt/lett**. Guppy counted –**ets** and –**etts** in Worcs only.

Willey L 'willow wood' OE, places in Ches, Herefords, Salop, Warwicks; or 'withy wood' OE, which comes to the same thing, place in Devon (both second elements might just be 'clearing'); or 'wood/clearing with a heathen temple' OE (cf. **Weedon**), place in Surrey. (Any link with F **William** is much less likely.) These places don't at all match with Guppy's count of the surname only in Lincs (around Grimsby). Family name of the barons Barnby.

Willgrass, Willgress, Willgross N 'wild pig' OE+ON.

William F 'will/resolve helmet' Germanic, normanized; naturally, the F was spread by the ruling classes after 1066, and its surname derivatives are very common, but the simple F is rare as a surname. Unlike **Roger** or **Richard** it had only one abbreviation, *Wil(l)*; *Bill* was not yet in use. **Williams** '(son) of W—'; widespread throughout England south of Lancs and Lincs, and very common in Wales (about seven per cent of its yeomen in Guppy's time), its Border, and Cornwall. Third commonest surname in England and Wales in 1853, and still the fifth in London (after **Smith, Jones, Brown,** and **Taylor**); fourth in USA in 1939. **Williamson** 'son of W—'. In curious contrast with –**s**, but with an even odder resemblance to the distribution of **Wilkinson**, it is a very northern name, with offshoots in Salop–Staffs, Bucks; but in addition it is common

F: *first name*   L: *local name*   N: *nickname*   O: *occupational name*

in Scotland, and found as far north as Shetland. 74th commonest surname in Scotland in 1958. Family name of the barons Forres.

Willicombe See **Wellcome**, in its L meaning; or from some lost 'willow valley' OE, or (as Wilcombe, in Charles, Devon) 'spring valley' OE.

Willie F dim. '**William**'; or see **Willey**.

Willing(s) F dim. '**Will/Willa**' (see **Willingale**), and '(son) of W—'. **Willing** is a Devon surname.

Willingale L 'the **Haugh** of Willa's gang' OE (this AS pioneer's name is related to *will/resolve*); places W— Doe and W— Spain in Essex.

Willis(s) F Forms of **Wills**, preserving the inflectional vowel (formerely –*e*-). **Willison** 'son of W—'. Guppy counted –**son** only in Bucks, but –**s** was scattered in Beds, Berks, Essex, Wilts–Dorset–Devon, Ches–Yorks–Co. Durham.

Willitt(s) See **Willett(s)**.

Willmett, Willmitt, Willmot(t) F dim. '**William**', with OF suffix –*ot*. Whereas the common surname **Willmot** is Norman, the Central French gives us the bird *guillemot*. Guppy found the principal members of this group, –**ot**/–**ott**, in Derbys, Herts, Somerset. **Willmetts** '(son) of W—'.

Willock F 'battle/creature game' OE (*Wiglāc*, cf. **Wyard**, **Laker**; or *Wihtlāc*, cf. *wight*). **Willocks, Willox** '(son) of W—'.

Willott See **Willett**.

Willoughby L 'farm in the willows' OE+ON. Ekwall remarks on the strange frequency of 'this hybrid name' – there are places in Leics, Lincs (four), Notts (three), Warwicks; yet Guppy counted it only in Berks and Cornwall. Family name of the earls of Ancaster and the barons Middleton. Mr J. L. Willoughby of Newton Ferrers has proved to me that the Cornish stock descend from Thomas Wilbye of Colchester, who got into paternity trouble, defected in 1647 to Cornwall, and there sired a race who were variously spelt **Wilby/ Wilaby/Willowby** and (in Illogan and Camborne registers alone) a dozen variant forms until 1728, when the present form settled down.

Willows L 'of (i.e. at) the willow' OE, or a plural. An old Lincs surname.

Willson Rare form of **Wilson**. Counted by Guppy only in Hunts–Cambs.

Wilmot(t), Wilmut Forms of **Willmot(t)**, –**ll**– being slightly commoner than –**l**–. Guppy assigns –**mot** mainly to Derbys.

Wilsher(e), Wilshire Slovenly versions of **Wiltshire**.

Wilson F 'son of Will'; found over all England, with huge numbers in the north. 11th commonest surname in England and Wales in 1853, fifth in Scotland in 1958 (rising three places in 100 years), 26th in Ireland in 1890, ninth in USA in 1939. A very few bearers may come from places W— in East Worlington, Devon ('altarstone' OE); in Cheriton Bishop, Devon ('Wolf Spear's farm' OE); and Leics ('Weevil/Beetle's farm' OE); but these L origins are of no importance compared with the F, one of the chief names of the English-speaking world, with even its own individual N *Tug*. Family name of the barons Moran and the barons Nunburnholme.

Wilton L The Wilts town is 'place/farm on the (River) Wylye (= ?tricky, liable to flood)' Keltic+OE; and another place in Wilts and one in Somerset are 'place by a spring/stream' OE; but those in Cumberland, Herefords, Norfolk, Yorks are 'place/farm in the willows' OE, though a couple may be 'wild/uncultivated place' OE. Guppy counted the surname only in Derbys, Cornwall.

Wiltshire L 'shire' OE 'dependent on **Wilton** (first meaning)', the county.

Wimbo(u)rne L 'pasture stream' OE; place (–orne) in Dorset.

Wimbush L '?reedy place at a ?pasture' OE; place (Wimbish) in Essex.

Wimpenny See **Winpenny**.

Wimple O 'wimple/veil(-maker)' OE, a metonym.

Winborn(e) See **Wimbo(u)rne**.

Winch L 'pulley, crane, windlass, well-head' OE; also, from same source, ?'sharp bend in a valley/stream'; but places in Norfolk were ?*Wynnwīc* 'Wick with a meadow' OE. Sometimes ?N 'lapwing' OE ('leap-turner', from its flight), though the force of such a N is not clear.

Winchester L 'Roman site' OE from Latin *castra* 'of Venta' Latin from Keltic related to Welsh *Gwent* (meaning connected with ?'love' or ?'kindred' or ? ?'white'); the Hants city. The rifle is named after its USA inventor Oliver F. W— (†1880).

Windaybank, Windebank, Windibank L 'windy hillside' OE; locality, or place (Windy Bank) in Lancs.

Windeatt A closer form than **Wingate** to OE *windgeat* (and cf. Wind Yeats in Westmorland).

Winder L 'wind shelter' ON; places in Cumberland, Westmorland (two), West Yorks, Lancs, and a Lancs surname. Sometimes perhaps O 'one who winds (things like yarn or thread)' OE+suffix.

F: *first name*   L: *local name*   N: *nickname*   O: *occupational name*

Windlesham L 'homestead on the ?winding stream' OE; place in Surrey.

Windmill L 'windmill' OE.

Window L 'window' OE; the name seems insignificant, since every dwelling had *some* sort of window, but this one may have been conspicuous (like an oriel). Or the surname could be O, for a glazier.

Windows If this is not related to **Window**, it may be L 'wind(ing)-house' OE, for a weaver.

Windrum L 'at the wind shelters' ON dative plural (see **Winder**).

Windsor L 'river-bank with a windlass/winch' (for pulling boats up) OE; places (also Winsor) in Berks, Devon, Dorset, Hants. But Guppy counted the surname only in Ches–Salop. The royal surname since 1917; and **Windsor-Clive** is the family name of the earls of Plymouth.

Windus See **Windows**. Here, too, belongs **Windust**.

Windybank See **Windaybank**.

Wine N 'friend' OE. **Wines** '(son) of W—'.

Winfield is the original spelling of some places now called **Wingfield**.

Winford L 'white/holy stream' OW, place in Somerset; but place in IoW is 'ford at the ?pasture' OE or even 'ford where there was contention' OE.

Wingate L 'windy pass (literally wind gate)' OE; places in Devon, Co. Durham.

Wingfield L 'pasture-ground' OE, places (North and South W—) in Derbys; places in Beds and Suffolk have an obscure first element. Family name of the viscounts Powerscourt. Chiefly a surname of Derbys (with **Winfield**) and (as **Wingfield-Digby**) Dorset.

Wink(s) See **Winch**; and '(son) of W—'.

Winn N 'friend' OE, or remains of a two-element F beginning 'Friend–'. Guppy counted it only in Lincs. Family name of the barons St Oswald.

Winnet(t) Perhaps 'windy pass' OE (see **Wingate**), in view of the place-name Winnats in Derbys.

Winpenny N 'gain a penny' OE, for a money-grubber.

Winser See **Windsor**.

Winskell, Winskill L 'shelter from the wind' ON; place (–i–) in Cumberland, as is Winscales.

Winslade L 'stream of (an AS called) Friend' OE; place in Hants, but chiefly a Somerset surname.

Winsley L '(AS called) Friend's wood/clearing' OE (cf. **Wine**), place in Wilts; or 'Friend's hill/mound' OE, place in West Yorks.

Winslow L '(AS called) Friend's burial-mound' OE (cf. **Wine**); place in Bucks.

Winson and **Winsor** See **Winston** and **Windsor**.

Winstanley L '(AS called) Joy Stone's wood/clearing' OE; place in Lancs, and a Lancs surname.

Winston L '(AS called) Friend's place/farm' OE (cf. **Wine, Winn**); the Glos hamlet (spelt Winson) in the Coln valley; it descended in the **Churchill** family, as a F, from Sir Henry W— of Standish, Glos. The places in Co. Durham, Suffolk have similar meaning, but the place in IoW is '(AS called) Joy Victory's place/farm' OE.

Winstone is linked with **Winston**, and perhaps with F 'joy stone' OE. Reaney also shows how a name of this sound was used in Wales to render 'White's place' Welsh *Trewin* as *Wynston*.

Winter N 'winter' OE – ?from birth in a hard one, or white hair, or lugubriousness. Guppy found the joke scattered – Co. Durham, Lincs–Norfolk, Somerset. **Winters** '(son) of W—'.

Winterbotham, Winterbottom L 'dell occupied in winter' or 'cold dell' OE; the place (–bottom) in Mere, Ches, is probably named from an owner.

Winterbourn(e), Winterburn L 'winter stream, stream dry in summer' OE; an amazing group of fifteen places (o(u)rne, with sub-titles) in Dorset alone; eight more in Wilts; and others in Berks, Glos, Kent, West Yorks.

Winterscale is the better spelling of **Wintersgill** L 'winter hut' ON (three places in West Yorks) spelt to look like a 'ravine' (**Gill**).

Winterton L 'farm used in winter' OE, place in Norfolk (its neighbour is **Somerton**); but the Lincs farm was settled by the gang of an AS with a F related to 'winter'.

Winthrop L '(AS called) Friend's **Thorp**' OE (cf. **Wine, Winn**) – but both elements possibly ON – place in Lincs; or '(Norseman or AS called) War Protector's **Thorp**' ON or OE, place in Notts; both Winthorpe, so the surname shows metathesis of the **–r–**.

Winton L 'grazing/willow(-copse)/(AS called) Friend's farm' OE; places in Westmorland/Lancs/North Yorks.

Wintour Form of **Winter**. Found chiefly in Glos.

Wintringham L 'homestead of the gang of (an AS called) **Winter**' OE; places in Hunts, East Yorks, and (Winter–) Lincs.

Wintrop, Wintrup See **Winthrop**.

Winyard See **Wynyard**.

Wisdom N 'wisdom, knowledge' OE; but abstract surnames are unusual.

F: *first name*   L: *local name*   N: *nickname*   O: *occupational name*

Wise N 'wise' OE (but now often German-Jewish, from *weiss* 'white').

Wiseman N 'wise man' OE, early used as a F; but Reaney shows it can have bad senses of (ironically) 'fool' and 'wizard, sorcerer'. Guppy counted it only in Essex, Norfolk.

Wish L 'marshy meadow' OE; locality, or place in Sussex.

Wishart F 'wise' ON 'hardy/brave' Germanic (or OF suffix *–ard*), or first element 'battle' Germanic; in OF (Norman dialect) form. Its eminence belongs to Scotland. Corrupted to **Wisher** and **Wisker**.

Witcher See **Whitcher**.

Witchurch L 'white/whitewashed/stone-built church' OE; places (Whitchurch) in a dozen counties from Salop to Devon.

Witcomb(e) L 'wide valley' OE, place (–e) in Glos; but place (–e) in Somerset is the same as **Withycombe**.

Withacombe See **Withycombe**.

Witham L 'homestead of the counsellor' or '(AS called) Wise's homestead' (cf. **Witty**) or even 'homestead in a bend' all OE; places in Essex, Lincs; place in Somerset has second meaning; also places in Lincs from the name of the River W— (first element ?'forest' Keltic).

Withecombe Same as **Withycombe**; place in Devon, and a Devon surname.

Witheridge L 'ridge with willows' OE; place in Devon, and a Devon surname.

Witherington L 'willow-copse farm' OE, place in Wilts; or 'Wither (? = Adversary)'s swine-pasture' OE, place (Witherenden) in Ticehurst, Sussex.

Withnell L 'hill with willows' OF; place in Lancs.

With(e)y L 'withy, willow' OE.

Withycombe L 'willow valley' OE (cf. *withy*, *withe*); places in Devon, Somerset.

Witley L 'wood/clearing in a (river-)bend' OE, place in Worcs; or '(AS called) Wise's wood/clearing' OE, place in Surrey; cf. **Witham**.

Witney L '(AS called) Wise's island' OE, with –n– for genitive of weak masculine name *Witta*; cf. **Witty**; the Oxon town – but cf. **Whitney**, though **Witney** is an Oxon surname and must have absorbed **Whitney** more often than *vice versa*.

Witt(s) Short-vowelled forms of **White(s)**, in various senses.

Witt(e)aker and **Wittington** See **Whitaker** and **Whittington**.

Witton L A dozen places in Northd–Co. Durham–North Yorks–Lancs–Ches, Warwicks–Worcs, Norfolk. Ekwall shows how some must be 'place by a **Wich**' (two are near Droitwich and Nantwich);

the Lancs place may be '(A S called) Wise's place/farm' (cf. **Witty**); others are 'place/farm by a wood'; all O E.

Witty N 'wise, skilful' O E (as in *use your wits*; the meaning 'facetious' is latish). Counted by Guppy only in East and North Yorks.

Wix See **Wick(es)**.

Wobey See **Walby, Waudby**.

Woddenhouse L 'wooden house' O E or 'house where there has been timber-cutting' O E.

Wodehouse See **Woodhouse**.

Woffenden, Woffendon, Woffinden, Woffindin See **Wolfenden**.

Wogan F dim. 'scowl/frown' Welsh *Gwgan*.

Wold See **Wald**.

Wolf(e), Wolff N 'wolf' O E (but reinforced by many German-Jewish immigrants, with same meaning).

Wolfenden L 'valley with an ?enclosure against wolves' O E; place in Lancs, and mainly a West Yorks–Lancs surname.

Wolford L ?'enclosure (cf. *ward*) against wolves' O E; place in Warwicks; that it is now in the Rural District of **Shipston**-on-Stour, where they washed sheep, shows how necessary it was.

Wolloms L 'curved/irregular (*wōh*) lanes/lands' O E (since there is no place *Woolhams*).

Wolseley L '(A S called) Wolf Victory's wood/clearing' O E; place in Staffs; cf. **Wolsey**.

Wolsey F 'wolf victory' O E, the origin of the surname of the cardinal from Ipswich. Rarely, N 'wolf's eye' O E. Or reduced from its derivative **Wolseley**.

Wolsoncroft, Wolstencroft, (or even) **Wolsten-Croft** L '(A S called) Wolf Stone's **Croft**' O E (cf. **Woolston**); lost place in Lancs.

Wolstenholme L '(A S called) Wolf Stone's **Holm**' O E + O N (cf. **Woolston**); place in Lancs.

Wolston L '(A S called) Wolf Powerful's place/farm' O E; place in Warwicks; or confused with the far commoner **Woolston**.

Wolverton See **Woolverton**.

Wombwell L 'spring/stream in a hollow' O E (cf. *womb*); place in West Yorks, and surname mainly of nearby Notts. First element may be owner's N 'Belly' O E/O N.

Wones L 'dwellings' M E, probably from O N *ván*.

Wonfor L 'waggon ford' O E; place (Wonford) in Thornbury, Devon (another place in Heavitree, Devon, is obscure).

Wonnacott L 'Wunna's cottage' O E (the F is of uncertain meaning); place in Sydenham Damerel, Devon.

F: *first name*   L: *local name*   N: *nickname*   O: *occupational name*

Wood L 'wood' OE, a surname as universal as woods were in medieval England. Rarely, however, N 'mad, frenzied' OE (Shakespeare's 'wood within this wood' in *Midsummer Night's Dream* means, rather, 'distracted, furious'); the basic meaning was 'inspired' – cf. the god *Woden* and his day, *Wednesday*. 14th commonest surname in England and Wales in 1853, 56th in Scotland in 1958. Family name of the earls of Halifax. **Woods** 'of (i.e. at) the wood' OE, or a plural; many family stocks, from many medieval woods; the N meaning of **Wood** may be involved in it sometimes.

Woodall See **Woodhall**. Counted by Guppy only in Ches.

Woodard F Apparently 'wood hard/hardy' OE. Also a reduced form of O 'wood-herd' OE – one who tends swine feeding in a wood on acorns or mast.

Woodbridge L 'wooden bridge' OE; locality, or places in Dorset, Suffolk.

Woodburn L 'stream in a wood' OE; locality, or place in Northd.

Woodbury L 'fort in a wood' OE, place in Devon; another Devon place could be this, or 'wooden fort' OE; W— Hill, Worcs, means 'old fort' OE; also places in Cambs, Somerset of one of the first two meanings.

Woodbyrne See **Woodburn**.

Woodchurch L 'wooden church' OE; locality, or places in Ches, Kent.

Woodcock N 'woodcock' OE; and, from the bird's supposed stupidity, 'simpleton, dupe'. But also absorbing L Woodcote/tt 'cottage in/by a wood' OE; places in six counties from Ches to Hants. (No evidence for O 'head woodman' by analogy with *cockfoster* 'head forester'.) Counted by Guppy only in Yorks, Salop, Leics, Norfolk, Cornwall.

Woodcraft, Woodcroft L 'Croft in/near a wood' OE; places (–o–) in Glos, Northants.

Woodd See **Wood**.

Wooden L 'wolves' valley' OE; place in Northd.

Woodend L 'end of the wood' OE; places in thirteen counties.

Woodey L 'enclosure in a wood' OE (cf. **Hay**); or a derivative of **Wood** in its rare N sense.

Woodfall L 'clearing in a wood' OE (cf. *felling*); place in Lancs; but meaning of surname may sometimes be '(sheep)fold in a wood' OE.

Woodford L 'ford in/by a wood' OE; places in ten counties from Ches to Cornwall.

Woodfull N 'wood-bird' OE (cf. *fowl*), used early as a F.

Woodgate L 'gate into a wood' OE.

Woodger O Commoner form of **Woodyer**.

431

Woodhall L 'hall in a wood, forest court-house' OE, places in six counties (twelve in Yorks); but one of the three places in Worcs is 'spring (cf. *well*) in a wood' OE.

Woodham L 'homestead in a wood' OE, places in Essex (three), Surrey; or 'river-meadow by a wood' OE, place in Bucks; or '(at) the woods' OE dative plural after lost preposition, place in Co. Durham.

Woodhead L 'top of the wood' OE; locality, or places in Ches–Derbys–West Yorks, Devon (three). Chiefly a West Yorks surname.

Woodhouse L 'house in a wood' OE; locality, or one of many places in West Yorks (a dozen), Derbys–Notts–Lincs (several in each), and twelve other counties. Or N 'faun, satyr, troll, woodwose' OE; the *wild man* was a frequent figure in pageants and heraldry, and the barons Wodehouse, earls of Kimberley, had as supporters to their arms two woodwoses. (There is definitely no meaning 'madhouse' based on the obsolete adjective *wood*; see **Wood**.) Guppy counted the surname in Herefords–Salop, Derbys. Family name of the viscounts Terrington.

Woodhurst L 'wooded **Hirst**' OE; place in Hunts, so called after an adjoining area (now Old Hurst) had been cleared.

Woodier Rarer form of **Woodyer**.

Woodiwiss N 'faun etc.' (see **Woodhouse**).

Woodland L 'woodland' OE; locality, or places from Co. Durham to Devon. Guppy counted it in Middx only.

Woodley L 'clearing/field in a wood' OE; the place-name occurs twice in Devon along with Woodleigh and in Berks, Ches. Guppy found it chiefly in Cornwall, where it must derive from the Devon places.

Woodman O 'woodman' OE; also used early as a F; common in Middx, Northd.

Woodmansee, Woodmansey L 'woodman's lake' OE; place (–ey) in East Yorks.

Woodroff(e) See **Woodruff**.

Woodrow L 'lane/row (of cottages) in a wood' OE; places in Wilts, Worcs.

Woodruff(e), Woodrup N 'woodruff (*Asperula odorata*)' OE, a sweet-scented herb, ?for one who used perfumes, or ?for one who should have.

Woodstock L 'place in the woods' OE; place in Oxon; see **Stock**, **Stokes**.

Woodthorpe L '**Thorp** in a wood' OE; places in Derbys, Leics, Lincs, Notts, West Yorks.

F: *first name*   L: *local name*   N: *nickname*   O: *occupational name*

Woodward O 'wood-keeper, forester' OE (the whole compound exists in OE). Very frequent Midland surname, especially in Worcs, with offshoots in Essex–Suffolk, Yorks. An affected pronunciation, as if **Woodard**, has nothing to recommend it.

Woodwell L 'spring/stream in a wood' OE.

Woodyat See **Woodgate**.

Woodyer O 'wood-hewer/-cutter' OE. **Woodyard** is given new 'meaning' by the mis-spelling.

Woof(f) See **Wolf**.

Wookey L 'snare, trap' OE; place in Somerset, and a Somerset surname. (A popular derivation from Welsh *ogof* 'cave' is now rejected, despite the famous W— Hole.)

Wool L 'spring/stream' (cf. *well*) OE, in dialect of Dorset especially, and of Somerset, West Sussex, West Surrey; locality, or place in Dorset.

Woolas(s) See **Woolhouse**.

Woolaway F 'wolf war' OE.

Wool(l)combe L 'spring/stream valley' OE *y* represented by south-western *u* spelt *oo*, place (one *l*) in Dorset; or for Woolacombe, Devon, same meaning or ?'wolves' valley' OE. A surname chiefly of Devon.

Woolcot(t) is probably an over-rounding of **Walcot(t)**, also corrupted to the Cornish form **Woolcock**.

Wooley and **Woolf(e)** See **Woolley** and **Wolf**.

Woolgar, Woolger F 'wolf spear' OE. Also spelt **Woolgard**.

Woolhouse L 'building for storing wool' OE. Chiefly a Northants surname.

Woollacott and **Woollam(s)** See **Woolcott** and **Wolloms**. Guppy counted **Woollams** only in Ches.

Woolland L 'pasture land' OE; place in Dorset (cf. first element of **Winton**, Westmorland), and a surname of nearby Devon.

Woollard F 'wolf guardian' OE. A Suffolk surname.

Woollatt F 'wolf Gēat' OE; Beowulf belonged to the Gēat tribe, commemorated in the title of the King of Sweden, *rex Sveorum Gothorumque* – 'and of the Goths'; see **Merriott**. Chiefly a Herts surname.

Wooler O 'wool-worker/-dealer' OE. Or L 'stream bank' OE (cf. **Wells, Over**); place (Wooler) in Northd.

Woolley L 'wood with wolves' OE, places in six counties; or 'hill with wolves' OE, place in Northd; or 'wood/clearing by a stream' OE, place in Somerset. The surname is found chiefly in Notts–Derbys–Ches–Salop–Staffs–Warwicks, Kent, which suits none of these places (save for a locality in Derbys).

Woolliams See **Wolloms**; the form must be influenced by **Williams**.

Woolman O 'wool-man (i.e. -merchant)' OE.

Woolmer L 'mere/pool frequented by wolves' OE, places in Hants, Wilts (Wolmer, Woolmore); or from a lost place in Lancs, 'moor frequented by wolves' OE. Or F 'wolf famous' OE.

Woolner, Woolno(u)th, Woolnough F 'wolf boldness' OE (the **-oth** ending is nearest to the original).

Woolrich, Woolridge F 'wolf powerful' OE *Wulfrīc*.

Woolsey See **Wolsey, Wolseley**.

Woolstenhulme See **Wolstenholme**.

Woolston(e) The names of a number of places, all OE, all with 'place/farm' (cf. **Town**) as their second element, all with –s– representing the *'s* of the owner, and all with the F of their AS owners as their first element: 'Wolf Victory' (cf. **Wolseley**), places in Devon, Lancs, Bucks, Glos; 'Wolf Guard', place in Somerset; 'Wolf', places in Hants, Somerset, Co. Durham (Wolviston); 'Wolf Powerful' (cf. **Woolrich**), place in Berks; or for **Wolston**. Or F 'wolf stone' OE, the name (*Wulfstān*) of an archbishop of York (†1023) and a canonized bishop of Worcester (†1095). Guppy found the name countable only in Norfolk.

Woolton L '(AS called) Wolf's place/farm' OE; two places in Lancs.

Woolven, Woolvin F 'wolf friend' OE (cf. **Winn, Wine**).

Woolverton L There are places Wolv– in Bucks, Hants, Warwicks, Worcs; Woolv– in Somerset; Wolf– in Norfolk; Woll– in Salop. All have final element OE *tūn* 'farm settlement'; the settler's first element is always 'Wolf' OE; the second elements vary, and are not always clear.

Woon L 'dwelling' ON (see **Wones**).

Woosnam See **Wolstenholme**.

Wooster See **Worcester**. Mainly a Bucks name.

Wootton L 'place/farm in/by a wood' OE; places in at least fifteen counties, and usually with distinctive additions. Guppy found the name grouped in Northants–Bucks–Beds–Herts, and in Notts, Kent, Wilts. Also spelt **Wootten**.

Worboys See **Warboys**.

Worcester L 'Roman site' OE from Latin *castra* 'of (a tribe called) the *Wigoran*', from a lost river-name *Wyre* ?'winding' Celtic; the Worcs city of which the bishop still signs *Wigorn*.

Worden L 'weir valley' OE, place in Lancs; but place in Devon is probably the same as **Worthen** (also a Devon place).

F: *first name* L: *local name* N: *nickname* O: *occupational name*

Wordsworth See **Wadsworth**.

Work(e) L '(building-)work, fortification' OE (as in **Wark**, *outwork*); the –e could show a dative after a lost preposition. Or perhaps O, for a man engaged in building.

Workman O 'workman, builder' OE compound; but it's an odd name, hardly distinguishing its bearer, and Reaney quotes one of our earliest dictionaries, giving 'ambidextrous' as the meaning of *werkemanne*. Guppy counted it only in Worcs.

Worle L 'wood-grouse wood' OE; place in Somerset.

Worlock Respelling of **Warlock**, after rounding of the –a– by the influence of the W– (cf. our *o* sound, not acknowledged by the spelling, in *war, wasp, was*, etc.).

Worm(s) N 'dragon, reptile, snake' OE. And '(son) of **W**—'.

Wormald L 'wild-boar spring' ON; three places (in Barkisland, Rishworth, and Scammonden) in West Yorks; this reiteration is against the first element's being an owner's name.

Wormeley Once an Ipswich, Suffolk, family; form of **Wormley**.

Wormleighton L 'leek plot on the ?bubbling/welling stream' OE; place in Warwicks. A Leics surname.

Wormley L 'wood/clearing/field with reptiles/snakes' OE; places in Herts, Lincs, Surrey.

Worrall, Worrell L 'Haugh (*halh*) with bog-myrtle' OE; place (–a–) in West Yorks; the same meaning as the peninsula of the Wirral, Ches.

Worster See **Worcester**.

Worsthorne L '(AS called) Worthy's thornbush' OE; place in Lancs.

Wort O 'vegetable(-grower)' OE, a metonym.

Worth L 'enclosure, fence, homestead' OE; locality, or one of the places in several counties, or one of the many now having –worth as the second element of a compound. Guppy counted the name in Ches, Lincs, Surrey.

Worthen L 'enclosure' OE (*–ign*); locality, or places in Devon, Salop (–thin), and a common place-name element in west Midlands; sometimes perhaps for **Worthing**, Norfolk, of same origin.

Worthing Usually L; cf. **Worthen**, and add W—, Sussex, 'family/folk of (an AS called) Worthy' OE. But also a F dim. based on this Old English F *Worth*, meaning 'worthy'.

Worthington L 'place/farm of the family/folk of (an AS called) Worthy' OE (cf. **Worthing**); but the first element could be the same as **Worthen**; places in Lancs, Leics, and the name fittingly found in Ches–Lancs and Leics–Notts.

Worthy L 'enclosure' OE (related to **Worth, Worthen**), a common element in south–west place-names; and places in Devon, Hants. Rarely N 'worthy' OE.

Wortley L 'clearing/field with plants/vegetables' OE (cf. *wort*, **Wort**), place in West Yorks; but another West Yorks place, near Leeds, has for its first element the F, akin to 'work', of an AS owner. Guppy counted the name in Norfolk only.

Worton L 'vegetable garden' OE (cf. **Wortley**), places in Oxon, Wilts, North Yorks; but places Nether and Over W—, Oxon, are 'place/farm on a bank/slope' OE (the first element being the second of **Windsor**).

Wotton L Same as **Wootton**; places in Bucks, Glos, Surrey. But counted by Guppy only in Devon.

Wouldham L '(AS called) ? ?Glorious's homestead' OE; place in Kent.

Wozencroft and **Wraight** See **Wolsoncroft** and **Wright**.

Wraith Northern form of **Wroth**, retaining OE *ā*.

Wrate Version of **Wright**; only two in the London TD, and family said to come from Norfolk.

Wrathall L No place now recorded, but could be 'nook where crosswort grows' OE *wrætt* + *halh*. A West Yorks surname.

Wraxall L The various places (also Wraxhall, Wroxhall, Roxhill) in six counties, formerly held to be 'buzzard's nook (*halh*; see **Haugh**)' OE, are now assigned to some other beast or bird of prey containing the OE stem *wroc*-. The most important family were Bristolians, from the north Somerset place.

Wray L 'felon-stream' (where they were executed by drowning) OE; stream and place in Devon. But the surname is mainly of York and East Yorks, so that 'corner, nook, remote place' ON, two places in Lancs and others (Wrea, Wreay) in Lancs, Cumberland, is much likelier. Or N, 'twisted, crooked' OE (cf. *awry*).

Wrayford, Wreford L ?'felon stream ford' OE, since the River **Wray** records judicial drowning, and these are Devon surnames.

Wren(n) N 'wren' OE; it was tiny, but it was the king of birds – shrewd, towny, and a singer; on the whole, a nice name. Guppy counted it (–n and –nn) in leafy Sussex only.

Wretham L 'homestead where crosswort/hellebore grows' OE; place in Norfolk.

Wride L 'bush, thicket' OE or (cf. *writhe*, *wreath*, and place Wryde in Cambs) 'twist, bend in a river' OE. Reaney supposes N 'a twister' also.

F: *first name*   L: *local name*   N: *nickname*   O: *occupational name*

Wright(e) O 'carpenter, joiner' OE, or almost any kind of 'maker, craftsman' – he *wrought*, i.e. worked, made; we are still familiar with a **Wheelwright** and a *playwright*, but there were once **Cheesewright**, **Sievewright**, **Cartwright**, etc. **Wrighte** is a very rare form, with the –e perhaps perpetuating the final –a of the OE word. **Wright** was the 13th commonest surname in England and Wales in 1853, and the 63rd in Scotland in 1958. **Wrightson** 'son of W—' OE; Guppy counted it only in East and North Yorks.

Wrigley L Second element probably as in **Leigh**; first OE but quite obscure; old hamlet W— Head in Manchester, Lancs, and a Lancs–Ches–West Yorks surname.

Wrixon Chiefly a Dorset form of **Wrightson**.

Wroath Good spelling of **Wroth**, with –oa– showing long open *o* from OE *ā*; but rare.

Wroe L 'corner, nook, remote place' ON; not a northern form like **Wray**, as the ON *á* has changed to Midland and south *ō*.

Wroth N 'angry, bad-tempered, fierce' OE. Counted by Guppy only in Devon.

Wyard F 'battle hardy/brave' OE. Often absorbed by **Wyatt**.

Wyatt F dim. 'Guy', in its Norman form, and quite the commonest of the **Guy** family, especially in Devon–Somerset–Glos, Hants, Norfolk. See **Wye**.

Wybar, Wyber, Wyberg(h), Wybrew, Wybrow F 'battle fortress' OE feminine.

Wyburn Despite the local pronunciation of Wythburn, Cumberland, originally 'willow valley' ON, the surname is a F 'war hero' OE (an A S of this name settled Wybunbury, Ches).

Wych(e) See **Wich**.

Wye F Norman dialect form of **Guy**. But perhaps more often L 'at the heathen temple' (cf. **Weedon**) OE ?locative case; place in Kent.

Wyke See **Wick(e)**. **Wykes** 'of (i.e. at) the W—', or a plural.

Wykeham L Same as **Wickham**; places in Hants, Lincs (three), North Yorks.

Wylam L '(at) the contrivances/machines/snares/fish-traps' (cf. *wile*) OE dative plural after lost preposition; place in Northd.

Wyl(e)y, Wylie See **Wiley**.

Wyman F 'battle protector' OE (for first element, cf. **Wyard**; for second, **Edmund**). Guppy counted it only in Northants.

Wymark F 'worthy to have a horse' Old Breton male and female.

Wymer F 'battle famous' OE; cf. **Wyard** and **Seamer**. But early confused with **Wymark**.

Wyndham L Usual pronunciation of place Wymondham, Norfolk, 'Wyman's homestead' OE. Family name of the barons Leconfield.

Wyne(s) See **Wine(s)**.

Wynn(e) The commoner of these is –e, which is normally N, the North Wales and Salop version (with initial **Gw—** mutated) of South Wales **Gwyn(n)**, **Gwynne** 'white, etc.'. But **Wynn(e)** will sometimes be a form of **Winn**. **Wynn** is the family name of the barons Newborough. **Wynnes** '(son) of **W—**'.

Wynyard L 'vineyard' OE (cf. **Vine**); but the place in Co. Durham is more likely to be 'pasture enclosure' OE (cf. first meaning of **Winton**).

Wyse See **Wise**.

F: *first name*   L: *local name*   N: *nickname*   O: *occupational name*

Y

Yale L 'fertile upland' Welsh *iâl*; Elihu **Y**—'s family was from Plas-Grono, near Wrexham, Denbs.

Yalland See **Yolland**.

Yandall, Yandell, Yandle See **Yeandle**.

Yapp N 'crooked, bent; deceitful; shrewd, smart' OE. Mainly a surname of Salop–Herefords.

Yarborough L 'earth fort' OE; places in Lincs, Somerset. A whist/bridge hand with nothing higher than a nine is named from a sporty earl of Y—.

Yard L Less likely to be 'yard, enclosure' OE than 'yardland, virgate, thirty acres' OE. **Yarde** 'at the yardland' shows dative after lost preposition.

Yardley L 'wood/clearing for getting sticks/spars/poles' (cf. *yard*) OE, places in Essex, Northants, Worcs; but place in Bucks is 'clearing for ploughing' OE. On the other hand, Guppy counted the surname only in Staffs, West Yorks.

Yarm L '(at) the yairs/dams/fishgarths' OE, –**m** showing dative plural after lost preposition; place in North Yorks.

Yarm(o)uth L 'mouth' OE 'of the (River) Yare (= ?babbler)' Keltic, place in Norfolk; or place in IoW with the first (river) element meaning ?'gravelly' OE.

Yarnold Chiefly a Worcs surname, said to be an early corruption of **Arnold** in its F or L meaning.

Yarrow L 'rough stream' Scots Gaelic, place in Selkirks; it is less likely to be the Lancs river-name (?'rough' Welsh) or the spots in Northd and Somerset.

Yarwood L Not an identifiable place; second element 'wood' OE, first '(River) Yare (= babbler)' Welsh, or 'gravel' OE *ēar*, or 'eagle' OE *earn*, or 'fish-trap' OE *gear*.

Yate L 'gate, gap' OE; locality, or place in Glos; cf. Symonds Yat, on the Wye. The OE noun began with a *y* sound, whereas its plural could begin with a *g* sound; cf. **Gate**. **Yates** 'of (i.e. at) the **Y**—'; common in the group Lancs–Ches–Derbys–Staffs–Salop–Herefords, and in Bucks.

Yaxley L 'cuckoo's wood' OE; place in Hunts.

Yeaman(s) See **Yeoman(s)**.

Yeandle L Perhaps a derivative of OE adjective *gēandele* 'steep'; no place is now so called, but this surname is common in Somerset, along with its versions in **Yand–**, **Yend–**, and **Yeandel**.

Yearling N 'yearling (year-old animal, or one in its second year)' OE; the reason for bestowal is obscure.

Yearsley L 'boar's wood' OE; place in North Yorks.

Yeat(e)s See **Yates**.

Yelland See **Yolland**; half a dozen places in Devon, and a Cornwall–Devon surname.

Yelverton L 'farm of (an AS called) ?Payment Peace' OE, place in Norfolk; the Devon place is too recent to make a surname – it was *Elleford* ('Ella's/elder-tree ford' OE) in 1291, and the farm remained *Elfordtown*, but the Great Western Railway used the dialect form Y— on building its station there in 1859. Elfordleigh, Plympton St Mary, Devon, is named after Thomas Elfforde, c. 1571.

Yemm N 'uncle' OE, in Forest of Dean dialect; cf. **Eames**.

Yendal, Yendell, Yendle, Yendole See **Yeandle**.

Yeo L 'river, stream' OE, here in Devon–Somerset dialect form; name of over twenty places in Devon, and a Devon–Cornwall surname.

Yeoland See **Yolland**.

Yeoman O 'yeoman, small freeholder', but the earlier use was 'servant, attendant' (with rank between sergeant and groom, or squire and page) ME from Germanic. **Yeomans** '(son) of Y—'. Scattered surnames – Guppy counted –n in East and North Yorks, Somerset, –ns in Derbys, Herefords.

Yerbury See **Yarborough**.

Yolland L 'old (?long-cultivated) land' OE; places (also **Yalland, Yelland**) in Devon.

Yong(e) Forms of **Young(e)**.

Yonwin F 'young friend' OE.

Yorath See **Iorwerth**.

York(e) L British *Eburac*– (from ?'yew-tree'), latinized, then mistakenly turned by the ASs into OE *Eoforwic* (as if to mean 'wild boar **Wick**'), and finally scandinavianized by the Vikings into York; the Yorks city. Guppy counted it in Northants only. **Yorke** is the family name of the earls of Hardwicke.

Yorkshire L 'county of **York**' second element OE. An uncommon surname.

Yorwerth See **Iorwerth**.

Youens F '(son) of **Ewan**'.

Youl See **Yule**.

Yould N 'old' OE, in south-western dialect.

Youlden, Youldon L 'old (?long-cultivated) hill' OE; places in Devon.

Youle, Youll F See **Yule**. **Youles** '(son) of Y—'.

F: *first name*   L: *local name*   N: *nickname*   O: *occupational name*

Young(e) N 'young' OE – perhaps usually in the sense of 'junior' to one's father; the **-e** could show a weak adjective after a lost definite article. **Young** occurs all over England, with its highest numbers in Co. Durham and in Glos–Somerset–Dorset–Hants, and was the 21st commonest surname in Scotland in 1958. Family name of the barons Kennet. **Youngs** '(son) of **Y—**'; found, like **Youngman**, in Norfolk–Suffolk.

Younger N 'younger, junior' OE – but Reaney cites a 1364 Fleming whose name was from Middle Dutch *jonghheer* 'young nobleman' (like the German *Junker*). Chiefly a Northd surname.

Younghusband O 'young farmer' OE; cf. **Husband**.

Youngman N 'young man' OE; a surname of Norfolk–Suffolk.

Youngmay N 'young lad' OE; and see other meanings of **May**.

Yoxall L '**Haugh** (*halh*) ?the size of a yoke (of oxen – fifty/sixty acres)' OE; place in Staffs. (The first element is apparently not 'cuckoo's' as in **Yaxley**, though this would give a pretty place-name resembling **Wraxall**.)

Yule N 'Christmas' OE and ON (really a pagan twelve-day festival); from birth or baptism then.

Z

Zeal South-west form, with initial *s*– voiced, of L 'sallow, willow' or 'hall' OE; places in Devon. Or of Ó 'seal(-maker)' or 'one who officially uses a seal' OF; a metonym. Also occurs as **Zeale**.

Zebedee F 'my gift' Greek respelling of Hebrew; the father of the Apostles James the Great and John.

Zeller South-east or -west form, with initial *s*– voiced, of **Seller**.

Zorkin N 'son of Pessimist' Irish, anglicized (if one can call it that) from *McDhuarcáin*.

Zouch See **Such**; the family strikingly left their name at Ashby de la Z—, Leics.

F: *first name*   L: *local name*   N: *nickname*   O: *occupational name*

BIBLIOGRAPHY

P. H. Reaney, *A Dictionary of British Surnames*, revised by R. M. Wilson (London, 1976).

C. W. Bardsley, *A Dictionary of English and Welsh Surnames* (London, 1901).

E. Weekley, *Surnames* (London, 1916).

H. B Guppy, *Homes of Family Names in Great Britain* (London, 1890).

T. F. G. Dexter, *Cornish Names* (London, 1926).

J. J. Kneen, *The Personal Names of the Isle of Man* (Douglas, 1937).

G. F. Black, *The Surnames of Scotland* (New York, 1946).

Annual Report of the Registrar-General for Scotland, 1962, No. 108 (Edinburgh, 1963).

E. MacLysaght, *Irish Families* (Dublin, 1957).

E. MacLysaght, *More Irish Families* (Galway and Dublin, 1960).

R. E. Matheson, *Special Report on Surnames in Ireland* (Dublin, 1894).

R. E. Matheson, *Varieties and Synonymes of Surnames and Christian Names in Ireland* (Dublin, 1901).

A. Dauzat, *Dictionnaire Étymologique des Noms de Famille et Prénoms de France* (Paris, 1951).

GPO Telephone Directory, 15 vols., 1962–1963.

G. Tengvik, *Old English Bynames* (Uppsala, 1938).

O. von Feilitzen, *The Pre-Conquest Personal Names of Domesday Book* (Uppsala, 1937).

M. T. Löfvenberg, *Studies on Middle English Local Surnames* (Lund, 1942).

G. Fransson, *Middle English Surnames of Occupation 1100–1350* (Lund, 1935).

E. Ekwall, *Variation in Surnames in Medieval London* (Lund, 1945).

E. Ekwall. *Early London Personal Names* (Lund, 1947).

Gillian Fellows Jensen, 'Some Observations on Scandinavian Personal Names in English Place-Names', *Saga-Book of the Viking Society for Northern Research*, Vol. XVI Part I (London, 1962).

Gillian Fellows Jensen, *Scandinavian Personal Names in Lincolnshire and Yorkshire* (Copenhagen, 1968).

Gillian Fellows Jensen, *Scandinavian Settlement Names in Yorkshire* (Copenhagen, 1972).

A. H. Smith, 'Early Northern Nick-Names and Surnames', *Saga-Book of the Viking Society for Northern Research*, Vol. XI (London, 1936).

BIBLIOGRAPHY

G. Kristensson, 'Studies on Middle English Local Surnames Containing Elements of French Origin', *English Studies* 50 (1969).

P. H. Reaney, *The Origin of English Surnames* (London, 1967).

G. Redmonds, *Yorkshire West Riding*, English Surname Series 1 (London, 1973).

B. Seltén, *The Anglo-Saxon Heritage in Middle English Personal Names: East Anglia 1100–1399* (Lund, 1972).

B. Seltén, 'Some Notes on Middle English By-Names in Independent Use', *English Studies* 46 (1965).

B. Seltén, *Early East-Anglian Nicknames: 'Shakespeare' Names* (Lund, 1969).

B. Seltén, *Early East-Anglian Nicknames: Bahuvrihi Names* (Lund, 1975).

E. G. Withycombe, *The Oxford Dictionary of English Christian Names*, third edition (Oxford, 1977).

General Register Office, *Census 1951, England and Wales: Index of Place-Names* (London, 1955).

E. Ekwall, *The Concise Oxford Dictionary of English Place-Names*, fourth edition (Oxford, 1960).

The volumes so far published of the English Place-Name Society.

W. F. H. Nicolaisen, *Scottish Place-Names* (London, 1976).

J. B. Johnston, *Place-Names of Scotland* (Edinburgh, 1892, and London, 1934).

W. J. Watson, *History of the Celtic Place-Names of Scotland* (Edinburgh and London, 1926).

A. Dauzat and C. Rostaing, *Dictionnaire Étymologique des Noms de Lieux en France* (Paris, 1963).

H. Kurath, S. M. Kuhn, etc., editors, *Middle English Dictionary* (Ann Arbor, Michigan, 1952–   ); it had reached *M* by 1977.

MORE ABOUT PENGUINS
AND PELICANS

Penguinews, which appears every month, contains details of all the new books issued by Penguins as they are published. From time to time it is supplemented by the *Penguin Stock List* which is our list of almost 5,000 titles.

A specimen copy of *Penguinews* will be sent to you free on request. Please write to Dept EP, Penguin Books Ltd, Harmondsworth, Middlesex, for your copy.

In the U.S.A.: For a complete list of books available from Penguins in the United States write to Dept CS, Penguin Books, 625 Madison Avenue, New York, New York 10022.

In Canada: For a complete list of books available from Penguins in Canada write to Penguin Books Canada Ltd, 2801 John Street, Markham, Ontario L3R 1B4.

ERIC PARTRIDGE

Abridged by Jacqueline Simpson

A DICTIONARY OF HISTORICAL SLANG

Eric Partridge's *Dictionary of Slang*, in which he assembled a striking collection of the rough words of past centuries and showed a remarkable knowledge of their use and origins, has been the standard work on the subject for years. This volume extracts the most valuable parts of that dictionary and includes all the expressions used or coined before 1914.

Nearly 50,000 entries recall the living speech of a world now largely lost. Often wry and flippant, occasionally 'blue', and sometimes uproariously comical, they recapture the rich idiom of English life through the ages, bringing back to mind the vigour of Elizabethan phrase, the ribald language of dockside and pub, the richer coinages of messdeck and barrack, the euphemisms and witticisms of the Victorian drawing-room, and the irrepressible wit of errand boys and costermongers.

'Even a casual perusal of the pages is extraordinarily instructive and entertaining, presenting the reader with so much out-of-the-way information' – *Sunday Times*

J. M. AND M. J. COHEN

THE PENGUIN DICTIONARY OF QUOTATIONS

This dictionary is designed for the casual reader. It sets out to give him the common stock of quotations from Shakespeare, the Bible and Paradise Lost, side by side with remarks and stray lines by almost unknown writers who have enriched the language with only a single phrase. Foreign languages are quoted in the original where the quotation is generally remembered in its foreign form, but an English translation is always provided. Modern authors have been drawn on for what the compilers believe to be their memorable sayings, and the ancients have been pruned of many lines that have gone into previous dictionaries of quotations, but which are now almost certainly forgotten. The reader, the writer, the after-dinner speaker, the crossword-puzzle solver and the browser – all will find what they want among the 12,000 or so quotations of this dictionary.